9
10. ✓
11 ✓
12 ✓
13
14 ✓
15 ✓

# MARKETING

Canadian Second Edition

# MARKETING
## Canadian Second Edition

**Gordon H. G. McDougall**
Wilfrid Laurier University

**Philip Kotler**
Northwestern University

**Gary Armstrong**
University of North Carolina

Prentice-Hall Canada Inc.
Scarborough, Ontario

**Canadian Cataloguing in Publication Data**

McDougall, Gordon H. G., 1942-
    Marketing

2nd ed.
First and 2nd authors in reverse order on 1st ed.
Includes bibliographical references and index.
ISBN 0-13-544685-6

1. Marketing.   2. Marketing - Management.
I. Kotler, Philip.   II. Armstrong, Gary.   III. Title.

HF5415.M33  1991          658.8          C91-094089-4

Prentice Hall, Inc., Englewood Cliffs, New Jersey
Prentice-Hall International, Inc., London
Prentice-Hall of Australia, Pty., Ltd., Sydney
Prentice-Hall of India Pvt., Ltd., New Delhi
Prentice-Hall of Japan, Inc., Tokyo
Prentice-Hall of Southeast Asia (Pte.) Ltd., Singapore
Editora Prentice-Hall do Brasil Ltda., Rio de Janeiro
Prentice-Hall Hispanoamericana, S.A., Mexico

ISBN 0-13-544685-6

Acquisitions Editor:  Jacqueline Wood
Developmental Editor:  Linda Gorman
Production Editor:  Kelly Dickson
Copy Editor:  Kateri Lanthier
Production Coordinator:  Florence Rousseau
Cover and Interior Design:  Monica Kompter
Page Layout and Illustrations:  Loates Electronic Design and Illustration
Photo Research:  Paulee Kestin/Photo Research

1     2     3     4     5     AGC     96     95     94     93     92

Printed and bound in the USA by Arcata Graphic Company

# Contents

4     Marketing Research and Information

# Preface

*Marketing* is designed to help students learn about the basic concepts and practices of modern marketing in an enjoyable and practical way. Marketing is all around us, and we all need to know something about it. Most students are surprised to find out how widely marketing is used. Marketing is used not only by manufacturing companies, wholesalers, and retailers, but by all kinds of individuals and organizations. Lawyers, accountants, and doctors use marketing to manage demand for their services. So do hospitals, museums, and performing arts groups. No politician can get the needed votes, and no resort the needed tourists, without developing and carrying out marketing plans.

People throughout these organizations need to know how to define and segment a market and develop need-satisfying products and services for chosen target markets. They must know how to price their offerings to make them attractive and affordable, and how to choose middlemen to make their products available to customers. And they need to know how to advertise and promote products so that customers will know about and want them. Clearly, marketers need a broad range of skills in order to sense, serve, and satisfy consumer needs.

Students also need to know marketing in their roles as consumers and citizens. Someone is always trying to sell us something, so we need to recognize the methods they use. And when students enter the job market, they must conduct a form of marketing research to find the best opportunities and the best ways to market themselves to prospective employers. Many will start their careers with marketing jobs in salesforces, in retailing, in advertising, in research, or in one of a dozen other marketing areas.

## Approach and Objectives

Several factors guided the development of *Marketing*. Most marketing students want a broad picture of its basics, but they don't want to drown in a sea of details. They want to know about important marketing principles and concepts, but also how these concepts are applied in actual marketing management practice. And they want a text that presents the complex and fascinating world of marketing in an easy to grasp, lively, and enjoyable way.

*Marketing* covers important marketing principles and concepts that are supported by research and evidence from economics, the behavioral sciences, and modern management theory. Yet it takes a practical, marketing management approach. Concepts are applied through examples of situations in which well-known and little-known companies assess and solve their marketing problems. Color illustrations, "Marketing Highlight" exhibits, and cases present further applications.

Finally, *Marketing* makes learning marketing easy and enjoyable. The book tells the stories that reveal the drama of modern marketing: The global strategy of Northern Telecom; Canadian Tire's future marketing plans; the abrupt rise and fall of New Coke; Campbell Soup's response to a changing environment; VS Services' approach to industrial markets; Procter & Gamble's segmentation strategy; Bombardier's ride through various life cycles; Sony's pricing decisions on its compact disc players; Mel Hurtig's pricing problems; Honest Ed's retail strategy; Quaker Oat's use of promotion tools; the Coke-Pepsi advertising battle; the impact of the Free Trade Agreement; and marketing's response to environmental issues. These and dozens of other examples and illustrations throughout each chapter reinforce key concepts and bring marketing to life for the student.

Thus *Marketing* gives the marketing student a complete, manageable, managerial introduction to the basics of marketing. Its style, level, and extensive use of examples and illustrations make the book easy to grasp and enjoyable to read.

## Changes in the Second Edition

The Second Edition of *Marketing* offers many improvements in content, style, and presentation that make the text even more effective and enjoyable than the First Edition. Dozens of new color photos and illustrations have been added to illuminate key points and make the text more visually appealing. Throughout, tables, figures, examples, and references have been thoroughly updated; many new examples have been added within the text material. This edition also includes more than 30 "Marketing Highlights" and chapter-opening examples to dramatize concepts and illustrate them with actual business applications. Most of the cases in the Second Edition have been either replaced or substantially revised.

The Second Edition of *Marketing* also includes substantial new or improved material on a wide range of topics: responding to the marketing environment, important new consumer markets, segmenting industrial markets, product quality and design, speeding up new-product development, test marketing, direct marketing, the increased use of "push" promotional strategies, public relations, consumer- and trade-promotion tools, inside selling and telemarketing, marketing strategies for service firms, marketing ethics and social responsibility, finding competitive advantages, and global marketing strategies.

## Learning Aids

Many aids are provided within this book to help students learn about marketing. The main features are:

- **Chapter Objectives** Each chapter begins with objectives that prepare the student for the chapter material and point out learning goals.
- **Opening Examples** Each chapter starts with a dramatic marketing story that

introduces the chapter material and arouses student interest.

- **Full-Color Figures, Photographs, and Illustrations** Throughout each chapter, key concepts and applications are illustrated with vivid full-color visual materials.
- **Marketing Highlights** Additional examples and important information are highlighted in boxed exhibits throughout the text.
- **Summaries** Each chapter ends with a summary which wraps up the main points and concepts.
- **Review Questions** Each chapter has a set of review questions covering the main chapter points.
- **Key Terms** Key Terms are highlighted within each chapter, and a list of key term definitions is provided at the end of each chapter.
- **Case Studies and Exercises** Cases and exercises for class or written discussion are provided at the end of the book. They challenge students to apply marketing principles to companies in various situations.
- **Appendices** Appendix A, "Marketing Arithmetic," provides additional, practical information for students. Appendix B, "Analyzing Cases," provides a guide for students in preparing the cases.
- **Glossary** At the end of the book, an extensive glossary provides quick reference to the key terms found in the book.
- **Indexes** A subject index, a name index and an index of companies and products—new to this edition—help students quickly find information and examples in the book.

## Supplements

A successful marketing course requires more than a well-written book. It requires a dedicated teacher and a complete set of supplemental learning and teaching aids. The following aids support *Marketing*:

- **Instructor's Manual** The comprehensive Instructor's Manual contains chapter overviews, lecture outlines, reviews of objectives and key terms, answers to chapter discussion questions, and analyses of all cases.
- **Test Item File** The Test Item File contains about 2000 multiple choice, true-false, and essay questions.
- **Computerized Test Item File** The computerized version of the Test Item File in IBM PC format is also available.
- **Study Guide** For each chapter, the Study Guide contains a chapter review, sample questions with answers to help students test their knowledge, and two sets of exercises that help students learn and apply chapter terms and concepts.
- **Color Transparencies** Providing additional information, these 140 transparencies include material not found in the text that can be easily integrated into lectures.
- **Transparencies** The Transparencies package includes over 100 transparencies.
- **Videos** Each ABC News video includes snippets from "20/20" and "Nightline" and illustrates a marketing concept by depicting real companies addressing real problems. Video topics include L.L. Bean, Shopping in the U.S.S.R., and the concern with oat bran. The videos are free upon adoption. Please contact your local Prentice-Hall representative for more information. A video guide is also available.

# Acknowledgments

In preparing the second Canadian edition of *Marketing*, I would like to acknowledge a number of people who assisted in the development of this book. First, a number of marketing colleagues at various universities and organizations who provided me with cases for this book; Marvin Ryder, Robert MacGregor, Arlene Bennett, Thomas Funk, Nancy Brown, William Braithwaite, Susan Hain, Dennis Anderson, Robert Wyckham, Sadrudin Ahmed, David Litvak, and John Yokom. Second, I am grateful for the excellent word processing services provided by Elsie Grogan, Janet Campbell, Lori Kapshey, Linda Okrucky, and Mavis Sheen at Wilfrid Laurier University. Third, the individuals at Prentice-Hall Canada—Yolanda de Rooy, Kelly Dickson, and Kateri Lanthier—who made the project enjoyable and worthwhile. I would also like to thank the reviewers: Deirdre Grondin of the University of New Brunswick, Pat Kolodziejski of Mohawk College, Anne Walker of Ryerson Polytechnic Institute, and Ken Wong of Queen's University. Finally, the financial support of the Office of Research at Wilfrid Laurier University is gratefully acknowledged.

I am dedicating the book to Betty, Michael, and Sandy.

Gordon H.G. McDougall

# CHAPTER 1

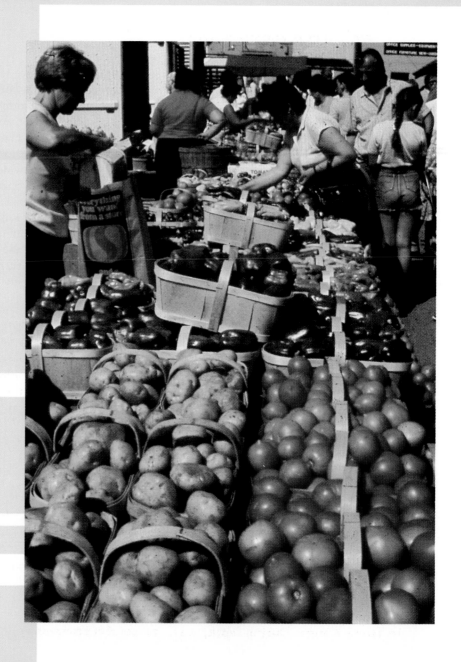

# Social Foundations of Marketing: Meeting Human Needs

## CHAPTER OBJECTIVES

After reading this chapter, you should be able to:
1. Define marketing and discuss its role in the economy.
2. Compare the four marketing management philosophies.
3. Explain how marketing can be used by different kinds of business and nonbusiness organizations.

Marketing touches all Canadians every day of our lives. We wake up to a Viking radio alarm clock (produced in Hong Kong), which is playing a Bryan Adams song followed by a Canadian Airlines commercial advertising a vacation flight to Florida. We brush our teeth with Crest, gargle with Listermint, shower with Zest (all products made by Canadian subsidiaries of U.S. parents). We put on our Pierre Cardin shirts (made in Canada but licenced from France), Harry Rosen suit (made in Italy), and Bass shoes (made in the United States). We pour some Maple Leaf milk and prepare a bowl of Cheerios (again, made by a Canadian subsidiary of a U.S. firm). We sweeten a cup of Nescafé (produced by the Canadian subsidiary of a European firm) with two teaspoons of Lantic sugar. We drive to work in a Mazda (made in Japan) and at lunchtime we purchase a T-shirt (made in Hong Kong). During work, we phone business firms in Vancouver, Montreal, and Halifax via a telecommunication system developed by Northern Telecom (a Canadian company) and fax a message to Australia (using a machine made in Canada). Arriving home we get our mail and find a Canadian Tire catalog, a letter from the Toronto-Dominion Bank offering various financial services, and coupons saving us money on our favorite brands. Later that night we watch Bill Cosby on cable television. Our day ends with CBC's "The National." As Canadians, we benefit from products from all over the world. Our marketing system has made these products available to us with little effort on our part. We support this standard of living, in part, by marketing the resources we have to other countries—Canada is in seventh place among the world's traders. Marketing is important to Canadians because of the global nature of our community.

The marketing system consists of many large and small companies, all seeking success. Two business researchers, Tom Peters and Robert Waterman, studied many successful companies to find out what made them tick. They reported the results in what became the best-selling business book of all time, *In Search of Excellence*.[1] They found that these companies shared a set of basic marketing principles: Each boasted a keen understanding of its customers, strongly defined markets, and the ability to motivate its employees to produce high quality and value for its customers.

In a second book, Tom Peters and Nancy Austin offered more stories about companies taking intelligent and effective measures to improve their customers' satisfaction.[2] They describe how IBM collects customer ratings of its sales and service people and gives awards to employees who best satisfy customers. They explain how The Limited studies women's clothing needs and creates the right store systems for different market segments.

Marketing has become a key factor in business success. The term marketing must be understood not merely in the old sense of making a sale—"selling"—but rather in the new sense of satisfying customer needs. Today's companies face increasingly stiff competition, and the rewards go to those who can best read customer wants and deliver the greatest value to their target consumers. In the marketplace, marketing skills separate the amateurs from the professionals.

In this chapter, we will define marketing and its core concepts, describe the major philosophies of marketing thinking and practice, discuss the goals of the marketing system, and explain how marketing is used by different kinds of organizations.

# WHAT IS MARKETING?

What does the term marketing mean? Most people mistakenly think of marketing only as selling and promotion. And no wonder—every day, Canadians are bombarded with television commercials, newspaper ads, direct mail, and sales calls. Someone is always trying to sell us something. It seems that we cannot escape death, taxes, or selling.

Therefore, many students are surprised to learn that selling is only the tip of the marketing iceberg. It is but one of several marketing functions, and often not the most important one. If the marketer does a good job of identifying consumer needs, developing good products, and pricing, distributing, and promoting them effectively, these goods will sell very easily.

Everyone knows about "hot" products that attract consumers in droves. When Trivial Pursuit was first offered for sale, when compact disc players were introduced to the Canadian market, when powerful portable computers were developed, and when McCain's introduced frozen pizza, the manufacturers of these products were swamped with orders. They had designed the "right" products—not "me-too" products that simply followed a trend, but ones offering new benefits. Peter Drucker, a leading management thinker, put it this way: "The aim of marketing is to make selling superfluous. The aim is to know and understand customers so well that the product or service fits them and sells itself."[3]

This does not mean that selling and promotion are unimportant, but rather that they are part of a larger "marketing mix," a set of marketing tools that work together to affect the marketplace. We define **marketing** as a social and managerial process by which individuals and groups obtain what they need and want through creating and exchanging products and values with others.[4]

To explain this definition, we will look at the following key terms: needs, wants, demands, products, exchange, transactions, and markets. These concepts are shown in Figure 1-1 and discussed below. As the figure shows, the core marketing concepts are linked, with each concept building on the one before it.

## Needs

The most basic concept underlying marketing is that of human needs. A **human need** is a state of felt deprivation. Humans have many complex needs. They include basic physical needs for food, clothing, warmth, and safety; social needs for belonging and affection; and individual needs for knowledge and self-expression.

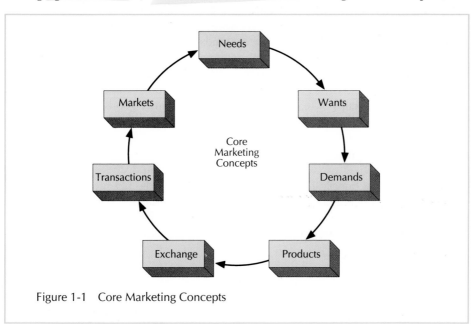

Figure 1-1   Core Marketing Concepts

These needs are not created by marketing, but are a basic part of human makeup.

When a need is not satisfied, a person will do one of two things—look for an object that will satisfy the need or try to reduce the need. People in industrial societies may try to find or develop objects that will satisfy their desires. In developing societies, people may have to focus on meeting basic needs or try to reduce their desires to what is available.

## Wants

A second basic concept in marketing is that of **human wants**—the form taken by human needs as they are shaped by culture and individual personality. A hungry person in Bali may want mangoes, suckling pig, and beans. A hungry person in Canada may want a hamburger, french fries, and a Coke. Wants are described in terms of objects that will satisfy needs. As a society evolves, the wants of its members expand. As people are exposed to more objects that arouse their interest and desire, producers try to provide more want-satisfying products and services.

Sellers often confuse wants and needs. A manufacturer of drill bits may think that the customer needs a drill bit, but what the customer really needs is a hole. These sellers suffer from "marketing myopia."[5] They are so taken with their products that they focus only on existing wants and lose sight of underlying customer needs. They forget that a physical product is only a tool to solve a consumer problem. These sellers have trouble if a new product comes along that serves the need better or more cheaply. The customer with the same need will want the new product.

## Demands

People may have almost unlimited wants but have limited resources. Thus they want to choose products that provide the most satisfaction for their money. When backed by buying power, wants become **demands.**

It is easy to list the demands in a society at a given time. In a single year, 26 million Canadians might purchase 5 billion eggs, 565 million kilograms of chicken, 314 million kilograms of ice cream, 1.6 billion kilograms of fresh fruit, 1 million cars, and 12 billion cups of tea. These and other consumer goods and services lead in turn to a demand for more than 16 million metric tons of steel, 10 million metric tons of newsprint, and many other industrial goods. These are a few of the demands in a $750 billion economy.

Consumers view products as bundles of benefits and choose products that give them the best bundle for their money. Thus a Mazda 323 means basic transportation, a low price, and fuel economy. A Mercedes means comfort, luxury, and status. Given their wants and resources, people choose the product whose benefits add up to the most satisfaction.

## Products

Human needs, wants and demands suggest that there are products available to satisfy them. A **product** is anything that can be offered to a market for attention, acquisition, use, or consumption, that might satisfy a want or need.

Suppose a person feels the need to be more attractive. We will call all the products that can satisfy this need the product choice set. The set may include such products as new clothes, hair styling services, a Caribbean suntan, and exercise classes. These products are not all equally desirable. The more available and less expensive products, such as clothing and a new haircut, are likely to be purchased first. As well, the closer the products come to matching the consumer's wants, the more successful the producer will be. Thus producers must know what consumers want and must provide products that come as close as possible to satisfying those wants.

The concept of product is not limited to physical objects. Anything capable of satisfying a need can be called a product. In addition to goods and services, products include persons, places, organizations, activities, and ideas. A consumer decides which entertainers to watch on television, places to go on a vacation, orga-

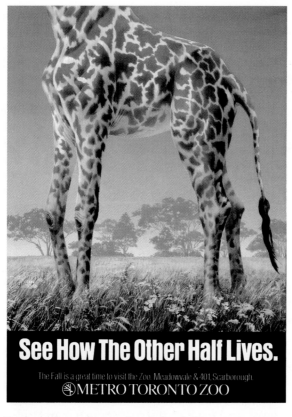

Products do not have to be physical objects. Here the "product" is a trip to the zoo.

nizations to contribute to, and ideas to support. To the consumer, these are all products. If the term product does not seem to fit at times, we can substitute terms such as satisfier, resource, or offer. All describe something of value to someone.

## Exchange

Marketing occurs when people decide to satisfy needs and wants through exchange. **Exchange** is the act of obtaining a desired object from someone by offering something in return. Exchange allows people to concentrate on making things they are good at making and trading them for needed items made by others. The society ends up producing much more than under any other alternative plan.

Exchange is the core concept of marketing.[6] For an exchange to take place, several conditions must be satisfied. Of course, there must be at least two parties, and each must have something of value to the other. Each party must want to deal with the other party and each must be free to accept or reject the other's offer. Finally, the parties must be able to communicate their decisions and to deliver the product or service.[7]

These conditions make exchange possible. Whether exchange actually takes place depends on whether the parties come to an agreement. If they agree, we conclude that the act of exchange leaves each party better off (or at least not worse off) because each was free to reject or accept the offer.

## Transactions

As exchange is the core concept of marketing, a transaction is its unit of measurement. A **transaction** consists of a trade of values between two parties. In a transaction, we must be able to say that A gives X to B and gets Y in return. For example, you pay Eaton's $400 for a television set. This is a classic monetary transaction, but not all transactions involve money. In a barter transaction, you might trade your old refrigerator in return for a neighbor's secondhand television set. A barter transaction can also involve trade between countries (see Marketing Highlight 1-1). A transaction involves at least two things of value—conditions that are agreed to—a time of agreement, and a place of agreement.

In the broadest sense, the marketer tries to bring about a response to some offer. The response may be more than "buying" or "trading" goods and services in the narrow sense. A political candidate wants a response called "votes," a church wants "membership," a social-action group wants "idea acceptance." Marketing consists of actions taken to obtain a desired response from a target audience toward some product, service, idea, or other object.

## Markets

The concept of transactions leads to the concept of a market. A **market** is the set of actual and potential buyers of a product. To understand the nature of a market, imagine a primitive economy with only four people: a fisherman, a hunter, a potter, and a farmer. Figure 1-2 shows three different ways in which these traders could meet their needs. In a self-sufficient economy, they gather the needed goods for themselves. Thus the hunter spends most of the time hunting, but also takes time to fish, make pottery, and farm to obtain the other goods. The hunter is therefore less efficient at hunting, and the same is true of the other three people.

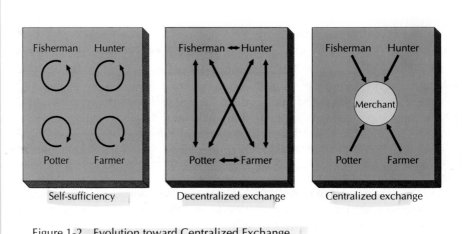

Figure 1-2  Evolution toward Centralized Exchange

# MARKETING HIGHLIGHT 1-1

## A New Form of Barter—Countertrade

In early times, barter was the method used to buy and sell—it involved the exchange of a specified amount of one product, like rice, for a specified amount of another, like fish. Marco Polo was recognized as one of the more famous "barterers," as he traded between countries.

Today, companies interested in selling in international markets may have to engage in a new form of barter, called countertrade. Countertrades are used where the buyer does not have access to a currency that is easily exchanged in international money markets. Typically, underdeveloped and developing countries (like India and Pakistan) and many Eastern European countries (including Russia and Hungary) do not have enough foreign currency available to purchase what they need. Russia, for example, has exchanged vodka for grain.

Countertrade can take several forms, from the simplest form, barter (vodka for grain), to counterpurchase, where the seller agrees to purchase a specified amount of goods for cash, to more sophisticated arrangements that include technology transfers.

Canadian companies wishing to do business with Eastern European and developing countries often engage in countertrade. For example, a Canadian company, Canadian Fracmaster, provides technology products for Siberian oil fields and receives oil from its Russian counterpart, Glavtyumenneftegaz. It is estimated that barter accounts for more than 20% of the annual $88 billion trade between Western nations and the East European nations. Predictions are that countertrade will account for 50% of all world trade by the end of the century.

Countertrade creates some problems for sellers, because they may have to market the products they receive (like vodka). However, firms interested in gaining a greater share of international markets may have to be prepared to return to one of the oldest forms of trade, the barter transaction.

**Sources:** Edward Cundiff and Marge Tharp Hilger, *Marketing in the International Environment*, 2nd ed., Englewood Cliffs, N.J.: Prentice-Hall, 1988, pp. 350-353; J. Alex Murray and Frank Horowitz, "Technology Offsets: Structuring a New Strategy for Industrial Benefits," *International Journal of Technology Management*, Vol. 3, No. 4, 1988, pp. 427-438; Gerhard Maier, "Costs and Benefits of International Barter," *Intereconomics*, May-June 1988, pp. 43-52; and Kenneth W. Banta, "Playing By Old Rules," *Time*, April 30, 1990, pp. 50-51.

In the second economy, decentralized exchange, each person sees the other three as potential "buyers" who make up a market. Thus the hunter may make separate trips to trade goods with the fisherman, the potter, and the farmer to exchange meat for their goods. In the third economy, centralized exchange, a new person called a merchant appears and locates in a central area called a marketplace. Each person brings goods to the merchant and trades for other needed goods. Thus the hunter transacts with one "market" to obtain all the needed goods, rather than with three other persons. Merchants and central marketplaces greatly reduce the total number of transactions needed to accomplish a given volume of exchange.[7]

As the number of people and transactions increases in a society, the number of merchants and marketplaces also increases. In advanced societies, markets need not be physical places where buyers and sellers interact. With modern communications and transportation, a merchant can advertise a product on late evening tele-

Markets bring buyers and sellers together to make transactions.

vision, take orders from hundreds of customers over the phone, and mail the goods to the buyers on the following day without having had any physical contact with the buyers. The development of fax machines allows buyers and sellers readily to communicate written orders and confirmations 24 hours a day.

A market can grow up around a product, a service, or anything else of value. For example, a labor market consists of people who are willing to offer their work in return for wages or products. Various institutions such as employment agencies and job-counselling firms will grow up around a labor market to help it function better. The money market is another important market that emerges to meet the needs of people so that they can borrow, lend, save, and protect money. The donor market emerges to meet the financial needs of nonprofit organizations.

## Marketing

The concept of markets finally brings us full circle to the concept of marketing. Marketing means working with markets to bring about exchanges for the purpose of satisfying human needs and wants. Thus we return to our definition of marketing as a process by which individuals and groups obtain what they need and want by creating and exchanging products and value with others.

Exchange processes involve work. Sellers must search for buyers, identify their needs, design good products, promote them, store and deliver them, and set prices. Such activities as product development, research, communication, distribution, pricing, and service are core marketing activities.

Although we normally think of marketing as being carried on by sellers, buyers also carry on marketing activities. Consumers are "marketing" when they search for the goods they need at prices they can afford. Company purchasing agents are "marketing" when they track down sellers and bargain for good terms. A seller's market is one in which sellers have more power and buyers have to be the more active "marketers." In a buyer's market, buyers have more power and sellers have to be more active "marketers."

In the early 1950s the supply of goods began to grow faster than the demand.

Marketing became identified with sellers trying to find buyers. This book will examine the marketing problems of sellers in a buyer's market.

# MARKETING MANAGEMENT

Those who engage in exchange activities learn over time how to market more effectively. We define **marketing management** as the analysis, planning, implementation, and control of programs designed to create, build, and maintain beneficial exchanges with target buyers for the purpose of achieving organizational objectives.

Demand management: Ontario Hydro presents tips for improving energy efficiency.

Most people think of a marketing manager as someone who finds enough customers for the company's current output. However, this view is too limited. Every organization has a desired level of demand for its products. At any time, there may be no demand, adequate demand, irregular demand, or too much demand. Marketing managers are concerned not only with finding and increasing demand, but also with changing or even reducing it. For example, managers at Ontario Hydro and British Columbia Hydro have developed marketing programs that encourage their customers to use less electricity. For these and other utilities, it is more economical to save energy than to build new generating plants.[8] Marketing management seeks to affect the level, timing, and nature of demand in a way that will help the organization achieve its objectives. Simply put, marketing management is demand management.

Marketing managers are people who are involved in marketing analysis, planning, implementation, and control activities. They include sales managers and salespeople, advertising executives, sales promotion people, marketing researchers, product managers, and pricing specialists. We will discuss these marketing jobs in Chapters 2 and 3.

# Marketing Management Philosophies

We have described marketing management as carrying out tasks to achieve desired exchanges with target markets. What philosophy should guide these marketing efforts? What weight should be given to the interests of the organization, customers, and society? Very often the interests of these groups conflict. Clearly, marketing activities should be carried out under some philosophy.

There are four alternative concepts under which organizations conduct their marketing activities: the production, selling, marketing, and societal marketing concepts.

## The Production Concept

The **production concept** holds that consumers will favor products that are available and highly affordable, and therefore management should focus on improving production and distribution efficiency.

The production concept is a reasonable philosophy in two types of situations. The first is when the demand for a product exceeds supply. Here management should look for ways to increase production.

The second situation is where the product's cost is high, and improved productivity is needed to bring it down. Henry Ford's whole philosophy was to perfect the production of the Model T so that its cost could be brought down and more people could afford it. He joked about offering people a car of any color as long as it was black. Today Texas Instruments (TI) follows this philosophy of increased production and lower costs in order to bring down prices. It won a major share of the hand-calculator market with this philosophy. However, lower prices and greater availability are not a guarantee of success. When TI used the same strategy in the digital watch market, it failed. Although they were priced low, customers did not find TI's watches very attractive. TI again tried the same strategy in the home computer market and lost over $300 million before it abandoned the field. [9]

# The Selling Concept

Many organizations follow the **selling concept,** which holds that consumers will not buy enough of the organization's products unless the organization undertakes a large selling and promotion effort.

The concept is typically practiced with "unsought goods," those that buyers normally do not think of buying, such as insurance, encyclopedias, and funeral plots. These industries must be good at tracking down prospective buyers and selling them on product benefits.

# The Marketing Concept

The **marketing concept** holds that achieving organizational goals depends on determining the needs and wants of target markets and delivering the desired satisfactions more effectively and efficiently than competitors. Surprisingly, this concept is a relatively recent business philosophy although certain marketing activities, like branding, have been practiced for over 100 years.[10] The marketing concept has been stated in colorful ways: "Find a need and fill it"; "Make what you can sell instead of trying to sell what you can make"; "We're not satisfied unless you are"; "Satisfaction guaranteed or your money refunded."

The selling concept and the marketing concept are frequently confused. Figure 1-3 compares the two concepts. The selling concept takes an inside-out perspective. It starts with the factory, focuses on the company's existing products, and calls for heavy selling and promoting to obtain profitable sales. In contrast, the marketing concept takes an outside-in perspective. It starts with the needs and wants of the company's target customers, coordinates all the activities affecting customers and makes profits by creating customer satisfaction. Under the marketing concept companies produce what consumers want, and in this way satisfy consumers and make profits.

Many companies have adopted the marketing concept. Procter & Gamble, IBM, Dylex, and McDonald's follow this concept faithfully (see Marketing Highlight 1-2). We also know that the marketing concept is practiced more among con-

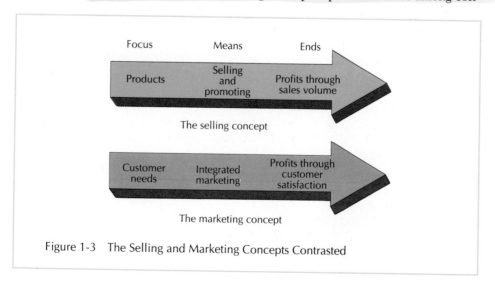

Figure 1-3   The Selling and Marketing Concepts Contrasted

# MARKETING HIGHLIGHT 1-2
## McDonald's Applies the Marketing Concept

McDonald's Corporation, the fast-food hamburger retailer, is a master marketer. In only three decades, McDonald's has served over 70 billion hamburgers to people in Canada and 51 other countries. With over 11,000 outlets, it commands over $16 billion in annual sales and a large share of the fast-food market. Credit for this leading position belongs to a strong marketing orientation. McDonald's knows how to serve people and adapt to changing consumer wants.

Before McDonald's, consumers could get hamburgers in restaurants or diners, but they often encountered poor hamburgers, slow and unfriendly service, unattractive decor, unclean conditions, and a noisy atmosphere. In 1955 Ray Kroc, a 52-year-old salesman of milkshake-mixing machines, became excited about a string of seven restaurants owned by Richard and Maurice McDonald. Kroc liked their fast-food restaurant concept and bought the chain for $2.7 million. Kroc decided to expand the chain by selling franchises to others.

McDonald's' marketing philosophy is captured in the motto of "Q.S.C. & V.," which stands for quality, service, cleanliness, and value. Customers enter a spotlessly clean restaurant, walk up to a friendly counterperson, receive a good-tasting hamburger within five minutes, and eat it there or take it out. There are no jukeboxes or telephones to create a teenage hangout. There are also no cigarette machines or newspaper racks. McDonald's is a family affair, appealing strongly to children.

In Canada, McDonald's opened in June 1967, with a single store in Richmond, British Columbia. George A. Cohon, president of McDonald's Restaurants of Canada Limited, opened a store in London, Ontario in November 1968, to mark entry into the Eastern Canadian market. In the early years, surprisingly, McDonald's lost money in Canada. Then in 1971, George Cohon made a dramatic move. He cut prices at McDonald's by 20% across the board. Sales jumped by 25% and have grown ever since.

As times changed, so did McDonald's. It expanded its sit-down sections, improved decor, launched a breakfast menu, added new food items (including pizza at select locations), and opened new outlets in high-traffic areas. For example, McDonald's was ready for Expo 86 in Vancouver. It had five restaurants on the Expo 86 site, including McBarge—a floating restaurant, and served between 60,000 and 70,000 customers every day. When the Toronto Skydome opened in 1989, McDonald's was there with a series of restaurants to cater to customers in the

The McDonald's motto is "quality, service, cleanliness, and value."

world's first retractable roof stadium. In Canada, McDonald's is a great marketing success story. More than one million Canadians a day visit one of the nearly 500 McDonald's restaurants. The company has 50,000 employees and makes annual purchases of more than 23 million kilograms of beef, 32 million kilograms of potatoes, 26 million dozen buns, and 10 million kilograms of chicken products.

George Cohon also has a unique place in the history of McDonald's—he is responsible for opening the first McDonald's in Moscow. After 14 years of perseverance, Mr. Cohon was present in Moscow in early 1990 when the largest McDonald's in the world (at 2,200 square metres) was opened as a joint venture between McDonald's Restaurants of Canada and Moscow's city council. The opening made headlines around the world. Mr. Cohon expects the restaurant will be the highest grossing McDonald's outlet, serving an average of 15,000 people a day.

McDonald's has mastered the art of serving consumers. It monitors product and service quality through continuous customer surveys, and puts great energy into improving hamburger production methods to simplify operations, bring down costs, and speed up service. McDonald's' focus on consumers has made it the world's largest food service organization.

**Sources:** John F Love and McDonald's Corporation, *McDonald's: Behind the Arches,* Toronto: Bantam Books, 1986; and Wynne Thomas, "Compelling Story of Common Sense Marketing," *Marketing,* November 24, 1986, pp. 11-12; and Gordon Pitts, "The Making of McMoscow," *Financial Post,* January 29, 1990, pp. 13, 16.

sumer goods companies than among industrial goods companies, and more among large companies than small companies. On the other hand, many companies claim they practice the concept, but do not. They have the forms of marketing—such as a marketing vice-president, product managers, marketing plans, marketing research—but not the substance.[11] Several years of hard work are needed to turn a sales-oriented company into a market-oriented company.[12]

Recently, critics have contended that the marketing concept, with its strong adherence to identifying and satisfying the needs and wants of buyers, may stifle product innovation. Two McGill researchers argue that:

> Inventors, scientists, engineers, and academics, in the normal pursuit of scientific knowledge, gave the world the telephone, the phonograph, the electric light, and in more recent times, the laser, xerography, instant photography, and the transistor. In contrast, worshippers of the marketing concept have bestowed upon mankind such products as new-fangled potato chips, feminine hygiene deodorant, and the pet rock.[13]

Market-driven behavior, which focuses entirely on the consumer, may be a factor in the economic decline of North America. Consider the following:

> Deferring to a market-driven strategy without paying attention to its limitations is, quite possibly, opting for customer satisfaction and lower risk in the short run at the expense of superior products in the future. Satisfied customers are crucially important, of course, but not if the strategy for creating them is responsible as well as for unnecessary product proliferation, inflated costs, unfocused diversification, and a lagging commitment to new technology and new capital equipment.[14]

Any business that is solely marketing oriented may be omitting some important dimensions in determining its future directions. For some firms the key to success may depend on technology or production. For example, technology is critical in the computer field. In pulp and paper and in steel, two important Canadian industries, lower production costs have more impact than any marketing techniques that could be used. While the marketing concept is an extremely valuable approach, in some situations other orientations may be more suitable.[15]

## The Societal Marketing Concept

The **societal marketing concept** holds that the organization should determine the needs, wants, and interests of target markets. It should then deliver the desired satisfactions more effectively and efficiently than competitors in a way that maintains or improves the consumer's and the society's well-being. The societal marketing concept is the newest of the marketing management philosophies.

The societal marketing concept questions whether the pure marketing concept is appropriate in an age of environmental problems, resource shortages, rapid population growth, worldwide inflation, and neglected social services.[16] It asks if the firm that senses, serves, and satisfies individual wants is always doing what is best for consumers and society in the long run. According to the societal marketing concept, the pure marketing concept overlooks possible conflicts between short-run consumer wants and long-run consumer welfare.

Consider the Coca-Cola Company. People see it as being a highly responsible corporation producing fine soft drinks that satisfy consumer tastes. Yet consumer and environmental groups have voiced concerns that Coke has little nutritional value, can harm teeth, contains caffeine, and adds to the litter problem with one-way disposable bottles.

Such concerns led to the societal marketing concept. The concept calls upon marketers to balance three considerations in setting their marketing policies. Originally, companies based their marketing decisions largely on short-run company profit. Over time, companies began to recognize the long-run importance of satisfying consumer wants, and introduced the marketing concept. Now they are beginning to think of society's interests when making decisions. Many companies are now considering the environmental impact of their decisions. The societal marketing concept calls for balancing all three considerations—company profits, consumer wants, and society's interests.[17]

# THE GOALS OF THE MARKETING SYSTEM

Marketing affects so many people in so many ways that it often stirs controversy. Some people intensely dislike modern marketing activity, charging it with ruining the environment, bombarding the public with senseless ads, creating unnecessary wants, and teaching greed to youngsters. Consider the following comments on advertising:

> The squandering of resources only begins the problem. The consumption binge which television has done so much to push has been fouling air, water, roads, streets, fields, and forests—a trend we failed or declined to recognize until almost irreversible. It has given us garbage statistics as staggering as our consumption statistics, and closely related to them.[18]

Others vigorously defend marketing and argue that marketing has been largely responsible for the high material standard of living in Canada. It is clear that various social commentators have vastly different views on the meaning and contributions of marketing. The major breakthrough in the last 30 years has been the recognition that sellers must not only take buyers' wants into account but must start with them.

Business is now going through another learning phase and is discovering that it must also take the interests of citizens into account. Marketing, at its highest level of practice, is a balanced serving of the combined interests of sellers, buyers, and citizens. This approach helps to ensure the long-run profitability and survival of businesses in an increasingly competitive and turbulent marketplace.

# THE RAPID ADOPTION OF MARKETING

Most people think that only large companies operating in capitalistic countries use marketing, but marketing actually occurs both inside and outside the business sector in all kinds of countries.

## In the Business Sector

In the business sector, different companies became interested in marketing at different times. A few U.S. companies, such as General Electric, General Motors, Sears, Procter & Gamble, and Coca-Cola, saw marketing's potential almost immediately. Marketing spread most rapidly in consumer packaged goods companies, consumer durables companies, and industrial equipment companies—in that order. The importance of marketing was quickly appreciated by many Canadian firms in these industries because of their close ties with U.S. companies and the similarity of the marketing systems. For example, in a survey of the chief executives of large Canadian companies, marketing experience was considered essential for the top position.[19] Producers of such commodities as steel, chemicals, and paper adopted marketing later, and many still have a long way to go.

Within the past decade consumer service firms, especially airlines and banks, have adopted modern marketing practices. Firms like the Toronto-Dominion Bank are now focusing on how to serve the customer best.[20] Marketing has also attracted the interest of insurance and financial service companies, such as Dominion Securities Pitfield, and they are learning to apply marketing effectively.

The latest business groups to take an interest in marketing are professionals such as lawyers, accountants, physicians, and architects. Until recently, professional associations have not allowed their members to engage in price competition, client solicitation, and advertising. Today accounting firms such as Clarkson Gordon are advertising to small businesses, and firms such as Price Waterhouse are advertising to the energy sector. Lawyers in some provinces are now advertising and competing on price. Dentists are devising new marketing techniques to increase their business, including advertising and accepting payment by credit cards. In Ontario, dentists and doctors are setting up offices in department stores and malls and offering extended hours.[21]

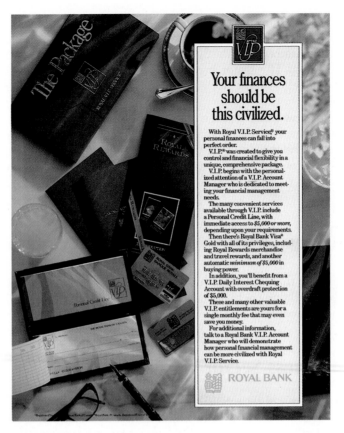

Consumer service firms, such as banks, have enthusiastically adopted marketing.

## In the International Sector

Marketing is practiced not only in North America, but in the rest of the world. In fact, several European and Japanese multinationals—companies like Nestlé, Siemens, Toyota, and Sony—often outperformed their North American competitors. Multinationals have spread modern marketing practices throughout the world. Because of recent and forthcoming events, such as the Free Trade Agreement with the United States, the dramatic changes in Eastern Europe, and the single European Community of 1992, multinationals are becoming more dominant. Marketing management is an important factor in achieving success on an international basis (see Marketing Highlight 1-3). With these changes, marketing is rapidly spreading through countries and organizations throughout the world.

## In the Nonprofit Sector

Marketing is currently attracting the interest of nonprofit organizations such as colleges, hospitals, police departments, museums, and symphony orchestras.[22] Consider the following developments:

# MARKETING HIGHLIGHT 1-3

## Canada's New Markets: The United States and the World

With over one-third of its gross national product in exports and a similar amount in imports, Canada is one of the world's leading trading nations. When the Free Trade Agreement (FTA) was signed with the United States in 1989, Canadian marketers were faced with new opportunities and threats. The major opportunity was access to the richest market in the world, the major threat was competition from U.S. firms within the Canadian market.

Today, Canadian companies can no longer focus on consumers and competitors within Canada. With the FTA and the formation of a single European market in 1992, Canadian companies must be able to compete internationally and many are doing just that. For example:

- Bombardier, the Montreal-based transportation and aerospace firm, now earns 80% of its $1.4 billion in net sales internationally. Laurent Beaudoin, the head of Bombardier, says, "the secret of being able to compete worldwide is to choose your niche, then exploit it by motivating your people through a highly decentralized organization."
- Northern Telecom, the world's fifth-largest equipment maker in telecommunications, sells its products in 70 countries and has a 7.5% share of the world market. Its keys to success include massive research and development spending and marketing teams that take into account local political and cultural factors to win orders. Paul Stern, the president, states that "the global company of the 1990s approaches the world as if it were a single market."
- McCain Foods, an international player in the food market, has 45 plants in eight countries producing such frozen foods as french fries, microwave breakfasts, orange juice, and pizza. Harrison McCain, the president, operates efficient plants and pays attention to what the customer wants. He says that McCain does best by sticking to the marketing of food products that save customers time and money.

**Source:** James Fleming, "Conquering Canadians," *Report on Business Magazine*, January 1990, pp. 30-32.

- Many universities in Canada are operating at a deficit because of declining enrollments and increasing costs. In Ontario, the possibility of closing smaller universities has been discussed for over a decade.
- Many cultural performance groups cannot attract large enough audiences. Even those that have seasonal ticket sellouts, such as the Winnipeg Symphony Orchestra, face huge operating deficits at the end of the year.
- Many nonprofit organizations that flourished in the earlier years of the century— the YMCA, Salvation Army, and Girl Guides—are re-examining their mission in an effort to reverse a decline in membership.

These organizations have marketplace problems. Their administrators are struggling to keep them alive in the face of changing consumer attitudes and reduced financial resources. Many such institutions have turned to marketing as a possible answer to their problems.

Governments are also showing an increasing interest in marketing. Canada Post has developed a number of marketing plans for its operations, and the federal government is the largest advertiser in Canada. Both federal and provincial gov-

# A child's *mind* is an *open* book.

As a parent, it is your responsibility to fill the pages of a child's mind with wonder and joy. Reading together is a delightful way of accomp-

lishing this and a means of ensuring that your child's future remains an open book.

Prepare a young mind for tomorrow. Open a book today.

**ABCANADA**

THE NETWORK TO PROMOTE LITERACY IN CANADA

Non-profit organizations have turned to marketing to promote their causes and to inform the public.

ernment agencies are involved in marketing energy conservation, anti-smoking, and other public causes. Other organizations, such as Crown corporations and marketing boards, are using marketing to solve some of their problems.

## PLAN OF THE BOOK

The following chapters will expand on the marketing topics introduced in this chapter. Chapter 2 discusses strategic planning and the marketing management process. Chapter 3 looks at how marketing strategies and programs are planned, implemented, and controlled by people in the organization's marketing department.

Chapters 4 and 5 look at the ways marketers seek attractive opportunities in the marketing environment. In Chapter 4 we discuss the importance of marketing research and information in preparing company and marketing plans, and in analyzing the marketing environment. Chapter 5 describes the actors and forces in the rapidly changing marketing environment.

Chapters 6, 7, and 8 examine the key characteristics of the company's markets. Chapter 6 examines consumer markets; Chapter 7 looks at organizational markets. Chapter 8 describes the art of selecting appropriate markets. The marketer first segments the market, then selects target segments and positions the company's products in chosen segments.

Chapters 9 through 17 look at the major marketing activities of the firm—designing, pricing, placing, and promoting products and services. In these chapters we will look at the various concepts that guide marketing managers and at the techniques they use to develop attractive offers and market them successfully.

The final three chapters look at topics of current interest. Chapter 18 discusses international marketing; Chapter 19 discusses services and nonprofit marketing. Chapter 20, "Marketing and Society," returns us to the basic question of marketing's role and purpose in society, its contributions, and its shortcomings.

The book ends with an appendix that presents the marketing arithmetic used by marketing managers when making many decisions.

# Summary

Marketing touches everyone's life. It is the means by which a standard of living is developed and made available to people. Many people confuse marketing with selling, but marketing occurs long before and after the selling event. Marketing actually combines many activities such as marketing research, product development, distribution, pricing, advertising, and personal selling. These activities are designed to sense, serve, and satisfy consumer needs while meeting the organization's goals.

Marketing is directed at satisfying needs and wants through exchange processes. The key concepts of marketing are needs, wants, demands, products, exchange, transactions, and markets. Marketing management is the analysis, planning, implementation, and control of programs designed to create, build, and maintain beneficial exchanges with target markets for the purpose of achieving organizational objectives. Marketers must be good at managing the level of demand, since actual demand can be different from what the organization wants.

Marketing management can be conducted under four different marketing philosophies. The production concept holds that consumers will favor products that are available at low cost, and therefore management's task is to improve production efficiency and bring down prices. The selling concept holds that consumers will not buy enough of the company's products unless they are stimulated through heavy selling and promotion. The marketing concept holds that a company should research the needs and wants of a well-defined target market and deliver the desired satisfactions. The societal marketing concept holds that the company should generate customer satisfaction and long- run societal well-being as the key to achieving organizational goals.

Interest in marketing is growing as more organizations in the business sector, in the international sector, and in the nonprofit sector recognize how marketing can improve performance.

# QUESTIONS FOR DISCUSSION

1. Why should you study marketing?

2. *In Search of Excellence* describes the marketing principles of many top companies. How can you apply these principles to market yourself and improve your chances of landing the job you want after graduation?

3. Economist John Kenneth Galbraith argues that the desires stimulated by marketing activities are not "genuine": "A man who is hungry need never be told of his need for food." Do you agree with this criticism? Why or why not?

4. Describe how the notions of products, exchanges, and transactions apply when you buy a soft drink from a vending machine. Do they also apply when you vote for a political candidate?

5. Many people dislike or fear some products and would not "demand" them at any price. For example, how might a health-care marketer manage the negative demand for such products as mammograms?

6. Identify organizations in your town that practice the production concept, and the selling concept. How could these organizations become more marketing-oriented?

7. The headline for an ad reads, "We don't just talk—we listen. That's what makes us a leader." In what ways can companies "listen" to consumers? How does this help them practice the marketing concept?

8. According to economist Milton Friedman, "Few trends could so thoroughly undermine the very foundations of our free society as the acceptance by corporate officials of a social responsibility other than to make as much money for their stockholders as possible." Do you agree or disagree? What are some drawbacks of the societal marketing concept?

9. Virtually all cigarette advertising is banned in Canada. Does this ban conflict with the goals of our marketing system? Does your answer depend on which goal you think appropriate for our society?

10. Why have many nonprofit organizations adopted marketing techniques in recent years? For example, how does your school market itself to attract new students?

# KEY TERMS

**Demands** Human wants that are backed by buying power.

**Exchange** The act of obtaining a desired object from someone by offering something in return.

**Human need** A state of felt deprivation in a person.

**Human want** The form taken by a human need as it is shaped by culture and individual personality.

**Market** The set of actual and potential buyers of a product.

**Marketing**  A social and managerial process by which individuals and groups obtain what they need and want through creating and exchanging products and value with others.

**Marketing concept**  The philosophy that achieving organizational goals depends on determining the needs and wants of target markets and delivering the desired satisfactions more effectively and efficiently than competitors.

**Marketing management**  The analysis, planning, implementation, and control of programs designed to create, build, and maintain beneficial exchanges with target buyers for the purpose of achieving organizational objectives.

**Product**  Anything that can be offered to a market for attention, acquisition, use, or consumption, that might satisfy a need or want.

**Production concept**  The philosophy that consumers will favor products that are available and highly affordable, and therefore management should focus on improving production and distribution efficiency.

**Selling concept**  The idea that consumers will not buy enough of the organization's products unless the organization undertakes a large selling and promotion effort.

**Societal marketing concept**  The idea that the organization should determine the needs, wants, and interests of target markets and deliver the desired satisfactions more effectively and efficiently than competitors in a way that maintains or improves the consumer's and society's well-being.

**Transaction**  A trade between two parties that involves at least two things of value —agreed-upon conditions—a time of agreement, and a place of agreement.

# REFERENCES

1. Thomas J. Peters and Robert H. Waterman, Jr., *In Search of Excellence: Lessons from America's Best-Run Companies* (New York: Harper & Row, 1982).

2. Thomas J. Peters and Nancy Austin, *A Passion for Excellence: The Leadership Difference* (New York: Random House, 1985).

3. Peter F. Drucker, *Management: Tasks, Responsibilities, Practices* (New York: Harper & Row, 1973), pp. 64-65.

4. Here are some other definitions: "Marketing is the performance of business activities that direct the flow of goods and services from producer to customer or user." "Marketing is getting the right goods and services to the right people at the right place at the right time at the right price with the right communication and promotion." "Marketing is the creation and delivery of a standard of living." For further definitions, see Ernest F. Cooke, C.L. Abercrombie, and J. Michael Rayburn, "Problems with the AMA's New Definition of Marketing Offer Opportunity to Develop an Even Better Definition," *Marketing Educator*, Spring 1986, pp. 1, 5.

5. See Theodore Levitt's classic article, "Marketing Myopia," *Harvard Business Review*, July-August 1960, pp. 45-56.

6. For more discussion on marketing as an exchange process, see Franklin S. Houston and Jule B. Gassenheimer, "Marketing and Exchange," *Journal of Marketing*, October 1987, pp. 3-18.

7. The number of transactions in a decentralized exchange system is given by $N(N-1)/2$. With four persons, this means $4(4-1)/2=6$ transactions. In a centralized exchange system, the number of transactions is given by N, here 4. Thus, a centralized exchange system reduces the number of transactions needed for exchange.

8. Craig McInnes, "Utilities Expect Profit From Conservation Push," *The Globe and Mail*, February 5, 1990, p. A4.

9. "Texas Instruments Shows U.S. Business How to Survive in the 1980s," *Business Week*, September 18, 1978, pp. 66ff; and "The Long-Term Damage from TI's Bombshell," *Business Week*, June 15, 1981, p. 36; and "Texas Instruments Cleans Up Its Act," *Business Week*, September 19, 1983, pp. 56-64.

10. For an interesting historical perspective on the evolution of marketing, see Ronald A. Fullerton, "How Modern is Modern Marketing? Marketing's Evolution and the Myth of the 'Production Era,'" *Journal of Marketing*, January 1988, pp. 108-125. For further information on the history of marketing thought see D.G. Brian Jones and David D. Monieson, "Early Development of the Philosophy of Marketing Thought," *Journal of Marketing*, January 1990, pp. 102-103.

11. Peter M. Banting and Randolph E. Ross, "The Marketing Masquerade," *Business Quarterly*, Spring 1974, pp. 19-27.

12. For more on the marketing concept, see Franklin S. Houston, "The Marketing Concept: What It Is and What It Is Not," *Journal of Marketing*, April 1986, pp. 81-87; Steven H. Star, "Marketing and Its Discontents," *Harvard Business Review*, November-December 1989, pp. 148-154; and Ajay K. Kohlie and Bernard J. Jaworski, "Market Orientation: The Construct, Research Propositions, and Managerial Implications," *Journal of Marketing*, April 1990, pp. 1-18.

13. Roger C. Bennett and Robert G. Cooper, "Beyond the Marketing Concept," *Business Horizons*, June 1979, p. 76.

14. Robert H. Hayes and William J. Abernathy, "Managing Our Way to Economic Decline," *Harvard Business Review*, July-August 1980, pp. 67-77.

15. Bennett and Cooper, "Beyond the Marketing Concept," p. 81.

16. Laurence P. Feldman, "Societal Adaptation: A New Challenge for Marketing," *Journal of Marketing*, July 1971, pp. 54-60; Martin L. Bell and C. William Emery, "The Faltering Marketing Concept," *Journal of Marketing*, October 1971, pp. 37-42; and Donald P. Robin and R. Eric Reidenbach, "Social Responsibility, Ethics, and Marketing Strategy: Closing the Gap Between Concept and Application," *Journal of Marketing*, January 1987, pp. 44-48.

17. Russell Abatt and Diane Sacks, "The Marketing Challenge: Toward Being Profitable and Socially Responsible," *Journal of Business Ethics*, July 1988, pp. 497-507.

18. Quotation appearing in Richard W. Pollay, "The Distorted Mirror: Reflections on the Unintended Consequences of Advertising," *Journal of Marketing*, April 1986, pp. 18-36.

19. Bruce Gates, "Marketing Skills Key in Quest For CEO's," *The Financial Post*, February 26, 1986, p. 24.

20. Jacquie McNish, "Dick Thomson's Born-Again Bankers," *Report on Business Magazine*, October 1989, pp. 51-60.

21. Robert MacKay, "The Dentists' New Marketing Push," *Financial Times*, November 24, 1980, pp. 19, 24; Kirk Makin, "Got Legal Woes? Hire Crazy Joe's," *Globe and Mail*, December 30, 1986, p. B1; and Joan Breckenridge, "Chain Offers Walk-in Legal Centres," *Globe and Mail*, November 12, 1986, p. B1; and Marina Strauss, "While You're Shopping, Go in for a Medical Too," *Globe and Mail*, March 2, 1987, p. B1, 12; and Stan Sutter, "Professionals Win Right to Advertise," *Marketing*, July 9, 1990, p. 2.

22. For a review of nonprofit marketing, see Christopher H. Lovelock and Charles B. Weinberg, "Public and Nonprofit Marketing Comes of Age," in *Review of Marketing*, 1978, eds. Gerald Zaltman and Thomas V. Bonoma (Chicago: American Marketing Association, 1978); and Philip Kotler and Alan R. Andreasen, *Strategic Marketing for Nonprofit Organizations* (Englewood Cliffs, N.J.: Prentice-Hall, 1987).

# CHAPTER 2

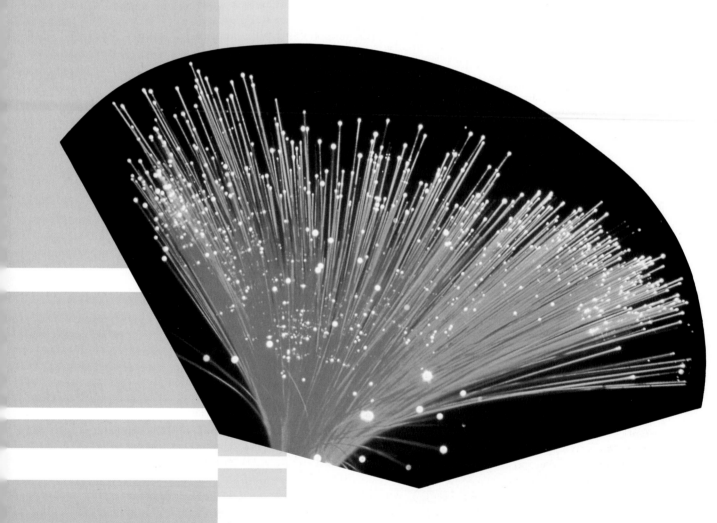

# Strategic Planning and the Marketing Management Process

## CHAPTER OBJECTIVES

After reading this chapter, you should be able to:
1. Explain company-wide strategic planning and its four steps.
2. Describe how companies develop mission statements and objectives.
3. Explain how companies evaluate and develop their "business portfolios."
4. Explain marketing's role in strategic planning.
5. Describe the marketing management process and the forces that influence it.

Northern Telecom, one of Canada's largest firms, has a new mission—to become the world's leading telecommunications equipment supplier by the end of the century. To accomplish that mission it has set company goals that include capturing ten percent of the global market, which translates into a growth rate of 15% per year. With sales in 1989 of over $7 billion, it will need sales of over $30 billion annually by the year 2000 to achieve the ten percent share.

Northern Telecom competes in a rapidly changing market where research and development is critical. Developing new products that merge the transmission of digitized data, voice, and picture signals through the use of fiber optics and microchips is not for the faint of heart. Ten years ago, 30 major telecommunication equipment manufacturers existed. Today 15 are in business (Northern Telecom is the fifth largest), and in ten years experts predict that there will be five globe-spanning giants. Northern Telecom's major competitors include firms from the United States, Japan, France, Sweden, and West Germany.

Northern Telecom's long-range plan includes transforming the company from a multinational company to a global corporation. As the president, Paul Stern, says: "We have no choice but to globalize. Our competitors are global and our best prospects for growth are global." This philosophy is reinforced by David Vice, vice-chairman of products and technology, who notes: "Even if you're a domestic company operating in a small market, if you are not thinking globally, somebody in France or Japan is thinking about increasing their activity in your market. You're going to have to face them at home, so you might as well face them elsewhere too."

Some of the growth strategies Northern Telecom has developed to achieve its long-term objectives include:

- **Product development**. Northern Telecom spends over $750 million in research and development each year. It recently announced a new group of products, under the umbrella of FiberWorld, which it hopes will allow the company to gain a greater share of the global market.
- **Market penetration.** A dominant player in the North American market, Northern Telecom plans to increase its share by maintaining its low cost position and superior research and development.
- **Market development.** Major efforts are underway to develop more foreign markets. Activities include joint developments with the Chinese and central office switch sales in the United Kingdom, the Caribbean, and Australia. Northern Telecom was the first foreign company to sell telecommunications equipment in Japan with

its 1986 sale of about $300 million in equipment to Nippon Telephone and Telegraph Corporation. Part of Northern Telecom's market development plan is to target niches in major markets around the world where it can be the major supplier.

Northern Telecom is also attempting to achieve greater cooperation and coordination between research and development, manufacturing, and marketing. While research and development are still central to the company, some projects put marketing people on equal footing with their counterparts in research and development and manufacturing. Northern Telecom did this in developing the Norstar office phone, which was launched in 1988. The product is now one of the top five phones in North America in terms of sales, and is exported to 24 countries.

Northern Telecom faces a formidable challenge, but it is one the company's executives feel they can meet. Through strategic planning and the development of growth strategies, top management has set a course of action to take one of Canada's largest companies into the next century.[1]

All companies must look ahead and develop long-term strategies to meet the changing conditions in their industries. No one strategy is best for all companies. Each company must find the game plan that makes the most sense given its situation, opportunities, objectives, and resources. The hard task of selecting an overall company strategy for long-run survival and growth is called strategic planning.

Marketing plays an important role in strategic planning. It provides information and other inputs to help prepare the strategic plan. In turn, strategic planning defines marketing's role in the organization. Guided by the strategic plan, marketing works with other departments in the organization to help achieve overall strategic objectives.

In this chapter, we will look first at the organization's overall strategic planning. Next we will discuss marketing's role in the organization as defined by the overall strategic plan. Then we will look at the marketing management process—the process that marketers undertake to carry out their role in the organization.

# Overview of Planning

## Benefits of Planning

Many companies operate without formal plans. In new companies, managers are so busy they have no time for planning. In mature companies, many managers argue that they have done well without formal planning and therefore planning cannot be too important. They resist taking the time to prepare a written plan. They argue that the marketplace changes too fast for a plan to be useful—it would end up collecting dust.

Yet formal planning can yield a number of benefits. It encourages management to think ahead systematically and improves coordination of company efforts. It forces the company to sharpen its objectives and policies and provides clearer performance standards for control. The argument that planning is less useful in a fast-changing environment makes little sense. In fact, the opposite is true: Sound planning helps the company to anticipate and respond quickly to environmental changes and to better prepare for sudden developments.

## Kinds of Plans

Companies usually prepare annual plans, long-range plans, and strategic plans. The annual plan describes the current marketing situation, company objectives, the marketing strategy for the year, action program, budgets, and controls. Top management approves this plan and uses it to coordinate marketing activities with production, finance, and other areas of the company.

The long-range plan describes the major factors and forces affecting the organization over the next several years. It includes long-term objectives, the major marketing strategies that will be used to attain them, and the resources required. This long-range plan is reviewed and updated each year so that the company always has a current long-range plan.

The company's annual and long-range plans deal with current businesses and how to keep them going. Management must also plan which businesses the company should stay in or drop and which new ones it should pursue. The environment is full of surprises, and management must design the company to withstand shocks. Strategic planning enables the firm to take advantage of opportunities by adapting to its constantly changing environment.

# Strategic Planning

Strategic planning sets the stage for the rest of the planning in the firm. We define **strategic planning** as the process of developing and maintaining a strategic fit between the organization's goals and capabilities and its changing marketing opportunities. It relies on developing a clear company mission, supporting objectives, a sound business portfolio, and coordinated functional strategies.

The steps in the strategic planning process are shown in Figure 2-1. At the

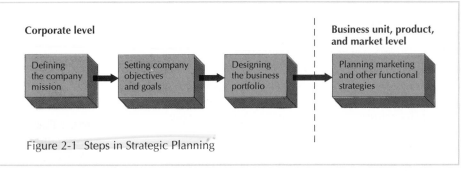

Figure 2-1 Steps in Strategic Planning

corporate level, the company first defines its overall purpose and mission. This mission is then turned into detailed supporting objectives that guide the whole company. Next, headquarters decides what portfolio of businesses and products is best for the company, and how much support to give each one. Each business and product unit must in turn develop detailed marketing and other departmental plans that support the company-wide plan. Thus, marketing planning occurs at the business-unit, product, and market levels. It supports company strategic planning with more detailed planning for specific marketing opportunities. We discuss each of the strategic planning steps in more detail below.

# Defining the Company Mission

An organization exists to accomplish something. At first it has a clear purpose or mission, but over time its mission may become unclear as the organization grows and adds new products and markets. Or the mission may remain clear, but some managers may no longer be committed to it. Or the mission may remain clear, but may no longer be the best choice given new conditions in the environment.

When management senses that the organization is drifting, it must renew its search for purpose. It is time to ask: What is our business? Who is the customer? What do consumers value? What will our business be? What should our business be? These simple-sounding questions are among the most difficult the company will ever have to answer. Successful companies continually raise these questions and answer them carefully and fully.

Many organizations develop formal mission statements that answer these questions. A **mission statement** is a statement of the organization's purpose—what it wants to accomplish in the larger environment. A clear mission statement acts as an "invisible hand" that guides people in the organization so that they can work independently and yet collectively toward overall organizational goals.

Companies traditionally defined their business in product terms, such as "We manufacture furniture," or in technological terms, such as "We are a chemical-processing firm." But market definitions of a business are better than product or technological definitions. Products and technologies eventually become outdated, but basic market needs may last forever. A market-oriented mission statement defines the business in terms of satisfying basic customer needs. Thus, Bell Canada is in the communication business, not the telephone business. Visa defines its business not as credit cards, but as allowing customers to exchange value—to exchange such assets as cash or deposit for virtually anything, anywhere in the world. Canadian Tire's mission is not to run retail stores but to provide a range of products and services that deliver value and convenience to consumers.

Management should avoid making its mission too narrow or too broad. A lead pencil manufacturer that says it is in the communication equipment business

Royal Bank Visa expresses its mission by emphasizing the privileges and conveniences offered by its Gold Card.

is stating its mission too broadly. Mission statements should be specific and realistic. Many mission statements are written for public relations purposes and lack specific, workable guidelines. The statement "We want to be the leading company in this industry producing the highest-quality products with the best service at the lowest prices" sounds good but it will not help the company make tough decisions.[2]

## Setting Company Objectives and Goals

The company's mission needs to be turned into detailed supporting objectives for each level of management. Each manager should have objectives and be responsible for reaching them.

For example, a major objective may be "to improve profits." Profits can be improved by increasing sales or reducing costs. Sales can be increased by increasing the company's share of the Canadian market and entering new foreign markets. These become the company's current marketing objectives.

Marketing strategies must be developed to support these marketing objectives. To increase its Canadian market share, the company could increase the product's availability and its promotion efforts. To enter new foreign markets, the company could cut prices. These are the broad marketing strategies.

Each marketing strategy should be spelled out in greater detail. For example, increasing the promotion will call for more salespeople and advertising, both of which will have to be carefully planned. In this way the firm's mission is translated into a set of objectives for the current period. The objectives should be as specific as possible. The objective to "increase our market share" is not as useful as to "increase our market share to 15% by the end of the second year."

## Designing the Business Portfolio

Guided by the company's mission statement and objectives, management must now plan its business portfolio. A company's **business portfolio** is the collection of businesses and products that make up the company. The best business portfolio carefully matches the company's strengths and weaknesses with opportunities in the environment. The company must (1) analyze its current business portfolio and decide which businesses should receive more or less investment, and (2) develop growth strategies for adding new products or businesses to the portfolio.

## Analyzing the Current Business Portfolio

The major tool in strategic planning is business portfolio analysis, whereby management evaluates the businesses that make up the company. The company will want to put strong resources into its more profitable businesses and phase down or drop its weaker business. It can keep its portfolio of businesses up to date by strengthening or adding growing businesses and withdrawing from declining businesses. For example, Bombardier withdrew from the locomotive and diesel engine business to concentrate its activities in other areas such as aerospace transportation.[3] Similarly, John Labatt disposed of its Catelli line of retail grocery products and its Chateau-Gai wine products to pursue more promising growth opportunities.[4]

Management's first step is to identify the key businesses making up the company. These can be called its strategic business units. A **strategic business unit (SBU)** is a unit of the company which has a separate mission and objectives, and which can be planned independently from other company businesses. An SBU can be a company division, a product line within a division, or sometimes a single product or brand. Identifying SBUs can be very difficult. In a large corporation, should SBUs be defined at the level of companies, divisions, product lines, or brands? Thus, defining basic business units for portfolio analysis is often a complex task.

The next step in business portfolio analysis calls for management to assess the attractiveness of its various SBUs and decide how much support each deserves. In some companies, this is done informally. Management looks at the company's collection of businesses or products and judges how much each SBU should contribute and receive. Other companies use formal portfolio planning methods.

The purpose of strategic planning is to find ways in which the company can best use its strengths to take advantage of attractive opportunities in the environment. Most standard portfolio analysis methods evaluate SBUs on two important dimensions—the attractiveness of the SBU's market or industry, and the strength of the SBU's position in that market or industry. The best-known of these portfolio planning methods was developed by the Boston Consulting Group, a leading management consulting firm.[5]

Using the Boston Consulting Group (BCG) approach, a company classifies all its SBUs in the growth-share matrix shown in Figure 2-2. On the vertical axis, market growth rate provides a measure of market attractiveness. On the horizontal axis, market share serves as a measure of company strength in the market. By dividing the growth-share matrix in the way indicated, four types of SBUs can be distinguished.

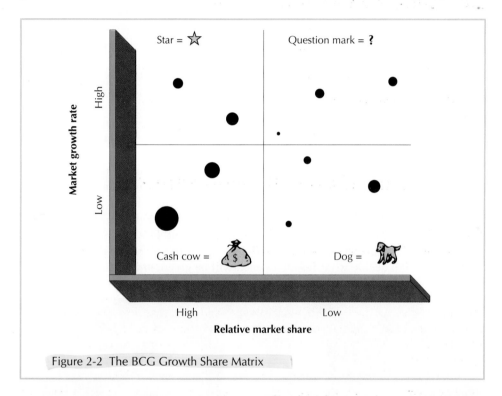

Figure 2-2 The BCG Growth Share Matrix

- **Stars**. Stars are high-growth, high-share businesses or products. They often need heavy investment to finance their rapid growth. Eventually their growth will slow down, and they will turn into cash cows.
- **Cash cows**. Cash cows are low-growth, high-share businesses or products. These established and successful SBUs need less investment to hold their market share. Thus they produce a lot of cash that the company uses to pay its bills and support other SBUs that need investment.
- **Question marks**. Question marks are low-share business units in high-growth markets. They require a lot of cash to hold their share, let alone increase it. Management has to think hard about which question marks it should try to build into stars and which should be phased out.
- **Dogs**. Dogs are low-growth, low-share businesses and products. They may generate enough cash to maintain themselves, but do not promise to be a large source of cash.

The ten circles in the growth-share matrix represent a company's ten current SBUs. The company has two stars, two cash cows, three question marks, and three dogs. The areas of each circle are proportional to the SBU's dollar sales. This company is in fair shape, although not in good shape. Fortunately, it has two good-sized cash cows whose income helps finance the company's question marks, stars, and dogs. The company should take some decisive action concerning its dogs and its question marks. The picture would be worse if the company had no stars, too many dogs, or only one weak cash cow.

Once it has classified its SBUs, the company must determine what role each will play in the future. One of four strategies can be pursued for each SBU. The company could invest more in the business unit in order to build its share. Second, it could invest just enough to hold the SBU's share at the current level. Third, it could harvest the SBU, increasing its short-term cash flow regardless of the long-term effect. Finally, the company could divest the SBU by selling it or phasing it out and using the resources elsewhere.

As time passes, SBUs change their position in the growth-share matrix. Each SBU has a life. Many SBUs start out as question marks, and move into the star category if they succeed. They later become cash cows as market growth falls, then finally turn into dogs toward the end of their life cycle. The company needs to add new products and units continually so that some of them will become stars and eventually cash cows to help finance the other SBUs.

The BCG and other formal methods that were developed in the 1970s revolutionized strategic planning.[6] However, such approaches have limitations. They can be difficult, time-consuming, and costly to implement. Management may find it difficult to define SBUs and measure market share and growth. In addition, these approaches focus on classifying current businesses, but provide little advice for future planning. Management must still use judgment to set the business objectives for each SBU, to decide what resources each will be given, and to figure out which new businesses should be added.

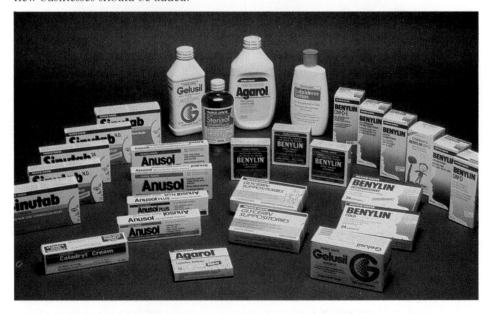

Formal approaches can also lead the company to place too much emphasis on market-share growth or growth through entry into attractive new markets. Using these approaches, many companies plunged into unrelated and new high-growth businesses that they did not know how to manage—with bad results. At the same time, they were often too quick to abandon, sell, or milk to death their healthy, mature businesses.

Some companies have dropped these formal methods to use more customized strategic planning approaches better suited to their situations. Most large Canadian companies use some form of strategic planning analysis.[7] Such analysis will not entirely solve the problem of finding the best strategy. But it can help management to better understand the company's overall situation, to see how each business or product contributes, to better assign resources to its businesses, and to better orient the company for future success. When used properly, strategic planning is just one important aspect of overall strategic management, a way of thinking about how to manage a business.[8]

# Developing Growth Strategies

Beyond evaluating current businesses, designing the business portfolio involves finding future businesses and products the company should consider. One useful device for identifying growth opportunities is the product/market expansion grid.[9] This grid is shown in Figure 2-3. We will apply it to a well-known company, Warner-Lambert Canada:

> Warner-Lambert Canada, the largest subsidiary of the U.S. firm Warner- Lambert, manufactures health care and consumer products. The company has annual sales in Canada of over $250 million. Warner-Lambert Canada operates three divisions, each manufacturing several products: Parke-Davis Consumer Health Group (health and beauty aids including Listerine mouthwash, Schick blades, and Bromo Seltzer); Adams Brand (confectionery products including Chiclets, Clorets, Rolaids, Halls, Dentyne, and Trident); and Parke-Davis Professional Health Group (ethical health care products including Lopid, Eryc, and Procan).

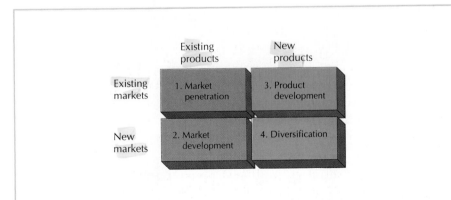

Figure 2-3 Market Opportunity Identification through the Product/Market Expansion Grid

## Market Penetration

First, Warner-Lambert Canada (WLC) management considers whether the company's major brands can achieve deeper **market penetration**—by increasing sales to present customers without changing the products in any way. For example, to increase Listerine sales, the company might cut prices, increase advertising, get Listerine into more stores, or obtain better shelf positions for Listerine. Basically, management would like to increase usage by current customers and attract customers of other brands to Listerine. WLC has been quite successful with market penetration as its Adams Brand group has at least a 50% share in each of four major categories—chewing gum, rolled candy, cough drops, and antacid tablets.

## Market Development

Second, WLC management considers possibilities for **market development**—identifying and developing new markets for current products.

For example, managers at WLC review demographic markets—infants, preschoolers, teenagers, young adults, senior citizens—to see if any of these groups can be encouraged to buy or buy more of its mouthwash. The managers look at institutional markets, such as hotels, airlines, and hospitals, to see if sales to these buyers can be increased. The managers also review geographical markets to see if these markets can be developed. All these are market development strategies.

Another company that has been quite successful with market penetration and other growth strategies is McCain (see Marketing Highlight 2-1).

Jell-O seeks further market penetration by suggesting a playful new approach to its product, and offering a mail-in premium.

# MARKETING HIGHLIGHT 2-1

## McCain - A World Leader Through Growth Strategies

In 1957, the McCain brothers, Harrison and Wallace, began manufacturing frozen french fries in a small plant in Florence, New Brunswick. Sales in the first year at $152,000, were modest—the french fries were sold as unbranded commodities to institutional buyers like restaurants and school cafeterias. Today, McCain Foods is the world's largest french fry processor with sales of over $2 billion, more than 40 factories around the world, and over 12,000 employees. Sales have doubled in the past five years. McCain's produces over one million kilograms of potato products every hour, along with a diverse assortment of frozen dinners, desserts, juice, fish, vegetables, and pizza. The story of how the McCain brothers achieved their success is a good example of growth strategies in action.

In the mid 1960s the McCain brothers were selling unbranded frozen french fries and vegetables to the food-services market in Eastern Canada and Britain. Eventually they decided to establish their own brand name and sell to the consumer market. By 1970 they had $40 million in sales, primarily in branded products. Over half of their sales were in Britain where they had set up a processing plant and their own sales force. As the concept of frozen french fries was new to Britain, McCains created a market for its own product (an example of market development).

An interesting aside is that while the McCains were active in the British market they had yet to penetrate Western Canada. In terms of distance, New Brunswick is closer to London, England (about 5,500 kilometres) than to Vancouver (over 6,000 kilometres).

As the years went by the McCains developed more international markets by first exporting, then setting up a local marketing and sales force team to push the brand and build volumes (market development), then constructing or acquiring a modern plant to become the dominant, low cost producer (market penetration). The McCains built a number of markets using french fries first, then growing through product development. After their french fries gain a firm hold, the McCains market the rest of their products, which include frozen green vegetables, frozen pizzas, frozen entrees, and frozen desserts, by piggybacking them on top of their high-volume french fries.

Now the company generates about 25% of its sales in Canada, 20% in the U.S., 40% in Western Europe, and about 15% in the rest of the world, including Australia. It controls over 50% of the frozen food market in Britain, holds a large share in France, and is gaining ground in Italy and Spain. Its branded french fries (called 1-2-3 in Europe and Oven Chips in Britain) are the leading brand in many countries in Western Europe.

The McCains foresee some opportunities for development when the European market becomes a single community in 1992, including unifying packaging and consolidating production. As well, they are keeping a close eye on Eastern Europe where new markets may open up. They sent a small team to Moscow to help McDonald's set up french fry processing for its fast-food outlets. Whatever the future holds, the McCains are likely to be increasing sales and profits through the growth strategies of market penetration, market development, and product development.

**Source:** Gordon Pitts, "McCain: Chip Wagon To The World," *Financial Post*, January 15, 1990, pp. 9, 14.

McCain consistency is worth its weight in gold.

McCain has entered foreign markets by introducing their french fries, then expanding to other products.

# Product Development

Third, the management considers **product development**—offering modified or new products to current markets. Listerine mouthwash could be offered in new sizes, or with new ingredients, or in new packaging, all representing possible product modifications. WLC could also launch new brands to appeal to different users, or it could launch other products that its current customers might buy. In fact, WLC launched a new brand of mouthwash, Listermint, and then modified the branch and relaunched it as Listermint, with Fluoride. These are product development strategies.

# Diversification

Fourth, WLC could consider **diversification**. It could start up or buy businesses entirely outside of its current products and markets. For example, the company could enter such "hot" industries as fitness equipment and health foods. Some companies try to identify the most attractive emerging industries. They feel that half the secret of success is to enter attractive industries instead of trying to be efficient in an unattractive industry.

# Planning Functional Strategies

The company's strategic plan establishes what kinds of businesses the company will be in and the company's objectives for each. Then, within each business unit, more detailed planning must take place. Each functional department—marketing, finance, accounting, purchasing, manufacturing, personnel, and others—plays an important role in the strategic-planning process. First, each department provides information for strategic planning. Then, management in each business unit prepares a plan that states the role that each department will play. The plan shows how all the functional areas will work together to accomplish strategic objectives.

Each functional department deals with different publics to obtain inputs the business needs, such as cash, labor, raw materials, research ideas, and manufacturing processes. For example, marketing brings in revenues by negotiating exchanges with consumers. Finance arranges exchanges with lenders and stockholders to obtain cash. The marketing and finance departments must therefore work together to obtain needed funds for the business. Similarly, the personnel department supplies labor, and purchasing obtains materials needed for operations and manufacturing.

# Marketing's Role in Strategic Planning

There is considerable overlap between overall company strategy and marketing strategy. Marketing looks at consumer needs and the company's ability to satisfy them; these same factors guide the company's mission and objectives. As most company strategy planning deals with marketing variables such as market share, market development, and growth, it is sometimes hard to separate strategic planning from marketing planning. In fact, in some companies, strategic planning is called "strategic marketing planning."

Marketing plays a key role in the company's strategic planning in several ways. First, marketing provides a guiding philosophy— company strategy should revolve around serving the needs of important consumer groups. Second, marketing provides inputs to strategic planners by helping to identify attractive market opportunities and to assess the firm's potential for taking advantage of them. Finally, marketing designs strategies within individual business units for reaching the unit's objectives.[10]

# Marketing and the Other Business Functions

There is sometimes much confusion about marketing's importance in the firm. In some firms it is just another function—all functions count in the company and none takes precedence. This view is illustrated in Figure 2-4A. If the company faces slow growth or a sales decline, marketing may temporarily become more important (Figure 2-4B).

Some marketers claim that marketing is the major function of the firm. They quote Drucker's statement: "The aim of the business is to create customers." They say it is marketing's job to define the company's mission, products, and markets and to direct the other functions in the task of serving customers (Figure 2-4C).

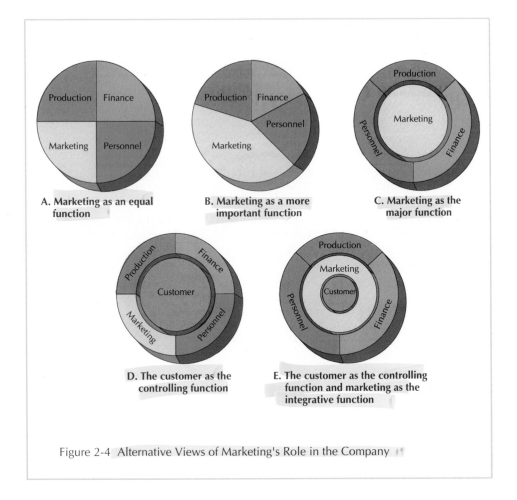

Figure 2-4 Alternative Views of Marketing's Role in the Company

Enlightened marketers, however, prefer to put the customer at the center of the company. They argue that all functions should work together to sense, serve, and satisfy the customer (Figure 2-4D).

Finally, some marketers say that marketing still needs to be in a central position to ensure that customers' needs are understood and satisfied (Figure 2-4E). These marketers argue that the firm cannot succeed without customers, so the key task is to attract and hold customers. Customers are attracted by promises and held through satisfaction, and marketing defines the promise and ensures its delivery. But because actual consumer satisfaction is affected by the performance of other departments, marketing must play an integrative role to help ensure that all departments work together toward consumer satisfaction.

# The Marketing Management Process

The strategic plan defines the company's overall mission and objectives. Within each business unit, marketing plays a role in helping to accomplish the overall strategic objectives. Marketing's role and activities in the organization are shown in Figure 2-5, which summarizes the entire marketing management process and the forces influencing company marketing strategy.

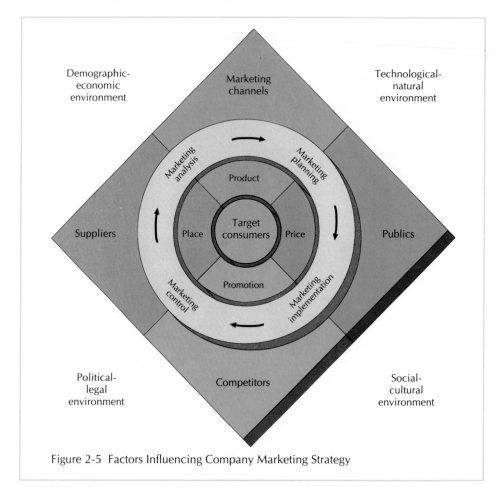

Figure 2-5  Factors Influencing Company Marketing Strategy

Target consumers stand in the center. The company identifies the total market, divides it into smaller segments, selects the most promising segments, and focuses on serving and satisfying these segments. It designs a marketing mix made up of factors under its control—product, price, place, and promotion. To find the best marketing mix and put it into action, the company engages in marketing analysis, planning, implementation, and control. Through these activities, the company watches and adapts to the marketing environment. We will now look briefly at each factor in the marketing management process. In later chapters, we will discuss each factor in more depth.

## Target Consumers

Sound marketing requires a careful analysis of consumers. Suppose a company is looking at possible markets for a potential new product. The company first needs to make a careful estimate of the current and future size of the market and its various segments. To estimate current market size, the company would identify all competing products, estimate their current sales, and determine whether the market is large enough.

Equally important is future market growth. Companies want to enter markets that show strong growth prospects. Growth potential may depend on the growth rate of certain age, income, and nationality groups that use the product more than others. Growth may also be related to larger developments in the environment, such as economic conditions, advances in technology, and life-style changes. For example, the future market for quality children's toys and clothing is strongly related to current birthrates, trends in consumer affluence, and projected family life styles. Forecasting—predicting what consumers are likely to do under a given set of conditions—is difficult, but it must be performed in order to make a decision about the market. The company's marketing information specialists will probably use complex techniques to measure and forecast demand.

Suppose the forecast looks good. The company now has to decide how to enter the market. Companies know that they cannot satisfy all consumers in a given market, at least not all consumers in the same way. There are too many different kinds of consumers with too many different kinds of needs. Some companies are in a better position to serve certain segments of the market. Therefore, each company must study the total market, and choose the segments it can profitably serve better than competitors. This involves three steps: market segmentation, market targeting, and market positioning.

### MARKET SEGMENTATION

The market consists of many types of customers, products, and needs, and the marketer has to determine which segments offer the best opportunity to achieve company objectives. Consumers can be grouped in various ways based on geographic factors (regions, cities), demographic factors (sex, age, income, education), psychographic factors (social classes, life styles), and behavioral factors (purchase occasions, benefits sought, usage rates). The process of classifying customers into groups with different needs, characteristics, or behavior is called **market segmentation**.

Every market is made up of market segments, but not all ways of segmenting the market are equally useful. For example, Bromo Seltzer would gain little by distinguishing between male and female users of the product category if both respond

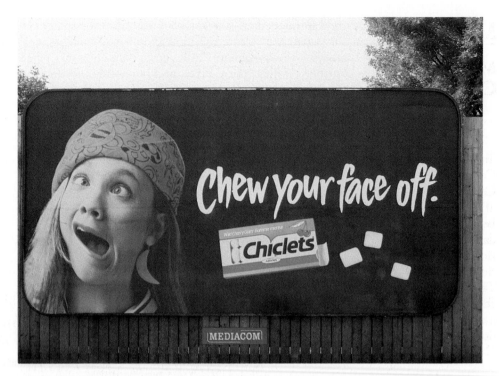

Adams Brand directs its Chiclets product advertising at the young teen market segment.

the same way to marketing stimuli. A **market segment** consists of consumers who respond in a similar way to a given set of marketing stimuli.

In the car market, consumers who choose the biggest, most comfortable car no matter what its price make up one market segment. Another market segment would be customers who care mainly about price and operating economy. It would be difficult to make one model of car that was the first choice of every consumer. Companies are wise to focus their efforts on meeting the distinct needs of one or more market segments. They should study the geographic, demographic, behavioral, and other characteristics of each market segment to evaluate its attractiveness as a marketing opportunity.

## MARKET TARGETING

After a company has defined market segments, it can enter one or many segments of a given market. **Market targeting** involves evaluating each market segment's attractiveness and selecting one or more segments to enter. A company with limited resources might decide to serve only one segment. This strategy limits sales but can be very profitable (see Marketing Highlight 2-2). Alternatively, a company might choose to serve several related segments, perhaps those that have different kinds of customers with the same basic wants. A large company might decide to offer a complete range of products to serve all the market segments.

Most companies enter a new market by serving a single segment, and if this proves successful, they add segments. Large companies eventually seek full market coverage. They want to be the "General Motors" of their industry. GM says that it makes a car for every "person, purse, and personality." The leading company normally has different products designed to meet the special needs of each segment.

# MARKETING HIGHLIGHT 2-2

## Market Segmentation and Targeting: Canadian Companies "Niche" the U.S. Market

With the advent of the Free Trade Agreement (FTA) between Canada and the U.S., many large Canadian firms and the Canadian subsidiaries of U.S. firms began rationalizing and consolidating manufacturing in preparation for the increased competition on both sides of the border. These firms were preparing for the massive battle where each market share point is worth millions of dollars. For many smaller Canadian companies, the opportunity to gain access to a small portion of the large U.S. market (246 million people) was exciting.

In fact, for years, many small Canadian firms have been successful in the U.S. by carefully segmenting the market and concentrating their efforts on a single segment. Rather than fighting with the giants, these companies pursue "nichemanship" because capturing a small segment in the U.S. means big business for many Canadian companies. For example, Canparts Automotive International saw a growing market in the U.S. for Japanese and European cars. It began supplying brake parts to this segment of the automobile after-market. Tanner Eye Ltd., located in Prince Edward Island, has a unique and profitable market niche. Tanner provides a covering for high quality eyeglass frames (mostly manufactured by others) with a thin layer of decorative leather facing. Other firms have secured market niches through their ability to deliver to specifications (International Submarine Engineering), through after-sales service (Shaver Poultry Breeding Farms), and through distribution capabilities (Seaboard Lumber Sales).

Successful small Canadian firms operating in the U.S. usually recognize that the U.S. consists of a number of regional markets, each with different customer and business demographics. These firms also recognize that because of their size, they need to find niches where their expertise protects them from direct competition. The rewards for these companies are often a dramatic increase in sales and profits. For example, Cognos Inc. is one of Canada's leading computer software manufacturers. A few years ago, it aligned itself with Hewlett-Packard and developed state-of-the-art products for particular niches. Today sales exceed $110 million on a world-wide basis.

As the FTA takes hold, many experts feel the name of the game in the 1990s for most Canadian companies is niche marketing. As few Canadian firms are in a position to sell their products nationwide in the U.S., niche marketing is the only practical way to enter that market. Selecting the right niche, whether geographic, demographic, or product line-related, will probably be the single most important decision for growing Canadian businesses.

**Sources:** Philip Rosson, Mary Brooks, Shyam Kamath, and Donald Patton, *Excellence in Exporting* (Ottawa: External Affairs Canada, 1985); *Tomorrow's Customers*, Clarkson Gordon/ Woods Gordon, 1989; and Jim de Wilde and Don Simpson, "Export Strategies For Innovative Canadian Firms: Finding Niches and Inventing Competitive Advantage," *Business Quarterly*, Summer 1988, pp. 72-76.

## MARKET POSITIONING

Once a company has decided which market segments to enter, it must decide what "positions" it wants to occupy in those segments. A product's position is the place the product occupies in consumers' minds relative to competing products. If a product is perceived to be exactly like another product on the market, consumers would have no reason to buy it.

Segmentation and targeting: Colgate-Palmolive identifies segments and serves a number of segments through targeting.

**Market positioning** is arranging for a product to occupy a clear, distinctive, and desirable place relative to competing products in the minds of target consumers. Thus marketers plan positions that distinguish their products from competing products, and that give them the greatest strategic advantage in their target markets.

For example, the Hyundai automobile is positioned on low price as "the car that makes sense"; Jaguar is positioned as "a blending of art and machine"; Saab is "the most intelligent car ever built." Procter and Gamble positions its Crest brand

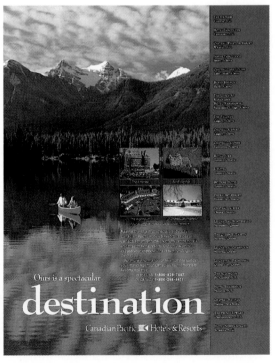

Canadian Pacific Hotels seek distinct target markets by creating separate ads for the business traveller and the vacation traveller.

as the "Family Dental Plan" toothpaste, and its Pearl Drops brand as the toothpaste that "cleans tobacco stains."

To plan a product's position, the company first identifies the existing positions of all the products and brands currently serving its market segments. Next the company determines what consumers want with respect to major product attributes. The company then selects a position based on its product's ability to satisfy consumer wants better than competitors' products. Finally, it develops a marketing program that communicates and delivers the product's position to target consumers.

## Developing the Marketing Mix

Once the company has decided on its positioning strategy, it is ready to begin planning the details of the marketing mix. The marketing mix is one of the major concepts in modern marketing. We define the **marketing mix** as the set of controllable marketing variables that the firm blends to produce the response it wants in the target market. The marketing mix consists of everything the firm can do to influence the demand for its product. The many possibilities can be collected into four groups of variables known as the "four P's": product, price, place, and promotion.[11] The particular marketing variables under each P are shown in Figure 2-6.

Product stands for the "goods-and-service" combination the company offers to the target market. Thus WLC's Listermint "product" consists of 500 milliliters of green liquid in a plastic package with a list of ingredients in both French and English.

Price stands for the amount of money customers have to pay to obtain the product. For Listermint, WLC suggests retail and wholesale prices, discounts, allowance, and credit terms. Its "price" has to be in line with the perceived value of the product, or buyers will purchase competing products.

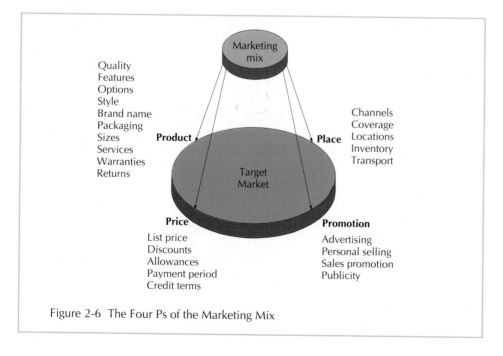

Figure 2-6 The Four Ps of the Marketing Mix

Place stands for company activities that make the product available to target consumers. Thus WLC chooses wholesalers and retailers, urges them to display and advertise the product, checks on shelf stock, and arranges product shipping and storage.

Promotion stands for activities that communicate the merits of the product and persuade target customers to buy it. Thus WLC buys advertising, hires salespeople, sets up sales promotions, and arranges publicity for Listermint.

An effective marketing program blends all the marketing mix elements into a coordinated program designed to achieve the company's marketing objectives.[12]

# Managing the Marketing Effort

The company wants to design and put into action the marketing mix that will best achieve its objectives in its target markets. This involves four marketing management functions—analysis, planning, implementation, and control. These functions are discussed briefly below and more fully in Chapter 3.

### MARKETING ANALYSIS

Managing the marketing function begins with a complete analysis of the company's situation. The company must analyze its markets and marketing environment to find attractive opportunities and avoid environmental threats. It must analyze company strengths and weaknesses, and current and possible marketing actions, to determine which opportunities it can best pursue. Marketing analysis feeds information and other inputs to each of the other marketing management functions.

### MARKETING PLANNING

Through strategic planning, the company decides what it wants to do with each business unit. Marketing planning involves deciding on marketing strategies that will help the company attain its overall strategic objectives. A detailed marketing plan is needed for each business, product, or brand. For example, suppose WLC decides that its Chiclets chewing gum should be built further because of its strong growth potential. The brand manager of Chiclets will then develop a marketing plan to carry out Chiclets' growth objective.

### MARKETING IMPLEMENTATION

Good marketing analysis and planning are only a start toward successful company performance—the marketing plans must be implemented well. It is often easier to design good marketing strategies then to put them into action.

People at all levels of the marketing system must work together to implement marketing strategy and plans. People in marketing must work closely with people in finance, purchasing, manufacturing, and other company departments. Many outside people and organizations must help with implementation—suppliers, resellers, advertising agencies, research firms, and the advertising media. All must work together effectively to implement the marketing program.

The implementation process consists of five elements—action programs, the company's organizational structure, decision and reward systems, human resources, and company climate and culture. To implement its marketing plans and strategies successfully, the company must blend these elements into a cohesive program.

These elements will be discussed more fully in Chapter 3.

## MARKETING CONTROL

Many surprises are likely to occur as marketing plans are being implemented. The company needs control procedures to make sure that its objectives will be achieved. Companies want to make sure that they are achieving the sales, profits, and other goals set in their annual plans. This control involves stating well-defined goals, measuring ongoing market performance, determining the causes of any serious gaps in performance, and deciding on the best corrective action to close the gaps. Corrective action could entail improving the ways in which the plan is being implemented or even changing the goals.

Companies should also stand back from time to time and look at their overall approach to the marketplace. The purpose is to make certain that the company's objectives, policies, strategies, and programs remain appropriate in the face of rapid environmental changes. Large companies such as Woodward's and National Sea Products fell on hard times because they did not watch the changing marketplace and make the proper adaptations. A major tool used for such strategic control is the marketing audit, which is described in Chapter 3.

# The Marketing Environment

Managing the marketing function would be hard enough if the marketer had to deal only with the controllable marketing mix variables. However, the company operates in a complex marketing environment that consists of uncontrollable forces to which it must adapt. The environment produces both threats and opportunities. The company must carefully analyze its environment so that it can avoid the threats and take advantage of the opportunities.

Companies may think that they have few opportunities, but they may simply be failing to think strategically about what business they are in and what strengths they have. Every company faces many opportunities. Companies can search for new opportunities casually or systematically. Many companies find new ideas by simply keeping their eyes and ears open to the changing marketplace. Other organizations use formal methods for analyzing the marketing environment.

Not all opportunities are right for every company. A marketing opportunity must fit the company's objectives and resources. Thus personal computers are an attractive industry, but not for every company. For example, we sense that personal computers would not be right for McDonald's. McDonald's seeks a high level of sales, growth, and profits from the fast-food business. Even though McDonald's has very large resources, it may lack the technical know-how, industrial marketing experience, and special distribution channels needed to sell personal computers successfully.

The company's marketing environment includes forces close to the company that affect its ability to serve its consumers, such as other company departments, channel members (such as retailers), suppliers, competitors, and publics. It also includes broader demographic/economic forces, political/legal forces, technological/ecological forces, and social/ cultural forces. The company must consider all of these actors and forces when developing and positioning its offer to the target market. The market environment is discussed more fully in Chapter 5.

# SUMMARY

Strategic planning involves developing a strategy for long-run survival and growth. Marketing helps in strategic planning, and the overall strategic plan defines marketing's role in the company. Marketers undertake the marketing management process to carry out their role in the organization.

Not all companies use formal planning or use it well. Yet formal planning offers several benefits, including systematic thinking, better coordination of company efforts, sharper objectives, and improved performance measurement, all of which can lead to improved sales and profits. Companies develop three kinds of plans—annual plans, long-range plans, and strategic plans.

Strategic planning sets the stage for the rest of company planning. The strategic planning process consists of developing the company's mission, objectives and goals, business portfolio, and functional plans.

Developing a sound mission statement is a challenging undertaking. The mission statement should be market-oriented, feasible, motivating, and specific if it is to direct the firm to its best opportunities. The mission statement then leads to supporting objectives and goals, in a system known as management by objectives.

From here, strategic planning calls for analyzing the company's business portfolio and deciding which businesses should receive greater or fewer resources. The company might use a formal portfolio planning method such as the BCG growth-share matrix. But most companies are now designing more customized portfolio planning approaches that better suit their unique situations.

Beyond evaluating current strategic business units, management must plan for growth into new businesses and products. The product-market expansion grid shows four avenues for growth. Market penetration involves more sales of current products to current customers. Market development involves identifying new markets for current products. Product development involves offering new or modified products to current markets. Finally, diversification involves starting businesses entirely outside of current products and markets.

Each of the company's functional departments provides inputs for strategic planning. Once strategic objectives have been defined, management within each business must prepare a set of functional plans that coordinates the activities of the marketing, finance, manufacturing, and other departments. Each department has a different idea about which objectives and activities are most important. The marketing department stresses the consumer's point of view. Marketing managers must understand the points of view of the other functions and work with other functional managers to develop a system of plans that will best accomplish the firm's overall strategic objectives.

To fulfill their role in the organization, marketers engage in the marketing management process. Consumers are at the center of the marketing management process. The company divides the total market into smaller segments and selects the segments it can best serve. It then designs its marketing mix to attract and satisfy these target segments. To find the best mix and put it into action, the company engages in marketing analysis, marketing planning, marketing implementation, and marketing control. Through these activities, the company watches and adapts to the marketing environment.

# QUESTIONS FOR DISCUSSION

1. In a series of job interviews, you ask three recruiters to describe the missions of their companies. One says, "To make profits." Another says, "To create customers." The third says, "To fight world hunger." What do these mission statements tell you about each company?

2. Choose a local radio station and describe what its apparent mission, objectives, and strategies are. What other things can the station do to accomplish its mission?

3. An electronics manufacturer obtains semiconductors from a company-owned subsidiary that also sells to other manufacturers. The subsidiary is smaller and less profitable than competing producers, and its growth rate has been below the industry average for five years. Into what cell of the BCG growth-share matrix does this strategic business unit fall? What should the parent company do with this SBU?

4. What market opportunities has McDonald's pursued in each of the four cells of the product/market expansion grid? What future opportunities would you suggest to McDonald's?

5. How can organizations forecast what consumers are likely to do in the future? Choose a recently released movie or compact disc and forecast its success. How much confidence do you have in your prediction?

6. Assume you want to start a business after graduation. What, for example, is the opportunity for a new music store selling records, tapes, and compact discs in your town? Briefly describe your target market or markets and the marketing mix you would develop for your store.

# KEY TERMS

**Business portfolio**  The collection of businesses and products that make up the company.

**Cash cows**  Low-growth, high-share businesses or products— established and successful units that generate cash that the company uses to pay its bills and support other business units that need investment.

**Diversification**  A strategy for expanding company growth by starting up or acquiring businesses outside the company's current products and markets.

**Dogs**  Low-growth, low-share businesses and products that may generate enough cash to maintain themselves, but do not promise to be a large source of cash.

**Market development**  A strategy for expanding company growth by identifying and developing new market segments for current company products.

**Market penetration**  A strategy for expanding company growth by increasing sales of current products to current market segments without changing the product in any way.

**Market positioning** Arranging for a product to occupy a clear, distinctive, and desirable place relative to competing products in the minds of target consumers.

**Market segment** A group of consumers who respond in a similar way to a given set of marketing stimuli.

**Market segmentation** The process of classifying customers into groups with different needs, characteristics, or behavior.

**Market targeting** The process of evaluating each market segment's attractiveness and selecting one or more segments to enter.

**Marketing mix** The set of controllable marketing variables that the firm blends to produce the response it wants in the target market.

**Mission statement** A statement of the organization's purpose, what it wants to accomplish in the larger environment.

**Product development** A strategy for expanding company growth by offering modified or new products to current market segments.

**Question marks** Low-share business units in high-growth markets that require a lot of cash to hold their share or build into stars.

**Stars** High-growth, high-share businesses or products. They often require heavy investment to finance their rapid growth.

**Strategic business unit (SBU)** A unit of the company that has a separate mission and objective, and which can be planned independently from other company businesses.

**Strategic planning** The process of developing and maintaining a strategic fit between the organizations' goals and capabilities and its changing marketing opportunities.

# References

1. Sources include: Gerry Blackwell, "Northern Lights," *Canadian Business*, March 1990, pp. 40-44; Michael Salter, "Shoot the Moon," *Report On Business Magazine*, August 1989, pp. 28-36; David Lake, "The New Europe," *Canadian Business*, March 1990, pp. 49-54; and Chuck Hawkins, "Is Paul Stern Tough Enough To Toughen Up Northern Telecom?" *Business Week*, August 14, 1989, pp. 84-85.

2. For more on mission statements, see David A. Aaker, *Strategic Market Management*, 2nd ed. (New York: John Wiley, 1988), Chap. 3; Laura Nash, "Mission Statements—Mirrors and Windows," *Harvard Business Review*, March-April 1988, pp. 155-56; and George S. Day, *Market Driven Strategy* (New York: The Free Press, 1990), Chap. 1.

3. Bombardier Inc., *Annual Report*, 1989.

4. John Labatt, *Annual Report*, 1989.

5. For additional reading on this and other portfolio analysis approaches, see Philippe Haspeslagh, "Portfolio Planning: Limits and Uses," *Harvard Business*

*Review*, January-February 1982, pp. 58-73; Yoram Wind and Vijay Mahajan, "Designing Product and Business Portfolios," *Harvard Business Review*, January-February 1981, pp. 155-65; Yoram Wind, Vijay Mahajan, and Donald J. Swire, "An Empirical Comparison of Standardized Portfolio Models," *Journal of Marketing*, Spring 1985, pp. 89-99; and Roger A. Kerin, Vijay Mahajan and P. Rajan Varadarajan, *Contemporary Perspectives on Strategic Marketing Planning* (New York: Allyn and Bacon, 1990), Chapters 1-3.

6. For examples of other formal methods and their use by Canadian companies, see Carolyn R. Farquhar and Stanley J. Shapiro, *Strategic Business Planning in Canada*, Conference Board of Canada, April 1983.

7. Farquar and Shapiro, *Strategic Business Planning in Canada*.

8. See Daniel H. Gray, "Uses and Misuses of Strategic Planning," *Harvard Business Review*, January-February 1986, pp. 89-96.

9. H. Igor Ansoff, "Strategies for Diversification," *Harvard Business Review*, September-October 1957, pp. 113-24.

10. For more reading on marketing's role, see Paul F. Anderson, "Marketing, Strategic Planning and the Theory of the Firm," *Journal of Marketing*, Spring 1982, pp. 15-26; and Yoram Wind and Thomas S. Robertson, "Marketing Strategy: New Directions for Theory and Research," *Journal of Marketing*, Spring 1983, pp. 12-25.

11. The four P classification was first suggested by E. Jerome McCarthy, *Basic Marketing: A Managerial Approach* (Homewood, IL: Irwin, 1960).

12. See Benson P. Shapiro, "Rejuvenating the Marketing Mix," *Harvard Business Review*, September-October 1985, pp. 28-34.

# CHAPTER 3

# Planning, Implementing, and Controlling Marketing Programs

## CHAPTER OBJECTIVES

After reading this chapter, you should be able to:
1. Identify the sections of a marketing plan and what each section contains.
2. Describe the elements of the marketing implementation process.
3. Compare different ways of organizing a marketing department.
4. Explain the three ways in which companies control their marketing activities.

Canadian Tire has an ambitious goal—to double its sales in Canada by 1995. The opportunity was identified by a detailed analysis of the Canadian market in 1988 and confirmed in 1989. With sales of $3 billion and earnings of $150 million the objective is a challenging one, but one that Canadian Tire managers feel they can meet.

Based on the analysis, which the company called Project Oracle, Canadian Tire has developed a plan to accomplish its goals. The plan will be a mix of products and services, organizational productivity, marketing innovation, and business partnerships. The plan calls for larger stores in key locations with a focus on product selection. The company plans to add about 400,000 square feet of retail space each year and by 1995 the company will have 450 stores (up from 414 in 1989).

Canadian Tire is constantly refining the breadth and depth of its product lines to meet customer's changing needs. It has test-marketed an installed home improvement business as it seeks to gain a share of the $12 billion Canadians spend annually on home renovations. It has also tested "Alex," a shopping service offering 500 Canadian Tire products via video display terminals in customers' homes. While the results were disappointing, a small investment provided insights into a potentially important market in the next decade. Canadian Tire is also testing the impact of on-line product information, which will allow customers quick access to the information they need to make purchase decisions. Productivity is being improved through the Seasonal Centre, where stores rotate seasonal goods without additional warehouse space. As well, Canadian

Tire is installing a new information system which provides store managers with a database of market share and comparative sales statistics. This allows the managers to improve promotions and in-store merchandising.

Recent marketing ideas tested include insurance products, owner-operated gas bars, free-standing auto service and product centers, and the installed home improvement business. In addition, a test market for a "car care" concept was developed in the north-central United States.

To enhance its business partner-ships, Canadian Tire is using electronic data interchange to automate product ordering, handling, payments, and invoicings. The result is improved productivity for Canadian Tire and its dealers.

Canadian Tire has set an ambitious goal. To achieve it, the company has developed marketing plans which have been and will be implemented over time. It evaluates the results and takes action to ensure the plans are on course. In this way, Canadian Tire plans to remain a leader in the future.[1]

In this chapter, we will look more closely at each marketing management function—analysis, planning, implementation, and control. Figure 3-1 shows the relationship between these marketing activities. The company first develops overall strategic plans. These companywide strategic plans are then translated into marketing and other plans for each division, product, and brand.

Through implementation, the company turns the strategic and marketing plans into action to achieve the company's strategic objectives. Marketing plans are implemented by people in the marketing organization who work with others inside and outside the company. Control consists of measuring and evaluating the results of marketing plans and activities and taking corrective action to make sure objectives are being reached. Marketing analysis provides the information and evaluation needed for all of the other marketing management activities.

To review all the factors that marketers must consider when designing marketing programs, we will discuss planning first. However, this does not mean that

Marketers must continuously plan their analysis, implementation, and control activities.

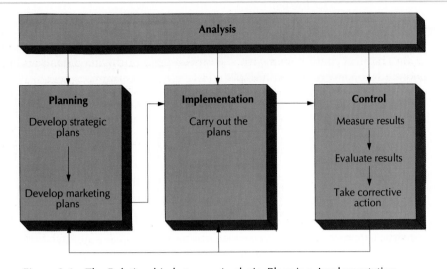

Figure 3-1    The Relationship between Analysis, Planning, Implementation, and Control

planning always comes first, or that planning ends before marketers move on to the other activities. Figure 3-1 shows that planning and the other activities are closely related. Marketers must plan their analysis, implementation, and control activities; analysis provides inputs for planning, implementation, and control; control provides feedback for future planning and implementation.

In the remainder of this chapter, we will discuss marketing planning, and how plans are implemented and controlled by people in the marketing department. In Chapter 4 we will examine many of the tools used in marketing analysis.

# MARKETING PLANNING

The strategic plan defines the company's overall mission and objectives. Within each business unit, functional plans must be prepared—including marketing plans. If the business unit consists of many product lines, brands, and markets, plans must be written for each.

What does a marketing plan look like? Our discussion will focus on product or brand plans. A product or brand plan should contain the following sections: executive summary, current marketing situation, threats and opportunities, strengths and weaknesses, objectives and issues, marketing strategies, action programs, budgets, and controls (see Figure 3-2).

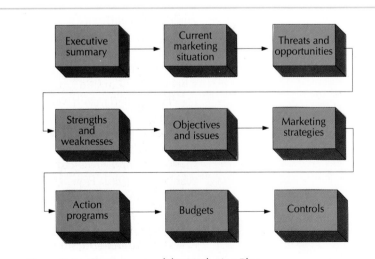

Figure 3-2    Components of the Marketing Plan

# Executive Summary

The marketing plan should open with a short summary of the main goals and recommendations to be presented in the plan. Here is a short example:

> The 1992 Marketing Plan seeks a significant increase over the preceding year in company sales and profits. The sales target is $80 million, a planned 20% sales gain. This increase is attainable because of the improved economic, competitive, and distribution picture. The target operating margin is $8 million, a 25% increase over last year. To achieve these goals, the sales promotion budget will be $1.6 million, or two percent of projected sales. The advertising budget will be $2.4 million, or three percent of projected sales... [More detail follows]

The executive summary helps top management to find the major points of the plan quickly. A table of contents should follow the executive summary.

# Current Marketing Situation

The first major section of the plan describes the target market and the company's position in it. The marketing planner provides the following information:

**Market description**. Here the market is defined, including the major market segments. The planner shows the size of the market (in units or dollars) in total and by segment for the past several years. The plan reviews customer needs and factors in the marketing environment that may affect customer purchasing.

**Product review**. Here the plan shows sales, prices, contribution margins and net profits for each of the major products in the product line for the past several years.

Table 3-1 shows an example of how data might be presented for a product line. Row 1 shows the total industry sales in units growing at five percent annually until 1991, when demand declined slightly. Row 2 shows the company's market share hovering around three percent, although it reached four percent in 1990. Row 3 shows the average price for the product rising about ten percent a year except the last year, when it rose four percent. Row 4 shows variable costs, such as materials and labor, rising each year. Row 5 shows that the gross contribution margin per unit—the difference between price (row 3) and unit variable cost (row 4)—rose the first few years and remained at $100 in the latest year. Rows 6 and 7 show sales volume in units and dollars, and row 8 shows the total gross contribution margin, which rose until the latest year, when it fell. Row 9 shows that overheads remained constant during 1988 and 1989 and increased to a higher level during 1990 and 1991 due to an increase in manufacturing capacity. Row 10 shows net contribution margin, that is, gross contribution margin less overhead. Rows 11, 12, and 13 show marketing expenditures on advertising and promotion, sales force and distribution, and marketing research. Finally, row 14 shows net operating profit after marketing expenses. The picture is one of increasing profits until 1991, when profits fell to about one-third of the 1990 level. Clearly the product manager needs to find a strategy for 1992 that will once again restore healthy growth in sales and profits to the product line.

**Competition.** Here the plan identifies major competitors and each of their strategies with respect to product quality, pricing, distribution, and promotion. The section also shows the market shares held by the company and each competitor. As an example, Table 3-2 provides market shares for the Canadian soft drink industry for a five year period. A company like Pepsi Canada would use this information, in part, to evaluate its past strategies and its competitors' strategies in preparing next year's plan.

**Distribution.** Here the plan describes recent sales trends and developments in the major distribution channels.

**TABLE 3-1**
**Historical Product Data**

| Variable | Columns | 1988 | 1989 | 1990 | 1991 |
|---|---|---|---|---|---|
| 1. Industry sales (in units) | | 200,000 | 210,000 | 220,500 | 220,000 |
| 2. Company market share | | 0.03 | 0.03 | 0.04 | 0.03 |
| 3. Average price per unit $ | | 200 | 220 | 240 | 250 |
| 4. Variable cost per unit $ | | 120 | 125 | 140 | 150 |
| 5. Gross contribution margin per unit $ | (3-4) | 80 | 95 | 100 | 100 |
| 6. Sales volume in units | (1x2) | 6,000 | 6,300 | 8,820 | 6,600 |
| 7. Sales revenue $ | (3x6) | 1,200,000 | 1,386,000 | 2,116,800 | 1,650,000 |
| 8. Gross contribution margin $ | (5x6) | 480,000 | 598,500 | 882,000 | 660,000 |
| 9. Overhead $ | | 200,000 | 200,000 | 350,000 | 350,000 |
| 10. Net contribution margin $ | (8-9) | 280,000 | 398,500 | 532,000 | 310,000 |
| 11. Advertising and promotion $ | | 80,000 | 100,000 | 100,000 | 90,000 |
| 12. Sales force and distribution $ | | 70,000 | 100,000 | 110,000 | 100,000 |
| 13. Marketing research $ | | 10,000 | 12,000 | 15,000 | 10,000 |
| 14. Net operating profit $ | (10-11-12-13) | 120,000 | 186,500 | 307,000 | 110,000 |

**TABLE 3-2**
**Market Share - Soft Drinks**

| PERCENT SHARE Brand | 1989 | 1988 | 1987 | 1986 | 1985 |
|---|---|---|---|---|---|
| Coke/Coke Classic | 20.0 | 19.7 | 19.0 | 20.0 | 20.8 |
| Pepsi | 18.3 | 17.7 | 18.4 | 17.2 | 18.4 |
| Diet Coke | 8.9 | 9.5 | 7.2 | 8.2 | 7.9 |
| 7-Up/Diet 7-Up | 7.8 | 8.2 | 13.8 | 13.2 | 10.7 |
| All Canada Dry | 9.2 | 8.8 | 8.6 | 7.9 | 8.6 |
| Sprite/Diet Sprite | 3.6 | 5.7 | 4.8 | 4.9 | 5.6 |
| Diet Pepsi | 5.7 | 5.4 | 5.2 | 4.7 | 4.1 |
| Other | 26.5 | 25.0 | 22.4 | 23.9 | 23.9 |
| Total Market | 100.0 | 100.0 | 100.0 | 100.0 | 100.0 |
| Total Market Size[1] (000,000 litres) | 2,606 | 2,520 | 2,211 | 2,086 | 2,071 |

**Source:** *Financial Times of Canada*, Annual presentation of market share data, various issues.

# Threats and Opportunities

This section requires the manager to look ahead for major threats and opportunities that the product might face in the external environment. The purpose is to make the manager anticipate important developments that can have an impact on the firm. Managers should list as many threats and opportunities as they can imagine. Suppose a major pet food marketer comes up with the following list:

1. A large competitor has just announced that it will introduce a new premium pet food line, backed by a huge advertising and sales promotion blitz.

2. Industry analysts predict that supermarket chain buyers will face more than 1,000 new grocery product introductions next year. Buyers are expected to accept only 20% of these new products and give each one only five months to prove itself.

3. Because of improved economic conditions over the past several years, pet ownership is increasing in almost all segments of the Canadian population.

4. The company's researchers have found a way to make a new pet food that is low in fat and calories yet highly nutritious and tasty. This product will appeal strongly to many of today's pet food buyers, who are almost as concerned about their pets' health as about their own.

5. Concern about proper pet care is increasing rapidly in Canada and pet owners are spending more on pet care.[2]

The first two items are threats. Not all threats call for the same attention or concern—the manager should assess how likely it is that each threat will occur, and how much harm it would cause. The manager should then focus on the most probable and harmful threats, and prepare plans in advance to meet them.

The last three items in the list are marketing opportunities. A **company marketing opportunity** is an attractive arena for marketing action in which the company could enjoy a competitive advantage.

## Strengths and Weaknesses

Strengths and weaknesses are inside factors, in contrast with opportunities and threats, which are outside factors. Company strengths point to certain strategies the company might be successful in using, while company weaknesses point to certain things the company needs to correct. For example, Canada Dry might list the following strengths for its products:

1. Canada Dry has an excellent distribution system.

2. Canada Dry produces a complementary range of soft drinks.

The company might list the following weaknesses:

1. Canada Dry has low brand awareness.

2. Canada Dry has higher prices, relative to competitive brands.

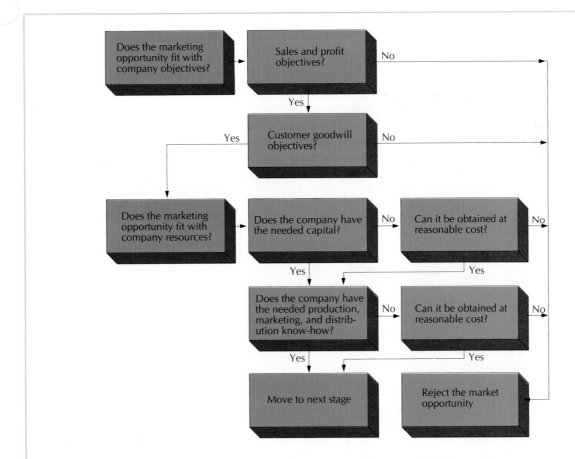

Figure 3-3   Evaluating a Company Marketing Opportunity in Terms of Company Objectives and Resources

A review of the company's strengths and weaknesses help the manager to assess each opportunity according to its potential attractiveness and the company's probability of success. Figure 3-3 shows that the company should pursue only the opportunities that fit its objectives and resources. Every company has objectives based on its business mission. In addition, each opportunity requires that the company have certain amounts of capital and know-how. Companies can rarely find ideal opportunities that exactly fit their objectives and resources. Developing opportunities involves risks. When evaluating opportunities, the manager must decide whether the expected returns justify this risk.

## Objectives and Issues

Having studied the product's threats, opportunities, strengths, and weaknesses, the manager can now set objectives and consider issues that will affect them. The objectives should be stated as goals that the company would like to reach during the plan's term. For example, the manager might want to achieve a 15% market share, a 20% pretax profit on sales, and a 25% pretax profit on investment. Suppose the current market share is only ten percent. This poses a key question: How can market share be increased? The manager will want to consider the major issues involved in trying to increase market share.

## Marketing Strategies

In this section, the manager outlines the broad marketing strategy or "game plan" for attaining the objectives. **Marketing strategy** is the marketing logic by which the business unit hopes to achieve its marketing objective. It consists of specific strategies for target markets, marketing mix, and marketing expenditure level.

Marketing strategy should spell out the market segments on which the company will focus. These segments differ in their needs and wants, responses to marketing, and profitability. The company would be smart to put its effort and energy into those market segments it can best serve from a competitive point of view. It should develop a marketing strategy for each targeted segment.

The manager should outline specific strategies for such marketing mix elements as new products, field sales, advertising, sales promotion, prices, and distribution. The manager should explain how each strategy responds to the threats, opportunities, strengths, weaknesses, and key issues spelled out earlier in the plan.

The manager should also map out the marketing budget that will be needed to carry out the marketing strategies. The manager knows that higher budgets will produce more sales, but is looking for the marketing budget that will produce the best profit picture.

## Action Programs

Marketing strategies should be turned into specific action programs that answer the following questions: What will be done? When will it be done? Who is responsible for doing it? How much will it cost? For example, the manager may want to step up sales promotion as a key strategy for winning market share. A sales promotion action plan should be drawn up that outlines special offers and their dates, trade shows entered, new point-of-purchase displays, and other promotions. The action plan shows when activities will be started, reviewed, and completed.

## Budgets

The action plans allow the manager to make a supporting marketing budget that is essentially a projected profit and loss statement. On the revenue side, it shows the forecasted number of units that could be sold and the average net price. On the expense side, it shows the cost of production, physical distribution, and marketing. The difference is the projected profit. Higher management will review the budget and approve or modify it. Once approved, the budget is the basis for materials buying, production scheduling, manpower planning, and marketing operations. Budgeting can be difficult, and budgeting methods range from simple "rules of thumb" to complex computer models.[3]

## Controls

The last section of the plan outlines the controls that will be used to monitor progress. Typically, goals and budgets are spelled out for each month or quarter. This means that higher management can review the results each period and spot businesses or products that are not meeting their goals. The managers of these businesses and products have to explain the problems and the corrective actions they will take.

# IMPLEMENTATION

Planning good strategies is only a start toward successful marketing. A brilliant marketing strategy will count for little if the company fails to implement it properly. **Marketing implementation** is the process that turns marketing strategies and plans into marketing actions in order to accomplish strategic marketing objectives.

Implementation involves day-to-day, month-to-month activities that effectively put the marketing plan to work. Whereas marketing planning addresses the what and who of marketing activities, implementation addresses the who, where, when, and how.

Many managers think that "doing things right" (implementation) is as important, or even more important, than "doing the right things" (strategy):

> A surprisingly large number of very successful large companies...don't have long-term strategic plans with an obsessive preoccupation on rivalry. They concentrate on operating details and doing things well. Hustle is their style and their strategy. They move fast and they get it right...Countless companies in all industries, young or old, mature or booming, are finally learning the limits of strategy and concentrating on tactics and execution.[4]

Implementation is difficult—it is often easier to think up good marketing strategies than to carry them out. In addition, managers often have trouble diagnosing implementation problems. It is usually hard to tell whether poor performance was caused by poor strategy, poor implementation, or both.[5]

# The Implementation Process

People at all levels of the marketing system must work together to implement marketing plans and strategies. People in the marketing department, in other company departments, and in outside organizations can either help or hinder marketing implementation. The company must find ways to coordinate all these actors and their activities.

The implementation process is shown in Figure 3-4.[6] The figure shows that marketing strategy and marketing performance are linked by an implementation system consisting of five related elements: action programs, an organization structure, decision and reward systems, human resources, and managerial climate and company culture.

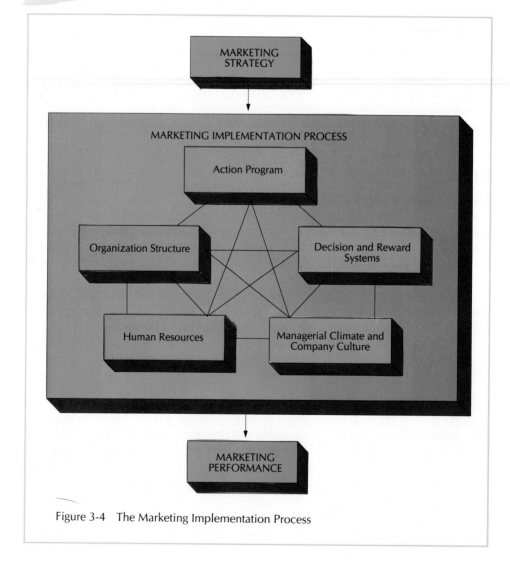

Figure 3-4   The Marketing Implementation Process

## THE ACTION PROGRAM

To implement marketing plans, people at all company levels make decisions and perform tasks. At Procter & Gamble, implementation of a plan to introduce a stream of high-quality new products requires day-to-day decisions and actions by many people inside and outside the organization. In the marketing organization, marketing researchers test new product concepts and scan the marketplace for new product ideas. For each new product, marketing managers make decisions about target segments, branding, packaging, pricing, promoting, and distributing. Salespeople are hired, trained and retrained, directed, and motivated.

Marketing managers work with other company managers to get support for promising new products. They talk with engineering about product design. They talk with manufacturing about production and inventory levels. They talk with finance about funding and cash flows, with the legal staff about patents and product safety issues, and with personnel about staffing and training needs. Marketing managers also work with outside people. They meet with advertising agency people to plan ad campaigns, and with the media to obtain publicity support. The salesforce urges retailers to advertise the new products, give them lots of shelf space, and use company displays.

The **action program** pulls all of these people and activities together. It identifies the decisions and actions needed to implement the marketing program. It also gives responsibility for these decisions and actions to specific people in the company. Finally, the action program provides a timetable that states when decisions must be made and when actions must be taken. The action program shows what must be done, who will do it, and how decisions and actions will be coordinated to reach the company's marketing objectives.

## THE ORGANIZATION STRUCTURE

The company's formal organization structure plays an important role in implementing marketing strategy. The structure breaks up the company's work into well-defined jobs, assigns these jobs to people and departments, and improves efficiency through specialization. The structure then coordinates these specialized jobs by defining formal ties between people and departments, and by setting lines of authority and communication.

Companies with different strategies need different organization structures. A small firm developing new products in a fast-changing industry might need a flexible structure that encourages individual action—a decentralized structure with lots of informal communication. A more established company in a more stable market might need a structure that provides more integration—a more centralized structure with well-defined roles and communication "through proper channels."[7]

In their study of successful companies, Peters and Waterman found the companies had many common structural characteristics that led to successful implementation.[8] For example, their structures tended to be more informal, decentralized, simple, and lean. In recent years, many large companies, including Procter & Gamble, have cut back unneeded layers of management and restructured their organizations to reduce costs and increase marketing flexibility.[9]

Some of the conclusions in the Peters and Waterman study have been questioned because the study focused on high-technology and consumer goods companies operating in rapidly changing environments.[10] The structures used by these companies may not be right for other types of firms in different situations. Many of the study's excellent companies will need to change their structures as their strategies and situations change.

## DECISION AND REWARD SYSTEMS

Decision and reward systems include formal and informal operating procedures that guide such activities as planning, information gathering, budgeting, recruiting and training, control, and personnel evaluation and rewards. Consider a company's compensation system. If it compensates managers for short-run results, they will have little incentive to work toward long-run objectives. Many companies are designing compensation systems that will overcome this problem. Here is an example:

> One company was concerned that its annual bonus system encouraged managers to ignore long-run objectives and focus on annual performance goals. To correct this, the company changed its bonus system to include rewards for both annual performance and for reaching "strategic milestones." Under the new plan, each manager works with planners to set two or three strategic objectives. At the end of the year, the manager's bonus is based on both operating performance and on reaching the strategic objectives. Thus the bonus system encourages managers to achieve more balance of the company's long-run and short-run needs.[11]

## HUMAN RESOURCES

Marketing strategies are implemented by people, so successful implementation requires careful human resources planning. At all levels, the company must fill its

structure and systems with people who have the necessary skills, motivation, and personal characteristics. Company personnel must be recruited, assigned, trained, and maintained.

The selection and development of executives and other managers are especially important for implementation. Different strategies call for managers with different personalities and skills. New venture strategies need managers with entrepreneurial skills, holding strategies require managers with organizational and administrative skills, and retrenchment strategies call for managers with cost-cutting skills. The company must carefully match its managers to the needs of the strategies to be implemented.

Marketing plans and strategies are of value only when they are properly implemented.

## MANAGERIAL CLIMATE AND COMPANY CULTURE

The company's managerial climate and company culture can make or break marketing implementation. **Managerial climate** is determined by the way company managers work with others in the company. Some managers take command, delegate little authority, and keep tight controls. Others delegate many responsibilities, encourage their people to take initiative, and communicate informally. No one managerial style is best for all situations. Different strategies may require different leadership styles. The style that is best varies with the company's structure, tasks, people, and environment.[12]

**Company culture** is a system of values and beliefs shared by people in an organization. It is the company's collective identity and meaning. The culture

**TABLE 3-3**
**Questions About the Marketing Implementation System**

### Organization Structure

What is the organization's structure?
What are the lines of authority and communication?
What is the role of task forces, committees, or similar mechanisms?

### Systems

What are the important systems?
What are the key control variables?
How do product and information flow?

### Action Program

What are the tasks to be performed and which are critical?
How are they accomplished, with what technology?
What strengths does the organization have?

### Human Resources

What are their skills, knowledge, and experience?
What are their expectations?
What are their attitudes toward the firm and their jobs?

### Climate and Culture

Are there shared values that are visible and accepted?
What are the shared values and how are they communicated?
What are the dominant management styles?
How is conflict resolved?

### Fit

Does each component above support marketing strategy?
Do the various components fit together well to form a cohesive framework for implementing strategy?

Source: Adapted from David A. Aaker, *Strategic Market Management* (New York: Wiley, 1988), p. 322 © 1988, John Wiley & Sons, Inc.

informally guides the behavior of people at all company levels. Peters and Waterman found that excellent companies have strong and clearly defined cultures.

> Without exception, the dominance and coherence of culture proved to be an essential quality of the excellent companies. Moreover, the stronger the culture and the more it was directed toward the marketplace, the less need there was for policy manuals, organization charts, or detailed procedures and rules. In these companies, people way down the line know what they are supposed to do in most situations because the handful of guiding values is crystal clear.[13]

Table 3-3 shows a list of questions companies should ask about each element of the implementation system. Successful implementation depends on how well the company blends the five activities into a cohesive program that supports its strategies.

# MARKETING DEPARTMENT ORGANIZATION

The company must design a marketing department that can carry out marketing analysis, planning, implementation, and control. In this section, we will focus on how marketing departments within companies are organized. If the company is very small, one person might end up doing all the marketing activities such as research, selling, advertising, customer service, and other activities. As the company expands, a marketing department organization emerges to plan and carry out marketing activities. In large companies, this department contains many marketing specialists. Thus General Mills has product managers, salespeople and sales managers, market researchers, advertising experts, and other specialists.

## Functional Organization

The **functional organization** is the most common form of marketing organization. Marketing specialists are in charge of different marketing activities, or functions. Figure 3-5 shows five specialists: marketing administration manager, advertising and sales promotion manager, sales manager, marketing research manager, and new products manager. Other specialists might include a customer service manager, a marketing planning manager, and a distribution manager.

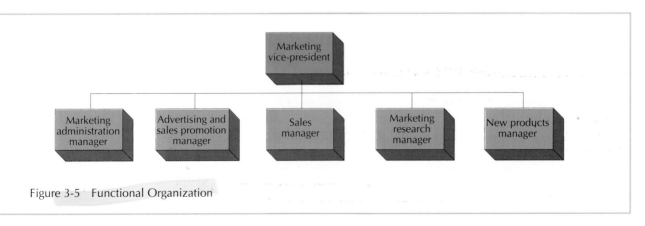

Figure 3-5  Functional Organization

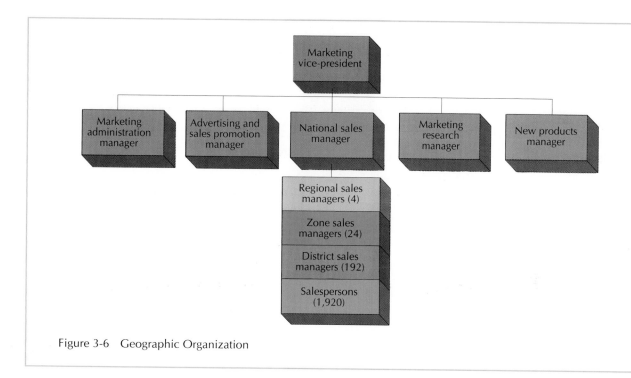

Figure 3-6    Geographic Organization

The main advantage of a functional marketing organization is that it is simple to administer. However, this form by itself is less and less effective as the company's products and markets grow. First, it becomes difficult to make plans for each different product or market, and products that are not favorites of the functional specialists get neglected. Second, as the functional groups compete with each other to gain more budget and status, top management has trouble coordinating all the marketing activities.

# Geographic Organization

A company selling all across the country often uses a **geographic organization** for its salesforce. Figure 3-6 shows one national sales manager, four regional sales managers, 24 zone sales managers, 192 district sales managers, and 1,920 salespeople. Geographic organization allows salespeople to settle into a territory, get to know their customers, and work with a minimum of travel time and cost.

# Product Management Organization

Companies with many products or brands often create a **product management organization**. The product or brand management organization is headed by a product manager. This manager supervises several product group managers, who in turn supervise product managers in charge of specific products (see Figure 3-7). The product manager's job is to develop and implement a complete strategy and marketing program for a specific product or brand. A product management organization makes sense if the company has many very different products.

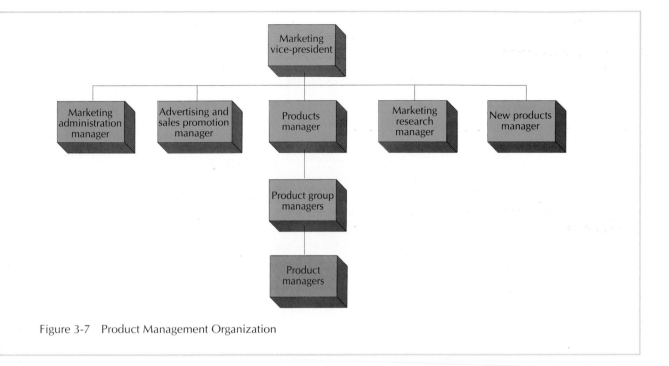

Figure 3-7    Product Management Organization

Product management first appeared in the Procter & Gamble Company in 1927. A new company soap, Camay, was not doing well, and a young P&G executive was assigned to give his exclusive attention to developing and promoting this product. He was successful, and the company soon added other product managers.

Since then, many firms, especially in the food, soap, toiletries, and chemical industries, have set up product management organizations. Because many of these firms, such as Colgate-Palmolive, Procter & Gamble, General Foods, and Bristol-Myers, operate in both Canada and the United States, the product management concept is common to both countries.[14] The Canadian subsidiary of General Foods, for example, uses a product management organization within each of its two major divisions, food services and groceries. Each product area within the grocery division has a group product manager. A group product manager might be in charge of cereals, pet foods, or beverages. Within the cereal product group, there are separate product managers for nutritional cereals, children's presweetened cereals, family cereals, and miscellaneous cereals. This organizational structure also extends to General Foods' subsidiaries, including Hostess Food Products, White Spot Limited, and Canterbury Foods.

The product management organization has many advantages. First, the product manager coordinates the whole marketing mix for the product. Second, the product manager can sense and react quickly to product problems. Third, smaller brands get more attention because they have their own product manager. Fourth, product management is an excellent training ground for young executives as it involves them in almost every area of company operations. For example, the presidents of 16 Canadian companies obtained some of their training at Procter & Gamble.[15]

However, a price is paid for these advantages. First, product management creates some conflict and frustration. Product managers are often not given enough authority to carry out their responsibilities effectively. Second, product managers become experts in their product but rarely become experts in any functions. Third, the product management system often costs more than expected due to higher payroll costs. Recently, companies have been rethinking the role of the product manager and some companies are redefining the manager's responsibilities.[16]

## Market Management Organization

Many companies sell one product line to many different types of markets. For example, IBM sells electric typewriters to consumer, business, and government markets. Stelco sells steel to the railroad, construction, and public utility industries. When different markets have different needs and preferences, a **market management organization** might be best for the company.

A market management organization is similar to the product management organization shown in Figure 3-7. Market managers are responsible for developing long-range and annual plans for the sales and profits in their markets. They have to coax help from marketing research, advertising, sales, and other functions. This system's main advantage is that the company is organized around the needs of specific customer segments.[17]

# MARKETING CONTROL

Because many surprises will occur during the implementation of marketing plans, the marketing department has to engage in constant marketing control. **Marketing control** is the process of measuring and evaluating the results of marketing strategies and plans, and taking corrective action to ensure that marketing objectives are attained.

There are three types of marketing control (see Table 3-4). Annual plan control involves checking ongoing performance against the annual plan, and taking corrective action when necessary. Profitability control involves determining the actual profitability of different products, territories, markets, and channels. Strategic control involves looking at whether the company's basic strategies are well matched to its opportunities.

## Annual Plan Control

The purpose of **annual plan control** is to ensure that the company achieves the sales, profits, and other goals set out in its annual plan. It involves the four steps shown in Figure 3-8. First, management must set monthly or quarterly goals in the annual plan.

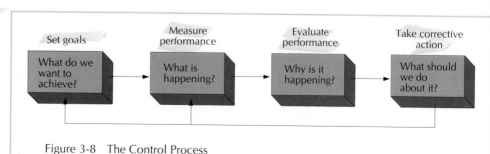

| Set goals | Measure performance | Evaluate performance | Take corrective action |

| What do we want to achieve? | What is happening? | Why is it happening? | What should we do about it? |

Figure 3-8   The Control Process

Second, management must measure its performance in the marketplace. Third, management must evaluate the causes of any differences between expected and actual performance. Fourth, management must take corrective action to close the gaps between its goals and its performance. This may require changing the action programs, or even changing the goals.

The four main control tools that management uses to check on performance are sales analysis, market-share analysis, marketing expense-to-sales analysis, and customer attitude tracking.

Sales analysis consists of measuring and evaluating actual sales in relation to sales goals. This might involve finding out whether specific products and territories are producing their expected share of sales. Suppose the company sells in three territories, and expected sales were 1,000 units, 500 units, and 2,000 units, respectively, adding up to 4,000 units. The actual sales volume was 1,400 units, 525 units, and 1,075 units. Thus territory one fell short by seven percent, territory two had a five percent surplus, and territory three fell short by four percent. Territory three is causing most of the trouble. The sales vice-president can check into territory three to see why performance is poor.

Company sales do not reveal how well the company is doing relative to competitors. A sales increase could be due to better economic conditions in which all companies gained, rather than to improved company performance in relation to its competitors. Management needs to use market share analysis to track the company's market share. If the company's market share goes up, it is gaining on competitors; if its market share goes down, it is losing to competitors. The information provided in Table 3-2 would be used to conduct a market share analysis.

**TABLE 3-4**
**Types of Marketing Control**

| Type of Control | Prime Responsibility | Purpose of Control | Approaches |
|---|---|---|---|
| I. Annual plan control | Top management Middle management | To examine whether the planned results are being achieved | Sales analysis Market-share analysis Marketing expense-to-sales ratios Customer attitude tracking |
| II. Profitability control | Marketing controller | To examine where the company is making and losing money | Profitability by: Product Territory Market segment Trade channel Order size |
| III. Strategic control | Top management Marketing auditor | To examine whether the company is pursuing its best marketing opportunities and doing this efficiently | Marketing audit |

Keeping track of sales and expenses.

Annual plan control requires making sure that the company is not over-spending to achieve its sales goals. Thus, marketing control also includes expense-to-sales analysis. Watching the ratio of marketing expenses to sales will help keep marketing expenses in line.

Alert companies use customer attitude tracking to check the attitudes of customers, dealers, and other marketing system participants. By becoming aware of changes in customer attitudes before they affect sales, management can take earlier action. The main customer attitude tracking systems are complaint and suggestion systems, customer panels, and customer surveys.

## Profitability Control

Besides annual plan control, companies also need **profitability control** to measure the profitability of their various products, territories, customer groups, channels, and order sizes. This information will help management determine whether any products or marketing activities should be expanded, reduced, or eliminated.

For example, suppose a lawnmower company wants to determine the profitability of selling its lawnmowers through three types of retail channels: hardware stores, garden supply shops, and department stores. Using profitability analysis, management would first identify all the expenses involved in selling, advertising, and delivering the product. Next, it would assign these expenses to each type of channel according to the effort and dollars spent on each channel. Finally, a profit and loss statement is prepared for each channel to see how much each is contributing to overall company profits.

If the analysis shows that one of the channels is unprofitable, the company can take one of many corrective actions. Suppose the company finds that it is actually losing money selling through garden supply shops. It might eliminate only the weakest garden supply shops. It might offer a program to train people in these shops to sell lawnmowers more effectively. The company could cut channel costs by reducing the sales calls and promotional aid going to garden supply shops. As a last resort, the company could drop the channel altogether.

# Strategic Control

From time to time, companies need **strategic control** to provide a critical review of their overall marketing effectiveness. Marketing strategies and programs can quickly become out of date. Each company should now and then reassess its overall approach to the marketplace, using a tool known as the marketing audit.[18] A **marketing audit** is a comprehensive, systematic, independent, and periodic examination of a company's environment, objectives, strategies, and activities to determine problem areas and opportunities and to recommend a plan of action to improve the company's marketing performance.

The marketing audit covers all major marketing areas of a business, not just a few trouble spots. It is normally conducted by an objective and experienced outside party who is independent of the marketing department. The marketing audit should be carried out periodically, not only when there is a crisis. It promises benefits for the successful company as well as for the company in trouble.

The marketing auditor should be given freedom to interview managers, customers, dealers, salespeople, and others who might throw light on marketing performance. Table 3-5 is a guide to the kinds of questions the marketing auditor will ask. Not all these questions are important in every situation. The auditor will develop a set of findings and recommendations based on this information. The findings may come as a surprise or even a shock to management. Management decides which recommendations make sense, and how and when to implement them.[19]

**TABLE 3-5**
**Parts of the Marketing Audit**

Part I—Marketing Environment Audit

The Macroenvironment

A. Demographic
1. What major demographic developments and trends pose opportunities or threats to this company?
2. What actions has the company taken in response to these developments and trends?

B. Economic
1. What major developments in income, prices, savings, and credit will impact the company?
2. What actions has the company been taking in response to these developments and trends?

C. Natural
1. What is the outlook for the cost and availability of natural resources and energy needed by the company?
2. What concerns have been expressed about the company's role in pollution and conservation, and what steps has the company taken?

D. Technological
1. What major changes are occurring in technology? What is the company's position in technology?
2. What major generic substitutes might replace this product?

E. Political
1. What laws now being proposed could affect marketing strategy and tactics?
2. What federal, provincial, and local actions should be watched? What is happening in pollution control, equal employment opportunity, product safety, advertising, price control, and other areas that affect marketing strategy?

F. Cultural
1. What is the public's attitude toward business and toward the products produced by the company?
2. What changes in consumer and business life styles and values might affect the company?

The Task Environment

A. Markets
1. What is happening to market size, growth, geographic distribution and profits?
2. What are the major market segments?

B. Customers
1. How do customers rate the company and its competitors on reputation, product quality, service, salesforce, and price?
2. How do different customer segments make their buying decisions?

C. Competitors
1. Who are the major competitors? What are their objectives and strategies, their strengths and weaknesses, their sizes and market shares?
2. What trends will affect future competition for this product?

D. Distribution and Dealers
1. What are the main channels for bringing products to customers?
2. What are the efficiency levels and growth potentials of the different channels?

E. Suppliers
1. What is the outlook for the availability of key resources used in production?
2. What trends are occurring among suppliers in their pattern of selling?

F. Marketing Service Firms
1. What is the cost and availability outlook for transportation services, warehousing facilities, and financial resources?
2. How effectively is the advertising agency performing?

G. Publics
1. What publics provide particular opportunities or problems for the company?
2. What steps has the company taken to deal effectively with each public?

Part II — Marketing Strategy Audit

A. Business Mission
1. Is the business mission clearly stated in market-oriented terms? Is it feasible?

B. Marketing Objectives and Goals
1. Are the corporate and marketing objectives stated in the form of clear goals to guide marketing planning and performance measurement?
2. Are the marketing objectives appropriate, given the company's competitive position, resources, and opportunities?

C. Strategy
1. What is the core marketing strategy for achieving the objectives? Is it sound?
2. Are enough resources (or too many) budgeted to accomplish the marketing objectives?
3. Are the marketing resources allocated optimally to market segments, territories, and products?

4. Are the marketing resources allocated optimally to the major elements of the marketing mix—such as product quality, service, salesforce, advertising, promotion, and distribution?

## Part III — Marketing Organization Audit

### A. Formal Structure
1. Does the marketing officer have adequate authority and responsibility over company activities that affect the customer's satisfaction?
2. Are the marketing activities optimally structured along functional, product, end user, and territorial lines?

### B. Functional Efficiency
1. Are there good communication and working relations between marketing and sales?
2. Is the product management system working effectively? Are product managers able to plan profits as well as sales volume?
3. Are there any groups in marketing that need more training, motivation, supervision, or evaluation?

### C. Interface Efficiency
1. Are there any problems between marketing and manufacturing, R&D, purchasing, or financial management that need attention?

## Part IV — Marketing Systems Audit

### A. Marketing Information System
1. Is the marketing intelligence system producing accurate, sufficient, and timely information about marketplace developments?
2. Is the marketing research being adequately used by company decision makers?

### B. Marketing Planning System
1. Is the marketing planning system effective?
2. Are sales forecasting and market potential measurement soundly carried out?
3. Are sales quotas set on a proper basis?

### C. Marketing Control Systems
1. Are control procedures adequate to ensure that the annual plan objectives are being achieved?
2. Does management periodically analyze the profitability of products, markets, territories, and channels of distribution?
3. Are marketing costs being examined periodically?

### D. New Product Development System
1. Is the company well organized to gather, generate, and screen new product ideas?
2. Does the company do adequate concept research and business analysis before investing in new ideas?
3. Does the company carry out adequate product and market testing before launching new products?

## Part V — Marketing Productivity Audit

### A. Profitability Analysis
1. What is the profitability of the company's different products, markets, territories, and channels of distribution?
2. Should the company enter, expand, contract, or withdraw from any business segments, and what should be the short- and long-run profit consequence?

B. Cost-Effective Analysis
1. Do any marketing activities seem to have excessive costs? Can cost- reducing steps be taken?

Part VI — Marketing Function Audits

---

A. Products
1. What are the product line objectives? Are these objectives sound? Is the current product line meeting the objectives?
2. Are there products that should be phased out?
3. Are there new products that are worth adding?
4. Would any products benefit from quality, feature, or style modifications?

B. Price
1. What are the pricing objectives, policies, strategies, and procedures? To what extent are prices set on cost, demand, and competitive criteria?
2. Do the customers see the company's prices as being in line with the value of its offer?
3. Does the company use price promotions effectively?

C. Distribution
1. What are the distribution objectives and strategies?
2. Is there adequate market coverage and service?
3. Should the company consider changing its degree of reliance on distributors, sales representatives, and direct selling?

D. Advertising, Sales Promotion, and Publicity
1. What are the organization's advertising objectives? Are they sound?
2. Is the right amount being spent on advertising? How is the budget determined?
3. Are the ad themes and copy effective? What do customers and the public think about the advertising?
4. Are the advertising media well chosen?
5. Is sales promotion used effectively?
6. Is there a well-conceived publicity program?

E. Sales Force
1. What are the organization's sales force objectives?
2. Is the sales force large enough to accomplish the company's objectives?
3. Is the sales force organized along the proper principles of specialization (territory, market, product)?
4. Does the sales force show high morale, ability, and effort?
5. Are the procedures adequate for setting quotas and evaluating performances?
6. How is the company's sales force rated in relation to competitors' sales forces?

# SUMMARY

This chapter has examined how marketing strategies are planned, implemented, and controlled.

Each business has to prepare marketing plans for its products, brands, and markets. The main components of a marketing plan are executive summary, current marketing situation, threats and opportunities, strengths and weaknesses, objectives and issues, marketing strategies, action programs, budgets, and controls.

It is often easier to plan good strategies than to carry them out. To be successful, companies must implement the strategies effectively. Implementation is the process that turns marketing strategies into marketing actions. The implementation process links marketing strategy and plans with marketing performance. The process consists of five related elements. The action program identifies crucial tasks and decisions needed to implement the marketing plan, assigns them to specific people, and sets up a timetable. The organization structure defines tasks and assignments, and coordinates the efforts of the company's people and units. The company's decision and reward systems guide activities such as planning, information, budgeting, training, control, and personnel evaluation and rewards. Well-designed action programs, organization structures, and systems can encourage good implementation.

Successful implementation also requires careful human resources planning. The company must recruit, allocate, develop, and maintain good people. It must carefully match its managers to the requirements of the marketing programs being implemented. The company's managerial climate and company culture can make or break implementation. Company climate and culture guide people in the company—good implementation relies on strong and clearly defined cultures that fit the chosen strategy.

Each element of the implementation system must fit company marketing strategy. Moreover, successful implementation depends on how well the company blends the five elements into a cohesive program that supports its strategies.

Most of the responsibility for implementation goes to the company's marketing department. Modern marketing departments are organized in a number of ways. The most common form is the functional marketing organization, in which marketing functions are headed by separate managers reporting to the marketing vice-president. Another form is the product management organization, in which products are assigned to product managers who work with functional specialists to develop and achieve their plans. Yet another form is the market management organization, in which major markets are assigned to market managers who work with functional specialists.

Marketing organizations carry out three types of marketing control. Annual plan control involves monitoring current marketing results to make sure that the annual sales and profit goals will be achieved. The main tools are sales analysis, market-share analysis, marketing expense-to-sales analysis, and customer attitude tracking. If underperformance is detected, the company can implement several corrective measures.

Profitability control calls for determining the actual profitability of the firm's products, territories, market segments, and channels. Strategic control makes sure that the company's marketing objectives, strategies, and systems fit with the current and forecasted marketing environment. It uses the marketing audit to determine marketing opportunities and problems and to recommend short-run and long-run actions to improve overall marketing performance.

# QUESTIONS FOR DISCUSSION

1. A junior member of your staff wonders how a 100- or 200- page marketing plan can be condensed into a useful one-page executive summary. What should go into the summary? What should be left out?

2. Describe some of the threats and opportunities facing the fast-food business. How should McDonald's and other chains respond to these threats and opportunities?

3. Overall, which is the most important part of the marketing management process—planning, implementation, or control?

4. What are the major advantages and disadvantages of organizing by function, geography, product, or market?

5. What are the relative advantages and disadvantages of customer attitude tracking when compared with the other annual plan control approaches?

6. IBM sells a wide range of information processing systems to individuals and organizations in North America and around the world. What organization should IBM use for its marketing department—functional, geographic, product-management, or market-management?

7. A friend who owns a restaurant thinks that it is less profitable than it ought to be. How could marketing control help your friend's restaurant be more successful?

8. Why should a university or college conduct a periodic marketing audit? Describe briefly how you would conduct an audit of your school and what you think the audit would reveal.

# KEY TERMS

**Action program** A detailed program that shows what must be done, who will do it, and how decisions and actions will be coordinated to implement marketing plans and strategy.

**Annual plan control** Evaluation and corrective action to ensure that the company achieves the sales, profits, and other goals set out in its annual plan.

**Company culture** A system of values and beliefs shared by people in an organization, the company's collective identity and meaning.

**Company marketing opportunity** An attractive arena for marketing action in which the company would enjoy a competitive advantage.

**Functional organization** An organization structure in which marketing specialists are in charge of different marketing activities or functions such as advertising, marketing research, sales management, and others.

**Geographic organization** An organization structure in which a company's national sales force (and perhaps other functions) specializes by geographic area.

**Managerial climate** The company climate resulting from the way managers work with others in the company.

**Market management organization** An organization structure in which market managers are responsible for developing plans for sales and profits in their specific markets.

**Marketing audit** A comprehensive, systematic, independent, and periodic examination of a company's environment, objectives, strategies, and activities to determine problem areas and opportunities and to recommend a plan of action to improve the company's marketing performance.

**Marketing control**  The process of measuring and evaluating the results of marketing strategies and plans, and taking corrective action to ensure that marketing objectives are attained.

**Marketing implementation**  The process that turns marketing strategies and plans into marketing actions in order to accomplish strategic marketing objectives.

**Marketing strategy**  The marketing logic by which the business unit hopes to achieve its marketing objectives. Marketing strategy consists of specific strategies for target markets, marketing mix, and marketing expenditure level.

**Product management organization**  An organization structure in which product managers are responsible for developing and implementing marketing strategies and plans for a specific product or brand.

**Profitability control**  Evaluation and corrective action to ensure the profitability of a company's various products, territories, customer groups, trade channels, and order sizes.

**Strategic control**  A critical review of the company's overall marketing effectiveness.

# REFERENCES

1. Information from Canadian Tire Corporation Limited, 1989 *Annual Report.*

2. For more on the pet food market in Canada, see Laura Medcalf, "Feast Not Famine in Pet-Food Marketing," *Marketing*, October 9, 1988, pp. 15-19; and Jo Marney, "Feeding Four-Footed Friends," *Marketing*, April 23, 1990, pp. 30-31.

3. For an interesting discussion of marketing budgeting methods and processes, see Nigel F. Piercy, "The Marketing Budgeting Process: Marketing Management Implications," *Journal of Marketing*, October 1987, pp. 45-59.

4. Amar Bhide, "Hustle as Strategy," *Harvard Business Review*, September-October 1986, p. 59.

5. For more on diagnosing implementation problems, see Thomas V. Bonoma, "Making Your Marketing Strategy Work," *Harvard Business Review*, March-April 1984, pp. 70-71.

6. This figure is styled after several models of organizational design components. For examples, see Jay R. Galbraith, *Organizational Design* (Reading, MA: Addison-Wesley, 1977); (Englewood Cliffs, NJ: Prentice-Hall, 1982), p. 95; David A. Aaker, *Strategic Market Management* (New York: Wiley, 1989), Chap. 17; and Carl R. Anderson, *Management Skills, Functions, and Organization Performance* (Dubuque, IA: Wm. C. Brown, 1984), pp. 409-13.

7. For an extensive discussion of the organizational structures and processes best suited for implementing different business strategies, see Orville C. Walker Jr., and Robert W. Ruekert, "Marketing's Role in the Implementation of Business Strategies: A Critical Review and Conceptual Framework," *Journal of Marketing*, July 1987, pp. 15-33.

8. See Thomas J. Peters and Robert H. Waterman, *In Search of Excellence: Lessons from America's Best-Run Companies* (New York: Harper & Row, 1982). For an excellent summary of the study's findings on structure, see Aaker, *Strategic Market Management*, pp. 154-157.

9. For more on Procter & Gamble's implementation process, see Brian Dumaine, "P&G Rewrites the Marketing Rules," *Fortune*, November 6, 1989, pp. 34-48.

10. See "Who's Excellent Now?" *Business Week*, November 5, 1984, pp. 76-78; and Daniel T. Carroll, "A Disappointing Search for Excellence," *Harvard Business Review*, November-December 1983, pp. 78-79ff.

11. This example is adapted from those found in Robert M. Tomasko, "Focusing Company Reward Systems to Help Achieve Business Objectives," *Management Review* (New York: AMA Membership Publications Division, American Management Associations, October 1982), pp. 8-12.

12. For an interesting discussion of management styles, see J.S. Ninomiya, "Wagon Masters and Lesser Managers," *Harvard Business Review*, March-April 1988, pp. 84-90.

13. Peters and Waterman, *In Search of Excellence*, pp. 75-76. For more information on organizational culture and marketing management, see Rohit Deshpande and Frederick E. Webster, Jr., "Organizational Culture and Marketing: Defining the Research Agenda," *Journal of Marketing*, January 19, 1989, pp. 3-15.

14. A.M. Ragab and A.W. Babcock, "An Investigation into the Practice of the Product Manager Concept by Selected Canadian Companies," in Brent Stidsen, ed., *Marketing in the 1970's and Beyond.* Proceedings, Marketing Division, Canadian Association of Administrative Sciences, Edmonton, 1975.

15. Jade Hemeon, "Inside Procter and Gamble," *Financial Times*, March 9, 1981, pp. 1, 21.

16. Dumain, "P&G Rewrites"; and Kevin T. Higgins, "Category Management," *Marketing News*, September 25, 1989, pp. 2, 19.

17. For a more complete discussion of marketing organization approaches and issues, see Robert W. Ruekert, Orville C. Walker, Jr., and Kenneth J. Roering, "The Organization of Marketing Activities: A Contingency Theory of Structure and Performance," *Journal of Marketing*, Winter 1985, pp. 13-25.

18. For details, see Philip Kotler, William Gregor, and William Rodgers, "The Marketing Audit Comes of Age," *Sloan Management Review*, Winter 1977, pp. 25-43.

19. For more on marketing control see Bernard J. Jaworski, "Toward a Theory of Marketing Control: Environmental Context, Control Types and Consequences," *Journal of Marketing*, July 1988, pp. 23-29; and Kenneth A. Merchant, "Progressing toward a Theory of Marketing Control: A Comment," *Journal of Marketing*, July 1988, pp. 40-44.

# CHAPTER 4

# Marketing Research and Information Systems

## CHAPTER OBJECTIVES

After reading this chapter, you should be able to:
1. Discuss the importance of information to the company.
2. Define the marketing information system and discuss its parts.
3. Describe the four steps in the marketing research process.
4. Identify the different kinds of information a company might use.
5. Compare the advantages and disadvantages of various methods of collecting information.

In 1985, the Coca-Cola Company made a spectacular marketing blunder. After 99 successful years, it set aside its long-standing rule—"don't mess with Mother Coke"—and dropped its original formula Coke! In its place came New Coke, which had a sweeter, smoother taste. The company boldly announced the new taste with a flurry of advertising and publicity in both Canada and the United States.

At first, amid the introductory fanfare, New Coke sold well in both countries. But sales soon went flat in the U.S., and the stunned public reacted. Coke began receiving more than 1,500 phone calls and many sacks of mail each day from angry consumers. A group called "Old Cola Drinkers" staged protests, handed out T-shirts, and threatened to start a class-action suit unless Coca-Cola brought back the old formula. Most marketing experts predicted that New Coke would be the "Edsel of the Eighties."

After just two months, the Coca-Cola Company brought old Coke back. Called Coke Classic, it sold side-by-side with New Coke on supermarket shelves. The company said that New Coke would remain its "flagship" brand, but consumers had a different idea. By the end of 1985, Classic was outselling New Coke in supermarkets by two to one. By the end of 1986 Coke Classic was the company's main brand and New Coke was the also-ran.

The situation was similar in Canada, but there was less of an emotional outburst from consumers. One reason was that Canadians had been drinking a sweeter blend of Coke, much like the new product, for over 45 years. In fact, when new Coke was introduced in Canada, the sweetness level was not changed and only a slight change was made in the ratio of syrup to carbonated water. The Canadian president of Coca-Cola said that Canadians had raised little outcry against old Coke's disappearance. However, a Canadian hot-line was established to let consumers tell Coca-Cola what they thought of the change. In three weeks, 575,000 Canadian callers said they wanted old Coke back. The company then re-introduced it as Coke Classic. As in the U.S., by the end of 1986 Coke Classic was outselling New Coke by a large margin. New Coke now holds less than two percent of the soft drink market.

Why was New Coke introduced in the first place? What went wrong? Many analysts blame the blunder on poor marketing research.

In the early 1980s, although Coke was still the leading soft drink, it was slowly losing market share to Pepsi in both Canada and the U.S. For years, Pepsi had successfully mounted the "Pepsi Challenge," a series of televised taste tests showing that consumers preferred the sweeter taste of Pepsi. In Canada, Coke's share of the $2.2 billion soft drink market fell from 28% in 1982 to 22% in 1984. The story was much the same in the U.S. market, which is ten times the size of the Canadian market. Coca-Cola had to do something to stop the erosion of its market share—the solution appeared to be a change in Coke's taste.

Coca-Cola began the largest new product research project in the company's history. It spent over two years and $4 million on research before settling on a new formula. It conducted some 200,000 taste tests in Canada and the U.S.—30,000 tests on the final formula alone. In the blind tests, 60% of consumers chose the new Coke over the old, and 52% chose it over Pepsi. Research showed that New Coke would be a winner and the company introduced it with confidence. So what happened?

Looking back, Coke's marketing research appears to have been too narrowly focused. The research looked only at taste; it did not explore how consumers felt about dropping the old Coke and replacing it with a new version. As one expert noted, the research consisted mostly of "blind comparisons, which took no account of the total product ... name, history, packaging, cultural heritage, image—a rich mix of tangible and intangible." Brand loyalty—that certain something that makes a consumer keep buying over and over again—is an elusive quality. It begins with the customer's preference for a product on the basis of objective reasons: the drink is sweeter, the paper towel is more absorbent. But when a branded product like Coke has been around for a long time it can become part of a person's self-image. The company failed to measure these deep emotional ties. Coke's symbolic meaning turned out to be more important to many consumers than its taste. More complete marketing research would have detected these strong emotions and explored how consumers feel about the product.

Coke's managers may also have used poor judgment in interpreting the research findings and planning strategies around them. For example, they took the finding that 60% of consumers preferred New Coke's taste to mean that the new product would win in the marketplace—as when a political candidate wins with 60% of the vote. But it also meant that 40% still wanted the old Coke. By dropping the old Coke, the company trampled the taste buds of its large core of loyal Coke drinkers who didn't want a change. The company might have been wiser to leave the old Coke alone and introduce New Coke as a brand extension, as was later done successfully with Cherry Coke.

The Coca-Cola Company has one of the largest, best managed, and most advanced marketing research operations in North America. Good marketing research has kept the company on top of the rough-and-tumble soft-drink market for decades. Nevertheless, marketing research is far from an exact science. Consumers are full of surprises, and anticipating them can be difficult. If the Coca-Cola Company can make a large marketing research mistake, any company can.[1]

In carrying out marketing analysis, planning, implementation, and control, marketing managers need information at almost every turn. They need information about customers, competitors, dealers, and other forces in the marketplace. One marketing executive put it this way: "To manage a business well is to manage its future; and to manage the future is to manage information."[2]

This chapter looks at how information is gathered and how it is organized in a useful way. Understanding consumers, the environment, competitive activities, and government intentions is a difficult task. Marketers often require substantial amounts of information to anticipate consumer and environmental changes. Although sellers always need more marketing information, the supply never seems sufficient. Marketers complain that they cannot gather enough of the accurate and useful information they need.

Marketing managers continually need more and better information. Companies have greater capacity to provide managers with information but often have not made good use of it. Many companies are now studying the information needs of their managers and designing information systems to meet these needs.

# THE MARKETING INFORMATION SYSTEM

A **marketing information system (MIS)** consists of people, equipment, and procedures to gather, sort, analyze, evaluate, and distribute information that is relevant, timely, and accurate to marketing decision makers. The marketing information system concept is illustrated in Figure 4-1. The MIS begins and ends with the marketing managers. First the MIS interacts with these managers to assess their information needs. Next, it develops the needed information from internal company records, marketing intelligence activities, and the marketing research process. Information analysis processes the information to make it more useful. Finally, the MIS distributes information to managers in the right form and at the right time to help them in marketing planning, implementation, and control.

We will now take a closer look at the functions of the company's marketing information system.

# ASSESSING INFORMATION NEEDS

A good marketing information system balances the information that managers would like to have against what they really need and what is feasible to offer. The company begins by interviewing managers to find out what information they would

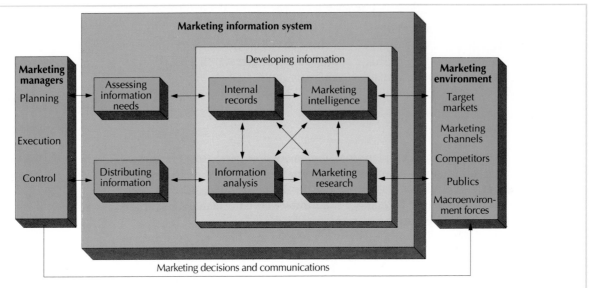

Figure 4-1    The Marketing Information System

like. But managers do not always need all the information they ask for, and they may not think carefully and ask for what they really need. Moreover, sometimes the MIS cannot supply all the information that managers request. However, with today's information technology, most companies can provide much more information than managers can actually use. Too much information can be as harmful as too little.

Busy managers may ignore vital information, or may not know to ask for some types of information. For example, managers might need to know that a competitor plans to introduce a new product during the coming year. Because they do not know about the new product, they do not think to ask about it. The MIS must watch the marketing environment and provide decision makers with information they should have in order to make key marketing decisions.

Sometimes the company cannot provide the needed information because it is not available or because of MIS limitations. For example, a brand manager might want to know how much competitors will change their advertising budgets next year and how these changes will affect industry market shares. The information on planned budgets is probably not available. Even if it is, the company's MIS may not be advanced enough to forecast resulting changes in market shares.

Finally, the company must decide whether the benefits of having an item of information are worth the costs of providing it. Both value and cost are often hard to assess. By itself, information has no worth—its value lies in how it is used. Although methods have been developed for calculating the value of information,[3] decision makers often rely on subjective judgment. Similarly, while the company can add up the costs of the people and equipment that make up a marketing information system, or the costs of a marketing research project, calculating the cost of a specific information item may be difficult.

The costs of obtaining, processing, storing, and delivering information can add up quickly. In many cases, additional information will do little to change or improve a manager's decision, or the costs of the information will exceed the

Information abounds—the problem is to give managers the *right* information at the *right* time.

returns from the better decision that results. For example, suppose a company estimates that launching a new product without any further information will yield a profit of $500,000. The manager believes that additional information will improve the marketing mix and allow the company to make $525,000. It would be foolish to pay $30,000 to obtain the extra information.

# Developing Information

The information needed by marketing managers can be obtained from internal company records, marketing intelligence, and marketing research. The information analysis system then processes this information to make it more useful for managers.

## Internal Records

Most marketing managers use internal records information and reports regularly, especially for making day-to-day planning, implementation, and control decisions. The company's accounting department provides financial statements and keeps detailed records of sales and orders, costs, and cash flows. Manufacturing reports on production schedules, shipments, and inventories. The salesforce reports information on reseller reactions and competitor activities. Information on customer satisfaction or service problems is provided by the customer service department. Research studies conducted for one department may provide useful information for several others. Managers can use information gathered from these and other sources within the company to evaluate performance and to detect problems and opportunities.

Here are some examples of how companies use internal records information in marketing decisions:

- Canadian Tire store managers, through the use of point-of-sale computer terminals, have instant access to sales patterns. The computers can trigger re-orders when needed to avoid stockouts and also to reduce or stop orders for slow-moving stock. Through this electronic data interchange (EDI), Canadian Tire has "linked" more than 370 stores and 130 vendors in its system. Store managers can select and stock more than 44,000 items through EDI.[4]
- Loblaws and A&P stores have installed computer scanners at the checkouts. The scanners supply the store managers with daily sales information on all products. The effect of the weekly advertisements is monitored through the total sales volume by store each day.
- Sears Canada has developed an on-line customer service program that involves placing personal computers, connected to the Sears mainframe computer, in more than 400 catalog stores so that customer orders can be processed on-line. Furthermore, the status of customer orders can be provided, regardless of when they were ordered and where they were being shipped from.

Information from internal records can usually be obtained more quickly and cheaply than information from other sources, but it also presents some problems. Because it was collected for other purposes, the information may be incomplete or in the wrong form for making marketing decisions. For example, accounting department sales and cost data used for preparing financial statements must be adapted for use in evaluating product, salesforce, or channel performance. In addition, the many different areas of a large company produce great amounts of information; keeping track of it all is difficult. The marketing information system must gather, organize, process, and index this mountain of information so that managers can find and use it easily and quickly.

# Marketing Intelligence

**Marketing intelligence** is everyday information about developments in the marketing environment that helps managers prepare and adjust marketing plans. The marketing intelligence system determines what intelligence is needed, collects it by searching the environment, and delivers it to the appropriate marketing managers.

Marketing intelligence can be gathered from many sources. Much intelligence can be collected from the company's own personnel— executives, engineers, scientists, purchasing agents, and the salesforce. Yet company people are often busy and fail to pass on important information. The company must convince its people of their importance as intelligence gatherers, train them to spot new developments, and urge them to report intelligence back to the company.

The company must also encourage suppliers, resellers, and customers to pass along important intelligence. Information on competitors can be obtained from what they say about themselves in annual reports, speeches, press releases, and advertisements. The company can also learn about competitors from what others say about them in business publications and at trade shows. Companies can also use the *Access to Information Act* to determine which competitors have received contracts with the Canadian federal government. In addition, the company can watch what competitors do—it can buy and analyze their products, monitor their sales, and check for new patents.

Companies also buy intelligence information from outside suppliers. A.C. Nielsen of Canada sells bimonthly data (based on a sample of 465 stores) on brand shares, retail prices, percentage of stores stocking the item, and percentage of stockout stores. The ISL Consumer Panel, on a quarterly basis, measures the purchasing behavior of over 3,000 Canadian households. The Daniel Starch Company regularly measures the readership of advertisements appearing in Canadian periodicals. Elliot Research Corporation provides estimates of advertising spending by brand and media.[5] Compusearch provides information on the consumer spending potential for a wide variety of product categories, including household furnishings, transportation, and recreation. Compusearch reports can be tailored to a specific business or a specific trading area, and can include a life style analysis. For a fee, companies can subscribe to one or more of many online databases or information-search services. A readily available online database exists to fill almost any marketing information need.[6]

Some companies set up an office to collect and circulate marketing intelligence. The staff scans major publications, summarizes important news, and sends news bulletins to marketing managers. It develops a file of intelligence information and helps managers to evaluate new information. These services greatly improve the quality of information available to marketing managers.

# Marketing Research

Managers cannot always wait for information to arrive in bits and pieces from the marketing intelligence system. They often require formal studies of specific situations. For example, *Maclean's* magazine would want to know current readers' attitudes toward format changes in the magazine. Or the Toronto-Dominion bank might want to know the effect of opening some of their branches on Saturday. In such situations, the marketing intelligence system will not provide the necessary detailed information. Furthermore, managers normally do not have the skill or time to obtain the information on their own. They need formal marketing research.

We define **marketing research** as the function that links the consumer, customer, and public to the marketer through information—information used to identify and define marketing opportunities and problems; to generate, refine, and evaluate marketing actions; to monitor marketing performance; and to improve understanding of the marketing process.[7] Marketing research specifies the information needed to address marketing issues, designs the method for collecting information, manages and implements the data-collection process, analyzes the results, and communicates the findings and their implications.[8]

Marketing researchers have steadily expanded their activities in Canada and the United States (see Table 4-1). The most common activities are market share analysis, measurement of market potentials, competitive product studies, and short-range forecasting. Firms in the United States generally spend more on marketing research and conduct more research than Canadian firms. The reason, in part, is the smaller size of both the Canadian economy and the Canadian firms.

Every marketer needs research. A company can do marketing research in its own research department or have some or all of it done outside. Whether a company uses outside firms depends on the skills and resources within the company. Fifty percent of large Canadian companies have their own marketing research depart-

**Table 4-1**
**Types of Marketing Research Performed by Companies in Canada and the United States**

| Type of Research | Percent Performing Research | |
|---|---|---|
| | Canada | U.S. |
| Promotion Research | | |
| A. Motivation research | 25 | 37 |
| B. Copy research | 33 | 50 |
| C. Media research | 36 | 57 |
| D. Studies of ad effectiveness | 42 | 65 |
| E. Studies of competitive advertising | 38 | 47 |
| Business Economics and Corporate Research | | |
| A. Short-range forecasting (up to 1 year) | 51 | 67 |
| B. Long-range forecasting (over 1 year) | 50 | 64 |
| C. Studies of business trends | 49 | 83 |
| D. Pricing studies | 50 | 60 |
| E. Plant and warehouse location studies | 35 | 23 |
| F. Acquisition studies | 41 | 53 |
| G. Export and international studies | 33 | 19 |
| H. Internal company employees | 39 | 54 |
| Product Research | | |
| A. New product acceptance and potential | 48 | 68 |
| B. Competitive product studies | 54 | 58 |
| C. Testing of existing products | 52 | 47 |
| D. Packaging research: design or physical characteristics | 41 | 31 |
| Sales and Market Research | | |
| A. Measurement of market potentials | 59 | 74 |
| B. Market share analysis | 61 | 79 |
| C. Establishment of sales quotas, territories | 54 | 26 |
| D. Distribution channel studies | 49 | 29 |
| E. Test markets | 35 | 45 |
| F. Sales compensation studies | 37 | 30 |
| G. Promotional studies of premiums, coupons, sampling, deals, etc. | 28 | 36 |

**Sources:** Thomas C. Kinnear and Ann Root, eds., *1988 Survey of Marketing Research* (Chicago: American Marketing Association, 1989), p. 43; Joyce Cheng, David Conway, and George Haines Jr., "Marketing Research in Canada: A 1985 Update," in *ASAC Marketing Proceedings*, Thomas G. Muller (ed), Whistler, 1986, p. 297.

ments. A company with no research department will have to buy the services of research firms. But even companies with their own departments often use outside firms to do special research tasks or special studies. In total, Canadian firms spend over $200 million annually on marketing research.[9]

# The Marketing Research Process

This section describes the four steps in the marketing research process (Figure 4-2): defining the problem and research objectives, developing the research plan, implementing the research plan, and interpreting and reporting the findings.

## DEFINING THE PROBLEM AND RESEARCH OBJECTIVES

The marketing manager and researcher must work closely together to define the problem carefully and agree on research objectives. The manager best understands the decision for which information is needed; the researcher best understands marketing research and how to obtain the information.

Managers must know enough about marketing research to help in the planning and to interpret research results. If they know little about marketing research, they may obtain the wrong information, reach the wrong conclusions, or ask for information that costs too much. Experienced marketing researchers who understand the manager's problem should also be involved at this stage. The researcher must be able to help the manager define the problem and to suggest ways that research can help the manager make better decisions.

Defining the problem and research objectives is often the hardest step in the research process. The manager may know that something is wrong, but not the specific causes. For example, managers of a discount retail store chain hastily decided that falling sales were caused by poor advertising, and ordered research to test the company's advertising. When this research showed that current advertising was reaching the right people with the right message, the managers were puzzled. It turned out that the chain was not delivering what the advertising promised. More careful problem definition would have avoided the cost and delay of doing advertising research. It would have suggested research on the real problem of consumer reactions to the products, service, and prices offered in the chain's stores.

When the problem has been carefully defined, the manager and researcher must set the research objectives. A marketing research project might have one of three types of objectives. Sometimes the objective is **exploratory**—to gather preliminary information that will help to better define the problem and suggest hypotheses. Sometimes the objective is **descriptive**—to describe things such as the market potential for a product or the demographics and attitudes of consumers who buy the product. Sometimes the objective is **causal**—to test hypotheses about cause-and-effect relationships. For example, would a ten percent decrease in price for an appliance manufacturer result in enough sales to increase profits? Managers often start with exploratory research and later follow with descriptive or causal research.

The statement of the problem and research objectives will guide the entire research process. The manager and researcher should put the statement in writing to be certain that they agree on the purpose and expected results of the research.

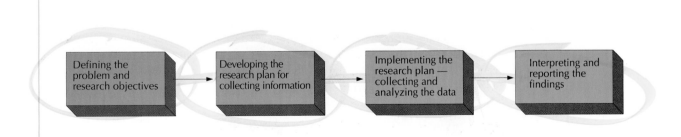

Figure 4-2   The Marketing Research Process

## DEVELOPING THE RESEARCH PLAN

The second step of the marketing research process calls for determining the information needed and developing a plan for gathering it efficiently and presenting the plan to marketing management. The plan outlines sources of secondary data and spells out the specific research approaches, contact methods, sampling plans, and instruments that researchers will use to gather primary data.

## DETERMINING SPECIFIC INFORMATION NEEDS

Research objectives must be translated into specific information needs. For example, suppose the Campbell Soup Company decides to do research to find out how Canadians will react to a new microwaveable breakfast.[10] This research might call for the following specific information:

- How Canadian consumers would respond to the idea of a microwaveable breakfast. (A growing market segment, called the "Chase-and-Grabbits," don't have time to cook. They eat fast foods when out and frozen foods at home.)

- The demographic, economic, and lifestyle characteristics of consumers who were interested in this type of breakfast. (Busy working couples and teenagers might find the convenience of the product attractive.)

- The number of microwave ovens in Canadian households. (Over 65% of Canadian households have microwave ovens.)

- Retailer reactions to the new product. (The average Canadian supermarket stocks around 20,000 products. Retailer support is critical for new product launches.)

- Forecasts of sales and profits for the new product. (Estimates of the market size, Campbell's share, and costs and revenues are required.)

Campbell managers will need information on the above topics, and many other types of information, in order to decide whether to introduce the new product.

## SURVEYS OF SECONDARY INFORMATION

To meet the manager's information needs, the researcher can gather secondary data, primary data, or both. **Secondary data** consist of information that already exists somewhere, having been collected for another purpose. **Primary data** consist of information collected for the specific purpose at hand.

Researchers usually start by gathering secondary data. Table 4-2 shows many secondary data sources, including internal and external sources. Secondary data can usually be obtained more quickly and at a lower cost than primary data. For example, a visit to the library might provide all the information Campbell needs on microwave oven

Researchers often find secondary data in a variety of external sources.

**Table 4-2**
**Sources of Secondary Data**

### A. Internal Sources

* Internal sources include company profit-and-loss statements, balance sheets, sales figures, sales call reports, invoices, inventory records, and prior research reports.

### B. Government Publications

* Statistics Canada, a major source of secondary data, provides information on virtually all aspects of the economy from the consumer price index to population projections. The Statistics Canada catalog provides details of both regular and special studies. Statistics Canada publications of particular interest to marketers include Market Research Handbook, Census publications, Canada Handbook, and Family Expenditures in Canada.
* At the provincial level, the department/ministry involved with industry, trade, and commerce is the most common source for business information. Provincial reports are referenced in the Profile Index.

### C. Periodicals and Books

* *Canadian Business Index* and *Canadian Periodical Index* list business and related articles appearing in a wide range of business and other publications.
* *Financial Post Survey of Industrials* provides an annual survey reviewing over 1,200 Canadian public companies.
* *Dun and Bradstreet Key Business Ratios in Canada* provides business ratios on 166 lines of retailing, wholesaling, manufacturing, and construction.
* *Sales and Marketing Management* presents the Canadian survey of buying power by province and metropolitan area.
* *Financial Post Canada Markets* provides an annual survey of complete demographics for Canadian urban markets.
* Marketing journals include the *Journal of Marketing, Journal of Consumer Research, Journal of Consumer Marketing,* and *Journal of Services Marketing.*
* Useful magazines and newspapers include *Marketing, Canadian Business, Globe and Mail Report on Business, Financial Post, Financial Times, Advertising Age, Marketing News, Business Week, Fortune,* and *Harvard Business Review.*

### D. Trade Association and Other Publications

* Canadian Advertising Rates and Data (CARD) provides a listing of virtually all media in Canada and the advertising rates for these media.
* Canadian Media Directors' Council Media Digest provides general information on the market and media habits of Canadians.
* Canadian Directory of Shopping Centers lists all important shopping centers and retail tenants in Canada, and includes data on gross volumes and market size.
* Tomorrow's Customers, a publication of Woods Gordon, examines trends in the Canadian marketplace.

### E. Commercial Data

Here are just three of the commercial firms selling data to subscribers:
* Print Media Bureau provides data on the readership of Canadian magazines.
* Maclean Hunter sells a wide range of secondary data on markets, including the drugstore market, the electronics market, and the furniture market.
* Bureau of Broadcast Measurement provides data on radio and television audiences and program ratings.
* Data bases are offered by a number of Canadian firms including Maclean Hunter (F.P. Online), the Conference Board (Conference Board) and the Globe and Mail (InfoGlobe).

Commercial research firms like Compusearch sell data on demographics and media audiences to subscribers.

ownership and usage. A study to collect primary information might take weeks or months and cost thousands of dollars. In addition, secondary sources can sometimes provide data that an individual company cannot collect on its own— information that is not directly available or would be too expensive to collect. For example, it would be too expensive for Campbell to conduct a continuing retail store audit to find out about the market shares, prices, and displays of existing competitors' brands like McCain's. But it can buy the A.C. Nielsen data, which provides this information from regular audits of supermarkets.

Secondary data also present problems. The needed information may not exist as researchers can rarely obtain all the data they need from secondary sources. For example, Campbell will not find existing information about a new product that it has not yet placed on the market. Even where the data can be found, they might not be usable. The researcher must evaluate secondary information carefully to make certain it is relevant, accurate, current, and impartial.

Secondary data provide a good starting point for research and often help to define the problem and research objectives. In most cases, however, secondary sources cannot provide all the needed information, and the company must collect primary data.

## PLANNING PRIMARY DATA COLLECTION

Good decisions require good data. Just as researchers must carefully evaluate the quality of the secondary information they obtain, they must also take great care in collecting primary data to ensure that they provide marketing decision makers with relevant, accurate, current, and unbiased information. Table 4-3 shows that designing a plan for primary data collection calls for decisions on research approaches, contact methods, sampling plan, and research instruments.

## RESEARCH APPROACHES

**Observational research** is the gathering of primary data by observing relevant people, actions, and situations. For example:

* A food products manufacturer sends researchers into supermarkets to find out the prices of competing brands or how much shelf space and display support retailers give its brands.
* A bank evaluates possible new branch locations by checking the locations of competing branches, traffic patterns, and neighborhood conditions.
* A maker of personal care products pretests its ads by showing them to people and measuring eye movements, pulse rates, and other physical reactions.
* A department store chain sends observers posing as customers to its stores to check on store conditions and customer service.
* A museum checks the popularity of various exhibits by noting the amount of floor wear around them.

Several companies sell information collected through mechanical observation. For example, A.C. Nielsen attaches "people meters" to television sets in selected homes to record who watches which programs. Nielsen then provides summaries of the size and demographic makeup of audiences for different television programs. The television networks use these ratings to judge program popularity and to set charges for advertising time. Advertisers use the ratings when selecting programs for their commercials.

Checkout scanners in retail stores also provide mechanical observation data. These scanners record consumer purchases in detail and several companies collect and process scanner data for client companies.

**Table 4-3**
**Planning Primary Data Collection**

| Research Approaches | Contact Methods | Sampling Plan | Research Instruments |
|---|---|---|---|
| Observation | Mail | Sampling unit | Questionnaire |
| Survey | Telephone | Sample size | Mechanical instruments |
| Experiment | Personal | Sampling procedure | |

Observational research can be used to obtain information that people are unwilling or unable to provide. In some cases, observation may be the only way to obtain the needed information. On the other hand, some responses simply cannot be observed: feelings, attitudes, motives, and personal behavior. Long-run or infrequent behavior is also difficult to observe. Because of these limitations, researchers often use observation in combination with other data collection methods.

**Survey research** is the approach best suited for gathering descriptive information. A company that wants to know about people's knowledge, attitudes, preferences, or buying behavior can often find out by asking them directly. Survey research can be structured or unstructured. Structured surveys use formal lists of questions asked of all respondents in the same way. Unstructured surveys let the interviewer probe respondents and guide the interview, according to their answers.

Survey research may be direct or indirect. In the direct approach, the researcher asks direct questions about behavior or thoughts—for example, "Why don't you buy clothes at Eaton's?" Using the indirect approach, the researcher might ask, "What kinds of people buy clothes at Eaton's?" From the response to this indirect question, the researcher may be able to discover why the consumer avoids Eaton's clothing—in fact, it may suggest reasons that influence the consumer subconsciously.

Survey research is the most widely used method for primary data collection, and it is often the only method used in a research study. The biggest advantage of survey research is its flexibility. It can be used to obtain many different kinds of information in many different marketing situations. Depending on the survey design, it may also provide information more quickly and at lower cost than the observational or experimental research.

Survey research also has some problems. Sometimes people are unable to answer survey questions because they cannot remember or never thought about what they do and why. Alternatively, people may be unwilling to answer questions asked by unknown interviewers or about things they consider private. Busy people may not take the time. Respondents may answer survey questions even when they do not know the answer in order to appear smarter or more informed or they may try to help the interviewer by giving pleasing answers. Careful survey design can help to minimize these problems.

Whereas observation is best suited for exploratory research and surveys for descriptive research, **experimental research** is best suited to gathering causal information. Experiments involve selecting matched groups of subjects, giving them different treatments, controlling unrelated factors, and checking for differences in group responses. Thus experimental research tries to explain cause-and-effect relationships. Observation and surveys may be used to collect information in experimental research.

Before adding pizza to the menu, researchers at McDonald's might use experiments to answer such questions as the following:

- How much will pizza increase McDonald's sales?
- How will pizza affect the sales of other menu items?
- Which advertising approach would have the greater effect on sales of pizza?
- How would different prices affect the sales of pizza?
- Should the new item be targeted toward adults, children, or both?

For example, to test the effects of two different prices, McDonald's could set up the following simple experiment. It could introduce pizza at one price in its restaurants in one city, and at another price in restaurants in another similar city. If the cities are very similar, and if all other marketing efforts for pizza are the same, then differences in sales in the two cities could be related to the price charged. More complex experiments could be designed to include other variables and other locations.

## CONTACT METHODS

Information can be collected by mail, telephone, or personal interview. Table 4-4 shows the strengths and weaknesses of each of these contact methods.

Mail questionnaires have many advantages. They can be used to collect large amounts of information at a low cost per respondent.

Respondents may give more honest answers to personal questions on a mail questionnaire than to an unknown interviewer in person or over the phone. No interviewer is involved to bias the respondent's answers.

Mail questionnaires also have some disadvantages. They are not very flexible: they require simple and clearly worded questions; all respondents answer the same questions in a fixed order; and the researcher cannot adapt the questionnaire based on earlier answers. Mail surveys usually take longer to complete, and the response rate—the number of people returning completed questionnaires—is often very low. The researcher often has little control over the mail questionnaire sample. Even with a good mailing list, it is often hard to control who fills out the questionnaire at the mailing address.

Telephone interviewing is the best method for gathering information quickly, and it provides greater flexibility than mail questionnaires. Interviewers can explain questions that are not understood. They can skip some questions or probe more on others, depending on the respondent's answers. Telephone interviewing allows greater sample control. Interviewers can ask to speak to respondents with the desired characteristics or even ask for them by name, and response rates tend to be higher than with mail questionnaires.

Telephone interviewing also has drawbacks. The cost per respondent is higher than with mail questionnaires, and people may not want to discuss personal questions with an interviewer. Using an interviewer increases flexibility, but also

Table 4-4
**Strengths and Weaknesses of the Three Contact Methods**

|  | Mail | Telephone | Personal |
|---|---|---|---|
| 1. Flexibility | Poor | Good | Excellent |
| 2. Quantity of data that can be collected | Good | Fair | Excellent |
| 3. Control of interviewer effects | Excellent | Fair | Poor |
| 4. Control of sample | Fair | Excellent | Fair |
| 5. Speed of data collection | Poor | Excellent | Good |
| 6. Response rate | Poor | Good | Good |
| 7. Cost | Good | Fair | Poor |

**Source:** Adapted with permission of Macmillan Publishing Company from *Marketing Research: Measurement and Method*, 4th ed., by Donald S. Tull and Del I. Hawkins. Copyright © 1987 by Macmillan Publishing Company.

In computer-assisted telephone interviewing, the interviewer enters respondents' answers directly into a computer.

introduces interviewer bias. The way interviewers talk, small differences in how they ask questions, and other differences may affect respondents' answers. Different interviewers may interpret and record responses differently, and under time pressures some interviewers might cheat by recording answers without asking questions.

Personal interviewing takes two forms, individual and group interviewing. Individual interviewing involves talking with people in their homes or offices, on the street, or in shopping malls. The interviewer must gain their cooperation, and the time involved can range from a few minutes to several hours. Sometimes a small payment is given to people in return for their time.

Group interviewing consists of inviting six to ten people to gather for a few hours with a trained interviewer to talk about a product, service, or organization. The interviewer needs objectivity, knowledge of the subject and industry, and some understanding of group and consumer behavior. The participants are normally paid a small sum for attending. The meeting is held in a pleasant place and refreshments are served to create an informal atmosphere. The interviewer starts with broad questions before moving to more specific issues, and encourages free and easy discussion, hoping that the group dynamics will bring out actual feelings and thoughts. At the same time, the interviewer "focuses" the discussion—hence the term focus group interviewing. The comments are recorded through note taking or on videotapes that are later studied to understand the consumers' buying process. Focus group interviewing is becoming one of the major marketing research tools for gaining insight into consumer thoughts and feelings. For example, Campbell's used focus groups to find out how Canadian consumers would respond to the idea of a microwaveable breakfast.

Personal interviewing is very flexible and can be used to collect large amounts of information. Trained interviewers can hold the respondent's attention for a long time and can explain difficult questions. They can guide interviews, explore issues, and probe as the situation requires. Personal interviews can be used with any type of questionnaire. Interviewers can show subjects some actual products, advertisements, and packages, and observe reactions and behavior. In most cases, personal interviews can be conducted fairly quickly.

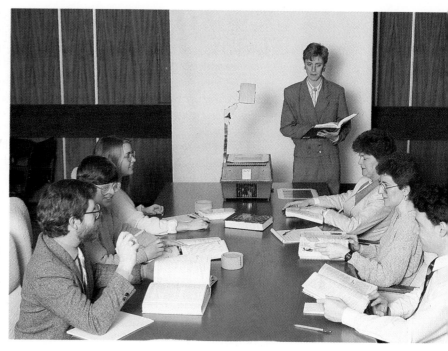

Focus group interviewing is now a major marketing research tool.

The main drawbacks of personal interviewing are costs and sampling problems. Personal interviews may cost three to four times as much as telephone interviews. Group interview studies usually use small sample sizes to keep time and costs down, and it may be difficult to generalize from the results. Because interviewers have more freedom in personal interviews, there is a greater problem of interviewer bias.

Which contact method is best depends on what information the researcher wants, and on the number and types of respondents to be contacted. Advances in computers and communications have had an impact on methods of obtaining information. For example, some research firms now do Computer Assisted Telephone Interviewing (CATI) using a combination of WATS lines and data-entry terminals. The interviewer reads a set of questions from a video screen and enters the respondent's answers right into the computer. This process eliminates data editing and coding, reduces errors, and saves time. Other research firms have set up terminals in shopping centers—respondents sit down at a terminal, read questions from a screen, and enter their own answers into the computer.[11]

## SAMPLING PLAN

Marketing researchers usually draw conclusions about large groups of consumers by studying a small sample of the total consumer population. A sample is a segment of the population elected to represent the population as a whole. Ideally, the sample should be representative so that the researcher can make accurate estimates of the thoughts and behaviors of the larger population.

Designing the sample calls for three decisions. First, who is to be surveyed (what sample unit)? This is not always obvious. For example, to study the decision-making process for a family automobile purchase, should the researcher interview the husband, wife, other family members, dealership salespeople, or all these people? The researcher must determine what information is needed and who is most likely to have it.

Second, how many people should be surveyed (what sample size)? Large samples give more reliable results than small samples. However, it is not necessary to sample the entire target market or even a large portion to get reliable results. If well chosen, samples of less than one percent of a population can often provide reliable data.

Third, how should the people in the sample be chosen (what sampling procedure)? They might be chosen at random from the entire population (a probability sample), or the researcher might select people who can easily provide information (a convenience sample). Alternatively, the researcher might interview a specified number of people in each of several demographic groups (a quota sample). These and other ways of drawing samples have different costs and time limitations, and different accuracy and statistical properties. Which method is best depends on the needs of the research project.

## RESEARCH INSTRUMENTS

In collecting primary data, marketing researchers have a choice of two main research instruments—the questionnaire and mechanical devices.

The questionnaire is by far the most common instrument. Broadly defined, a questionnaire consists of a set of questions presented to a respondent for his or her answers. The questionnaire is very flexible as there are many ways to ask questions. Questionnaires need to be carefully developed and tested before they can be used on a large scale. It is usually possible to spot several errors in a carelessly prepared questionnaire (see Marketing Highlight 4-1).

In preparing a questionnaire, the marketing researcher must decide what questions to ask, the form of the questions, the wording of the questions, and the ordering of the questions. Questionnaires too often leave out questions that should be answered, and include questions that cannot, will not, or need not be answered. Each question should be checked to see that it contributes to the research objectives.

The form of the question can influence the response. Marketing researchers distinguish between closed-end and open-end questions. Closed-end questions include all the possible answers, and subjects make choices among them. Figure 4-3 shows the most common forms of closed-end questions. Open-end questions allow respondents to answer in their own words. The questions take various forms; the main ones are shown in Figure 4-3. Open-end questions often reveal more because respondents are not limited in their answers and, as a result, are especially useful in exploratory research where the researcher is trying to find out how people think, rather than measuring how many people think in a certain way. Closed-end questions, on the other hand, provide answers that are easier to interpret and tabulate.

Care should be used in the wording of questions. The researcher should use simple, direct, and unbiased wording. The questions should be pretested before they are widely used. Care should also be taken in the ordering of questions. If possible, the first question should create interest. Difficult or personal questions should be asked last so that respondents do not become defensive. The questions should come up in a logical order.

Although questionnaires are the most common research instrument, mechanical instruments are also used. For example, a galvanometer measures the strength

# MARKETING HIGHLIGHT 4-1

## A "Questionable" Questionnaire

Suppose the following questionnaire had been prepared by a summer camp director to be used in interviewing parents of prospective campers. How do you feel about each question?

1. *What is your income to the nearest hundred dollars?*

   People don't necessarily know their income to the nearest hundred dollars nor do they want to reveal their income that closely. Furthermore, a questionnaire should never open with such a personal question.

2. *Are you a strong or a weak supporter of overnight summer camping for your children?*

   What do "strong" and "weak" mean?

3. *Do your children behave themselves well in a summer camp?*

   Yes ( ) No ( )

   "Behave" is a relative term. Besides, will people want to answer this? Furthermore, is "yes" or "no" the best way to allow a response to the question? Why is the question being asked in the first place?

4. *How many camps mailed literature to you last April? This April?*

   Who can remember this?

5. *What are the most salient and determinant attributes in your evaluation of summer camps?*

   What are "salient and determinant attributes"? Don't use big words on me.

6. *Do you think it is right to deprive your child of the opportunity to grow into a mature person through the experience of summer camping?*

   Loaded question. How can one answer "yes," given the bias?

of a subject's interest or emotions aroused by exposure to an ad or picture. The galvanometer picks up the minute degree of perspiration that accompanies emotional arousal. The tachistoscope flashes an ad to a subject at exposures ranging from less than one-hundredth of a second to several seconds. After each exposure, the respondents describe everything they recall. Eye cameras are used to study respondents' eye movements to determine at what points their eyes land first, and how long they linger on a given item. The audiometer is an electronic device attached to television sets in homes to record when the set is on and to which channel it is tuned.

### PRESENTING THE RESEARCH PLAN

At this stage, the marketing researcher should summarize the research plan in a written proposal. A written proposal is especially important when the research project will be large and complex, or when an outside firm carries out the research. The proposal should cover the management problems to be addressed, the research objectives, the information to be obtained, the sources of secondary information or methods for collecting primary data, and how the results will help management decision making. The proposal should also include research costs. A written research plan or proposal ensures that the marketing manager and researchers have considered all important aspects of the research, and that they agree on why and how the research will be done.

## IMPLEMENTING THE RESEARCH PLAN

The researcher next puts the marketing research plan into action. This involves collecting, processing, and analyzing the information. Data collection can be done by the company's marketing research staff or by outside firms. The company keeps more control over the collection process and data quality by using its own staff. However, outside firms that specialize in data collection can often do the job more quickly and at lower cost.

| | | Closed-End Questions |
|---|---|---|
| Name | Description | Example |
| Dichotomous | A question offering two answer choices. | Do you eat breakfast? <br> Yes ❏   No ❏ |
| Multiple choice | A question offering three or more answer choices. | With whom do you usually eat dinner? <br><br> No one ❏   Children only ❏ <br><br> Spouse ❏   Business associates/friends/relatives ❏ <br><br> Spouse and children ❏   An organized tour group ❏ |
| Likert scale | A statement where respondent shows the amount of agreement/disagreement. | Campbell Soup produces good quality products. <br><br> Strongly disagree 1 ❏   Disagree 2 ❏   Neither agree nor disagree 3 ❏   Agree 4 ❏   Strongly agree 5 ❏ |
| Semantic differential | A scale is inscribed between two bipolar words, and the respondent selects the point that represents the direction and intensity of his or her feelings. | Campbell Soup <br><br> Large [x] ...... Small <br> Experienced ...... [x] .. Inexperienced <br> Modern ... [x] .... Old-fashioned |
| Importance scale | A scale that rates the importance of some attribute from "not at all important" to "extremely important." | A hot breakfast to me is: <br><br> Extremely important 1   Very important 2   Somewhat important 3   Not very important 4   Not at all important 5 |
| Rating scale | A scale that rates some attribute from "poor" to "excellent." | Campbell's Soups are: <br><br> Excellent 1   Very good 2   Good 3   Fair 4   Poor 5 |

| Open-End Questions | | |
|---|---|---|
| Name | Description | Example |
| Completely unstructured | A question that respondents can answer in an almost unlimited number of ways. | "What is your opinion of Campbell's Soup?" |
| Word association | Words are presented, one at a time, and respondents mention the first word that comes to mind. | "What is the first word that comes to your mind when you hear the following?" Soup_____ Breakfast_____ Campbell_____ |
| Sentence completion | Incomplete sentences are presented, one at a time, and respondents complete the sentence. | "When I choose what to eat for breakfast, the most important consideration in my decision is _____ _____" |
| Story completion | An incomplete story is presented, and respondents are asked to complete it. | "I had a really good breakfast last week. This aroused in me the following thoughts and feelings." Now complete the story. |

Figure 4-3   Types of Questions

The data collection phase of the marketing research process is generally the most expensive and the most subject to error. The researcher should watch the fieldwork closely to make sure that the plan is correctly implemented. The researcher can also help to guard against problems with contacting respondents, with respondents who refuse to cooperate or who give biased or dishonest answers, and with interviewers who make mistakes or take shortcuts.

The collected data must be processed and analyzed to pull out important information and findings. Data from questionnaires is checked for accuracy and completeness, and coded for computer analysis. The researcher applies standard computer programs to prepare tabulations of results and to compute averages and other measures for the major variables.

## INTERPRETING AND REPORTING THE FINDINGS

The researcher must now interpret the findings, draw conclusions, and report them to management. It is important for the researcher not to overwhelm managers with numbers and fancy statistical techniques. The researcher should present major findings that are relevant to the major decisions faced by management.

However, interpretation should not be left only to the researchers. They are often experts in research design and statistics, but the marketing manager knows more about the problem and the decisions that must be made. In many cases, findings can be interpreted in different ways, and discussions between researchers and managers will help highlight the best interpretations. The manager will also want to check that the research project was properly carried out and that all the necessary analysis was done. Or, after seeing the findings, the manager may have additional questions that can be answered using the collected research data. Finally, the manager is the one who must ultimately decide what action the research suggests.

The researchers may even make the data directly available to marketing managers so that they can perform new analyses and test new relationships on their own.

Interpretation is an important phase of the marketing process. The best research is meaningless if the manager blindly accepts incorrect interpretations from the researcher. Similarly, managers may have biased interpretations—they tend to accept research results that show what they expected and to reject those that they did not expect or hope for. Thus, managers and researchers must work together closely when interpreting research results, and both share responsibility for the research process and resulting decisions.

## Marketing Research in Smaller Organizations

In the last section we have looked at the marketing research process—from defining research objectives to interpreting and reporting results—as a lengthy, formal process carried out by large marketing companies. However, many small businesses and nonprofit organizations also use marketing research. Almost any organization can find informal, low-cost alternatives to the formal and complex marketing research techniques used by research experts in large firms (see Marketing Highlight 4-2).

## Information Analysis

Information gathered by the company's marketing intelligence and marketing research systems often requires further analysis. Managers may need help to apply the research to marketing problems and decisions. This might include more advanced statistical analysis to learn more about the relationships within a set of data and their statistical reliability. Such analysis allows management to go beyond means and standard deviations in the data, and allows managers to answer such questions as:

- What are the major variables affecting my sales and how important is each one?
- If I raise my price ten percent and increased my advertising expenditures 20%, what would happen to sales?
- What are the best predictors of consumers who are likely to buy my brand versus my competitor's brand?
- What are the best variables for segmenting my market, and how many segments exist?

Information analysis might also involve a collection of mathematical models that will help marketers make better decisions. Each model represents some real system, process, or outcome. These models can help answer the questions of what if and which is best. In the past 20 years, marketing scientists have developed a great number of models to help marketing managers make better marketing mix decisions, design sales territories and sales call plans, select sites for retail outlets, develop optimal advertising mixes, and forecast new product sales.[12]

## Distributing Information

Marketing information has no value until managers use it to make better marketing

# MARKETING HIGHLIGHT 4-2

## Marketing Research in Small Businesses and Nonprofit Organizations

Managers of small businesses and nonprofit organizations often think that marketing research can be done only by experts in large companies with big research budgets. However, many of the marketing research techniques discussed in this chapter can also be used less formally by smaller organizations, at little or no expense.

Managers of small businesses and nonprofit organizations can obtain good marketing information simply by observing their environment. For example, retailers can evaluate new locations by observing vehicle and pedestrian traffic. They can visit competing stores to check on facilities and prices. They can evaluate their customer mix by recording how many and what kinds of customers shop in the store at different times. Competitor advertising can be monitored by collecting advertisements from local media.

Managers can conduct informal surveys using small convenience samples. The director of an art museum can learn what patrons think about new exhibits by conducting informal "focus groups"— inviting small groups to lunch and having discussions on topics of interest. Retail salespeople can talk with customers visiting the store; hospital officials can interview patients. Restaurant managers might make random phone calls during slack hours to interview consumers about where they eat out and what they think of various restaurants in the area.

Managers can also conduct their own simple experiments. For example, by changing the themes in regular fundraising mailings and watching the results, a nonprofit manager can find out much about which marketing strategies work best. By varying newspaper advertisements, a store manager can learn the effects of aspects such as ad size and position, price coupons, and media used.

Small organizations can obtain most of the secondary data available to large businesses. In addition, many associations, local media, chambers of commerce, and government agencies provide special help to small organizations. Local newspapers often provide information on local shoppers and their buying patterns.

Sometimes volunteers and colleges are willing to help carry out research. Nonprofit organizations can often use volunteers from local service clubs and other sources. Many colleges are seeking small businesses and nonprofit organizations to serve as cases for projects in marketing research classes.

Thus, secondary data collection, observation, surveys, and experiments can be used effectively by small organizations with small budgets. Although such informal research is less complex and costly, it must still be done carefully. Managers must carefully think through the objectives of the research, formulate questions in advance, recognize the biases introduced by smaller samples and less skilled researchers, and conduct the research systematically. If carefully planned and implemented, such low-cost research can provide reliable information for improving marketing decision making.

decisions. The information gathered through marketing intelligence and marketing research must be distributed to the right marketing managers at the right time. Most companies have centralized marketing information systems that provide managers with regular performance reports, intelligence updates, and reports on the results of studies. Managers need these routine reports for making regular planning, implementation, and control decisions. However, marketing managers may also need particular information for special situations and on-the-spot decisions. For

# MARKETING HIGHLIGHT 4-3

## Information Networks: Decentralizing the Marketing Information System

New information technologies are making it possible to help managers obtain, process, and send information directly through machines rather than relying on the services of information specialists. The last decade's centralized information systems are giving way to systems that take information management out of the hands of staff specialists and put it into the hands of managers. Many companies are developing information networks that link separate technologies such as word processing, data processing, and image processing into a single system.

For example, envision the working day of a future marketing manager. On arriving at work, the manager turns to a desk-top computer and reads any messages that arrived during the night, reviews the day's schedule, checks the status of an ongoing computer conference, reads several intelligence alerts, and browses through abstracts of relevant articles from the previous day's business press. To prepare for a late-morning meeting of the new-products committee, the manager calls up a recent marketing research report from microfilm storage to the screen, reviews relevant sections, edits them into a short report, sends copies electronically to other committee members who are also connected to the information network, and has the computer file a copy on microfilm. Before leaving for the meeting, the manager uses the computer to make lunch reservations at a favorite restaurant and to buy airline tickets for next week's trip to Halifax.

The afternoon is spent preparing sales and profit forecasts for the new product discussed at the morning meeting. The manager obtains test-market data from company data banks and information on market demand, sales of competing products, and expected economic conditions from external data bases to which the company subscribes. These data are used as inputs for the sales-forecasting model stored in the company's model bank. The manager "plays" with the model to see how different assumptions affect predicted results.

At home later that evening, the manager uses a laptop personal computer to contact the network, prepare a report on the product, and send copies to the computers of other involved managers, who can read them first thing in the morning. When the manager logs off, the computer automatically sets the alarm clock and puts out the cat.

example, a sales manager having trouble with a major customer wants a summary of the account's sales and profitability over the past year. As another example, a retail store manager whose store has run out of a best-selling product wants to know the current inventory levels in the chain's other stores. In companies with centralized information systems, these managers must request the information from the MIS staff and wait; often the information arrives too late to be useful.

Recent developments in information handling have caused a revolution in information distribution. With advances in microcomputers, software, and communications, many companies are decentralizing their marketing information systems. They are giving managers direct access to information stored in the system.[13] In some companies, marketing managers can use a microcomputer to tie into the company's information network.[14] From any location, they can obtain information from internal records or outside information services, analyze the information using statistical packages and models, prepare reports on a word processor, and communi-

New technologies enable managers to access an information network.

cate with others in the network through telecommunications (see Marketing Highlight 4-3).

Such systems offer exciting prospects. They allow the managers to get the information they need directly and quickly, and to tailor it to their own needs. As more managers develop the skills needed to use such systems, and as improvements in the technology make them more economical, more and more marketing companies will use decentralized marketing information systems.

# SUMMARY

In carrying out their marketing responsibilities, marketing managers need a great deal of information. Despite the growing supply of information, managers often lack enough information of the right kind or have too much of the wrong kind. To overcome these problems, many companies are taking steps to improve their marketing information systems.

A well-designed marketing information system begins and ends with the user. It first assesses information needs by interviewing marketing managers and surveying their decision environment to determine what information is desired, needed, and feasible to offer.

The MIS next develops information and helps managers to use it more effectively. Internal records provide information on sales, costs, inventories, cash flows, and accounts receivable and payable. Such data can be obtained quickly and cheaply, but must often be adapted for marketing decisions. The marketing intelligence system supplies marketing executives with everyday information about developments in the external marketing environment. Intelligence can be collected from company employees, customers, suppliers, and resellers, or by monitoring published reports, conferences, advertisements, competitor actions, and other activities in the environment.

Marketing research involves collecting information relevant to a specific marketing problem facing the company. Every marketer needs marketing research, and many companies have their own marketing research departments. Marketing research involves a four-step process. The first step consists of the manager and researcher carefully defining the problem and setting the research objectives. The objectives may be exploratory, descriptive, or causal. The second step consists of developing the research plan for collecting data from primary and secondary sources. Primary data collection calls for choosing a research approach (observation, survey, experiment), choosing a contact method (mail, telephone, personal), designing a sampling plan (who to survey, how many to survey, and how to choose them) and developing research instruments (questionnaire, mechanical). The third step consists of implementing the marketing research plan by collecting, processing, and analyzing the information. The fourth step consists of interpreting and reporting the findings. Further information analysis helps marketing managers to apply the information and provides advanced statistical procedures and models to develop more rigorous findings from information.

Finally, the marketing information system distributes information gathered from internal sources, marketing intelligence, and marketing research to the right managers at the right times. More and more companies are decentralizing their information systems through distributed processing networks that allow managers to have direct access to information.

# QUESTIONS FOR DISCUSSION

1. What are some kinds of information that managers want? What kinds of information is a marketing information system likely to provide?

2. As a salesperson calling on industrial accounts, you would learn a lot that could help decision makers in your company. What kinds of information would you pass on? How would you decide whether something is worth reporting?

3. List some internal and environmental factors that can influence the focus and scope of a company's marketing research program.

4. The president of a campus organization has asked you to investigate its declining membership. How would you apply the four steps in the marketing research process to this project?

5. You are a research supplier, designing and conducting studies for a variety of companies. What is the most important thing you can do to ensure that your clients will get their money's worth from your services?

6. What research problem did Coca-Cola appear to be investigating prior to the introduction of New Coke? What problem should Coke have investigated?

7. What type of research would be appropriate in the following situations?

   a. Kellogg wants to investigate the impact of children on parents' decisions to buy breakfast foods.

b. Your college bookstore wants some insights into students' feelings about its merchandise, prices, and services.

c. McDonald's must decide on the best location for a new outlet in a fast-growing suburb.

d. Gillette wants to determine whether a new line of children's deodorant will be profitable.

8. A recently completed study shows that most customers use more of your company's brand of shampoo than they need in order to clean their hair. Company advertising encourages overuse, which wastes customers' money but increases sales. Although you suggested to the product manager that the advertising be modified, no changes were made. Assuming you are in the research department, what should you do now?

# KEY TERMS

**Causal research** Marketing research to test hypotheses about cause-and-effect relationships.

**Descriptive research** Marketing research to better describe marketing problems, situations, or markets—such as the market potential for a product, or the demographics and attitudes of consumers.

**Experimental research** The gathering of primary data by selecting matched groups of subjects, giving them different treatments, controlling related factors, and checking for differences in group responses.

**Exploratory research** Marketing research to gather preliminary information that will help to better define problems and suggest hypotheses.

**Marketing information system (MIS)** A structure of people, equipment, and procedures to gather, sort, analyze, evaluate, and distribute information that is relevant, timely, and accurate to marketing decision makers.

**Marketing intelligence** Everyday information about developments in the marketing environment that helps managers prepare and adjust marketing plans.

**Marketing research** The function that links the consumer, customer, and public to the marketer through information— information used to identify and define marketing opportunities and problems; to generate, refine, and evaluate marketing actions; to monitor marketing performance; and to improve understanding of the marketing process.

**Observational research** The gathering of primary data by observing relevant people, actions, and situations.

**Primary data** Information collected for the specific purpose at hand.

**Sample** A segment of the population selected for marketing research to represent the population as a whole.

**Secondary data** Information that already exists somewhere, having been collected for another purpose.

**Survey research**  The gathering of primary data by asking people questions about their knowledge, attitudes, preferences, and buying behavior.

# REFERENCES

1. Based on numerous sources, including "Coke 'Family' Sales Fly as New Coke Stumbles," *Advertising Age*, January 17, 1986, p. 1ff; Scott Scredon and Marc Frons, "Coke's Man on the Spot," *Business Week*, July 29, 1985, pp. 56-61; Cathryn Matherwell, "Canada Getting Coke Classic," *Globe and Mail*, July 24, 1985, p. B5; Patricia Winters, "For New Coke, What Price Success?" *Advertising Age*, March 20, 1989, pp. 51-52; Marc Rice, "New Coca-Cola a Classic Mistake," *Toronto Star*, May 8, 1989, p. B2, and Andrew Cohen, "Escalating Cola Wars Leave Bitter After Taste," *Financial Post*, July 13, 1985, p. 5. The quoted material is from Jack Honomichl, "Missing Ingredients in 'New' Coke's Research," *Advertising Age*, July 22, 1985, p. 1ff and Anne B. Fisher, "Coke's Brand Loyalty Lesson," *Fortune*, August 5, 1985, pp. 44-46.

2. Marion Harper, Jr., "A New Profession to Aid Management," *Journal of Marketing*, January 1961, p. 1.

3. Donald S. Tull and Del I. Hawkins, *Marketing Research: Measurement and Method*, 4th ed. (New York: MacMillan, 1987), pp. 40-41, 750- 760.

4. Serge Fortier, "EDI Efficiency," *Retail Directions*, January/February 1989, pp. 21-22.

5. For further information on advertising research in Canada, see René Y. Darmon, Michel Laroche, and K. Lee McGown, *Marketing Research in Canada* (Toronto: Gage, 1989), Chap. 15.

6. See Tim Miller, "Focus: Competitive Intelligence," *Online Access Guide*, March/April 1987, pp. 43-57.

7. The American Marketing Association officially adopted this definition in 1987.

8. For an excellent overview of the marketing research process, see Vincent P. Barabba, "The Marketing Research Encyclopedia," *Harvard Business Review*, January-February, 1990, pp. 105-116.

9. See Joyce Cheng, David Conway, and George Haines Jr., "A Comparison of Business Use of Marketing Research in Canada and the United States," in ASAC *Marketing Proceedings*, Thomas E. Muller (ed.), Whistler, 1986, p. 297; and Jared Mitchell, "The Truth is Not for the Squeamish," *Report on Business Magazine*, March 1987, pp. 74-76. For an historical perspective see A.B. Blankenship, Chuck Chaprapani, and W. Harold Poole, *A History of Marketing Research in Canada*, Professional Marketing Research Society, Toronto, 1985.

10. This example is based on Campbell's introduction of microwaveable breakfasts to the Canadian market. See Pat Davis, "The Soul of a New Instant Breakfast," *Report on Business Magazine*, September 1988, pp. 78-92. Campbell's launched the Swanson frozen breakfast line in 1987, but soon after the launch, the market became cluttered with competitive brands and Campbell's decided to exit the business.

11. For more on computer-assisted interviewing, see John P. Liefeld, "Response

Effects in Computer-Administered Questioning," *Journal of Marketing Research*, November 1988, pp. 405-409.

12. For more on statistical analysis, consult a standard text such as Darmon, Laroche, and McGown, *Marketing Research in Canada*. For a review of marketing models, see Gary L. Lilien and Philip Kotler, *Marketing Decision Making: A Model Building Approach* (New York: Harper & Row, 1983); also see John D. C. Little, "Decision Support Systems for Marketing Managers," *Journal of Marketing*, Summer 1979, pp. 9-26.

13. See Peter Nulty, "How Personal Computers Change Managers' Lives," *Fortune*, September 3, 1984, pp. 38-48; "Marketing Managers No Stranger to the PC," *Sales & Marketing Management*, May 13, 1985; and "Make Way for the Salesman's Best Friend," *Sales & Marketing Management*, February 1988, pp. 53-56.

14. For further information on the use of microcomputers in marketing research see René Y. Darmon, Michel Laroche, and K. Lee McGown, *Marketing Research in Canada* (Toronto: Gage, 1989), Appendix 1.

# CHAPTER 5

# The Marketing Environment

## CHAPTER OBJECTIVES

After reading this chapter, you should be able to:
1. Describe the environmental forces that affect a company's ability to serve its customers.
2. Explain how changes in the demographic and economic environments affect marketing decisions.
3. Identify the major trends in a firm's natural and technological environments.
4. Discuss the key changes occurring in the political and cultural environments.

Understanding the changing Canadian environment is a difficult task for many marketers. Shifting demographics are creating new opportunities and threats in the marketplace. For example, between 1986 and 1996, the number of Canadians under 35 years of age will decline by seven percent and the number over 35 will increase by 25%. The biggest increase will occur as the Baby Boomers enter middle age—there will be 1.6 million more adults in the 35 to 49 age group, an increase of 32% from 1986.

Not only is the median age of the population shifting, but Canadians are getting married later in life, the average family size is declining, the number of working mothers is increasing, and the divorce rate is increasing. Ignoring these changes can lead to dire consequences in the marketplace—as the Campbell Soup Company learned in the early 1980s.

By 1982, Campbell Soup had become a stodgy, conservative company with declining sales in the highly competitive packaged foods industry. As the market changed, consumers didn't want just a can of soup, they also wanted increased convenience, sophistication, and variety. Per capita consumption of soup had decreased and Campbell was losing share in a declining market. The story was the same for TV dinners and tomato juice, as market share for Campbell was flat or declining in these product categories.

In 1983, Campbell hired a new president who was given the task of turning the company around. The president, David Clark, defined the company's mission as operating in the "well-being" business and focused on meeting and responding to the ever-changing needs of Canadian consumers. Campbell's objective was to be in the top five percent of all Canadian packaged goods companies. To accomplish this goal it dramatically increased research and development and marketing expenditures to support the launching of new products and repositioning of existing products. Many of these products were targeted at the growing, health-conscious, convenience food market which is prepared to pay more for value-added, higher quality products. As well, products were designed to satisfy the needs of those Canadians who were eating four meals a day, with the last two meals consisting of lighter convenience foods.

The new and rejuvenated products in Campbell's line include:
- Chunky Soups—"The Soup That Eats Like a Meal."
- Special Request Soups—with one-third less salt than regular soup.
- Prego Spagetti Sauce—a premium sauce.
- Le Menu and Le Menu Light—premium-quality frozen food dinners.
- V-8 Juice—repackaged and positioned as a drink that is nutritious and delicious.

In 1988, David Clark outlined a five-year strategy in which Campbell dedicated itself to being the best food company in Canada. As well, the company has recognized a major change in the environment—the Free Trade Agreement with the United States—which will lead to a much more cost-competitive North American marketplace. The plan will include the merger of a number of production plants in Canada and the U.S. (Campbell U.S. owns 70% of Campbell in Canada) with the new plants being able to serve the entire market. As Mr. Clark noted: "Instead of 400 people in the Toronto plant manufacturing six million cases of canned goods each year, I can foresee 600 people producing 12 to 14 million cases with half shipped to the United States."

By closely monitoring the changing Canadian consumer environment and the larger North American environment, Campbell has been able to identify and capture new opportunities in the marketplace. Since 1983, sales, market share, and profits have steadily increased; these increases strongly indicate that Campbell is on the right track in adapting to developments in the marketing environment.[1]

The marketing environment consists of uncontrollable forces that surround the company. To be successful, the company must adapt its marketing mix to trends and developments in this marketing environment. A company's **marketing environment** consists of the actors and forces outside the firm that affect marketing management's ability to develop and maintain successful transactions with its target customers. The changing and uncertain marketing environment deeply affects the company. Instead of changing slowly and predictably, the environment can produce major surprises and shocks. Which oil companies in 1971 would have predicted the end of cheap energy in the years that followed, the changes in the government's position on Canadian ownership of the oil industry, the decline in world oil prices in 1985, or the price increases of 1990? How many managers at Gerber Foods foresaw the end of the baby boom? Which companies foresaw the opportunities provided by the dramatic changes in Eastern Europe? How many Canadian companies were prepared for the Free Trade Agreement with the United States? The marketing environment offers both opportunities and threats, and the company must use its marketing research and marketing intelligence systems to monitor the changing environment.

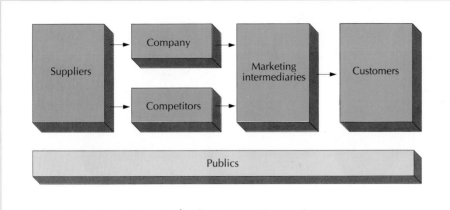

Figure 5-1    Major Actors in the Company's Microenvironment

The marketing environment is made up of a microenvironment and a macroenvironment. The **microenvironment** consists of the forces close to the company that affect its ability to serve its customers—the company, marketing channel firms, customer markets, competitors, and publics. The **macroenvironment** consists of the larger societal forces that affect the whole microenvironment—demographic, economic, natural, technological, political, and cultural forces. We will first look at the company's microenvironment and then at its macroenvironment.

# THE COMPANY'S MICROENVIRONMENT

The job of marketing management is to create attractive products for its target markets. However, marketing management's success will be affected by the rest of the company, middlemen, competitors, and various publics. These actors in the company's microenvironment are shown in Figure 5-1. Marketing managers cannot simply focus on the target market's needs. They must also watch all actors in the company's microenvironment. This chapter will examine the company, suppliers, middlemen, customers, competitors, and publics—in that order. We will illustrate the role and impact of these actors by referring to Pro Cycle of Quebec, a large Canadian bicycle producer. Pro Cycle markets three major brands of bicycles: Velo Sport, Peugeot, and C.C.M.

The forces in Pro Cycle's microenvironment affect the marketing of its bicycles.

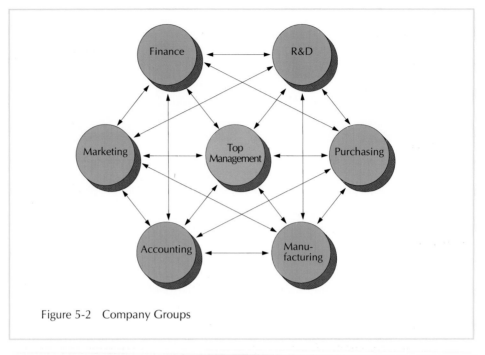

Figure 5-2   Company Groups

# The Company

In making marketing plans, marketing management at Pro Cycle takes into account other company groups such as top management, finance, research and development (R&D), purchasing, manufacturing, and accounting (see Figure 5-2). Top management at Pro Cycle consists of the bicycle division's general manager, the executive committee, the chief executive officer, the chairman of the board, and the board of directors. These higher levels of management set the company's mission, objectives, broad strategies, and policies. Marketing managers must make decisions within the plans made by top management. Marketing plans must be approved by top management before they can be implemented.

Marketing managers must also work closely with other company departments. Finance is concerned with finding and using funds to carry out the marketing plan. R&D focuses on the problems of designing safe, attractive bicycles or new products such as mountain bicycles. Purchasing obtains supplies and materials, while manufacturing is responsible for producing the desired number of bicycles. Accounting measures revenues and costs to help marketing judge how well it is achieving its objectives. All these departments have an impact on the marketing department's plans and actions.

# Suppliers

**Suppliers** are firms and individuals that provide the resources needed by the company to produce goods and services. For example, in order to produce bicycles, Pro Cycle must obtain steel, aluminum, rubber tires, gears, seats, and other materials from Canadian and foreign suppliers. It must also obtain labor, equipment, fuel, electricity, computers, and other factors of production.

Developments with suppliers can seriously affect marketing. Marketing managers need to watch price trends of their key inputs. Rising supply costs may force price increases that can harm the company's sales volume. Marketing managers must also watch supply availability. Supply shortages, labor strikes, and other events can mean lost sales in the short run, and damage to customer goodwill in the long run.

# Marketing Intermediaries

**Marketing intermediaries** are firms that help the company to promote, sell, and distribute its goods to final buyers. They include middlemen, physical distribution firms, marketing service agencies, and financial intermediaries.

## MIDDLEMEN

Middlemen are business firms that help the company find customers or make sales to them. These include wholesalers and retailers who buy and resell merchandise (they are often called resellers). Pro Cycle's primary method of marketing bicycles is to sell them to dealers, who resell them at a profit.

Why does Pro Cycle use middlemen? The answer is that middlemen perform important functions more cheaply than Pro Cycle can by itself. They stock bicycles in locations convenient to customers. They show and deliver bicycles when consumers want them. They advertise the bikes, and negotiate terms of sale. Pro Cycle finds it better to work through middlemen than to try to own and operate its own massive system of outlets.

Selecting and working with middlemen is not easy. No longer do manufacturers have many small, independent middlemen from which to choose. They now face large and growing middlemen organizations. Most bicycles are being sold through large corporate chains (such as Eaton's and Canadian Tire) and large wholesalers, retailers, and voluntary chains. These groups have great power to dictate terms or shut the manufacturer out of large markets. Manufacturers must work hard to get "shelf space."

## PHYSICAL DISTRIBUTION FIRMS

Physical distribution firms help the company to stock and move goods from their origin to their destination. Warehouses are firms that store and protect goods before they move to the next destination. Transportation firms include railroads, trucking companies, airlines, ships, and other companies that specialize in moving goods from one location to another. A company has to decide on the best ways to store and ship goods, balancing such considerations as cost, delivery, speed, and safety.

## MARKETING SERVICES AGENCIES

Marketing services agencies—marketing research firms, advertising agencies, media firms, and marketing consulting firms—help the company to target and promote its products to the right markets. When the company decides to use one of these agencies, it must choose carefully, since these firms vary in creativity, quality, service, and price. The company has to review the performance of these firms regularly and consider replacing those that no longer perform well.

## FINANCIAL INTERMEDIARIES

Financial intermediaries include banks, credit companies, insurance companies, and other companies that help finance transactions or insure against the risks associated with the buying and selling of goods. Most firms and customers depend on these intermediaries to finance their transactions. The company's marketing performance can be seriously affected by rising credit costs or limited credit or both. For this reason, the company has to develop strong relationships with important financial institutions.

# Customers

The company needs to study its customer markets closely. There are basically five types of customer markets. These are shown in Figure 5-3 and defined below:

- Consumer markets: individuals and households that buy goods and services for personal consumption.
- Industrial markets: organizations that buy goods and services for further processing or for use in their production process.
- Reseller markets: organizations that buy goods and services in order to resell them at a profit.
- Government markets: government agencies that buy goods and services in order to produce public services or transfer these goods and services to others who need them.
- International markets: foreign buyers, including consumers, producers, resellers, and governments.

Pro Cycle may sell bicycles in all these markets. It might sell some bicycles directly to consumers through factory outlets. Producers might purchase the bicycles to deliver goods or ride around the plant. It might sell bicycles to bicycle wholesalers and retailers who resell them to consumer and producer markets. It could sell bicycles to government agencies. Pro Cycle might also sell bicycles to foreign consumers, producers, resellers, and governments. Each market type has special characteristics that call for careful study by the seller.

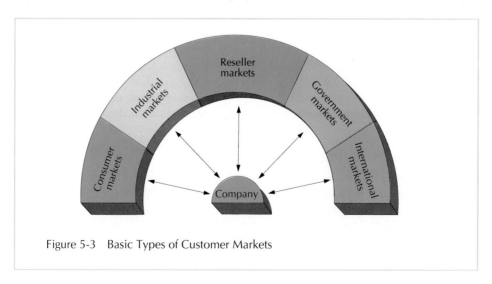

Figure 5-3   Basic Types of Customer Markets

# Competitors

Every company faces a wide range of competitors. The marketing concept states that, to be successful, the company must satisfy the needs and wants of consumers better than the competition. Therefore, marketers must do more than simply adapt to the needs of target consumers. They must also adapt to the strategies of competitors who are serving the same target consumers (see Marketing Highlight 5-1). Companies must gain strategic advantage by strongly positioning their offerings against competitors' offerings in the minds of consumers.

No single competitive marketing strategy is best for all companies. Each firm must consider its size and industry position compared to competitors. Large firms with dominant positions in an industry can use certain strategies that smaller firms cannot afford, but being large is not enough. There are both winning and losing strategies for large firms, and small firms can find strategies that give them better rates of return than large firms. Both large and small firms must find marketing strategies that best position them against competitors in their markets.

In deciding on a marketing strategy Pro Cycle must consider competition from large Canadian firms like TI Raleigh Industries and Victoria Precision, as well as from smaller specialty builders such as Cycles Marinoni and Bicycle-sport. Competition also comes from Canadian firms that import bicycles from around the world, including Italy, Taiwan, South Korea, and Japan. Pro Cycle must analyze a variety of both foreign and domestic competitors as it considers its strategy.

# Publics

The company's marketing environment also includes various publics. A **public** is any group that has an actual or potential interest in or impact on an organization's ability to achieve its objectives. Every company is surrounded by seven types of publics (see Figure 5-4):

• **Financial publics.** Financial publics influence the company's ability to obtain funds. Banks, investment houses, and stockholders are the major financial publics. Pro Cycle seeks the goodwill of these groups by issuing annual reports and showing the financial community that its house is in order.

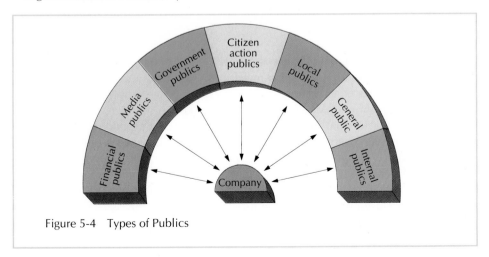

Figure 5-4  Types of Publics

# MARKETING HIGHLIGHT 5-1

## Analyzing Competitors

Knowing one's competitors is critical to effective marketing planning. The company's success is determined, in part, by outperforming the competition. At the very least, the company needs to know four things about the competition:

- Who are the key competitors?

  Identify those competitors who operate in the same segments. These are competitors who offer similar products and services to the same customers at similar prices. The key competitors with McDonald's include Burger King, Wendy's, and Harvey's. McDonald's may also want to consider other fast food companies who specialize in pizza (e.g. Pizza Pizza, Pizza Hut), chicken (e.g. Kentucky Fried Chicken), and other fast foods.

- What are the competitors' marketing strategies?

  Competitors' strategies can be inferred by their actions with respect to product, price, promotion, and distribution. For example, a dramatic increase in advertising for Molson Canadian in Ontario would signal that Molson's is attempting to gain market share, probably at the expense of Labatt's.

- What are the competitor's relative strengths and weaknesses?

  Competitor performance—in terms of sales, market share, profits and return on investment—will help to identify strengths and weaknesses. As well, a review of competitors' resources and competencies in the areas of marketing, operations, research and development, finance, and general management will assist in this task. For example, Proctor-Silex has continually gained share in the Canadian coffee maker market at the expense of Black & Decker and other brands. A review of Proctor-Silex's strategy, performance, and competen-

cies will help companies like Black & Decker identify their own strengths and weaknesses.

- What are the competitor's likely future strategies?

  The previous analysis should help in predicting what competitors are likely to do in the future. As well, management judgment and experience is useful in making predictions about competitors' future strategies.

  Information sources for competitive analysis include: (1) published sources (annual reports, business magazines, industry associations), (2) syndicated services (e.g. A.C. Neilson for market share, other services for advertising expenditures), (3) company employees (the company's salesforce can monitor competitors' actions in the marketplace), (4) competitors' products (analyzing the composition of products), and (5) market research (conducting surveys of consumer's perception of competing products).

- **Media publics.** Media publics are those that carry news, features, and editorial opinion. They include newspapers, magazines, and radio and television stations. Pro Cycle is interested in getting more and better media coverage.
- **Government publics.** Management must take government developments into account. Pro Cycle's marketers must respond to issues of product safety, truth-in-advertising, dealers' rights, and others. Pro Cycle must consider joining with other bicycle manufacturers to lobby for better laws.
- **Citizen action publics.** A company's marketing decisions may be questioned by consumer organizations, environmental groups, minority groups, and others. For example, parent groups are lobbying for greater safety in bicycles. Pro Cycle has the opportunity to be a leader in product safety design. Pro Cycle public relations department can help it to stay in touch with consumer groups.

- **Local publics.** Every company has local publics such as neighborhood residents and community organizations. Large companies usually appoint a community relations officer to deal with the community, attend meetings, answer questions, and contribute to worthwhile causes.
- **General public.** A company needs to be concerned about the general public's attitude toward its products and activities. The public's image of the company affects its buying. To build a strong "corporate citizen" image, Pro Cycle will lend its officers to community fund drives, make large contributions to charity, and set up systems for consumer complaint handling.
- **Internal publics.** A company's internal publics include blue-collar workers, white-collar workers, volunteers, managers, and the board of directors. Large companies develop newsletters and other methods of communication to inform and motivate their internal publics. When employees feel good about their company, this positive attitude spills over to external publics.

A company can prepare marketing plans for its major publics as well as its customer markets. Suppose the company wants some response from a particular public, such as that public's goodwill, favorable word of mouth, or donations of time or money. The company would have to design an offer to this public that is attractive enough to produce the desired response. The results of some of the microenvironment forces on the Canadian bicycle industry have been quite dramatic. The remaining Canadian manufacturers will continue to face many challenges due to the dynamics of these forces (See Marketing Highlight 5-2).

## The Company's Macroenvironment

The company and its suppliers, marketing intermediaries, customers, competitors, and publics all operate in a larger macroenvironment of forces that shape opportunities and pose threats to the company. The company must watch and respond to these forces, which are "uncontrollables." The macroenvironment consists of the six major forces shown in Figure 5-5. The remaining sections of this chapter will examine these forces and show how they affect marketing plans.

# Demographic Environment

**Demography** is the study of human populations in terms of size, density, location, age, sex, race, occupation, and other statistics. The demographic environment is of major interest to marketers because people make up markets. The most important demographic trends are described here.[2]

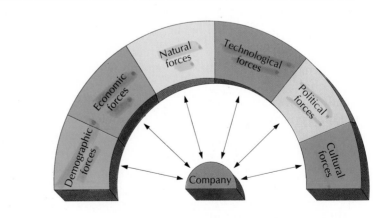

Figure 5-5    Major Forces in the Company's Macroenvironment

# MARKETING HIGHLIGHT 5-2

## The Canadian Bicycle Business: Dynamics of Microenvironment Forces

About 1.1 million bicycles are sold every year in Canada, but the companies that manufacture and market them have changed dramatically in the past few years. Consider how the following microenvironment forces have affected the industry.

- **Suppliers.** Most of the companies that manufactured bicycles in Canada purchased many of the components (e.g. gears, frames) from foreign suppliers in Italy, Japan, Taiwan, and South Korea. In 1984, the import duty on bicycles was reduced from 19.6% to 13.2%. Now companies like Cycles Talisman, which assembled low-cost bicycles in Canada, can no longer compete in the private brand market for the low-end department store. It has stopped assembling bicycles and is now importing them. Companies like Motokov Canada, which imports over 30,000 Czechoslovakian and Taiwanese bicycles each year, have benefited from the lower import duty.

- **Middlemen.** Mass merchandisers, including Eaton's and Canadian Tire, are shifting away from private brands. Ten years ago, 75% of all bicycles sold were private brands (typically retailing for under $100). Now less than 60% are private brands. In fact, Canadian Tire is pouring over $3 million into promoting professional and amateur cycling in Canada and

has joined forces with the Niagara Bicycle Corporation to sell the Steve Bauer line of bicycles, named after the well-known Canadian cyclist. Niagara designed the bicycles in Canada and manufactured them in Italy, Japan, and Taiwan.

- **Customers.** The consumer market is shifting into two distinct segments: the casual, recreation market which is primarily concerned with price, and the more serious market which is more concerned with value. Experts think that the "price" market will be dominated by low-cost imports, whereas there are opportunities for Canadian manufacturers at the upper end. For example, Pro Cycle produces about 275,000 bicycles each year and 75% are targeted towards the "value" market. Pro Cycle also exports about one-third of its bicycles, mainly to the U.S.

- **Competitors.** Companies who manufacture bicycles in Canada face competition not only from other Canadian firms but also from European and Asian imports which account for about 30% of the

market. Thus, Canadian manufacturers must be aware of such factors as import duties, the value of the Canadian dollar, and freight costs from foreign countries. The competition has proven to be tough and a number of Canadian manufacturers have gone under, including C.C.M. (its assets were purchased by Pro Cycle), Sekine, Mikado, and Talisman.

- **Publics.** The government public has affected the industry through the reduction in import duties and the movement to free trade with the U.S. As well, Pro Cycle has benefited from grants of $3.5 million from the

Steve Bauer makes a personal appearance to support Canadian Tire's promotion of cycling. The company markets a line of bicycles with his name.

federal government for machinery and retooling.

Thus, microenvironmental forces have a substantial impact on the bicycle industry. Like many other Canadian industries, bicycles are faced with environments that are not bound by borders— Canadian firms must now face the opportunities and threats provided by global markets and competitors.

**Sources:** Mark Evans, "Canada's Last Bicycle Makers Still Optimistic About Survival," *Financial Post*, June 26, 1989, p. 5; Oliver Bertin, "Two Canadian Bike Makers Done in by Asian Imports," *Globe and Mail*, June 6, 1989, p. B7; Oliver Bertin, "Bicycle Maker Gavin Co. Wheels Out of Receivership," *Globe and Mail*, August 31, 1989, p. B5; and Mark Toljagir, "Wheeler Dealer," *Canadian Business*, August 1989, pp. 15-18.

## CHANGING AGE STRUCTURE OF THE CANADIAN POPULATION

The single most important demographic trend in Canada is the changing age structure of the population. The Canadian population is getting older for two reasons. First, there is a slowdown in the birthrate, so there are fewer young people to pull the population's average age down. Second, life expectancy is increasing, so there are more older people to pull the average age up.

The Canadian population stood at 26 million in 1991 and may increase to 28 million by the year 2001. During the **baby boom** that followed World War II and lasted until the early 1960s, the annual birthrate reached an all-time high. The baby boom created a "bulge" in the age distribution—about one-third of the nation's population are "boomers." Because of its sheer size, most major demographic and socioeconomic changes occurring during the next half decade will be tied to the baby-boom generation (see Marketing Highlight 5-3).

The baby boom was followed by a "birth dearth," and by the mid-1970s the birthrate had fallen sharply. The annual number of births forecast for the early 1990s is about 380,000, compared to a peak of 479,000 in 1959. This decrease was caused by smaller family sizes resulting from the desire to improve personal living standards, the increasing desire of women to work outside the home, and improved birth control.

The second factor in the general aging of the population is increased life expectancy. Current average life expectancy is 75 years; 73 for males and 80 for females. This increasing life expectancy and the declining birthrate are producing an aging population. The Canadian median age is now 32 and by the year 2000 more than half the population will be over the age of 37.

The changing age structure of the population is resulting in different growth rates for various age groups in the 1986 to 1996 decade (see Figure 5-6). These differences will strongly affect the targeting strategies of marketers. Growth trends for the six age groups are summarized below.

- **Children.** The number of infants to nine year olds will decline by 10% in the decade. This will mean that markets for baby toys, clothes, furniture, and food will decline in the next few years.
- **Youths.** The number of ten to 19 year olds will drop slightly during the decade. This means slower sales growth for jeans manufacturers, movie and record companies, colleges, and others who target the teen market.
- **Young adults.** This group will decline during the 1980s and in the next decade, as the "birth dearth" generation moves in. Marketers who sell to the 20 to 34 age group—furniture makers, life insurance companies, sports equipment manufacturers—can no longer rely on increasing market size for increases in sales. They will have to work for bigger shares of smaller markets.

# MARKETING HIGHLIGHT 5-3

## The Baby Boomers

At the end of World War II, a baby boom began in Canada that lasted until 1966. During those years, an average of over 400,000 births per year were recorded, reaching a high of 479,000 in 1959. About one in three Canadians was born during that time, so the baby boomers make up a large part of Canada's population. They have become one of the biggest forces shaping the marketing environment.

The boomers have presented a moving target, creating new markets as they grew through their infant, preadolescent, teenage, young-adult, and now middle-age years. They created markets for baby products and toys in the 1950s; jeans, records, and cosmetics in the 1960s; fun and informal fashions in the 1970s; and fitness, new homes, and childcare in the 1980s.

Today, the baby boomers are starting to gray at the temples and spread at the waist. They are also reaching their peak earning and spending years. They are settling into home ownership, starting to raise families, and maturing into the most affluent generation in history. Thus, they constitute a lucrative market for housing, furniture and appliances, low-cal foods and beverages, physical fitness products, high-priced cars, convenience products, and financial services.

The baby boomer parents of today are generally older, better educated, and more affluent than previous generations. With an increase in working couples, disposable income is high, and with fewer children (an average of 1.7 per family), there is more money to spend on each child. In fact, even though there were fewer kids between the ages of five and 13 in 1986 than in 1980, spending on these kids increased by 12% a year. The "kid" market (from infancy-13) is estimated to be worth $3.6 billion. Numerous companies have sprung up to tap this market, including children's bookstores, upscale children's clothing, and quality toys.

As the baby boomers move through the household-formation and child-rearing stages, the companies that are likely to prosper are those that can "help them around the house," offer kitchen and bathroom products, and offer travel packages to child-oriented destinations. As well, many are concerned about the environment and its effect on the quality of life for their children. This concern will be reflected in their buying behavior and their attitudes towards marketing.

Because more than 60% of married women with children work outside the home, and a majority of these are baby boomers, they are interested in upscale baby products and "make-it-snappy" products. The baby boomers have been a potent market force for the last 40 years, and they will continue to be for the next 40.

**Sources:** Barrie McKenna, "Leading the Pack," *The Financial Post*, September 12, 1988, p. 17; Terry Brodie, "Going Absolutely Ga-Ga Over Kids Biz," *Financial Times of Canada*, February 22, 1988, p. 18; Jo Marney, "Canada's Baby Boom: The Sequel," *Marketing*, May 9, 1988, pp. 38-39; Jennifer Hunter, "Baby, It's Yours," *Report on Business Magazine*, January 1989, pp. 44-47; Kenneth Kidd, "Catering to Kids," *Toronto Star*, December 6, 1987, pp. F1, F2; Leonard Kubas, "Radio Aims at Baby Boomers," *Marketing*, March 21, 1988, p. 26; John Lorinc, "The Next Wave," *Canadian Business*, August 1990, pp. 59-60; and Thomas E. Muller, "Forecasting Baby-Boomer Demand For Recreation Products," in John Liefeld, (ed.), *Marketing* (Whistler, ASAC Proceedings, 1990), pp. 218-227.

The baby boomers are a prime target for marketers.

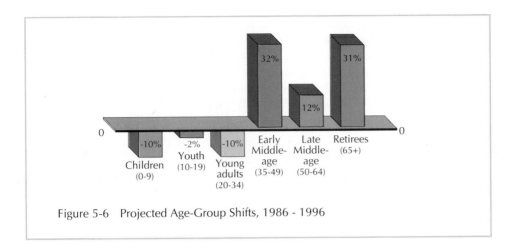

Figure 5-6   Projected Age-Group Shifts, 1986 - 1996

- **Early middle age.** The baby boom generation will be moving into the 35 to 49 age group, creating huge increases. This group is a major market for larger homes, new automobiles, clothing, entertainment, and investments.
- **Late middle age.** The 50 to 64 age group will increase over the decade. This group is a major market for eating out, travel, clothing, and recreation.
- **Retirees.** The over-65 group will increase by 31% over the decade, and will continue to grow. This group has a demand for retirement communities, quieter forms of recreation, single-portion food packaging, and medical goods and services.

Thus the changing age structure of the Canadian population will strongly affect future marketing decisions.

## THE CHANGING CANADIAN FAMILY

The Canadian ideal of the two-children, two car suburban family has been losing some of its luster. There are many forces at work. People are marrying later and having fewer children. The average age of couples marrying for the first time has been rising over the years and now stands at 25 years for males and 23 for females. Couples with no children under 18 now make up about 40% of all families. Of those families that have children, the average number of children is 2.2, down from 3.5 in 1955. There has also been an increase in the number of mothers working outside the home. More than half of the mothers with pre-school children hold a job. In dual-parent families, their incomes constitute 40% of the household's income, and influence the purchase of higher-quality goods and services. Marketers of tires, automobiles, insurance, and travel services are increasingly directing their advertising to working women. All these changes are accompanied by a shift in the traditional roles and values of husbands and wives, with the husband assuming more domestic functions such as shopping and childcare. As a result, husbands are becoming more of a target market for food and household appliance marketers.

Finally, the number of non-family households is increasing. Many young adults leave home and move into apartments. Other adults choose to remain single. Still others are divorced or widowed people living alone. This has meant that the rate of household formation has increased faster than the growth in population. Between 1976 and 1986, the population grew by 11% while households grew by 29%. Between 1986 and 1996, it is estimated that the population will grow by seven percent while households will grow by 16%.

Today, over 32% of all households are non-family households or single-parent households. In Canada, over 1.8 million people live alone (20% of all households). This group needs smaller apartments, inexpensive and smaller appliances, furniture, and furnishings, and food that is packaged in smaller sizes.

## GEOGRAPHIC SHIFTS IN POPULATION

Canadians are a mobile people. About one out of ten, or 2.6 million Canadians, move each year. Among the major trends are the following:

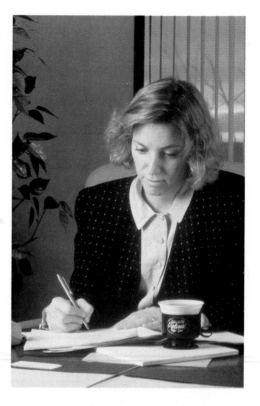

As more married women enter or return to the workforce, more husbands take on domestic responsibilities, including shopping for food and household goods.

- **Movement West then East.** In the 1980s, when Canada's population increased by nine percent, British Columbia's population increased by 15%, followed by Ontario (12%), the Prairies (12%), Quebec (seven percent), and the Maritimes (three percent). However, by 1996 it is projected that Canada's population will increase by less than four percent to 27.3 million. The greatest growth will be experienced by the Maritimes (six percent) followed by Ontario (four percent). These shifts in population are caused, in part, by the economic climates in the various regions of Canada. The population shifts offer opportunities for home builders and retailers in the faster growth areas and threats for the same marketers in the lower growth regions.
- **Movement from rural to urban areas.** People have been moving from rural to urban areas for over a century. Cities show a faster pace of living, more commuting, higher incomes, and greater variety of goods and services than can be found in the small towns and rural areas across Canada. The largest cities, such as Toronto, Montreal, and Vancouver, account for most of the sales of expensive furs, perfumes, luggage, and works of art. These cities also support the opera, ballet, and other forms of "high culture." Recently, however, there has been a slight shift of population back to small towns and rural areas.
- **Movement from the city to the suburbs.** Cities have become surrounded by suburbs. Statistics Canada calls concentrated urban areas Census Metropolitan Areas (CMAs). About 56% of the nation's population live in the 23 CMAs. The CMAs constitute the primary market focus of many firms. The 23 CMA markets with future projections are listed in Table 5-1. Companies use the CMAs in researching the best geographical segments for their products and in deciding where to buy advertising time.

A large number of Canadians live in the suburbs. Suburbs are characterized by more casual, outdoor living, greater neighbor interaction, higher incomes, and

**TABLE 5-1**
**The Top 23 CMA Markets in Canada, 1986 and 1996E**

| Rank 1986 | Rank 1996E | CMA | Population 1986 | Population 1996E |
|---|---|---|---|---|
| 1 | 1 | Toronto | 3,074,000 | 3,310,000 |
| 2 | 2 | Montreal | 2,910,000 | 2,959,000 |
| 3 | 3 | Vancouver | 1,339,000 | 1,512,000 |
| 4 | 4 | Ottawa-Hull | 781,000 | 860,000 |
| 5 | 5 | Calgary | 696,000 | 904,000 |
| 6 | 6 | Edmonton | 673,000 | 790,000 |
| 7 | 7 | Quebec | 622,000 | 699,000 |
| 8 | 8 | Winnipeg | 622,000 | 664,000 |
| 9 | 9 | Hamilton | 597,000 | 626,000 |
| 10 | 10 | St. Catharines-Niagara | 324,000 | 342,000 |
| 11 | 11 | Kitchener | 310,000 | 337,000 |
| 12 | 12 | Halifax | 299,000 | 333,000 |
| 13 | 14 | London | 299,000 | 320,000 |
| 14 | 13 | Victoria | 266,000 | 323,000 |
| 15 | 15 | Windsor | 238,000 | 227,000 |
| 16 | 16 | St. John's | 177,000 | 218,000 |
| 17 | 17 | Oshawa | 165,000 | 196,000 |
| 18 | 18 | Regina | 165,000 | 179,000 |
| 19 | 19 | Sudbury | 151,000 | 144,000 |
| 20 | 20 | Saskatoon | 148,000 | 160,000 |
| 21 | 21 | St. John | 133,000 | 141,000 |
| 22 | 23 | Chicoutimi-Jonquière | 130,000 | 130,000 |
| 23 | 22 | Thunder Bay | 127,000 | 135,000 |

**Source:** *Marketing Research Handbook 1990*, Statistics Canada, #63-224.

younger families. Suburbanites buy station wagons, home workshop equipment, garden furniture, lawn and gardening tools, and outdoor cooking equipment. Retailers have acknowledged the suburbs by building branch department stores and suburban shopping centers.

## A BETTER-EDUCATED AND MORE WHITE-COLLAR POPULATION

In 1981, 36% of Canadian adults had completed some post-secondary education and by 1990, that number had increased to 40% or over 8 million adults. Currently, over 800,000 Canadians are enrolled in colleges and universities. The rising number of educated people will increase the demand for quality products, books, magazines, and travel. It suggests a decline in television viewing, because college-educated consumers watch less TV than the population at large.

The workforce is becoming more white-collar. Forty percent of Canadian workers are employed in white collar jobs (sales, clerical) and 25% of the workforce are in professional, managerial, and administrative occupations. One-third of the workforce are in blue collar occupations. The category with the greatest annual increase in employment in the past decade was professionals, followed by white-collar, and then blue-collar workers.

Demographic trends are highly reliable for the short and intermediate run. There is little excuse for a company to be suddenly surprised by a demographic development. Companies can list the major demographic trends, then spell out what the trends mean for them.[3]

# Economic Environment

The **economic environment** consists of factors that affect consumer purchasing power and spending patterns. Markets require buying power as well as people. Total purchasing power depends on current income, prices, savings, and credit. Marketers should be aware of major trends in income and of changing consumer spending patterns.

## CHANGES IN INCOME

Real income per capita declined during the early 1980s as inflation, high interest rates, and high unemployment reduced the amount of money people had to spend. As a result, many Canadians turned to more cautious buying. To save money, they bought more store brands and fewer national brands. Some companies introduced economy versions of their products and turned to price appeals in their advertising. Some consumers postponed purchases of durable goods, while others purchased them out of fear that prices would be higher the next year. Many families began to feel that a large home, two cars, foreign travel, and private higher education were beyond their reach.

In recent years economic conditions improved then declined. Current projections suggest that real income will rise modestly through the mid-1990s. The baby boom generation will be moving into its prime wage-earning years, and the number of small families headed by dual-career couples will increase greatly. It is forecast that by 1995, over 75% of the women in the 25 to 44 age group will be working outside the home and 50% of the 45-64 age group will be employed. These more affluent groups will demand higher quality and better service, and they will be willing to pay for it. These consumers will spend more on time-saving products and services, travel and entertainment, physical fitness products, cultural activities, and continuing education.

Marketers should pay attention to income distribution as well as average income. Income distribution in Canada is still very skewed. At the top are upper-class consumers, whose spending patterns are not affected by current economic events. These consumers are a major market for luxury goods. There is a comfortable middle class that is somewhat careful about its spending but is able to afford expensive clothes, minor antiques, and a small boat or cottage. The working class sticks close to the basics of food, clothing, and shelter and must try hard to save. Finally, the underclass (people on welfare and many retirees) have to count their pennies when making even the most basic purchases.

In 1987, about six percent of working Canadians made over $50,000 annually, 11% made between $35,000 and $50,000, 14% made between $25,000 and $35,000, 23% made between $15,000 and $25,000, and 46% made less than $15,000. Income differences also exist between the various regions of Canada because of local economic activity and employment levels. The median family income in Newfoundland is about 24% less than in Ontario. As well, the median family income is 18% higher in Canadian cities with a population of over 100,000 than it is in rural communities. Marketers need to take these geographic differences into account when planning their programs.

## CHANGING CONSUMER SPENDING PATTERNS

Table 5-2 shows the consumer spending patterns for major goods and services categories between 1960 and 1990. Food, housing, household operations, and transportation use up most household income. Over time, however, the food, clothing, and personal care bills of households have been falling, while the housing, transportation, and recreational bills have been increasing. Some of these changes were noted over a century ago by Ernest Engel, who studied how people shifted their spending as their income rose. He found that as family income rises, the percentage spent on food declines, the percentage spent on housing and household operations remains constant, and the percentage spent on other categories and savings increases. Engel's laws have generally been supported by more recent studies.

Changes in such major economic variables as income, cost of living, interest rates, and savings and borrowing patterns have a large impact on the marketplace. Companies monitor these variables with economic forecasting. Businesses do not have to be wiped out by a downturn in economic activity. With adequate warning, they can take steps to reduce their costs and ride out the economic storm.

# Natural Environment

The **natural environment** contains natural resources that are needed as inputs by marketers, or that are affected by marketing activities.

During the 1960s, public concern grew over whether the natural environment was being damaged by the industrial activities of modern nations. Popular books raised concerns about shortages of natural resources, and about the damage to water, earth, and air caused by certain industrial activity. Watchdog groups such as Pollution Probe sprang up, and legislators proposed measures to protect the environment. Marketers should be aware of the following two trends in the natural environment.

## INCREASED CONSUMER CONCERN

The 1990s are being referred to as the "decade of the environment." More Canadian consumers are joining the "Green" revolution and basing their consumer and life-style decisions on the effect these will have on the environment. In ever-increasing numbers, Canadians are now participating in recycling programs, purchasing "environmentally friendly" products, and supporting environmental groups. These groups, such as Pollution Probe, the Consumers Association of Canada and Greenpeace, have focused attention on companies they feel are damaging the environment and lobbied governments for better laws to protect the environment. New laws governing emission standards, product contents, and hazardous waste have been enacted, often as a result of pressure from these organized groups.

**TABLE 5-2**
**Percentage Distribution of Consumption Expenditures, 1960, 1970, 1980, and 1990 Estimate**

| Expenditure | 1960 | 1970 | 1980 | 1990E |
|---|---|---|---|---|
| Food, beverages, tobacco | 25.3 | 22.3 | 20.3 | 20.0 |
| Housing | 17.7 | 19.6 | 18.4 | 19.8 |
| Household operations | 10.2 | 9.5 | 9.2 | 8.5 |
| Transportation | 13.1 | 13.8 | 14.7 | 14.5 |
| Medical-care expenses | 6.4 | 3.5 | 3.3 | 3.5 |
| Clothing and footwear | 8.6 | 8.1 | 6.9 | 6.8 |
| Recreation and education | 5.9 | 8.9 | 10.2 | 12.5 |
| Personal business | 4.8 | 6.1 | 9.1 | 8.5 |
| Personal care | 7.4 | 8.0 | 7.3 | 7.4 |
| Other | .6 | .2 | .5 | .5 |

**Sources:** Lawrence R. Small, ed., *Handbook of Canadian Markets*, 1979, The Conference Board of Canada, Ottawa, October 1979 and *Market Research Handbook*, 1990 Statistics Canada, #63-224.

Marketers unwilling to respond to these consumer concerns will face an uncertain future. It appears that neither consumers nor governments will continue to tolerate companies who pollute the environment. On the other hand, the public's concern creates a marketing opportunity for alert companies. It creates a large market for pollution control solutions such as scrubbers and recycling centers. It leads to a search for new ways to produce and package goods that do not cause environmental damage.

Many companies today are responding to consumer concerns. Loblaws with their Green product line, Procter & Gamble with their environpaks, and the Body Shop with their entire business philosophy are examples of firms that are focusing on environmental issues.

## GOVERNMENT INTERVENTION IN NATURAL RESOURCE MANAGEMENT

Various government agencies, at both the federal and provincial level, play an active role in environmental protection. At the federal level, the government has passed the Canadian Environmental Protection Act dealing with toxic substances, the Office of Waste Management is focusing on waste reduction and recycling, and the Environmental Choice program has developed the Ecologo, the environmental equivalent of the Good Housekeeping Seal of Approval. At the provincial level, various programs and legislation have focused on improving the environment, including community assistance for recycling programs.

Today, marketing management must pay attention to the natural environment. Business can expect strong controls from government and pressure groups. Instead of opposing regulation, business should help develop solutions to the environmental problems facing the nation.

# Technological Environment

Another force shaping people's destiny is technology. The **technological environment** consists of forces that affect new technology, creating new product and market opportunities. Technology has released such wonders as penicillin, open-heart surgery, and the birth control pill. In contrast, it has produced such horrors as the hydrogen bomb, nerve gas, and the submachine gun. Technology has also produced such mixed blessings as the automobile, television, and white bread. Our attitude toward technology depends on whether we are more impressed with its wonders or with its blunders.

Every new technology replaces an older technology. Transistors hurt the vacuum-tube industry, photocopiers hurt the carbon-paper business, the auto industry hurt the railroads, and television hurt the movies. When older industries fought or ignored new technologies, their businesses declined.

Successful firms recognize that consumers have basic enduring needs they are attempting to satisfy. New technologies often allow the consumer to satisfy these needs in a better way. For example, the superior sound of a compact disc player versus the record player allowed consumers to better satisfy an entertainment need. New technologies create new markets and opportunities. The marketer should watch the following trends in technology.

## FASTER PACE OF TECHNOLOGICAL CHANGE

Many of today's common products were not available even a hundred years ago. Sir John A. MacDonald did not know of automobiles, airplanes, phonographs, radios, or the electric light. Sir Robert Laird Borden did not know of television, home freezers, automatic dishwashers, room air conditioners, antibiotics, or electronic computers. William Lyon MacKenzie King did not know of photocopiers, synthetic detergents, taperecorders, birth control pills, or earth satellites. John Diefenbaker did not know of personal computers, digital watches, VCRs, or word processors. Companies that do not keep up with technological change will soon find their products out of date, and will miss new product and market opportunities.

## UNLIMITED OPPORTUNITIES

Scientists today are working on a wide range of new technologies that will revolutionize our products and production processes. The most exciting work is being done in biotechnology, solid-

Protecting the natural environment: Alcan helped to found the Blue Box recycling program.

state electronics, robotics, and materials science.[4] Scientists today are working on the following promising new products and services:

| | | |
|---|---|---|
| Practical solar energy | Commercial space shuttle | Correction of simple vision problems with lasers |
| Cancer cures | Small but powerful superconductors | Electric cars |
| Chemical control of mental health | Household robots that do cooking and cleaning | Electronic anesthetic or pain killing |
| Desalinization of seawater | Nonfattening, tasty, nutritious foods | Voice and gesture controlled computers |

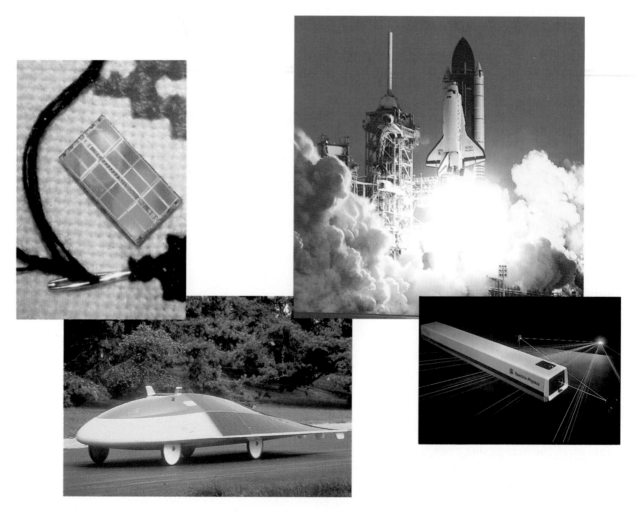

Technology brings exciting new products and services.

Scientists also speculate on fantasy products, such as small flying cars, single-person rocket belts, three-dimensional television, space colonies, and human clones. The challenge in each case is not only technical but commercial—to make practical, affordable versions of these products.

# R&D Budgets

In order to capture the potential offered by innovation, companies and governments must invest in research and development (R&D). In contrast to the United States, where R&D expenditures are about 2.8% of the gross domestic product, Canada spends around 1.3% of its gross domestic product on R&D. While this amounted to over $8 billion in 1989, most industrialized nations spend over two percent of gross national product on R&D.[5] As one example, the level of R&D as a percentage of industrial output is about five times lower in Canada than in the U.S.[6] As well, Canada is importing more technology than it is exporting, which is creating an increasing trade deficit in advanced technology goods such as computers and electronics.[7]

The result of this low R&D activity in Canada is a deficiency in the innovative capability of many Canadian firms. These firms, particularly the subsidiaries of multinationals, frequently rely on parent companies to transfer technology to Canada. This leads to Canadian firms following technology rather than being in the forefront.[8] The industries that spend the most on R&D in Canada are in the "high-tech" sector; notably communications, computer hardware and software, and aerospace. They typically invest five percent to ten percent of sales on R&D, versus less than two percent for resource industries. For example, Northern Telecom spends over $900 million annually to be on the leading edge of the telecommunications equipment market.

Marketers need to understand the changing technological environment and how new technologies can serve human needs. They need to work closely with R&D people to encourage more market-oriented research. With new ideas, they must be alert to possible negative aspects that might harm the users and bring about distrust and opposition.

# Political Environment

Marketing decisions are strongly affected by developments in the political environment. The **political environment** is made up of laws, government agencies, and pressure groups that influence and limit various organizations and individuals in society. We will look at the main political trends and what they mean to marketing management.

## LEGISLATION REGULATING BUSINESS

Legislation affecting business has increased steadily over the years. This legislation has been enacted for a number of reasons. The first is to protect companies from each other. Business executives all praise competition but try to neutralize it when it touches them. For example, the old Combines Investigation Act contained a section that made it an indictable offense to form a merger by which competition in an industry is lessened against the interests of the public (i.e. consumers, produc-ers, or others). The enforcement of this section of the Act was not successful.[9] In 1986, the federal government enacted the Competition Act which contained new provisions for mergers and anti-competitive conduct. Since that time, the Bureau of Competitive Policy has reviewed over 350 merger applications including the "big four": the Canada Safeway purchase of Woodward's Food Floors, Imperial Oil's purchase of Texaco Canada, the merger of Molson and Carling O'Keefe, and Pacif-ic Western Airlines' purchase of Wardair. In two of the cases—Safeway and Imperi-al Oil—changes were made before the mergers were approved. For example, Imperial Oil had to sell over 600 service stations and provide stronger supply guar-antees for independent stations.[10]

The second purpose of government regulation is to protect consumers from unfair business practices. Some firms, if left alone, would make poor products, tell lies in their advertising, and deceive through their packaging and pricing. Unfair consumer practices have been defined and are enforced by various agencies, such as the Department of Consumer and Corporate Affairs at the federal level. In addi-tion, various provincial consumer departments have been established to protect consumers. Many managers become incensed with each new consumer law, while others welcome consumer protection and look for the new opportunities it pre-sents.

The third purpose of government regulation is to protect the interests of soci-ety against unrestrained business behavior. Profitable business activity does not always create a better quality of life. Regulation arises to make certain that firms take responsibility for the social costs of their production or products.

New laws and their enforcement will continue to increase. Business execu-tives must watch these developments when planning their products and marketing programs. Marketers need to know about the major laws protecting competition, consumers, and society. The main federal laws are listed in Table 5-3. In addition, each province has its own set of laws for marketing activities. In Quebec, for exam-ple, Bill 101 requires that all labels have the same information in French as in English.

## Growth of Public Interest Groups

The number and power of public interest groups have increased during the past three decades. The most successful is Ralph Nader's Public Citizen group, a "watch-dog" for consumer interests. Nader built consumerism into a major social force, first with his successful attack on unsafe automobiles and then through investigations of meat processing, truth-in-lending, auto repairs, insurance, and X-ray equipment. In Canada, the Consumers Association of Canada has led the fight to improve pack-ages and labelling, standards for hockey helmets, children's car seats, inspection of meat plants, and many other consumer areas.[11] Other Canadian consumer interest groups that have had an impact on marketing activities include Greenpeace, Pollu-tion Probe, and Energy Probe. Many of these groups are focusing their attention on environmental issues and using various tactics, such as boycotts and demonstra-tions, to draw attention to problem areas. Marketers need to consider the influence of these groups when making decisions that will have an impact on the environ-ment.

# Cultural Environment

The **cultural environment** is made up of institutions and other forces that affect society's basic values, perceptions, preferences, and behavior. People grow up in a particular society that shapes their basic beliefs and values. They absorb a world view that defines their relationship to themselves and others. The following cultural characteristics can affect marketing decision making.

## PERSISTENCE OF CULTURAL VALUES

People in every society hold many beliefs and values. Their core beliefs and values usually persist over time. For example, most Canadians believe in work, the institution of marriage, charity, and honesty. These beliefs shape more specific attitudes and behaviors found in everyday life. Core beliefs and values are passed on from parents to children and are reinforced by schools, churches, business, and government.

Secondary beliefs and values are more open to change. Believing in marriage is a core belief, while believing that people should get married early is a secondary belief. Family planning marketers could argue more effectively that people should get married later rather than that they should not get married at all. Marketers have some chance of changing secondary values, but little chance of changing core values.

---

**TABLE 5-3**
**Major Federal Legislation Affecting Marketing**

---

The Competition Act

---

The Competition Act is a major legislative act affecting the marketing activities of companies in Canada. Specific sections and the relevant areas are:

- Section 34: Pricing—Forbids a supplier to charge different prices to competitors purchasing like quantities of goods (price discrimination). Forbids price-cutting that lessens competition (predatory pricing).
- Section 36: Pricing and Advertising—Forbids advertising prices that misrepresent the "usual" selling price (misleading price advertising).
- Section 38: Pricing—Forbids suppliers to require subsequent resellers to offer products at a stipulated price (resale price maintenance).
- Section 33: Mergers—Forbids mergers by which competition is, or is likely to be, lessened to the detriment of, or against, the interests of the public.

Other selected Acts that have an impact on marketing activities:

- National Trade Mark and True Labelling Act—established the term "Canada-Standard" or "C.S." as a national trade mark; requires certain commodities to be properly labelled or described in advertising for the purpose of indicating material content or quality.
- Consumer Packaging and Labelling Act—provides a set of rules to ensure that full information is disclosed by the manufacturer, packer, or distributor. Requires that all prepackaged products bear the quantity in French and English in metric as well as traditional Canadian standard units of weight, volume, or measure.
- Motor Vehicle Safety Act—established mandatory safety standards for motor vehicles.
- Food and Drug Act—prohibits the advertisement and sale of adulterated or misbranded foods, cosmetics, and drugs.

## SUBCULTURES

In Canada there are at least two major social groups, English and French. While these two share some common core beliefs and values, major differences also exist. For example, French consumers in Quebec have a predisposition to rely more on their senses—touch, taste, smell, hearing—when making a purchase decision. The French consumer also tends to be "conservative" in purchasing, an expression of low risk-taking behavior. Finally, these two values combine to produce a third, called "non-price rationale," which means that consumers who are satisfied with a brand will not switch because of price considerations.[12] Other major differences between these two cultures will be discussed in the next chapter.

Along with the two major cultures, a large number of subcultures exist in Canada. These are groups of individuals who hold different beliefs and values from the cultural mainstream. For example, immigrants form subcultures because they have had different experiences and may have different beliefs and values. Sizeable communities of Italian, Ukrainian, German, and Chinese consumers exist in Canada. These communities are often served by their own newspapers and radio stations. Marketing to these groups requires special efforts because of the different patterns of consumer wants and behaviors.

## SHIFTS IN SECONDARY CULTURAL VALUES

Although core values are fairly persistent, cultural swings do take place. Consider the impact of the hippies, the Beatles, Elvis Presley, Michael Jackson, Bruce Springsteen, Madonna, and other culture heroes on young people's hairstyles, clothing, and sexual norms. Marketers have a keen interest in anticipating cultural shifts in order to spot new marketing opportunities or threats. For example, the percentage of people who value physical fitness and well-being has been going up steadily over the years, especially in the under-30 group and the upscale group. Marketers will want to cater to this trend with appropriate products and communication appeals.

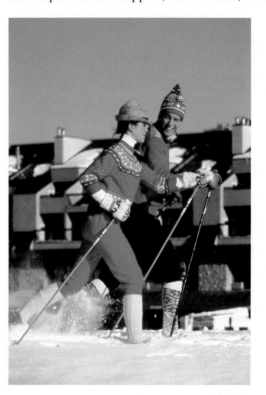

Secondary cultural values: The shift toward physical fitness and well-being has created a need for new products and services.

# Summary

The company must start with the marketing environment when searching for opportunities and monitoring threats. The marketing environment consists of all the actors and forces that affect the company's ability to transact effectively with the target market. The company's marketing environment can be divided into the microenvironment and the macroenvironment.

The microenvironment consists of five components. The first is the company's internal environment—its several departments and management levels—as it affects marketing management's decision making. The second component includes the marketing channel firms that cooperate to improve the value of the product: the suppliers and marketing intermediaries (middlemen, physical distribution firms, marketing service agencies, financial intermediaries). The third component consists of the five types of markets in which the company can sell: the consumer, producer, reseller, government, and international markets. The fourth component consists of the competitors facing the company. The fifth component consists of all the publics that have an actual or potential interest in or impact on the organization's ability to achieve its objectives: financial, media, government, citizen action, and local, general, and internal publics.

The company's macroenvironment consists of major forces that shape opportunities and pose threats to the company: demographic, economic, natural, technological, political, and cultural.

The demographic environment shows a changing age structure in the Canadian population, a changing Canadian family, geographic population shifts, and a better-educated and more white-collar population. The economic environment shows changes in real income and changing consumer spending patterns. The natural environment shows coming shortages of certain raw materials, increased pollution levels, and increasing government intervention in natural resource management. The technological environment shows rapid technological change, unlimited opportunities for innovation, concentration on minor improvements rather than major discoveries, and increased regulation of technological change. The political environment shows increasing business regulation and the growth of public interest groups. The cultural environment shows the endurance of core values.

# Questions for Discussion

1. Some companies purchase in such large volumes that they can dictate terms to their suppliers. What are the advantages and disadvantages of marketing to companies that can "make or break" you as a supplier?

2. How would an automobile manufacturer's marketing mix vary for different types of customer markets? Compare marketing mixes in the consumer, industrial. reseller, government, and international automobile markets.

3. You are communications director for a small regional airline. What publics might be affected by a report that your company had a considerably less frequent maintenance schedule than your competitors? How would you respond to this report?

4. Recent life-style studies show a growing feeling that "meal preparation should take as little time as possible." What products and businesses are being affected by this trend? What future marketing opportunities does it suggest?

5. If Everready developed a battery that made electric cars feasible, how do you think auto manufacturers would respond to this technological development? What kind of company would be the first to market an electric car to the general public?

6. A major alcoholic beverage marketer plans to introduce an "adult soft drink"—a socially acceptable drink that would be cheaper and lower in alcohol than wine coolers. What cultural and other factors might affect the success of this product?

7. Discuss steps that a hospital could take to "manage" its different environments.

# KEY TERMS

**Baby boom**  The major increase in the annual birthrate following World War II and lasting until the early 1960s. The "baby boomers," now moving into middle age, are a prime target for marketers.

**Cultural environment**  Institutions and other forces that affect society's basic values, perceptions, preferences, and behaviors.

**Demography**  The study of human populations in terms of size, density, location, age, sex, race, occupation, and other statistics.

**Economic environment**  Factors that affect consumer purchasing power and spending patterns.

**Macroenvironment**  The larger societal forces that affect the whole microenvironment—demographic, economic, natural, technological, political, and cultural forces.

**Marketing environment**  The actors and forces outside the firm that affect marketing management's ability to develop and maintain successful transactions with its target customers.

**Marketing intermediaries**  Firms that help the company to promote, sell, and distribute its goods to final buyers; they include middlemen, physical distribution firms, marketing service agencies, and financial intermediaries.

**Microenvironment**  The forces close to the company that affect its ability to serve its customers—the company, market channel firms, customer markets, competitors, and publics.

**Natural environment**  Natural resources that are needed as inputs by marketers or that are affected by marketing activities.

**Political environment**  Laws, government agencies, and pressure groups that influence and limit various organizations and individuals in society.

**Public**  Any group that has an actual or potential interest in or impact on an organization's ability to achieve its objectives.

**Suppliers**  Firms and individuals that provide the resources needed by the company and its competitors to produce goods and services.

**Technological environment**  Forces that create new technologies, creating new product and market opportunities.

# REFERENCES

1. From various sources, including Campbell Soup Company Ltd., Annual Reports; "Marketing's New Look," *Business Week*, January 26, 1987, pp. 64-69; Oliver Bertin, "New Lines, Marketing Add Spice to Campbell Soup," *Globe and Mail*, June 3, 1985, p. B3; Tessa Eilmott, "Campbell Blends Corporate Vision Into Its Product Mix," *Financial Post*, November 23, 1985, p. 26; Oliver Bertin, "Campbell Soup to Merge Units in North America," *Globe and Mail*, February 28, 1990, p. B1; Mark Evans, "Campbell Canada On Expansion Kick," *Financial Post*, January 15, 1990, p. 17; and Don Hogarth, "Campbell Soup to Cut 3,000 in Big Shakeup," *Financial Post*, July 2, 1990, p. 1.

2. The statistical data in this chapter are drawn from: *Marketing Research Handbook 1990*, Statistics Canada, Catalogue 63-224; *Canadian Markets 1988/89*, Financial Post; and *Tomorrow's Customers*, 22nd ed., Clarkson Gordon/Woods Gordon, 1989.

3. For more on the effects of demographics on consumer spending patterns, see William L. Marr and Douglas J. McCready, "The Effects of Demographic Structure on Expenditure Patterns in Canada," Institute for Research on Public Policy, Ottawa, June 1989.

4. See Gene Bylinsky, "Technology in the Year 2000," *Fortune*, July 18, 1988, pp. 92-98.

5. David Crane, "Here Come the R&D Crusaders," *Toronto Star*, October 15, 1989, pp. F1-F2; and "Ranking the World's Big Spenders on R&D," *Business Week*, June 15, 1990, p. 195.

6. Geoffrey Rowan, "Canadian Technology Trade Looks Bleak, Experts Say," *Globe and Mail*, May 20, 1989, p. A1.

7. Geoffrey Rowan, *ibid*, pp. F1-F2.

8. Catharine G. Johnston, *Globalization: Canadian Companies Compete*, Conference Board of Canada, Report 50-90-E, 1990.

9. Jan Austen, "The Competition Cop's Tricky Balancing Act," *Financial Times of Canada*, January 30, 1989, p. 12.

10. Peter Foster, "Takeover Horror," *Report on Business Magazine*, May 1989, pp. 55-65 and Drew Fagan, "Tribunal Allows Texaco Deal," Globe and Mail, February 4, 1990, pp. B1, B4.

11. For an interesting view of how Consumers Association of Canada members differ from the "average" consumer, see Jacques C. Bourgeois and James G. Barnes, "Viability and Profile of the Consumerist Segment," *Journal of Consumer Research*, March 1979, pp. 217-228.

12. Madeleine Saint-Jacques, "The French-Canadian Market," in *Advertising in Canada: Its Theory and Practice*, eds. Peter T. Zarry and Robert D. Wilson (Toronto: McGraw-Hill Ryerson, 1981), pp. 349-368.

# CHAPTER 6

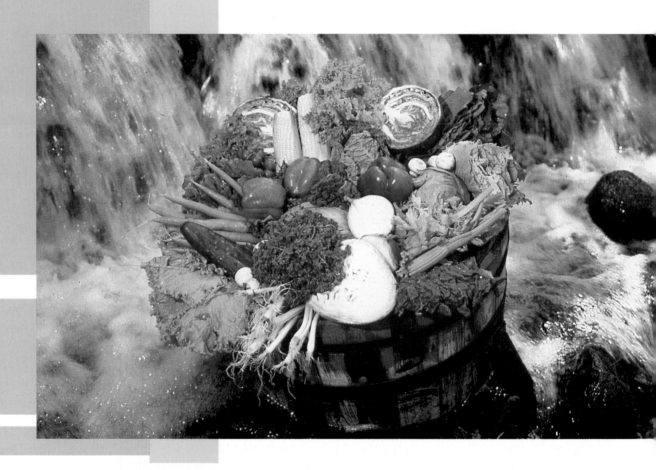

# Consumer Markets and Consumer Buying Behavior

## CHAPTER OBJECTIVES

After reading this chapter, you should be able to:
1. Define the consumer market, and construct a simple model of consumer buying behavior.
2. Name the four major factors that influence consumer buying behavior.
3. List the stages in the buyer decision process.

The well-known slogan "You are what you eat" is causing concern among many marketers in the Canadian food industry. Due to shifts in demographics—in particular the aging of the Canadian population, changes in lifestyles, and new family structures—consumers are modifying their eating habits. Consider the following:

- Canada is a greying society—the average age of Canadians is increasing and by 1996 almost 7.6 million Canadians (28% of the population) will be over 50 years old. As well, there will be a seven percent decline in the number of Canadians under 35. Older people need fewer calories than younger people, so total consumption of food is likely to decline in the future.
- The "well-being" syndrome is important for many Canadians and this translates to desire for physical fitness, good nutrition, and a healthy lifestyle. Consumers are concerned about what and how much they eat.

These demographic changes and other factors are causing a revolution in Canada's $50 billion food business. Those companies that respond quickly to changing consumer trends are gaining sales and profits. Campbell Soup is one of them. In the past four years, Campbell Soup has introduced Le Menu (high quality frozen food line), Le Menu Light (calorie reduced), and Swanson Gourmet (for the value-conscious market), and now holds 28% share of the Canadian frozen prepared meat market.

Some companies have ignored or been slow to catch on to these trends. The meat industry, particularly beef producers, did not realize how much consumers were changing their eating habits. In 1976, consumption of red meats (beef, pork, and lamb) peaked at an annual per capita amount of 51.4 kilograms. Ten years later it had declined to 38.3 kilograms, which translates into lost revenues of about $2.6 billion for the red meat industry. Meat producers are finally responding to the trends. Pork producers have developed the "light" pork steak, a boneless, fat-trimmed chop made from lean, grain-fed pigs, that contains only half the calories of the "old" pork chop. Beef producers are now paid more for leaner beef because a serving of lean beef has 13% less cholesterol then chicken and ten percent less than cod. Indications are that pork and beef per capita consumption is now stabilizing.

The marketers of fish, a product that has less fat and fewer calories than meat, have also been winners. Moreover, the fat in fish is polyunsaturated, as opposed to the saturated fats in meat. As well, per capita consumption of chicken has increased because of its nutritional value. Occasionally chicken producers can't keep up with demand.

Sales of diet foods are also soaring as more Canadians become concerned about the "battle of the bulge." While retail food sales grew by only four percent in 1989, five products—low calorie soft drinks, artificial sweetners, calorie reduced salad dressings, diet frozen dinners, and low calorie yogurts—increased by nine percent and accounted for more than $800 million in sales.

Marketers who fail to understand consumers and how their behaviors change over time will face a troubled future. Consumers need food, but what they buy is determined by their wants. Today, many want foods that fit an active, healthy lifestyle. Marketers who match these wants are more likely to survive and prosper than those who don't.[1]

Marketers have to be extremely careful in analyzing consumer behavior. Buying behavior is never simple, yet understanding it is the essential task of marketing management.

This chapter will explore the dynamics of consumer behavior and the consumer market. The **consumer market** consists of all the individuals and households who buy goods and services for personal consumption.

The discussion will focus on the Canadian consumer market. In a later chapter, international markets will be considered. However, it is important to note that approximately one-third of all the goods and services that Canadians produce are sold in other countries. The Canadian consumer market is only one-tenth the size of the American consumer market, and Canada has less than one percent of the world's population. While it makes sense to start with the Canadian consumer market, many firms consider Canada just one of many markets in which they could operate. In particular, because of the Free Trade Agreement between Canada and the United States, many Canadian firms consider North America as their market.[2]

In 1990 the Canadian consumer market consisted of about 26 million people, who consumed over $410 billion worth of goods and services— over $15,000 worth for every man, woman, and child. Each year this market grows by over 250,000 persons and another $30 billion.[3]

Consumers vary tremendously in age, income, education level, and tastes. Marketers have found it worthwhile to develop products and services tailored to the needs of specific consumer groups. If a market segment is large enough, some

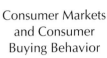

Linguistic and cultural differences affect the approach
to advertising in the French market.

companies may set up special marketing programs to serve this market. Here are
two examples of special consumer groups:

• **French consumers.** Constituting the second largest ethnic group in Canada (26%
of the population) are over 6,000,000 French-speaking consumers, most of whom
live in Quebec, Ontario, and New Brunswick. These consumers differ from other
Canadians in a number of ways, some of which are discussed in Marketing Highlight 6-1. Appealing to the French consumer requires knowledge of language, culture, and socio-economic characteristics of this target market. Some firms have
taken English ad campaigns and had a literal translation done. This approach can
be disastrous. For example, "car wash" literally translated meant "car enema" in
French (lavement d'auto); "chicken to take out" has ended up as "chicken to go
out with" (poulet pour sortir).[4]

• **University students as consumers.** This group of over 420,000 consumers represents a total market of $3.8 billion. On average they spend $188 a month on discretionary items such as compact discs, tapes, stereo equipment, and other forms
of entertainment. Downhill skiing is a popular recreation activity. As well, about
40% own cars and 23% own a computer. The one problem for marketers is that
students cannot easily be reached by media as they are classified as light television
viewers and radio listeners. Most read the campus and daily newspapers but few
read national magazines (only 16% on average read Maclean's).[5]

Other consumer submarkets, for example, women, seniors, or a cultural community like the Italians, also provide good opportunities for tailored marketing programs.

The 26 million consumers in Canada buy an incredible variety of goods and
services. We will now look at how consumers make their choices among these
products.

# A MODEL OF CONSUMER BEHAVIOR

Consumers make many buying decisions every day. Most large companies research
consumer buying decisions in great detail. They want to answer questions about

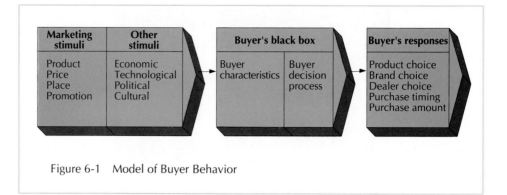

Figure 6-1    Model of Buyer Behavior

what consumers buy, where they buy, how and how much they buy, when they buy, and why they buy. Marketers can study consumer purchases to find answers to most of these questions. But learning about the whys of consumer buying behavior and the buying-decision process is not so easy— the answers are often locked deep within the consumer's head.

The central question is this: How do consumers respond to various marketing stimuli the company might use? The company that really understands how consumers will respond to different product features, prices and advertising appeals has a great advantage over its competitors. Therefore companies and academics have heavily researched the relationship between marketing stimuli and consumer response. Their starting point is the stimulus-response model shown in Figure 6-1. This figure shows that marketing and other stimuli enter the consumer's "black box" and produce certain responses. Marketers must figure out what is in the buyer's "black box."

On the left in Figure 6-1, marketing stimuli consist of the four Ps—product, price, place, and promotion. Other stimuli include major forces and events in the buyer's environment—economic, technological, political, and cultural. All these stimuli enter the buyer's black box, where they are turned into a set of observable buyer responses shown on the right—product choice, brand choice, dealer choice, purchase timing, and purchase amount.

The marketer wants to understand how the stimuli are changed into responses inside the consumer's black box. The black box has two parts. First, the buyer's characteristics influence how he or she perceives and reacts to the stimuli. Second, the buyer's decision process itself affects outcomes. This chapter looks first at buyer characteristics as they affect buying behavior. It then examines the buyer decision process.

# Buyer Characteristics Affecting Consumer Behavior

Consumer purchases are strongly influenced by cultural, social, personal, and psychological characteristics. These factors are shown in Figure 6-2. For the most part they cannot be controlled by the marketer, but they must be taken into account. We want to examine the influence of each factor on a buyer's behavior. We will illustrate these characteristics for the case of a hypothetical consumer named Betty

# MARKETING HIGHLIGHT 6-1

## Are There Really Major Cultural Differences Between English and French Consumers?

Various studies that have looked at the differences between French and English consumers (or Quebec consumers and the rest of Canada) have reached conclusions such as:

- French-Canadian families serve more home-made soup than English-Canadian families.
- French-Canadian homemakers buy more packaged soups and cake mixes than canned soups and ready-made cakes.
- Quebec consumers drink more soft drinks per capita than the rest of Canada.
- French Canadians drink less Canadian whisky than does the rest of Canada.
- The French Canadian, compared to other Canadians, shops less in chain stores and malls.
- French-Canadian buyers of new cars search less (in terms of number of cars considered, time, number of test drives) than do English Canadians.

These differences exist for three possible reasons: (1) true cultural differences, (2) socio-economic differences, or (3) differences in marketing strategies —particularly distribution— in Quebec. Few researchers have examined differences in culture or consumer behavior in the French market beyond socio-economic and marketing differences. For example, many of the studies ignored the fact that the population in Quebec has less formal education than other Canadians. In 1976, 31% of the Quebec population had less than nine years of formal schooling, while in the rest of Canada, only 23% of the population had as little schooling. In 1986, 24% of the Quebec population had less than nine years of schooling; for Canada it was 18%. Education, a determinant of social class, has been shown to influence some types of product choice and usage levels. However, were the differences in buying behavior due to cultural or educational differences? Similarly, many of the early studies did not control for income when there were substantial differences between Quebec (lower average income) and the rest of Canada. For example, in 1955, personal income per capita in Quebec was 85% of the national average, in 1965 it was 88%, in 1973 it was 90%, and in 1988 was 89%. Again, the level of income has an effect on consumer behavior.

Four studies did consider cultural differences while controlling for income or education level. Their conclusions were that consumption patterns are different between Quebec and Ontario households (Palda, Thomas) and that both French males and females held different activities, interests, opinions, and behaviors than their English counterparts (Tigert). For example, the French-Canadian female is more oriented toward home, family, and kitchen, more interested in baking, and more fashion and appearance conscious. As a result, French-speaking, compared to English-speaking families, use more staples, less frozen vegetables, consume more soft drinks, beer, and wine, and consume less hard liquor (Schaninger, et al.).

Some differences may also be due to marketing strategies. In Quebec, wine and beer are sold in "mom and pop" corner grocery stores. These products are significant "traffic generators" for these stores, with consumers buying many other food products in addition to their beverages. As a result, the major supermarket chains hold a lower market share of total foods sales than in other provinces. This and other external factors account for some differences in preferences and purchasing behavior.

It is dangerous to assume that an identical marketing strategy will have the same results with both English and French consumers. While retail sales per capita were virtually the same in Quebec as the national average, there were differences in how the money was spent. Quebec consumers spent more than the rest of Canadian consumers in food stores (nine percent more), hardware stores (50% more), and furniture, appliance, television, and radio stores (37% more). The Quebec consumers spent less on motor vehicles (two percent less). Some of these differences in spending patterns are due to culture. The marketer must also consider the media habits of Quebeckers; they watch more television than do other Canadians and listen to more radio. The marketer can get an understanding of these differences and the implications for strategy through specific research studies on the French market.

**Sources:** Bruce Mallen, "How Different is the French-Canadian Market?" *The Business Quarterly*, Fall 1967, pp. 59-66; E. Clifford , "Tippers Reflect Diverse Tastes of National Mosaic," *Globe and Mail*, June 30, 1979; Morris B. Holbrook and John A. Howard, "Frequently Purchased Non-durable Goods and Services," in *Selected Aspects of Consumer Behavior* (Washington: National Science Foundation, 1977), pp. 189-222; William L. Marr and Donald G. Paterson, *Canada: An Economic History* (Toronto: Macmillan of Canada, 1980), p. 426; Kristian S. Palda, "A Comparison of Consumer Expenditures in Quebec and Ontario," *Canadian Journal of Economics and Political Science*, February 1967, p. 26; Dwight R. Thomas, "Culture and Consumer Consumption: Behavior in English and French Canada," *Proceedings*, Marketing Division, CAAS Conference, Edmonton, 1975; Douglas J. Tigert, "Can a Separate Marketing Strategy for French Canada be Justified: Profiling English-French Markets Through Life Style Analysis," in Donald N. Thompson and David S.R. Leighton (eds.), *Canadian Marketing: Problems and Prospects* (Toronto: Wiley Publishers of Canada, 1973), pp. 113-142; Gail Chiasson, "The Quebec Market," *Marketing*, various issues, Charles M. Schaninger, Jacques C. Bourgeois, and W. Christian Buss, "French-English Canadian Subcultural Consumption Differences," *Journal of Marketing*, Spring 1985, pp. 82-92; Canadian Markets, *Financial Post*, various issues; Gurprit S. Kindra, Michel Laroche, and Thomas E. Muller, *Consumer Behaviour in Canada* (Toronto: Nelson, 1989), Chap. 8; T.K. Clarke and F.G. Crane, *Consumer Behaviour in Canada* (Toronto: Harcourt Brace Jovanovich, 1990), Chap. 5; Barrie McKenna, "Quebec Tastes Blending with the Rest of the Country," *Globe and Mail*, July 3, 1989, p. B1; and Thomas E. Muller and Christopher Bolger, "Search Behavior of French and English Canadians in Automobile Purchase," *International Marketing Review*, Winter 1985, pp. 21-30.

Smith. Betty Smith is a married college graduate who works as a brand manager in a leading consumer packaged-goods company. She currently wants to find a new leisure time activity that will offer some contrast to her working day. This need has led her to consider buying a camera and taking up photography. Many characteristics in her background will affect the way she goes about looking at cameras and choosing a brand.

## CULTURAL FACTORS

Cultural factors exert the broadest and deepest influence on consumer behavior. We will look at the role played by the buyer's culture, subculture, and social class.

**CULTURE** **Culture** is the most basic influence on a person's wants and behavior. Human behavior is largely learned. The child growing up in a society learns basic values, perceptions, wants, and behaviors from the family and other key institutions.

Betty Smith's desire for a camera is a result of being raised in a modern society where camera technology and a whole set of consumer learnings and values have developed. Betty knows what cameras are. She knows how to read instructions on how to operate cameras, and her society has accepted the idea of women photographers. In another culture, for example, an aboriginal tribe in central Australia, a camera may mean nothing. It may simply be a curiosity.

Marketers are always trying to spot cultural shifts in order to imagine new products that might be wanted. For example, the cultural shift toward greater concern with health and fitness has created a huge industry for exercise equipment and clothing, lighter and more natural foods, and health and fitness services. The shift toward informality has resulted in more demand for casual clothing, simpler home

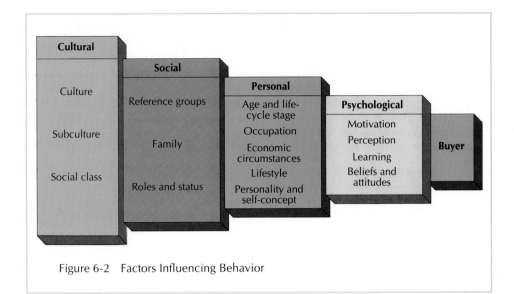

Figure 6-2   Factors Influencing Behavior

furnishings, and lighter entertainment. The increased desire for leisure time has resulted in more demand for convenience products and services such as microwave ovens and fast food.

**SUBCULTURE**   Each culture contains smaller **subcultures,** or groups of people with shared value systems based on common life experiences and situations. Nationality groups such as the Italians, Portuguese, and Germans are found within large communities and have distinct ethnic tastes and interests. Religious groups such as the Catholics, Protestants, Moslems, and Jews are subcultures with their own preferences and taboos. Racial groups such as the Chinese have distinct culture styles and attitudes. Geographical areas such as parts of the Maritimes have distinct subcultures with characteristic life styles.

Betty Smith's interest in various goods will be influenced by her nationality, religion, race, and geographical background. These factors will affect her food preferences, clothing choices, recreation, and career goals. Subcultures attach different meanings to picture taking, which could affect Betty's interest in cameras and the brand she buys.

**SOCIAL CLASS**   Almost every society has some form of social class structure. **Social classes** are relatively permanent and ordered divisions in a society whose members share similar values, interests, and behaviors. Social scientists have identified the seven social classes shown in Table 6-1.[6]

Social class is not indicated by a single factor such as income, but is measured as a combination of occupation, income, education, wealth, and other variables. Marketers are interested in social class because people within a given social class tend to have similar behavior, including buying behavior.

Social classes show distinct product and brand preferences in such areas as clothing, home furnishings, leisure activity, and automobiles. Betty Smith's social class may affect her camera decision. She may have come from a higher social class background. In this case, her family probably owned an expensive camera and may have dabbled in photography. The fact that she thinks about "going professional" is also in line with a higher social class background.

**TABLE 6-1**
**Characteristics of Seven Major Social Classes**

1. Upper Uppers (less than 1 percent).

The social elite who live on inherited wealth and have well-known family backgrounds. They give large sums to charity, own more than one home, and send their children to the finest schools. They are a market for jewelry, antiques, homes, and vacations. They often buy and dress conservatively. While small as a group, their consumption decisions trickle down and are imitated by the other social classes.

2. Lower Uppers (about 2 percent).

People who have earned high income or wealth from the professions or business. They usually come from the middle class. They tend to be active in social and civic affairs and to buy the symbols of status for themselves and their children, such as expensive homes, schools, yachts, swimming pools, and automobiles. They want acceptance in the upper-upper stratum, which is more likely to be achieved by their children than themselves.

3. Upper Middles (12 percent).

People who possess neither family status nor unusual wealth. They are primarily concerned with "career." They have attained positions as professionals, independent businesspeople, and corporate managers. They believe in education and want their children to develop professional or administrative skills so that they will not drop into a lower stratum. They are joiners and highly civic-minded. They are the quality market for good homes, clothes, furniture, and appliances.

4. Middle Class (31 percent).

The middle class are average-pay, white- and blue-collar workers who live on "the better side of town" and try to "do the proper things." Often, they buy products that are popular to keep up with the trends. Most are concerned with fashion, seeking the better brand names. Better living means owning a nice home in a safe neighborhood with good schools. The middle class believes in spending more money on worthwhile experiences for their children and directing them toward a college education.

5. Working Class (38 percent).

The working class consists of average-pay, blue-collar workers and those who lead a "working class life style," whatever their income, school background, or job. The working class maintains close family ties, drawing on relatives for advice on purchases, and for assistance in times of trouble. The working class may maintain sharper sex-role divisions. Car preferences include standard size and larger cars, rejecting domestic and foreign compacts.

6. Upper Lowers (9 percent).

Upper lowers are working, not on welfare, although their living standard is just above poverty. They perform unskilled work for very poor pay, although they strive toward a higher class. Often, upper lowers have limited education. Although they fall near the poverty line financially, they manage to "present a picture of self-discipline."

7. Lower Lowers (7 percent).

Lower lowers are on welfare, visibly poverty-stricken, and usually out of work or have "the dirtiest jobs." Often, they are not interested in finding a job and are permanently dependent on public aid or charity for income. They have few valuable possessions and only basic clothing. They may have difficulty in finding affordable or permanent living accommodations.

**Sources:** See Richard P. Coleman, "The Continuing Significance of Social Class to Marketing," *Journal of Consumer Research*, December 1983, pp. 265-80; and Richard P. Coleman and Lee P. Rainwater, *Social Standing in America: New Dimension of Class* (New York: Basic Books, 1978).

## SOCIAL FACTORS

A consumer's behavior is also influenced by social factors, such as the consumer's reference groups, family, and social roles and status. Because these socal factors can strongly affect consumer responses, companies must take them into account when designing marketing strategies.

**REFERENCE GROUPS**   A person's behavior is influenced by many reference groups. **Reference groups** are groups that have a direct (face-to-face) or indirect influence on the person's attitudes or behavior. Reference groups that have a direct influence and to which a person belongs are called membership groups. Some are primary groups with whom there is regular informal interaction, such as family, friends, neighbors, and co-workers. Some are secondary groups, which are more formal and have less regular interaction. They include organizations such as religious groups, professional associations, and trade unions.

People are also influenced by groups to which they do not belong. An aspirational group is one to which the individual wishes to belong. For example, a teenage hockey player may aspire to play someday for the Edmonton Oilers. He identifies with this group although there is no face-to-face contact.

Marketers try to identify the reference groups of their target markets. Reference groups influence a person in at least three ways. They expose the person to new behaviors and life styles. They influence the person's attitudes and self-concept because he or she wants to "fit in." They also create pressures to conform that may affect the person's product and brand choices.

The importance of group influence varies across products and brands. It tends to be strongest when the product is visible to others whom the buyer respects.[7] Purchases of products that are bought and used privately are not much affected by group influences because neither the product nor the brand will be noticed by others. If Betty Smith buys a camera, both the product and the brand will be visible to others she respects. Her decision to buy the camera and her brand choice may be strongly influenced by some of her groups. Friends who belong to a photography club may influence her to buy a good camera.

**FAMILY** **Family** members can have a strong influence on the buyer's behavior. The family is the most important consumer buying organization in society and it has been researched extensively. Marketers are interested in the roles and influence of the husband, wife, and children in the purchase of different products and services. Five different roles and influences can be identified:

1. Initiator. The initiator is the person who first suggests or thinks of buying the particular product or service.

2. Influencer. An influencer is a person whose views or advice carry some weight in making the final decision.

3. Decider. The decider is a person who ultimately determines any part of or the entire buying decision: whether to buy, what to buy, how to buy, when to buy, or where to buy.

4. Buyer. The buyer is the person who makes the actual purchase.

5. User. The user is the person(s) who consumes or uses the product or service.

Depending on the product and situation, individual family members exert different amounts of influence.

Husband-wife involvement varies widely by product category. The wife has traditionally been the main buyer for the family, especially for food and clothing. This situation is changing with the increased number of working wives and the willingness of husbands to do more of the family purchasing. Marketers of basic products would therefore be making a mistake to continue to think of women as the main or only purchasers of their product.

In the case of expensive products and services, husbands and wives more often make joint decisions. In the case of Betty Smith buying a camera, her husband will play an influencer role. He may have an opinion about her purchase of a camera and the kind of camera to buy. At the same time, she will be the primary decider, purchaser, and user.

The ways in which families make decisions also depend on whether or not the household has children. In a study of where and when to take a vacation, it was found that although Canadian husbands tended to dominate the "vacation" decision in families with children, joint decision making was more prevalent in couples with no children.[8] As a result, marketers might consider different approaches to "couples" versus "families" in promoting vacation travel.

**ROLES AND STATUS** A person may belong to many groups—family, clubs, organizations. The person's position in each group can be defined in terms of role and status. With her parents, Betty Smith plays the role of daughter; in her family, she plays the role of wife; in her company, she plays the role of brand manager. A **role** consists of the activities people are expected to perform according to the persons around them. Each of Betty's roles will influence some of her buying behavior.

Each role carries a **status** reflecting the general esteem given to it by society. The role of brand manager has more status in this society than the role of daughter. As a brand manager, Betty will buy the kind of clothing that reflects her role and status.

## PERSONAL FACTORS

A buyer's decisions are also influenced by personal characteristics such as the buyer's age and life-cycle stage, occupation, economic situation, life style, personality, and self-concept.

**AGE AND LIFE-CYCLE STAGE**   People change the goods and services they consume over their lifetimes. They eat baby food in the early years, a wide variety of foods in the growing and mature years, and special diets in the later years. People's taste in clothes, furniture, and recreation is also age-related.

Buying is also shaped by the stage of the **family life cycle**—the stages through which families might pass as they mature over time. The stages of the family life cycle are listed in Table 6-2. Marketers often define their target markets in terms of life-cycle stages and develop appropriate products and marketing plans.[9]

Some changes in this family life cycle concept have been suggested because a number of demographic shifts have altered the composition of the "typical" Canadian family.[10] Three major shifts have occurred. First, the overall decline in family size will mean that the "full nest" stages may no longer be the predominant portion of the family life cycle. Second, the tendency to delay the time of first marriage will increase the amount of time women and men spend in the bachelor stage. Third, the increased rate of divorces in Canada, from about 3,000 in 1960 to over 70,000 in 1990 suggests that a new category of "divorced" should be incorporated into the stages. To illustrate, the number of single-parent families in Canada, because of divorce or other reasons, exceeds 12% of all households or more than 850,000 families.[11] With the changing sizes of these stages and the development of new stages, new opportunities are appearing for marketers, including a dramatic increase in the demand for day care facilities.

**OCCUPATION**   A person's occupation affects the purchase of goods and services. A blue-collar worker may buy work clothes, work shoes, lunch boxes, and bowling recreation. A company president may buy expensive clothes, air travel, country club membership, and a large sailboat. Marketers try to identify the occupational groups that have an above-average interest in their products and services. A company can even specialize in making products needed by a given occupational group. As an example, Mark's Work Wearhouse has targeted part of its retail offering to meet the needs of workers in physical occupations, such as construction workers.

**ECONOMIC SITUATION**   A person's economic situation will greatly affect product choice. The economic situation consists of spendable income, savings, assets, borrowing power, and attitude toward spending versus saving. For example, a study of Canadian buyers of furniture and appliances found that financial constraints lead consumers to search longer and delay major purchases.[12] Thus, Betty Smith can consider buying an expensive Nikon if she has enough spendable income, savings, or borrowing power. Marketers of income-sensitive goods closely watch trends in personal income, savings, and interest rates. If economic indicators point to a recession, marketers can take steps to redesign, reposition, and reprice their product.

**LIFE STYLE**   People coming from the same subculture, social class, and even occupation may have quite different life styles. **Life style** is a person's pattern of living as expressed in his or her activities, interests, and opinions.

Life style captures something more than the person's social class or personality. It profiles a person's whole pattern of acting and interacting in the world. The

**TABLE 6-2**
**An Overview of the Family Life Cycle and Buying Behavior**

| Stage in Family Life Cycle | Buying or Behavioral Pattern |
| --- | --- |
| 1. Bachelor stage: Young single people not living at home | Few financial burdens. Fashion opinion leaders. Recreation-oriented. Buy basic kitchen equipment, basic furniture, cars, equipment for the mating game, vacations. |
| 2. Newly married couples: Young, no children | Better off financially than they will be in near future. Highest purchase rate and highest average purchase of durables. Buy cars, refrigerators, stoves, sensible and durable furniture, vacations. |
| 3. Full nest I: Youngest child under six | Home purchasing at peak. Liquid assets low. Dissatisfied with financial position and amount of money saved. Interested in new products. Like advertised products. Buy washers, dryers, TV, baby food, chest rubs and cough medicines, vitamins, dolls, wagons, sleds, skates. |
| 4. Full nest II: Youngest child six or over | Financial position better. More wives work. Less influenced by advertising. Like larger-sized packages, multiple-unit deals. Buy many foods, cleaning materials, bicycles, music lessons, pianos. |
| 5. Full nest III: Older married couples with dependent children | Financial position still better. More wives work. Some children get jobs. Hard to influence with advertising. High average purchase of durables. Buy new and more tasteful furniture, auto travel, unessential appliances, boats, dental services, magazines. |
| 6. Empty nest I: Older married couples, no children living with them, head in labor force | Home ownership at peak. Most satisfied with financial position and money saved. Interested in travel, recreation, self-education. Make gifts and contributions. Not interested in new products. Buy vacations, luxuries, home improvements. |
| 7. Empty nest II: Older married, no children living at home, head retired | Drastic cut in income. Keep home. Buy medical appliances, medical care products that aid health, sleep and digestion. |
| 8. Solitary survivor, in labor force | Income still good but likely to sell home. |
| 9. Solitary survivor, retired | Same medical and product needs as other retired group; drastic cut in income. Special need for attention, affection, and security. |

**Source:** William D. Wells and George Gubar, "Life Cycle Concepts in Marketing Research," *Journal of Marketing Research*, November 1966, pp. 355-63, here p. 362. Also see Patrick E. Murphy and Willam A. Staples, "A Modernized Family Life Cycle," *Journal of Consumer Research*, June 1979, p. 12-22; and Janet Wagner and Sherman Hanna, "The Effectiveness of Family Life Cycle Variables in Consumer Expenditure Research," *Journal of Consumer Research*, December 1983, pp. 281-91.

Mark's Work Warehouse targets the needs of workers in physically demanding occupations.

technique of measuring life styles is known as psychographics.[13] It involves measuring dimensions related to activities, interests, and opinions. Using these measures, 14 Canadian life style types have been identified, such as "Sue, the social single" and "Steve, the hard hat."[14]

People's life styles affect their buying behavior. Betty Smith, for example, can choose to live the role of a capable homemaker, a career woman, or a free spirit—or all three. She plays several roles, and the way she blends them expresses her life style. If she becomes a professional photographer, this would change her life style, in turn changing what and how she buys. When preparing strategies, marketers must search for relationships between the product or brand and life style groups.[15]

**PERSONALITY AND SELF-CONCEPT**   Each person's distinct personality will influence his or her buying behavior. **Personality** refers to the unique psychological characteristics that lead to relatively consistent and lasting responses to one's own environment. Personality is usually described in terms of such traits as self-confidence, sociability, affiliation, and achievement.[16] Personality can be useful in analyzing consumer behavior for some product or brand choices. For example, a beer company may discover that heavy beer drinkers tend to be very sociable and aggressive. This suggests a possible brand image for the beer, and the type of people to show in the advertising.

Many marketers use a concept related to personality—a person's self-concept (also called self-image). All of us have a complex mental picture of ourselves. For example, Betty Smith may see herself as outgoing, creative, and active. Therefore, she will favor a camera that projects the same qualities. If the Nikon is promoted as a camera for outgoing, creative, and active people, then its brand image will match her self-image. Marketers should try to develop brand images that match the self-image of the target market.[17]

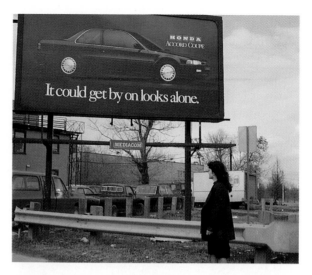

An advertisement can lead a person to recognize a need.

## PSYCHOLOGICAL FACTORS

A person's buying choices are also influenced by four major psychological factors—motivation, perception, learning, and beliefs and attitudes.

**MOTIVATION** We saw that Betty Smith became interested in buying a camera. Why? What is she really seeking? What needs is she trying to satisfy?

A person has many needs at any given time. Some needs are biological, arising from states of tension such as hunger, thirst, or discomfort. Other needs are psychological, arising from states of tension such as the need for recognition, esteem, or belonging. Most of these needs will not be strong enough to motivate the person to act at a given time. A need becomes a motive when it is aroused to a sufficient level of intensity. A **motive (or drive)** is a need that is sufficiently pressing to direct the person to seek satisfaction of the need. Psychologists have developed theories of human motivation. Two of the most popular—the theories of Sigmund Freud and Abraham Maslow—have quite different meanings for consumer analysis and marketing.

**FREUD'S THEORY OF MOTIVATION** Freud assumes that people are largely unconscious of the real psychological forces shaping their behavior. He suggests that people repress many urges as they grow up. These urges are never eliminated or under perfect control; they emerge in dreams, in slips of the tongue, in neurotic and obsessive behavior, or ultimately in psychoses.

According to Freud's theory, a person does not fully understand his or her motivation. If Betty Smith wants to purchase an expensive camera, she may describe her motive as wanting a hobby or career. At a deeper level, she may be purchasing the camera to impress others with her creative talent. At a still deeper level, she may be buying the camera to feel young and independent again.

Motivational researchers collect in-depth information from small samples of consumers to uncover the deeper motives for their product choices. They use various "projective techniques" to throw the ego off guard—techniques such as word association, sentence completion, picture interpretation, and role playing. Motivation researchers have reached some interesting and sometimes odd conclusions about what may be in the buyer's mind regarding certain purchases. They have suggested that:

- Consumers resist prunes because they are wrinkled-looking and remind people of sickness and old age.
- Smoking is an adult version of thumbsucking.
- People prefer vegetable shortening to animal fats because the latter arouse a sense of guilt over killing animals.

**MASLOW'S THEORY OF MOTIVATION**    Abraham Maslow sought to explain why people are driven by particular needs at particular times.[18] Why does one person spend lots of time and energy on personal safety and another on acquiring the esteem of others? His answer is that human needs are arranged in a hierarchy, from the most pressing to the least pressing. Maslow's hierarchy of needs is shown in Figure 6-3.

The hierarchy, in order of importance, consists of physiological needs, safety needs, social needs, esteem needs, and self-actualization needs. A person will try to satisfy the most important needs first. When the most important need is satisfied, it will stop being a motivator for the present time, and the person will be motivated to satisfy the next most important need.

For example, a starving man (need 1) will not take an interest in the latest happenings in the art world (need 5), nor in how he is seen or esteemed by others

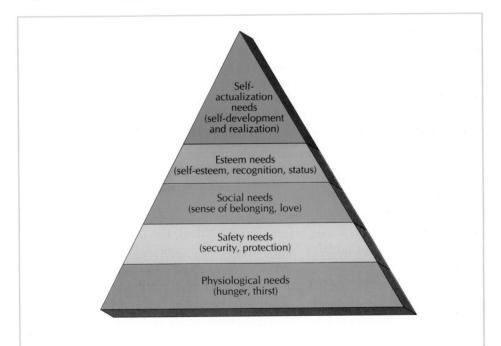

Adapted from *Motivation and Personality*, Second edition, Abraham H. Maslow, Copyright © 1970 by Abraham H. Maslow. Reprinted by permission of Harper & Row, Publishers, Inc.

Figure 6-3   Maslow's Hierarchy of Needs

(needs 3 or 4), nor even in whether he is breathing clean air (need 2). But as each important need is satisfied, the next most important need will come into play.

What light does Maslow's theory throw on Betty Smith's interest in buying a camera? We can guess that Betty has satisfied her physiological, safety, and social needs; they do not motivate her interest in cameras. Her camera interest might come from a strong need for more esteem from others, or it might come from a need for self-actualization. She wants to be a creative person and express herself through photography.

**PERCEPTION**   A motivated person is ready to act. How the motivated person acts is influenced by his or her perception of the situation. Two people with the same motivation and in the same situation may act quite differently because they perceive the situation differently. Betty Smith might consider a fast-talking camera salesperson loud and phony. Another camera buyer might consider the same salesperson intelligent and helpful.

Why do people have different perceptions of the same situation? All of us learn about a stimulus by the flow of information through our five senses: sight, hearing, smell, touch, and taste. However, each of us receives, organizes, and interprets this sensory information in an individual way. **Perception** is the process by which people select, organize, and interpret information to form a meaningful picture of the world.

People can form different perceptions of the same stimulus because of three perceptual processes: selective exposure, selective distortion, and selective retention.

**SELECTIVE EXPOSURE**   People are exposed to a great amount of stimuli every day. For example, the average person may be exposed to over 1500 ads a day. It is impossible for a person to pay attention to all these stimuli. Most will be screened out. Selective exposure means that marketers have to work especially hard to attract the consumer's attention. Their message will be lost on most people who are not in the market for the product. Even people who are in the market may not notice the message unless it stands out from the surrounding sea of other ads.

**SELECTIVE DISTORTION**   Even stimuli that consumers notice do not always come across in the intended way. Each person tries to fit incoming information into his or her existing mind set. Selective distortion describes the tendency of people to twist information into personal meanings. Betty Smith may hear the salesperson mention some good and bad points about a competing camera brand. Since she already has a strong leaning toward Nikon, she is likely to distort the points in order to conclude that Nikon is the better camera. People tend to interpret information in a way that will support what they already believe.

**SELECTIVE RETENTION**   People will forget much that they learn. They tend to retain information that supports their attitudes and beliefs. Because of selective retention, Betty is likely to remember good points mentioned about the Nikon and forget good points mentioned about competing cameras. She remembers Nikon's good points because she "rehearses" them whenever she thinks about choosing a camera.

These three perceptual factors—selective exposure, distortion, and retention—mean that marketers have to work hard to get their messages through. This explains why marketers use so much drama and repetition in sending messages to their market.

**LEARNING**  When people act, they learn. **Learning** describes changes in an individual's behavior arising from experience. Most human behavior is learned. Learning theorists say that learning occurs through the interplay of drives, stimuli, cues, responses, and reinforcement.

We saw that Betty Smith has a drive for self-actualization. A drive is a strong internal stimulus that calls for action. Her drive becomes a motive when it is directed toward a particular stimulus object, in this case a camera. Betty's response to the idea of buying a camera is conditioned by the surrounding cues. Cues are minor stimuli that determine when, where, and how the person responds. Seeing cameras in a shop window, hearing of a special sales price, and being encouraged by her husband are all cues that can influence Betty's response to the impulse to buy a camera.

Suppose Betty buys the camera. If the experience is rewarding, the probability is that she will use the camera more and more. Her response to cameras will be reinforced. Then the next time she buys a camera, or binoculars, or a similar product, the probability is greater that she will buy a Nikon.

The practical significance of learning theory for marketers is that they can build up demand for a product by associating it with strong drives, using motivating cues, and providing positive reinforcement.

**BELIEFS AND ATTITUDES**  Through acting and learning, people acquire their beliefs and attitudes. These in turn influence their buying behavior. A **belief** is a descriptive thought that a person has about something. Betty Smith may believe that a Nikon takes great pictures, stands up well under hard use, and costs $550. These beliefs may be based on real knowledge, opinion, or faith. They may or may not carry an emotional charge. For example, Betty Smith's belief that a Nikon camera is heavy may or may not matter to her decision.

Marketers are very interested in the beliefs that people carry in their heads about specific products and services. These beliefs make up product and brand images, and people act on their beliefs. If some of the beliefs are wrong and prevent purchase, the marketer would want to launch a campaign to correct these beliefs.

People have attitudes regarding almost everything: religion, politics, clothes, music, food, and so on. An **attitude** describes a person's relatively consistent evaluations, feelings, and tendencies toward some object or idea. Attitudes put people into a frame of mind to like or dislike things, moving toward or away from them. Thus Betty Smith may hold such attitudes as "Buy the best," "The Japanese make the best products in the world," and "Creativity and self-expression are among the most important things in life." The Nikon camera therefore fits well into Betty's existing attitudes. A company would benefit greatly from researching the various attitudes people have that might bear on its product.

Attitudes are very difficult to change. A person's various attitudes fit into a pattern, and to change one attitude may require difficult adjustments in many others. A company would be well advised to fit its products into existing attitudes, rather than to try to change people's attitudes. There are exceptions, of course, where the great cost of trying to change attitudes may pay off.

We can now appreciate the many individual characteristics and forces acting on consumer behavior. The person's choice is the result of the complex interplay of cultural, social, personal, and psychological factors. Many of these factors cannot be influenced by the marketer. However, they are useful in identifying the buyers who may be more interested in the product.

# THE BUYER DECISION PROCESS

Now that we have looked at all the influences that affect buyers, we are ready to look at how consumers make buying decisions. Figure 6-4 shows the buyer decision process consisting of five stages: problem recognition, information search, evaluation of alternatives, purchase decision, and postpurchase behavior. This model emphasizes that the buying process starts long before the actual purchase and continues long after the purchase. It encourages the marketer to focus on the entire buying process, rather than just the purchase decision.

The decision process model seems to imply that consumers pass through all five stages with every purchase they make. Whether or not a consumer passes through all five stages or skips or reverses some of these stages depends on the complexity of the product for the consumer. There are great differences between buying toothpaste, a tennis racket, an expensive camera, and a new car. It has been suggested that consumer buying can be viewed as a problem-solving activity, and that there are three types of buying situations.[19]

## Routinized Response Behavior

The simplest type of buying behavior occurs in the purchase of low-cost, frequently purchased items. Buyers have very few decisions to make as they are well acquainted with the product class, know the major brands, and have fairly clear preferences among the brands. They do not always buy the same brand because choice can be influenced by stockouts, special deals, and a wish for variety. In general, however, buyers' operations are routinized, and they are not likely to give much thought, search, or time to the purchase. The goods in this class are often called low involvement goods. Buyers often have a low interest in this class of goods and frequently purchase a particular brand through habit.

The marketer's task in this situation is twofold. With respect to current customers, the marketer should provide positive reinforcement. The brand's quality, stock level, and value must be maintained. With respect to potential customers, the marketer must break their normal buying habits by cues that call attention to the brand and its value in relation to the buyers' preferred brands. These cues include new features or benefits, point-of-purchase displays, price specials, and premiums.

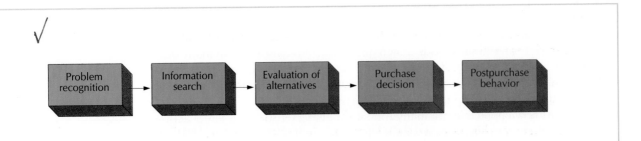

Figure 6-4   Buyer Decision Process

# Limited Problem Solving

Buying is more complex when buyers confront an unfamiliar brand in a familiar product class that requires information before making a purchase choice. For example, people thinking about buying a new tennis racket may hear about a new oversized brand called the Prince. They may ask questions and look at ads to learn more about the new brand concept before choosing. This approach is described as limited problem solving because buyers are fully aware of the product class and the qualities they want, but are not familiar with all the brands and their features.

The marketer recognizes that consumers are trying to reduce risk through information gathering. The marketer must design a communication program that will increase the buyer's brand comprehension and confidence.

# Extensive Problem Solving

Buying reaches its greatest complexity when buyers face an unfamiliar product class and do not know what criteria to use. For example, a man may become interested in buying a citizen-band receiver for the first time. He had heard brand names such as Cobra, Panasonic, and Lloyd's, but lacks clear brand concepts. He does not even know what product-class-attributes to consider in choosing a good citizen-band receiver. He is in a state of extensive problem solving.

The marketer of products in this class, often called high-involvement goods, must understand the information-gathering and evaluation activities of prospective buyers. The marketer's task is to facilitate the buyer's learning of the attributes of the product class, their relative importance, and the high standing of the brand on the more important attributes.

We will use the model in Figure 6-4 because it shows all considerations that arise when a consumer faces a new and complex purchase situation. We will use this model to follow Betty Smith in order to understand how she became interested in buying an expensive camera and the stages she went through to make the final choice.

# Problem Recognition

The buying process starts when the buyer recognizes a problem or need. The buyer senses a difference between his or her actual state and a desired state. The need can be triggered by internal stimuli. One of the person's normal needs—hunger, thirst, sex— rises to a high enough level and becomes a drive. From previous experience, the person has learned how to cope with this drive and is motivated toward objects that he or she knows will satisfy this drive.

A need can also be triggered by external stimuli. Betty Smith passes a bakery and the sight of freshly baked bread stimulates her hunger; she admires a neighbor's new car; she watches a television commercial for a Caribbean vacation. All of these can lead her to recognize a problem or need.

The marketer at this stage needs to determine the factors and situations that usually trigger consumer problem recognition. The marketer should research consumers to find out what kinds of needs or problems arose, what brought them about, and how they led to this particular product.

Betty Smith might answer that she felt the need for a new hobby when her busy season at work slowed down. She thought of cameras after talking to a friend about photography. By gathering such information, the marketer can identify the stimuli that most often trigger interest in the product and develop marketing programs that involve these stimuli.

# Information Search

An aroused consumer may or may not search for more information. If the consumer's drive is strong and a satisfying product is near at hand, the consumer is likely to buy it then. If not, the consumer may simply store the need in memory and search for information bearing on the need.

At one level, the buyer may simply have heightened attention. Here Betty Smith simply becomes more receptive to information about cameras. She pays attention to camera ads, cameras used by friends, and conversations about cameras. Alternatively, Betty may actively search for information by looking for reading material, phoning friends, and gathering product information in other ways. How much searching she does will depend upon the strength of her drive, the amount of information she starts with, the ease of obtaining more information, the value she places on additional information, and the satisfaction she gets from searching.

The degree of search that is undertaken can also be explained in part by perceived risk.[20] In many situations consumers are concerned that they make the right product and brand choice. They cannot be certain about the performance and psychosocial consequences of their purchase decision. This uncertainty produces anxiety or perceived risk. The three most common types of perceived risk are: financial—"Can I afford to purchase this product?"; performance—"Will this product work and continue to work to my satisfaction when I get it home?"; and social—"Will my family or friends, or reference groups approve of my purchase decision?"

Consumers develop strategies for reducing perceived risk. For example, consumers may search for more information in an attempt to make the "right" purchase decision. Consumers may look for a lower-priced brand to reduce financial risk, they may read Canadian Consumer or Consumer Reports to determine product reliability and to reduce performance risk, or they may take along a friend or a "purchase pal" to obtain social approval and reduce social risk. Consumers may also use other strategies to reduce perceived risk, including delaying the purchase, purchasing national brands from well-known retailers, and buying brands that have warranties. Marketers need to understand the factors that provoke perceived risk in the consumer and attempt to provide information and support that will help reduce that risk.

The consumer can obtain information from any of several sources. These include:

- **Personal sources:** family, friends, neighbors, acquaintances
- **Commercial sources:** advertising, salespeople, dealers, packaging, displays
- **Public sources:** mass media, consumer-rating organizations
- **Experiential sources:** handling, examining, using the product

The relative influence of these information sources varies with the product and the buyer. Generally the consumer receives the most information about a product from commercial sources, which are dominated by the marketer. The most effective sources, however, tend to be personal sources. Commercial sources normally inform the buyer, but personal sources legitimize or evaluate products for the buyer. For example, doctors normally learn of new drugs from commercial sources, but turn to other doctors for evaluation information.

As a result of gathering information, the consumer increases his or her awareness and knowledge of the available brands and their features. In looking for information, Betty Smith found out about the many camera brands available. The information also helped her drop certain brands from consideration. A company must design its marketing mix to make prospects aware of and knowledgeable about its brand. If it fails to do this, the company must also learn which other brands customers consider, so that it knows its competition and can plan its appeals.

The marketer should carefully identify consumers' sources of information and the importance of each source. Consumers should be asked how they first heard about the brand, what information they received, and the importance they place on different information sources. This information is critical in preparing effective communication for target markets.

## Evaluation of Alternatives

We have seen how the consumer uses information to arrive at a set of final brand choices. Now the question is: How does the consumer choose among the alternative brands? The marketer needs to know how the consumer processes information to arrive at brand choices. Unfortunately, there is no simple and single evaluation process used by all consumers, or even by one consumer in all buying situations. There are several evaluation processes.

Certain basic concepts will help explain consumer evaluation processes. First, we assume that each consumer sees a product as a bundle of product attributes. For cameras, these attributes include picture quality, ease of use, camera size, price, and others. Consumers will vary as to which of these attributes they consider relevant, and will pay the most attention to those attributes connected with their needs.

Second, the consumer will attach a different degree of importance to the attributes. That is, each consumer attaches importance to each attribute according to his or her unique needs and wants.

Third, the consumer is likely to develop a set of brand beliefs about where each brand stands on each attribute. The set of beliefs held about a particular brand is known as the brand image. The consumer's beliefs may vary from the true attributes because of his or her experience and the effect of selective perception, selective distortion, and selective retention.

Fourth, the consumer is assumed to have a utility function for each attribute. The utility function shows how the consumer expects total product satisfaction to vary with different levels of different attributes. For example, Betty Smith may expect her satisfaction from a camera to increase with better picture quality; to peak with a medium-weight camera as opposed to a very light or very heavy one; and to be higher for a 35-mm camera than for a 135-mm camera. If we combine the attribute levels where the utilities are highest, they make up Betty's ideal camera. The camera would also be her preferred camera if it were available and affordable.

Fifth, the consumer arrives at attitudes toward the different brands through an evaluation procedure. Consumers have been found to use one or more of several evaluation procedures, depending on the consumer and the buying decision.

We will illustrate these concepts with Betty Smith's camera buying situation. Suppose Betty has narrowed her choices to four cameras, and that she is primarily interested in four attributes —picture quality, ease of use, camera size, and price. Betty has formed beliefs about how each brand rates on each attribute. The marketer would like to be able to predict which camera Betty will buy.

Clearly, if one camera rated best on all the attributes, we could predict that Betty would choose it. However, the brands vary in appeal. Some buyers will make their choice using only one attribute, and their choices are easy to predict. If Betty wants picture quality above everything, she would buy the camera that she thinks has the best picture quality. Most buyers, however, consider several attributes, each with different importance. If we knew the weight of importance that Betty assigns to each of the four attributes, we could predict her camera choice more reliably.

Marketers should study buyers to find out how they actually evaluate brand alternatives. With this knowledge, the marketer could take steps to influence the buyer's decision. Suppose Betty is inclined to buy a Nikon camera because she rates it highly on picture quality and ease of use. What strategies might another camera maker, say Minolta, use to influence people like Betty? There are several. Minolta

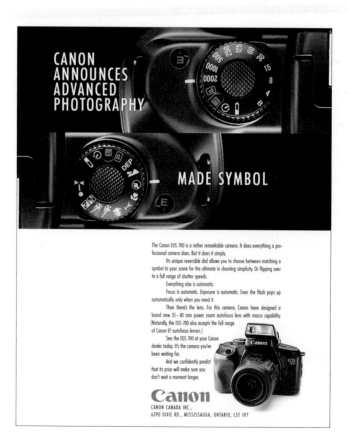

Convenience and high quality at a competitive price are the attributes promised by Canon in this camera ad.

could modify its camera so that it delivers better pictures or other features that consumers like Betty want. It could try to change buyers' beliefs about how its camera rates on key attributes, especially if consumers currently underestimate the camera's qualities. It could try to change buyers' beliefs about Nikon and other competitors. Finally, it could try to change the list of attributes that buyers consider, or the importance attached to these attributes. For example, it might advertise that all good cameras have about equal picture quality, and that its lighter weight, lower priced camera is a better buy for people like Betty.

## Purchase Decision

In the evaluation stage, the consumer ranks brands in the choice set and forms purchase intentions. Generally the consumer will buy the most preferred brand, but two factors can come between the purchase intention and the purchase decision. These factors are shown in Figure 6-5.[21]

The first is the attitudes of others. If Betty Smith's husband feels strongly that Betty should buy the lowest-priced camera to keep down expenses, the chances of Betty buying more expensive cameras may be reduced. How much another person's attitudes will affect Betty's choices depends on the strength of the other person's attitudes toward her buying decision, and Betty's motivation to comply with the other person's wishes. The more intense the other person's attitudes and the closer the other person is to Betty, the greater effect the other person's attitudes will have.

Purchase intention is also influenced by unexpected situational factors. The consumer forms a purchase intention based on such factors as expected family income, expected price, and expected benefits from the product. When the consumer is about to act, unexpected situational factors may arise to change the purchase intention. Betty Smith may lose her job, some other purchase may become more urgent, or a friend may report being disappointed in that camera.

Thus preferences and even purchase intentions do not always result in actual purchase choice. They direct purchase behavior, but may not fully determine the outcome.

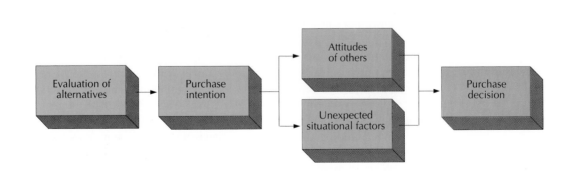

Figure 6-5   Steps between Evaluation of Alternatives and a Purchase Decision

# Postpurchase Behavior

The marketer's job does not end when the product is bought. After purchasing the product, the consumer will be satisfied or dissatisfied, and will engage in postpurchase actions of interest to the marketer. What determines whether the buyer is satisfied or dissatisfied with a purchase? The answer lies in the relationship between the consumer's expectations and the product's perceived performance.[22] If the product matches expectations, the consumer is satisfied; if it falls short, the consumer is dissatisfied.

Consumers base their expectations on messages they receive from sellers, friends, and other information sources. If the seller exaggerates the product's performance, the consumer's expectations will not be met, which leads to dissatisfaction. The larger the gap between expectations and performance, the greater the consumer's dissatisfaction. This suggests that the seller should make product claims that faithfully represent the product's performance so that buyers are satisfied.

Satisfaction with the product will affect later behavior. A satisfied consumer is more likely to buy the product the next time and will speak well of the product to others. According to marketers, "A satisfied customer is our best advertisement."

Almost all major purchases result in **cognitive dissonance**, or discomfort caused by postpurchase conflict. Consumers are satisfied with the benefits of the chosen brand and glad to avoid the drawbacks of the brands not purchased. On the other hand, every purchase involves compromise. Consumers feel uneasy about acquiring the drawbacks of the chosen brand and about losing the benefits of the brands not purchased. Thus, consumers feel at least some postpurchase dissonance for every purchase. They will often take steps after the purchase to reduce this dissonance.[23]

Dissatisfied consumers may take any of several actions. They may return the product, or complain to the company and ask for a refund or exchange. They may go to a lawyer, or complain to other groups that might help them get satisfaction. Alternatively, buyers may simply stop buying the product or may bad-mouth it to friends and others. In all these cases, the seller loses something.

Marketers can take steps to reduce consumer postpurchase dissatisfaction and to help customers feel good about their purchase. Automobile companies can send a letter to new car owners congratulating them on having selected a fine car. The companies can place ads showing satisfied owners driving their new cars. They can obtain customer suggestions for improvements and list the location of available services. They can write instruction booklets that reduce dissatisfaction, and send owners a magazine full of articles describing the pleasures of owning the new car.

Postpurchase communications to buyers have been shown to result in fewer product returns and order cancellations. Paying careful attention to customer dissatisfactions can help the company to spot and correct problems, resulting in increased postpurchase satisfaction for future buyers.

Understanding the consumer's needs and buying power is the foundation of successful marketing. By understanding how buyers go through problem recognition, information search, evaluation of alternatives, the purchase decision, and postpurchase behavior, the marketer can pick up many clues about how to meet the buyer's needs. By understanding the various participants in the buying process and the major influences on their buying behavior, the marketer can develop an effective marketing program to support an attractive offer to the target market.

# SUMMARY

Markets have to be understood before marketing strategies can be developed. The consumer market buys goods and services for personal consumption. It consists of many submarkets, such as the French-speaking population and university students, that may require special marketing programs.

Consumer behavior is influenced by the buyer's characteristics and by the buyer's decision process. Buyer characteristics include four major factors: cultural, social, personal, and psychological.

Culture is the basic determinant of a person's wants and behavior. Marketers try to track cultural shifts that might suggest new ways to serve consumers. Subcultures are "cultures within cultures" that have distinct values and life styles. Social classes are subcultures whose members have similar social prestige based on occupation, income, education, wealth, and other variables. People with different cultural, subcultural, and social class characteristics have different product and brand preferences. Marketers may want to focus their marketing programs on the special needs of certain groups.

Social factors also influence a buyer's behavior. A person's reference groups—family, friends, social organizations, professional associations—strongly affect product and brand choices. The person's position within each group can be defined in terms of role and status. A buyer chooses products and brands that reflect his or her role and status.

The buyer's age, life-cycle stage, occupation, economic circumstances, life style, personality, and other personal characteristics influence his or her buying decisions. Young consumers have different needs and wants from older consumers; the needs of young married couples differ from those of retirees; consumers with higher incomes buy differently from those who have less to spend. Consumer life styles—the whole pattern of acting and interacting in the world—are also an important influence on buyers' choices.

Finally, consumer buying behavior is influenced by four major psychological factors—motivation, perception, learning, and attitudes. Each of these factors provides a different perspective for understanding the workings of the buyer's "black box."

In buying something, the buyer goes through a decision process consisting of problem recognition, information search, evaluation of alternatives, purchase decision, and postpurchase behavior. The marketer must understand the buyer's behavior at each stage and what influences are operating. This helps the marketer to develop effective marketing programs for the target market.

# QUESTIONS FOR DISCUSSION

1. What factors could you add to the model in Figure 6-1 to make it a more complete description of consumer behavior?

2. A new method of packaging wine in cardboard boxes offers more consumer convenience than traditional bottles: Instead of a cork, an airtight dispenser allows servings of desired amounts while keeping the remaining wine fresh for

weeks. How will the factors shown in Figure 6-2 work for or against the success of this packaging innovation?

3. What does each part of the following pairs of items tell you about a person's social class:

   a. An annual income of $30,000/an annual income of $40,000?

   b. Floors covered with Oriental rugs/a house with wall-to-wall carpeting?

   c. Shopping at Sears/shopping at Simpson's?

   d. A college degree/a high-school degree?

4. Ads sponsored by Rockers Against Drunk Driving feature popular recording artists telling listeners not to drink and drive. What social factors will probably contribute to the success or failure of this campaign?

5. In designing the advertising for a soft drink, which would be more helpful—information about consumer demographics or consumer life styles? How would you use each type of information?

6. One suggestion arising from motivations research is that shaving represents a loss of masculinity to men, which is reasserted by the sting of an aftershave. Does this idea make sense? If so, what are the implications for marketing men's toiletries?

7. Which levels of Maslow's hierarchy could be appealed to in marketing the following: (a) popcorn, (b) the armed forces, (c) a college education?

8. One advertising agency president says "Perception is reality." What does he mean by this? How is perception important to marketers?

9. How can understanding attitudes help in designing marketing strategies? Give examples.

10. Relate the five stages of the buyer-decision process to your most recent purchase of any kind. Now compare these stages with the steps involved in your most recent purchase of a pair of shoes.

11. When planning to go to a movie, what information sources do you use in deciding which one to see? Do you use the same sources to decide which movies to rent on videotape?

# KEY TERMS

**Attitude**  A person's consistently favorable or unfavorable evaluations, feelings, and tendencies toward some object or idea.

**Belief**  A descriptive thought that a person has about something.

**Cognitive dissonance**  Postpurchase consumer discomfort caused by after-purchase conflict.

**Consumer market**  The set of all final consumers—individuals and households who buy goods and services for personal consumption.

**Culture**  The set of basic values, perceptions, wants, and behaviors learned by a member of society from family and other important institutions.

**Family life cycle** The stages through which families might pass as they mature over time.

**Learning** Changes in an individual's behavior arising from experience.

**Life style** A person's pattern of living as expressed in his or her activities, interests, and opinions.

**Motive (or drive)** A need that is sufficiently pressing to direct the person to seek satisfaction of the need.

**Perception** The process by which people select, organize, and interpret information to form a meaningful picture of the world.

**Personality** The unique psychological characteristics that lead to relatively consistent and lasting responses to one's own environment.

**Reference groups** Groups that have a direct (face-to-face) or indirect influence on the person's attitudes or behavior.

**Role** The activities people are expected to perform according to the people around them.

**Social classes** Relatively permanent and ordered divisions in a society whose members share similar values, interests, and behaviors.

**Status** The general esteem given to a role by society.

**Subculture** A group of people with shared value systems based on common life experiences and situations.

# REFERENCES

1. See Daniel Stoffman, "Hungry Competition," *Canadian Business*, December 1986, pp. 46-50, 149; Barbara Wickens, "The Dangers of Dieting," *Maclean's*, October 9, 1989, pp. 48-51; Jim McElgrenn, "Beefing It Up," *Marketing*, August 28, 1989, pp. 10, 13; and Carolyn Green, "Diet Industry is No Lightweight," *Financial Post*, February 19, 1990, p. 36.

2. *Tomorrow's Customers*, 22nd Ed., Clarkson Gordon/Woods Gordon, 1989.

3. Estimates based on *Market Research Handbook 1990*, Statistics Canada, Catalogue 63-224.

4. Madeleine Saint-Jacques, "The French Canadian Market," in *Advertising in Canada: Its Theory and Practice*, eds. Peter T. Zarry and Robert T. Wilson (Toronto: McGraw-Hill Ryerson, 1981), pp. 349-368.

5. Marina Strauss, "University Students Now Wealthier, More Serious," *Globe and Mail*, June 24, 1989, p. B-3; and "Average University Student Profiled by Campus Plus," *Marketing*, August 19, 1985, p. 5.

6. This classification was originally developed by W. Lloyd Warner and Paul S. Lundt in *The Social Life of a Modern Community* (New Haven, CT: Yale University Press, 1941). For a summary of more recent classifications, see Richard P. Coleman, "The Continuing Significance of Social Class to Marketers," *Journal of Consumer Research*, December 1983, pp. 265-280.

7. William O. Bearden and Michael J. Etzel, "Reference Group Influence on Product and Brand Purchase Decisions," *Journal of Consumer Research*, September 1982, p. 185.

8. Pierre Filiatrault and J.R. Brent Ritchie, "Joint Purchasing Decisions: A Comparison of Influence Structure in Family and Couple Decision-Making Units," *Journal of Consumer Research*, September 1980, pp. 131-140. For more on family decision making, see James F. Engel, Roger D. Blackwell, and Paul W. Miniard, *Consumer Behavior*, 6th Ed., (Chicago: Dryden Press, 1990) Chap. 6.

9. In some cases, income is more important than family life cycle. See Janet Wagner and Sherman Hanna, "The Effectiveness of Family Life Cycle Variables in Consumer Expenditure Research," *Journal of Consumer Research*, December 1983, pp. 281-291.

10. Patrick E. Murphy and William A. Staples, "A Modernized Family Life Cycle," *Journal of Consumer Research*, June 1979, pp. 12-22.

11. *Market Research Handbook 1990*, Statistics Canada, Catalogue 63-224.

12. John D. Claxton, Joseph N. Fry and Bernard Portis, "A Taxonomy of Prepurchase Information Gathering Patterns," *Journal of Consumer Research*, December 1974, pp. 35-42.

13. See William D. Wells, "Psychographics: A Critical Review," *Journal of Marketing Research*, May 1975, pp. 196-213; Stephen C. Cosmas, "Life Styles and Consumption Patterns," *Journal of Consumer Research*, March 1984, pp. 453-455; John L. Lastovicka, "On the Validation of Lifestyle Traits: A Review and Illustration," *Journal of Marketing Research*, February 1982, pp. 126-138.

14. Jan Pearson, "Social Studies," *Canadian Business*, December 1985, pp. 67-73. For further examples of lifestyle profiles of Canadians, see John Chaplin, "Psychographics: Pigeonholes for Consumers," Marketing, October 16, 1989, pp. 28-29.

15. Gurprit S. Kindra, Michel Laroche, and Thomas E. Muller, *Consumer Behaviour in Canada* (Toronto: Nelson, 1989), Chap. 6.

16. See Raymond L. Horton, "Some Relationships Between Personality and Consumer Decision-Making," *Journal of Marketing Research*, May 1979, pp. 244-45; and Joseph T. Plummer, "How Personality Makes a Difference," *Journal of Advertising Research*, January 1985, pp. 27-31.

17. See M. Joseph Sirgy, "Self-Concept in Consumer Behavior; A Critical Review," *Journal of Consumer Research*, December 1982, pp. 287-300.

18. Abraham H. Maslow, *Motivation and Personality*, 2nd ed. (New York: Harper & Row, 1970), pp. 80-106.

19. For example, see Engel, Blackwell, and Miniard, *Consumer Behavior*, Chap 16.

20. See Raymond A. Bauer, "Consumer Behavior as Risk Taking" in *Risk Taking and Information Handling in Consumer Behavior*, ed. Donald F. Cox (Boston: Division of Research, Harvard Business School, 1967); James W. Taylor, "The Role of Risk in Consumer Behavior", *Journal of Marketing*, April 1974, pp. 54-60; Gilles Laurent and Jean-Noel Kapferer, "Measuring Consumer Involvement Profiles," *Journal of Marketing Research*, February 1985, pp. 41-53; Robert N. Stone and Frederick W. Winter, "Risk: Is it Still Uncertainty Times Consequences?" in Russell W. Belk et. al. ed., 1987 AMA Winter Educators' Conference Proceedings (Chicago: American Marketing Association, 1987), pp. 261-265.

21. See Jagdish N. Sheth, "An Investigation of Relationships Among Evaluative Beliefs, Affect, Behavioral Intention, and Behavior," in *Consumer Behavior: Theory and Application*, John U. Farley, John A. Howard, and L. Winston Ring, eds. (Boston: Allyn & Bacon, 1974), pp. 89-114.

22. See Priscilla A. LaBarbara and David Mazursky, "A Longitudinal Assessment of Consumer Satisfaction/Dissatisfaction: The Dynamic Aspect of the Cognitive Process," *Journal of Marketing Research*, November 1983, pp. 393-404.

23. See Leon Festinger, *A Theory of Cognitive Dissonance* (Stanford: Stanford University Press, 1957).

# CHAPTER 7

# Organizational Markets and Organizational Buyer Behavior

## CHAPTER OBJECTIVES

After reading this chapter, you should be able to:
1. Explain how organizational markets differ from consumer markets.
2. Identify the major factors that influence organizational buyer behavior.
3. List and define the steps in the industrial buying decision process.
4. Explain how resellers and government buyers make their buying decisions.

There is a good chance that when a Canadian buys a soft drink or coffee from a vending machine, it is from VS Services. There is also a good chance that when a high-school student has a meal in the school cafeteria, when a patient or resident in a hospital, nursing, or retirement home has a meal, or when a traveler has a bite to eat at the airport in Winnipeg, Montreal, Moncton, or Fredericton, that the meal is from VS Services.

VS Services concentrates on organizational markets—satisfying the needs of industry and government by offering such "products" as food services, catering services, linen and laundry services, office cleaning, and office catering services. Their major markets are hospitals and nursing homes, public and private schools, colleges and large universities, correctional facilities, and various industrial and business clients. These organizational markets offer tremendous potential for growth: VS Services has sales of over $350 million, and sales have tripled in the last decade.

Successful strategies in the industrial market are often similar to those taken in the consumer market, but there are some differences. Take VS Services' approach to the education market. If most high-school students had their way, the cafeterias would serve the McDonald's type of menu. If most school boards had their way, the cafeterias would serve only "wholesome" food. Both groups want a good price. To be selected for a school, a food service firm has to please both types of consumers—recognizing that they are dealing with organizations and individuals. VS Services introduced the Rainbow Program, which color-codes foods into four groups, each color representing a specific food group providing different basic nutritional requirements. By selecting one of the variety of dishes offered under each of the rainbow colors, students can choose foods they like while making sure they are receiving a nutritious meal. VS Services have also designed the "Itza Pizza" program and the "Gretel's Bake Shop" program for the educational market. The Campus Food Service division prepares and serves over 100,000 meals daily for the educational market.

Other programs, such as "Chef Plan," are focused on the office/factory market; the client list includes General Motors, Toyota, Northern Telecom, and Montreal Trust. The company's one concern in this market is that the Free Trade Agreement with the U.S. has resulted in the streamlining of Canadian branch operations with the loss of cafeteria volume for VS Services. However, with its emphasis on high standards and levels of service, the company is confident of its future growth.

The four major markets in which VS Services operates—health care, work, education, and leisure and recreation—require the company to consider a wide range of needs of both consumers and organizations. Thus VS Services faces the same challenges as consumer marketers, and some additional challenges.[1]

In one way or another most large companies sell to other organizations. Many industrial companies sell most of their products to organizations—companies such as Bombardier, Dofasco, Alcan, and countless other large and small firms. Even large consumer products companies do organizational marketing. For example, Canada Packers makes many familiar products for final consumers, such as Tenderflake lard and Maple Leaf bacon. To sell these products to final consumers, Canada Packers must first sell them to the wholesale and retail organizations that serve the consumer market. Canada Packers also makes products, such as specialty chemicals, that are sold only to other companies.

Organizations make up a vast market. In fact, industrial markets involve many more dollars and items than consumer markets. Figure 7-1 shows the large number of transactions needed to produce and sell a simple pair of shoes. Hide dealers sell to tanners, who sell leather to shoe manufacturers, who sell shoes to wholesalers, who in turn sell shoes to retailers, who finally sell them to consumers.

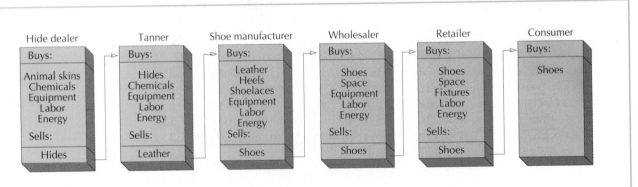

Figure 7-1    Organizational Transactions Involved in Producing and Distributing a Pair of Shoes

Each party in the chain buys many other goods and services as well. It is easy to see why there is more organizational buying than consumer buying—many sets of organizational purchases are made for only one set of consumer purchases.

**Organizational buying** is the decision-making process by which formal organizations establish the need for purchased products and services, and identify, evaluate, and choose among alternative brands and suppliers. Companies that sell to other organizations must do their best to understand organizational buyer behavior.

# ORGANIZATIONAL MARKETS

We will examine three types of organizational markets: the industrial market, the reseller market, and the government market.

## The Industrial Market

The **industrial market** consists of all the individuals and organizations that acquire goods and services that enter into the production of other products and services, which are then sold, rented, or supplied to others. The industrial market is huge: It consists of over 1 million organizations that generate an annual value added of over $150 billion and constitute a buying market for the goods of most firms.

## The Reseller Market

The **reseller market** consists of all the individuals and organizations that acquire goods for the purpose of reselling or renting them to others at a profit. The reseller market includes over 62,000 wholesaling firms and 160,000 retailing firms that combine to purchase over $400 billion worth of goods and services a year.[2] Resellers purchase goods for resale and goods and services

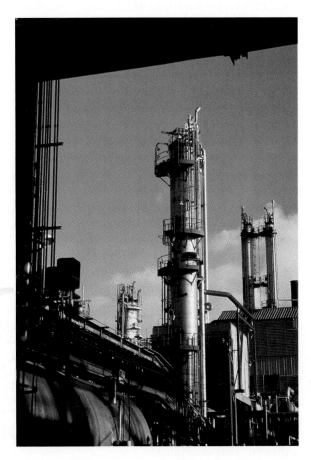

Industrial buyers purchase the raw materials that companies use to make other products.

for conducting their operations. In their role as purchasing agents for their own customers, resellers purchase a vast variety of goods for resale—indeed, they purchase everything produced except for the few classes of goods that producers sell directly to customers.

## The Government Market

The **government market** consists of governmental units—federal, provincial, and municipal—that purchase or rent goods and services for carrying out the main functions of government. Governments, including crown corporations, purchase about $100 billion worth of products and services, or 14% of the gross domestic product.³ Federal, provincial, and municipal government agencies buy an amazing range of products and services. They buy airplanes, paintings, chalkboards, furniture, toiletries, clothing, fire engines, vehicles, and fuel. Governments represent a tremendous market for many producers or resellers.

# CHARACTERISTICS OF ORGANIZATIONAL MARKETS

In some ways, organizational markets are similar to consumer markets as both involve people who assume buying roles and make purchase decisions to satisfy needs. In many ways, however, organizational markets differ from consumer markets.⁴ The main differences are in market structure and demand, the nature of the buying unit, and the types of decisions and the decision process.

## Market Structure and Demand

The organizational marketer normally deals with far fewer, larger buyers than the consumer marketer. The Michelin Tire Company's fate in the industrial market depends on getting orders from one of the large automakers. In contrast, when Michelin sells replacement tires to consumers, its potential market includes the owners of 12 million cars currently in use. Even in large organizational markets, a few buyers normally account for most of the purchasing.

Organizational markets are also more geographically concentrated. Seventy-one percent of the manufacturing establishments in Canada are concentrated in Ontario (42%) and Quebec (29%). These plants produce 77% of the output of Canadian manufacturers.⁵ In fact, an even more narrow geographic area within these two provinces, referred to as the Windsor-Quebec corridor, contains most of the manufacturing plants.

Organizational demand is derived demand—it ultimately comes from the demand for consumer goods. General Motors buys steel because consumers buy cars. If consumer demand for cars drops, so will the demand for steel and all the other products used to make cars.

Many organizational markets have inelastic demand. Total demand for many industrial products is not much affected by price changes, especially in the short run. A drop in the price of leather will not cause shoe manufacturers to buy much more unless it results in lower shoe prices, which increase consumer demand.

Finally, organizational markets have more fluctuating demand. The demand for many industrial goods and services tends to change more often and more quickly than the demand for consumer goods and services. A small percentage increase in consumer demand can cause large increases in industrial demand. Sometimes a rise of only ten percent in consumer demand can cause as much as a 200% rise in industrial demand in the next period.

## The Nature of the Buying Unit

Compared with consumer purchases, organizational purchases usually involve more buyers and more professional purchasing. Organizational buying is often done by trained purchasing agents who spend their work lives learning how to buy better. The more complex the purchase, the more likely that several people will participate in the decision-making process. Buying committees made up of technical experts and top management are common in the buying of major goods.[6] This means that organizational marketers must have well-trained salespeople to deal with well-trained buyers.

## Types of Decisions and the Decision Process

Organizational buyers usually face more complex buying decisions than consumer buyers. Purchases often involve large sums of money, complex technical and economic considerations, and interactions among many people at many levels of the buyer's organization. Because the purchases are more complex, organizational buyers may take longer to make their decisions. A company buying a large computer system may take many months or more than a year to select a supplier.

The organizational buying process tends to be more formalized than the consumer buying process. Large organizational purchases usually call for detailed product specifications, written purchase orders, careful supplier searches, and formal approval. The purchase process may be spelled out in detail in policy manuals.

Finally, in the organizational buying process, buyer and seller are often much more dependent on each other. Consumer marketers usually stay at a distance from their customers. But organizational marketers may roll up their sleeves and work closely with their customers during all stages of the buying process—from helping customers to define the problem, to finding solutions, to after-sale operation.

They often customize their offerings to individual customer needs. In the short run, sales go to suppliers who meet the buyers' immediate product and service needs. But organizational marketers must also build close long-run relationships with customers. In the long run, sales are kept by meeting current needs and thinking ahead to meet the customer's future needs.[7] For example, Budd Canada has introduced a computer-aided design and manufacturing system which allows the company to respond more efficiently and rapidly to customer needs. This technology provides the ability to take customer specifications for component parts and then design and manufacture quality products.[8]

Two recent trends have increased the dependency between buyers and sellers. First, many buyers such as automobile manufacturers are developing a new form of

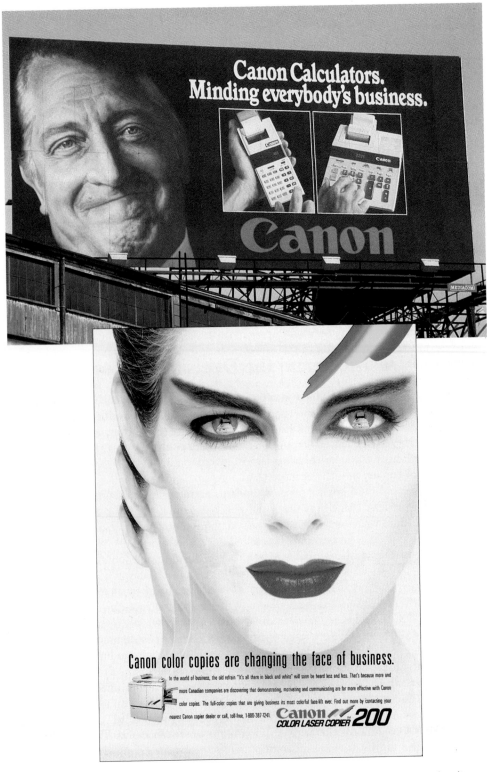

Canon addresses current business needs, in its ad for calculators, and anticipates the direction of business needs, in its ad for color copiers.

relationship with their suppliers, referred to as "just-in-time" (JIT). JIT requires the supplier to deliver to the manufacturer precisely the necessary units in the necessary quantities at the necessary time while meeting specific quality standards.[9] JIT means that buyer and seller work closely to achieve a high degree of coordination. Second, "reverse marketing" is a situation where the buyer takes charge and aggressively searches out sellers who can satisfy the buyer's requirements. Typically, reverse marketing results in close buyer-seller relationships and benefits for both parties.[10]

# A MODEL OF ORGANIZATIONAL BUYER BEHAVIOR

In trying to understand organizational buyer behavior, marketers must answer some hard questions. What kinds of buying decisions do organizational buyers make? How do they choose among suppliers? Who makes the decisions? What is the organizational buying decision process? What factors affect organizational buying decisions?

At the most basic level, marketers want to know how organizational buyers will respond to various marketing stimuli. A simple model of organizational buyer behavior is shown in Figure 7-2.[11] The figure shows that marketing and other stimuli affect the organization and produce certain buyer responses. The marketing stimuli consist of the four Ps: product, price, place, and promotion. The other stimuli consist of major forces in the environment: economic, technological, political, cultural, and competitive. All these stimuli enter the organization and are turned into buyer responses: product or service choice, supplier choice, order quantities,

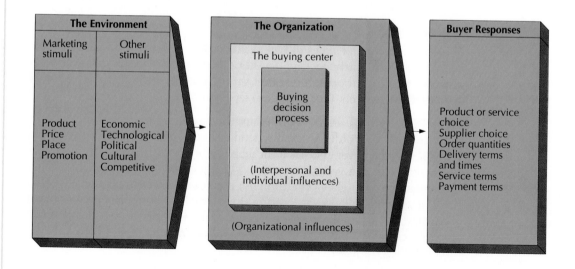

Figure 7-2   A Model of Organizational Buyer Behavior

delivery times and terms, service terms, and payment terms. To design good marketing mix strategies, the marketer must understand what happens within the organization to turn the stimuli into purchase responses.

Within the organization, the buying activity consists of two major parts—the buying center (made up of all the people involved in the buying decision) and the buying decision process. The figure shows that the buying center and the buying decision process are influenced by internal organizational, interpersonal, and individual factors as well as by external environmental factors.

We will look at the various elements in this organizational buyer behavior model. For now we will focus on the largest and most important organizational market—the industrial market. Later in the chapter we will consider the special characteristics of reseller and government buyer behavior.

# INDUSTRIAL BUYER BEHAVIOR

The model in Figure 7-2 suggests four questions about industrial buyer behavior:

- What buying decisions do industrial buyers make?
- Who participates in the buying process?
- What are the major influences on buyers?
- How do industrial buyers make their buying decisions?

## What Buying Decisions Do Industrial Buyers Make?

The industrial buyer faces a whole set of decisions in making a purchase. The number of decisions depends on the type of buying situation.

### MAJOR TYPES OF BUYING SITUATIONS

There are three major types of buying situations.[12] At one extreme is the straight rebuy, which is a fairly routine decision. At the other extreme is the new task, which may call for thorough research. In the middle is the modified rebuy, which requires some research. (For examples, see Figure 7-3).

**STRAIGHT REBUY** In a straight rebuy, the buyer reorders something without any modifications. The order is usually handled on a routine basis by the purchasing department. The buyer chooses from suppliers on its "list," based on its past buying satisfaction with the various suppliers. The "in" suppliers try to maintain product and service quality. They often propose automatic reordering systems so that the purchasing agent will save reordering time. The "out" suppliers try to offer something new or exploit dissatisfaction so that the buyer will consider them. "Out" suppliers try to get their foot in the door with a small order and then enlarge their purchase share over time.

**MODIFIED REBUY** In a modified rebuy, the buyer wants to modify product specifications, prices, terms, or suppliers. The modified rebuy usually involves more decision participants. "In" suppliers may become nervous and have to put their best

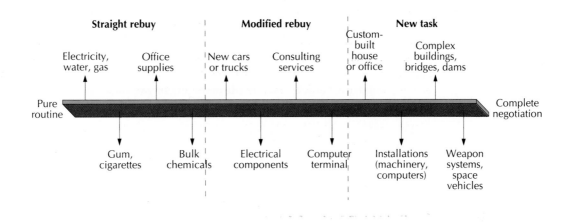

From *Marketing Principles*, Third edition, Ben M. Enis. Copyright © 1980, Scott, Foresman and Company. Reprinted by permission.

Figure 7-3   Three Types of Industrial Buying Situations

foot forward to protect the account. "Out" suppliers see it as an opportunity to make a better offer to gain some new business.

**NEW TASK**   A company faces a new task when it buys a product or service for the first time. The greater the cost or risk, the larger the number of decision participants and the greater their information seeking. The new task situation is the marketer's greatest opportunity and challenge. The marketer not only tries to reach as many key buying influences as possible, but also provides help and information.

## THE ROLE OF SYSTEMS BUYING AND SELLING

Many buyers prefer to buy a whole solution to their problem and not make all the separate decisions involved. This solution, called **systems buying**, began with government buying of major systems. Instead of buying and putting all the components together, the government would ask for bids from suppliers who would assemble the package or system. The winning supplier would be responsible for buying and assembling the subcomponents.

Sellers have increasingly recognized that buyers like to purchase in this way and have adopted the practice of systems selling as a marketing tool.[13] Systems selling has two parts. First, the supplier sells a group of interlocking products. For example, the supplier would sell not only glue, but applicators and dryers as well. Second, the supplier sells a system of production, inventory control, distribution, and other services to meet the buyer's need for a smooth-running operation. Systems selling is a key industrial marketing strategy for winning and holding accounts. The contract often goes to the firm that provides the most complete system that meets the customer's needs.

# Who Participates in the Industrial Buying Process?

Who does the buying of the billions of dollars worth of goods and services needed by the industrial market? The decision-making unit of a buying organization is called its **buying center**, defined as "all those individuals and groups who participate in the purchasing decision-making process, who share some common goals and the risks arising from the decisions."[14]

The buying center includes all members of the organization who play a role in the purchase decision process:

1. **Users.** Users are the members of the organization who will use the product or service. In many cases the users initiate the buying process and play an important role in defining the purchase specifications.

2. **Influencers.** Influencers are those members inside and outside of the organization who directly or indirectly influence the buying decision. They often help define specifications and also provide information for evaluating alternatives. Technical personnel are particularly important as influencers.

3. **Buyers.** Buyers are organizational members with formal authority for selecting the supplier and arranging the terms of purchase. Buyers may help shape product specifications, but they play their major role in selecting vendors and negotiating within the purchase constraints. In more complex purchases, the buyers might include high-level officers of the company participating in the negotiations.

4. **Deciders.** Deciders are organizational members who have either formal or informal power to select or approve the final suppliers. In the routine buying of standard items, the buyers are often the deciders. In more complex buying, the officers of the company are often the deciders.

5. **Gatekeepers.** Gatekeepers are members of the organization who control the flow of information to others. For example, purchasing agents often have authority to prevent salespeople from seeing users or deciders. Other gatekeepers include technical personnel and even switchboard operators. The main impact of gatekeepers is their influence on the inflow of information about buying alternatives.

The buying center is not a fixed and formally identified unit within the buying organization. It is a set of buying roles assumed by different people for different purchases. Within the organization, the size and makeup of the buying center will vary for different products and for different buying situations. The buying center concept presents a major marketing challenge. The industrial marketer has to figure out: Who is involved in the decision? What decisions do they affect? What is their relative degree of influence? What evaluation criteria does each decision participant use? Consider the following example:

> McGaw sells disposable surgical gowns to hospitals. It tries to identify the hospital personnel involved in this buying decision. The decision participants turn out to be (1) the vice-president of purchasing, (2) the operating room administrator, and (3) the surgeons. Each party plays a different role. The vice-president of purchasing analyzes whether the hospital should buy disposable gowns or reusable gowns. If analysis favors disposable gowns, then the operating room administrator compares competing products and prices and makes a choice. This administrator considers the gown's absorbency, antiseptic quality, design, and

cost, and normally buys the brand that meets requirements at the lowest cost. Finally, surgeons affect the decision later by reporting their satisfaction or dissatisfaction with the brand.

# What Are the Major Influences on Industrial Buyers?

Industrial buyers are subject to many influences when they make their buying decisions. Some marketers assume that the major influences are economic. They think that buyers will favor the supplier who offers the lowest price, or the best product, or the most service. They concentrate on offering strong economic benefits to buyers. Other marketers see the buyers as responding to personal motives. The buyers may seek favors, or attention, or risk reduction. This view suggests that industrial marketers should look mostly at the human and social factors in the buying situation.

Industrial buyers actually respond to both economic and personal factors. When offers from suppliers are very similar, industrial buyers have little basis for rational choice. Since they can meet organizational goals with any supplier, buyers can consider personal factors. Where competing products differ greatly, industrial buyers are more accountable for their choice and pay more attention to economic factors.

The various groups of influences on industrial buyers— environmental, organizational, interpersonal, and individual—are listed in Figure 7-4 and described below.[15]

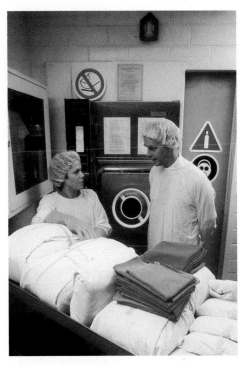

Hospital personnel include product users and influencers, who will affect the purchase of supplies such as surgical gowns.

## ENVIRONMENTAL FACTORS

Industrial buyers are heavily influenced by factors in the current and expected economic environment, such as the level of primary demand, the economic outlook, and the cost of money. As the level of economic uncertainty rises, industrial buyers stop making new investments and attempt to reduce their inventories.

An increasingly important environmental factor is the impact of decisions on the environment. Industrial buyers are now considering the ecological consequences of their actions, particularly in the area of packaging (see Marketing Highlight 7-1). Industrial buyers are also affected by technological, political, and competitive developments in the environment. The industrial marketer has to watch these factors, determine how they will affect the buyer, and try to turn these problems into opportunities.

## ORGANIZATIONAL FACTORS

Each buying organization has its own objectives, policies, procedures, structure, and systems. The industrial marketer has to know these organizational factors as thoroughly as possible. Questions such as these arise: How many people are involved in the buying decision? Who are they? What are their evaluative criteria?

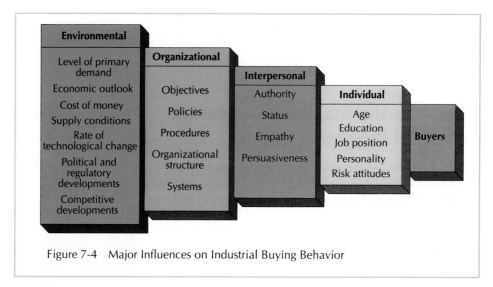

Figure 7-4    Major Influences on Industrial Buying Behavior

What are the company's policies and limits on the buyers? For example, Canadian industrial buyers are likely to have more people involved in the decision than their U.S. counterparts.[16] For the industrial marketer who focuses on Canada, more effort is required to identify the organizational influences.

## INTERPERSONAL FACTORS

The buying center usually includes many participants; each affects and is affected by the others. In many cases, the industrial marketer will not know what kinds of group dynamics take place during the buying process. As one writer notes: "Managers do not wear tags that say "decision maker" or "unimportant person." The powerful are often invisible, at least to vendor representatives."[17]

The buying center participant with the highest rank does not always have the most influence. Participants may have influence in the buying decision because they control rewards and punishments, because they are well liked, or because they have special expertise.[18] Interpersonal factors are often very subtle. Where possible, industrial marketers try to understand these factors and design strategies that take them into account.

## INDIVIDUAL FACTORS

Each participant in the buying decision process brings in personal motives, perceptions, and preferences. These individual factors are affected by age, income, education, professional identification, personality, and attitudes toward risk. Buyers have different buying styles. Some of the younger, higher-educated buyers are "computer freaks" and make in-depth analyses of competitive proposals before choosing a supplier. Other buyers are "tough guys" from the "old school" and play the sellers off against each other for the best deal.

# How Do Industrial Buyers Make Their Buying Decisions?

We now come to the issue of how industrial buyers move through the purchasing process. We can identify eight stages of the industrial buying process.[19] They are

# MARKETING HIGHLIGHT 7-1

## A Major Environmental Factor: Protecting the Environment

Canadian businesses are coming under increasing pressure to consider the impact of their decisions on the environment. With the 1990s the "decade of the environment" began, and many industrial buyers are now responding to the challenge, particularly companies involved in the packaging industry. For example, Alcan Aluminum is increasing its recycling capacity in Canada and the U.S. to ensure the acceptability of aluminum cans. By improving recyclability of aluminum products, Alcan not only reduces the solid waste problem but also provides more low capital source of metal for Alcan's own needs—a clear case of doing well by doing good.

Consumer Packaging is Canada's largest manufacturer of glass and plastic containers. The company is particularly susceptible to changing consumer attitudes to the environment —which will influence the derived demand for the company's products. While glass containers will continue to be accepted by consumers if the industry has appropriate recycling programs, plastic containers could suffer declines in sales if consumers shift their preference to glass, aluminum, steel, or paper.

Environmental issues are becoming more important in industrial buyers' decisions as consumers and governments demand that companies behave in a socially responsible manner. The buyers will reflect this change by purchasing environmentally friendly products ranging from recycled paper to non-toxic chemicals to biodegradable containers.

listed in Table 7-1. The table shows that buyers facing the new task buying situation will go through all the stages of the buying process. Buyers making modified or straight rebuys will skip some of the stages. We will examine these steps for the typical new task buying situation.

## PROBLEM RECOGNITION

The buying process begins when someone in the company recognizes a problem or need that can be met by acquiring a good or a service. Problem recognition can result from internal or external stimuli. Internally, the most common events leading to problem recognition are the following:

- The company decides to launch a new product and needs new equipment and materials to produce this product.
- A machine breaks down and needs new parts.
- Some purchased material turns out to be unsatisfactory, and the company searches for another supplier.
- A purchasing manager sees a chance to get better prices or quality.

Externally, the buyer may get some new ideas at a trade show, or see an ad, or receive a call from a salesperson who offers a better product or a lower price.

## GENERAL NEED DESCRIPTION

Having recognized a need the buyer next prepares a description of the general characteristics and quantity of the needed item. For standard items, this is not

**Table 7-1**
**Major Stages of the Industrial Buying Process in Relation to Major Buying Situations**

| Stages of the Buying Process | Buying Situations | | |
|---|---|---|---|
| | New Task | Modified Rebuy | Straight Rebuy |
| 1. Problem recognition | Yes | Maybe | No |
| 2. General need description | Yes | Maybe | No |
| 3. Product specification | Yes | Yes | Yes |
| 4. Supplier search | Yes | Maybe | No |
| 5. Proposal solicitation | Yes | Maybe | No |
| 6. Supplier selection | Yes | Maybe | No |
| 7. Order routine specification | Yes | Maybe | No |
| 8. Performance review | Yes | Yes | Yes |

**Source:** Adapted from Patrick J. Robinson, Charles W. Faris, and Yoram Wind, *Industrial and Creative Marketing* (Boxton: Allyn & Bacon, 1967), p.14.

much of a problem. For complex items, the buyer will work with others —engineers, users, consultants—to define the item. They will want to rank the importance of reliability, durability, price, and other attributes desired in the item.

The industrial marketer can help the buying company in this phase. Often the buyer is not aware of the value of different product characteristics. An alert marketer can help the buyer define the company's needs.

## PRODUCT SPECIFICATION

The buying organization next develops the item's technical product specifications. Often, a value analysis engineering team will be put to work on the problem. **Value analysis** is an approach to cost reduction in which components are carefully studied to determine if they can be redesigned or standardized or made by cheaper methods of production. The team will decide on the best product characteristics and specify them accordingly. Sellers can also use value analysis as a tool for breaking into an account. By showing a better way to make an object, outside sellers can turn straight rebuy situations into new task situations in which their company has a chance for business.

## SUPPLIER SEARCH

The buyer now conducts a supplier search to find the best vendors. The buyer can look at trade directories, do a computer search, or phone other companies for recommendations. Some vendors will not be considered because they are not large enough to supply the needed quantity or because they have a poor reputation for delivery and service. The buyer will end up with a small list of qualified suppliers.

The newer the buying task, and the more complex and costly the item, the greater the amount of time spent in searching for suppliers. The supplier's task is to get listed in major directories and build a good reputation in the marketplace.

Salespeople should watch for companies in the process of searching for suppliers and make certain that their firm is considered.

## PROPOSAL SOLICITATION

In the proposal solicitation stage, the buyer will invite qualified suppliers to submit proposals. Some suppliers will send only a catalog or a sales representative. If the item is complex or expensive, the buyer will need detailed written proposals from each potential supplier. The buyer will review the suppliers when they make their formal presentations.

Industrial marketers must therefore be skilled in researching, writing, and presenting proposals. Their proposals should be marketing documents, not just technical documents. Their presentations should inspire confidence, and help their companies stand out from the competition.

## SUPPLIER SELECTION

The members of the buying center now review the proposals and select a supplier(s). In supplier selection, they will consider not only the technical competence of the various suppliers, but also their ability to deliver the item on time and provide necessary services. The buying center will often draw up a list of the desired supplier attributes and their relative importance. These attributes could include quality, price, repair service, technical capability, delivery capability, reputation, financial position, and geographic location. The members of the buying center will rate the suppliers against these or other attributes and identify the most attractive suppliers.

Buyers may attempt to negotiate with preferred suppliers for better prices and terms before making the final selections. In the end, they may select a single supplier or a few suppliers, depending on their needs and the type of product involved.

## ORDER ROUTINE SPECIFICATION

The buyer now prepares an order routine specification. It includes the final order with the chosen supplier(s), listing the technical specifications, quantity needed, expected time of delivery, return policies, warranties, and so on. In the case of maintenance, repair, and operating items, buyers are increasingly using blanket contracts rather than frequent or periodic purchase orders. Writing a new purchase order each time stock is needed is expensive. In addition, if the buyers wrote fewer and larger purchase orders they would have to carry more inventory, which would add to carrying costs.

A blanket contract creates a long-term relationship in which the supplier promises to resupply the buyer as needed at agreed prices for a set time period. The stock is held by the seller and the buyer's computer automatically prints out an order to the seller when stock is needed. Blanket contracting leads to more single-source buying and the buying of more items from that single source. This locks the supplier in tighter with the buyer and makes it difficult for other suppliers to break in unless the buyer becomes dissatisfied with prices or service.

## PERFORMANCE REVIEW

In this stage the buyer reviews supplier performance. The buyer may contact users and ask them to rate their satisfaction. The performance review may lead the buyer to continue, modify, or drop the seller. The seller's job is to monitor the same factors used by the buyer to make sure that the seller is giving the expected satisfac-

# MARKETING HIGHLIGHT 7-2

## Customer Satisfaction — Xerox Scores High

A few years ago Xerox Canada thought that customer silence meant customer satisfaction. After losing market share to competitors, primarily from Japan, who were picking up Xerox's dissatisfied customers, Xerox made some changes that included improving quality and increasing customer satisfaction. In 1989, Xerox Canada received the first national Quality Award from the federal government, as it was judged the best company at keeping its customers happy.

Xerox Canada got serious about product quality in 1987. In surveys of Xerox customers, 93% now say they are willing to recommend Xerox to business associates based on their experiences with the company's service or product installation. That figure was up five percent in 1988 and 1989, since Xerox Canada made quality a priority. Xerox, like many other companies, has found that it pays to do things right the first time and to keep checking with the customer to make sure it is right.

In one study of customer satisfaction, it was found that:

- If a company's unhappy customers had no easy way to register a complaint, 90% of them would find another supplier without attempting to complain (ten percent would give repeat business and suffer silently).
- If a company's unhappy customers had a clear route for complaints, 80% of them would find another supplier (20% would stay).
- When a problem was resolved after a complaint, only 50% of the unhappy customers sought a new supplier. When it was resolved quickly, only 20% of the customers were lost.

Industrial marketers need to make sure that their customers are satisfied. The rewards are increased profits and market share—the goals of many marketers.

**Source:** Geoffrey Rowan, "Xerox Canada First Winner of Federal Government Award for Quality," *Globe and Mail*, November 8, 1989, p. B3.

Xerox has deliberately made customer satisfaction a priority.

tion. Many sellers today realize the importance of ensuring customer satisfaction (see Marketing Highlight 7-2).

We have described the buying stages that would operate in a new task buying situation. In the modified rebuy or straight rebuy situation, some of these stages would be compressed or bypassed. The eight-stage model provides a simple view of the industrial buying decision process. The actual process is usually much more complex.[20] Each organization buys in its own way, and each buying situation has unique requirements. Different buying center participants may be involved at different stages of the process. Although certain buying process steps usually occur, buyers do not always follow them in the same order, and they may add other steps. Often, buyers repeat certain stages more than once.

# RESELLER BUYER BEHAVIOR

In most ways, reseller buyer behavior is like industrial buyer behavior. Reseller organizations have buying centers whose participants interact to make a variety of buying decisions. Their buying decision process starts with problem recognition and ends with decisions about which products to buy from which suppliers and under what terms. The buyers are affected by a wide range of environmental, organizational, interpersonal, and individual factors.

However, there are some important differences between industrial and reseller buying behavior. Resellers differ in the types of buying decisions they make, who participates in the buying decision, and how they make their buying decisions.

## What Buying Decisions Do Resellers Make?

Resellers serve as purchasing agents for their customers, so they buy products and brands they think will appeal to their customers. They have to decide what product assortment to carry, what vendors to buy from, and what prices and terms to negotiate. The assortment decision is very important because it positions the reseller in the marketplace. The reseller's assortment strategy will strongly affect its choice of which products to buy and which suppliers to buy from.

Resellers can carry products from only one supplier, or several related products or lines from a few suppliers, or a scrambled assortment of unrelated products from many suppliers. Therefore, a camera store might carry only Kodak cameras; many brands of cameras; cameras, radios, tape recorders, and stereo equipment; or all these plus stoves and refrigerators. The reseller's assortment will affect its customer mix, marketing mix, and supplier mix.

## Who Participates in the Reseller Buying Process?

Who does the buying for wholesale and retail organizations? The reseller's buying center may include one or many participants assuming different roles. Some will have formal buying responsibility, and some will be behind-the-scenes influencers. In small "mom and pop" firms, the owner usually takes care of buying decisions. In large reseller firms, buying is a specialized function and a full-time job. The buying center and buying process vary for different types of resellers.

Consider supermarkets. In the headquarters of a supermarket chain, specialist buyers have the responsibility for developing brand assortments and listening to new brand presentations made by salespeople. In some chains these buyers have the authority to accept or reject new items. In many chains, however, they are limited to screening "obvious rejects" and "obvious accepts"; otherwise they must bring new items to the chain's buying committee for approval. Even when an item is accepted by a buying committee, chain-store managers may not carry it.

# How Do Resellers Make Their Buying Decisions?

For new items, resellers use roughly the same buying process described for industrial buyers. For standard items, resellers simply reorder goods when the inventory gets low. The orders are placed with the same suppliers as long as their terms, goods, and services are satisfactory. Buyers will try to renegotiate prices if their margins drop due to rising operating costs. In many retail lines, the profit margin is so low (one to two percent on sales in supermarkets, for example) that a sudden drop in demand or rise in operating costs will drive profits into the red.

Resellers consider many factors besides costs when choosing products and suppliers. Other criteria include expected consumer acceptance of the product, the amount of promotion the supplier will provide, merchandising help given by the supplier, purchase discounts, and others. Sellers stand the best chance when they can report strong evidence of consumer acceptance, present a well-designed advertising and sales promotion plan, and provide strong financial incentives to the retailer.

Several studies have attempted to rank the major criteria used by buyers, buying committees, and store managers. In one study of Canadian non-food retail chain buyers such as Shoppers' Drug Mart, Sears, Canadian Tire, and Eaton's, the major criteria used in their decision to accept a new product were:[21]

- Expected profit contribution
- Supplier's ability to fill repeat orders quickly
- Product quality
- Retailer or dealer markup
- Product's meeting of government regulations
- Competitive price

**Table 7-2**
**Vendor Marketing Tools Used With Resellers**

Vendor Marketing Tools Used With Resellers

*Cooperative advertising*, where the vendor agrees to pay a portion of the reseller's advertising costs for the vendor's product.

*Preticketing*, where the vendor places a tag on each product listing its price, manufacturer, size, identification number, and color: these tags help the reseller reorder merchandise as it is being sold.

*Stockless purchasing*, where the vendor carries the inventory and delivers goods to the reseller on short notice.

*Automatic reordering systems*, where the vendor supplies forms and computer links for automatic reordering of merchandise by the reseller.

*Advertising aids*, such as glossy photos, broadcast scripts.

*Special prices* for storewide promotion.

*Return and exchange priveledges* for the reseller.

*Allowances for merchandise markdowns* by the reseller.

*Sponsorship of in-store demonstrations*.

- Supplier's known track record
- Potential market volume
- Manufacturer's initial supply capabilities
- Product's fitting into new trends in the market

Sellers are facing increasingly advanced buying on the part of resellers. They need to understand the changing needs of resellers and to develop attractive offers that help resellers serve their customers better. Table 7-2 lists several marketing tools used by sellers to make their offer to resellers more attractive.

# GOVERNMENT BUYER BEHAVIOR

Although government buying and industrial buying are similar in many ways, they do have differences that must be understood by companies wishing to sell products and services to governments.[22] To succeed in the government market, sellers must locate key decision makers, identify the factors that affect buyer behavior, and understand the buying decision process.

## Who Participates in the Government Buying Process?

Who does the buying of the billions of dollars of goods and services? Government buying organizations are found at the federal, provincial, and local levels. At the federal level, all government departments instigate the purchase of goods and supplies, although some of the purchasing for these departments is handled by the Department of Supply and Services. Its major function is to obtain goods and services of the best quality for the best price. At the provincial and municipal level, departments also have their own buying organizations that determine what is to be purchased and from whom.

## What Are the Major Influences on Government Buyers?

Government buyers are affected by environmental, organizational, interpersonal, and individual factors. A unique aspect of government buying is that it is carefully watched by outside publics. At the federal level, members of parliament in the Opposition frequently query government expenditures. Probably the most visible watchdog is the Auditor General who provides an annual review of government buying and makes suggestions as to improvement in the efficiency of public spending. Many private groups also watch government agencies to see how they spend the public's money.

Because spending decisions are subject to public review, government organizations get involved in much paperwork. Elaborate forms must be filled out and signed before purchases are approved. The level of bureaucracy is high, and marketers have to find a way to cut through the red tape. Noneconomic criteria are playing a growing role in government buying. The new criteria come out of government reform programs and call for favoring firms that are Canadian-owned or located in particular regions of the country.

# How Do Government Buyers Make Their Buying Decisions?

Government buying practices often seem complex and frustrating to suppliers. However, the ins and outs of selling to government can be mastered in a short time. The government is generally helpful in spreading information about its buying needs and procedures. Government is often as anxious to attract new suppliers as the suppliers are to find customers. The federal government provides the Government Business Opportunities bulletin on a weekly basis which lists major federal requirements and contracts awarded to firms by federal departments and agencies.[23] As well, the federal and provincial governments offer a guide to their purchasing policies.[24]

Government buying procedures fall into two types: the open bid and the negotiated contract. Open bid buying means that the government office invites bids from qualified suppliers for carefully described items, generally awarding a contract to the lowest bidder. At the federal level, the Department of Supply and Services publishes lists of all contracts open for bidding in a daily magazine and on an electronic bulletin board.[25] The supplier must consider whether it can meet the specifications and accept the terms. For standard items, such as fuel or school supplies, the specifications are not a hurdle, although they may be a hurdle for non-standard items. The government office is usually required to award the contract to the lowest bidder on a winner-take-all basis. In some cases, allowance is made for the supplier's better product or reputation for completing contracts.

In negotiated contract buying, the agency works with one or more companies and negotiates a contract with one of them covering the project and terms. This occurs primarily with complex projects— those involving major research and development cost and risk, or those for which there is little competition. The contract can be reviewed and renegotiated if the supplier's profits seem too high.

For a number of reasons, many companies that sell to the government have not been marketing-oriented. Total government spending is determined by elected officials rather than by the efforts of marketing. The government buying has emphasized price, making suppliers invest their effort in technology to bring costs down. Where the product's characteristics are carefully specified, product differentiation is not a marketing factor. Furthermore, advertising and personal selling are of little importance in winning bids on an open bid basis.

# SUMMARY

Organizations make up a vast market. There are three major types of organizational markets—the industrial market, the reseller market, and the government market.

In many ways, organizational markets are like consumer markets, but in other ways they are much different. Organizational markets usually have fewer and larger buyers who are more geographically concentrated. Organizational demand is derived, largely inelastic, and more fluctuating. More buyers are usually involved in the organizational buying decision, and organizational buyers are better trained and more professional than consumer buyers. Organizational purchasing decisions are more complex and the buying process is more formal.

The industrial market includes firms and individuals that buy goods and services in order to produce other goods and services for sale or rental to others.

Industrial buyers make decisions that vary with the three types of buying situations—straight rebuys, modified rebuys, and new tasks. The decision-making unit of a buying organization, called the buying center, may consist of many people playing many roles. The industrial marketer needs to know: Who are the major participants? In what decisions do they exercise influence? What is their relative degree of influence? What evaluation criteria does each decision participant use? The industrial marketer also needs to understand the major environmental, organizational, interpersonal, and individual influences on the buying process. The buying process itself consists of eight stages: problem recognition, general need description, product specification, supplier search, proposal solicitation, supplier selection, order routine specification, and performance review. As industrial buyers become more sophisticated, industrial sellers must upgrade their marketing efforts.

The reseller market consists of individuals and organizations that acquire and resell goods produced by others. Resellers have to decide on their assortment, suppliers, prices, and terms. In small wholesale and retail organizations, buying may be carried on by one or a few individuals; in large organizations, by an entire purchasing department. With new items, the buyers go through a buying process similar to the one shown for industrial buyers; and with standard items, the buying process consists of routines for reordering and renegotiating contracts.

The government market is a vast one that annually purchases billions of dollars of products and services for defense, education, public welfare, and other public needs. Government buying practices are highly specialized and specified, with open bidding or negotiated contracts characterizing most of the buying. Government buyers operate under the watchful eye of the Auditor General and many private watchdog groups. Hence they tend to fill out more forms, require more signatures, and respond more slowly in placing orders.

# QUESTIONS FOR DISCUSSION

1. In what ways can your school be considered an industrial marketer? What are its products and who are its customers?

2. How does the geographic concentration of organizational markets influence the marketing efforts of firms selling to organizational buyers?

3. Which of the three major types of buying situations—straight rebuy, modified rebuy, and new task—are represented by the following: (a) Chrysler's purchase of computers that adjust engine performance to changing driving conditions, (b) Volkswagen's purchase of spark plugs for its line of Jettas, and (c) Honda's purchase of light bulbs for its Acura division?

4. If a university wants to introduce polo as a varsity sport, what elements would a systems seller include in a proposal to start the program and make it succeed?

5. How could a marketer of office equipment identify the buying center for a law firm's purchase of dictaphone equipment for its partners?

6. What major environmental factors would affect the purchase of radar speed detectors by provincial and local police forces?

7. What are the advantages and disadvantages of buying from single suppliers instead of multiple suppliers?

8. Compare the major buying influences on industrial, reseller, and government buyers.

# Key Terms

**Buying center**  All the individuals and groups that participate in the organizational buying decision process.

**Government market**  Governmental units—federal, provincial, and municipal—that purchase or rent goods and services for carrying out the main functions of government.

**Industrial market**  All the individuals and organizations that acquire goods and services that enter into the production of other products and services that are in turn sold, rented, or supplied to others.

**Organizational buying**  The decision-making process by which formal organizations establish the need for purchased products and services, and identify, evaluate, and choose among alternative brands and suppliers.

**Reseller market**  All the individuals and organizations that acquire goods for the purpose of reselling or renting them to others at a profit.

**Systems buying**  Buying a whole solution to a problem and not making all the separate decisions involved.

**Value analysis**  An approach to cost reduction in which components are carefully studied to determine if they can be redesigned or standardized or made by cheaper methods of production.

# References

1. Information obtained from VS Services Annual Report, various years.

2. *Marketing Research Handbook*, 1990, Statistics Canada, Catalogue 63-224.

3. *Marketing Research Handbook*, 1990, Statistics Canada.

4. Some authors argue that there are more similarities than differences. See Edward F. Fern and James R. Brown, "The Industrial/Consumer Marketing Dichotomy: A Case of Insufficient Justification," *Journal of Marketing*, Spring 1984, pp. 68-77.

5. *Canadian Markets 1988/89*, *Financial Post*, Toronto, Maclean Hunter, 1989.

6. Thomas V. Bonoma, "Major Sales: Who Really Does The Buying?" *Harvard Business Review*, May-June 1982, pp. 111-119.

7. See Barbara Bund Jackson, "Build Customer Relationships That Last," *Harvard Business Review*, November-December 1985, pp. 120-128.

8. Budd Canada Inc., *Annual Report*, 1989.

9. Gary L. Frazier, Robert E. Speckman, and Charles R. O'Neal, "Just-in-Time Exchange Relationships in Industrial Markets," *Journal of Marketing*, October, 1988, pp. 52-67 and Charles R. O'Neal, "JIT Procurement and Relationship Marketing," *Industrial Marketing Management*, 18, 1989, pp. 55-63.

10. Michiel R. Leenders and David L. Blenkhorn, *Reverse Marketing: The New Buyer-Seller Relationship* (New York: The Free Press, 1988).

11. For a discussion of other organizational buyer behavior models, see Raymond L. Horton, *Buyer Behavior: A Decision-Making Approach* (Columbus, OH: Charles E. Merrill, 1984), Chap. 16.

12. Patrick J. Robinson, Charles W. Faris, and Yoram Wind, *Industrial Buying Behavior and Creative Marketing* (Boston: Allyn & Bacon, 1967). Also see Erin Anderson, Weyien Chu, and Barton Weitz, "Industrial Purchasing: An Empirical Exploration of the Buyclass Framework," *Journal of Marketing*, July 1987, pp. 71-86.

13. For more on systems selling, see Robert R. Reeder, Edward G. Brierty, and Betty H. Reeder, *Industrial Marketing: Analysis, Planning and Control* (Englewood Cliffs, NJ: Prentice Hall, 1987), pp. 247-50.

14. Frederick E. Webster, Jr. and Yoram Wind, *Organizational Buying Behavior* (Englewood Cliffs, NJ: Prentice-Hall 1972), p. 6. For more reading on buying centers, see Bonoma, "Major Sales," and Donald W. Jackson, Jr., Janet E. Keith, and Richard K. Burdick, "Purchasing Agents' Perceptions of Industrial Buying Center Influence: A Situational Approach," *Journal of Marketing*, Fall 1984, pp. 75-83 and John R. Ronchetta, Jr., Michael D. Hutt, and Peter H. Reingen, "Embedded Influence Patterns in Organizational Buying Systems," *Journal of Marketing*, October 1989, pp. 51-62.

15. Webster and Wind, *Organizational Buying Behavior*, pp. 33-37.

16. Paul A. Dion and Peter Banting, "What Industrial Marketers can Expect From U.S.-Canada Free Trade," *Industrial Marketing Management*, 19, 1990, pp. 77-80.

17. Bonoma, "Major Sales," p. 114.

18. Ajay Kohli, "Determinants of Influence in Organizational Buying: A Contingency Approach," *Journal of Marketing*, July 1989, pp. 50-65

19. Robinson, Faris, and Wind, *Industrial Buying*.

20. Wesley J. Johnson and Thomas V. Bonoma, "Purchase Process for Capital Equipment and Services," Industrial Marketing Management, 10, (1981), pp. 261.

21. David L. Blenkhorn and Peter M. Banting, "Non-Food Retail Chain New Product Adoption Decision Criteria," in Robert Wyckham (ed.), *Proceedings of the Marketing Division* (Halifax: ASAC, 1981), pp.28-35; and Peter M. Banting and David L. Blenkhorn, "The Mind of the Retail Buyer," *Management Decision*, 26, 6, 1988, pp. 29-36.

22. For more reading on similarities and differences, see Jagdish N. Sheth, Robert F. Williams, and Richard M. Hill, "Government and Business Buying: How Similar Are They?" *Journal of Purchasing and Materials Management*, Winter 1983, pp. 7-13.

23. *Government Business Opportunities*, Supply and Services, Ottawa. For more details on various aspects of marketing to governments, see "Selling to Government," *Financial Post*, March 28, 1988, pp. 37-40.

24. See *Selling to Government: A Guide to Government Procurement in Canada*, Supply and Services, Ottawa.

25. Patricia Lush, "Ottawa to Open Bidding System For Goods, Services," *Globe and Mail*, April 18, 1990, p. B8.

# CHAPTER 8

# Market Segmentation, Targeting, and Positioning

## CHAPTER OBJECTIVES

After reading this chapter, you should be able to:
1. Define market segmentation, market targeting, and market positioning.
2. List and discuss the major bases for segmenting consumer and industrial markets.
3. Explain how companies identify attractive market segments and choose a market-coverage strategy.
4. Describe how companies can position their products for maximum advantage in the marketplace.

Procter & Gamble makes six different brands of laundry detergent (Tide, Ultra Cheer, Bold, Dreft, Ivory Snow, and Oxydol). It also sells five brands of hand soap (Zest, Coast, Ivory, Safeguard, and Camay), five shampoos (Vidal Sassoon, Head & Shoulders, Ivory, Pantene, and Pert), two liquid dishwashing detergents (Joy and Ivory), one brand of toothpaste and two dental adhesives (Crest, Fasteeth, and Fixadent), shortening (Crisco and Fluffo), fabric softener (Downy and Bounce), household cleaners (Spic & Span, Mr. Clean, and Comet), and disposable diapers (Pampers and Luvs). Thus, P&G brands compete with one another on the same supermarket shelves.

But why would P&G introduce several brands in one category instead of concentrating its resources on a single leading brand? The answer lies in the fact that different people want different mixes of benefits from the products they buy. Take laundry detergents as an example. People use laundry detergents to get their clothes clean. But they also want other things from their detergents—attributes such as economy, bleaching power, fabric softening, fresh smell, strength or mildness, and lots of suds. We all want some of these benefits from our detergent, but we may have different priorities for each benefit. To some people, cleaning and bleaching power are most important; to others, fabric softening is most important; still others want a mild, fresh-scented detergent. Thus, there are groups—or segments—of laundry detergent buyers, and each segment seeks a special combination of benefits.

Procter & Gamble has identified at least six important laundry segments, and it has developed a different brand designed to meet the special needs of each segment. The P&G brands are positioned for different segments as follows:

- Tide is the "extra action," all-purpose detergent for extra tough laundry jobs. It is a family detergent—"It gets out the dirt kids get into," "Tide's in, dirt's out." As well, Tide is offered as Liquid Tide (for quicker dispersal), Tide with Bleach (for convenience), and Phosphate Free Tide (for environmental concern).
- Ultra Cheer is specially formulated for use in hot, warm, or cold water. It's "all tempera-Cheer." It is also compact and contains no phosphates.
- Bold 3 originally "powered out dirt." Now it's the detergent plus fabric softener. It "cleans, softens and controls static."
- Dreft is formulated for baby's diapers and clothes and it contains borax, "nature's natural sweetener."
- Ivory Snow is "Ninety-nine and forty-four one hundredths percent pure." It's the mild, gentle soap for diapers and baby clothes."
- Oxydol contains bleach. It's for "sparkling whites, a full power detergent with color-safe bleach."

By segmenting the market and having several different detergent brands, P&G has an attractive offering for consumers in all important preference groups. All P&G brands combined hold more than a 45% share of the Canadian laundry detergent market—much more than any single brand could obtain by itself.[1]

The term market has acquired many meanings over the years. In its original meaning, a market was a location where buyers and sellers gathered to exchange goods and services. To an economist, a market consists of all the buyers and sellers who transact over some good or service. Thus, the soft drink market consists of major sellers such as Coca-Cola, Pepsi-Cola, and 7-Up and all the consumers who buy soft drinks. To a marketer, a **market** is the set of all actual and potential buyers of a product.

Organizations that sell to consumer and industrial markets recognize that they cannot appeal to all buyers in those markets, or at least not to all buyers in the same way. The buyers are too numerous, widely scattered, and varied in needs and buying practices. Different companies will be in better positions to serve certain segments of the market. Each company has to identify the parts of the market that it can serve best.

Sellers have not always practiced this philosophy. Their thinking passed through three stages:

- **Mass marketing**. In mass marketing the seller mass-produces, mass-distributes, and mass-promotes one product to all buyers. At one time Coca-Cola produced only one drink for the whole market, hoping it would appeal to everyone. The argument for mass marketing is that it should lead to the lowest costs and prices and create the largest potential market.
- **Product-differentiated marketing**. Here the seller produces two or more products that have different features, styles, quality, sizes, and so on. Today Coca-Cola produces several soft drinks packaged in different sizes and containers. They are designed to offer variety to buyers rather than appeal to different market segments.
- **Target marketing**. Here the seller identifies market segments, selects one or more of these segments, and develops products and marketing mixes tailored to each

segment. For example, approximately 50% of all soft drinks sold in Canada are Coca-Cola products. Coca-Cola has achieved this share by target marketing. Coca-Cola Classic is aimed at the over 20's; Coke is aimed at the teen market; Diet Coke at the diet-conscious drinkers; and Caffeine Free Diet Coke at the older consumer who is concerned with health and wellness issues. As well, Coca Cola Beverages markets a wide range of brands including Sprite, Minute Maid, Canada Dry, Schweppes, and A&W to capture different segments. This target marketing adds up to over $930 million in annual sales (over 200 million cases) and a dominant share of the Canadian soft drink market.[2]

Today's companies are moving away from mass marketing and product- differentiated marketing toward target marketing. Target marketing more effectively helps sellers find marketing opportunities. The sellers can develop the right product for each target market. They can adjust their prices, distribution channels, and advertising to reach the target market efficiently. Instead of scattering their marketing effort ("shotgun" approach), they can focus it on the buyers who have the greater purchase interest ("rifle" approach).

Target marketing calls for three major steps (Figure 8-1). The first is **market segmentation**, dividing a market into distinct groups of buyers who might call for separate products or marketing mixes. The company identifies different ways to segment the market and develops profiles of the resulting market segments. The second step is **market targeting**, evaluating each segment's attractiveness and selecting one or more of the market segments to enter. The third step is market positioning, setting the competitive positioning for the product and a detailed marketing mix. This chapter will describe the principles of market segmentation, market targeting, and market positioning.

# MARKET SEGMENTATION

Markets consist of buyers, which differ in one or more ways. They may differ in their wants, resources, locations, buying attitudes, and buying practices. Any of these variables can be used to segment a market.

Because buyers have unique needs and wants, each is potentially a separate market. Ideally, a seller might design a separate marketing program for each buyer. For example, a company like Hayes-Dana, which produces new and replacement components for cars and trucks, faces only a few buyers in the market for new components, namely car and truck manufacturers. Hayes-Dana treats each buyer, such as Ford, as a separate market. Using such complete market segmentation, they customize their products and

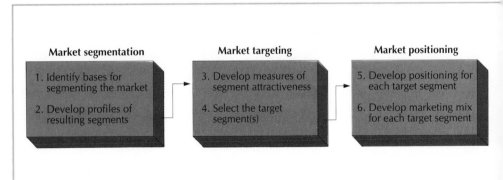

Figure 8-1   Steps in Market Segmentation, Targeting, and Positioning

marketing programs to satisfy each specific customer.

However, most sellers do not find complete segmentation worthwhile. Instead, most sellers look for broad classes of buyers who differ in their product needs or buying response. For example, Ford Motors has found that high and low income groups differ in their car buying needs and wants. It also knows that young consumers' needs and wants differ from those of older consumers. Thus, Ford has designed specific models for different income and age groups—in fact, it sells models for segments with varied combinations of age and income. For example, Ford designed its Probe for younger, middle income consumers. Age and income are only two of many bases that companies use for segmenting their markets.

## Bases for Segmenting Consumer Markets

There is no single way to segment a market. A marketer has to try different segmentation variables, alone and in combination, hoping to find the best way to view the market structure. Table 8-1 outlines the major variables that might be used in segmenting consumer markets. Here we will look at the major geographic, demographic, psychographic, and behavior variables used in segmenting consumer markets.

**TABLE 8-1**
**Major Segmentation Variables for Consumer Markets**

| Variable | Typical Breakdowns |
| --- | --- |
| *Geographic:* | |
| Region | Maritimes, Ontario, Quebec (Windsor-Quebec corridor), Prairies, British Columbia |
| City | Under 1000, 1000-2999, 3000-4999, 5000-9999, 10,000-14,999, 15,000-24,000, 25,000-49,999, 50,000-99,999, 100,000-199,999, 200,000-299,999, 300,000-399,999, 400,000-499,999, over 500,000 |
| Density | Urban, suburban, rural |
| Climate | Pacific, Prairie, Central, Atlantic |
| *Psychographic:* | |
| Social class | Lower lowers, upper lowers, lower middles, upper middles, lower uppers, upper uppers |
| Life style | Use of one's time, values, beliefs; belongers, achievers |
| Personality | Compulsive, gregarious, authoritarian, ambitious |
| *Behavioristic:* | |
| Purchase occasion | Regular occasion, special occasion |
| Benefits sought | Quality, service, economy |
| User status | Nonuser, ex-user, potential user, first-time user, regular user |

| | |
|---|---|
| Usage status | Light user, medium user, heavy user |
| Loyalty status | None, medium, strong, absolute |
| Readiness stage | Unaware, aware, informed, interested, desirous, intending to buy |
| Attitude toward product | Enthusiastic, positive, indifferent, negative, hostile |
| *Demographic:* | |
| Age | Under 6, 6-11, 12-19, 20-34, 35-49, 50-64, 65+ |
| Sex | Male, female |
| Family size | 1-2, 3-4, 5+ |
| Family life cycle | Young, single; young, married, no children; young, married, youngest child under 6; young, married, youngest child 6 or over; older, married, with children; older, married, no children under 18; older, single; other |
| Income | Under $1,000, 1,000-1,999, 10-14,999, 15,000-24,999, 25,000-34,999, 35,000-49,999 and 50,000 and over |
| Occupation | Professional and technical; managers, officials, and proprietors; clerical,sales; craftspeople; operatives; farmers; retired; students; homemakers; unemployed |
| Education | Grade school or less; some high school; graduated high school; some university; graduated university |
| Religion | Catholic, Protestant, Jewish, Lutheran, other |
| Race | White, black, asian, brown |
| Nationality | Canadian, American, British, French, German, Eastern European, Scandinavian, Italian, Latin American, Middle Eastern, Japanese, Chinese |

## GEOGRAPHIC SEGMENTATION

**Geographic segmentation** divides the market into different geographical units such as nations, provinces, regions, counties, cities, or neighborhoods. The company decides to operate in one or a few geographical areas, or to operate in all areas but pay attention to geographical differences in needs and wants. For example, gasoline is sold nationally by Petro Canada or Shell but is modified by region to accommodate differences in climate. Many beers in Canada are brewed and sold on a regional basis, such as Moosehead in the Maritimes and Uncle Ben's in British Columbia.

## DEMOGRAPHIC SEGMENTATION

**Demographic segmentation** divides the market into groups based on demographic variables such as age, sex, family size, family life cycle, income, occupation, education, religion, race, and nationality. Demographic factors are the most popular bases for segmenting consumer groups. One reason is that consumer needs, wants, and usage rates often vary closely with demographic variables. Another is that demographic variables are easier to measure than most other types of variables.

Even when market segments are first defined using other bases such as personality or behavior, their demographic characteristics must be known in order to assess the size of the target market and to reach it efficiently. Here we will show how certain demographic factors have been used in market segmentation.

### AGE AND LIFE-CYCLE STAGE

Consumer needs and wants change with age. Some companies offer different products or use different marketing approaches for various age and life-cycle segments. For example, Life Stage vitamins come in four versions, each designed for the special needs of specific age segments—chewable Children's Formula for children from four to 12 years old, Teen's Formula for teenagers, and two adult versions (Men's Formula and Women's Formula). Johnson & Johnson developed Affinity Shampoo for women over 40 to help overcome age-related hair changes.

National Trust, of Toronto, has offered a special savings account for children under 14 that includes a discount on a subscription to *Owl* magazine. Many retailers also recognize the importance of age. Firms such as Eaton's and the Bay hold Seniors Days. Others, including Canadian Airlines International and Air Canada, provide special discounts for people over 65 in an attempt to attract consumers from this rapidly growing age segment.

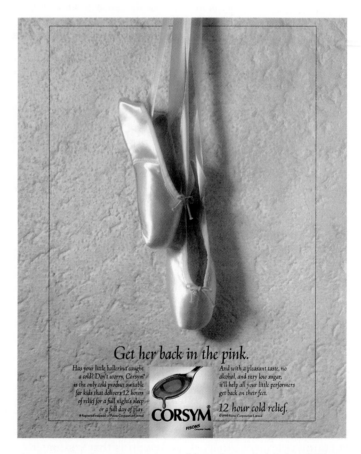

Age segmentation: Corsym is a cold product suitable for children, marketed here in an ad designed to appeal both to young girls and their parents.

## SEX

Sex segmentation has long been used in clothing, hairdressing, cosmetics, and magazines. Occasionally other marketers will notice an opportunity for sex segmentation. The deodorant market provides a good example. Most deodorant brands are used by men and women alike. Procter and Gamble, however, developed Secret as the brand specially formulated for a woman's chemistry, and packaged and advertised the product to reinforce the female image. The automobile industry is also beginning to see the potential for sex segmentation. In the past, cars were designed to appeal to male and female family members. With more working women and women car owners, however, some manufacturers are designing cars especially for women drivers. Studies conducted by General Motors of Canada have identified the prime female market for Camaro as being between the ages of 27 and 35, with some buyers as young as 22. As well, 35% of the buyers of the sporty Mazda RX-7 in Canada are female.[3] Chrysler Canada has targeted the Le Baron for career and professional women under 40 and hopes to capture more of the younger working women car buyers with its Plymouth Turismo and Dodge Charger.[4]

## INCOME

Income segmentation has long been used by the marketers of such products and services as automobiles, boats, clothing, cosmetics, and travel. Many companies target affluent consumers with luxury goods and convenience services. Stores like Ports International offer exclusive fashion for the upper-income market.

But not all companies using income segmentation target the affluent. Many companies such as Zellers and Fields (divisions of the Hudson's Bay Company) and Bi-Way (a division of Dylex) target lower-income consumers. Zellers, the discount department store chain, focuses on the budget-minded consumer by emphasizing low prices. It generates sales of over $2 billion annually.

## PSYCHOGRAPHIC SEGMENTATION

In **psychographic segmentation**, buyers are divided into different groups based on social class, life style, or personality characteristics. People in the same demographic group can have very different psychographic profiles.

**SOCIAL CLASS**   We described the six basic social classes in Chapter 6 and showed that social class has a strong effect on preferences in cars, clothes, home furnishings, leisure activities, reading habits, and retailers. Many companies design products or services for specific social classes, building in features that appeal to the target social class.

**LIFE STYLE**   We saw in Chapter 6 that people's interest in various goods is affected by their life styles and that the goods they buy express their life styles. Marketers are increasingly segmenting their markets by consumer life styles. For example, a manufacturer of men's blue jeans will want to design jeans for a specific male life style group—the "active achiever," the "pleasure seeker," the " homebody," the "blue-collar outdoorsman," or the "business leader." Each group would require different jeans designs, prices, advertising, and outlets. Unless the company states which specific life style group it is aiming at, its jeans may not appeal to any life style group at all.

Various research companies in Canada provide life style segments based on a combination of geography, demographic, attitudes, values, and interest informa-

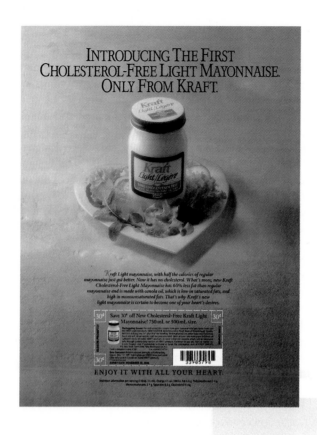

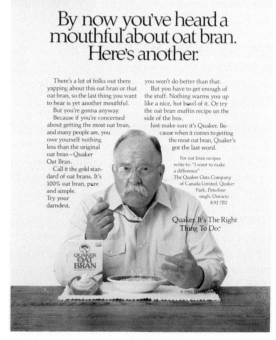

Kraft and Quaker Oats market their products at consumers concerned with a healthy lifestyle.

tion. The Goldfarb six lifestyle segments include the "old-fashioned puritans" who are conservative, traditional individuals and the "aggressive achievers" who are confident, success-oriented people. The Thompson Lightstone Canadian lifestyles include the "active/convenience" group described as the typical "yuppie" and the "traditional home/family-oriented" group who are preoccupied with family life and their children. Marketers can use this information to identify potential segments and targets for their products.[5] Many Canadian marketers, including Kellogg's, Kraft, and Quaker Oats, are designing products that are focused on consumers who want a healthy lifestyle.

PERSONALITY    Marketers have also used personality variables to segment markets. They give their products personalities that correspond to consumer personalities. Successful market segmentation strategies based on personality have been used for such products as women's cosmetics, cigarettes, insurance, and liquor.[6] In one interesting study it was found that blood donors are often low in self-esteem, low risk takers, and more concerned about their health; nondonors tend to be the opposite on all these dimensions.[7] This suggests that social agencies should use different marketing approaches for keeping current donors and attracting new ones.

## BEHAVIOR SEGMENTATION

In **behavior segmentation**, buyers are divided into groups based on their knowledge, attitudes, uses, or responses to a product. Many marketers believe that behavior variables are the best starting point for building market segments.

### OCCASIONS

Buyers can be grouped according to occasions when they get an idea, make a purchase, or use a product. For example, air travel is triggered by occasions related to business, vacation, or family. Airlines such as Air Canada and Canadian International can specialize in serving people who are flying for one of these occasions.

Occasion segmentation can help firms build up product usage. For example, eggs are most often consumed at breakfast. The Canadian Egg Marketing Agency can promote eating eggs at lunch or dinner. Some holidays—Mother's Day and Father's Day for example—were promoted partly to increase the sale of candy, flowers, cards, and other gifts.

Occasion segmentation: Ikea advertises its clocks as Christmas presents.

### BENEFITS SOUGHT

A powerful form of segmentation is to group buyers according to the different benefits that they seek from the product.

Benefit segmentation requires finding out the major benefits people look for in the product class, the kinds of people who look for each benefit, and the major brands that deliver each benefit. One of the best examples of benefit segmentations was conducted in the toothpaste market (see Table 8-2). Research found four benefit segments: those seeking economy, protection, cosmetic, and taste benefits. Each benefit group had special demographic, behavior, and psychographic characteristics. For example, decay prevention seekers had large families, were heavy toothpaste users, and were conservative. Each segment also favored certain brands. A toothpaste company can use these results to clarify which benefit segment it is appealing to, its characteristics, and the major competitive brands. The company can also search for a new benefit and launch a brand that delivers this benefit.[8]

An interesting application of benefit segmentation was the study conducted by the Canadian Government Office of Tourism.[9] A survey of Americans who were potential vacation travelers to Canada identified six benefit segments as illustrated in Table 8-3. Through the use of advanced statistical techniques, a "perceptual map" can be constructed that links the benefits people are looking for, the kinds of people looking for each benefit, and the products or services that can deliver the benefits. A perceptual map of vacation travelers is illustrated in Figure 8-2.

Because of their relatively low vacation expenditures, segments I and II offered less attractive business potential than was offered by the other segments. Moreover, Canadian vacations could not provide an opportunity to visit with

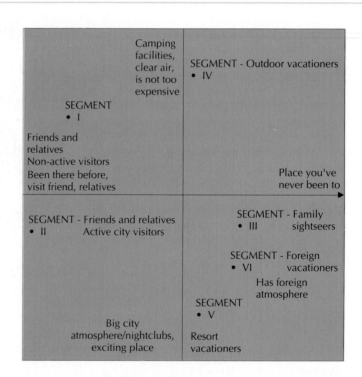

Source: Shirley Young, Leland Ott and Barbara Feigin, "Some Practical Considerations in Marketing Segmentation," *Journal of Marketing Research*, August 1978, p. 407.

Figure 8-2  A Perceptual Map of Vacation Benefits and Segments

## Table 8-2
## Benefit Segmentation of the Toothpaste Market

| Benefit Segments | Demographics | Behavior | Psychographics | Favored Brands |
|---|---|---|---|---|
| Economy (low price) | Men | Heavy users | High autonomy, value oriented | Brands on sale |
| Medicinal (decay prevention) | Large families | Heavy users | Hypochondriac, conservative | Crest |
| Cosmetic (bright teeth) | Teens, young adults | Smokers | High sociability, active | Aqua-Fresh, Ultra Brite |
| Taste (good tasting) | Children | Spearmint lovers | High self-involvement, hedonistic | Colgate Aim |

**Source:** Adapted from Russell I. Haley, "Benefit Segmentation: A Decision Oriented Research Tool," *Journal of Marketing*, July 1963, pp. 30-35. See also Russell I. Haley, " Benefit Segmentation: Backwards and Forwards," *Journal of Advertising Research*, February-March 1984, pp. 19-25.

## Table 8-3
## Benefit Segmentation of the Vacation Travel Market in Canada

| | |
|---|---|
| Segment I | Friends and relatives—nonactive visitor (29%). These vacationers seek familiar surroundings where they can visit friends and relatives. They are not very inclined to participate in any activity. |
| Segment II | Friends and relatives—active city visitor (12%). These vacationers also seek familiar surroundings where they can visit friends and relatives, but they are more inclined to participate in activities—especially sightseeing, shopping, and cultural and other entertainment. |
| Segment III | Family sightseers (six percent). These vacationers are looking for a new vacation place which would be a treat for the children and an enriching experience. |
| Segment IV | Outdoor vacationer (19%). These vacationers seek clean air, rest and quiet, and beautiful scenery. Many are campers and availability of recreation facilities is important. Children are also an important factor. |
| Segment V | Resort vacationer (19%). These vacationers are most interested in water sports (e.g. swimming) and good weather. They prefer a popular place with a big city atmosphere. |
| Segment VI | Foreign vacationer (26%). These vacationers look for vacations in a place they have never been before with a foreign atmosphere and beautiful scenery. Money is not of major concern but good accommodation and service are. They want an exciting, enriching experience. |

**Source:** Shirley Young, Leland Ott, and Barbara Feigin, "Some Practical Considerations in Marketing Segmentation," *Journal of Marketing Research*, August 1978, p. 408.

friends and relatives. The other segments had vacation needs and desires that could be delivered by various areas of Canada through different types of vacations. For each of these segments, data from the questionnaire were used to determine a profile in terms of behavior, psychographics, travel incentives, and image of a Canadian vacation.

## USER STATUS

Many markets can be segmented into nonusers, ex-users, potential users, first-time users, and regular users of a product. High market share companies are particularly interested in attracting potential users, while smaller firms will try to attract regular users to their brand. Potential users and regular users require different kinds of marketing appeals.

## USAGE RATE

Markets can also be segmented into light-user, medium-user, and heavy-user groups. Heavy users are often a small percentage of the market but account for a high percentage of total buying. Figure 8-3 shows usage rates for some popular consumer products. Product users were divided into two groups—a light user half and a heavy user half—according to their buying rates for the specific products. Using beer as an example, the figure shows that 41% of the households studied buy beer. But the heavy user half accounted for 87% of the beer consumed—almost seven

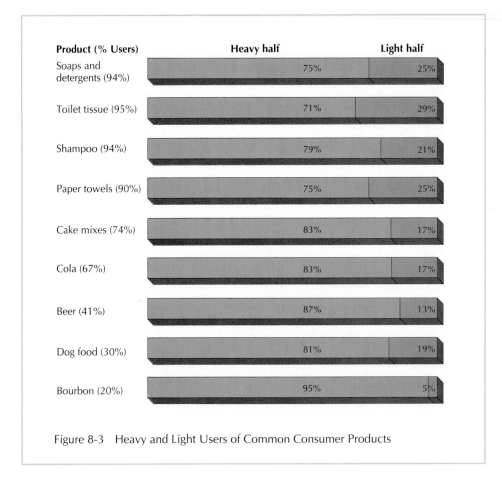

Figure 8-3   Heavy and Light Users of Common Consumer Products

times as much as the light user half. Clearly, a beer company would prefer to attract one heavy user to its brand over several light users. Most beer companies target the heavy beer drinker, using appeals such as Molson's "what beer's all about."

## LOYALTY STATUS

A market can also be segmented by consumer loyalty. Consumers can be loyal to brands (Black Label), stores (Eaton's), and companies (McCain Foods). Buyers can be divided into groups according to their degree of loyalty. Some consumers are completely loyal— they buy one brand all the time. Others are somewhat loyal— they are loyal to two or three brands of a given product, or favor one brand but buy others. Still other buyers show no loyalty to any brand. They want something different each time they buy, or always buy the brand on sale.

A company can learn a lot by analyzing loyalty patterns in its market. It should study its own loyal customers. Colgate finds that its loyal buyers are more middle class, have larger families, and are more health conscious. This pinpoints the target market for Colgate. By studying its less loyal buyers, the company can pinpoint which brands are most competitive with its own. If many Colgate buyers also buy Crest, Colgate can attempt to improve its positioning against Crest, possibly by using direct comparison advertising. By looking at customers who are shifting away from its brand, the company can learn about its marketing weaknesses. As for nonloyals, the company can attract them by putting its brand on sale.

## BUYER READINESS STATE

At any time, people are in different stages of readiness to buy a product. Some people are unaware of the product, some are aware, some are informed, some are interested, some want the product, and some intend to buy. The relative numbers make a big difference in designing the marketing program. Suppose provincial health care officials want women to take an annual Pap test to detect cervical cancer. At the beginning, most women may be unaware of the Pap test. The marketing effort should go into high-awareness-building advertising, using a simple message. If successful, the advertising should then dramatize the benefits of the Pap test and the risks of not taking it, in order to move more women into the stage of wanting to take the test. Facilities should be readied for handling the large number of women who may be moved to take the examination. In general, the marketing program must be adjusted to the changing distribution of buyer readiness.

## ATTITUDE

People in a market can be enthusiastic, positive, indifferent, negative, or hostile toward a product. Door-to-door workers in a political campaign use the voter's attitude to determine how much time to spend with the voter. They thank enthusiastic voters and remind them to vote; they spend no time trying to change the attitudes of negative and hostile voters. They reinforce those who are positive and try to win the vote of the indifferent voters. In such marketing situations, attitudes can be effective segmentation variables.[10]

# Bases for Segmenting Industrial Markets

Industrial markets can be segmented with many of the same variables used in consumer market segmentation. Industrial buyers can be segmented geographically and by several behavior variables: benefits sought, user status, usage rate, loyalty status, readiness stage, and attitudes. Yet there are also some new variables. These include industrial customer demographics (industry, company size), operating characteristics, purchasing approaches, and personal characteristics.[11]

By going after segments instead of the whole market, the company has a much better opportunity to deliver value to consumers and to receive maximum rewards for its close attention to segmented consumer needs. Thus, Michelin and other tire companies should decide which industries they want to serve. Manufacturers seeking original-equipment tires vary in their needs. Makers of luxury and high-performance cars want higher-grade tires than makers of economy models. The tires needed by aircraft manufacturers must meet much higher safety standards than tires needed by farm tractor manufacturers.

Within the chosen industry, a company can further segment by customer size or geographic location. The company might set up separate systems for dealing with larger or multiple-location customers. For example, Steelcase, a major producer of office furniture, first segments customers into ten different industries, including banking, insurance, and electronics. Then, company salespeople work with independent Steelcase dealers to handle smaller local or regional Steelcase customers in each segment. But many national, multiple-location customers, such as Esso or Northern Telecom, have special needs that may reach beyond the scope of individual dealers. So Steelcase uses national accounts managers to help its dealer network handle its national accounts.

Within a certain target industry and customer size, the company can segment by purchase approaches and criteria. For example, government, university, and industrial laboratories typically differ in their purchase criteria for scientific instruments. Government labs need low prices (because they have difficulty getting funds to buy instruments) and service contracts (because they can easily get money to maintain instruments). University labs want equipment that needs little regular service because they do not have service people on their payrolls. Industrial labs need highly reliable equipment because they cannot afford downtime.

In general, industrial companies do not focus on one segmentation variable but use a combination of many. One aluminum company used a series of four major variables. It first looked at which end-use market to serve: automobile, residential, or beverage containers. Choosing the residential market, it determined the most attractive product application: semifinished material, building components, or mobile homes. Deciding to focus on building components, it next considered the best customer size to serve and chose large customers. The company further segmented the large-customer/ building components market. It saw customers falling into three benefit groups—those who bought on price, those who bought on service, and those who bought on quality. Because the company offered excellent service, it decided to concentrate on the service-seeking segment of the market.

## Requirements for Effective Segmentation

Clearly, there are many ways to segment a market, and not all segmentations are effective. For example, buyers of table salt could be divided into blond and brunette customers. However, hair color does not affect the purchase of salt. Furthermore, if all salt buyers buy the same amount of salt each month, believe all salt is the same, and want to pay the same price, the company would not benefit from segmenting this market.

To be useful, market segments must have the following characteristics:

- **Measurability:** the degree to which the size and purchasing power of the segments can be measured. Certain segmentation variables are difficult to measure. An illustration would be the size of the segment of teenage smokers who smoke primarily to rebel against their parents.
- **Accessibility:** the degree to which the segments can be reached and served. Suppose a perfume company finds that heavy users of its brand are single women who often stay out late and socialize a lot. Unless this group lives or shops at certain places and is exposed to certain media, they will be difficult to reach.
- **Substantiality:** the degree to which the segments are large or profitable. A segment should be the largest possible homogeneous group worth going after with a tailored marketing program. It would not pay, for example, for an automobile manufacturer to develop cars for people whose height is less than four feet.
- **Actionability:** the degree to which effective programs can be designed for attracting and serving the segments. A small airline, for example, identified seven market segments, but its staff was too small to develop separate marketing programs for each segment.

Substantiality is a problem faced by Canadian marketers because of the relatively small size of the Canadian market. With a population of 26 million, many segments are not large and/or profitable enough for a company to pursue. The problem is also complicated by the geographic dispersion of the population, which increases the costs of distribution and advertising. To overcome these problems some Canadian companies have selected wider segments and developed strategies that appeal to a more general target market.[12]

# Market Targeting

Marketing segmentation reveals the market segment opportunities facing the company. The company now has to decide on how many segments to cover and how to identify the best segments.

## Three Market-Coverage Alternatives

The company can adopt one of three market-coverage strategies, known as undifferentiated marketing, differentiated marketing, and concentrated marketing. These strategies are shown in Figure 8-4 and discussed below.

## Undifferentiated Marketing

Using an undifferentiated marketing strategy, a firm might decide to ignore market segment differences and go after the whole market with one market offer. By focusing on what is common in the needs of consumers, rather than on what is different, the company designs a product and marketing program that appeals to the most buyers. The company relies on mass distribution and mass advertising, and aims to give the product a superior image in people's minds.

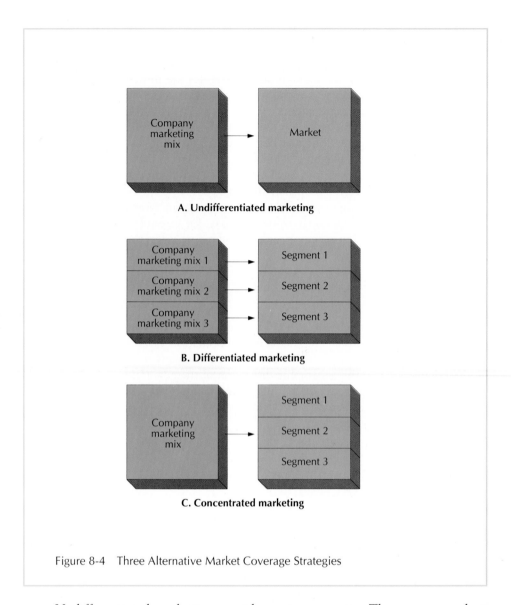

A. Undifferentiated marketing

B. Differentiated marketing

C. Concentrated marketing

Figure 8-4   Three Alternative Market Coverage Strategies

Undifferentiated marketing provides cost economies. The narrow product line keeps down production, inventory, and transportation costs. The undifferentiated advertising program keeps down advertising costs. The absence of segment marketing research and planning lowers the costs of marketing research and product management. In Canada, some companies use this approach because of the small size of the total market.

However, most modern marketers have strong doubts about undifferentiated marketing. It is very difficult to develop a product or brand that will satisfy all consumers. Firms using undifferentiated marketing typically develop an offer aimed at the largest segments in the market. When several firms do this, there is heavy competition in the largest segments and less satisfaction in the smaller ones. The result is that the larger segments may be less profitable because they attract heavy competition. Recognition of this problem has resulted in a greater interest on the part of companies in smaller segments of the market.

# Differentiated Marketing

Using a differentiated marketing strategy, the firm decides to target several market segments and designs separate offers for each. General Motors tries to produce a car for every "purse, purpose, and personality." By offering product and marketing variations, it hopes for higher sales and a stronger position within each market segment. The company also hopes that a stronger position in several segments will strengthen consumers' overall identification of the company with the product category. In addition, General Motors hopes for greater repeat purchasing because the company's offer better matches the customer's desire.

A growing number of companies have adopted differentiated marketing. Here is an excellent example.

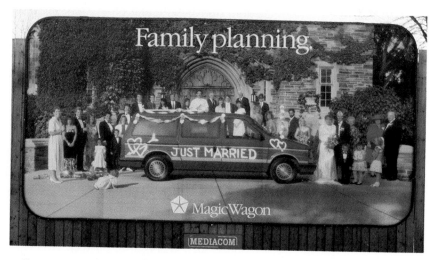

Differentiated marketing: Chrysler creates different vehicles for different market segments.

- Dylex Limited operates a number of different retail chains, each appealing to a different market segment. Its clothing stores sell high-priced men's wear (Harry Rosen), medium-priced men's wear (Tip Top, Big Steel), and moderate-priced men's wear (Thrifty's). Often these stores will all be located in the same mall. Putting the stores near each other does not hurt them because they are aimed at different segments of the men's clothing market. Dylex also uses the strategy in women's wear (Fairweather, Town and Country, Suzy Shier, and Braemar).[13]

Differentiated marketing typically creates more total sales than undifferentiated marketing. Procter & Gamble Canada gets a higher total market share with five brands of hand soap than it could with only one. However, it also increases the costs of doing business. Modifying a product to meet different market segment requirements usually involves some R&D, engineering, or special tooling costs. It is usually more expensive to produce ten units of ten different products than 100 units of one product. Developing separate marketing plans for the separate segments requires extra marketing research, forecasting, sales analysis, promotion planning, and channel management. In addition, trying to reach different market segments with different advertising increases promotion costs. Therefore, the company must weigh increased sales against increased costs when deciding on a differentiated marketing strategy.

# Concentrated Marketing

A third possibility—concentrated marketing—is especially appealing when company resources are limited. Instead of going after a small share of a large market, the company goes after a large share of one or a few submarkets. Many examples of concentrated marketing can be found in Canada, particularly in areas where the companies focus on international markets. Fletcher's Fine Foods concentrates on premium pork products and sells over 60% of its products in the U.S.; Virtual Prototypes designs control and display systems for aircraft and other systems—95% of its sales are outside Canada.[14] Through concentrated marketing the company achieves a strong market position in the segments it serves, owing to its greater knowledge of the needs of the segments, and the special reputation it acquires. The company also enjoys many operating economies because of specialization in production, distribution, and promotion. If the segment is chosen well, the company can earn a high rate of return on its investment.

At the same time, concentrated marketing involves higher than normal risks. The particular market segment can turn sour or competitors may decide to enter the same segment. For these reasons, many companies prefer to diversify in several market segments.

## Choosing a Market-Coverage Strategy

The following factors need to be considered in choosing a market-coverage strategy:

- **Company resources**. When the firm's resources are limited, concentrated marketing makes the most sense.
- **Product variability**. Undifferentiated marketing is more suitable for homogeneous products such as grapefruit or steel. Products that can vary in design, such as cameras and automobiles, are more suited to differentiation or concentration.
- **Product stage in the life cycle**. When a firm introduces a new product, it is practical to launch only one version, and undifferentiated marketing or concentrated marketing makes the most sense. In the mature stage of the product life cycle, differentiated marketing starts to make more sense.
- **Market variability**. If buyers have the same tastes, buy the same amounts, and react the same way to marketing efforts, undifferentiated marketing is appropriate.
- **Competitive marketing strategies**. When competitors segment the market, undifferentiated marketing can be disastrous. Conversely, when competitors use undifferentiated marketing, a firm can gain by using differentiated or concentrated marketing.

## Identifying Attractive Market Segments

Suppose a firm decides on undifferentiated or concentrated marketing. It must now identify the most attractive segments to target. The company first needs to collect data on various market segments. The data would include current dollar sales, projected sales-growth rates, expected profit margins, strength of competition, and marketing channel needs. Often, the company will want to target segments with large current sales, a high growth rate, a high profit margin, weak competition, and simple marketing channel requirements. Usually, no segments will be best in all these areas, and trade-offs will have to be made. Moreover, the largest, fastest growing segments are not always the most attractive ones for every company. The largest segment is not attractive unless the company has the skills and resources to serve its needs effectively.

After the company assesses the characteristics and requirements of the various segments, it must ask which segments best fit its own business strengths. For example, the home computer market is large and very attractive to Carter Data Systems, but the company has had little experience selling computers to consumers and lacks the retail distribution and promotion resources needed to challenge IBM and Apple directly in the home segment. On the other hand, Carter has developed special products and a separate salesforce for the government and higher education market segments. Thus, the company focuses on less-crowded segments in which it has the necessary business strengths to succeed. It targets the segments in which it has the greatest strategic advantage.

# Market Positioning

Once a company has decided which segments of the market it will enter, it must decide what "positions" it wants to occupy in those segments.

## What is Market Positioning?

A product's **position** is the way the product is defined by consumers on important attributes—the place the product occupies in consumers' minds relative to competing products. Thus Tide is positioned as an all-purpose, family detergent; Era is positioned as a concentrated liquid; Arctic Power is positioned as a cold-water detergent. Datsun and Toyota are positioned on economy; Mercedes and Cadillacs are positioned on luxury.[15]

Consumers are overloaded with information about products and services. They cannot re-evaluate products every time they make a buying decision. To simplify buying decision making, consumers organize products into categories—they "position" products, services, and companies in their minds. A product's position is a complex set of consumer perceptions, impressions, and feelings that consumers hold for the product compared with competing products. Consumers position products with or without the help of marketers. However, marketers do not want to leave their products' positions to chance. They plan positions that will give their products the greatest advantage in selected target markets, and they design marketing mixes to create the planned positions.

## Positioning Strategies

The marketer can follow several positioning strategies.[16] It can position its product on specific product attributes: Hyundai advertises its low price; Saab promotes performance. Products can also be positioned on the needs they fill or the benefits they offer: Crest reduces cavities; Aim tastes good. Products can also be positioned according to usage occasions. In the summer, Gatorade can be positioned as a beverage for replacing athletes' body fluids; in the winter, it can be positioned as the drink to use when a doctor recommends drinking plenty of liquids. Another approach is to position the product for certain classes of users. Johnson & Johnson improved the market share for its baby shampoo from 3% to 14% by repositioning the product as one for adults who wash their hair often and need a gentle shampoo.

A product can be positioned directly against a competitor. In its famous "We're number two, so we try harder" campaign, Avis successfully positioned itself against larger Hertz. A product may also be positioned away from competitors—7-Up became the number-three soft drink when it was positioned as the "un-cola," the fresh and thirst-quenching alternative to Coke and Pepsi.

Finally, the product can be positioned for different product classes. For example, some margarines are positioned against butter, others against cooking oils. Camay hand soap is positioned with bath oils rather than with soap. Marketers often use a combination of these positioning strategies. For example, Johnson & Johnson's Affinity shampoo is positioned as a hair conditioner for women over 40 (product class and user). Arm & Hammer baking soda has been positioned as a deodorizer for refrigerators or garbage disposals (product class and usage situation).

## Choosing and Implementing a Positioning Strategy

Some firms will find it easy to choose their positioning strategy. For example, a firm well known for quality in certain segments will go for this position in a new segment if there are enough buyers seeking quality. But in many cases, two or more firms will go after the same position. Then, each will have to find other ways to set

Hewlett Packard positions its computers as more adaptable than those of its competitors, and therefore distinct.

itself apart, such as promising "high quality for lower cost" or "high quality and more technical service." That is, each firm must build a unique bundle of competitive advantages that appeal to a substantial group within the segment.

The positioning task consists of three steps: identifying a set of possible competitive advantages upon which to build a position, selecting the right competitive advantages, and effectively communicating and delivering the chosen position to the market.

A company differentiates itself from competitors by bundling competitive advantages. It gains competitive advantage either by offering consumers lower prices than competitors or by providing more benefits to justify higher prices.[17] Thus, the company must do a better job than competitors of keeping costs and prices down or of offering better value to consumers. The company has to compare its prices and products with those of competitors and look for possible improvements. To the extent that it can do better than its competitors, it has achieved a competitive advantage.

Not every company will find many opportunities for gaining competitive advantages. Some companies will find many minor advantages that are easily copied by competitors and therefore highly perishable. The solution for these companies is to keep identifying new potential advantages and introducing them one by one to keep competitors off-balance. These companies do not expect to gain a single major permanent advantage, but rather many minor ones that can be introduced to win market share over a period of time.

Suppose a company is fortunate enough to discover several potential competitive advantages. It must now choose the ones on which it will build its positioning strategy. Some competitive advantages can be quickly ruled out because they are too slight, too costly to develop, or too inconsistent with the company's profile. In general, the company wants to develop those competitive advantages that are most important to consumers, that fit within its mission and resources, that give it the greatest advantage over competitors, and that competitors will find hardest to match.

Once they have chosen a position, companies must take strong steps to communicate and deliver it to target consumers. All the company's marketing mix efforts must support the positioning strategy. Positioning the company calls for concrete action, not just talk. Thus, if the company decides to build a position on better service, it should hire and train more service people, find retailers who have a good reputation for service, and develop sales and advertising messages that broadcast its superior service.

The company's positioning decisions determine who its competitors will be. When setting its positioning strategy, the company should look at its competitive strengths and weaknesses as compared with those of competitors and select a position in which it attains a strong competitive advantage.

# SUMMARY

Sellers can take three approaches to a market. Mass marketing is the decision to mass-produce and mass-distribute one product and attempt to attract all kinds of buyers. Product differentiation is the decision to produce two or more market offers differentiated in style, features, quality, or size in order to offer variety to the market and set the seller's products apart from competitor's products. Target marketing is the decision to identify the different groups that make up a market and to develop products and marketing mixes for selected target markets. Sellers today are moving away from mass marketing and product differentiation toward target marketing because the latter is more helpful in spotting market opportunities and developing more effective products and marketing mixes.

The key steps in target marketing are market segmentation, market targeting, and market positioning. Market segmentation is the act of dividing a market into distinct groups of buyers who might merit separate products or marketing mixes. The marketer tries different variables to see which give the best segmentation opportunities. For consumer marketing, the major segmentation variables are geographic, demographic, psychographic, and behavioral. Industrial markets can be segmented by industrial demographics, operating characteristics, purchasing approaches and personal characteristics. The effectiveness of the segmentation analysis depends upon finding segments that are measurable, accessible, substantial, and actionable.

Next, the seller has to target the best market segments. The first decision is how many segments to cover. The seller can ignore segment differences (undifferentiated marketing), develop different market offers for several segments (differentiated marketing), or go after one or a few market segments (concentrated marketing). Much depends on company resources, product and market variability, product life-cycle stage, and competitive marketing strategies.

If the company decides to enter one segment, which one should it be? Market segments can be evaluated on their objective attractiveness and on company business strengths needed to succeed in that market segment.

Once a company has decided what segments to enter, it must decide on its market-positioning strategy—on what position to occupy in its chosen segments. It can position its products on specific product attributes, according to usage occasion, for certain classes of uses, or by product class. It can position against competitors or away from competitors. The positioning task consists of three steps: identifying a set of possible competitive advantages upon which to build a position, selecting the right competitive advantages, and effectively communicating and delivering the chosen position to the market.

# QUESTIONS FOR DISCUSSION

1. Describe how Ford has moved from mass marketing to product-variety marketing to target marketing. Can you give examples of other companies whose marketing approaches have evolved over time?

2. What variables are used in market segmentation for beer? Are the same variables used to segment the soft-drink market?

3. If you were manager of a mass-transit company, how would you use benefit segmentation to appeal to different groups of potential riders?

4. Some industrial suppliers make above-average profits by offering service, selection, and reliability—at a premium price. How do these suppliers segment the market to find customers willing to pay more for these benefits?

5. Are some characteristics of market segments more important than others, or are

measurability, accessibility, substantiality, and actionability equally important? Why?

6. Explain which of the following marketers is likely to use undifferentiated marketing: (a) a retired home economics teacher who opens a clothing store, (b) an agricultural cooperative that promotes the use of potatoes and onions, (c) a foreign manufacturer that begins exporting automobiles to Canada, (d) an accounting firm that offers walk-in tax consulting.

7. What roles do product attributes and perceptions of attributes play in positioning a product? Can an attribute common to several competing brands contribute to a successful positioning strategy?

8. A recently developed fabric has the look and feel of cotton but is comfortably stretchable. What segment would you target with a line of casual pants made from this fabric? How would you position these pants?

# KEY TERMS

**Behavior segmentation** Dividing a market into groups based on their knowledge, attitudes, uses, or responses to a product.

**Demographic segmentation** Dividing the market into groups based on demographic variables such as age, sex, family size, family life cycle, income, occupation, education, religion, race, and nationality.

**Geographic segmentation** Dividing a market into different geographical units such as nations, provinces, regions, counties, cities, or neighborhoods.

**Market** The set of all actual and potential buyers of a product.

**Market positioning** Formulating a competitive positioning for a product and a detailed marketing mix.

**Market segmentation** Dividing a market into distinct groups of buyers who might require separate products or marketing mixes.

**Market targeting** Evaluating each market segment's attractiveness and selecting one or more segments to enter.

**Product position** The way the product is defined by consumers on important attributes—the place the product occupies in consumers' minds relative to competing products.

**Psychographic segmentation** Dividing a market into different groups based on social class, life style, or personality characteristics.

# REFERENCES

1. From various sources, including: "Who's on First," *Financial Times*, various issues, and Gordon H.G. McDougall and Douglas Snetsinger, "Arctic Power," in *Canadian Marketing: Cases and Exercises* (Toronto: McGraw-Hill, 1988), pp. 368-384.

2. Coca-Cola Beverages, Annual Report, 1990.

3. Edward Clifford, "Sporty Cars Attracting More Women Buyers," *Globe and Mail*, January 30, 1984, p. B1.

4. Rob Wilson, "Chrysler's Come a Long Way, Baby," *Marketing*, January 27, 1986, pp. 1, 3.

5. "How to Define Target Audience Segments," *Marketing*, June 20, 1988, p. 7, and John Chaplin, "Pigeon Holes for Consumers," *Marketing*, October 16, 1989, p. 28.

6. For further discussion of personality and buyer behavior, see James F. Engel, Roger D. Blackwell and Paul Miniard, *Consumer Behavior*, 6th ed. (Chicago: Dryden Press, 1990), Chap. 12.

7. John J. Burnett, "Psychographic and Demographic Characteristics of Blood Donors," *Journal of Consumer Research*, June 1981, pp. 62-66.

8. For more reading on benefit segmentation, see Russell I. Haley, "Benefit Segmentation: Backwards and Forwards," *Journal of Advertising Research*, February-March 1984, pp. 19-25.

9. Shirley Young, Leland Ott, and Barbara Feigen, "Some Practical Considerations in Market Segmentation," *Journal of Marketing Research*, August 1978, pp. 405-412.

10. For more on consumer segmentation variables, see Yoram Wind, "Issues and Advances in Segmentation Research," *Journal of Marketing Research*, August 1978, pp. 317-37; Terry Elrod and Russell S. Winer, "An Empirical Evaluation of Aggregation Approaches for Developing Market Segments," *Journal of Marketing*, Fall 1982, pp. 56-63; and Lynn R. Kahle, "The Nine Nations of North America and the Value Basis of Geographic Segmentation," *Journal of Marketing*, April 1986, pp. 37-47.

11. For more on industrial segmentation variables, see Benson P. Shapiro and Thomas V. Bonoma, "How to Segment Industrial Markets," Harvard Business Review, May-June 1984, pp. 104-110; Peter Doyle and John Saunders, "Market Segmentation and Positioning in Specialized Industrial Markets," *Journal of Marketing*, Spring 1985, pp. 24-32; and Cornelius A. de Kluyver and David B. Whitlark, "Benefit Segmentation for Industrial Products," *Industrial Marketing Management*, 15, 1986, pp. 273-286.

12. For a review of segmentation issues in Canada, see John Oldland, "The Closing Window of Market Segmentation," *Marketing*, May 5, 1986, p. 14; "Emerging Trends in Market Segmentation," *Marketing*, May 12, 1986; and "Segmentation: Where Does the Future Lie?," *Marketing*, May 19, 1986, p. 30. For an example of retail bank segmentation in Canada, see Michel Laroche and Thomas Taylor, "An Empirical Study of Major Segmentation Issues in Retail Banking," *International Journal of Bank Marketing*, 6, 1, 1988, pp. 31-48.

13. Information obtained from annual reports, Dylex Limited.

14. Catherine G. Johnston, *Globalization: Canadian Companies Compete*, Conference Board of Canada, Report 50-90-E, 1990.

15. For more reading on positioning, see Yoram Wind, "New Twists for Some Old Tricks," *The Wharton Magazine*, Spring 1980, pp. 54-39; David A. Aaker and J. Gary Shansby, "Positioning Your Product," *Business Horizon*, May-June 1982,

pp. 56-62; and Regis McKenna, "Playing for Position," *Inc.*, April 1985, pp 92-97.

16. See Wind, "New Twists," p. 36; and Aaker and Shansby, "Positioning Your Product," pp. 67-58.

17. See Michael Porter, *Competitive Advantage* (New York: Free Press, 1985), Chap. 2. For a good discussion of the concept of competitive advantage and methods for assessing it, see George S. Day and Robin Wensley, "Assessing Advantage: A Framework for Diagnosing Competitive Superiority," *Journal of Marketing*, April 1988, pp. 1-20.

# CHAPTER 9

# Designing Products: Products, Brands, Packaging, and Services

## CHAPTER OBJECTIVES

After reading this chapter, you should be able to:

1. Define product and the major classifications of consumer and industrial products.
2. Explain why companies use brands and identify the major branding decisions.
3. Describe the role of product packaging.
4. Discuss the decisions companies make when developing product lines and mixes.

When is ketchup more than just ketchup? When it's Heinz, of course! When is a headache tablet more than a headache tablet? When it's Aspirin. These are two classic examples of brands representing the product type almost as a generic term. In many cases these brand names become thoroughly entrenched in the consumer's mind and gain market dominance. Any competitor is at a severe disadvantage and must engage in a strategy that will make the brand stand out, in the hope of capturing some portion of the remaining market. One way of accomplishing this is through distinctive packaging. The success of L'eggs pantyhose, Janitor in a Drum, and André's Cask Wines are, in part, due to unique packaging strategies.

When a company differentiates its product through packaging, that strategic element alone will not lead to success. While Heinz used packaging to revitalize interest by introducing the Keg O'Ketchup, this packaging strategy was employed in conjunction with the other parts of the marketing mix, which Heinz executed exceptionally well.

A small Toronto-based company, Grenadier Chocolate, had a product it felt could compete successfully with the chocolate-milk drink mixes marketed by the industry leaders: Cadbury's, Nestlé's (Quik), and Hershey's. Grenadier entered the marketplace with a liquid milk mix, branded Milk Mate, in a plastic bottle. The product was physically differentiated from its major competition (bottle versus can, liquid versus solid). The shopper could easily relate to the bottled liquid form as many home products were packaged in this manner. Milk Mate's physical difference certainly made it eye-catching and somewhat appealing on the shelf; however, the shopper would be breaking long-established purchase and consumption habits by buying Milk Mate rather than an old familiar brand like Nestlé's Quik.

Along with a unique package and a differentiated product form, Milk Mate had to provide definite benefits or value to the consumer. Without some tangible benefits the incentive to switch brands might be too low. Milk Mate advertised the product extensively, focusing on a number of benefits including:

• Convenience—no awkward measuring as in the powdered form.

• No waste—doesn't solidify in chunks like the powder.

• No mess—no spoons on counters, in glasses.

• Dissolves easily.

• Kid proof—no mess, no waste, convenient.

• Same value—equal or lower cost per serving.

The advertising themes pointed out the advantages of the unique product form, as well as stressing the cost equivalency with the powdered-milk mixes on a per-serving basis. This promotional strategy attempted to reduce the risk in changing brands.

Milk Mate proved to be a successful new product entry into the market, a somewhat rare event in situations where there are well-established brands. Milk Mate was a differentiated, competitive product with a well-designed marketing strategy that included some excellent packaging ideas.

Milk Mate's success is based on developing an original and attractive product concept for its target market. Grenadier Chocolate is not just selling a milk modifier, but an augmented product that has achieved acceptance by the market. Marketers do not believe that "a product is a product is a product." Constructing the product concept is an important first step in marketing mix planning.[1]

Milk Mate's unique package helps it to compete with established products.

The chapter begins with the question, what is a product? We will then look at ways to classify products in consumer and industrial markets, and look for links between types of products and marketing strategies. Next, we will see that each product involves several decisions beyond basic product design, such as branding, packaging, and the offering of product support services. Finally, we will move from decisions about individual products to decisions about building product lines and product mixes.

# WHAT IS A PRODUCT?

A Wilson tennis racquet, a Superclips haircut, a Bryan Adams concert, a Club Med vacation, a two-ton truck, Head skis, and a telephone answering service are all products. We define product as follows: A **product** is anything that can be offered to a market for attention, acquisition, use, or consumption that might satisfy a want or need. It includes physical objects, services, persons, places, organizations, and ideas.[2]

Product planners need to think about the product on three levels. The most basic level is the core product, which answers the question, what is the buyer really buying? The core product stands at the center of the total product, as illustrated in Figure 9-1. It consists of the problem-solving services or core benefits that consumers obtain when they buy a product. A woman buying lipstick buys more than lip color. Charles Revson of Revlon saw this early: "In the factory, we make cosmetics; in the store, we sell hope." Theodore Levitt pointed out that buyers "do not buy quarter-inch drills; they buy quarter-inch holes." When designing products, marketers must first define the core benefits the product will provide to customers.

The product planner must next build an actual product around the core product. Actual products may have as many as five characteristics: quality level, fea-

This ad presents the Sony Handycam as a bundle of tangible and intangible features and services that deliver a core benefit.

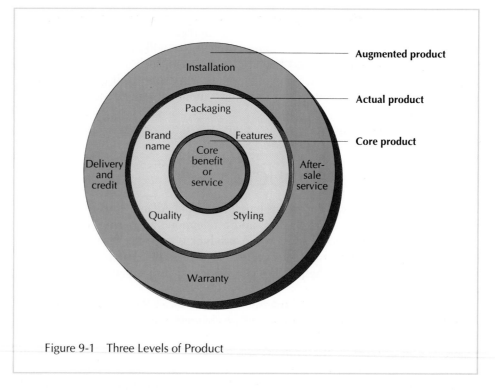

Figure 9-1   Three Levels of Product

tures, styling, brand name, and packaging. For example, Sony's Handycam Camcorder is an actual product. Its name, parts, styling, features, packaging, and other attributes have all been carefully combined to deliver the core benefit—a convenient, high quality way to capture important moments.

Finally, the product planner must build an augmented product around the core and actual products by offering additional consumer services and benefits. Sony must offer more than a camcorder—it must provide consumers with a complete solution to their picture-taking problems. Thus, when consumers buy a Sony Handycam, they get more than just the camcorder itself. Sony and its dealers might also give buyers a warranty on parts and workmanship, free lessons on how to use the camcorder, quick repair services when needed, and a toll-free telephone number to call if they have problems or questions. To the consumer, all of these augmentations become an important part of the total product.

A product is more than a simple set of tangible features. In fact, some products (a haircut or a doctor's exam) have no tangible features. Consumers see products as complex bundles of benefits that satisfy their needs. When developing products, marketers must first identify the core consumer needs the product will satisfy. They must then design the actual product and find ways to augment the product to create the bundle of benefits that will best satisfy consumers.

# Product Classifications

In seeking marketing strategies for individual products, marketers have developed several product classification schemes based on product characteristics.

# Durable Goods, Nondurable Goods, and Services

Products can be classified into three groups according to their durability or tangibility:[3] **Nondurable goods** are tangible goods normally consumed in one or a few uses. Examples include beer, soap, and salt. **Durable goods** are tangible goods that normally survive many uses. Examples include refrigerators, machine tools, and clothing. **Services** are activities, benefits, or satisfactions that are offered for sale. Examples include haircuts and repairs. Because of the growing importance of services in our society, we will look at them more closely in Chapter 19.

## Consumer Goods Classification

**Consumer goods** are those bought by final consumers for personal consumption. Marketers usually classify these goods based on consumer shopping habits. Consumer goods include convenience, shopping, specialty, and unsought goods (see Figure 9-2).[4]

**Convenience goods** are consumer goods that the customer usually buys frequently, immediately, and with a minimum of comparison and buying effort. Examples include tobacco products, soap, and newspapers. Convenience goods can be further divided into staples, impulse goods, and emergency goods. Staples are goods that consumers buy on a regular basis, such as Heinz ketchup, Crest toothpaste, or Five Roses flour. Impulse goods are purchased without any planning or search effort. These goods are normally available in many places because consumers seldom look for them. Therefore, candy bars and magazines are often placed next to checkout counters because shoppers may not have thought of buying them. Emergency goods are purchased when a need is urgent—umbrellas during a rainstorm, boots and shovels during the first winter snowstorm. Manufacturers of emergency goods will place them in many outlets to avoid losing the sale when the customer needs these goods.

**Shopping goods** are consumer goods that the customer, in the process of selection and purchase, usually compares on such bases as suitability, quality, price, and style. Examples include furniture, clothing, used cars, and major appliances. In defining and providing examples of shopping goods the marketer should remember that the description is for the typical customer. Many people do compare prices and brands, and shop around when purchasing furniture and appliances. For example, one study of Canadian furniture buyers found that the average buyer made about five store visits and sought information from two different sources before purchasing furniture.[5] However, some buyers went to only one store and did very little comparison shopping before buying. For these buyers, the process was more similar to routinized response behavior than limited or extensive problem solving. Marketing to these atypical buyers might emphasize convenience and ease of shopping.

Convenience goods
— Staple goods
— Impulse goods
— Emergency goods

Shopping goods

Specialty goods

Unsought goods

Figure 9-2   Classification of Consumer Goods

Shopping goods can be divided into uniform and nonuniform goods. The buyer sees uniform shopping goods as being similar in quality but different enough in price to justify shopping comparisons. The seller has to "talk price" to the buyer. But in shopping for clothing, furniture, and more nonuniform goods, product features are often more important to the consumer than the price. If the buyer wants a new suit, the cut, fit, and look are likely to be more important than small price differences. The seller of nonuniform shopping goods must therefore carry a wide assortment to satisfy individual tastes and must have well-trained salespeople to give information and advice to customers.

**Specialty goods** are consumer goods with unique characteristics or brand identification for which a significant group of buyers is willing to make a special purchase effort. Examples include specific brands and types of fancy goods, cars, stereo components, photographic equipment, and men's suits. A Mercedes, for example, is a specialty good because buyers are willing to travel a great distance to buy one. Buyers do not compare specialty goods. They only invest time to reach the dealers carrying the wanted products. The dealers do not need convenient locations, but they must let buyers know their locations.

Types of consumer products: convenience, shopping, and specialty goods.

**Unsought goods** are consumer goods that the consumer does not know about or knows about but does not normally think of buying. New products such as smoke detectors and compact disc players are unsought goods until the consumer is made aware of them through advertising. The classic examples of known but unsought goods are life insurance and encyclopedias. By their very nature, unsought goods require a lot of advertising, personal selling, and other marketing efforts. Some of the most advanced personal selling methods have developed out of the challenge of selling unsought goods.

## Industrial Goods

**Industrial goods** are those bought by individuals and organizations for further processing or for use in conducting a business. The distinction between a consumer good and an industrial good is based on the purpose for which the product is purchased. If a consumer buys a lawnmower for use around the home, the lawnmower is a consumer good. If the same consumer buys the same lawnmower for use in a landscaping business, the lawnmower is an industrial good.

Industrial goods can be classified in terms of how they enter the production process and their cost. There are three groups: materials and parts, capital items, and supplies and services (see Figure 9-3).

**Materials and parts** are industrial goods that enter the manufacturer's product completely. They fall into two classes: raw materials and manufactured materials and parts. Raw materials include farm products (wheat, livestock, fruits and vegetables) and natural products (fish, lumber, crude petroleum, iron ore). Each is marketed somewhat differently. Farm products are supplied by many small producers who turn them over to marketing intermediaries, who in turn process and sell them. In Canada, this intermediary function is frequently provided by a marketing board.

Over 100 marketing boards have been established in Canada by producers to perform a variety of marketing functions. Some boards provide a means of buying and selling the products, such as the Pork Board in Ontario, which operates auction yards for its members. Other boards not only provide all the distribution functions but also control both production levels and prices for the products. For example, in the dairy industry and the egg industry the marketing board governs how much a farmer can produce and at what prices the products will be sold. These two boards also actively promote their products. While there has been considerable controversy concerning the role of marketing boards in the Canadian economy, the boards have helped improve the distribution efficiency of farmers.[6]

Natural products usually have great bulk and low unit value and require lots of transportation to move them from producer to user. There are fewer and larger producers, who tend to market them directly to industrial users. Many of these natural products, like lumber and iron ore, are sold primarily on the basis of price because industrial users see little difference between iron ore from one company versus another.

Manufactured materials and parts include component materials (iron, yarn, cement, wires) and component parts (small motors, tires, castings). Component materials are usually processed further—for example, pig iron is made into steel and yarn is woven into cloth. Component parts enter the finished product completely with no further change in form, as when small motors are put into vacuum cleaners

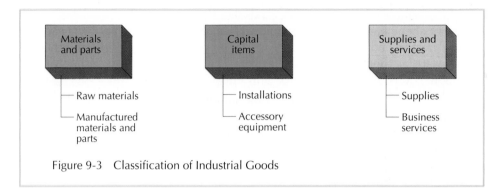

Figure 9-3   Classification of Industrial Goods

and tires are added to automobiles. Most manufactured materials and parts are sold directly to industrial users. Price and service are the major marketing factors, and branding and advertising tend to be less important.

**Capital items** are industrial goods that enter the finished product partly. They include two groups: installations and accessory equipment. Installations consist of buildings (factories, offices) and fixed equipment (generators, drill presses, computers, elevators). Because installations are major purchases, they are usually bought directly from the producer after a long decision period.

Accessory equipment includes portable factory equipment and tools (hand tools, lift trucks) and office equipment (typewriters, desks). These products do not become part of the finished product. They have a shorter life than installations and simply aid in the production process. Most accessory equipment sellers use middlemen because the market is spread out geographically, the buyers are numerous, and the orders are small.

**Supplies and services** are industrial goods that do not enter the finished product at all. Supplies include operating supplies (lubricants, coal, typing paper, pencils) and maintenance and repair items (paint, nails, brooms). Supplies are the convenience goods of the industrial field because they are usually purchased with a minimum effort or comparison. Business services include maintenance and repair services (window cleaning, typewriter repair), and business advisory services (legal, management consulting, advertising). These services are usually supplied under contract. Maintenance services are often provided by small producers, and repair services are often available from the manufacturers of the original equipment.

We have seen that a product's characteristics will have a major effect on marketing strategy. At the same time, marketing strategy will also depend on such factors as the product's stage in the life cycle, the number of competitors, the degree of market segmentation, and the condition of the economy.

# Individual Product Decisions

In the following section, we will look at decisions relating to the development and marketing of individual products. We will also examine decisions about product attributes, branding, packaging, and labeling.

### PRODUCT ATTRIBUTE DECISIONS

Developing a product involves defining the benefits that the product will offer. These benefits are communicated and delivered by tangible product attributes, such as quality, features, and design. Decisions about these attributes will greatly affect consumer reactions to a product. Below, we discuss the issues involved in each decision.

## PRODUCT QUALITY

In developing a product, the manufacturer has to choose a quality level that will support the product's position in the target market. Quality is one of the marketer's major positioning tools. Product quality stands for the ability of a product to perform its function. It includes the product's overall durability, reliability, precision, ease of operation and repair, and other valued attributes. Some of these attributes can be measured objectively. From a marketing point of view, however, quality should be measured in terms of buyers' perceptions.

To some companies, improving quality means using better quality control to reduce defects that annoy consumers. But strategic quality management means more than this. It means gaining an edge over competitors by offering products that better serve consumers' needs and preferences for quality. As one analyst suggests, "Quality is not simply a problem to be solved; it is a competitive opportunity."[7]

The theme of quality is now attracting stronger interest among consumers and companies. Canadian consumers have been impressed with the product quality in Japanese automobiles and electronics and in European automobiles, clothing, and food. Many consumers are favoring apparel that lasts and stays in style longer instead of trendy clothes. They are more interested in fresh and nutritious foods and gourmet items and less interested in soft drinks, sweets, and TV dinners. A

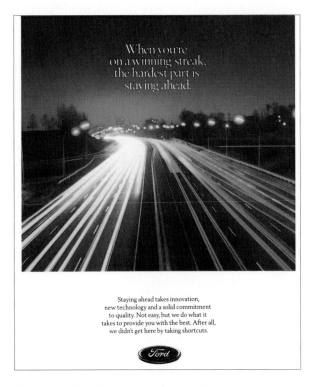

When you're on a winning streak, the hardest part is staying ahead.

Staying ahead takes innovation, new technology and a solid commitment to quality. Not easy, but we do what it takes to provide you with the best. After all, we didn't get here by taking shortcuts.

Ford

Product quality themes are now attracting stronger interest among consumers and companies.

number of companies are catering to this growing interest in quality. Ford, with its "Quality is Job 1" marketing campaign, is an excellent example of a company that mounted a quality drive and is reaping the benefits in increased market share and profitability.

Companies must do more than simply build quality into their products; they must also communicate product quality. The product's look and feel should communicate its quality level. Quality is also communicated through other elements of the marketing mix. A high price usually signals a premium-quality product. The product's brand name, packaging, distribution, and promotion also announce its quality. All of these elements must work together to communicate and support the brand's image.[8]

At the same time, we should not leap to the conclusion that the firm should design the highest quality possible. Not all consumers want or can afford the high levels of quality offered in such products as a Rolls-Royce or a Rolex watch. The manufacturer must choose a quality level that matches target market needs and the quality levels of competing products.

## PRODUCT FEATURES

A product can be offered with varying features. A "stripped-down" model—one without any extras—is the starting point. The company can create higher-level models by adding more features. Features are a competitive tool for differentiating the company's product from competitors' products. Some companies are very innovative in adding new features. Being the first producer to introduce a needed and valued new feature is one of the most effective ways to compete.

How can a company identify new features and decide which ones to add to its product? The company should periodically survey buyers who have used the product and ask these questions: How do you like the product? What specific features of the product do you like most? What features could we add to improve the product? How much would you pay for each feature? The answers will provide the company with a rich list of feature ideas. The company can then assess each feature's customer value versus its company cost. Features that customers value little in relation to costs should be dropped; those that customers value highly in relation to costs should be added.

## PRODUCT DESIGN

Another way to add product distinctiveness is through product design. Some companies have reputations for outstanding design, such as Black & Decker in cordless appliances and tools, Steelcase in office furniture and systems, and Angstrom in audio equipment. Many companies, however, lack a "design touch." Their product designs function poorly or are dull or common-looking. Yet design can be one of the most powerful competitive weapons in a company's marketing arsenal. Well-designed products win attention and sales:

> They stand out in the material landscape. The sleek, elegant lines of a liquid black automobile as it slips around a curve. A baby bottle carefully crafted to fit the tiny fingers of an infant. The hidden power of trim, triangular speakers as they pulsate with music. The difference is design, that elusive blend of form and function, quality and style, art and engineering.[9]

Design is a larger concept than style. Style simply describes the appearance of a product. Styles can be eye-catching or yawn-inspiring. A sensational style may grab attention, but it does not necessarily make the product perform better. In some cases, it might even result in worse performance: A chair may look great yet be extremely uncomfortable. Unlike style, design is more than skin-deep—it goes to the very heart of a product. Good design contributes to a product's usefulness as well as its looks. A good designer considers appearance but also creates products that are easy, safe, inexpensive to use and service, and simple and economical to produce and distribute.

Several companies are now waking up to the importance of design. The radical new design of the Ford Probe—with its sleek styling, passenger comforts, engineering advances, and efficient manufacturing—has made the car a huge success. Outstanding design was a major factor in the success of Black & Decker's family of cordless power tools. Good design can attract attention, improve product performance, cut production costs, and give the product a strong competitive advantage in the target market.[10]

## BRAND DECISIONS

Consumers view a brand as an important part of the product, and branding can add value to the product. For example, most consumers would perceive a bottle of Chanel No. 5 as a high quality, expensive perfume. But the same perfume in an unmarked bottle would be viewed as lower in quality even though the fragrance is identical. Therefore, branding decisions are an important part of product strategy.

First, we should become familiar with the language of branding. Here are some key definitions: A **brand** is a name, term, sign, symbol, or design, or a combination of them intended to identify the goods or services of one seller or group of sellers and to differentiate them from those of competitors. A **brand name** is that part of a brand that can be vocalized—the utterable. Examples are Avon, Chevrolet, and UBC. A **brand mark** is that part of a brand that can be recognized but is not utterable, such as a symbol, design, or distinctive coloring or lettering. Examples are the Air Canada maple leaf and the Royal Bank lion. A **trademark** is a brand or part of a brand that is given legal protection—it protects the seller's exclusive rights to use the brand name or brand mark. Finally, a **copyright** is the exclusive legal right to reproduce, publish, and sell the matter and form of a literary, musical, or artistic work.[11]

Here are some well-known brand marks.

Branding creates difficult decisions for the marketer. The key decisions are shown in Figure 9-4 and discussed below.

### BRANDING DECISION

The company must first decide whether it should put a brand name on its product. Branding has become so strong that today hardly anything is sold unbranded. Salt is packaged in branded containers, oranges are stamped with growers' names, common nuts and bolts are packaged with a distributor's label, and automobile parts, such as spark plugs, tires, and filters, bear brand names that differ from those of the automakers.

Recently there has been a return to "no branding" of certain consumer goods. These "generics" are plainly packaged with no manufacturer called a national brand). Alternatively, the manufacturer may sell the product to middlemen who put on a private brand (also called middlemen brand, distributor brand, or dealer brand). The manufacturer may also sell identification (see Marketing Highlight 9-1). The intent of generics is to bring down the cost to the consumer by saving on

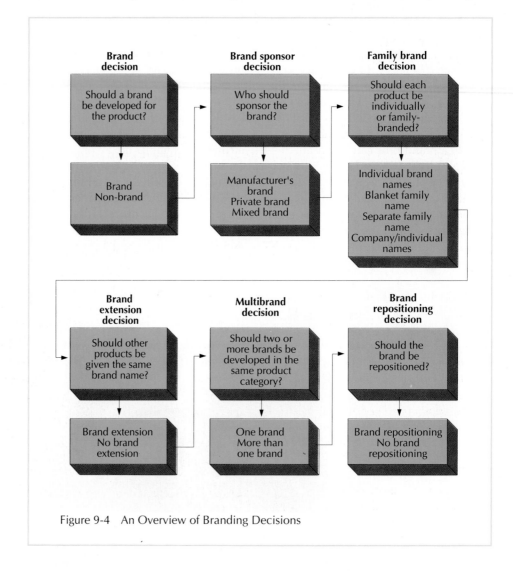

Figure 9-4   An Overview of Branding Decisions

# MARKETING HIGHLIGHT 9-1

## Generics: The Growth and Decline of "No-Brand, No Frills" Products

Generics were first introduced in North America in 1977 by Jewel Food Stores, a large Chicago-based supermarket chain. Generics are unbranded, plainly packaged, less expensive versions of common products such as spaghetti, paper towels, and canned peaches. They offer prices as much as 40% lower than national brands. The lower price is made possible by lower-quality ingredients, lower-cost packaging, and lower advertising costs.

Two Canadian supermarkets, Dominion and Loblaws, followed Jewel Stores and both introduced generics early in 1978. However, Loblaws quickly became the leader in generic sales. In the 15 months that generic products first went on the shelf, Loblaws sold over 30 million no-name items and expanded the line to 120 products. By 1983 Loblaws carried over 500 generic products, which accounted for about 10% of their grocery volume. Of the total no-name products Loblaws introduced, about 60% ranked highest in dollar sales in their categories.

The price savings of generics appeal strongly to consumers, but product quality remains an important factor in consumers' buying decisions. Generics have sold better in product areas where consumers care less about quality or see little quality difference between generics and national brands. Areas such as paper products, frozen foods, peanut butter, canned vegetables, plastic bags, disposable diapers, and dog food have been hardest hit by generics. Generics have had less success in such areas as health and beauty aids, where consumers are less willing to trade quality for price.

Although generics are probably here to stay, it appears that they peaked in 1983. Since then, the market share for generics has dropped. This decline resulted partly from an improved economy—prices stabilized and consumers had more income in the late 1980s than they did when generics exploded in the late 1970s and early 1980s.

When economic conditions improved, Loblaws introduced the "President's Choice" brands—a group of products that were manufactured specifically for Loblaws and that competed directly with national brands. Recently, Loblaws introduced the "Green" product line—a group of environmentally friendly products. Thus, another reason for the decline in generics is the increased attention that Loblaws has given to other store brands. With the recession of the early 1990s, however, Loblaws began to promote its generic products once more, and redesigned their packaging.

The overall decline in generics has also resulted from better marketing strategies by brand-name manufacturers. These marketers have responded by emphasizing brand image and

Consumers have the choice of generic or branded products.

quality. Another strategy is to cut costs and pass the savings along to consumers through lower prices and greater values. The brand-name manufacturer can also introduce lower-quality, lower-priced products that compete directly with generic products. In the United States, Procter & Gamble, for example, introduced its line of Banner paper products. Although this line offered lower quality than other P&G brands, it offered greater quality than generics at a competitive price.

The brand-name marketers must convince consumers that their product's higher quality is worth the extra cost. Branded products that offer a large quality difference will not be hurt much by generics. Those most threatened are weak national brands and lower-price store brands that offer little additional quality. Why pay 20 to 40% more for a branded item, when its quality is not much different from that of its generic cousin?

**Sources:** Martha R. McEnally and Jon M. Hawes, "The Market for Generic Brand Grocery Products: A Review and Extension," *Journal of Marketing*, Winter 1984, pp. 75-83; Bernard Portis, Terry Deutscher, and Jorgen Rasmussen, "Trial and Satisfaction with Generic Grocery Products in Canada," ASAC Conference, Marketing Division Proceedings (Montreal: 1980), pp. 280-288; and Ben Fiber, "Loblaws Focuses on Own Products," *Globe and Mail*, June 9, 1986, p. B1; Brian F. Harris and Roger A. Strang, "Marketing in the Age of Generics," *Journal of Marketing*, Fall 1985, pp. 70-81.

packaging and advertising. Although the popularity of generics peaked in the early 1980s, the issue of whether or not to brand is very much alive today.

This raises the questions: Why have branding in the first place? Who benefits? How do they benefit? At what cost? Branding helps buyers in many ways. Brand names tell the buyer something about product quality. Buyers who always buy the same brand expect that they will get the same quality each time they buy. Brand names also increase the shopper's efficiency. Imagine a buyer going into a supermarket and finding thousands of unlabeled products. Finally, brand names help call consumers' attention to new products that might benefit them. Brands become the basis upon which a whole story can be built about the new product's special qualities.[12]

Branding also gives the seller several advantages. The brand name makes it easier for the seller to process orders and track down problems. The seller's brand name and trademark provide legal protection of unique product features, which would otherwise be copied by competitors. Branding lets the seller attract a loyal and profitable set of customers. Branding also helps the seller to segment markets— P&G can offer five soap brands, not just one general product for all consumers.

## BRAND SPONSOR DECISION

In deciding to brand a product, the manufacturer has three sponsorship options. The product may be launched as a manufacturer's brand, under its own brand name, or under a private label. Kellogg's and IBM sell almost all their output under their own brand names. Camco, the largest manufacturer of major home appliances in Canada, sells all its output under various distributors' names. Laura Secord makes puddings both under its own name and under a no-name or generic name. By adopting this approach, Laura Secord has come to hold the leading share among branded puddings as well as in the generic field.

Manufacturers' brands have dominated the Canadian scene. Consider such well-known brands as Campbell's soup and Heinz ketchup. Recently, however, large retailers and wholesalers have developed their own brands. Canadian Tire, Eaton's, Simpsons, The Bay, Loblaws, and other store chains are promoting their own brands.

## FAMILY BRAND DECISION

Manufacturers who brand their products face several further choices. There are at least four brand-name strategies:

1. **Individual brand names.** This policy is followed by Canada Packers (Maple Leaf, York, Domestic, Dial, and Devon).
2. **A blanket family name for all products.** This policy is followed by Heinz and Philips.
3. **Separate family names for all products.** This policy is followed by Sears Canada (Kenmore for appliances and Craftsman for tools).
4. **Company trade name combined with individual product names.** This policy is followed by Kellogg's (Kellogg's Rice Krispies and Kellogg's Raisin Bran).

Procter & Gamble uses the strategy of individual brand names, which allows its brands to compete in various market segments.

What are the advantages of an individual brand-names strategy? A major advantage is that the company does not tie its reputation to the product's acceptance. If the product fails, it does not hurt the company's name.

Using a blanket family name for all products also has some advantages. The cost of introducing the product will be less, because there is no need for heavy advertising to create brand recognition and preference. Furthermore, sales will be strong if the manufacturer's name is good. For example, new soups introduced under the Campbell brand name get instant recognition.

When a company produces very different products, it may not be best to use one blanket family name. Swift Canada uses separate family names for its turkeys (Butterball) and fertilizers (Vigoro). Companies will often invent different family brand names for different quality lines within the same product class. Thus Loblaws sells a first-grade, second-grade, and third-grade set of brands—President's Choice, Loblaws, and No-Name.

Finally, some manufacturers want to use their company name along with an individual brand name for each product. The company name adds familiarity to the new product, while the individual name sets it apart from other company products. Thus Quaker Oats in Quaker Oats Cap'n Crunch taps the company's reputation for breakfast cereal while Cap'n Crunch sets apart and dramatizes the new product.

### BRAND-EXTENSION DECISION

A brand-extension strategy is any effort to use a successful brand name to launch new or modified products. Procter & Gamble put its Ivory name on dishwashing detergent, liquid hand soap, and shampoo with excellent results, and it used the strength of the Tide name to launch unscented and liquid laundry detergents. Brand extension saves the manufacturer the high cost of promoting new names and creates instant brand recognition of the new product. At the same time, if the new product fails, it may hurt consumer attitudes toward the other products carrying the same brand name.

### MULTIBRAND DECISION

A seller uses a multibrand strategy when it develops two or more brands in the same product category. This marketing practice was pioneered by P&G when it introduced Cheer as a competitor for its already successful Tide. Although Tide's sales dropped slightly, the combined sales of Cheer and Tide were higher. P&G now produces six detergent brands and three versions of Tide.

Manufacturers use multibrand strategies for several reasons. First, they can gain more shelf space, thus increasing the retailer's dependence on their brands. Second, few consumers are so loyal to a brand that they will not try another. The only way to capture the "brand switchers" is to offer several brands. Third, creating new brands develops healthy competition within the manufacturer's organization. Managers of different General Motors brands compete to outperform each other. Fourth, a multibrand strategy positions brands on different benefits and appeals, and each brand can attract a separate following.

### BRAND REPOSITIONING DECISION

However well a brand is initially positioned in a market, the company may have to reposition it later. A competitor may launch a brand next to the company's brand and cut into its market share, or customer wants may shift, leaving the company's brand in less demand. Marketers should consider repositioning existing brands before introducing new ones. In this way they can build on existing brand recognition and consumer loyalty. Repositioning may require changing both the product and its image. P&G repositioned Bold detergent by adding a fabric softening ingredient. A brand can also be repositioned by changing only the product's image. Ivory Soap was repositioned without change from a "baby soap" to an "all natural soap" for adults who want healthy-looking skin.

## SELECTING A BRAND NAME

The brand name should be carefully chosen. A good brand name can add greatly to a product's success. Most large marketing companies have developed a formal brand-name selection process. Finding the best brand name is a difficult task. It begins with a careful review of the product and its benefits, the target market, and proposed marketing strategies.

Among the desirable qualities for a brand name are the following: (1) It should suggest something about the product's benefits and qualities. Examples: Beautyrest, Craftsman, Sunkist, Spic and Span, Zest. (2) It should be easy to pronounce, recognize, and remember. Examples: Tide, Crest, Visa. (3) It should be distinctive. Examples: Mustang, Kodak.

Once chosen, the brand name must be protected. Many firms try to build a brand name that will eventually become identified with the product category. Such brand names as Frigidaire, Kleenex, Levi's, Jell-O, Scotch Tape, and Fiberglas have succeeded in this way. However, their very success may threaten the company's rights to the name. Cellophane, nylon, and shredded wheat are now names that any seller can use.

# PACKAGING DECISIONS

Many products offered to the market have to be packaged. Some marketers have called packaging a fifth P, along with price, product, place, and promotion. Most marketers, however, treat packaging as an element of product strategy.

**Packaging** includes the activities of designing and producing the container or wrapper for a product. The package may include the product's immediate container (for example, the bottle holding Old Spice After-Shave Lotion); a secondary package that is thrown away when the product is about to be used (the cardboard box containing the bottle of Old Spice); and the shipping package necessary to store, identify, and ship the product (a corrugated box carrying six dozen bottles of Old Spice). Labelling is also part of packaging and consists of printed information appearing on or with the package.

Traditionally, packaging decisions were based mostly on cost and production factors; the primary function of the package was to contain and protect the product. In recent times, however, numerous factors have made packaging an important marketing tool. An increase in self-service means that packages must now perform many sales tasks, from attracting attention, to describing the product, to making the sale.[13]

Companies are realizing the power of good packaging to create instant consumer recognition of the company or brand. Every film buyer immediately recognizes the familiar yellow packaging of Kodak film. Innovative packaging can also give the company an advantage over competitors. When Imperial Oil switched from packaging motor oil in cans to plastic, the change was enthusiastically received by both service station operators and consumers. Chateau-Gai Wines packaged San Gabriel wine in a box made of polyethylene, foil, and cardboard, and it became a Canadian best-seller.[14]

Developing a good package for a new product requires many decisions. The first task is to establish the packaging concept. The packaging concept states what the package should be or do for the product. Should the main functions of the package be to offer product protection, introduce a new dispensing method, suggest certain qualities about the product or the company, or something else? Decisions must be made on specific elements of the package—size, shape, materials, color, text, and brand mark. These various elements must work together to support the product's position and marketing strategy. The package must be consistent with the product's advertising, pricing, distribution, and other marketing strategies.

Companies usually consider several different package designs for a new product. To select the best package, the company must test the various designs to find the one that stands up best under normal use, that dealers find easiest to handle, and that consumers respond to most favorably. After selecting and introducing the package, the company must check it regularly in the face of changing consumer preferences and advances in technology. In the past, a package design might last for 15 years before changes were needed. In today's rapidly changing environment, most companies must recheck their packaging every two or three years. Keeping a package up to date usually requires only minor, but regular, changes—changes so subtle that they go unnoticed by most consumers.

Cost remains an important packaging consideration. Developing the packaging for a new product may cost a few hundred thousand dollars and take from a few months to a year. Converting to a new package may cost millions, as the major Canadian breweries learned when they entered the "packaging" wars that resulted in reduced profits for two years.[15] Marketers must weigh packaging costs against consumer perceptions of value added by the packaging, and against the role of packaging in helping to attain marketing objectives. In making packaging decisions, the company must also heed growing societal concerns about packaging and make decisions that serve society's interests as well as customer and company objectives (see Marketing Highlight 9-2).

# PRODUCT-SUPPORT SERVICE DECISIONS

Customer service is another element of product strategy. A company's offer to the marketplace usually includes some services. Services can be a minor or a major part of the total offer. In fact, the offer can range from a pure good on the one hand to a pure service on the other. In Chapter 19 we discuss services as products themselves. Here we will discuss product-support services. More and more companies are using product-support services as a major tool for gaining competitive advantage.

Good customer service is good for business. It costs less to keep the goodwill of existing customers than to attract new customers or woo back lost customers. Firms that provide high-quality service usually outperform their less service-oriented competitors. Four Seasons Hotels, the Toronto-based chain, consistently leads the hotel industry in occupancy rates and repeat business by providing excellent customer service, right down to identifying guests' preferences for tea.[16] A recent

# MARKET HIGHLIGHT 9-2
## Packaging and Public Policy

Packaging is attracting more and more public attention. Marketers should heed the following issues in making their packaging decisions.

### Fair Packaging and Labelling
The public is concerned with packaging and labelling that might be false and misleading. Both the federal and provincial governments have responded to this concern by providing a considerable amount of legislation in regard to packaging. It is estimated that there are over 100 regulations in place affecting packages of all shapes and sizes. The following are the four main pieces of legislation.

- The Consumer Packaging and Labelling Act requires the net weight to be in metric units and the identity of the product to be on the main display surface in English and French.
- The Food and Drug Act requires ingredient listings in descending order of product importance, and, for perishable products, a "best before" date stamp must be included. All information must be in English and French.
- The Hazardous Products Act applies to products, listed on a schedule, that are considered to be a hazard to public health or safety. For those consumer products, the degree of hazard is identified with a series of symbols that warns of any potential danger, in English and French.
- Bill 101 (Province of Quebec) requires information on the package or product to be in French, and any other language cannot occupy more space than the French listings.

Other legislation that directly affects the package and/or label includes the National Trademark and True Labelling Act and the Textile Labelling Act.

### Excessive Cost
Critics have claimed that excessive packaging raises prices. They point to secondary "throwaway" packaging and question its value to the consumer. It is estimated that packaging is an $8 billion-a-year business in Canada, and many would argue that packaging costs of approximately 22% of net sales in the food-processing business are too high. Marketers respond that they want to keep packaging costs down and that critics do not understand all the functions of the package.

### Scarce Resource
The growing concern over shortages of paper, aluminum, and other materials suggests that industry should try harder to reduce its packaging. For example, the growth of non-returnable glass containers has resulted in the use of up to 17 times as much glass as with returnable containers. The throwaway bottle is also an energy waster, which can be ill-afforded in this time of energy management. All provinces have passed laws prohibiting or taxing non-returnable containers.

### Pollution
As much as 40% of the total solid waste in this country is made up of package material. Many packages end up in the form of broken bottles and bent cans littering the streets and countryside. All this packaging creates a major problem in solid waste disposal, requiring huge amounts of labor and energy.

These packaging questions have mobilized public action and interest in new laws that might further affect marketing decision making in the packaging area. Marketers must be equally concerned. They must try to design fair, economical packages for their products.

For more on packaging and public policy, see *The Canadian Green Consumer Guide*, Pollution Probe Foundation of Canada (Toronto: McClelland & Stewart, 1989).

study compared the performance of businesses that had high customer ratings of service quality with those that had lower ratings. It found that the high-service businesses managed to charge more, grow faster, and make more profits.[17] Clearly, marketers need to think carefully about their service strategies.

## Deciding on the Service Mix

A company should design its product and support services to meet the needs of target customers. Thus, the first step in deciding what product-support services to offer is to determine both what services target consumers value and their relative importance. Customers will vary in the value they assign to different services. Some will stress credit and financing services, fast and reliable delivery, or quick installation. Others will put more weight on technical information and advice, training in product use, or after-sale service and repair.

The marketer needs to survey customers to find out the main services that might be offered and their importance. For example, Canadian buyers of industrial equipment ranked 13 service elements in the following order of importance: (1) delivery reliability, (2) prompt price quotation, (3) technical advice, (4) discounts, (5) after-sales service, (6) sales representation, (7) ease of contact, (8) replacement guarantee, (9) wide range of manufacturer, (10) pattern design, (11) credit, (12) test facilities, and (13) machining facilities.[18] These importance rankings suggest that in this market the seller should at least match competition on delivery reliability, prompt price quotation, technical advice, and other services deemed most important by customers.

Products can often be designed to reduce the amount of required servicing. Thus, companies need to coordinate their product-design and service-mix decisions. For example, the Canon home copier uses a disposable toner cartridge that greatly reduces the need for service calls. Kodak and 3M are designing products that can be "plugged in" to a central diagnostic facility that performs tests, locates troubles, and fixes equipment over telephone lines. Thus, a key to successful service strategy is to design products that rarely break down and, if they do, are easily fixable with little service expense.

## Delivering Product-Support Services

Finally, companies must decide how they want to deliver product- support services to customers. For example, consider the many ways Maytag might offer repair services on its major appliances. It could hire and train its own service people and locate them across the country. It could arrange with distributors and dealers to provide the repair services. Or it could leave it to independent companies to provide these services.

Most equipment companies start out adopting the first alternative, providing their own service. They want to stay close to the equipment and know its problems. They also find that they can make good money running the "parts and service business." As long as they are the only supplier of the needed parts, they can charge a premium price. Indeed, some equipment manufacturers make over half of their profits in after-sale service.

Over time, producers typically shift more of the maintenance and repair ser-

GE provides product-support service at the customer's home.

vice to authorized distributors and dealers. These middlemen are closer to customers, have more locations, and can offer quicker if not better service. The producer still makes a profit on selling the parts but leaves the servicing cost to middlemen.

Still later, independent service firms emerge. For example, over 40% of all auto service work is now done outside of franchised automobile dealerships by independent garages and chains such as Midas Muffler and Sears. Such independent service firms have emerged in most industries. They typically offer lower cost or faster service than the manufacturer or authorized middlemen.

Ultimately, some large customers start to handle their own maintenance and repair services. Thus, a company with several hundred personal computers, printers, and related equipment might find it cheaper to have its own service people on-site.

## The Customer Service Department

Given the importance of customer service as a marketing tool, many companies have set up strong customer service departments to handle complaints and adjustments, credit service, maintenance service, technical service, and consumer information. For example, many companies have set up hot lines to handle consumer complaints and requests for information. By keeping records on the types of requests and complaints, the customer service department can press for needed changes in product design, quality control, high-pressure selling, and so on. An active customer service department coordinates all the company's services, creates consumer satisfaction and loyalty and helps the company to further set itself apart from competitors.[19]

Product line: Hewlett Packard's peripherals are compatible with the Macintosh computer.

# PRODUCT LINE DECISIONS

We have looked at product strategy decisions—branding, packaging, and services—for individual products. However, product strategy also calls for building a product line. A **product line** is a group of products that are closely related, either because they function in a similar manner, are sold to the same customer groups, are marketed through the same types of outlets, or fall within given price ranges.

Thus General Motors produces a line of cars, and Revlon produces a line of cosmetics. Each product line needs a marketing strategy. Marketers face a number of tough decisions on product line length and product line featuring.

## Product Line Length Decision

Product line managers have to decide on product line length. The line is too short if the manager can increase profits by adding items; the line is too long if the manager can increase profits by dropping items. Product line length is influenced by company objectives. Companies that want to be positioned as full-line companies or are seeking high market share and market growth will carry longer lines. They are less concerned when some items fail to add to profits. Companies that are keen on high profitability will carry shorter lines consisting of selected items.

Product lines tend to lengthen over time. The company must plan this growth carefully. It can systematically increase the length of its product line in two ways: by stretching its line and by filling its line.

# Product Line Stretching Decision

Every company's product line covers a certain range of the products offered by the industry as a whole. For example, BMW automobiles are located in the medium-high price range of the automobile market. Product line stretching occurs when a company lengthens its product line beyond its current range. As shown in Figure 9-5, the company can stretch its line downward, upward, or both ways.

## DOWNWARD STRETCH

Many companies initially locate at the high end of the market and later stretch their lines downward. A company may stretch downward for any number of reasons. It may find faster growth taking place at the low end. The company may have first entered the high end to establish a quality image and intended to roll downward. The company may add a low-end product to plug a market hole that would otherwise attract a new competitor. The company may be attacked at the high end and respond by invading the low end.

## UPWARD STRETCH

Companies at the lower end of the market may want to enter the higher end. They may be attracted by a faster growth rate or higher margins at the higher end, or

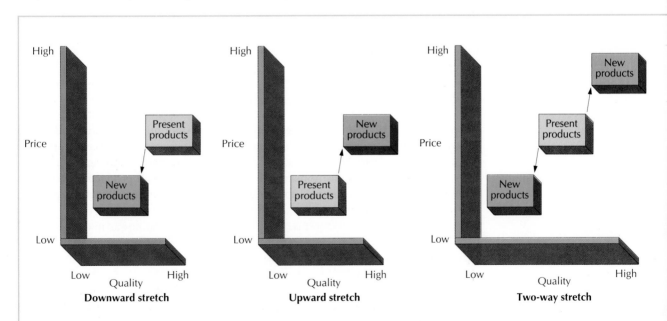

Figure 9-5    Product Line Stretching Decision

they may simply want to position themselves as full-line manufacturers.

An upward stretch decision can be risky. The higher-end competitors not only are well entrenched, but may also strike back by entering the lower end of the market. Prospective customers may not believe that the newcomer can produce quality products. Finally, the company's salespeople and distributors may lack the talent and training to serve the higher end of the market.

### TWO-WAY STRETCH

Companies in the middle range of the market may decide to stretch their lines in both directions. Sony did this to hold off copycat competitors for its Walkman line of personal tape players. Sony introduced its first Walkman in the middle of the market. As imitative competitors moved in with lower-priced models, Sony stretched downward. At the same time, to add luster to its lower-priced models and to attract more affluent consumers, Sony stretched the Walkman line upward. It now sells more than 100 models, ranging from a plain-vanilla playback-only version for $32 to a high-tech, high-quality $450 version that both plays and records.

## Product Line Filling Decision

A product line can also be lengthened by adding more items within the present range of the line. Companies have several reasons for product line filling: reaching for extra profits, trying to satisfy dealers, trying to use excess capacity, trying to be the leading full-line company, and trying to plug holes to keep out competitors. Thus, Sony has added solar-powered and waterproof Walkmans and an ultra-light model that attaches to a sweatband for joggers, bicyclers, tennis players, and other exercisers.

Line filling is overdone if it results in cannibalization and customer confusion. The company should make sure that new product items are noticeably different from present items.

# Product Mix Decisions

An organization with several product lines has a product mix. A **product mix** (also called product assortment) is the set of all product lines and items that a particular seller offers for sale to buyers.[20] Avon's product mix consists of four major product lines: cosmetics, jewelry, fashions, and household items. Each product line consists of several sublines. For example, cosmetics break down into lipstick, rouge, powder, and so on. Each line and subline has many individual items. Altogether, Avon's product mix includes 1,300 items. A large supermarket handles as many as 14,000 items; a typical K mart stocks 15,000 items; and Canadian Tire holds over 25,000 different automobile items in each of its supply depots, which can be shipped to any of their more than 400 stores within two days.

A company's product mix can be described as having a certain width, length, depth, and consistency. These concepts are illustrated in Table 9-1 in connection with selected Procter & Gamble Canada consumer products.

The width of P&G's product mix refers to how many different product lines the company carries. Table 9-1 shows a product mix width of six lines. (In fact,

**Table 9-1**
**Product Mix Width and Product Line Length Shown for
Procter & Gamble Products**

| | | | Product Mix Width → | | |
|---|---|---|---|---|---|
| Detergents | Toothpaste | Bar Soap | Deodorants | Disposable Diapers | Shampoo |
| Ivory Snow 1932 | Crest 1961 | Ivory 1916 | Secret 1965 | Pampers 1972 | Head & Shoulders 1964 |
| Dreft 1948 | Fasteeth 1970 | Camay 1927 | | Luvs 1983 | Vidal Sassoon 1977 |
| Tide 1948 | Fixodent 1970 | Zest 1958 | | Always 1984 | |
| Cheer 1951 | | Safeguard 1965 | | Attends 1985 | Pert 1981 |
| Oxydol 1958 | | | | | Pantene 1981 |
| Bold 3 1981 | | Coast 1979 | | | Ivory 1986 |
| Liquid Tide 1987 | | Liquid Ivory 1984 | | | |
| Tide With Bleach 1989 | | | | | |

*Product Line Length*

Courtesy:  Procter and Gamble Canada.  Does not include all products of P&G.

P&G produces many more lines, including mouthwash, cough and cold products, shortening, and others.)

The length of P&G's product mix refers to the total number of items the company carries. In Table 9-1, it is 27. We can also compute the average length of a line at P&G by dividing the total length (here 27) by the number of lines (here 6), or 4.5. The average P&G product line as represented in Table 9-1 consists of 4.5 brands.

The depth of P&G's product mix refers to how many versions are offered of each product in the line. Thus if Crest comes in three sizes and two formulations (regular and mint), Crest has a depth of six. By counting the number of versions within each brand, the average depth of P&G's product mix can be calculated.

The consistency of the product mix refers to how closely related the various product lines are in end use, production requirements, distribution channels or in some other way. P&G's product lines are consistent in so far as they are consumer goods that go through the same distribution channels. The lines are less consistent insofar as they perform different functions for the buyers.

These four dimensions of the product mix provide a method for defining the company's product strategy. The company can increase its business in four ways. The company can add new product lines, thus widening its product mix. In this way, its new lines build on the company's reputation in its other lines. The company can lengthen its existing product lines to become a more full-line company. The company can add more product versions to each product and thus deepen its product mix. Finally, the company can pursue more product line consistency or less, depending upon whether it wants to have a strong reputation in a single field or in several fields.

Thus product strategy calls for complex decisions on product mix, product line, branding, packaging, and service strategy. These decisions must be made with a full understanding of consumer wants and competitors' strategies.

# SUMMARY

Product is a complex concept that must be carefully defined. Product strategy calls for making coordinated decisions on product items, product lines, and the product mix.

Each product item offered to customers can be looked at on three levels. The core product is the essential service the buyer is really buying. The actual product is the features, styling, quality, brand name, and packaging of the product offered for sale. The augmented product is the actual product plus the various services offered with it, such as warranty, installation, maintenance, and free delivery.

There are several ways to classify products. For example, all products can be classified according to their durability (nondurable goods, durable goods, and services). Consumer goods are usually classified according to consumer shopping habits (convenience, shopping, specialty and unsought goods). Industrial goods are classified according to their cost and how they enter the production process (materials and parts, capital items, and supplies and services).

Companies have to develop brand policies for the product items in their lines. They must decide whether to brand at all, whether to do manufacturing or private branding, whether to use family brand names or individual brand names, whether to put out several competing brands, and whether to reposition any of the brands.

Products require packaging decisions to create such benefits as protection, economy, convenience, and promotion. Marketers have to develop a packaging concept and test it to make sure it achieves the desired objectives and is compatible with public policy.

Companies have to develop product-support services that are desired by customers and effective against competitors. The company has to decide on the most important services to offer and the best ways to deliver those services.

Most companies produce not a single product but a product line. A product line is a group of products related in function, customer purchase needs, or distribution channels. Each product line requires a product strategy. Line stretching raises the question of whether a line should be extended downward, upward, or both ways. Line filling raises the question of whether additional items should be added within the present range of the line.

Product mix describes the set of product lines and items offered to customers by a particular seller. The product mix can be described by its width, length, depth, and consistency. The four dimensions of the product mix are the tools for developing the company's product strategy.

# QUESTIONS FOR DISCUSSION

1. What are the core, actual, and augmented products of the educational experience offered by universities?

2. How would you classify the products offered by restaurants—as nondurable goods or as services?

3. Compare the number of retail outlets for each type of consumer good (convenience, shopping, specialty, unsought) in a particular geographic area. Give examples.

4. In recent years, automakers have tried to reposition many brands at the high-quality end of the market. How well have they succeeded? What else could they do to change consumer perceptions?

5. Why are many people willing to pay more for branded products than for unbranded products? What does this fact say about the value of branding?

6. Think of several products you buy regularly and recommend improvements in their packaging or labelling. If the packaging change added to the product's cost, how much more would you be willing to pay for the improvement?

7. Describe some service decisions that the following marketers must make: (a) a small women's clothing store, (b) bank, (c) a supermarket.

8. Describe the product mix of hospitals in your area. Are their mixes wide or deep? How could they stretch lines upward or downward?

# KEY TERMS

**Brand** A name, term, sign, symbol, or design, or a combination of them intended to identify the goods or services of one seller or group of sellers and to differentiate them from those of competitors.

**Brand mark** That part of a brand that can be recognized but is not utterable, such as a symbol, design, or distinctive coloring or lettering.

**Brand name** That part of a brand that can be vocalized.

**Capital items** Industrial goods that enter the finished product partly, including installations and accessory equipment.

**Consumer goods** Goods bought by final consumers for personal consumption.

**Convenience goods** Consumer goods that the customer usually buys frequently, immediately, and with the minimum of comparison and buying effort.

**Copyright** The exclusive legal right to reproduce, publish, and sell the matter and form of a literary, musical, or artistic work.

**Durable goods** Tangible goods that normally survive many uses.

**Industrial goods** Goods bought by individuals and organizations for further processing or for use in conducting a business.

**Materials and parts** Industrial goods that enter the manufacturer's product completely, including raw materials and manufactured materials and parts.

**Nondurable goods** Tangible goods normally consumed in one or a few uses.

**Packaging** The activities of designing and producing the container or wrapper for a product.

**Product** Anything that can be offered to a market for attention, acquisition, use, or consumption that might satisfy a want or need.

**Product line** A group of products that are closely related, either by function, customer group, retail outlet, or price range.

**Product mix** The set of all product lines and items that a particular seller offers for sale to buyers.

**Services** Activities, benefits, or satisfactions that are offered for sale.

**Shopping goods** Consumer goods that the customer, in the process of selection and purchase, usually compares on such bases as suitability, quality, price, and style.

**Specialty goods** Consumer goods with unique characteristics or brand identification for which a significant group of buyers is willing to make a special purchase effort.

**Supplies and services** Industrial goods that do not enter the finished product at all.

**Trademark** A brand or part of a brand that is given legal protection—it protects the seller's exclusive rights to use the brand name or brand mark.

**Unsought goods** Consumer goods that the consumer does not know about or knows about but does not normally think of buying.

# References

1. For a detailed discussion of the introduction of Milk Mate, see "Grenadier Chocolate Company Limited" in Charles B. Weinberg and Gordon H.G. McDougall, *Canadian Marketing: Cases and Exercises*, 2nd Ed. (Toronto: McGraw-Hill Ryerson) 1991, pp. 484-490.

2. See *Marketing Definitions: A Glossary of Marketing Terms*, compiled by the Committee on Definitions of the American Marketing Association (Chicago: American Marketing Association, 1960).

3. The three definitions can be found in *Marketing Definitions*.

4. The first three definitions can be found in *Marketing Definitions*. For more information on the classification of products, see Patrick E. Murphy and Ben M. Enis, "Classifying Products Strategically," *Journal of Marketing*, July 1986, pp. 24-42.

5. John D. Claxton, Joseph N. Fry, and Bernard Portis, "A Taxonomy of Prepurchase Information Gathering Patterns," *Journal of Consumer Research*, December 1974, pp. 35-42.

6. For those interested in the pros and cons of marketing boards in Canada, see J.D. Forbes, D.R. Hughes and T.K. Warley, *Economic Intervention and Regulation in Canadian Agriculture*, Economic Council of Canada (Ottawa: Supply and Services Canada, 1982); R.M.A. Lyons, "Marketing Boards: The Irrelevance and Irreverence of Economic Analysis," in Donald N. Thompson, et al. (eds.), *Macromarketing: A Canadian Perspective* (Chicago: American Marketing Association, 1980), pp. 196-224; John Spears, "Guardians of Farm Prices Face Critics," *Toronto Star*, November 9, 1986, p. F1-2; and Philip DeMont, "Free Trade's Threat to the Marketing Boards," *Financial Times*, August 21, 1989, p. 17.

7. David A. Garvin, "Competing on Eight Dimensions of Quality," *Harvard Business Review*, November-December 1987, p. 109. Also see Robert Jacobson and David A. Aaker, "The Strategic Role of Product Quality," *Journal of Marketing*, October 1987, pp. 31-44.

8. For a discussion of consumer perceptions of quality, see Valarie A. Zeithaml, "Consumer Perceptions of Price, Quality, and Value: A Means-End Model and Synthesis of Evidence," *Journal of Marketing*, July 1988, pp. 2-22.

9. Bruce Nussbaum, "Smart Design: Quality Is the New Style," *Business Week*, April 11, 1988, pp. 102-8.

10. For more on design, see Philip Kotler, "Design: A Powerful but Neglected Strategic Tool," *Journal of Business Strategy*, Fall 1984, pp. 16-21; Robert A. Abler, "The Value-Added of Design," *Business Marketing*, September 1986, pp. 96-103; and Nussbaum, "Smart Design: Quality Is the New Style."

11. The first four definitions can be found in *Marketing Definitions*.

12. See Allan J. Magrath, "Strengthen Brands With 8 Essential Elements," *Marketing News*, January 8, 1990, p. 36.

13. Charles A. Moldenhauer, "Packaging Designers Must Be Cognizant of Right Cues If the Consumer Base Is to Expand," *Marketing News*, March 30, 1984, p. 14; and Elliot C. Young, "Judging a Package by Its Cover," *Madison Avenue*, August 1983, p. 17.

14. Jennifer Hunter, "Drug Tampering Cases Put Spotlight on Packaging," *Globe and Mail*, December 12, 1983, p. B3. See also: Janet Marchant, "Packager, Contain Thyself," in *Readings in Canadian Marketing*, U. De Brentane and M. Laroche (eds), Kendall/Hunt, Dubuque, Iowa, 1983, pp. 106-109.

15. Jaimie Hubbard, "The Soaring Cost of Selling Beer," *Financial Post*, June 28, 1986, p. 11.

16. Patricia Sellers, "Getting Customers to Love You," *Fortune*, March 13, 1989, pp. 38-49.

17. Bro Uttal, "Companies That Serve You Best," *Fortune*, December 7, 1987, pp. 98-116; and "Customer Service: Up the Bottom Line," *Sales & Marketing Management*, January 1989, p. 19.

18. Peter G. Banting, "Customer Service in Industrial Marketing: A Comparative Study," *European Journal of Marketing* 10, 3, 1976, p. 140.

19. For more examples of how companies have used customer service as a marketing tool, see "Making Service a Potent Marketing Tool," *Business Week*, June 11, 1984, pp. 164-70; Bill Kelley, "Five Companies That Do It Right—And Make It Pay," *Sales & Marketing Management*, April 1988, pp. 57-64; and Kevin T. Higgins, "Business Marketers Make Customer Service Job for All," *Marketing News*, January 1, 1989, pp. 1-2.

20. This definition can be found in *Marketing Definitions*.

# CHAPTER 10

# Designing Products: New Product Development and Product Life Cycle

## CHAPTER OBJECTIVES

After reading this chapter, you should be able to:
1. List and define the steps in new product development.
2. Explain how companies find and develop new product ideas.
3. Describe the stages of the product life cycle.
4. Explain how marketing strategy changes during a product's life cycle.

When a new product hits the market and "takes off," the rewards can be tremendous. Unfortunately, when the market cools, the results are often disastrous. Just ask the managers of Bombardier Inc. of Montreal, a company that experienced a number of ups and downs riding the snowmobile life cycle. The good years were the early 1970s. Bombardier was the market leader in snowmobile sales with the Ski-Doo, and in 1971-72 had an excellent year when the total market was 400,000 units. Then the oil crisis hit in 1973-74 and the market took a nose dive. It began a product diversification program in 1974 to reduce its dependence on one product. This program, described by some as helter-skelter, went first into other leisure products—motorcycles and sailboats. These new product ventures were not particularly successful and Bombardier lost $12 million in 1974.

The next diversification move, in late 1974, involved retooling some snowmobile capacity to make subway cars for the city of Montreal. Next, Bombardier purchased a manufacturer of diesel locomotives. Thus, in 1976 Bombardier was in two chancy businesses, snowmobiles and mass transit. By early 1981, it was engaged in the development, manufacture, and sale of a number of different recreational vehicles, trucks, railway cars, heat transfer products, all-terrain vehicles, aerospace components, marine and stationary engines, medium-speed diesel engines, and surface condensers for use in nuclear and fossil-fuel electrical stations.

In the past few years, Bombardier's marketing strategy has become more refined. Its global strategy and mission is to concentrate its activities in sectors such as aerospace, transportation equipment, defence, and motorized consumer products where the company is able to maintain or achieve a leadership position.

To achieve its mission, Bombardier changed its product line by:

- building graffiti-proof subway cars for New York City in 1982, which was the largest Canadian transit export deal,
- purchasing Canadair in 1986 from the federal government. To date it has sold over 200 Challenger jets, a commuter/business aircraft,
- designing monorail cars through a Florida subsidiary (TGI) and selling them to Disneyworld in 1987,
- designing the regional jet in 1989, a new stretched version of the Challenger, for longer, lightly travelled commuter routes,
- purchasing Short Brothers in 1989, a civil and military aircraft manufacturer in Northern Ireland which provides access to the European market,
- purchasing Learjet in 1990, the leading builder of small business jets in the U.S.

Today, Bombardier is a global empire of jets and trains. It is regarded as a world power in mass transit and sells subway cars to customers around the world from plants in Canada, the U.S., and Europe. It manufactures business aircraft and builds structural components for Boeing and the European Airbus. In the future, railcars built by a Belgian subsidiary will shuttle passengers under the English Channel, and it is well positioned to take advantage of opportunities resulting from the single market of Europe 1992. As well, it is planning to develop TGV, the "Train grande vitesse," a 300 kilometer per hour intercity train that will be part of a high-speed rail system for the Quebec City-Windsor corridor. Finally, the product that started it all, the Ski-Doo, is making a comeback. The market for snowmobiles is growing again and new versions of the Ski-Doo are dominating both the North American and European market (through a joint venture with a company in Finland). As well, the company developed and launched the Sea-Doo, a personal watercraft product to meet the needs of a new growth market.

Bombardier's strategy seems to be paying off. After suffering an $18.5 million loss in 1982, it has turned a profit every subsequent year, and sales are now over $1.3 billion. But for companies like Bombardier who market high technology products, the pressure is always there to pick the right products for the future.[1]

A company like Bombardier has to be good at identifying and developing new products. It also has to be good at managing them in the face of changing tastes, technologies, and competition. Every product seems to go through a life cycle—it is born, goes through several phases and eventually dies as younger products come along that better serve consumer needs.

This product life cycle presents two major challenges. First, because all products eventually decline, the firm must find new products to replace aging ones (the problem of new product development). Second, the firm must understand how its products age, and adapt its marketing strategies as products pass through life-cycle stages (the problem of product life-cycle strategies). We will first look at the problem of finding and developing new products, and then at how to manage them successfully over their life cycle.

# NEW PRODUCT DEVELOPMENT STRATEGY

Given rapid changes in tastes, technology, and competition, a company cannot rely only on its existing products. Customers want and expect new and improved products. Competition will do its best to provide them. Every company needs a new product development program.

A company can obtain new products in two ways. One is through acquisition, by buying a whole company (for example, Bombardier's purchase of Canadair and Learjet), a patent, or a license to produce someone else's product. As the cost of developing and introducing a major new product climbed rapidly in the 1980s, many large companies decided to acquire existing brands rather than to create new ones. Following this direction, Procter & Gamble acquired Richardson-Vicks, R.J. Reynolds bought Nabisco, and Pepsico took over 7-Up.

The company can also obtain new products through **new product development**, by setting up its own research and development department. By new products we mean original products, product improvements, product modifications, and new brands that the firm develops through its own R&D efforts. In this chapter, we will concentrate on new product development.

Innovation can be very risky. Ford lost $350 million on its Edsel automobile; RCA lost a staggering $580 million on its SelectaVision video-disc player; Xerox's venture into computers was a disaster; and the Concorde aircraft will never pay back its investment. One study found that the new product failure rate was 40% for consumer products, 20% for industrial products, and 18% for services.[2] A recent study of 700 consumer and industrial firms found an overall success rate for new products of only 65%.[3]

Why do many new products fail? There are several reasons. A high-level executive might push a favorite idea in spite of poor marketing research findings. An idea may be good, but the market size may have been overestimated. The actual product may not be designed as well as it should have been. A product might be incorrectly positioned in the market, priced too high, or advertised poorly. Sometimes the costs of product development are higher than expected, or the competitors fight back harder than expected.

A major reason for failure of new industrial products in Canada is a poor marketing effort.[4] The marketing problems include inadequate attention to customer requirements, inadequate assessment of competitors' strengths, a lack of market research to identify product deficiencies, and pricing the new product too high.

Companies face a problem—they must develop new products, but the odds weigh heavily against success. The solution lies in strong new product planning, and in setting up a systematic new product development process for finding and nurturing new products. The major steps in this process are shown in Figure 10-1 and described below.

## Idea Generation

New product development starts with **idea generation**, a systematic search for new ideas. A company typically has to generate many ideas in order to find a few good ones. The search for new product ideas should be systematic rather than haphazard. Otherwise the company will expand energy in generating ideas that are not neces-

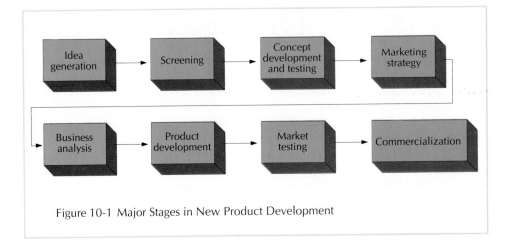

Figure 10-1 Major Stages in New Product Development

sarily suited to its business. For example, Canadian firms with no systematic approach in formal planning often are reactive and less satisfied with the entire process.[5]

Top management can avoid this error by carefully defining its new product development strategy. It should state what products and markets to emphasize. Management should also state what the company wants from the new products, whether it is high cash flow, market share, or some other objective. It should state the effort to be devoted to developing original products, changing existing products, and imitating competitors' products.

To obtain a flow of new product ideas, the company must tap many sources. Major sources of new product ideas include:

- **Internal sources.** One study of 100 large Canadian companies found that over 60% of all new product ideas come from within the company.[6] The company can find new ideas through formal research and development. It can seek advice and input from its scientists, engineers, and manufacturing people. Company executives can brainstorm for new product ideas. The company's salespeople are another good source because they are in daily contact with customers.
- **Customers.** A study of Canadian high technology firms found that most of the new product ideas come from watching and listening to customers.[7] In part, this reflected the close relationship these firms had established with their customers. Consumer needs and wants can be looked at through consumer surveys. The company can analyze customer questions and complaints to find new products that can better solve consumer problems. Company engineers or salespeople can meet with customers to get suggestions.
- **Competitors.** New product ideas can come from analyzing competitors' products. Companies buy competing new products, take them apart to see how they work, analyze their sales, and decide whether the company should bring out a new product of its own. The company can also watch competitors' ads and other communications to get clues about their new products.
- **Distributors and suppliers.** Resellers are close to the market and can pass along information about consumer problems and new product possibilities. Suppliers can tell the company about new concepts, techniques, and materials that can be used to develop new products.
- **Other sources.** Other idea sources include trade magazines, shows, and seminars;

government agencies; new product consultants; advertising agencies; marketing research firms; university and commercial laboratories; and inventors.

# Idea Screening

The purpose of idea generation is to create a large number of ideas. The aim of the succeeding stages is to reduce the number of ideas. The first idea-reducing stage is **idea screening**. The purpose of screening is to spot good ideas and drop poor ones as soon as possible. Product development costs rise greatly in later stages. The company will want to proceed only with the product ideas that will turn into profitable products.

Most companies require their executives to write up new product ideas on a standard form that can be reviewed by a new product committee. They describe the product, the target market, and the competition, and make some rough estimates of market size, product price, development time and costs, manufacturing costs, and rate of return. They answer the questions: Is this idea good for our particular company? Does it mesh well with the company's objectives and strategies? Do we have the people, skills, and resources to make it succeed? Many companies have well designed systems for rating and screening new product ideas.

# Concept Development and Testing

Surviving ideas must now be developed into product concepts. It is important to distinguish between a product idea, a product concept, and a product image. A **product idea** is an idea for a possible product that the company can see itself offering to the market. A **product concept** is a detailed version of the idea stated in meaningful consumer terms. A **product image** is the way consumers picture an actual or potential product.

# Concept Development

As part of its effort to forecast the future demand for electrical power, British Columbia Hydro was interested in forecasting the usage of electrically powered vehicles by commercial fleets.[8] The utility decided to study fleet owners' reactions to electric trucks that had certain operating characteristics including speed, range, operation costs, price, and pollution standards. The electric truck is a product idea. Customers, however, do not buy a product idea; they buy a product concept. The marketer's task is to develop this idea into some alternative product concepts, find out how attractive each concept is to customers, and choose the best one.

Among the product concepts tested for the electric truck were:

1. Speed of 64 km/h and a range of 64 km.
2. Operating costs of 5¢ per 1.6 km.
3. Price $8,000.
4. Pollution level zero.
5. Electric propulsion system.

# Concept Testing

**Concept testing** calls for testing these concepts with a group of target consumers. The concepts may be presented through word or picture descriptions. In this case, the consumers were the fleet personnel directly responsible for the vehicle purchase decisions. To increase the realism of the study, the consumers attended a seminar where they were shown an electrically powered van and given instructions on its operation. They were asked to evaluate the electric truck concept against a conventional truck. The relative importance of various vehicle characteristics were determined by asking the consumers to rank a set of alternatives from most to least desirable. This required the consumer to "trade off" various characteristics—a situation faced by all buyers in real life. For example, consumers may be asked to decide whether they prefer an increased range (e.g., 100 km) or an increased payload (e.g., 1,100 kg).[9]

The reaction of consumers in this situation was that electric vehicles would only be more desirable than conventional vehicles if they were sold at the same price as the conventional vehicle and were not constrained by limited speed or range. At the time of the study, it was not possible to build these characteristics into an electric vehicle.

# Marketing Strategy Development

Let's assume that a similar study was conducted on a personal electric car, and that consumers reacted favorably to the following product concept:

> An efficient, fun-to-drive, electric-powered car in the subcompact class that seats four. Great for shopping trips and visits to friends. Costs half as much to operate as similar gasoline-driven cars. Goes up to 80 km/h and does not need to be recharged for 160 km. Priced at $8,000.

The next step is **marketing strategy development**, designing an initial marketing strategy for introducing this car into the market.

The marketing strategy statement consists of three parts. The first part describes the target market, the planned product positioning, and the sales, market share, and profit goals for the first few years. Thus:

> The target market is households that need a second car for shopping trips and visits to friends. The car will be positioned as more economical to buy and operate, and more fun to drive, than cars now available to this market. The company will aim to sell 20,000 cars in the first year, at a loss of not more than $3 million. The second year will aim for sales of 30,000 cars and a profit of $5 million.

The second part of the marketing strategy statement outlines the product's planned price, distribution, and marketing budget for the first year:

> The electric car will be offered in three colors and will have optional air conditioning and power-drive features. It will sell at a retail price of $10,000, with 15% off the list price to dealers. Dealers who sell over ten cars per month will get an additional discount of five percent on each car sold that month. An advertising budget of $2 million will be split 50:50 between national and local advertising. Advertising will empha-

size the car's economy and fun. During the first year, $100,000 will be spent on marketing research to find out who is buying the car and their satisfaction levels.

The third part of the marketing strategy statement describes the planned long-run sales and profit goals and marketing mix strategy over time:

> The company intends to capture a three percent long-run share of the total auto market and realize an after-tax return on investment of 15%. To achieve this, product quality will start high and be improved over time. Price will be raised in the second and third years if competition permits. The total advertising budget will be raised each year by about ten percent. Marketing research will be reduced to $60,000 per year after the first year.

## Business Analysis

Once management has decided on the product concept and marketing strategy, it can evaluate the business attractiveness of the proposal. **Business analysis** involves a review of sales, costs, and profit projections to find out whether they satisfy the company's objectives. If they do, the product can move to the product development stage.

To estimate sales, the company should look at the sales history of similar products and survey market opinion. It should estimate minimum and maximum sales to learn the range of risk. After preparing the sales forecast, management can estimate the expected costs and profits for the product. The costs are estimated by the R&D, manufacturing, accounting, and finance departments. The planned marketing costs are included in the analysis. The company then uses the sales and costs figures to analyze the new product's financial attractiveness.

## Product Development

If the product concept passes the business test, it moves into **product development**. Here R&D or engineering develop the product concept into a physical product. Until this point, the product concept existed only as a word description, a drawing, or a crude mockup. This step calls for a large jump in investment. It will show whether the product idea can be turned into a workable product.

The R&D department will develop one or more physical versions of the product concept. It hopes to find a prototype that meets the following criteria: (1) consumers see it as having the key features described in the product concept statement; (2) it performs safely under normal use; (3) it can be produced for the budgeted costs.

Developing a successful prototype can take days, weeks, months, or even years. The prototype must have the required functional features and also convey the intended psychological characteristics. The electric car, for example, should strike consumers as being well built and safe. Management must learn how consumers decide how well a car is built. For example, some consumers slam the door to hear its "sound." If the car does not have "solid-sounding" doors, consumers will think it is poorly built.

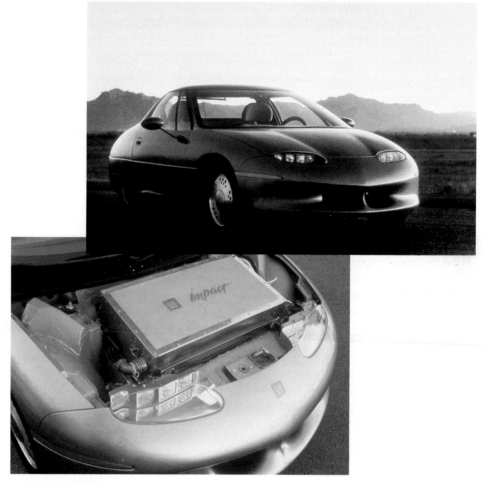

GM has developed an electric car.

When the prototypes are ready, they must be tested. Functional tests are conducted under laboratory and field conditions to make sure that the product performs safely and effectively. The new car must start well; it must be comfortable; it must be able to go around corners without overturning. Consumer tests are conducted, asking consumers to test-drive the car and rate the car and its attributes.

## Test Marketing

If the product passes functional and consumer tests, the next step is test marketing. **Test marketing** is the stage where the product and marketing program are introduced into more realistic market settings.

Test marketing lets the marketer get experience with marketing the product, find potential problems, and learn where more information is needed before going to the great expense of full introduction. The basic purpose of test marketing is to test the product itself in real market situations. However, test marketing also allows the company to test the entire marketing program for the product—the positioning strategy, advertising, distribution, pricing, branding and packaging, and budget levels. The company uses test marketing to learn how consumers and dealers will react to handling, using, and repurchasing the product. Test marketing results can be used to make better sales and profit forecasts.

The amount of test marketing needed varies with each new product. Test marketing costs can be enormous, and it takes time that competitors may use to gain an advantage. When the costs of developing and introducing the product are low or when management is already confident that the new product will succeed, the company may do little or no test marketing. Minor modifications of current products or copies of successful competitor products might not need testing. When introducing the new product requires a large investment, or when management is not sure of the product or marketing program, the company may do a lot of test marketing.

## Commercialization

Market testing gives management the information needed to make a final decision about whether to launch the new product. If the company goes ahead with **commercialization**, it will face high costs. The company will have to build or rent a manufacturing facility. It may have to spend, in the case of a new consumer packaged good, between $1 million and $5 million for advertising and sales promotion alone in the first year. When Diet Coke was launched in Canada, total promotion expenditures were close to $4 million, including about $1 million spent on sampling.[10] Cheesebrough-Pond's spent over $3 million in television advertising to launch Pears Shampoo and Conditioner and over 4 million Canadian homes received product samples and coupons.[11] Gillette spent more than $200 million in a 19 country marketing launch for its new Sensor shaving system, including $7.5 million in Canada.[12]

## Product Launching

In launching a new product, the company must make four decisions.

### WHEN?

The first decision is whether it is the right time to introduce the new product. If sales of the electric car will cannibalize the sales of the company's other cars, its introduction may be delayed. If the electric car can be improved further, the company may wait to launch it next year. The company may also want to wait if the economy is down.

### WHERE?

The company must decide whether to launch the new product in a single location, one region, several regions, the national market, or the international market. Few companies have the confidence, capital, and capacity to launch new products into full national distribution. They will develop a planned market rollout over time. Small companies, in particular, will select an attractive city and put on a blitz campaign to enter the market. They will enter other cities one at a time.

Large companies will introduce their product into a whole region and then move to the next region. Companies with national distribution networks, such as auto companies, will often launch their new models in the national market.

### TO WHOM?

Within the rollout markets, the company must target its distribution and promotion to the best prospect groups. The company has already profiled the prime prospects in earlier market testing. It must now fine-tune its market identification, looking especially for early adopters, heavy users, and opinion leaders.

### HOW?

The company must develop an action plan for introducing the new product into the selected markets. It must spend the marketing budget on the marketing mix and various other activities. Thus the electric car's launch may be supported by a publicity campaign, and then by offers of gifts to draw more people to the showrooms. The company must prepare a separate marketing plan for each new market.

In making these decisions, management should be guided by the findings in the field known as innovation diffusion and adoption theory (see Marketing Highlight 10-1). These findings clearly point out the high risks involved in new-product development and the careful planning that is needed to launch a new product successfully.[13]

# PRODUCT LIFE-CYCLE STRATEGIES

After launching the new product, management wants the product to enjoy a long and prosperous life. Although they do not expect the product to sell forever, management wants to earn a decent profit to cover all the effort and risk that went into

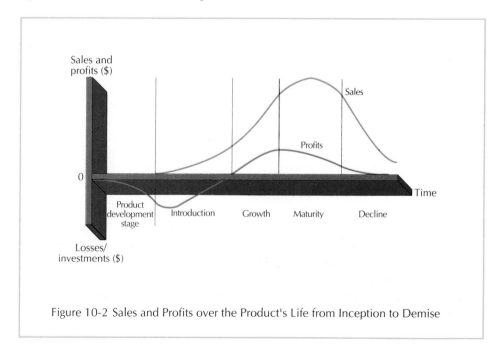

Figure 10-2 Sales and Profits over the Product's Life from Inception to Demise

# MARKETING HIGHLIGHT 10-1

## Major Findings of Innovation Diffusion and Adoption

In launching a new product, a firm should be guided by the major findings in the field of innovation diffusion and adoption theory. These findings are:

### Stages of Adoption
Individual consumers go through a series of stages of acceptance in the process of adopting a new product. The stages are awareness, interest, evaluation, trial, and adoption. Thus the manufacturer of a new electric car must think about what can be done to move people efficiently through each stage. For example, if people have awareness and interest but are not coming into a dealer's showrooms, the manufacturer must develop promotional incentives to attract people into the showrooms.

### Consumer Adopter Types
People differ greatly in their readiness to try new products. There are innovators (the first 2.5% of the individuals to adopt a new product), early adopters (the next 13.5%), early majority (the next 34%), late majority (the next 34%), and laggards (the last 16%). The electric car manufacturer should try to identify the characteristics of people who are likely to be early adopters, such as having a high income and being active in the community, and should then focus its promotion on this group.

### Role of personal influence
Personal influence plays a major role in the adoption of new products. The statements of other people about a new product carry heavy weight with a prospect, especially if the product is risky or costly. The electric car manufacturer will want to research what opinion leaders and early buyers say to others about the new electric car and to correct as soon as possible any product features that will give rise to complaints. The manufacturer may also want to use a "testimonial advertising" approach in which some attractive sources assure other people that the electric car is reliable and fun to drive.

### Innovation characteristics
Certain characteristics of the innovation strongly affect the rate of adoption. The main ones are the innovation's relative advantage over other products, compatibility with the person's life style, complexity, divisibility into small trial units, and communicability. Thus an electric car will be more appealing to the extent that it saves buyers a lot of money, fits their life style, is simple to operate, can be test driven, and is easy to understand.

**Source:** These and other ideas are elaborated in Everett M. Rogers, *Diffusion of Innovation*, 3rd ed. (New York: Free Press, 1983). For a recent review, see Vijay Mahajan, Eitan Muller, and Frank M. Bass, "New Product Diffusion Models in Marketing: A Review and Directions For Research," *Journal of Marketing*, January 1990, pp. 1-26.

---

it. Management is aware that each product will have a life cycle, although the exact shape and length is not known in advance.

The sales and profit patterns in a typical **product life cycle (PLC)** are shown in Figure 10-2. The product life cycle is marked by five distinct stages:

1. Product development begins when the company finds and develops a new product idea. During product development, sales are zero and the company's investment costs add up.

2. Introduction is a period of slow sales growth as the product is being introduced in the market. Profits are nonexistent in this stage because of the heavy expenses of product introduction.

3. Growth is a period of rapid market acceptance and increasing profits.

4. Maturity is a period of slowdown in sales growth because the product has achieved acceptance by most of the potential buyers. Profits level off or decline because of increased marketing outlays to defend the product against competition.

5. Decline is the period when sales fall off quickly and profits drop.

Not all products follow this S-shaped product life cycle. Some products are introduced and die quickly. Others stay in the mature stage for a long time. Some enter the decline stage, and then are cycled back into the growth stage through strong promotion or repositioning.[14]

The PLC concept can describe a product class (gasoline-powered automobiles), a product form (station wagons), or a brand (the Ford Probe). The PLC concept applies differently in each case. Product classes have the longest life cycles. The sales of many product classes stay in the mature stage for long time. Product forms, on the other hand, tend to have the standard PLC shape. Product forms such as the "dial telephone" and "cream deodorants" pass through a regular history of introduction, rapid growth, maturity, and decline. A specific brand's life cycle can change quickly because of changing competitive attacks and responses. The life cycles of several toothpaste brands are shown in Figure 10-3.

The PLC concept can also be applied to what are known as styles, fashions, and fads. Their special life-cycle features are described in Marketing Highlight 10-2.

The PLC concept can be applied by marketers as a useful framework for describing how products and markets work. However, the use of the PLC concept to forecast product performance or to develop marketing strategies presents some practical problems.[15] For example, managers may have trouble identifying a product's current life-cycle stage, when it will move into the next stage, and the factors

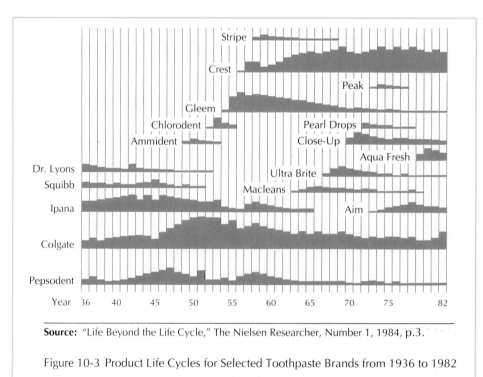

**Source:** "Life Beyond the Life Cycle," The Nielsen Researcher, Number 1, 1984, p.3.

Figure 10-3 Product Life Cycles for Selected Toothpaste Brands from 1936 to 1982

# MARKETING HIGHLIGHT 10-2

## Style, Fashion, and Fad Cycles

In markets where style and fashion are influential, sales cycles occur. Marketers need to understand and predict them.

A style is a basic and distinctive mode of expression appearing in a field of human activity. For example, styles appear in homes (colonial, ranch, Cape Cod), clothing (formal, casual), and art (realistic, surrealistic, abstract). Once a style is invented, it may last for generations, coming in and out of vogue. A style exhibits a cycle showing several periods of renewed interest.

A fashion is a currently accepted or popular style in a given field. For example, the "preppie look" in the clothing of the late 1970s gave way to the "loose and layered look" of the mid- to late 1980s. Fashions pass through many stages. First, a small number of consumers take an interest in something new to set themselves apart from other consumers. Then, other consumers take an interest out of a desire to copy the fashion leaders. Next, the fashion becomes very popular and is adopted by the mass market. Finally, the fashion fades away as consumers start moving toward other fashions that are beginning to catch their eye. Thus fashions tend to grow slowly, remain popular for a while, then decline slowly.

Fads are fashions that enter quickly, are adopted with great zeal, peak early, and decline very fast. Their acceptance cycle is short, and they tend to attract only a limited following. They often have a novel or quirky aspect, as when people start buying Rubik's Cubes or Trivial Pursuit games. Fads appeal to people who are searching for excitement or who want to set themselves apart from others or have something to talk about to others. Fads do not survive for long because they normally do not satisfy a strong need or satisfy it well. It is difficult to predict whether something will only be a fad, and if so, how long it will last—a few days, weeks, or months. The amount of media attention it receives, along with other factors, will influence its duration.

that affect how the product will move through the stages. In practice, it is very hard to forecast the sales level at each PLC stage, the length of each stage, and the shape of the PLC curve.

Using the PLC concept to develop marketing strategy can be difficult because strategy is both a cause and result of the product's life cycle. The product's current PLC position suggests the best marketing strategies, and the resulting marketing strategies affect product performance in later life-cycle stages. Yet when used carefully the PLC concept can help in developing good marketing strategies for different stages of the product life cycle.

We looked at the product development stage of the product life cycle in the first part of the chapter. We now look at strategies for each of the other life-cycle stages.

## Introduction Stage

The **introduction stage** starts when the new product is first distributed and made available for purchase. Introduction takes time, and sales growth is apt to be slow.

An introduction ad for a new service.

Such well-known products as instant coffee, frozen orange juice, and powdered coffee creamers lingered for many years before they entered a stage of rapid growth.

In this stage, profits are negative or low because of low sales and high distribution and promotion expenses. Much money is needed to attract distributors and "fill the pipelines." Promotion spending is high to inform consumers of the new product and encourage them to try it.[16]

There are only a few competitors, and they produce basic versions of the product, since the market is not ready for product refinements. The firms focus their selling on those buyers who are ready to buy, usually the higher-income groups.

## Growth Stage

If the new product satisfies the market, it will enter the **growth stage**, and sales will start climbing quickly. The early adopters will continue to buy, and later buyers will

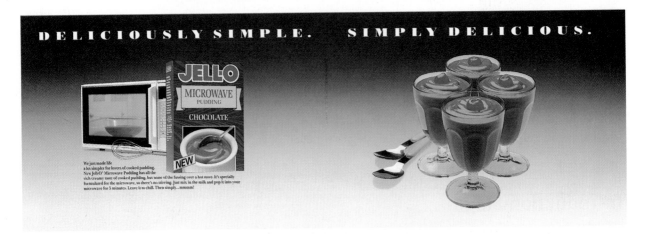

Jell-O introduces a variation on its established product.

start following their lead, especially if they hear favorable word of mouth. New competitors will enter the market attracted by the opportunities for profit. They will introduce new product features, and expand the market. The increase in competitors leads to an increase in the number of distribution outlets, and sales will jump just to build reseller inventories. Prices remain where they are or fall only slightly. Companies keep their promotion spending at the same or a slightly higher level to meet competition and continue educating the market.

Profits increase during this growth stage as promotion costs are spread over a large volume and unit manufacturing costs fall due, in part, to the "experience curve" effect.[17] The firm uses several strategies to sustain rapid market growth as long as possible. It improves product quality and adds new product features and models. It enters new market segments and new distribution channels. It shifts some advertising from building product awareness to building product conviction and purchase and lowers prices at the right time to attract more buyers.

The firm in the growth stage faces a tradeoff between high market share and high current profit. By spending a lot of money on product improvement, promo-

3 M has expanded its marketing mix over the years, so that it now markets over a thousand product varieties.

tion, and distribution, it can capture a dominant position. The firm gives up maximum current profit at this stage but it hopes to make up the profit in the next stage.

## Maturity Stage

At some point a product's sales growth will slow down, and the product will enter a **maturity stage**. This maturity stage normally lasts longer than the previous stages, and it poses strong challenges to marketing management. Most products are in the maturity stage of the life cycle, and therefore most of marketing management deals with the mature product.

The slowdown in sales growth results in many producers with many products to sell. This overcapacity leads to greater competition. Competitors begin marking down prices, and they increase their advertising and sales promotions. They also increase their R&D budgets to find better versions of the product. These steps mean a drop in profit, and some of the weaker competitors start dropping out. The industry eventually contains only well-established competitors.

During the maturity stage, companies modify the features and styles of their products.

Product managers should not simply defend the product. A good offense is the best defense. They should consider modifying the market, product, and marketing mix.

## MARKET MODIFICATION

Here the manager tries to increase the consumption of the current product. The manager looks for new users and market segments, as well as for ways to increase usage among present customers. The manager may want to reposition the brand to appeal to a larger or faster-growing segment.

## PRODUCT MODIFICATION

The product manager can also change product characteristics—such as product quality, features, or style—to attract new users and more usage.

A strategy of quality improvement aims at increasing the performance of the product—its durability, reliability, speed, or taste. This strategy is effective when the quality can be improved, buyers believe the claim of improved quality, and enough buyers want higher quality.

A strategy of feature improvement adds new features that expand the product's usefulness, safety, or convenience. Feature improvement has been successfully used by Japanese makers of watches, calculators, and copying machines. For example, Sony continues to add new playing features to its Walkman line of miniature stereo players.

A strategy of style improvement aims to increase the attractiveness of the product. Thus car manufacturers restyle their cars to attract buyers who want a new look.

## MARKETING MIX MODIFICATION

The product manager can also try to improve sales by changing one or more marketing mix elements. Prices can be cut to attract new users and competitors' customers. A better advertising campaign can be sought. Aggressive sales promotion such as trade deals, cents-off, gifts, and contests can be used. The company can move into larger market channels, if these channels are growing, using mass merchandisers. The company can offer new or improved services to the buyers.

# Decline Stage

The sales of most product forms and brands eventually dip. The sales decline may be slow, as in the case of porridge; or rapid, as for the pet rock. Sales may plunge to zero, or they may drop to a low level where they continue for many years. This is the **decline stage**.

Sales decline for many reasons, including technological advances, shifts in consumer tastes, and increased competition. As sales and profits decline, some firms withdraw from the market. Those that remain may reduce the number of their product offerings. They may drop smaller market segments and marginal trade channels, cut the promotion budget, and reduce their prices further.

Carrying a weak product can be very costly to the firm, and not only in profit terms. There are many hidden costs—the weak product may take up too much of management's time. Frequent price and inventory adjustments are often necessary for a weak product. It requires advertising and salesforce attention that might better be used to make the "healthy" products more profitable. Its failing reputation

**Table 10-2**
**Product Life Cycle: Characteristics and Responses**

|  | Introduction | Growth | Maturity | Decline |
|---|---|---|---|---|
| *Characteristics* |  |  |  |  |
| Sales | Low | Fast growth | Slow growth | Decline |
| Profits | Negligible | Peak levels | Declining | Low or zero |
| Cash flow | Negative | Moderate | High | Low |
| Customers | Innovative | Mass market | Mass market | Laggards |
| Competitors | Few | Growing | Many rivals | Declining number |
|  |  |  |  |  |
| *Responses* |  |  |  |  |
| Strategic focus | Expand market | Market penetration | Defend share | Productivity |
| Mktg. expenditures | High | High (declining %) | Falling | Low |
| Mktg. emphasis | Product | Brand preference | Brand loyalty awareness | Selective |
| Distribution | Patchy | Intensive | Intensive | Selective |
| Price | High | Lower | Lowest | Rising |
| Product | Basic | Improved | Differentiated | Unchanged |

**Source:** Peter Doyle, "The Realities of the Product Life Cycle," *Quarterly Review of Marketing* (UK), Summer 1976, p.5.

can cause customer concerns about the company and its other products. The biggest cost may well lie in the future. Keeping weak products delays the search for replacement products, creates a lopsided product mix, and hurts current profits, weakening the company's foothold on the future.

For these reasons, companies need to pay more attention to their aging products. The first task is to identify those products in the declining stage by regularly reviewing the sales, market shares, cost, and profit trends on each of its products. For each declining product, management has to decide whether to maintain, harvest, or drop the product. Management may decide to maintain its brand without change in the hope that competitors will leave the industry. For example, Procter & Gamble remained in the declining liquid-soap business as others withdrew, and it made good profits. Alternatively, management may decide to reposition the brand in hopes of moving it back into the growth stage of the product life cycle, as Clairol did with Ban deodorant. It relaunched Ban with a $2.5 million promotion campaign targeted at "stylish" women in the hopes of gaining a greater share of the $100 million deodorant market in Canada.[18]

Management may decide to harvest the product, which means reducing various costs (plant and equipment, maintenance, R&D, advertising, sales force), and hoping that sales hold up fairly well for a while. If successful, harvesting will increase the company's profits in the short run. If management decides to drop the product from the line, it can sell the product to another firm or simply liquidate it at salvage value. If the company plans to find a buyer, it will not want to run down the product through harvesting.[19]

The key characteristics of each stage of the product life cycle are summarized in Table 10-2. The table also lists the marketing responses made by companies in each stage.[b]

# SUMMARY

Organizations need to develop new products and services. Their current products face limited life spans and must be replaced by newer products. However, new products can fail—the risks of innovation are as great as the rewards. The key to successful innovation lies in strong planning and a systematic new product development process.

The new product development process consists of eight stages: idea generation, idea screening, concept development and testing, marketing, and commercialization. The purpose of each stage is to decide whether the idea should be further developed or dropped. The company wants to minimize the chances of poor ideas moving forward and good ideas being rejected.

Each product has a life cycle marked by a changing set of problems and opportunities. The sales of the typical product follow an S-shaped curve made up of five stages. The cycle begins with the product development stage when the company finds and develops a new product idea. The introduction stage is marked by slow growth and low profits as the product is being pushed into distribution. If successful, the product enters a growth stage marked by rapid sales growth and increasing profits. During this stage the company tries to improve the product, enter new market segments and distribution channels, and reduce its prices slightly. Then comes a maturity stage in which sales growth slows down and profits stabilize. The company seeks strategies to renew sales growth, including market, product, and marketing mix modification. Finally, the product enters a decline stage where sales and profits fall off. The company's task during this stage is to identify the declining product and decide whether to maintain, harvest, or drop it. In the latter case, the product can be sold to another firm or liquidated for salvage value.

# QUESTIONS FOR DISCUSSION

1. Before videotape cameras were available for home use, Polaroid introduced Polavision, a system for making home movies that did not require laboratory processing. Like most other home-movie systems, Polavision cassettes lasted only a few minutes and did not record sound. Despite the advantage of "instant developing" and heavy promotional expenditures, Polavision never gained wide acceptance. Given Polaroid's record of new-product successes, why did Polavision fail?

2. List as many new-product ideas for your favorite fast-food chain as you can. Which of these ideas have the best chance of succeeding?

3. Less than one-third of all new-product ideas come from customers. Does this low

percentage conflict with the philosophy of "find a need and fill it"?

4. What factors would you consider in choosing cities for test-marketing a new snack? Would your home town be a good test market?

5. NutraSweet, the NutraSweet Company's brand name for aspartame, was approved in 1981. In 1992, the company's patent expires, and other companies will be able to sell their own brands of aspartame. Describe NutraSweet's probable product life cycle from 1980 to 1999.

6. How can a company distinguish products with long life cycles from fads and fashions? What current products do you consider fads or fashions likely to disappear soon?

7. Compare the relative spending levels on promotion at the different stages of a product's life cycle. What types of promotion are best used at each stage?

# KEY TERMS

**Business analysis**  A review of the sales, costs, and profit projections for a new product to find out whether they satisfy the company's objectives.

**Commercialization**  Introducing a new product into the market.

**Concept testing**  Testing new product concepts with a group of target consumers to find out if the concepts have strong consumer appeal.

**Decline stage**  The product life cycle stage in which a product's sales decline.

**Growth stage**  The product life cycle stage when the product's sales start climbing quickly.

**Idea generation**  The systematic search for new product ideas.

**Idea screening**  Screening new product ideas in order to spot good ideas and drop poor ones as soon as possible.

**Introduction stage**  The product life cycle stage in which the new product is first distributed and made available for purchase.

**Marketing strategy development**  Designing an initial marketing strategy for a new product based on the product concept.

**Maturity stage**  The stage in the product life cycle where sales growth slows or levels off.

**New product development**  The development of original products, product improvements, product modifications, and new brands through the firm's own R&D efforts.

**Product concept**  A detailed version of the new product idea stated in meaningful consumer terms.

**Product development**  Developing the product concept into a physical product in order to ensure that the product idea can be turned into a workable product.

**Product idea**  An idea for a possible product that the company can see itself offering to the market.

**Product image**  The way consumers picture an actual or potential product.

**Product life cycle (PLC)**  The course of a product's sales and profits over its lifetime. It involves five distinct stages: product development, introduction, growth, maturity, and decline.

**Test marketing**  The stage of new product development in which the product and marketing program are tested in more realistic market settings.

# REFERENCES

1. Written by the author, based on material in Peter Menyasz, "Bombardier's Formula for Growth," *Financial Times*, November 28, 1983, p. 5; Matthew Horsmeen, "Car Venture Revs Up," *Financial Post*, June 21, 1986, pp. 1, 2; Alan D. Gray, "Bombardier Step Into the Billion-Dollar Class," *Financial Times*, August 25, 1986, p. 6; David Stewart-Patterson, "Ottawa Selling Canadian to Bombardier," *Globe and Mail*, August 19, 1986, pp. B1, B2; Christian Allard, "The Fast Track," *Canadian Business*, January 1990, pp. 29-34; James Daw, "All Eyes on the Jet," *Toronto Star*, January 28, 1990, pp. F1, F5; Ken Romain, "Bombardier Buying Learjet Corp. For $75 Million (U.S.)," *Globe and Mail*, April 10, 1990, pp. B1, B10; and Bombardier Inc., Annual Report, 1989.

2. David S. Hopkins and Earl L. Bailey, "New Product Pressures," *Conference Board Record*, June 1971, pp. 16-24.

3. New Product Management for the 1980s (New York: Booz, Allen & Hamilton, 1982). For a review of studies on new product failure rates see C. Merle Crawford, "New Product Failure Rates," *Research Management*, September, 1979, pp. 9-13.

4. See Robert G. Cooper, "The Dimensions of Industrial New Product Success and Failure," *Journal of Marketing*, Summer 1979, pp. 93-103; Roger J. Calantone and Roger G. Cooper, "New Product Scenarios: Prospects for Success," *Journal of Marketing*, Spring 1981, pp. 48-60; and R.G. Cooper and E.J. Kleinschmidt, "New Products: What Separates Winners From Losers?" *Journal of Product Innovation Management 4*, 1987, pp. 169-184.

5. David A. Boag and Brenda L. Rinholm, "New Product Management Practices of Small High Technology Firms," *Journal of Product Innovation Management 6*, 1989, pp. 109-122.

6. Russell M. Knight, "Corporate Innovation and Entrepreneurship: A Canadian Study," *Journal of Product Innovation Management 4*, 1987, pp. 284-297.

7. H. Allan Conway and Norm W. McGuinness, "Idea Generation in Technology-Based Firms," *Journal of Product Innovation Management 4*, 1986, pp. 276-291.

8. The following example is taken from George Hargreaves, John D. Claxton, and Frederick H. Siller, "New Product Evaluation: Electric Vehicles for Commercial Applications," *Journal of Marketing*, January 1976, pp. 74-77.

9. For more on product concept testing, see William L. Moore, "Concept Testing," *Journal of Business Research*, 10, 1982, pp. 279-94; and David A. Schwartz, "Concept Testing Can Be Improved — and Here's How," *Marketing News*, January 6, 1984, pp. 22-23.

10. James Walker, "Diet Coke's Success Formula," *Financial Times*, August 22, 1983, pp. 2, 6.

11. Martin Mehr, "Aiming For Number One," *Marketing*, August 7, 1989, p. 2.

12. Randy Scotland, "Gillette Launches System Globally," *Marketing*, October 9, 1989, p. 1.

13. For more on new product development, see F. Axel Johne and Patricia A. Snelson, "Success Factors in Product Innovation: A Selective Review of the Literature," *Journal of Product Innovation Management*, 5, 1988, pp. 114-128.

14. For an interesting example of the product life cycle, see Steven C. Wheelwright and W. Earl Sasser, Jr., "The New Product Development Map," *Harvard Business Review*, May-June 1989, pp. 112-125.

15. See George S. Day, "The Product Life Cycle: Analysis and Applications Issues," *Journal of Marketing*, Fall 1981, pp. 60-67; John E. Swan and David R. Rink, "Fitting Market Strategy to Varying Product Life Cycles," *Business Horizons*, January-February 1982, pp. 72-76; Sak Onkvisit and John J. Shaw, "Competition and Product Management: Can the Product Life Cycle Help?" *Business Horizons*, July-August 1986, pp. 51-62; and Mary Lambkin and George S. Day, "Evolutionary Processes in Competitive Markets: Beyond the Product Life Cycle," *Journal of Marketing*, July 1989, pp. 4-20.

16. For more on promotion and the PLC, see Gerald J. Tallis and Claes Fornell, "The Relationship Between Advertising and Product Quality Over the Product Life Cycle: A Contingency Theory," *Journal of Marketing Research*, February 1988, pp. 64-71.

17. The experience curve describes the rate at which costs fall as a function of accumulated production experience. See "Selling Business a Theory of Economics," *Business Week*, September 8, 1973, pp. 86-88; Walter Kiechel III, "The Decline of the Experience Curve," *Fortune*, October 5, 1981, pp. 46-48; George S. Day and David B. Montgomery, "Diagnosing the Experience Curve," *Journal of Marketing*, Spring 1983, pp. 44-58; Bruce D. Henderson, "The Application and Misapplication of the Experience Curve," *Journal of Business Strategy*, Winter 1984, pp. 3-9; and William W. Alberts, "The Experience Curve Doctrine Reconsidered," *Journal of Marketing*, July 1989, pp. 36-49.

18. Ian Timberlake, "2.5 Million Backs Ban's Relaunch," *Marketing*, August 25, 1986, p. 3.

19. See Laurence P. Feldman and Albert L. Page, "Harvesting: The Misunderstood Market Exit Strategy," *Journal of Business Strategy*, Spring 1985, pp. 79-85.

20. For further reading on the product life-cycle concept, see Theodore Levitt, "Exploit the Product Life Cycle," *Harvard Business Review*, November-December 1965, pp. 81-94; Nariman K. Dhalla and Sonia Yuspeh, "Forget the Product Life Cycle Concept!" *Harvard Business Review*, January-February 1976, pp. 102-12; the special section of articles on the product life cycle in the Fall 1981 issue of the *Journal of Marketing*; D.R. Rink and J.E. Swan, "Product Life Cycle

Research: A Literature Review," *Journal of Business Research*, September 1979, pp. 219-42; Carl R. Anderson and Carl P. Zeithaml, "Stages of the Product Life Cycle, Business Strategy, and Business Performance," *Academy of Management Journal*, March 1984, pp. 5-24; and Mary Lambkin and George S. Day, "Evolutionary Processes in Competitive Markets: Beyond the Product Life Cycle," *Journal of Marketing*, July 1989, pp. 4-20.

# CHAPTER 11

# Pricing Products: Pricing Considerations and Approaches

## CHAPTER OBJECTIVES

After reading this chapter, you should be able to:

1. Discuss how marketing objectives and mix strategy, costs, and other internal company factors affect pricing decisions.
2. List and discuss factors outside the company that affect pricing decisions.
3. Explain how price setting depends on consumer perceptions of price and on the price-demand relationship.
4. Compare the three general pricing approaches.

A consumer buying a compact disc player faces a bewildering array of models and prices. Over 20 brands and 60 models are sold in Canada, ranging from a stripped-down player selling for less than $200 to a player that fits into the trunk of a car, changes up to ten compact discs through remote control, and sells for over $1,500. The consumer must decide whether the extra features on the more expensive models, such as shuffle play and linear remote tracking, are worth the higher price.

Consumers may have trouble choosing among the different prices, but manufacturers probably have more trouble setting the prices. Consider the case of Gendis Inc., the company selling Sony products in Canada. Through a joint venture, Gendis owns 51% of Sony Canada and Toyko-based Sony Corp. holds the remaining 49%. Man-agers at Gendis must consider many factors in their complex price-setting process. They first consider the company's overall marketing objectives and the role of price in the marketing mix. Should Gendis price to maximize current profits on compact disc players, or to maximize long-run market share? Should it use a high-price/low-volume strategy or a low-price/high-volume strategy?

When setting compact disc player prices, Gendis must also consider costs. These include the manufacturing costs, shipping, and import duties, and the costs of storing, stocking, selling, and customer services. Gendis must price its compact disc players to cover these costs, plus a target profit. However, if Gendis considers only costs when setting prices, it ignores important demand and competitive factors.

The total demand for compact disc players has increased dramatically in Canada. Beginning in 1985 when 60,000 units were sold, sales have sky-rocketed — total sales in 1989 were 530,000 units, and in that year about 12% of all Canadian households owned a compact disc player. This increased demand is due in part to rapidly falling prices for the players. Gendis must determine how to price its players so that consumers will consider and buy their units. Consumer-oriented pricing starts with knowing consumer perceptions of each model's value. If Gendis charges more than the product's value as perceived by buyers, its compact disc players will sell poorly. If it charges less, its players will sell very well but will provide less revenue.

Gendis must also consider the quality and prices of competitors' compact disc players. If Sony players are similar to those of its major competitors, but Sony charges more, it risks losing sales. If it sets prices much lower than those of comparable products, it will win sales from competitors but lose profit opportunities.

Thus Gendis sets the prices of its basic compact disc players on the basis of costs, demand, and competitors' prices. For each player in its product line Gendis must determine how consumers value different features and what features consumers prefer. Gendis has decided to use a premium price strategy for its line of compact disc players. Gendis sees the target market for Sony products, including compact disc players, as consumers who want "reliability, reputation, after-sale service and support" and are willing to pay for that "comfort." This strategy has paid off as Gendis sales of Sony products exceed $200 million in Canada each year.[1]

All profit organizations and many nonprofit organizations must set prices on their products or services. Price goes by many names. You pay rent for your apartment, tuition for your education, and a fee to your physician or dentist. A transportation company charges you a fare, the local bank charges you interest on a credit card, and the company that insures your car charges you a premium. Your regular lawyer may ask for a retainer to cover her services. The price of an executive is a salary, the price of a salesperson may be a commission, and the price of a worker is a wage.[2] Simply defined, **price** is the amount of money charged for a product or service. More broadly, price is the sum of the values consumers exchange for the benefits of having or using the product or service.

Price is the only element in the marketing mix that produces revenue; the other elements represent costs. However, many companies do not handle pricing well. The most common mistakes are pricing that is too cost-oriented, is not revised often enough to reflect market changes, does not take the rest of the marketing mix into account, and is not varied enough for different product items and market segments.

In this chapter and the following one, we will look at the problem of setting prices. This chapter will look at the factors marketers must consider when setting prices, and at general pricing approaches. In the next chapter, we will examine pricing strategies for new product pricing, product-mix pricing, initiating and responding to price changes, and adjusting prices for buyer and situational factors.

# FACTORS TO CONSIDER WHEN SETTING PRICES

The company's pricing decisions are affected by many internal company factors and external environmental factors. These factors are shown in Figure 11-1. Internal factors include the company's marketing objectives, marketing mix strategy, costs, and organization. External factors include the nature of the market and demand, competition, and other environmental factors.

## Internal Factors Affecting Pricing Decisions

### MARKETING OBJECTIVES

Before setting price, the company must decide on its strategy for the product. If the company has selected its target market and positioning carefully, then its marketing mix strategy (including price) will be fairly straightforward. For example, if Sony wants to produce high quality stereo and video components for the higher-income segments, this suggests charging higher prices. Thus pricing strategy is largely determined by past decisions on market positioning.

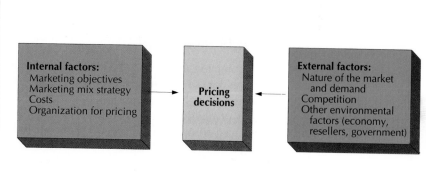

Figure 11-1 Factors Affecting Price Decisions

At the same time, the company may seek additional objectives. The clearer a firm is about its objectives, the easier it is to set a price. Examples of common objectives are survival, current profit maximization, market share maximization, and product quality leadership.

### SURVIVAL

Companies set survival as their major objective if troubled by too much manufacturing capacity, heavy competition, or changing consumer wants. To keep the plant going, a company must set a low price in the hopes that it will increase demand. Profits are less important than survival. In recent years, troubled companies such as Chrysler resorted to large price rebate programs in order to survive. As long as their prices cover variable costs and some fixed costs, they can stay in business until conditions change or other problems are corrected.

### CURRENT PROFIT MAXIMIZATION

Many companies want to set a price that will maximize current profits. They estimate what the demand and costs will be at different prices, and choose the price that will produce the maximum current profit, cash flow, or return on investment. In all cases, the company wants to maximize current financial outcomes rather than long-run performance.

## MARKET SHARE LEADERSHIP

Many companies want to obtain the dominant market share. They believe that the company with the largest market share will enjoy the lowest costs and highest long-run profit. To become the market share leader, they set prices as low as possible. A variation of this objective is to pursue a specific market share gain. For example, if a company wants to increase its market share from ten percent to 15% in one year, it will search for the price and marketing program to achieve this objective.

## PRODUCT QUALITY LEADERSHIP

A company might decide it wants to have the highest quality product on the market. This normally calls for charging a high price to cover the high product quality and high cost of R&D. Michelin, the tire manufacturer, is a good example of a firm seeking product quality leadership. It continually introduces new tire features and longer- lasting tires, and prices its tires at a premium.

## OTHER OBJECTIVES

A company might use price to attain other, more specific, objectives. It can set prices low to prevent competition from entering the market, or set prices at competitors' levels to stabilize the market. Prices can be set to keep the loyalty and support of resellers, or to avoid government intervention. Prices can be temporarily reduced to create excitement about a product or to draw more customers into a retail store. One product may be priced to help the sales of other products in the company's line. Thus pricing may play an important role in helping to accomplish the company's objectives at many levels.

## MARKETING MIX STRATEGY

Price is only one of the marketing mix tools that the company uses to achieve its marketing objectives. Price decisions must be coordinated with product design, distribution, and promotion decisions to form a consistent and effective marketing program. Decisions made for other marketing mix variables may affect pricing decisions. For example, producers who use many resellers and expect these resellers to support and promote their products may have to build larger reseller margins into their prices. The decision to develop a high-quality position will mean that the seller must charge a higher price to cover higher costs.

The company often makes its pricing decision first and then bases other marketing mix decisions on the price it wants to charge. For example, Hyundai, Honda, and other makers of low-budget cars discovered a market segment for affordable cars and designed models to sell within the price range that this segment was willing to pay. Here was a key product positioning factor that defined the product's market, competition, and design. The intended price determined what product features could be offered and what production costs could be incurred.

Thus, the marketer must consider the total marketing mix when setting prices. If the product is positioned on nonprice factors, then decisions about quality, promotion, and distribution will strongly affect price. If price is a key positioning factor then price will strongly affect decisions on the other marketing mix elements. In most cases, the company will consider all the marketing mix decisions together when developing the marketing program.

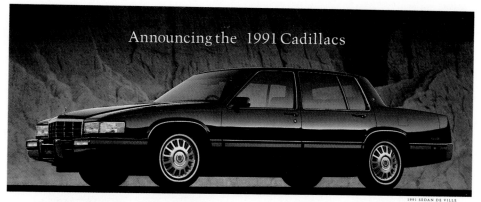

# Announcing the 1991 Cadillacs

1991 SEDAN DE VILLE

## Canada's most successful luxury automobiles gain new stature.

SUBSTANCE BEHIND THE STYLE

Behind the new styling of the 1991 Cadillac Fleetwood and De Ville lies the full-size, six-passenger luxury afforded by the longest wheelbase of any front-drive sedans.

A new, more powerful, 4.9 litre V8 generates 200 horsepower to let you pass and merge with confidence. A new electronically controlled, four-speed automatic transmission assures

impressively smooth shifts, even at highway speeds. Fleetwood and De Ville afford you the largest interiors of any front-drive sedans.

Computer Command Ride, a new speed-sensitive suspension, softens the ride for added comfort in city driving, then firms automatically at highway speeds for impressive stability and control.* The reassuring control of sophisticated anti-lock brakes are standard, helping to maintain steering control on a variety of road surfaces.

Plus a no-deductible, 3 year/100,000 km complete vehicle coverage warranty and a no charge scheduled maintenance program.* 1991 Cadillacs, Canada's most successful luxury automobiles.

CADILLAC STYLE

*See your dealer for terms of this limited warranty
*Optional on 1991 Sedan De Ville.

Cadillac positions its sedans on luxury, quality, and other nonprice factors—the price reflects this position.

## COSTS

Costs set the floor for the price that the company can set for its product. The company wants to charge a price that covers all its costs for producing, distributing, and selling the product, plus a fair rate of return for its effort and risk.

A company's costs take two forms, fixed and variable. **Fixed costs** (also known as overhead) are costs that do not vary with production or sales level. A company must pay bills each month for rent, heat, interest, and executive salaries, whatever the company's output. Fixed costs are incurred no matter what the production level.

**Variable costs** vary directly with the level of production. Each issue of Maclean's magazine involves a cost of paper, ink, and other inputs. These costs tend to be the same for each unit produced. They are called variable because their total varies with the number of units produced.

**Total costs** are the sum of the fixed and variable cost for any given level of production. Management wants to charge a price that will at least cover the total production costs at a given level of production.

The company must watch its costs carefully. If it costs the company more than it does competitors to produce and sell a product, the company will have to charge a higher price or make less profit, putting it at a competitive disadvantage.

## ORGANIZATIONAL CONSIDERATIONS

Management must decide who, within the organization, should set prices. Companies handle pricing in a variety of ways. In small companies, prices are often set by top management rather than by the marketing or sales department. In large companies, pricing is typically handled by divisional or product line managers. In industrial markets, salespeople may be allowed to negotiate with customers within certain price ranges. Even here, top management sets the pricing objectives and policies and often approves the prices proposed by lower-level management or salespeople.[3] In industries where pricing is a key factor (steel, railroads, pulp and paper, oil), companies will often have a pricing department to set prices or help others in setting the best prices. This department reports to the marketing department or top management.

# External Factors Affecting Pricing Decisions

## THE MARKET AND DEMAND

Costs set the floor for prices, and the market and demand set the ceiling. Both consumer and industrial buyers balance the price of a product or service against the benefits of owning it. Thus, before setting prices, the marketer must understand the relationship between price and demand for its product.

In this section, we will look at how the price-demand relationship varies for different types of markets and at how buyer perceptions of price affect the pricing decision. Then we will discuss methods for measuring the price-demand relationship.

## PRICING IN DIFFERENT TYPES OF MARKETS

The seller's pricing freedom varies with different types of markets. Economists recognize four types of markets, each presenting a different pricing challenge.

Under **pure competition**, the market consists of many buyers and sellers trading in a uniform commodity such as wheat, copper, or financial securities. No single buyer or seller has much effect on the going market price. A seller cannot charge more than the going price, because buyers can obtain as much as they need at this price. Sellers would not charge less than the market price, because they can sell all they want at the market price. If the price and profits rise, new sellers can easily enter the market. Sellers in these markets do not spend much time on marketing strategy since the role of marketing research, product development, pricing, advertising, and sales promotion is small as long as the market stays purely competitive.

Under **monopolistic competition**, the market consists of many buyers and sellers who trade over a range of prices rather than a single market price. The reason for the price range is that sellers are able to differentiate their offers to the buyers. Either the physical product can be varied in quality, features, or style, or the accompanying services can be varied. Buyers see differences in sellers' products and will pay different prices. Sellers try to develop differentiated offers for different customer segments and freely use branding, advertising, and personal selling, in addition to price, to set their offers apart. Because there are many competitors, each firm is less affected by competitors' marketing strategies than in oligopolistic markets.

Under **oligopolistic competition**, the market consists of a few sellers who are highly sensitive to each other's pricing and marketing strategies. The product can be uniform (steel, aluminum) or nonuniform (cars, computers). There are few sellers because it is difficult for new sellers to enter the market. Each seller is alert to competitors' strategies and moves. If a steel company like Dofasco slashes its price by ten percent, buyers will quickly switch to this supplier. Other steelmakers, like

In monopolistic competition, as in the small electronics product field, many sellers compete over a wide range of products.

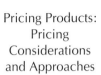
Stelco, will have to respond by lowering their prices or increasing their services. An oligopolist is never sure that it will gain anything permanent through a price cut. On the other hand, if the oligopolist raised the price, the competitors might not follow this lead. The oligopolist would have to retract its price increase or risk losing customers to competitors.

A **pure monopoly** consists of one seller. The seller may be a government monopoly (Canada Post), a private regulated monopoly (Hydro Quebec), or a private nonregulated monopoly (as Du Pont became when it introduced nylon). Pricing is handled differently in each case. A government monopoly can pursue a variety of pricing objectives. It might set a price below cost because the product is important to buyers and they cannot afford to pay full cost. Alternatively, the price might be set to cover costs or to produce fair revenues, or it might be set quite high to slow down consumption. In a regulated monopoly, the government permits a company, such as Bell Canada, to set rates that will yield a "fair return," one that will let the company maintain and expand its plant as needed.

## CONSUMER PERCEPTIONS OF PRICE AND VALUE

In the end, the consumer will decide whether a product's price is right. When setting prices, the company must consider consumer perceptions of price and how these perceptions affect consumers' buying decisions. Pricing decisions, like other marketing mix decisions, must be buyer-oriented:

> Pricing requires more than mere technical expertise. It requires creative judgment and a keen awareness of buyers' motivations...the key to effective pricing is the same one that opens doors...in other marketing functions: a creative awareness of who buyers are, why they buy, and how they make their buying decisions. The recognition that buyers differ in these dimensions is as important for effective pricing as it is for effective promotion, distribution, or product development.[4]

When consumers buy a product, they exchange something of value (the price) to get something of value (the benefits of having or using the product). Effective, buyer-oriented pricing involves understanding what value consumers place on the benefits they receive from the product and setting a price that fits this value. The benefits include both actual and perceived benefits. When a consumer buys a meal at a fancy restaurant, it is easy to figure out the value of the meal's ingredients. But it is very hard, even for the consumer, to measure the value of other satisfactions such as taste, a plush environment, relaxation, conversation, and status. These values will vary for different consumers and for different situations. As an example, when Domino's Pizza began operations in Canada, it conducted market surveys to determine what value Canadian consumers would attach to quality and service, the key "ingredients" of Domino's marketing strategy. The surveys revealed that consumers were willing to pay for these factors. Domino's charges a premium price for their pizzas and has captured 40% of the market in some areas of Ontario.[5]

Marketers must try to look at the consumer's reason for buying the product, and set price according to consumer perceptions of the product's value. Because consumers vary in the values they assign to different product features, marketers often vary their pricing strategies for different price segments. They offer different sets of product features at different prices. For example, jeans makers may offer lower-priced, rugged jeans for consumers who value utility and durability, and higher-priced designer jeans for customers who value fashion and status.

Buyer-oriented pricing means that the marketer cannot design a product and marketing program, and only then set the price. Good pricing begins with analyz-

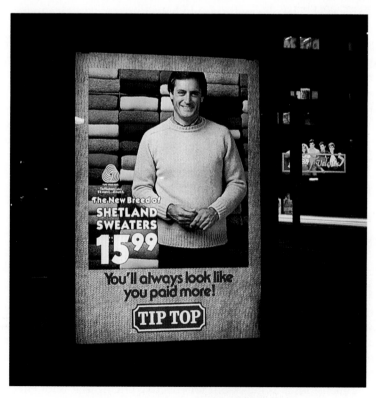

Tip Top positions its men's clothes on price and economy.

ing consumer needs and price perceptions. Price must be considered along with the other marketing mix variables before the marketing program is set.[6]

## ANALYZING THE PRICE-DEMAND RELATIONSHIP

Each price the company might charge will lead to a different level of demand. The relation between the price charged and the resulting demand level is shown in the familiar **demand curve** in Figure 11-2A. The demand curve shows the number of units the market will buy in a given time period at different prices that might be charged. In the normal case, demand and price are inversely related. That is, the higher the price, the lower the demand. Therefore, the company would sell less if it raised its price from $P_1$ to $P_2$. Consumers with limited budgets will probably buy less of the item if its price is too high.

Most demand curves slope downward in either a straight or a curved line, as in Figure 11-2A. But for prestige goods, the demand curve sometimes slopes upward, as in Figure 11-2B. A perfume company found that by raising its price from $P_1$ to $P_2$, it sold more perfume rather than less. Consumers thought the higher price meant a better or more desirable perfume. However, if too high a price is charged ($P_3$), the level of demand will be lower than at $P_2$.

Most companies try to measure their demand curves. The type of market makes a difference. In a monopoly, the demand curve shows the total market demand resulting from different prices. If the company faces competition, its demand at different prices will depend on whether competitors' prices stay constant or change with the company's prices. Here, we will assume that competitors' prices remain constant. Later in this chapter, we will discuss what happens when competitors' prices change.

The measurement of a demand curve requires an estimation of demand at different prices. In measuring the price-demand relationship, the market researcher must not allow other factors affecting demand to vary. If a company raised its advertising budget when it lowered its price, we would not know how much of the increased demand was due to the lower price and how much to the increased advertising.

Economists show the impact of nonprice factors on demand through shifts of the demand curve, rather than movements along the demand curve. Suppose the

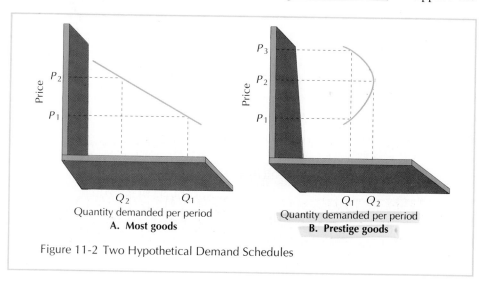

Figure 11-2 Two Hypothetical Demand Schedules

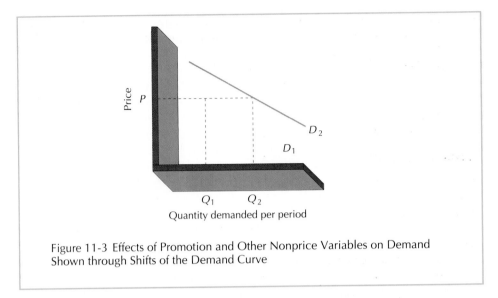

Figure 11-3 Effects of Promotion and Other Nonprice Variables on Demand Shown through Shifts of the Demand Curve

initial demand curve in Figure 11-3 is $D_1$. The seller is charging P and selling $Q_1$ units. Now suppose the economy suddenly improves, or the seller doubles its advertising budget. The higher demand is reflected through an upward shift of the demand curve from $D_1$ to $D_2$. Without changing the price P, the seller's demand is now $Q_2$.

## PRICE ELASTICITY OF DEMAND

Marketers need to know **price elasticity**, or how responsive demand will be to a change in price. Consider the two demand curves in Figure 11-4. In Figure 11-4A a price increase from $P_1$ to $P_2$ leads to a relatively small drop in demand from $Q_1$ to $Q_2$. In Figure 11-4B the same price increase leads to a large drop in demand from $Q_1$ to $Q_2$. If demand hardly changes with a small change in price, we say the demand is inelastic. In this case, buyers are less price sensitive. If demand changes a lot, we say the demand is elastic. Here buyers are more price sensitive.

What determines the price elasticity of demand? Buyers are less price sensitive

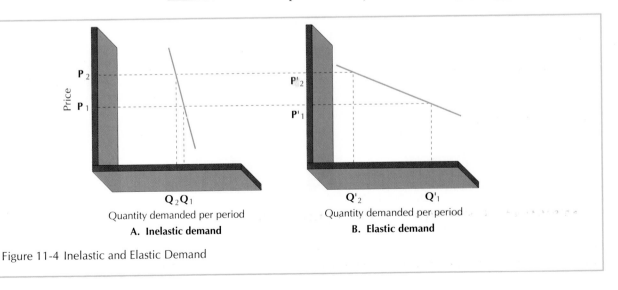

Figure 11-4 Inelastic and Elastic Demand

when the product is unique or when it is high in quality, prestige, or exclusiveness. They are also less price sensitive when substitute products are hard to find or when they cannot easily compare the quality of substitutes. Finally, buyers are less price sensitive when the total expenditure for a product is low relative to their income or when the cost is shared by another party.[7]

If demand is elastic rather than inelastic, sellers will consider lowering their price. A lower price will produce more total revenue. This makes sense as long as the extra costs of producing and selling more do not exceed the extra revenue.

## COMPETITORS' PRICES AND OFFERS

Additional external factors affecting the company's pricing decisions are competitors' prices and their possible reactions to the company's pricing moves. Consumers evaluate a product's price and value against the prices and values of comparable products. In addition, the company's pricing strategy may affect the nature of the competition it faces—a high-price, high-margin strategy may attract competition, whereas a low-price, low-margin strategy may stop competitors or drive them out of the market.

The company needs to learn the price and quality of each competitor's offer. This can be done in several ways. The firm can send out comparison shoppers to price and compare competitors' offers. The firm can get competitors' price lists and buy competitors' equipment and take it apart. The firm can also ask buyers how they view the price and quality of each competitor's offer.

Once the company is aware of competitors' prices and offers, it can use them as a starting point for its own pricing. If the firm's offer is similar to a major competitor's offer, the firm will have to price close to the competitor or lose sales. If the firm's offer is not as good, the firm will not be able to charge as much as the competitor. If the firm's offer is better, the firm can charge more than the competitor. Basically, the firm will use price to position its offer relative to competitors.

## OTHER EXTERNAL FACTORS

When setting prices, the company must also consider other factors in its external environment. For example, economic conditions can have a strong impact on the results of the firm's pricing strategies. Economic factors such as inflation, boom or recession, and interest rates affect pricing decisions because they affect both the costs of producing a product and consumer perceptions of the product's price and value.

The company must consider what impact its prices will have on other parties in its environment. How will resellers react to various prices? The company should set prices that give resellers a fair profit, encourage their support, and help them to sell the product effectively. The government is another important external influence on pricing decisions. Marketers need to know the laws affecting price and to make sure their pricing policies are legal. The major laws affecting price are summarized in Marketing Highlight 11-1.

# GENERAL PRICING APPROACHES

The price the company charges will be somewhere between one that is too low to produce a profit and one that is too high to produce any demand. Figure 11-5 summarizes

# MARKETING HIGHLIGHT 11-1
## Price Decisions and Public Policy

In 1986, the new federal Competition Act was enacted and the existing pricing laws were incorporated into this act. The laws cover price discrimination, predatory pricing, discriminatory promotional al-lowances, misleading price advertising, and resale price maintenance.

### Price Discrimination
Under section 34a of the Act it is illegal for a supplier to charge different prices to competitors purchasing similar quantities of goods.

### Predatory Pricing
Sections 34b and 34c of the Act prohibit pricing practices that can substantially lessen competition. The sections do not preclude price-cutting at the retail level.

### Discriminatory Promotional Allowances
Section 35 of the Act makes it illegal for sellers or their customers to receive or seek any type of promotional allowance, such as discounts or rebates, not offered on a proportional basis.

### Misleading Price Advertising
Under Section 36 of the Act it is illegal to misrepresent the regular price at which a product is usually sold. The federal government has actively enforced this section and hundreds of convictions have occurred since the addition of this legislation in 1960. Companies convicted of misleading price advertising are fined and the cases are published to inform the public.

### Resale Price Maintenance
Section 38 of the Act prohibits manufacturers from requiring resellers to sell their products at a stipulated price.

---

the major considerations in setting price. Product costs set a floor to the price; consumer perceptions of the product's value set the ceiling. The company must consider competitors' prices and other external and internal factors to find the best price between these two extremes.

Companies set prices by selecting a general pricing approach that includes one or more of these three sets of factors. We will look at the following approaches: the cost-based approach (cost-plus pricing, breakeven analysis, and target profit pricing), the buyer-based approach (perceived-value pricing), and the competition-based approach (going-rate and sealed-bid pricing).

## Cost-Based Pricing

### COST-PLUS PRICING

The simplest pricing method is **cost-plus pricing**, which means adding a standard markup to the cost of the product. An appliance retailer might pay a manufacturer $20 for a toaster and mark it up to sell at $30, which is a 50% markup on cost. The retailer's gross margin is ten dollars. If the store's operating costs amount to eight dollars per toaster sold, the retailer's profit margin will be two dollars.[8]

The manufacturer who made the toaster could also have used cost-plus pricing. If the manufacturer's standard cost of producing the toaster was $16, it might have added a 25% markup, setting the price to the retailer at $20. Construction companies calculate job bids by estimating the total project cost and adding a standard markup for profit. Lawyers and other professionals typically price by adding a

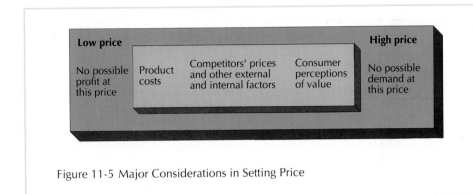

| Low price | | | | High price |
|---|---|---|---|---|
| No possible profit at this price | Product costs | Competitors' prices and other external and internal factors | Consumer perceptions of value | No possible demand at this price |

Figure 11-5 Major Considerations in Setting Price

standard markup to their costs. Some sellers tell their customers they will charge them cost plus a specified markup; for example, aerospace companies price this way to the government.

Markups vary a lot among different goods. Some common markups (on price, not cost) are 62% for bakeries, 50% for jewelry stores, and 20% for supermarkets.[9] In the retail grocery industry, coffee, canned milk, and sugar tend to have low markups, while frozen foods, jellies, and some canned products have high markups. The varying markups reflect differences in unit costs, sales, turnover, and manufacturers' brands versus private brands. Markups are generally higher on seasonal items (to cover the risk of not selling), specialty items, slower- moving items, items with high storage and handling costs, and items with inelastic demand.

Does the use of standard markups to set prices seem logical? Generally, any pricing method that ignores current demand and competition is not likely to lead to the best price. The retail graveyard is full of merchants who insisted on using standard markups after their competitors had gone into discount pricing.

Still, markup pricing remains popular for many reasons. First, sellers are more certain about costs than about demand. By tying the price to cost, sellers simplify pricing—they do not have to make frequent adjustments as demand changes. Second, where all firms in the industry use this pricing method, prices tend to be similar, and price competition is minimized. Third, many people feel that cost-plus pricing is fairer to both buyers and sellers. Sellers do not take advantage of buyers when buyers' demand becomes great, yet the sellers earn a fair return on their investment.

## BREAKEVEN ANALYSIS AND TARGET PROFIT PRICING

Another cost-oriented pricing approach is **breakeven pricing** or a variation called target profit pricing. The firm tries to determine the price at which it will break even or make the profit it is seeking. Target pricing is used by General Motors, which prices its automobiles to achieve a 15 to 20% profit on its investment. This pricing method is also used by public utilities, which are constrained to make a fair return on their investment.

Target pricing uses the concept of a breakeven chart. A breakeven chart shows the total cost and total revenue expected at different levels of sales. Figure 11-6 shows a hypothetical breakeven chart and analysis. Fixed costs are $6 million, regardless of sales volume. Variable costs of five dollars per unit are added to fixed costs to form total costs, which rise with volume. The total revenue curve starts at zero and rises with each unit sold. The slope of the total revenue curve also reflects

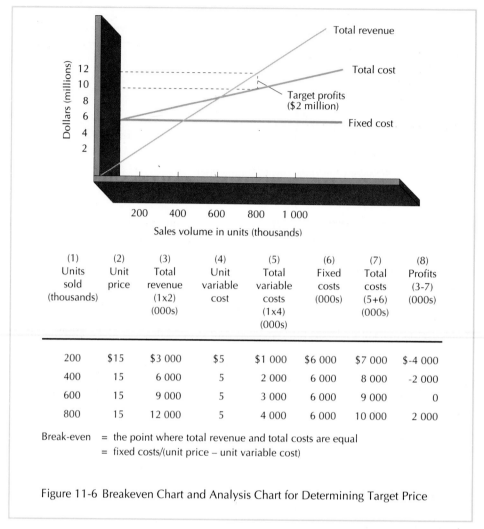

| (1) Units sold (thousands) | (2) Unit price | (3) Total revenue (1x2) (000s) | (4) Unit variable cost | (5) Total variable costs (1x4) (000s) | (6) Fixed costs (000s) | (7) Total costs (5+6) (000s) | (8) Profits (3-7) (000s) |
|---|---|---|---|---|---|---|---|
| 200 | $15 | $3 000 | $5 | $1 000 | $6 000 | $7 000 | $-4 000 |
| 400 | 15 | 6 000 | 5 | 2 000 | 6 000 | 8 000 | -2 000 |
| 600 | 15 | 9 000 | 5 | 3 000 | 6 000 | 9 000 | 0 |
| 800 | 15 | 12 000 | 5 | 4 000 | 6 000 | 10 000 | 2 000 |

Break-even = the point where total revenue and total costs are equal
= fixed costs/(unit price – unit variable cost)

Figure 11-6 Breakeven Chart and Analysis Chart for Determining Target Price

the price. Here the price is $15 (for example, the company's revenue is $12 million on 800,000 units, or $15 per unit).

At $15, the company must sell at least 600,000 units to break even; that is, for total revenue to cover total cost. If the company wants a target profit of $2 million, it must sell at least 800,000 units at a price of $15 each to obtain the $12 million in total revenue needed to cover costs ($10 million) plus profits ($2 million). If the company is willing to charge a higher price, say $20, it will not need to sell as many units to break even or to achieve its target profit.

However, as the price increases, demand decreases and the market may not buy even the lower volume needed to break even at the higher price. Much depends on the relationship between price and demand. For example, suppose the company calculates that, given its current fixed and variable costs, it must charge a price of $30 for the product in order to earn its desired target profit. But marketing research shows that few consumers will pay more than $25 for the product. In this case, the company has to trim its costs in order to lower the breakeven point so that it can charge the lower price that consumers expect. Thus, although breakeven analysis and target profit pricing can help the company to determine minimum prices needed to cover expected costs and profits, they do not take the price-demand relationship into account. When using this method, the company must also consider the impact of price on the sales volume needed to realize target profits and the likelihood that the needed volume will be achieved at each possible price.

## Buyer-Based Pricing

An increasing number of companies are basing their prices on the product's perceived value. **Perceived value pricing** uses buyers' perception of value, not the seller's cost, as the key to pricing. The company uses the nonprice variables in the marketing mix to build up perceived value in the buyers' minds. Price is set to match the perceived value.

Consider the various prices different restaurants charge for the same item. A consumer who wants a cup of coffee and a slice of apple pie may pay $1.50 in a fast-food outlet, $3.00 at a family restaurant, $5.00 at a hotel coffee shop, $7.00 for hotel room service, and $9.00 at an elegant restaurant. Each succeeding restaurant can charge more because of the value added by the atmosphere.

Any company using perceived-value pricing must find out the value in the buyers' minds for different competitive offers. In the last example, consumers could be asked how much they would pay for the same coffee and pie in the different surroundings. Sometimes consumers could be asked how much they would pay for each benefit added to the offer. If the seller charges more than the value perceived by buyers, the company's sales will suffer. Many companies overprice their products, and their products sell poorly. Other companies underprice. Although their products sell very well, they produce less revenue than if price was raised to the perceived value level.[10]

## Competition-Based Pricing

### GOING-RATE PRICING

In **going-rate pricing**, the firm bases its price largely on competitors' prices, with less attention paid to its own costs or demand. The firm might charge the same, more, or less than its major competitors. In oligopolistic industries that sell a commodity such as steel, paper, or fertilizer, firms normally charge the same price. The smaller firms "follow the leader." They change their prices when the market leader's prices change, rather than when their own demand or cost changes. Some firms may charge more or less, but they hold the amount of difference constant. Thus minor gasoline retailers usually charge a cent per litre less than the major oil companies, without letting the difference increase or decrease.

Going-rate pricing is quite popular. Where demand elasticity is difficult to measure, firms feel that the going price represents the collective wisdom of the industry concerning the price that will yield a fair return. They also feel that holding to the going price will avoid harmful price wars.

### SEALED-BID PRICING

Competition-based pricing is also used when firms bid for jobs. Using **sealed-bid pricing**, the firm bases its price on how it thinks competitors will price rather than on its own costs or demand. The firm wants to win the contract, and this requires pricing lower than the other firms. Yet the firm cannot set its price below a certain level. It cannot price below cost without harming its position. On the other hand, the higher it sets its price above its costs, the lower its chance of getting the contract.

# Summary

In spite of the increased role of nonprice factors in the modern marketing process, price remains an important element in the marketing mix. Many internal and external factors influence the company's pricing decisions. Internal factors include the firm's marketing objectives, marketing mix strategy, cost, and organization for pricing.

The pricing strategy is largely determined by the company's target market and positioning objectives. Common pricing objectives include survival, current profit maximization, market-share leadership, and product quality leadership.

Price is only one of the marketing mix tools the company uses to accomplish its objective, and pricing decisions affect and are affected by product design, distribution, and promotion decisions. Price decisions must be carefully coordinated with the other marketing mix decisions when designing the marketing program.

Costs set the floor for the company's price—the price must cover all the costs of making and selling the product, plus a fair rate of return. Management must decide who within the organization is responsible for setting price. In large companies, some pricing authority may be delegated to lower-level managers and salespeople, but top management usually sets pricing policies and approves proposed prices. Production, finance, and accounting managers also influence pricing.

External factors that influence pricing decisions include the nature of the market and demand, competitors' prices and offers, and other external factors such as the economy, reseller needs, and government actions. The seller's pricing freedom varies with different types of market. Pricing is specially challenging in markets characterized by monopolistic competition or oligopoly.

In the end, the consumer decides whether the company has set the right price. The consumer weighs the price against the perceived values of using the product—if the price exceeds the sum of the value, consumers will not buy the product. Consumers differ in the values they assign to different product features, and marketers often vary their pricing strategies for different price segments. When assessing the market and demand, the company estimates the demand schedule, which shows the probable quantity purchased per period at alternative price levels. The more inelastic the demand, the higher the company can set its price. Demand and consumer value perceptions set the ceiling for prices.

Consumers compare a product's price to the price of competitors' products. The company must learn the price and quality of competitors' offers and use them as a starting point for its own pricing.

The company can select one or a combination of three general pricing approaches: the cost-based approach (cost-plus or breakeven analysis and target profit pricing), the buyer-based (perceived-value pricing) approach, and the competition-based (going-rate or sealed-bid pricing) approach.

# QUESTIONS FOR DISCUSSION

1. Certain "inexpensive" products that waste energy, provide few servings per container, or require frequent maintenance may cost much more than products selling for higher prices. How can marketers use cost information to gain a competitive edge in pricing and promoting products?

2. Dofasco, a major sheet metal producer, has developed a process for galvanizing steel sheets so that they can be painted—something previously impossible. Such sheets could be used to prevent rust in car body parts. What price setting factor should Dofasco consider in pricing this new product?

3. What different kinds of firms might have the different marketing objectives of survival, profit maximization, market share leadership, and product quality leadership? Give examples.

4. Which type of cost is more relevant in setting the price of a product—fixed costs or variable costs?

5. What are the major factors influencing price setting in each of these four market types—pure competition, monopolistic competition, oligopolistic competition, and pure monopoly? Give examples of these market types and describe the prices of products available in each.

6. In a supermarket, which will have the higher price elasticity of demand—hamburger or steak? If the demand for steak is elastic, what effect would raising its price have on meat department profits?

7. In test markets, Procter & Gamble replaced 450 gram packages of regular Folgers coffee with 360 gram "fast roast" packages. The fast roasting processing allows Procter & Gamble to use fewer green coffee beans per pack without affecting flavor or the number of servings per package. What pricing approach was appropriate for setting the price of this coffee—cost-based, buyer-based, or competition-based?

8. You have inherited an automatic car wash with annual fixed costs of $50,000 and variable costs of $0.50 per car. You believe people will pay one dollar to have a car washed. What would be your breakeven volume at that price?

9. Sales of Gordon's gin increased when prices were raised 22% over a two- year period. What does this fact say about the demand curve and the elasticity of demand for Gordon's gin? What does it suggest about perceived-value pricing in marketing alcoholic beverages?

10. Columnist Jack Howard jokes that federal law requires this message under the sticker price of new cars: WARNING TO STUPID PEOPLE: DO NOT PAY THIS AMOUNT. Why is a car's sticker price generally higher than its actual selling price? How do car dealers set the actual prices of their cars?

# KEY TERMS

**Breakeven pricing** Setting price to break even on the costs of making and marketing a product.

**Cost-plus pricing**  Adding a standard markup to the cost of the product.

**Demand curve**  A curve that shows the number of units the market will buy in a given time period at different prices that might be charged.

**Fixed costs**  Costs that do not vary with production or sales level.

**Going-rate pricing**  Setting price based largely on following competitors' prices rather than on company cost or demand.

**Monopolistic competition**  A market in which many buyers and sellers trade over a range of prices rather than a single market price.

**Oligopolistic competition**  A market in which there are a few sellers who are highly sensitive to each other's pricing and marketing strategies.

**Perceived-value pricing**  Setting price based on buyers' perception of value rather than on the seller's cost.

**Price**  The amount of money charged for a product or service, or the sum of the values consumers exchange for the benefits of having or using the product or service.

**Price elasticity**  A measure of the responsiveness of demand to changes in price.

**Pure competition**  A market in which many buyers and sellers trade in a uniform commodity—no single buyer or seller has much effect on the going market price.

**Pure monopoly**  A market in which there is a single seller—it may be a government monopoly, a private regulated monopoly, or a private nonregulated monopoly.

**Sealed-bid pricing**  Setting price based on how the firm thinks competitors will price rather than on its own costs or demand—used when a company bids for jobs.

**Total costs**  The sum of the fixed and variable cost for any given level of production.

**Variable costs**  Costs that vary directly with the level of production.

# REFERENCES

1. From various sources, including Renate Lerch, "Sony Not Afraid of Competition," *The Financial Post*, April 26, 1986, p. 45; Gendis Inc., *Annual Report*, various issues; and *Household Facilities and Equipment 1989*, Statistics Canada, Catalogue 64-202.

2. David J. Schwartz, *Marketing Today: A Basic Approach* (3rd ed.) (New York: Harcourt Brace Jovanovich, 1981), pp. 270-273.

3. See P. Ronald Stephenson, William L. Cron, and Gary L. Frazier, "Delegating Pricing Authority to the Sales Force: The Effects on Sales and Profit Performance," *Journal of Marketing*, Spring 1979, pp. 21-28.

4. Thomas Nagle, "Pricing as Creative Marketing," *Business Horizons*, July-August 1981, p. 19.

5. Shonee McKay, "Pricing Strategies: How to Choose the One That's Right For

You," *Canadian Business*, July 1986, pp. 69-71.

6. See Thomas T. Nagle, *The Strategy and Tactics of Pricing* (Englewood Cliffs, NJ: Prentice-Hall, 1987), pp. 1-9; and Allan Magrath, "Tactical Steps to Competitive Pricing," *Marketing*, June 26, 1989, pp. B10, B16; and Allan Magrath, "Price - An Effective Marketing Tool," *Marketing*, September 18, 1989, p. B13, B17.

7. Nagle, *The Strategy and Tactics of Pricing*, Chap. 3.

8. The arithmetic of markups and margins is discussed in Appendix A, "Marketing Arithmetic."

9. *Market Research Handbook*, 1990, Statistics Canada, Catalogue 63-224.

10. For more on value-based pricing see John L. Forbis and Nitin T. Mehta, "Value-Based Strategies for Industrial Products," *Business Horizons*, May-June 1981, pp. 32-42; and Ely S. Lurin, "Make Sure Product's Price Reflects Its True Value," *Marketing News*, May 8, 1987, p. 8.

# CHAPTER 12

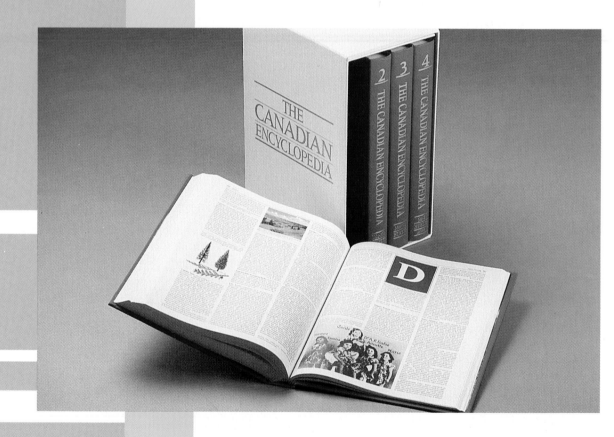

# Pricing Products:
# Pricing Strategies

## CHAPTER OBJECTIVES

After reading this chapter, you should be able to:
1. Describe the major strategies for pricing new products.
2. Discuss how companies find a set of prices that maximizes the profits for the total product mix.
3. Explain how companies adjust their prices to take into account different types of customers and situations.
4. Tell why companies decide to change their prices.

One of the most successful books published in Canada was the first edition of *The Canadian Encyclopedia*, a three-volume set that provided comprehensive information on Canada. Mel Hurtig, the owner of Hurtig Publishers, was responsible for this massive work, which sold 155,000 copies. He began planning for the second edition shortly after the first edition was published in 1985.

The second edition of *The Canadian Encyclopedia*, a four-volume set, cost $8.5 million to produce and a sales target of 150,000 copies was set. Approximately $750,000 was spent to advertise and promote the second edition, which was launched in the fall of 1988. The marketing plan was as follows:

— Extensive prepublication promotion to all bookstores in Canada (this activity started in 1987).
— An introductory retail price of $175, later to increase to $225.

— A rebate to customers who had purchased the first edition. They could trade in the first edition and receive a $50 credit on the second edition, reducing the price to $125.
— Varying discounts to retailers, depending on the volume purchased. Coles, one of the leading book retailers in Canada, ordered 20,000 copies and received a 55% discount (Coles' cost was $78.75). Small bookstores that ordered fewer than five copies received a 30% discount (the cost to these retailers was $122.50).

Mel Hurtig had expected that some retailers would offer the book at less than the recommended retail price of $175, but was not prepared for what happened. Coles deep-discounted the book to $99, a retail price that was less than that for which the small bookstores could buy the book from Hurtig. W.H. Smith, another large chain, quickly followed suit and the result was that the two chains sold a large number of copies of *The Canadian Encyclopedia* during the Christmas season and also brought extra traffic into their stores.

However, the small independent bookstores were extremely angry and began returning their copies to Hurtig. All told, Hurtig issued $800,000 in refunds to these stores. The book was still profitable but less so than had been expected, as 23,000 sets of the 113,000 printed remained unsold as of early 1989.

Hurtig tried to avoid this problem when he published *The Junior Encyclopedia*. The set, targeted at eight to 15 year olds, had an introductory price of $159.95, that later rose to $189.95. This time, Hurtig did not sell the set through retailers. Instead, *Junior* was sold through the mail. Hurtig invited bookstores to display and take orders for the book. The bookstore received $20 for every order they took. This way Hurtig got more of the price but the book cost more to market—promoting *Junior* cost over $3 million, including a direct mail campaign that cost over $1 million. Hurtig later modified the plan because of the threat of a postal strike and sold the encyclopedia through bookstores.

Setting prices is an important issue and marketers have to consider the reactions of distributors as well as consumers. As Mel Hurtig learned, there may be long-term consequences to short-term actions.[1]

In this chapter, we will look at pricing dynamics. A company does not set a single price, but develops a pricing structure that covers different items in its line. This pricing structure changes over time as products move through their life cycles. The company adjusts product prices to reflect changing costs and demand, and to account for variations in buyers and situations. As the competitive environment changes, at times the company considers initiating price changes and at other times responds to price changes by other companies.

This chapter will examine the major pricing strategies available to management.[2] We will look at new product pricing strategies for products in the introductory stage of the product life cycle; product-mix pricing strategies for related products in the mix; price-adjustment strategies that account for customer differences and changing situations; and strategies for initiating and responding to price changes.

# New Product Pricing Strategies

Pricing strategies usually change as the product passes through the product life cycle. The introductory stage is especially challenging. We can distinguish between pricing a real product innovation that is patent-protected and pricing a product that imitates existing products.

## Pricing an Innovative Product

Companies introducing a new patent-protected innovative product can choose between market-skimming pricing and market penetration pricing.

## MARKET-SKIMMING PRICING

Many companies that invent new products set high prices initially to "skim" the market. Du Pont is a prime user of **market skimming pricing**. On its new discoveries—cellophane, nylon—it finds the highest price it can charge given the benefits of its new product over other products customers might buy. Du Pont sets a price that makes it just worthwhile for some segments of the market to adopt the new material. After the initial sales slow down, it lowers the price to draw in the next price-sensitive layer of customers. In this way, Du Pont skims a maximum amount of revenue from the various segments of the market. Market skimming was also used when Trivial Pursuit was introduced in Canada. After production levels increased to match demand, both the price of the game and the new card sets were lowered.

Market skimming makes sense only under certain conditions. First, the product's quality and image must support the higher price and enough buyers must want the product at that price. Second, the costs of producing a small volume cannot be so high that they cancel the advantage of charging more. Finally, competitors should not be able to enter the market easily and undercut the high price.

## MARKET PENETRATION PRICING

Other companies set a low price on their innovative product, hoping to attract a large number of buyers and win a large market share. Texas Instruments (TI) is a prime user of this **market penetration pricing**. TI will build a large plant, set its price as low as possible, win a large market share, realize falling costs through experience curve effects, and cut its price further as costs fall.[3]

Several conditions favor setting a low price. The market must be highly price-sensitive so that a low price produces more market growth. Production and distribution costs must fall as production volume increases, and the low price must help to keep out the competition.[4]

## Pricing an Imitative New Product

A company that plans to develop an imitative new product faces a product-positioning problem. It must decide where to position the product on quality and price. Figure 12-1 shows nine possible price-quality strategies. If the existing market leader has taken Box One by producing the premium product and charging the highest price, the newcomer might prefer to use one of the other strategies. The newcomer could design a high-quality product and charge a medium price (Box Two), design an average-quality product and charge an average price (Box Five), and so on. The newcomer must consider the size and growth rate of the market in each box and the competitors it would face.

# PRODUCT MIX PRICING STRATEGIES

The strategy for setting a price on a product has to be changed when the product is part of a product mix. In this case the firm looks for a set of prices that maximizes the profits on the total product mix. Pricing is difficult because the various products have

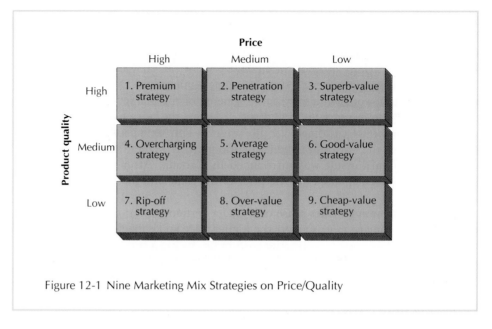

Figure 12-1 Nine Marketing Mix Strategies on Price/Quality

related demand and costs, and face different degrees of competition. We will look at four situations.

## Product Line Pricing

Companies usually develop product lines rather than single products. For example, Panasonic offers five different color video sound cameras, ranging from a simple one weighing 2.1 kilograms to a complex one weighing 2.9 kilograms that includes automatic focusing, fade control, and a two-speed zoom lens. Each successive camera in the line offers more features. In product line pricing, management must decide on the price steps to set between the various cameras.

The price steps should take into account cost differences between the cameras, customer evaluations of the different features, and competitors' prices. If the price difference between two successive cameras is small, buyers will buy the more advanced camera, and this will increase company profits if the cost difference is smaller than the price difference. If the price difference is large, customers will buy the less advanced camera.

In many industries, sellers use well-established price points for the products in their line. Thus men's clothing stores might carry men's suits at three price levels: $185, $285, and $385. The customers will associate low-, average-, and high-quality suits with the three price "points." Even if the three prices are raised a little, men will normally buy suits at their preferred price point. The seller's task is to establish perceived quality differences that support the price differences.

## Optional Product Pricing

Many companies offer to sell optional or accessory products along with their main product. A car buyer can order electric windows, defoggers, and cruise control.

**THE SONY 8MM HANDYCAMS. TRY ONE ON FOR SIZE.**

On the left, the wondrous Sony F77 8mm Handycam,™ a prime example of the Sony Video8 technology which, with its infinitely superior picture quality has helped revolutionize video recording. When it comes to innovative features, the F77 is clearly a leader.

On the right, the wondrously small Sony TR7 8mm Handycam, a prime example of the Sony miniaturization technology that made the Sony Traveller into the world's favourite travelling companion. Less than 2 pounds in weight and small enough to hold in the palm of one hand, or slip into pocket, purse or portfolio, the TR7 is a mini-video studio with many of the features of its big

brother on the left, including, of course, the outstanding Sony broadcast picture quality, that enabled the TR7 to shoot its own TV commercials.

And in between—though not shown here—a vast array of other wondrous Sony 8mm Handycams with a diversity of comprehensive features sufficient to satisfy all your video requirements. Please come and view these many wonders for yourself and try them on for size. One will fit you.

CELEBRATING 35 YEARS IN CANADA
**SONY.**
SONY OF CANADA LTD.

TM HANDYCAM is a trademark of Sony Corp.

Here Sony advertises two products from its wide product line.

Pricing these options is a sticky problem. Automobile companies have to decide which items to build into the base price and which items to offer as options. General Motors' normal pricing strategy is to advertise a stripped-down model for $10,000 to pull people into showrooms, but to devote most of the showroom space to showing loaded cars at $12,000 or $14,000.

The economy model is stripped of so many comforts and conveniences that most buyers reject it. When GM launched its new front-wheel drive J-cars in the early 1980s, it took a clue from the Japanese automakers and included in the sticker price many useful items previously sold only as options. Now the advertised price represented a well-equipped car.

## Captive Product Pricing

Companies in some industries make products that must be used with the main product. Examples of captive products are razor blades and camera film. Producers of the main products (razors and cameras) often price them low and set high markups on the supplies. Thus Kodak prices its cameras low because it makes its money on selling film. Those camera makers who do not sell film have to price their cameras higher in order to make the same overall profit.

## By-Product Pricing

In producing processed meats, petroleum products, chemicals, and other products, there are often by-products. If the by-products have no value and getting rid of them is costly, this will affect the pricing of the main product. The manufacturer will seek a market for these by-products and should accept any price that covers more than the cost of storing and delivering them. This will let the seller reduce the main product's price to make it more competitive.

## Product-Bundle Pricing

Using product-bundle pricing, sellers often combine several of their products and offer the bundle at a reduced price. Thus, theaters and sports teams sell season tickets at less than the cost of single tickets; hotels sell specially priced packages that include room, meals and entertainment; automobile companies sell attractively priced options packages. Price bundling can promote the sales of products consumers might not otherwise buy, but the combined price must be low enough to get them to buy the bundle.[5]

# PRICE-ADJUSTMENT STRATEGIES

Companies adjust their basic price to account for various customer differences and changing situations. We will look at the following adjustment strategies: discount pricing and allowances, discriminatory pricing, psychological pricing, promotional pricing, and geographical pricing.

## Discount Pricing and Allowances

Most companies will adjust their basic price to reward customers for certain acts, such as early payment of bills, volume purchases, and off-season buying. These price adjustments—called discounts and allowances—are described below.[6]

### CASH DISCOUNTS

A **cash discount** is a price reduction to buyers who pay their bills promptly. A typical example is "2/10, net 30," which means that payment is due within 30 days, but the buyer can deduct two percent if the bill is paid within ten days. The discount must be granted to all buyers meeting these terms. Such discounts are customary in many industries and help to improve the sellers' cash situation and reduce credit collection costs and bad debts.

### QUANTITY DISCOUNTS

A **quantity discount** is a price reduction to buyers who buy large volumes. A typical example is "ten dollars per unit for less than 100 units; nine dollars per unit for 100 or more units." Quantity discounts must be offered to all customers and must not exceed the seller's cost savings associated with selling large quantities. These savings include lower selling, inventory, and transportation expenses. Discounts provide an incentive to the customer to buy more from a given seller rather than to buy from many sources.[7]

## FUNCTIONAL DISCOUNTS

A **functional discount** (also called a trade discount) is offered by the seller to trade channel members who perform certain functions such as selling, storing, and record keeping. Manufacturers may offer different functional discounts to different trade channels because of the varying services they perform, but manufacturers must offer the same functional discounts within each trade channel. Functional discounts, while a common practice in the U.S., are illegal in Canada under the price discrimination provisions of The Competition Act (see Marketing Highlight 11-1, Chapter 11).

## SEASONAL DISCOUNTS

A **seasonal discount** is a price reduction to buyers who buy merchandise or services out of season. Seasonal discounts allow the seller to keep production steady during the year. Ski manufacturers will offer seasonal discounts to retailers in the spring and summer to encourage early ordering. Hotels, motels, and airlines will offer seasonal discounts in their slower selling periods.

While ski resorts charge top prices in winter, they often offer discounts in other seasons.

## ALLOWANCES

Allowances are other types of reductions from the list price. For example, trade-in allowances are price reductions given for turning in an old item when buying a new one. **Trade-in allowances** are most common in the automobile industry and are also given for some other durable goods. **Promotional allowances** are payments or price reductions to reward dealers for participating in advertising and sales-support programs.

## DISCRIMINATORY PRICING

Companies will often adjust their basic prices to allow for differences in customers, products, and locations. In **discriminatory pricing**, the company sells a product or service at two or more prices, where the difference in prices is not based on differences in costs. Discriminatory pricing takes several forms:

- **Customer segment pricing.** Different customers pay different prices for the same product or service. For example, museums will charge a lower admission for students and senior citizens.
- **Product-form pricing.** Different versions of the product are priced differently, but not according to differences in their costs. A dishwasher with a formica top might be priced at $460 and the same dishwasher with a wooden top might be priced at $480. Yet the wooden top only cost five dollars more to make than the formica top.
- **Location pricing.** Different locations are priced differently even though the cost of offering each location is the same. A theater varies its seat prices because of audience preferences for certain locations.
- **Time pricing.** Prices are varied seasonally, by the day, and even by the hour. Public utilities vary their prices to commercial users by time of day and weekend versus weekday. Bell Canada offers lower "off-peak" charges and resorts give seasonal discounts.

For discriminatory pricing to be an effective strategy for the company, certain conditions must exist. The market must be segmentable, and the segments must show different degrees of demand. Members of the segment paying the lower price should not be able to turn around and resell the product to the segment paying the higher price. Competitors should not be able to under-sell the firm in the segment being charged the higher price. Nor should the cost of segmenting and watching the market exceed the extra revenue obtained from price discrimination. The practice should not lead to customer resentment and ill-will. Finally, the discriminatory pricing used must be legal. With the current deregulation taking place in certain industries (such as airlines), companies in these industries have used more discriminatory pricing. Consider the price discrimination used by airlines:

> At one point, the passengers on a plane bound from Toronto to Vancouver were paying as many as eight different fares for the same flight due to the heated-up competition between Air Canada and Canadian Airlines. Many of the fares were aimed at segments of the market. The eight possible fares were: (1) $641 one-way for first class; (2) $485 one-way for executive class; (3) $458 one-way for economy class; (4) $435 one-way special economy class; (5) $504 for a return fare if the ticket was purchased 14 days in advance; (6) $299 for a return fare if the ticket was purchased 21 days in advance; (7) $229 for a one-way youth

standby; and (8) $366 for a return fare for senior citizens if the ticket was purchased 14 days in advance.

# Psychological Pricing

Price says something about the product. For example, many consumers use price to judge quality. A $50 bottle of perfume may contain only $3 worth of scent, but people are willing to pay $50 because the price seems to indicate something special.

In using **psychological pricing**, sellers consider the psychology of prices and not simply the economics. A study of the relationship between price and quality perceptions of cars found that consumers perceive higher- priced cars as having higher quality.[8] By the same token, higher-quality cars are perceived to be even higher priced than they actually are! When consumers can judge the quality of a product by examining it or by calling on past experience with it, they use price less to judge quality. But when consumers cannot judge quality because they lack the information or skill, price becomes an important quality signal.[9]

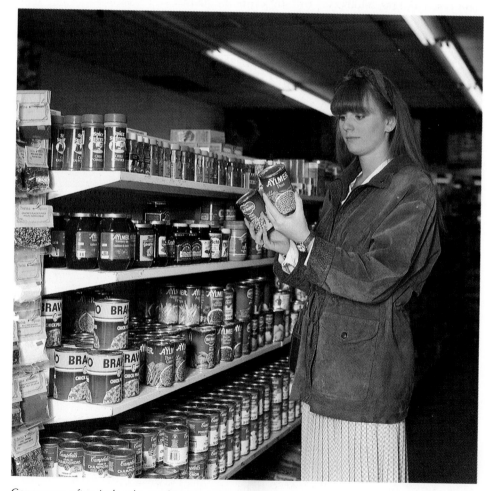

Consumers often judge the quality of products by the prices charged.

Another aspect of psychological pricing is the reference price. Buyers carry reference prices in their minds and refer to them when they look at a given product. The reference price might be formed by noting current prices, remembering past prices, or assessing the buying situation. Sellers can influence or use consumers' reference prices when setting prices. For example, a company could display its product next to more expensive ones in order to imply that it belongs in the same class. Department stores often sell women's clothing in separate departments differentiated by price. Clothing found in the more expensive department is assumed to be of better quality. Supermarkets, like Loblaws, can place less expensive store brands next to more expensive national brands to show the "bargain" store brand. Companies can also influence consumers' reference prices by stating high manufacturer's suggested prices, by indicating that the product was originally priced much higher, or by pointing to a competitor's higher price.

Even small differences in price can suggest product differences to consumers. Consider a stereo priced at $300 compared to one priced at $299.95. The actual price difference is only five cents, but the psychological difference can be much greater. For example, some consumers will see the $299.95 as a price in the $200 range rather than the $300 range. The $299.95 will more likely be seen as a bargain price, and the $300 price will suggest more quality.

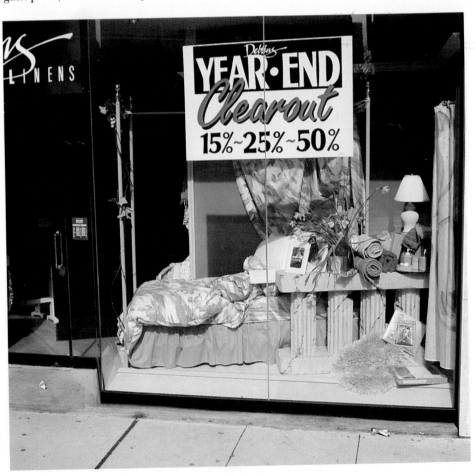

# Promotional Pricing

With **promotional pricing**, companies will temporarily price their products below the list price, and sometimes even below cost. Promotional pricing takes several forms. Supermarkets and department stores will price a few products as loss leaders to attract customers to the store in the hope that they will buy other items at normal markups. Sellers will also use special-event pricing in certain seasons to draw in more customers. Thus white sales are promotionally priced every January to attract shopping-weary customers into the stores. Manufacturers will sometimes offer cash rebates to consumers who buy the product from dealers within a specified time. The manufacturer sends the rebate directly to the customer. These rebates have recently been popular with automakers, and with durable goods and small appliance producers. The seller may simply offer discounts from normal prices to increase sales and reduce inventories. One study of Canadian consumers' reactions to retail "price-offs" found that consumers thought the "best deal in town" was more likely when substantial savings were announced (for example, 50% off), and depended upon the particular store doing the advertising (for example, a discount store).[10]

# Geographical Pricing

The company must decide how to price its products to customers located in different parts of the country. Should the company charge higher prices to distant customers to cover the higher shipping costs, but thereby risk losing their business? Or should the company charge the same to all customers regardless of location? We will look at five geographical pricing strategies for the following hypothetical situation:

> The Peerless Paper Company is located in Vancouver, British Columbia, and sells paper products to customers all over Canada and the United States. The cost of freight is high and affects the companies from which customers buy their paper. Peerless wants to establish a geographical pricing policy. It is trying to determine how to price a $100 order to three specific customers: Customer A (Edmonton); Customer B (San Francisco, California); and Customer C (Toronto).

## FOB ORIGIN PRICING

Peerless can ask each customer to pay the shipping cost from the Vancouver factory to the customer's location. All three customers would pay the same factory price of $100, with Customer A paying, say, ten dollars for shipping, Customer B paying $15, and Customer C paying $25. With **FOB origin pricing**, the goods are then placed free on board a carrier, at which point the title and responsibility pass to the customer, who pays the freight from the factory to the destination.

Supporters of FOB pricing feel that it is the fairest way to assess freight charges, because each customer picks up its own cost. The disadvantage, however, is that Peerless will be a high-cost firm to distant customers. If Peerless's main competitor is in Ontario, this competitor would outsell Peerless in Ontario. In fact, the competitor would outsell Peerless in most of the East, while Peerless would dominate the West. A vertical line could be drawn on a map connecting the cities where the two companies' price plus freight would just be equal. Peerless would have the price advantage west of this line, and its competitor would have the price advantage east of this line.

## UNIFORM DELIVERED PRICING

**Uniform delivered pricing** is the opposite of FOB pricing. Here the company charges the same price plus freight to all customers regardless of their location. The freight charge is set at the average freight cost. Suppose the average freight cost is $15. Uniform delivered pricing therefore results in a high charge to the Edmonton customer (who pays $15 freight instead of ten dollars) and a lower charge to the Toronto customer (who pay $15 instead of $25). The Edmonton customer would prefer to buy paper from another local paper company that uses FOB origin pricing. On the other hand, Peerless has a better chance to win the Toronto customer. Other advantages are that uniform delivered pricing is fairly easy to administer and lets the firm advertise its price nationally.

## ZONE PRICING

**Zone pricing** falls between FOB origin pricing and uniform delivered pricing. The company sets up two or more zones. All customers within a zone pay the same total price, and this price is higher in the more distant zones. Peerless might set up a West zone and charge ten dollars freight to all customers in this zone; a South zone and charge $15; and an East zone and charge $25. In this way, the customers within a given price zone receive no price advantage from the company. Customers in Edmonton and Regina pay the same total price to Peerless. The complaint, however, is that the Edmonton customer is paying part of the Regina customer's freight cost. In addition, a customer just on the east side of the line dividing the West and East pays much more than one just on the west side of the line, although they may be within a few miles of each other.

## BASING-POINT PRICING

**Basing-point pricing** allows the seller to select a particular city as a basing point and charge all customers the freight cost from that city to the customer location, regardless of the city from which the goods are actually shipped. For example, Peerless might set Winnipeg as the basing point and charge all customers $100 plus the freight from Winnipeg to their location. This means that an Edmonton customer pays the freight cost from Winnipeg to Edmonton even though the goods may be shipped from Vancouver. Using a basing-point location other than the factory raises the total price to customers near the factory and lowers the total price to customers far from the factory.

If all the sellers used the same basing-point city, delivered prices would be the same for all customers, and price competition would be eliminated. Such industries as sugar, cement, steel, and automobiles used basing-point pricing for years, but this method is less popular today. Some companies set up multiple basing points to create more flexibility. They would quote freight charges from the basing-point city nearest to the customer.

## FREIGHT ABSORPTION PRICING

The seller who is anxious to do business with a certain customer or geographical area might use **freight absorption pricing**. This involves absorbing all or part of the actual freight charges in order to get the business. The seller might reason that if it can get more business, its average costs will fall and more than compensate for the extra freight cost. Freight absorption pricing is used for market penetration and also to hold on to increasingly competitive markets.

# Price Changes

## Initiating Price Changes

After developing their price structures and strategies, companies will face occasions when they will want to cut or raise prices.

### INITIATING PRICE CUTS

Several situations may lead a firm to consider cutting its price. One situation is excess capacity. Here the firm needs more business and cannot get it through increased sales effort, product improvement, or other measures. In the late 1970s many airline companies dropped "follow-the-leader pricing" and aggressively cut prices to boost their sales. But as the airline industry learned in recent years, cutting prices to increase share in an industry with excess capacity can lead to price wars.

Another situation is falling market share in the face of strong price competition (see Marketing Highlight 12-1). Several industries—automobiles and consumer electronics—have been losing market share to Japanese competitors whose high quality products carry lower prices than Canadian products. This may lead Canadian firms to more aggressive pricing action.

Companies will also cut prices in a drive to dominate the market through lower costs. Either the company starts with lower costs than its competitors, or it cuts prices in the hope of gaining market share that will lead to falling costs through larger volume.

### INITIATING PRICE INCREASES

Many companies have had to raise prices in recent years. They do this knowing that the price increases will be resented by customers, dealers, and the company's own salesforce. Yet a successful price increase can greatly increase profits. For example, if the company's profit margin is three percent of sales, a one percent price increase will increase profits by 33% if sales volume is unaffected.

A major factor in price increases is cost inflation. Rising costs squeeze profit margins and lead companies to regular rounds of price increases. In anticipation of further inflation, companies often raise their prices by more than the cost increase. Companies do not want to make long-run price agreements with customers—they fear that cost inflation will eat up their profit margins. Another factor leading to price increases is overdemand. When a company cannot supply all its customers' needs, it can raise its prices, ration products to customers, or both. Prices can be raised almost invisibly by dropping discounts and adding higher-priced units to the line, or prices can be pushed up openly.

### BUYER REACTIONS TO PRICE CHANGES

Whether the price is raised or lowered, the action will affect buyers, competitors, distributors, and suppliers, and may interest government as well.

# MARKETING HIGHLIGHT 12-1

## Price Competition Comes to the Beer Business

In the spring of 1989, Ontario beer drinkers were offered a bargain: U.S. beer at low prices. The beer was on sale at Ontario liquor stores—the only outlets that sell it in the province—for two dollars less per six-pack than Canadian beer. Customer reaction was quick. People began drinking Lone Star and Milwaukee's Best at about $4.50 a six-pack instead of Labatt's Blue or Molson Canadian at $6.60 a six-pack. The U.S. share of the Ontario market leaped to seven percent—prior to that, U.S. beers held less than two percent of the market.

Molson and Labatt also had a quick reaction—they got the Ontario government to add a handling charge of $.70 a six-pack to the U.S. imports, and they dropped their price on a six-pack by $.35. Within days, the sale of U.S. beer declined by over 40%. Now, the Ontario liquor stores faced a problem. They had a backlog of 48 million cans of U.S. beer sitting in warehouses. The liquor stores slashed prices by about 20% to get rid of the excess inventory. After the inventory problem was cleared up, the average price of a U.S. six-pack was about $5.40, about $1.20 less than Canadian beers.

Consumers in Alberta and British Columbia might have been surprised by all this fuss. About one-third of all the beer sold in these provinces is discount beer because cheap U.S. beer has been on store shelves for years. The Canadian breweries responded in these two provinces with their own discount versions; Labatt's Lucky Lager and Molson Old Style Pilsener retail at about $4.95 a six-pack, with the lowest price U.S. brand, Rainier, at $4.55. U.S. beers hold about a ten percent share of the B.C. market.

The Canadian beer business is worth over $5 billion annually, and Molson and Labatt, the two Canadian breweries that control about 95% of the market, clearly want to keep it to themselves. But some United States breweries have different ideas. Where Molson and Labatt are willing to compete on nonprice factors, like advertising, the U.S. firms want to compete on price. U.S. brewers can produce beer more cheaply than the Canadian firms because they have larger, more efficient plants. In part, Labatt and Molson cannot be blamed because, in the past, provincial regulations required them to set up breweries in every province, resulting in small, inefficient plants.

Both Labatt and Molson are rationalizing their plants to become more efficient producers. In the future, they are likely to face more competition in the form of lower priced imports. In the meantime, the U.S. government has launched a trade action against beer marketing practices in Canada. As well, many consumers have sent the Canadian breweries a clear message—brand loyalty only goes so far and then price becomes an important factor.

**Sources:** Michael Harrison, "Brewing Beer Wars," *Maclean's*, July 10, 1990, pp. 34-36; Marina Strauss, "Cheap Beer Dumped by U.S., Canadian Breweries Complain," *Globe and Mail*, May 27, 1989, p. B1; and Marina Strauss, "Canadian Beer Marketing Draws Complaint in U.S.," *Globe and Mail*, May 16, 1990, p. B3.

Customers do not always put a straightforward interpretation on price changes. Customers may view a price cut in several ways. They may think the item is about to be replaced by a later model, or that it has some fault and is not selling well. They may think that the firm is in financial trouble and may not stay in business to supply future parts. Alternatively, they may believe that the price will come down even further and it will pay to wait. They may believe that quality has been reduced.

A price increase, which would normally lower sales, may carry some positive associations for the buyers. They may think that the item is very "hot" and may be unobtainable unless it is bought soon. They may think the item is an unusually good value, or, alternatively and negatively, that the seller is greedy and is charging what the traffic will bear.

## COMPETITOR REACTIONS TO PRICE CHANGES

A firm considering a price change has to worry about competitors' as well as customers' reactions. Competitors are likely to react where the number of firms is small, the product is uniform, and the buyers are well informed.

How can a firm figure out the likely reactions of its competitors? Assume that a firm faces one large competitor. If the competitor reacts in a set way to price changes, the reaction can be anticipated. However, if the competitor treats each price change as a fresh challenge, and reacts according to its self-interest, the company will have to figure out what makes up the competitor's self-interest at the time.

The problem is complex because the competitor can interpret a company price cut in many ways. It might think that the company is trying to steal the market, or that the company is doing poorly and is trying to boost its sales, or that the company wants the whole industry to cut prices to increase total demand.

When there are several competitors, the company must guess each competitor's likely reaction. If all competitors behave alike, the company needs to analyze only a typical competitor. If the competitors do not behave alike because of differences in size, market shares, or policies, then separate analyses are necessary. If some competitors will match the price change, there is good reason to expect that the rest will also match it.

# Responding to Price Changes

Here we reverse the question and ask how a firm should respond to a price change by a competitor. The firm needs to consider several issues. Why did the competitor change the price? Did it want to steal the market, use excess capacity, meet changing cost conditions, or lead an industry-wide price change? Does the competitor plan to make the price change temporary or permanent? What will happen to the company's market share and profits if it doesn't respond? Are other companies going to respond? If so, what are the responses of the competitor and other firms likely to be to each possible reaction?

Besides these issues, the company must make a broader analysis. The company has to consider the product's stage in the life cycle, its importance in the company's product mix, the intentions and resources of the competitor, the price and value sensitivity of the market, the behavior of costs with volume, and the company's other opportunities.

The company cannot always make an extended analysis of its alternatives at the time of a price change. The competitor may have spent much time preparing this decision, but the company may have to react within hours or days. About the only way to cut down reaction time is to plan ahead for possible competitors' price changes and possible responses. Reaction programs for meeting price changes are most often used in industries where price changes occur often and where it is important to react quickly. Examples can be found in the meatpacking, lumber, and oil industries.

# SUMMARY

Pricing is a dynamic process. Companies design a pricing structure that covers all their products. They change the structure over time, and adjust it to account for different customers and situations.

Pricing strategies usually change as a product passes through its life cycle. In pricing innovative new products, the company can follow a skimming policy by setting prices high initially to "skim" the maximum amount of revenue from various segments of the market. Alternatively, the company can use penetration pricing by setting a low initial price to win a large market share. When introducing an imitative product, the company can decide on one of nine price-quality strategies.

When the product is part of a product mix, the firm searches for a set of prices that will maximize the profits from the total mix. The company decides on the price zones for items in its product line and on the pricing of optional products, captive products, and by-products.

Companies apply a variety of price-adjustment strategies to account for differences in consumer segments and situations. One is geographical pricing, where the company decides how to price for distant customers, choosing from such alternatives as FOB pricing, uniform delivered pricing, zone pricing, basing-point pricing, and freight absorption pricing. A second is discount pricing and allowances, where the company establishes cash discounts, quantity discounts, functional discounts, seasonal discounts, and allowances. A third is discriminatory pricing, where the company sets different prices for different customers, product forms, places, or times. A fourth is psychological pricing, where the company adjusts the price to better communicate a product's intended position. A fifth is promotional pricing, where the company decides on loss-leader pricing, special-event pricing, and psychological discounting.

When a firm considers initiating a price change, it must consider customers' and competitors' reactions. Customers' reactions are influenced by the meaning customers see in the price change. Competitors' reactions flow from a set reaction policy or a fresh analysis of each situation. The firm initiating the price change must also anticipate the probable reactions of suppliers, middlemen, and government.

The firm that faces a price change initiated by a competitor must try to understand the competitor's intent and the likely duration of the change. If swiftness of reaction is desirable, the firm should preplan its reactions to different possible price actions by competitors.

# QUESTIONS FOR DISCUSSION

1. Describe which strategy—market skimming or market penetration—is used by these companies in pricing their products: (a) McDonald's; (b) Curtis Mathes (television and other home electronics); (c) Bic Corporation (pens, lighters,

shavers and related products); (d) IBM. Are these the right strategies for these companies?

2. A by-product of manufacturing tennis balls is the "dead" ball—a ball that does not bounce high enough to meet standards (a minimum of 135 cm when dropped from 254 cm onto a concrete surface). What strategy should be used for pricing these balls?

3. What types of discount-pricing tactics might a manufacturer of snow skis use in dealing with the retail outlets carrying its product?

4. Analyze different pricing strategies at movie theaters. To which market segments are these different strategies designed to appeal?

5. A clothing store sells men's suits at three price levels—$180, $250, and $340. If shoppers use these levels as reference prices in comparing suits, consider the effect of adding a new line of suits at a cost of $280. Would sales of the $250 suits probably increase, decrease, or stay the same?

6. A garden supply company located in Saskatoon uses catalogs to sell seeds and bulbs to gardeners in every part of the country. What geographical-pricing strategy should this company use for maximum profits?

7. Increases in the worldwide supply of cocoa have led to decreases in the price of cocoa and lowered production costs for chocolate products. What impact will this reduction have on chocolate prices? If manufacturers expect the price of cocoa to go back up next year, what approach should they take if they want to cut prices?

8. If McDonald's cut the price of a Big Mac to only 99 cents, how would competing hamburger chains probably react? Would they react the same way if the price decrease were for Chicken McNuggets rather than Big Macs?

# KEY TERMS

**Basing-point pricing** A geographic pricing strategy in which the seller designates some city as a basing point and charges all customers the freight cost from that city to the customer location, regardless of the city from which the goods are actually shipped.

**Cash discount** A price reduction to buyers who pay their bills promptly.

**Discriminatory pricing** Selling a product or service at two or more prices, where the difference in prices is not based on differences in costs.

**FOB origin pricing** A geographic pricing strategy in which goods are placed free on board a carrier, and the customer pays the freight from the factory to the destination.

**Freight absorption pricing** A geographic pricing strategy in which the company absorbs all or part of the actual freight charges in order to get the business.

**Functional discount** A price reduction offered by the seller to trade channel members who perform certain functions such as selling, storing, and record keeping.

**Market penetration pricing** Setting a low price for a new product in order to attract a large number of buyers and a large market share.

**Market skimming pricing** Setting a high price for a new product to skim maximum revenue from the segments willing to pay the high price.

**Promotional allowance** A payment or price reduction to reward dealers for participating in advertising and sales-support programs.

**Promotional pricing** Temporarily pricing products below the list price, and sometimes even below cost, to increase short-run sales.

**Psychological pricing** A pricing approach which considers the psychology of prices and not simply the economics—the price is used to say something about the product.

**Quantity discount** A price reduction to buyers who buy large volumes.

**Seasonal discount** A price reduction to buyers who buy merchandise or services out of season.

**Trade-in allowance** A price reduction given for turning in an old item when buying a new one.

**Uniform delivered pricing** A geographic pricing strategy in which the company charges the same price plus freight to all customers regardless of their location.

**Zone pricing** A geographic pricing strategy in which the company sets up two or more zones—all customers within a zone pay the same total price, and this price is higher in the more distant zones.

# REFERENCES

1. Sources include: Tamsim Carlisle, "Hurtig Unbowed by Discount Damage," *Financial Post*, September 24, 1988, p. 6; William French, "Shock Waves Continue After Coles Prices Cut," *Globe and Mail*, November 8, 1988, p. A23; Diana Shepard, "A Million Dollar Promotion and Satisfaction Guaranteed," *Quill and Quire*, July 1987, p. 48; Diana Shepard, "Coles Discounting Shocks Industry," *Quill and Quire*, November 1988, p. 4; Mel Hurtig, "Deep Discounting: Learning Lessons the Hard Way," *Quill and Quire*, November 1988, p. 30; Susan Lazasruk, "Hurtig Faces Bank Hurdle for Junior Encyclopedia," *Globe and Mail*, May 14, 1990, p. C8; and "Hurtig Alters Plan; Will Sell Encyclopedia in Stores," *Globe and Mail*, October 24, 1990, p.C5.

2. For a comprehensive review of pricing strategies, see Gerard J. Telles, "Beyond The Many Faces of Price: An Integration of Pricing Strategies," *Journal of Marketing*, October 1986, pp. 146-160.

3. See Bruce D. Henderson, "The Application and Misapplication of the Experience Curve," *Journal of Business Strategy*, Winter 1984, pp. 3-9.

4. For more information on pricing new products, see William H. Redmond, "Effects of New Product Pricing on the Evolution of Market Structure," *Journal of Product Innovation Management*, 6, 1989, pp. 99-108.

5. See Telles, "Beyond the Many Faces of Price," p. 155; and Thomas T. Nagle,

*The Strategy and Tactics of Pricing* (Englewood Cliffs, NJ: Prentice Hall, 1987), pp. 170-172.

6. For an overview of price discounts, see George S. Day and Adrian B. Ryans, "Using Price Discounts for a Competitive Advantage," *Industrial Marketing Management*, February 1988, pp. 1-14.

7. For more on quantity discounts, see James B. Wilcox, Rod D. Howell, Paul Kuzdrall, and Robert Britney, "Price Quantity Discounts: Some Implications for Buyers and Sellers," *Journal of Marketing*, July 1987, pp. 60-70.

8. Gary M. Erickson and Johny K. Joansson, "The Role of Price on Multi-Attribute Product Evaluations," *Journal of Consumer Research*, September 1986, pp. 195-199.

9. For more on this subject, see David J. Curry and Peter C. Riesz, "Prices and Price Quality Relationships: A Longitudinal Analysis," *Journal of Marketing*, January 1988, pp. 36-51; and Valarie A. Zeithaml, "Consumer Perceptions of Price, Quality and Volume: A Means-End Model and Synthesis of Evidence," *Journal of Marketing*, July 1988, pp. 2-22.

10. J.N. Fry and G.H.G. McDougall, "Consumer Appraisal of Retail Price Advertisements," *Journal of Marketing*, July 1974, pp. 64-67. See also, John Liefeld and Louise A. Heslop, "Reference Prices and Deception in Newspaper Advertising," *Journal of Consumer Research*, March 1985, pp. 868-876.

# CHAPTER 13

# Placing Products: Distribution Channels and Physical Distribution

## CHAPTER OBJECTIVES

After reading this chapter you should be able to:
1. Explain why companies use distribution channels and the functions these channels perform.
2. Discuss how channel members interact, and how they organize to do the work of the channel.
3. Identify the major distribution channel alternatives open to a company.
4. Tell how companies select, motivate, and evaluate channel members.
5. Discuss the issues firms face when setting up physical distribution systems.

Getting your product to market in Canada is easy—if your manufacturing plant is in Toronto and your market is Southern Ontario. National distribution, however, is harder and more expensive. Here are several elements that make distribution in Canada somewhat unique:

- The distance from coast to coast is 6,400 km and most of our population is in a narrow 300-km band across the country. In fact, most Canadians live in one of five population clusters.
- Because of the geography, on a per capita basis, Canada has twice the mileage of railway mainline as the United States and 40% more surfaced highway.
- Most of Canada's manufacturing is located in Quebec and Ontario (79%), while many large Western markets are thousands of kilometers away.
- About three-quarters of Canada's population resides in urban areas, the remaining 25% in areas that often have few transportation facilities.
- Transportation alternatives for many Canadian firms are limited: there are only two major railways, two major airlines, one crosscountry highway, and only regional and seasonal connecting waterways.

Some significant managerial implications result from these unique aspects of Canadian distribution:

- Firms deciding to operate on a national basis will face not only relatively high transportation costs but also additional costs such as: greater working capital requirements, because goods are in transit longer;

greater communication costs for personnel visiting markets and greater costs of transmitting information to and from distant markets; and extra packaging costs.
- For some firms it may be more profitable to limit their market coverage. This can be done in two ways: distribution only to the urban areas of Canada, or limited distribution to a specific geographic area such as Ontario and Quebec.

- Firms located outside Ontario and Quebec have a difficult time competing in these markets because of their higher distribution costs, yet most of Canada's buying power is contained in these two provinces.
- Because of the distances involved in reaching many Canadian markets, firms may lose some control over their ability to supply and service their customers at the level they consider appropriate.[1]

Marketing channel decisions are among the most important decisions faced by management. The company's channel decision directly affects every other marketing decision. The company's pricing depends on whether it uses large, high-quality dealers or medium-size, medium-quality dealers. The firm's salesforce decisions depend on how much selling and training the dealers will need. Whether a company develops or acquires certain new products may depend on how well these products fit the abilities of channel members.

Distribution channel decisions often involve long-term commitment to other firms. A furniture manufacturer can easily change its advertising, pricing or promotion programs. It can scrap old product designs and introduce new ones as market taste demands. But when it sets up a distribution channel with independent dealers, it cannot readily replace this channel with company-owned branches if conditions change. Therefore management must design its channels carefully, with an eye on tomorrow's likely selling environment as well as today's.[2]

In this chapter we will examine four major issues: What is the nature of distribution channels? How do channel firms interact and organize to do the work of the channel? What problems do companies face in designing and managing their channels? What role does physical distribution play in attracting and satisfying customers? In the next chapter we will look at distribution channel issues from the viewpoint of retailers and wholesalers.

# THE NATURE OF DISTRIBUTION CHANNELS

Most producers use middlemen to bring their products to market. They try to forge a distribution channel. A **distribution channel** is the set of firms and individuals that take title, or assist in transferring title, to a good or service as it moves from the producer to the consumer or industrial user.

## Why Are Middlemen Used?

Why do producers give some of the selling job to middlemen? Although they must give up some control over how and to whom the products are sold, producers gain certain advantages from using middlemen. These advantages are described below.

Many producers lack the financial resources to carry out direct marketing. For example, Ford of Canada sells its automobiles through over 750 independent dealers. Even Ford would be hard pressed to raise the cash to buy out its dealers. Similarly, Beaver Lumber Company, which had only company-owned stores until 1977, decided that it could obtain greater market penetration without stretching its financial resources by introducing franchise stores. Now Beaver Lumber, a division of Molson Companies, has over 120 franchise stores that account for most of the company's sales.

Direct marketing would require many producers to become middlemen for the products of other producers in order to achieve mass-distribution economies. For example, the Adams Division of Warner-Lambert Canada would not find it practical to set up small retail gum shops around the country or to sell gum door to door or by mail order. It would have to sell gum along with many other small products and would end up in the drugstore and foodstore business. Adams finds it easier to work through a network of privately owned distributors.

Even producers who can afford to set up their own channels can often earn a greater return by increasing their investment in their main business. If a company earns a 20% rate of return on manufacturing and foresees only a ten percent return on retailing, it will not want to do its own retailing.

The decision to use middlemen often rests on their greater efficiency in making goods available to target markets. Through their contacts, experience, specialization, and scale of operation, middlemen usually offer the firm more than it can achieve on its own.

Figure 13-1 shows one way that using middlemen can be economical. Part A

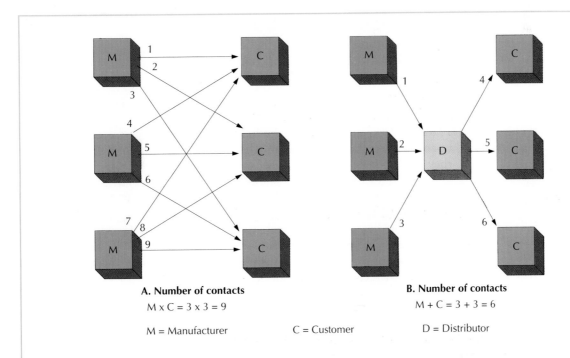

**A. Number of contacts**

$M \times C = 3 \times 3 = 9$

M = Manufacturer          C = Customer

**B. Number of contacts**

$M + C = 3 + 3 = 6$

D = Distributor

Figure 13-1 How a Distributor Reduces the Number of Channel Transactions

shows three producers each using direct marketing to reach three customers. This requires nine different contacts. Part B shows the three producers working through one distributor, who contacts the three customers. This system requires only six contacts. In this way, middlemen reduce the amount of work that must be done.

From the economic system's point of view, the role of middlemen is to transform the assortment of products made by producers into the assortments wanted by consumers. Producers make narrow assortments of products in large quantities, but consumers want broad assortments of products in small quantities. In the distribution channels, middlemen buy the large quantities from many producers and break them down into the smaller quantities and broader assortments wanted by consumers. Thus, middlemen play an important role in matching supply and demand.

## Distribution Channel Functions

A distribution channel moves goods from producers to consumers. It overcomes the major time, place, and possession gaps that separate goods and services from those who would use them. Members of the marketing channel perform many key functions:

*help to complete transaction*

- **Research**—gathering of information needed for planning and aiding exchange.
- **Promotion**—developing and spreading persuasive communications about the offer.
- **Contact**—finding and communicating with prospective buyers.
- **Matching**—shaping and fitting the offer to the buyer's needs, including such activities as manufacturing, grading, assembling, and packaging.
- **Negotiation**—reaching an agreement on price and other terms of the offer so that ownership or possession can be transferred.

*help fulfill the completed transaction*

- **Physical distribution**—transporting and storing goods.
- **Financing**—acquiring and using funds to cover the costs of the channel work.
- **Risk taking**—assuming the risks of carrying out the channel work.

The first five functions help to complete transactions; the last three help fulfill the completed transactions.

The question is not whether these functions need to be performed (they must be), but rather who is to perform them. All the functions have three things in common: they use up scarce resources, they can often be performed better through specialization, and they can be shifted among channel members. To the extent that the manufacturer performs them, its costs go up and prices have to be higher. When some functions are shifted to middlemen, the producer's costs and prices are lower, but the middlemen must add a charge to cover their work. In dividing up the work of the channel, the various functions should be assigned to the channel members who can perform them most efficiently and effectively to provide satisfactory assortments of goods to target consumers.

## Number of Channel Levels

Distribution channels can be described by the number of channel levels. Each middleman that performs some work in bringing the product and its ownership closer to the final buyer is a channel level. Since the producer and the final consumer

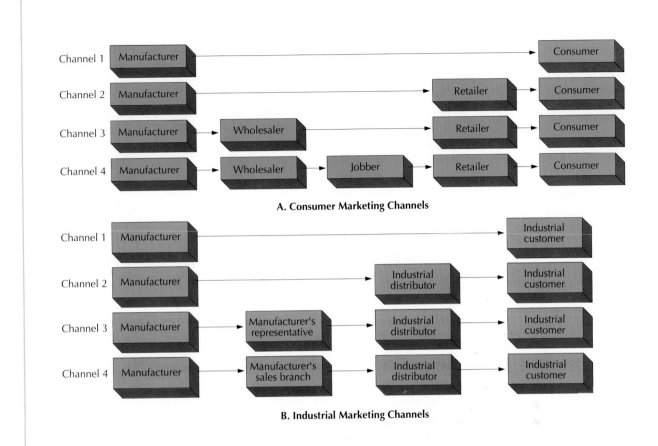

**A. Consumer Marketing Channels**

**B. Industrial Marketing Channels**

Figure 13-2 Consumer and Industrial Marketing Channels

both perform some work, they are part of every channel. We will use the number of intermediary levels to indicate the length of a channel. Figure 13-2A shows several consumer distribution channels of different lengths.

Channel 1, called a direct-marketing channel, has no intermediary levels. It consists of a manufacturer selling directly to consumers. For example, Avon sells its products door-to-door and Statistics Canada sells various reports through mail order. Channel 2 contains one middleman level. In consumer markets, this level is typically a retailer. For example, large retailers such as Sears and Eaton's sell televisions, cameras, tires, furniture, major appliances, and many other products that they buy directly from manufacturers. Channel 3 contains two middleman levels. In consumer markets, these levels are typically a wholesaler and a retailer. This channel is often used by small manufacturers of food, drug, hardware, and other products. Channel 4 contains three middleman levels. In the meatpacking industry, for example, jobbers usually come between wholesalers and retailers. The jobber buys from wholesalers and sells to smaller retailers who are not generally served by larger wholesalers. Distribution channels with more levels are sometimes found, but less often. From the producer's point of view, a greater number of levels means less control. In addition, of course, the more levels, the greater the channel's complexity.

Figure 13-2B shows some common industrial distribution channels. The industrial-goods producer can use its own salesforce to sell directly to industrial customers. It can also sell to industrial distributors who in turn sell to industrial customers. It can sell through manufacturer's representatives or its own sales branches to industrial customers, or use them to sell through industrial distributors. Thus zero, one-, and two-level distribution channels are common in industrial goods markets.

All the institutions in the channel are connected by several types of flows. These include the physical flow of products, the flow of ownership, payment flow, information flow, and promotion flow. These flows can make complex even channels with only one or a few levels.

# CHANNEL BEHAVIOR AND ORGANIZATION

Distribution channels are more than simple collections of firms tied together by various flows. They are complex behavioral systems in which people and companies interact to accomplish individual, company, and channel goals. Some channel systems consist of only informal interactions among loosely organized firms; others consist of formal interactions guided by strong organizational structures. Channel systems do not stand still—new types of middlemen surface and whole new channel systems evolve. Here we will look at channel behavior and at how members organize to do the work of the channel.

## Channel Behavior

A distribution channel is made up of dissimilar firms that have banded together for their common good. Each channel member is dependent on the other channel members. A Ford dealer depends on the Ford Motor Company to design cars that meet consumer needs. In turn, Ford depends on the dealer to attract consumers, persuade them to buy Ford cars, and service the cars after the sale. The Ford dealer also depends on other dealers to provide good sales and service that will uphold the reputation of Ford and its dealer network. In fact, the success of individual Ford dealers will depend on how well the entire Ford distribution channel competes with the channels of other auto manufacturers.

Each channel member plays a role in the channel and specializes in performing one or more functions. IBM's role is to produce personal computers that consumers will like and to create demand through national advertising. Computerland's role is to display these computers in a convenient location, answer the buyers' questions, close sales, and provide service. The channel will be most effective when each member is assigned the tasks it can do best.

Ideally, because the success of individual channel members depends on overall channel success, all channel firms should work smoothly together. They should understand and accept their roles, coordinate their goals and activities with those of other channel members, and cooperate to attain overall channel goals. Manufacturers, wholesalers, and retailers should work together to produce greater profit than they could obtain individually. By cooperating, they can more effectively sense, serve, and satisfy the target market.

But individual channel members rarely take such a broad view. They are usually more concerned with their own short-run goals and their dealings with firms next to them in the channel. Cooperating to achieve overall channel goals sometimes means giving up individual company goals. Though channel members are dependent on one another, they often act alone in their own short-run best interests. They often disagree on the roles each should play—on who should do what and for what rewards. Such disagreements over goals and roles generate channel conflict.

Horizontal conflict is conflict between firms at the same level of the channel. Some Ford dealers in Montreal may complain about other dealers in the city stealing sales from them by being too aggressive in their pricing and advertising, or by selling outside their assigned territories. Some Harvey's franchises might complain about other Harvey's franchises cheating on ingredients, giving poor service, and hurting the overall Harvey's image.

Vertical conflict is even more common and refers to conflicts between different levels of the same channel. For example, General Motors came into conflict with its dealers some years ago when trying to enforce policies on service, pricing, and advertising. For the channel as a whole to perform well, each channel member's role must be specified, and channel conflict must be managed. Cooperation, assigning roles, and conflict management in the channel are attained through strong channel leadership. The channel will perform better if it contains a firm, agency, or mechanism that has the power to assign roles and manage conflict.

In a large, single company, the formal organization structure assigns roles and provides needed leadership. But in a distribution channel made up of independent firms, leadership and power are not formally set. Traditionally, distribution channels have lacked the leadership needed to assign roles and manage conflict. In recent years, however, new types of channel organizations have appeared that provide stronger leadership and improved performance. We will look now at these organizations.[3]

## Channel Organization

Historically, distribution channels have been loose collections of independently owned and managed companies, each showing little concern for overall channel performance. These conventional distribution channels have lacked strong leadership and have been troubled by damaging conflict and poor performance.

## Growth of Vertical Marketing Systems

One of the biggest recent developments has been the vertical marketing systems that have emerged to challenge conventional marketing channels. Figure 13-3 contrasts the two types of channel arrangement.

A **conventional distribution channel** consists of an independent producer(s), wholesaler(s), and retailer(s). Each is a separate business seeking to maximize its own profits, even at the expense of profits for the system as a whole. No channel member has much control over the other members, and there are no formal means for assigning roles and resolving channel conflict.

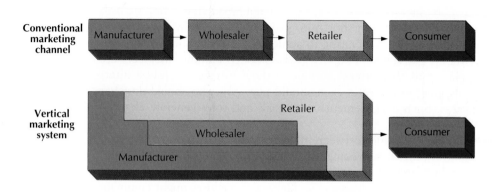

Figure 13-3 Comparison of Conventional Distribution Channel with Vertical Marketing System

By contrast, a **vertical marketing system (VMS)** consists of the producer(s), wholesaler(s), and retailer(s) acting as a unified system. One channel member either owns the others, has contracts with them, or has so much power that they all cooperate.[4] The vertical marketing system can be dominated by the producer, wholesaler, or retailer. The VMS came into being to control channel behavior and manage the channel conflict. It achieves economies through size, bargaining power, and elimination of duplicated services.

We will now look at the three major types of VMS shown in Figure 13-4. Each type uses a different means for setting up leadership and power in the channel. In a corporate VMS, coordination and conflict management are attained through common ownership at different levels of the channel. In a contractual VMS, they are attained through contractual agreements among channel members. In an administered VMS, leadership is assumed by one or a few dominant channel members.

## CORPORATE VMS

A **corporate VMS** combines successive stages of production and distribution under single ownership. For example, Bata Shoes, the largest shoe company in the world, has over 5,000 company-owned retail stores. In addition, Bata also sells shoes through independent retailers in a conventional distribution channel.

## CONTRACTUAL VMS

A **contractual VMS** consists of independent firms at different levels of production and distribution who join together through contracts to obtain more economies or sales impact than they could achieve alone. Contractual VMSs have expanded rapidly in recent years. There are three types of contractual VMSs.

Wholesaler-sponsored voluntary chains are systems in which wholesalers organize voluntary chains of independent retailers to help them compete with large chain organizations. The wholesaler develops a program in which independent retailers standardize their selling practices and achieve buying economies that let

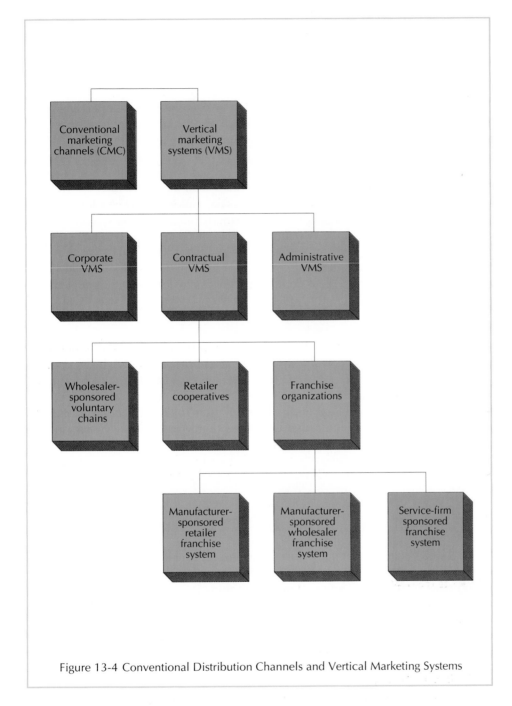

Figure 13-4 Conventional Distribution Channels and Vertical Marketing Systems

the group compete effectively with chain organizations. Examples include Federated Co-operatives and Co-op Atlantic.

Retailer cooperatives are systems in which retailers organize a new, jointly owned business to carry on wholesaling and possibly production. Members buy most of their goods through the retailer co-op and plan their advertising jointly. Profits are passed back to members in proportion to their purchases. Nonmember retailers may also buy through the co-op but do not share in the profits. Examples include The Red River Co-op and The Scotsburn Co-operative.

In franchise organizations, a channel member called a franchiser might link several stages in the production distribution process. Franchising has been the fastest growing retailing form in recent years. Ahough the basic idea is an old one, some forms of franchising are quite new.

There are three forms of franchises. The first is the manufacturer-sponsored retailer franchise system, as found in the automobile industry. Ford, for example, licenses dealers to sell its cars—the dealers are independent business people who agree to meet various conditions of sales and service. The second is the manufacturer-sponsored wholesaler franchise system, as found in the soft-drink industry. Coca-Cola, for example, licenses bottlers (wholesalers) in various markets who buy its syrup concentrate and then carbonate, bottle, and sell it to retailers in local markets. The third is the service-firm-sponsored retailer franchise system. Here a service firm organizes a whole system for bringing its service to consumers. Examples are found in the auto rental business (Hertz, Tilden), fast-food service business (McDonald's, Harvey's, Burger King), and the personal care business (Colours, First Choice haircutting). The various contractual VMSs are discussed in more detail in Chapter 14.

### ADMINISTERED VMS

An **administered VMS** coordinates successive stages of production and distribution, not through common ownership or contractual ties, but through the size and power of one of the parties. Manufacturers of a top brand can obtain strong trade cooperation and support from resellers. Thus Procter & Gamble, Arrow, and Campbell Soup can command unusual cooperation from resellers regarding displays, shelf space, promotions, and price policies. Large retailers like Canadian Tire and Sears Canada can exert a strong influence on manufacturers that supply the products they sell.

# CHANNEL DESIGN DECISION

We will now look at several channel decision problems facing manufacturers. In designing marketing channels, manufacturers have to struggle between what is ideal and what is available. A new firm usually starts by selling in a limited market area. Since it has limited capital, it usually uses only a few existing middlemen in each market. For example, the majority of manufacturing firms start out in Ontario or Quebec, which have both 62% of the retail buying power and 62% of Canada's population.[5] In these provinces the number of middlemen is fairly extensive and the major problem may be to convince one or more of the middlemen to handle the line.

If the new firm is successful, it might branch out to new markets. Again, the manufacturer will tend to work through the existing middlemen, although this might mean using different types of marketing channels in different areas. In the smaller markets the firm might sell directly to retailers; in the larger markets it might sell through distributors. In one part of the country it might grant exclusive franchises because the merchants normally work this way; in another, it might sell through all outlets willing to handle the merchandise. The manufacturer's channel system thus evolves to meet local opportunities and conditions.

Designing a channel system calls for analyzing customer-service needs, setting the channel objectives and constraints, identifying the major channel alternatives, and evaluating them.

## Analyzing Consumer Service Needs

Designing the distribution channel starts with finding out what services consumers in various target segments want from the channel. The necessary level of channel services depends on the answers to several questions.[6] Do consumers want to buy from nearby locations or will they buy from more distant centralized locations by traveling, phoning, or buying through the mail? The more decentralized the channel, the greater the service it provides. Do consumers want immediate delivery or are they willing to wait? Faster delivery means greater service from the channel. Do consumers value breadth of assortment or do they prefer specialization? The greater the assortment provided by the channel, the higher its service level. Finally, do consumers want many add-on services (delivery credit, repairs, installation) or will they obtain these elsewhere? More add-on services mean a higher level of channel service.

Thus, to design an effective channel, the designer must know the service levels desired by consumers. But providing all the desired services may not be possible or practical. The company and its channel members may not have the resources or skills needed to provide all the desired services. Providing higher levels of service also means higher costs for the channel and higher prices for consumers. The company must balance consumer service needs against not only the feasibility and costs of meeting these needs but also customer price preferences. The success of discount retailing shows that consumers are often willing to accept lower service levels if a lower service level means lower prices.

## Setting the Channel Objectives and Constraints

Channel objectives should be stated in terms of the desired service level of target consumers. Usually, a company can identify several segments wanting different levels of channel service. The company should decide which segments to serve and the best channels to use in each case. In each segment, the company wants to minimize the total channel cost of delivering the desired service level.

The company's channel objectives are also influenced by the nature of its products, company policies, middlemen, competitors, and environment. Product characteristics greatly affect channel design. For example, perishable products require more direct marketing to avoid delays and too much handling. Bulky products, such as building materials or soft drinks, require channels that minimize shipping distance and amount of handling.

Company characteristics also play an important role. For example, a company's size and financial situation determine which marketing functions it can handle itself and which it gives to middlemen. A company marketing strategy based on speedy customer delivery affects the functions that the company wants its middlemen to perform, the number of its outlets, and the choice of its transportation methods.

Middlemen characteristics also influence channel design. In general, middle-

Product characteristics affect channel decisions: fresh flowers must be delivered quickly, with a minimum of handling.

men differ in their abilities to handle promotion, customer contact, storage, and credit. The company may have trouble finding middlemen who are willing and able to perform the needed tasks.

When designing its channels, a company will want to consider competitors' channels. It may want to compete in or near the same outlets that carry competitors' products. Thus, food companies want their brands to be displayed next to competing brands; Burger King wants to locate near McDonald's. In other industries, producers may avoid the channels used by competitors. Avon decided not to compete with other cosmetics makers for scarce positions in retail stores and instead set up a profitable door-to-door selling operation.

Finally, environmental factors such as economic conditions and legal constraints affect channel-design decisions. For example, in a depressed economy, producers want to distribute their goods in the most economical way, using shorter channels and dropping unneeded services that add to the final price of the goods. Legal regulations in the Competition Act prevent channel arrangements that "may tend to substantially lessen competition."

# Identifying the Major Alternatives

When the company has defined its channel objectives, it should next identify its major channel alternatives in terms of types of middlemen, number of middlemen, and the responsibilities of each channel member.

## Types of Middlemen

The firm should identify the types of middlemen available to carry on its channel work. For example, suppose a manufacturer of test equipment developed an audio device that detects poor mechanical connections in any machine with moving parts. Company executives felt that this product would have a market in all industries where electric, combustion, or steam engines were made or used. The market would include such industries as aviation, automobile, railroad, food canning, construction, and oil. The company's salesforce was small, and the problem was how best to reach these different industries. The following channel alternatives might emerge from management discussion:

**Company salesforce.** Expand the company's direct salesforce. Assign salespeople to territories and have them contact all prospects in the area. Alternatively, develop separate company salesforces for the different industries.

**Manufacturers' agency.** Contract manufacturers' agencies—independent firms whose salesforces handle related products from many companies—in different regions or industries to sell the new test equipment.

**Industrial distributors.** Find distributors in the different regions or industries who will buy and carry the new line. Give them exclusive distribution, good margins, product training, and promotional support.

Companies should also search for more innovative distribution channels. This happened when IBM (Canada) decided to merchandise its typewriter products and related supplies by catalog in addition to using its regular sales force. IBM sent the catalog to every Canadian customer who had bought an IBM typewriter. Within five months, 20% of IBM's total typewriter orders were being generated through catalog sales, five times more than the company anticipated.[7] In another example of a new channel, a group decided to merchandise books through the mail in the now famous Book-of-the-Month Club.

Sometimes a company has to develop a channel other than the one it prefers because of the difficulty or cost of using the preferred channel. The decision sometimes turns out extremely well. For example, the U.S. Time Company first tried to sell its inexpensive Timex watches through regular jewelry stores. But most jewelry stores refused to carry them. The company then managed to get its watches into mass-merchandising outlets. This turned out to be a wise decision because of the rapid growth of mass merchandising.

## Number of Middlemen

Companies have to decide on the number of middlemen to use at each level. Three strategies are available.

Soft drinks, candy, and convenience products are sold through intensive distribution.

## INTENSIVE DISTRIBUTION

Producers of convenience goods and common raw material typically seek intensive distribution—that is, stocking their product in as many outlets as possible. These goods must be available where and when consumers want them. Chewing gum and candy, for example, sell in over 300,000 outlets to provide maximum brand exposure and convenience.

## EXCLUSIVE DISTRIBUTION

Some producers purposely limit the number of middlemen handling their products. The extreme form of this limiting is **exclusive distribution**, where a limited number of dealers are given the exclusive right to distribute the company's products in their territories. Exclusive distribution is often found in the distribution of new automobiles, major appliances, and prestige women's clothing. By granting exclusive distribution, the manufacturer hopes for stronger selling support from distributors and more control over middlemen's prices, promotion, credit, and services. Exclusive distribution often enhances the product's image and allows higher markups.

## SELECTIVE DISTRIBUTION

Between intensive and exclusive distribution is **selective distribution**—the use of more than one but less than all the middlemen who are willing to carry the company's products. The company does not have to spread its efforts over many outlets, including many marginal ones. It can develop a good working relationship with the selected middlemen and expect a better than average selling effort. Selective distribution lets the producer gain good market coverage with more control and less cost than intensive distribution. Most television, furniture, and small appliance brands are distributed selectively.

Suppose a producer has identified several possible channels and wants to select the one that will best satisfy the firm's long-run objectives. Each alternative should be evaluated against economic, control, and adaptive criteria.

Using economic criteria, the company compares the likely profitability of the different channel alternatives. It estimates the sales that each channel would produce, and the costs of selling different volumes through each channel. The company must also consider control issues. Using distributors usually means giving them some control over the marketing of the product, and some distributors take more control than others. Other things being equal, the company prefers to keep as much control as possible. Finally, channels often involve long-term commitments to other firms, making it hard to adapt the channel to the changing marketing environment. The company wants to keep the channel as flexible as possible. To be considered, a channel involving a long commitment should be greatly superior on economic or control grounds.

# CHANNEL MANAGEMENT DECISIONS

Once the company has reviewed its channel alternatives and decided on the best channel design, it must implement and manage the chosen channel. Channel management calls for selecting and motivating individual middlemen and evaluating their performance over time.

## Selecting Channel Members

Producers vary in their ability to attract qualified middlemen. Some producers have no trouble signing up middlemen. In some cases, the promise of exclusive or selective distribution for a desirable product will draw enough applicants.

At the other extreme are producers who have to work hard to line up enough qualified middlemen. When Polaroid started, it could not convince photography stores to carry its new cameras and had to go to mass-merchandising outlets. Small food producers often find it difficult to persuade grocery stores to carry their products.[8]

## Motivating Channel Members

Once selected, middlemen must be continually motivated to do their best. The producer must sell not only through the middlemen, but to them. Most producers see the problem as finding ways to gain middlemen's cooperation.[9] They will use the carrot-and-stick approach. As positive motivators, producers may offer higher margins, special deals, premiums, cooperative advertising allowances, display allowances, and sales contests. At times they will use negative motivators such as threatening to reduce margins, slow down delivery, or end the relationship. The weakness of this approach is that the producer has not really studied the needs, problems, strengths, and weaknesses of the distributors.

More advanced companies try to forge a long-term partnership with their distributors. The manufacturer develops a clear sense of what it wants from its distributors and what its distributors can expect. The manufacturer seeks an agreement from its distributors on their roles and responsibilities, and rewards them accordingly.

## Evaluating Channel Members

The producer must regularly check middlemen's performance against such standards as reaching sales quotas, average inventory levels, customer delivery time, treatment of damaged and lost goods, cooperation in company promotion and training programs, and services to the customer.

The producer typically sets sales quotas for the middlemen. After each period, the producer might circulate a list showing the sales performance of each middleman. This list should motivate middlemen at the bottom to do better and middlemen at the top to keep up their performance. Each middleman's sales performance can be compared with performance in the last period. The average percentage improvement for the group can be used as a norm.

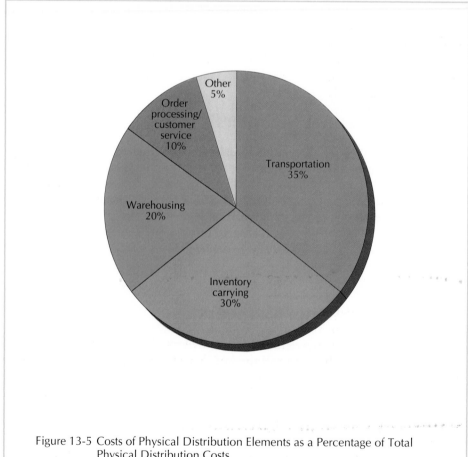

Figure 13-5 Costs of Physical Distribution Elements as a Percentage of Total Physical Distribution Costs

Manufacturers need to be sensitive to their dealer. Those who treat their dealer lightly risk not only losing the dealer's support, but also provoking some legal actions. Marketing Highlight 13-1 describes various legal aspects pertaining to manufacturers and their channel members.

# PHYSICAL DISTRIBUTION DECISIONS

We are now ready to look at physical distribution—how companies store, handle, and move goods so that they will be available to customers at the right time and place. Customers are greatly affected by the seller's physical distribution system. Here we will consider the nature, objectives, systems, and organizational aspects of physical distribution.

## Nature of Physical Distribution

The main elements of the physical distribution mix are shown in Figure 13-5. **Physical distribution** involves planning, implementing, and controlling the physical flow of materials and final goods from points of origin to points of use to meet the needs of customers at a profit.

Physical distribution decisions are important in Canada because of the tremendous distances between many markets. Poor physical distribution decisions result in high costs. In one study of Canadian firms, most of them did not have the necessary cost data available to make coordinated physical-distribution decisions.[10] Not enough use is being made of modern decision tools for coordinating inventory levels, transportation modes, and plant, warehouse, and store locations.

Physical distribution is not only a cost, it is a potent tool in demand creation. Companies can attract more customers by giving better service or lower prices through better physical distribution. Companies lose customers when they fail to supply goods on time. When John Labatt Limited introduced Budweiser beer in Canada it did not have enough inventory on hand to supply the unexpected demand. Many customers had to settle for other brands when Budweiser was out of stock, resuing in lost sales for Labatt.

## The Physical Distribution Objective

Many companies state their objective as getting the right goods to the right places at the right time for the least cost. Unfortunately, no physical distribution system can both maximize customer service and minimize distribution costs. Maximum customer service implies large inventories, the best transportation, and many warehouses, all of which raise distribution cost. Minimum distribution cost implies cheap transportation, low inventories, and few warehouses.

The company cannot simply let each physical distribution manager keep down his or her costs. Physical distribution costs interact, often in an inverse way. For example, low inventory levels reduce inventory carrying costs. But they also increase costs from stockouts, back orders, paperwork, special production runs, and high-cost fast-freight shipments.

The starting point for designing the system is to study what customers want and what competitors are offering. Customers want several things from suppliers: on-time delivery, sufficiently large inventories, ability to meet emergency needs, careful handling of merchandise, good after-sale service, and willingness to take back or quickly replace defective goods. The company has to research the importance of these services to customers. For example, selection and availability are very important services in the auto parts business. Canadian Tire has acknowledged this by building four large depots in Edmonton, Toronto, Montreal, and Moncton. Twenty-five thousand auto parts are available through these depots for shipment to over 400 Canadian Tire Stores, and delivery is made anywhere in the country within two days of receiving an order.

The company must look at competitors' service standards when setting its own as it will normally want to offer at least the same level of service. But the objective is to maximize profits, not sales. The company has to look at the costs of providing higher levels of service. Some companies offer less service and charge a lower price. Other companies offer more service than competitors and charge a high price to cover their higher cost.

The company ultimately must set physical distribution objectives to guide its planning. For example, Coca-Cola wants "to put Coke within an arm's length of desire." Companies go further and define standards for each service factor. One appliance manufacturer has set the following service standards: to deliver at least 95% of the dealer's order within seven days of order receipt, to fill the dealer's order with 99% accuracy, to answer dealer questions on order status within three hours, and to ensure that damage to merchandise in transit does not exceed one percent.

Given a set of objectives, the company is ready to design a physical distribution system that will minimize the cost of attaining these objectives. The major decision issues are: (1) How should orders be handled? (order processing) (2) Where should stocks be located? (warehousing) (3) How much stock should be kept on hand? (inventory) and (4) How should goods be shipped? (transportation). We will now look at these four issues.

## Order Processing

Physical distribution begins with a customer order. The order department prepares invoices and sends them to various departments. Items out of stock are back-ordered. Shipped items are accompanied by shipping and billing documents with copies going to various departments.

The company and customers benefit when these steps are carried out quickly and accurately. Ideally, salespeople send in their orders every evening, in some cases phoning them in. The order department processes these quickly. The warehouse sends the goods out as soon as possible. Bills go out as soon as possible. The computer is often used to speed up the order-shipping-billing cycle.

## Warehousing

Every company has to store its goods while they wait to be sold. A storage function is needed because production and consumption cycles rarely match. For example, many agricultural commodities are produced seasonally, but demand is continuous. The storage function overcomes differences in needed quantities and timing.

The company must decide on the best number of stocking locations. More stocking locations mean that goods can be delivered to customers more quickly. However, warehousing costs increase. In making the decision about the number of stocking locations, the company must balance the

An automated warehouse.

level of customer service against distribution costs.

Some company stock is kept at or near the plant, and the rest is located in warehouses around the country. The company might own private warehouses and rent space in public warehouses. Companies have more control in owned warehouses, but warehouses tie up their capital and are less flexible if desired locations change. Public warehouses, on the other hand, charge for the rented space and provide additional services (at a cost) for inspecting goods, packaging them, shipping them, and invoicing them. In using public warehouses, companies have a wide choice of locations and warehouse types.

Companies use either storage warehouses or distribution centers. Storage warehouses store goods for moderate to long periods of time. Distribution centers receive goods from various plants and suppliers and move them out as soon as possible. They are large and highly automated warehouses designed to receive goods from various plants and suppliers, take orders, fill them efficiently, and deliver goods as quickly as possible. For example, Canadian Tire has recently opened a new distribution center in Toronto which will process over 200,000 cartons and 120 truckloads of shipments each day. The facility, over 102,000 square metres in size, is fully automated and uses computer-directed carts that automatically guide merchandise from one section of the warehouse to another.[11]

## Inventory

Inventory levels also affect customer satisfaction. Marketers would like their companies to carry enough stock to fill all customer orders right away. However, it costs too much for a company to carry this much inventory. Inventory costs increase at an increasing rate as the customer service level approaches 100%. Management would need to know whether sales and profits would increase enough to justify larger inventories.

Inventory decisions involve knowing when to order, and how much to order. In deciding when to order, the company balances the risks of running out of stock against the costs of carrying too much stock. In deciding how much to order, the company needs to balance order-processing costs against inventory carrying costs. Larger average order size means fewer orders and lower order-processing costs, but it also means larger inventory-carrying costs.

## Transportation

Marketers need to take an interest in their company's transportation decisions. The choice of transportation carriers affects the pricing of the products, delivery performance, and the condition of the goods when they arrive, all of which will affect customer satisfaction.

In shipping goods to its warehouses, dealers, and customers, the company can choose among four transportation modes: rail, water, truck, and air. Each transportation mode's characteristics are summarized in Table 13-1 and discussed in the following paragraphs.

### RAIL

Because most of Canada's population is contained in a belt that is less than 300 km

**TABLE 13-1**
**Characteristics of Major Transportation Modes**

| Transportation Mode | 1988 Tonne-Kilometers (Billions) | Revenues (Billions) | Typical Shipped Products |
|---|---|---|---|
| Rail | 260.0 | $6.5 | Farm products, minerals, coal, chemicals, autos |
| Water | N/A | $2.2 | Oil, grain, sand, gravel, metallic ores, coal |
| Truck | 57.6 | $9.7 | Clothing, books, computers, paper goods |
| Air | 1.4 | N/A | Technical instruments, perishable food |

**Source:** *Transportation in Canada*, Transport Canada, TP10451-E, May, 1990.

wide but 6,400 km long, railway remains the nation's largest transportation carrier in terms of tonne-kilometers. Railways are one of the most cost-effective modes of transportation for shipping carload quantities of bulk products—coal, wheat, minerals, and forest products—over long land distances. In Canada, the rate costs for shipping merchandise by rail are quite complex, and require an historical perspective to be understood. The shipper's lowest rate comes from shipping carload rather than less-than-carload quantities. Manufacturers will often get together and combine shipments to common destinations to take advantage of lower rates. The Canadian railways have a number of customer-oriented services, including new kinds of equipment to handle categories of merchandise more efficiently, and flatcars that permit the carrying of truck trailers by rail (piggyback)

## WATER

A large amount of goods moves by ships and barges on coastal and inland waterways. The cost of water transportation is very low for shipping bulky, low-value, nonperishable products such as sand, coal, grain, oil, and metallic ores. On the other hand, water transportation is the slowest transportation mode and is sometimes affected by the weather. The St. Lawrence Seaway, for example, is closed for most of the winter season.

## TRUCK

Trucks have steadily increased their share of transportation, and total revenues are close to $10 billion. They account for the largest portion of transportation within cities as opposed to between cities. Trucks are highly flexible in their routing and time schedules. They can move goods door to door, saving shippers the need to

Marketers can choose among four transportation modes: rail, water, truck, and air.

**TABLE 13-2**

**Transportation Modes Ranked according to Major Shipper Criteria (1 = Highest Rank)**

| | Speed (door-to-door delivery time) | Dependability (meeting schedules on time) | Capability (ability to handle various products) | Availability (no. of geographic points served) | Cost (per ton-kil.) |
|---|---|---|---|---|---|
| Rail | 3 | 3 | 2 | 2 | 2 |
| Water | 4 | 4 | 1 | 4 | 1 |
| Truck | 2 | 1 | 3 | 1 | 3 |
| Air | 1 | 2 | 4 | 3 | 4 |

**Source:** See Carl M. Guelzo, *Introduction to Logistics Management* (Englewood Cliffs, N.J.: Prentice-Hall, 1986), p. 46.

transfer goods from truck to rail and back again at a loss of time and risk of theft or damage. Trucks are efficient for short hauls of high-value merchandise. Their rates are competitive with railway rates in many cases, and trucks can usually offer faster services.

### AIR

Air carriers transport relatively little of the nation's goods but are becoming more important as a transportation mode. Ahough air freight rates are much higher than rail or truck rates, air freight is ideal where speed is needed or distant markets have to be reached. Among the most frequently airfreighted products are perishables (fresh fish, cut flowers) and high-value, low-bulk items (technical instruments, jewelry). Companies find that air freight reduces inventory levels, number of warehouses, and costs of packaging.

## Choosing Transportation Modes

Until the mid-1980s, routes, rates, and service in the transportation industry were heavily regulated by the federal government. Today, most of these regulations have been eased. Deregulation has caused rapid and substantial changes. Railroads, ships, trucks, and airline companies are now much more competitive, flexible, and responsive to the needs of their customers. These changes have resulted in better services and lower prices for shippers. But such changes also mean that marketers must do better transportation planning if they want to take full advantage of new opportunities in the changing transportation environment.[12]

In choosing a transportation mode for a product, shippers consider as many as five criteria. Table 13-2 ranks the various modes on these criteria. If a shipper needs speed, air and truck are the prime choices. If the goal is low cost, then water might be best. Trucks appear to offer the most advantages, which explains their growing share.

Shippers are increasingly combining two or more modes of transportation, thanks to containerization. Containerization consists of putting the goods in boxes or trailers that are easy to transfer between two transportation modes.[13] Piggyback describes the use of rail and trucks; fishyback, water and trucks; trainship, water and rail; and airtruck, air and truck. Each combination offers advantages to the shipper. For example, piggyback is cheaper than trucking alone, and yet provides flexibility and convenience. Canadian Pacific, with extensive investments in most of these modes of transportation, can offer a manufacturer many of these combinations for shipping products.

## Organizational Responsibility for Physical Distribution

We can see that decisions on warehousing, inventory, and transportation require much coordination. A growing number of companies have set up a permanent committee made up of managers responsible for different physical distribution activities. This committee meets often to set policies for improving overall distribution efficiency. The goal is to coordinate the company's physical distribution and marketing activities in order to create high market satisfaction at a reasonable cost. One study of Canadian manufacturing firms concluded that only about one in five companies had made serious attempts to centralize or coordinate their physical distribution activities.[14] Among the reasons cited for these findings was the lack of internal pressure for adopting more centralization.

# SUMMARY

Distribution channel decisions are among the most complex and challenging decisions facing the firm. Each channel system creates a different level of sales and cost. Once a distribution channel has been chosen, the firm must usually stick with it for a long time. The chosen channel will strongly affect and be affected by the other elements in the marketing mix.

Each firm needs to identify alternative ways to reach the market. They vary from direct selling to using one, two, three, or more intermediary channel levels. Marketing channels face continual and sometimes dramatic change. An important trend is the growth of vertical marketing systems. This trend affects channel cooperation, conflict, and competition.

Channel design calls for identifying the major channel alternatives in terms of the types of intermediaries, the number of intermediaries, and the channel responsibilities. Each channel alternative has to be evaluated according to economic, control, and adaptive criteria. Channel management calls for selecting qualified middlemen and motivating them. Individual channel members must be evaluated regularly.

Just as the marketing concept is receiving increased recognition, more business firms are paying attention to the physical distribution concept. Physical distribution is an area of potentially high cost savings and improved customer satisfaction. When order processors, warehouse planners, inventory managers, and transportation managers make decisions, they affect each other's cost and ability to handle demand. The physical distribution concept calls for treating all these decisions within a unified framework. The task is to design physical distribution systems that minimize the total cost of providing a desired level of customer services.

# QUESTIONS FOR DISCUSSION

1. The Book-of-the-Month Club has been successfully marketing books by mail for over 50 years. Why do so few publishers sell their own books by mail?

2. How many channel levels are commonly used by these companies: (a) H & R Block, (b) Sears, (c) Procter & Gamble, (d) Carrier (a maker of air conditioning equipment)?

3. What organizations are needed to conduct the flows of products, ownership, payment, information, and promotion from the manufacturer to the customer? Are these organizations part of the distribution channel?

4. How is the leader chosen in a distribution channel? How much power does the leader have in getting other members to work for the overall good of the channel instead of solely for their own good?

5. Why is franchising such a fast-growing form of retail organization?

6. Describe the channel-service needs of the following groups: (a) consumers buying computers for home use, (b) retailers buying computers to resell to consumers, (c) purchasing agents buying computers for company use. What different channels would a computer manufacturer design to satisfy these different needs?

7. Which distribution strategies—intensive, selective, or exclusive—are used for the following products: (a) Piaget watches, (b) Acura automobiles, (c) Snickers candy bars?

8. How do physical distribution decisions differ from channel decisions?

9. When planning inventory levels, what consequences of running out of stock must be considered?

# KEY TERMS

**Administered VMS** A vertical marketing system that coordinates successive stages of production and distribution, not through common ownership or contractual ties, but through the size and power of one of the parties.

**Contractual VMS** A vertical marketing system in which independent firms at different levels of production and distribution join together through contracts to obtain more economies or sales impact than they could achieve alone.

**Conventional distribution channel** A channel consisting of an independent producer(s), wholesaler(s), and retailer(s), each a separate business seeking to maximize its own profits, even at the expense of profits for the system as a whole.

**Corporate VMS** A vertical marketing system that combines successive stages of production and distribution under single ownership.

**Distribution channel** The set of firms and individuals that take title, or assist in transferring title, to a good or service as it moves from the producer to the consumer or industrial user.

**Exclusive distribution** Giving a limited number of dealers the exclusive right to distribute the company's products in their territories.

**Intensive distribution** Stocking the product in as many outlets as possible.

**Physical distribution** The tasks involved in planning, implementing, and controlling the physical flow of materials and final goods from points of origin to points of use to meet the needs of customers at a profit.

**Selective distribution** The use of more than one but less than all the middlemen who are willing to carry the company's products.

**Vertical marketing system (VMS)** A distribution channel structure in which the producer(s), wholesaler(s), and retailer(s) act as a unified system.

# References

1. Prepared from various sources, including: James D. Forbes, "Some Managerial Implications of Canada's Unique Distribution System," in Donald N. Thompson and Davis S.R. Leighton, eds., *Canadian Marketing: Problems and Prospects* (Toronto: Wiley, 1973), pp. 145-159; Gerald Byers and Charles S. Mayer, "Physical Distribution in Canada," and Ronald E. Turner, "Canadian Freight Transportation Modes," both in Donald N. Thompson, ed., *Problems in Canadian Marketing* (Chicago: American Marketing Association, 1975), pp. 85-110, and pp. 111-30.

2. See Louis W. Stern and Frederick D. Sturdivant, "Customer-Driven Distribution Systems," *Harvard Business Review*, July-August 1987, p. 34-41.

3. For an excellent summary of channel conflict and power, see Louis W. Stern and Adel I. El-Ansary, *Marketing Channels* (2nd ed.) (Englewood Cliffs, NJ: Prentice-Hall, 1982), pp. 291-92, Chaps. 6 and 7.

4. See Bert C. McCammon, Jr., "Perspectives for Distribution Programming," in Louis P. Bucklin, ed., *Vertical Marketing Systems* (Glenview, IL: Scott Foresman, 1970), pp. 32-51.

5. "Canadian Markets 1988/89," *Financial Post*, Toronto: Maclean Hunter, 1989.

6. See Stern and Sturdivant, "Customer-Driven Distribution Systems," p. 35.

7. Jade Hemeon, "More Firms Turn to Direct Mail," *Financial Times*, March 2, 1981, p. 10.

8. For more on selecting channel members, see Allan J. Magrath and Kenneth G. Hardy, "Selecting Sales and Distribution Channels," *Industrial Marketing Management*, 16, 1987, pp. 273-278, and Kenneth G. Hardy and Allan J. Magrath, *Marketing Channel Management* (Glenview, IL: Scott Foresman, 1988).

9. See Bert Rosenbloom, *Marketing Channels: A Management View* (Hinsdale, IL: Dryden Press, 1978), pp. 192-203.

10. Douglas M. Lambert and Robert H. Quinn, "Increasing Profitability By Managing the Distribution Factor," *Business Quarterly*, Spring 1981, pp. 56-64.

11. Canadian Tire Corporation Limited, *Annual Report*, 1989.

12. See Lewis M. Schneider, "New Era in Transportation Strategy," *Harvard Business Review*, July-August 1987, p. 34-41.

13. For more discussion, see Norman E. Hutchinson, *An Integrated Approach to Logistics Management* (Englewood Cliffs, NJ: Prentice-Hall, 1987), p. 69.

14. Gerald Byers and Charles S. Mayer, "Physical Distribution Management in Canada," in Donald N. Thompson, ed., *Problems in Canadian Marketing* (American Marketing Association, 1977), pp. 85-110.

# CHAPTER 14

# Placing Products: Retailing and Wholesaling

## CHAPTER OBJECTIVES

After reading this chapter, you should be able to:
1. Explain the roles of retailers and wholesalers in the distribution channel.
2. Describe the major types of retailers and give examples of each.
3. Identify the major types of wholesalers and give examples of each.
4. Explain the marketing decisions facing retailers and wholesalers.

Metropolitan Toronto is the largest single retail market in Canada, with sales of over $28 billion each year. Torontonians have the widest selection of products and stores in the nation. Every large retail chain operates in Toronto, aggressively pursuing consumers for an increased share of this massive market. The department stores have tried to blanket the market by moving out to where the consumer lives and locating in the large suburban malls. Eaton's, Simpsons, K mart, and Sears have been at the leading edge of the suburban shift. As well, Eaton's and The Bay have helped revitalize the core, with the Eaton Centre being the flagship of retailing in downtown Toronto.

In the midst of all the clamor and glamor of the "Store Wars" in Toronto sits the unusual retail concept espoused by Ed Mirvish and institutionalized as Honest Ed's. Ed Mirvish has very few basic beliefs when it comes to business and retailing. One of his principal beliefs, and perhaps the main strategy of Honest Ed's, is to "go against the trends."

Honest Ed's central tactic is to give the customer bargains without frills. When you think of modern department stores, located downtown or in the suburbs, you think of their extensive services. Honest Ed's has none. The modern department store is spacious, with wide aisles, expansive display areas, and neatly organized goods. Honest Ed's is packed with goods in functional stacks arranged along narrow aisles in one 14,000 square metre location.

The modern department store has its own credit card system and may also accept Master Card and Visa. The credit system is convenient for the customer and helps increase potential sales. At Honest Ed's, it's strictly cash.

Modern department stores are aware that they are operating in a very competitive environment. Their advertising is high-powered, multi-media, and slick. They issue catalogs and flyers, and their TV and radio spots highlight seasonal specials and nationwide sales extravaganzas. Honest Ed laughs at himself in newspaper ads and clogs them with a multitude of products, accentuating the low price.

When he opened Honest Ed's in 1948, Ed Mirvish introduced the discount house to Canada. One might assume that Honest Ed's customers probably are from the lower income groups. However, shopping at Honest Ed's is an event, an experience, and all income groups are attracted to this landmark at Bathurst and Bloor Streets. While it is a method of retailing that is certainly more appropriate for particular segments of the population, a customer's age, affluence, cus-toms, habits, and tastes are meaningless at Honest Ed's. The distinctive concept—good prices and no frills—defines a target market that cuts across age and income groups. Honest Ed's customers love a good bargain and that is all he promises and delivers. The strategy is simple, but it works. On busy days up to 20,000 customers will visit the store, helping to ring up sales of more than $50 million each year. Ed Mirvish has used the profits from this store to purchase the Royal Alexandra Theatre in Toronto, open restaurants, and engage in a wide variety of other activities.

Honest Ed's remains a unique retail concept in a world that has seen many rapid and dramatic changes in retailing. It is a simple and honest concept that has worked for over 30 years.

"Ed never spanked his kid. (But his prices hit bottom)."

This chapter looks at retailing and wholesaling. In the first section we look at retailing's nature and importance, major types of retailers, decisions retailers make, and the future of retailing. In the second section, we discuss the same topics for wholesalers.

# RETAILING

What is retailing? We all know that Eaton's and The Bay are retailers, but so are Avon representatives, the local Holiday Inn, and a doctor seeing patients. We define **retailing** as all activities involved in selling goods or services directly to final consumers for their personal, non-business use. Many institutions—manufacturers, wholesalers, retailers—do retailing. But most retailing is done by retailers, businesses whose sales come primarily from retailing. Retailing can be done by person, mail, telephone, or vending machines; in stores, on the street, or in the consumer's home. Retailing is a major industry in Canada. Total retail sales exceed $170 billion and over 1,300,000 people are employed in retailing.

Much of Canada's retailing is concentrated in a few large retail chains. Seventeen retail chains, including Sears Canada, The Bay, Safeway Stores, Loblaws, Steinberg, Eaton's, Woolworth, Canadian Tire, Provigo, and Dylex, have sales of over $1 billion annually. These and other retail chains have a tremendous amount of buying power and can frequently dictate terms and conditions to many of their suppliers. The Bay, in particular, with its controlling interest in Fields, Zellers, Simpsons, and Marshall Wells, and its large minority interest in Robinsons, can have a significant influence on manufacturers in Canada.

At the other end of the spectrum are the independent stores, usually owner-operated, and often described as "mom and pop" stores. Their importance and market share have been declining since the 1950s, although in recent years they have increased their share of total retail sales.[1] One reason for the turnaround of the independents is that many have banded together in voluntary retail groups.[2] These groups can provide increased buying power and expertise that would not be available to an independent operating alone.

# TYPES OF RETAILERS

Retailers come in all shapes and sizes, and new retailing forms keep emerging. Retailers can be classified by one or more of several characteristics: amount of service, product line sold, relative prices, nature of business premises, control of outlets, and type of store cluster. These classification elements and the corresponding retailer types are shown in Table 14-1 and discussed below.

## Amount of Service

Different products need different amounts of service, and customers' service preferences vary. Some customers will pay retailers for more service; others would rather have fewer services and pay a lower price. Thus several types of retailers have evolved offering different levels of service. Table 14-2 shows three levels of service and the retailers that use them.

**TABLE 14-1**
**Different Ways to Classify Retail Outlets**

| Amount of Service | Product Line Sold | Relative Price Emphsis | Nature of Business Premises | Control of Outlets | Type of Store Cluster |
|---|---|---|---|---|---|
| Self-service | Specialty store | Discount store | Direct marketing | Corporate chain | Central business district |
| Limited service | Department store | Warehouse | Direct selling | Voluntary chain and cooperative | Regional shopping center |
| Full service | Supermarket | Catalog showroom | Automatic vending | Franchise organization | Community shopping center |
| | Convenience store | | | | |
| | Combination store and superstore | | | | Neighborhood shopping center |

Self-service retailing grew rapidly in the 1930s. Customers were willing to carry out their own "locate-compare-select" process to save money. Today self-service is the basis of all discount operations and is typically used by sellers of convenience goods and nationally branded, fast-moving shopping goods.

Limited-service retailers such as Zellers provide more sales assistance because they carry more shopping goods for which customers need more information. They also offer additional services such as credit and merchandise return that are not usually offered by low-service stores. Their increased operating costs result in higher prices.

In full-service retailing, found in specialty stores and first-class department stores, salespeople assist customers in every phase of the locate-compare-select process. Full-service stores usually carry more specialty goods and slower-moving items such as cameras, jewelry, and fashions, for which customers like to be "waited on." They provide more liberal return policies, various credit plans, free delivery, home servicing, and extras such as lounges and restaurants. More services result in higher operating costs, which are passed along to customers as higher prices.

## Product Line Sold

Retailers can be classified by the length and breadth of their product assortments. Among the most important types of stores are the specialty store, department store, supermarket, convenience store, and superstore.

### SPECIALTY STORE

A **specialty store** carries a narrow product line with a deep assortment within that line. Examples include clothing stores, sporting goods stores, furniture stores, florists, and bookstores. Specialty stores can be further classified by the narrowness of their product lines. A clothing store is a single-line store, a men's clothing store is a limited-line store, and a men's custom shirt store is a superspecialty store. The increasing use of market segmentation, market targeting, and product specialization has resulted in the rapid growth of specialty stores such as Athlete's World (sportswear and shoes), Pennington's (clothes for large women), and Computerland (personal computers).

The shopping center boom has also contributed to the recent growth of specialty stores. Specialty stores often occupy 60 to 70% of the total shopping center space. Although most specialty stores are independently owned, chain specialty stores show the strongest growth. The most successful chain specialty stores zero in on specific target market needs.

Suzy Shier is a young women's fashion clothing store chain operated by Dylex Limited. Suzy Shier specializes in moderately priced clothes for the single working woman in the 18 to 35 age group. Merchandise selection and pricing decisions are based on market research conducted to identify Suzy Shier customers and their needs. Having defined its target market carefully, Suzy Shier is able to achieve a number of advantages. It can continually study the fashion interests of 18- to 35-year-old women, it can pretest new fashion ideas, it can build a unique image, it can aim its advertising carefully, and it can locate in shopping centers in areas with the right demographics.

**TABLE 14-2**
**Classification of Retailers Based on the Amount of Customer Service**

| | Decreasing Services ←————————→ Increasing Services | | |
|---|---|---|---|
| | **Self-Service** | **Limited Service** | **Full Service** |
| **Attributes** | Very few services<br>Price appeal<br>Staple goods<br>Convenience goods | Small variety of services<br>Shopping goods | Wide variety of services<br>Fashion merchandise<br>Specialty merchandise |
| **Examples** | Warehouse retailing<br>Grocery stores<br>Discount retailing<br>Variety stores<br>Mail-order retailing<br>Automatic vending | Door-to-door sales<br>Department stores<br>Telephone sales<br>Variety stores | Specialty stores<br>Department stores |

**Source:** Adapted from Larry D. Redinbaugh, *Retailing Management: A Planning Approach* (New York: McGraw-Hill, 1976), p. 12.

## DEPARTMENT STORE

A **department store** carries a wide variety of product lines, typically clothing, home furnishings, and household goods. Each line is operated as a separate department managed by specialist buyers or merchandisers.

Department stores have been a dominant force in retailing and are well-known by most Canadians. Since 1979, however, department stores have lost ground to other types of retailers. Several factors led to this decline, including greater competition from specialty stores, lack of clearly defined target markets, and reduced customer service. Some of the department stores are trying to arrest

Specialty stores, such as Suzy Shier, can focus on the needs and tastes of a specific market segment.

this trend by redesigning their stores (Sears) or repositioning them (Woodwards, Simpsons).[3]

## SUPERMARKET

**Supermarkets** are large, low-cost, low-margin, high-volume, self-service stores that carry a wide variety of food, laundry, and household products. Seven supermarket chains control over one-half of the retail food industry in Canada and each of the chains tends to be concentrated in a particular geographic area. For example, Safeway is the dominant chain in Western Canada with sales of around $4 billion annually. In Ontario, A&P is the dominant chain, followed by Loblaws, which also controls Zehr's. The other chain with a strong market position in Ontario is the Oshawa Group (with IGA and Food City). In Quebec, Metro-Richelieu, Steinberg, and Provigo are the market leaders. Sobey's and Loblaws are dominant in the Maritimes. Sobey's also has a substantial interest in Provigo.

Supermarkets have faced a number of challenges in recent years including the growth of fast-food outlets (McDonald's, Kentucky Fried Chicken, Pizza Pizza). Canadians are now spending over 35% of their total food budgets outside of food stores. In response, supermarkets have increased the number of their private brands (including generics), added more high-margin nonfood items, and added "takeout" delicatessens and bakery departments. As well, they are building larger stores and using "scrambled merchandising" strategies. Today many supermarkets are selling prescriptions, appliances, tapes, sporting goods, hardware, garden supplies, and even cameras, hoping to find high-margin lines to improve profit.

## CONVENIENCE STORE

**Convenience stores** are small stores that carry a limited line of high-turnover convenience goods. Examples include 7-Eleven, Mac's, and Beckers. These stores locate near residential areas and remain open long hours and seven days a week. Convenience stores must charge high prices to make up for higher operating costs and lower sales volume, but they satisfy an important consumer need. Consumers use convenience stores for "fill-in" purchases at off hours or when time is short, and they are willing to pay for the convenience. There are approximately 4,800 convenience stores in Canada, like Mac's, Beckers, and 7-Eleven, which have total sales in excess of $2 billion annually.[4]

## SUPERSTORE AND COMBINATION STORE

These two types of stores are larger than the conventional supermarket. **Superstores** are about twice the size of regular supermarkets and carry a large assortment of routinely purchased food and nonfood items. They offer such services as laundry, dry cleaning, shoe repair, video rentals, gasoline bars, and bargain lunch counters. An example is the Calgary Co-op, which has 12 superstores in Calgary each about twice the size of the average supermarket. Total annual sales exceed $370 million and the Co-op holds more than a 35% share of the Calgary retail food market.[5]

**Combination stores** are combined food and drug stores. Their average size is over 100,000 square feet and they are the latest weapon in the supermarket wars in Canada. Companies like Loblaws, Ferme Carnaval, and Safeway are opening "super-combos" from Halifax to Vancouver. They offer the consumer a wide selection of food, nonfood, and drug products at discount prices. Total sales from one super-combo store can exceed $75 million annually, up to seven times more than a conventional supermarket.[6]

A Loblaws Superstore.

## SERVICE BUSINESS

For some businesses, the "product line" is actually a service. Service retailers include hotels and motels, banks, airlines, colleges, hospitals, movie theaters, bowling alleys, restaurants, repair services, hair salons, and dry cleaners. Service retailers in Canada are growing faster than product retailers, and each service industry has its own retailing drama. Banks look for new ways to distribute their services, including automatic tellers, direct deposit, and telephone banking. The amusement industry has spawned Disney World, Canada's Wonderland, and other theme parks. H&R Block has built a franchise network to help consumers pay as little as possible to the government.

# Relative Prices

Retailers can also be classified by their prices. Most retailers charge regular prices and offer normal-quality goods and customer service. Some offer higher-quality goods and service at higher prices. Discount stores run lower-cost, lower-service operations and sell goods for lower prices. Here we will look at discount stores and two offshoots, warehouse stores and catalog showrooms.

## DISCOUNT STORE

A **discount store** sells standard merchandise at lower prices by accepting lower margins and selling higher volumes. The use of occasional discounts or specials does not make a discount store. A true discount store regularly sells its merchandise at lower prices, offering mostly national brands, not inferior goods.

Competition in recent years, particularly from specialty stores and combination stores, has created problems for many discount retailers. For example, K mart, a general merchandise discount chain in Canada, has shown slow profit growth in the last few years.

## WAREHOUSE STORE

A **warehouse store** is a no-frills, reduced-service store that seeks high volume through low prices. One of its most interesting forms is the furniture showroom warehouse. Conventional furniture stores have run warehouse sales for years to clear out old stock. However, this new concept has been most clearly developed in Canada by Leon's Furniture and The Brick. Shoppers enter a large warehouse usually located in a low-rent suburban area. They enter the showroom section containing room settings of attractively displayed furniture and appliances. Customers select goods and place orders with salespeople. By the time the customer pays, leaves, and drives to the loading dock, the merchandise is ready. Leon's 23 company-owned outlets and 21 franchises sell over $240 million each year with aggressive advertising, numerous sales, and a good product assortment.[7]

## CATALOG SHOWROOM

A **catalog showroom** sells a wide selection of high-markup, fast- moving, brand-name goods at discount prices. These include jewelry, power tools, cameras, luggage, small appliances, toys, and sporting goods. Catalog showrooms make their money by cutting costs and margins to provide low prices that will attract a higher volume of sales. The catalog showroom industry is led by companies such as Consumers Distributing.

Emerging in the late 1960s, catalog showrooms became one of retailing's hottest new forms. But catalog showrooms have been struggling in recent years to hold their share of the retail market. Department stores and discount retailers now run regular sales that match showroom prices.

# Nature of Business Premises

Most goods and services are sold through stores, but nonstore retailing has been growing rapidly in Canada. Here we examine three types of nonstore retailing: direct marketing, direct selling, and automatic vending.

## DIRECT MARKETING

Direct marketing uses various advertising media to interact directly with consumers, generally calling for the consumer to make a direct response. We will now look at the four major forms of direct marketing: direct-mail and catalog marketing, telemarketing, and electronic shopping.

## DIRECT-MAIL AND CATALOG MARKETING

Direct-mail marketing involves single mailings that include letters, ads, samples, foldouts, and other "salespeople on wings" sent to prospects on mailing lists. Mailing lists are developed from customer lists or obtained from mailing list houses that provide names of people fitting almost any description—the superwealthy, university students, veterinarians, pet owners, or just about anyone else.[8]

Direct mail is becoming increasingly popular because it permits high target market selectivity, can be personalized, is flexible, and allows easy measurements of results. Although the cost-per-thousand people reached is higher than with such mass media as television or magazines, the people who are reached are much better prospects. Organizations ranging from IBM Canada to Eaton's, from the National Ballet of Canada to the United Way, all use direct mail as a means of marketing their products and services. Direct mail has proved very successful in promoting magazines, books, records, and insurance. Major charities use direct mail to raise over $350 million in Canada each year. It is estimated that the average household

Catalogs are an important promotion tool for many retailers.

in Canada receives 106 pieces of direct mail each year.[9] Direct mail is popular with marketers because it can be a very cost-effective form of advertising and it is much easier to analyze the sales results of direct mail than those of broadcast media.

Catalog marketing involves selling through catalogs mailed to a select list of customers or made available in stores. Sears Canada, the industry leader, sends out 18 editions of its catalogs each year to over 3.7 million households and generates between 30 and 40% of its total sales through catalog sales. Other Canadian retailers, notably Canadian Tire and Beaver Lumber, use catalogs as part of their marketing mix, although the customer visits the store to purchase items shown in the catalog.

## TELEMARKETING

**Telemarketing**—using the telephone to sell directly to consumers—has become the major direct marketing tool. Telemarketing blossomed in the late 1960s with the introduction of inward and outward Wide Area Telephone Service (WATS). With IN WATS, marketers can use toll-free 800 numbers to receive orders from television and radio ads, direct mail, or catalogs. With OUT WATS, they can use the phone to sell directly to consumers and businesses.

Some telemarketing systems are fully automated. For example, automatic dialing and recorded message players (ADRMPs) self-dial numbers, play a voice-activated advertising message, and take orders from interested customers on an answering machine device or by forwarding the call to an operator. Telemarketing is used in business marketing as well as consumer marketing. In a study of Canadian industrial firms using telemarketing, most perceived their telemarketing efforts as successful.[10]

## TELEVISION MARKETING

**Television marketing** is used in two different ways to market products directly to consumers. The first is through direct-response advertising. Direct-response marketers air television spots, often 60 or 120 seconds long, that persuasively describe a product and give customers a toll-free number for ordering. Direct-response advertising works well for magazines, books, small appliances, records and tapes, collectibles, and many other products.

Home shopping channels, another form of television direct marketing, are television programs—or even entire channels—dedicated to selling goods and services. The Canadian Home Shopping Network broadcasts 24 hours a day on cable television. It has met with limited success in Canada.

## ELECTRONIC SHOPPING

The major form of electronic shopping is videotex. Videotex is a two-way system that links consumers with the seller's computer data banks by cable or telephone lines. The videotex service makes up a computerized catalog of products offered by producers, retailers, banks, travel organizations, and others. Consumers either use an ordinary television set that has a special keyboard device connected to the system by two-way cable, or they hook into the system by telephone using a home computer. For example, a consumer wanting to buy a new compact disc player could request a list of all CD brands in the computerized catalog, compare brands, and order one by using a charge card—all without leaving home.

Videotex is still a new idea. One system, developed by Bell Canada and Telecommerce, has been introduced in Toronto and Montreal, but its future is uncertain.

## AUTOMATIC VENDING

**Automatic vending** through coin-operated machines generates annual sales of over $360 million in Canada.[11] Today's machines use space-age and computer technology to sell a wide variety of impulse goods—cigarettes, beverages, candy, newspapers, foods and snacks, french fries, hosiery, cosmetics, paperbacks, T-shirts, and insurance policies.

Vending machines are found in factories, offices, lobbies, retail stores, and gasoline stations. They increasingly supply entertainment services—pinball machines, jukeboxes, and electronic computer games. Automatic teller machines provide bank customers with chequing, savings, withdrawals, and funds-transfer services.

Vending machines offer 24-hour selling, self-service, and less damaged goods. But automatic vending is a more costly channel, and prices of vended goods are often 15 to 20% higher than in other retail methods. Customers must put up with machine breakdowns, out-of-stocks, and the fact that merchandise cannot be returned.

## DOOR-TO-DOOR RETAILING

**Door-to-door retailing**, which started centuries ago with roving peddlers, has grown into a substantial industry. In Canada, over 200,000 people are involved in selling door-to-door, office-to-office, or at home sales parties. The leading direct sales companies in Canada are Avon, Mary Kay Cosmetics, and Shaklee.

Door-to-door selling companies have sometimes been accused of pyramid selling, which is illegal under the Competition Act. The main feature of a pyramid sales company is that money is made through recruiting "representatives" and having them purchase the product. In such cases the product is sold through a number of recruiters rather than to the "final consumer."[12] Instances of pyramid selling have created a certain amount of distrust for direct sales firms.

The advantages of door-to-door selling are consumer convenience and personal attention, but the high costs of hiring, training, paying, and motivating the salesforce result in higher prices. Door-to-door selling has a somewhat uncertain future. The increase in the number of single- person and working-couple households decreases the chances of finding anyone at home. Recent advances in interactive telecommunication make it likely that the door-to-door salesperson may be replaced in the future by the household television or home computer.

# Control of Outlets

Retailing institutions can be classified by form of ownership. Independent retail stores account for about 57% of all retail sales. Here we will look at several other forms of ownership—the corporate chain, voluntary chain, and retailer cooperative and franchise organization.

## CORPORATE CHAIN

The chain store is one of the most important retail developments of this century. In the general merchandise field and in food retailing, corporate chain stores control a substantial share of the market. A chain store has been defined by Statistics Canada as an organization operating four or more retail outlets in the same kind of business, under the same legal ownership.[13] Beginning in 1869 with Timothy Eaton, generally acknowledged as being the "father of the department store" in Canada, department stores have been a dominant force in retailing in Canada. By 1929, three chains accounted for 80% of all department store sales.[14] Since then the level of concentration declined as more competitors entered the market.

Today, the six largest department store chains—The Bay, Sears Canada, Woolworth, Kmart, Woodwards, and Eaton's—have total sales exceeding $16 billion annually. These chains control a substantial portion of sales, store locations, buying power, and financial resources in this market. Their dominance has been created by aggressive marketing, merchandising practices, central buying, and efficient distribution.

A similar picture exists in food retailing in Canada but with an interesting twist. The giant supermarket chains—A&P, Safeway, Loblaws, Provigo, Steinberg, The Oshawa Group—have frequently achieved growth through vertical integration. For example, George Weston Limited controls Loblaws and also controls, either directly or through subsidiaries like Loblaws, bakeries, flour mills, cookie and biscuit factories, chocolate bar firms, dairies, sugar companies, fish canneries, oyster farms, grocery wholesalers, tea manufacturers, and grocery outlets in the United States, to name a few of their activities. This extensive vertical integration in the food industry allows Weston to achieve both economies of scale and control over the channel of distribution. George Weston Limited is now the sixth largest company in Canada, with sales of over $10.5 billion annually.

A number of specialty retail chains have also grown rapidly in recent years—Canadian Tire in the automotive and hardware business, Dylex, the Grafton Group, Reitman's, and Dalmys in the clothing field, and Beaver Lumber in the home improvement area. These specialty chains have many advantages over independents. Their size allows them to buy in large quantities at lower prices. They can afford to hire corporate-level specialists to deal with such areas as pricing, promotion, merchandising, inventory control, and sales forecasting. In addition, chains gain promotional economies because their advertising costs are spread over many stores and a large sales volume.

## VOLUNTARY CHAIN AND RETAILER COOPERATIVE

The great success of corporate chains caused many independents to band together in one of two forms of contractual associations. One is the voluntary chain—a wholesaler- sponsored group of independent retailers that engage in group buying and common merchandising. Examples include Federated Co-operatives, a Western Canadian chain that supplies over 300 retail stores and generates annual sales of over $1.5 billion.[15] The other is the retailer cooperative—a group of independent retailers that band together and set up a jointly owned central wholesale operation and conduct joint merchandising and promotion efforts. Examples include the Red River Co-op and The Scotsburn Co-operative. These organizations give independents the buying and promotion economies they need to meet the prices of corporate chains.

## FRANCHISE ORGANIZATION

A **franchise** is a contractual association between a manufacturer, wholesaler, or service organization (the franchiser) and independent business people who buy the right to own and operate one or more units in the franchise system (franchisees). The main difference between a franchise and other contractual systems (voluntary chains and retail cooperatives) is that franchise systems are normally based on some unique product or service, or on a method of doing business, or on a trade name, goodwill, or patent that the franchiser has developed. Franchising is one of the fastest-growing segments of retailing in Canada and accounts for about 45% of all retail sales. Experts predict that by the year 2000, franchises will account for 60% of retail sales.

Virtually anything and everything is now being franchised in Canada, from records to rent-a-wreck, from real estate to repair shops. Leading the way are firms such as Canadian Tire, McDonald's, Shoppers Drug Mart, Scott's (Kentucky Fried Chicken), Coca-Cola, and Pepsi-Cola, all with sales of over $400 million annually.

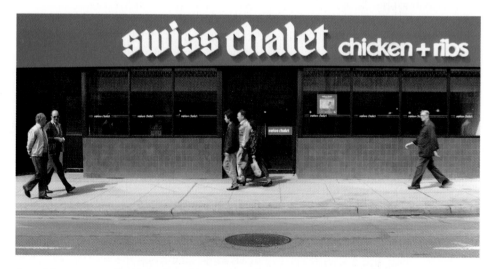

Franchises are a major form of retailing in Canada.

Cara is one of the leading franchise companies as combined sales from Swiss Chalet and Harvey's are above $400 million a year. About one-half of the total retail sales through the more than 50,000 franchise outlets are accounted for by automobile and truck dealers and soft drink bottlers.[16]

# Type of Store Cluster

Most stores today cluster together to increase their customer pulling power and to give consumers the convenience of one-stop shopping. The main types of store clusters are the central business district and the shopping center.

## CENTRAL BUSINESS DISTRICT

Central business districts were the main form of retail cluster until the 1950s. Every large city and town had a central business district with department stores, specialty stores, banks, and movie theaters. When people began to move to the suburbs,

The Eaton Centre is a "mini-downtown" within Toronto's downtown core.

these central business districts, with their traffic and parking problems, began to lose business. Downtown merchants opened branches in suburban shopping centers, and the decline of the central business districts continued. In the past decade, many cities have joined with merchants to try to revive downtown shopping areas by building malls and underground parking. Many central business districts have made a comeback; others remain in a slow and possibly irreversible decline.

### SHOPPING CENTER

A **shopping center** is a group of retail businesses planned, developed, owned, and managed as a unit, and related in location, size, and type of store to the trade area that it serves. The regional shopping center is the largest and most dramatic of the shopping centers. A regional shopping center is like a mini-downtown. It contains from 40 to 100 or more stores and pulls customers from a wide area. In its early form, the regional shopping center had two strong department stores "anchoring" the ends, with specialty stores in between. With this design, consumers could easily compare products at various specialty and department stores. Regional centers have added new types of retailers over the years—dentists, health clubs, and even branch libraries. Larger regional malls now have several department stores and several shopping levels. Probably the most famous regional mall in Canada is the West Edmonton Mall, which has a children's zoo, circus rides, and a variety of other activities to attract and entertain shoppers in Alberta. It is the world's largest shopping, fashion, and entertainment center with over 800 stores located in the mall.

A community shopping center contains 15 to 50 retail stores. The center normally contains a primary store (usually a branch of a department or variety store), a supermarket, specialty stores, convenience goods stores, professional offices, and sometimes a bank. The primary store usually locates at the middle of the center.

Most shopping centers are neighborhood shopping centers that contain five to 15 stores. They are close and convenient for consumers. They usually contain a supermarket as the anchor store and several service stores—a dry cleaner, self-service laundry, drugstore, a hair stylist shop, a hardware, or other stores located in an unplanned strip.

In 1987, for the first time, Canadians spent more money in the 3,270 shopping centers than in all other retail outlets combined.[17] Current trends suggest that shopping centers will steadily increase their share of total retail sales.

# RETAILER MARKETING DECISIONS

We will now look at the major marketing decisions retailers must make about their target markets, product assortment and services, price, promotion, and place.

## Target Market Decision

Retailers must first define the target market, and decide how they will be positioned in the target market. The retailer's positioning guides all other retailer marketing decisions. Product assortment, services, pricing, advertising, store decor, and other decisions must all support the retailer's position in its market segment.

Some stores define their target markets quite well. A women's apparel store in Montreal positions itself as "fashions for the discriminating woman" and targets upper-income women between the ages of 30 and 35 living within 30 minutes' driving time of the store. But many retailers fail clearly to define their target markets and positions. They try to have "something for everyone" and end up not satisfying any market well. Even large department stores like Eaton's must define their major target markets so that they can design effective strategies for serving these markets.

## Product Assortment and Services Decision

Retailers have to decide on three major product variables: product assortment, services mix, and store atmosphere.

The retailer's product assortment must match what target shoppers expect. In fact, assortment becomes a key element in the competitive battle with other retailers.

Stores create distinct atmospheres to match their target markets.

**TABLE 14-3**
**Typical Retail Services**

| Primary Services | Supplementary Services | |
|---|---|---|
| Alterations | Baby strollers | Packaging and gift wrapping |
| Complaint handling | Bill payment | Product locater |
| Convenient store hours | Bridal registries | Restaurants or snack counters |
| Credit | Cheque cashing | Shopping consultants |
| Delivery | Children's playrooms | Shopping information |
| Fitting rooms | Demonstrations | Shows, displays, and exhibits |
| Installation and assembly | Layaway | Special ordering |
| Merchandise returns and adjustments | Lost and found | Wheelchairs |
| Parking | Personal shopping | |
| Rest rooms | Package checkrooms | |
| Service and repair | | |
| Telephone ordering | | |

The retailer has to decide on product assortment width and depth. Thus a restaurant can offer a narrow and shallow assortment (small lunch counter), a narrow and deep assortment (delicatessen), a wide and shallow assortment (cafeteria), or a wide and deep assortment (large restaurant). Another product assortment element is the quality of the goods. The customer is interested not only in the range of choice, but also in the quality of the products.

However, no matter what the store's product assortment and quality level, there will always be competitors with similar assortments and quality. Thus, the retailer must search for other ways to differentiate itself from similar competitors. It can use any of several product-differentiation strategies. For one thing, it can offer merchandise that no other competitor carries—its own private brands or national brands on which it holds exclusives. Thus, Loblaws offers the President's Choice label. Second, the retailer can feature blockbuster merchandising events—Eaton's is known for its Trans Canada sale. Finally, the retailer can differentiate itself by offering a highly targeted product assortment—Pennington's carries fashion for larger women.

Retailers also must decide on the services mix to offer customers. The old "mom and pop" grocery stores offered home delivery, credit, and conversation, services that today's supermarkets have dropped. The services mix is one of the key tools of nonprice competition for setting one store apart from another. Table 14-3 lists some of the major services full-service retailers can offer.

The store's atmosphere is a third element in its product arsenal. Every store has a physical layout that makes moving around hard or easy. Every store has a "feel"; one store is crowded, another is charming, a third is plush, a fourth is somber. The store must have a planned atmosphere that suits the target market and moves them to buy. A bank should be quiet, solid, and peaceful, and a nightclub should be bright, loud, and vibrating.

## Price Decision

A retailer's prices are a key positioning factor and must be decided in relation to its target market, its product and service assortment, and its competition. All retailers would like to charge high markups and achieve high volume, but the two seldom go together. Most retailers seek either high markups on lower volume (most specialty stores) or low markups on higher volume (mass merchandisers and discount stores).

Retailers must also pay attention to pricing tactics. Most retailers will put low prices on some items to serve as "traffic builders" or "loss leaders." On some occasions, they run storewide sales. On others, they plan markdowns on slower-moving merchandise. For example, shoe retailers expect to sell 50% of their shoes at the normal markup, 25% at a 40% markup, and the remaining 25% at cost.

## Promotion Decision

Retailers use the normal promotion tools of advertising, personal selling, sales promotion, and publicity to reach consumers. Retailers advertise in newspapers, magazines, radio, and television. Advertising may be supported by circulars and direct mail pieces. Personal selling requires careful training of salespeople in how to greet customers, meet their needs, and handle their complaints. Sales promotion may include in-store demonstrations, contests, and visiting celebrities. Publicity is always available to retailers who have something interesting to say.

## Place Decision

Retailers often say that there are three critical factors in retailing success: location, location, and location. A retailer's location is a key factor in its ability to attract customers. The costs of building or leasing facilities also have a major impact on the retailer's profits. Thus site location decisions are among the most important the retailer makes. Small retailers may have to settle for whatever locations they can find or afford. Large retailers usually employ specialists who select locations using advanced site-location methods.[18]

# THE FUTURE OF RETAILING

Several trends will affect the future of retailing. The slowdown in population and economic growth means that retailers will no longer have sales and profit growth through natural expansion in current and new markets. Growth will have to come from increasing their shares of current markets. But greater competition and new types of retailers will make it more difficult for retailers to improve their market shares. Consumer demographics, life styles, and shopping patterns are changing rapidly. To be successful, retailers will have to choose target segments carefully and position themselves strongly.[19] As well, Canadian retailers may face increased competition from U.S. retailers as the Free Trade Agreement reduces the trade barriers between Canada and the United States. Some Canadian retailers are responding by entering the U.S. market (see Marketing Highlight 14-1).

# MARKETING HIGHLIGHT 14-1

## North America: One Retail Market?

With the Free Trade Agreement promising easier access between Canada and the United States, retailers from both countries are eyeing the "other side of the fence" for growth opportunities. With the U.S. retail market approximately ten times the size of the Canadian market, some Canadian retailers see future growth coming from the U.S. However, these retailers should be prepared for increased competition in Canada from their U.S. counterparts.

Some experts feel that Canada's retail sector will be reshaped in the 1990s as more U.S. retailers expand into Canada. Specialty chains such as Lenscrafter, Pier 1 Imports, the Gap, and Toys R Us have all entered the Canadian market, and predictions are that more chains will come. Many Canadian retailers have tried the U.S. market but few have been successful. In fact, nearly two dozen have entered—including Canadian Tire, Dylex, and Pennington's—and most have either withdrawn from the market or are struggling with sustained losses. The reasons for these failures are varied, but two stand out: Canadian retailers misjudged either the U.S. consumer or the intensely competitive nature of U.S. retail markets. Some Canadian retailers have succeeded, including People's Jewellers, which through its purchase of Zale is now the second largest chain of jewellery stores in North America. People's success is explained in part by its patience in learning about the U.S. market.

In the future, retailers in both countries are likely to face increased competition as trade barriers are eliminated and North America becomes open to all retailers, north and south of the border.

**Sources:** Jim McElgreen, "Canada Headed For Retail Invasion," *Marketing*, October 2, 1988, p. 2; Kenneth Kidd, "U.S. Market Tough, Retailers Find," *Globe and Mail*, November 4, 1989, p. B1; Gerry Blackwell, "Looking For That Pot of Gold," *Challenges*, Summer 1989, pp. 22-25; Henry W. Lane and Terry Hildebrand, "How To Survive in U.S. Retail Markets," *Business Quarterly*, Winter, 1990, pp. 62-66; and Eric Reguly, "Something for Everyone Pays Off Big For Peoples," *Financial Post*, April 16, 1990, p. 9.

Rising costs will make more efficient operation and smarter buying essential to successful retailing. New methods such as computerized checkout and inventory control will help cut costs and provide new ways to serve consumers better.

Many retailing innovations are partially explained by the wheel of retailing concept.[20] According to this concept, many new types of retailing forms begin as low-margin, low-price, low-status operations. They challenge established retailers that have become "fat" over the years by letting their costs and margins increase. The new retailers' success leads them to upgrade their facilities and offer more services. This raises their costs and forces them to increase their prices. Eventually, the new retailers become like the conventional retailers they replaced. The cycle begins again when still newer types of retailers evolve with lower costs and prices.

New retail forms will continue to emerge to meet new consumer needs and new situations. But the life cycle of new retail forms is getting shorter. Department stores took about 100 years to reach the mature stage of the life cycle; more recent forms reach maturity in about ten years. Retailers can no longer sit back with a successful formula. To remain successful, they must keep adapting.

# WHOLESALING

**Wholesaling** includes all activities involved in selling goods and services to those buying for resale or business use. A retail bakery does wholesaling when it sells pastry to the local hotel. However, we will define as **wholesalers** firms engaged primarily in wholesaling activity.

Wholesalers buy mostly from producers and sell mostly to retailers, industrial consumers, and other wholesalers. But why are wholesalers used at all? For example, why would a producer use wholesalers rather than sell directly to retailers or consumers? The answer is that wholesalers are often better at performing one or more of the following channel functions:

- **Selling and promoting.** Wholesalers' salesforces help manufacturers reach many small customers at a low cost. The wholesaler has more contacts and is often better trusted by the buyer than the distant manufacturer.
- **Buying and assortment building.** Wholesalers can select items and build assortments needed by their customers, thus saving the customers much work.
- **Bulk breaking.** Wholesalers save their customers money by buying in carload lots and breaking bulk (breaking large lots into small quantities).

A specialty wholesaler.

- **Warehousing.** Wholesalers hold inventories, thereby reducing the inventory costs and risks of suppliers and customers.
- **Transportation.** Wholesalers can provide quicker delivery to buyers because they are closer.
- **Financing.** Wholesalers finance their customers by giving credit, and they finance their suppliers by ordering early and paying bills on time.
- **Risk bearing.** Wholesalers absorb some risk by taking title and bearing the cost of theft, damage, spoilage, and obsolescence.
- **Market information.** Wholesalers give information to suppliers and customers about competitors, new products, and price developments.
- **Management services and advice.** Wholesalers often help retailers to train their salesclerks, improve store layouts and displays, and set up accounting and inventory control systems.

## Types of Wholesalers

Wholesalers fall into three major groups (see Table 14-4): merchant wholesalers, brokers and agents, and manufacturers' sales branches and offices. We will now look at each of these groups of wholesalers.

### MERCHANT WHOLESALERS

**Merchant wholesalers** are independently owned businesses that take title to the merchandise they handle. Merchant wholesalers are of two broad types: full-service and limited-service wholesalers.

**FULL-SERVICE WHOLESALERS** Full service wholesalers provide a full set of services such as carrying stock, using a salesforce, offering credit, making deliveries, and providing management assistance. They are either wholesale merchants or industrial distributors.

Wholesale merchants sell mostly to retailers and provide a full range of services. They vary in the width of their product line. Some carry several lines of

**TABLE 14-4**
**Classification of Wholesalers**

| Merchant Wholesalers | Brokers and Agents | Manufacturers' Sales Branches and Offices |
|---|---|---|
| Full-service | Brokers | Sales branches and offices |
|     Wholesale merchants | Agents | Purchasing offices |
|     Industrial distributors | | |
| Limited-service wholesalers | | |
|     Cash-and-carry wholesalers | | |
|     Truck wholesalers | | |
|     Drop shippers | | |
|     Rack jobbers | | |
|     Producers' cooperatives | | |
|     Mail-order wholesalers | | |

goods to meet the needs of both general merchandise retailers and single-line retailers. Others carry one or two lines of goods in a greater depth of assortment. Examples are hardware wholesalers, drug wholesalers, and clothing wholesalers. Some specialty wholesalers carry only part of a line in great depth. Examples are health food, seafood, and automotive parts wholesalers. They offer customers deeper choice and greater product knowledge. Most of Canada's major food retailers, including Loblaws and Safeway, operate separate wholesale units that supply their own stores plus independent supermarkets and convenience stores.

Industrial distributors are merchant wholesalers who sell to producers rather than to retailers. They provide inventory, credit, delivery, and other services. They may carry a broad range of merchandise, a general line, or a specialty line. Industrial distributors may focus on such lines as MRO items (maintenance, repair, and operating supplies), OEM items (original equipment supplies such as ball bearings, motors), or equipment (such as hand and power tools, and forklift trucks).

**LIMITED-SERVICE WHOLESALERS** Limited service wholesalers offer fewer services to their suppliers and customers. There are several types of limited service wholesalers.

Cash-and-carry wholesalers have a limited line of fast-moving goods, sell to small retailers for cash, and normally do not deliver. A small fish store retailer, for example, normally drives at dawn to a cash-and-carry fish wholesaler and buys several crates of fish, pays on the spot, drives the merchandise back to the store, and unloads it.

Truck wholesalers (also called truck jobbers) perform a selling and delivery function. They carry a limited line of goods (such as milk, bread, snack foods), which they sell for cash as they make their rounds of supermarkets, small groceries, hospitals, restaurants, factory cafeterias, and hotels.

Drop shippers operate in bulk industries such as coal, lumber, and heavy equipment. They do not carry inventory or handle the product. Once an order is received, they find a producer who ships the goods directly to the customer. The drop shipper takes title and risk from the time the order is accepted to the time it is delivered to the customer. Because drop shippers do not carry inventory, their costs are lower and they can pass on some savings to customers.

Rack jobbers serve grocery and drug retailers, mostly in the area of nonfood items. These retailers do not want to order and maintain displays of hundreds of nonfood items. The rack jobbers send delivery trucks to stores, and the delivery person sets up racks of toys, paperbacks, hardware items, health and beauty aids, or other items. They price the goods, keep them fresh, and set up and keep inventory records. Rack jobbers sell on consignment, which means that they retain title to the goods and bill the retailers only for the goods sold to consumers. Thus they provide such services as delivery, shelving, inventory, and financing. They do little promotion because they carry many branded items that are highly advertised.

Mail-order wholesalers send catalogs to retail, industrial, and institutional customers offering jewelry, cosmetics, special foods, and other small items. Their main customers are businesses in small outlying areas. They have no salesforce to call on customers.

## BROKERS AND AGENTS

Brokers and agents differ from merchant wholesalers in two ways: they do not take title to goods, and they perform only a few functions. Their main function is to aid in buying and selling, and for these services they earn a commission on the selling price. Like merchant wholesalers, they generally specialize by product line or customer types.

BROKERS   A **broker** brings buyers and sellers together and assists in negotiation. Brokers are paid by the party that hired them. They do not carry inventory, get involved in financing, or assume risk. The most familiar examples are food brokers, real estate brokers, insurance brokers, and security brokers.

AGENTS Agents represent buyers or sellers on a more permanent basis. There are several types. Manufacturers' agents (also called manufacturers' representatives) are the most numerous type of agent wholesaler. They represent two or more manufacturers of related lines. They have a formal agreement with each manufacturer covering prices, territories, order-handling procedures, delivery and warranties, and commission rates. They know each manufacturer's product line and use their wide contacts to sell the products. Manufacturers' agents are used in such lines as apparel, furniture, and electrical goods. Most manufacturers' agents are small businesses, with only a few employees who are skilled salespeople. They are hired by small producers who cannot afford to maintain their own field salesforces, and by large producers who want to open new territories or sell in areas that cannot support a full-time salesperson.

Selling agents contract to sell a producer's entire output when the manufacturer is either not interested in doing the selling or feels unqualified. The selling agent serves as a sales department and has considerable influence over prices, terms, and conditions of sale. The selling agent normally has no territory limits. Selling agents are found in such product areas as textiles, industrial machinery and equipment, coal and coke, chemicals, and metals.

Purchasing agents generally have a long-term relationship with buyers. They make purchases for buyers, and often receive, inspect, warehouse, and ship goods to the buyers. One type consists of resident buyers in major apparel markets, who look for apparel lines that can be carried by small retailers located in small cities. They know a lot and provide helpful market information to clients as well as obtaining the best goods and prices available.

Commission merchants (or houses) are agents that take physical possession of products and negotiate sales. They are not normally used on a long-term basis. They are used most often in agricultural marketing by farmers who do not want to sell their own output and do not belong to cooperatives. The commission merchant would take a truckload of farm products to a central market, sell it for the best price, deduct a commission and expenses, and pay the balance to the farmer.

## MANUFACTURERS' SALES BRANCHES AND OFFICES

The third major type of wholesaling is done in **manufacturers' sales branches and offices** by sellers or buyers themselves, rather than through independent wholesalers. There are two types.

Manufacturers often set up their own sales branches and offices to improve inventory control, selling, and promotion. Sales branches carry inventory and are found in such industries as lumber and automotive equipment and parts. Sales offices do not carry inventory and are most often found in dry goods and notion industries. Many retailers set up purchasing offices in major market centers such as Toronto and Vancouver. These purchasing offices perform a role similar to that of brokers or agents, but are part of the buyer's organization.

# WHOLESALER MARKETING DECISIONS

Wholesalers also make decisions about target markets, product assortments and services, pricing, promotion, and place.

## Target Market Decision

Wholesalers, like retailers, need to define their target market and not try to serve everyone. They can choose a target group by size of customer (only large retailers), type of customer (convenience food stores only), need for service (customers who need credit), or other factors. Within the target group, they can identify the more profitable customers in order to design stronger offers and build better relationships with these customers. They can propose automatic reordering systems, set up management training and advising systems, or even sponsor a voluntary chain. They can discourage less profitable customers by requiring larger orders or adding charges to smaller ones.

## Product Assortment and Services Decision

The wholesaler's "product" is its assortment. Wholesalers are under great pressure to carry a full line and stock enough for immediate delivery, but this can damage profits. Wholesalers today are cutting down on the number of lines they carry, choosing to carry only the more profitable ones. Wholesalers are also rethinking which services count most in building strong customer relationships and which should be dropped or charged for. The key is to find the mix of services most valued by their target customers.

## Pricing Decision

Wholesalers usually mark up the cost of goods by a standard percentage, say 20%. Expenses may run 17% of the gross margin, leaving a profit margin of three percent. In grocery wholesaling the average profit margin is often less than two percent. Wholesalers are now trying new pricing approaches. They may cut their margin on some lines in order to win important new customers. They will ask suppliers for a special price break when they can turn it into an increase in the supplier's sales.

## Promotion Decision

Most wholesalers are not promotion-minded. Their use of trade advertising, sales promotion, publicity, and personal selling is largely scattered and unplanned. Many are behind the times in personal selling—they still see selling as a single salesperson talking to a single customer instead of a team effort to sell, build, and service major accounts. Wholesalers also need to adopt some of the nonpersonal promotion techniques used by retailers. They need to develop an overall promotion strategy and to make greater use of supplier promotion materials and programs.

## Place Decision

Wholesalers typically locate in low-rent, low-tax areas, and put little money into their physical setting and offices. Their materials-handling and order-processing systems are often out of date. To meet rising costs, large and progressive wholesalers are turning to the automated warehouse. Orders are fed into a computer, and the items are picked up by mechanical devices and automatically taken to the shipping platform where they are assembled. Many wholesalers are turning to computers and wordprocessing machines to carry out accounting, billing, inventory control, and forecasting. Progressive wholesalers are adapting their services to the needs of target customers and finding cost-reducing methods of doing business.

# Summary

Retailing and wholesaling consist of many organizations bringing goods and services from the point of production to the point of use.

Retailing, one of the major industries in Canada, includes all the activities involved in selling goods or services directly to final consumers for their personal, nonbusiness use. Retailers can be classified in several ways: by the amount of service they provide (self-service, self-selection, limited service, or full service); product line sold (specialty stores, department stores, supermarkets, convenience stores, combination stores, and superstores); relative prices (discount stores, warehouse stores, and catalog showrooms); nature of the business premises (direct marketing, direct selling, and automatic vending); control of outlets (corporate chains, voluntary chains, retailer cooperatives, and franchise organizations); and type of store cluster (central business districts and shopping centers). Retailers make decisions on their target market, product assortment and services, pricing, promotion, and place. They need to find ways to improve their management and increase their productivity.

Wholesaling includes all the activities involved in selling goods or services to those who are buying for the purpose of resale or for business use. Wholesalers help manufacturers deliver their products to the many retailer and industrial users across the nation. Some of the many functions of wholesalers include selling and promoting, buying and assortment building, bulk-breaking, warehousing, transporting, financing, risk bearing, supplying market information, and providing management service and advice.

Wholesalers fall into three groups. Merchant wholesalers take possession of the goods. They can be subclassified as full-service wholesalers (wholesale merchant, industrial distributors) and limited-service wholesalers (cash-and-carry wholesalers, truck wholesalers, drop shippers, rack jobbers, and mail order wholesalers). Agents and brokers do not take possession of the goods but are paid a commission for aiding buying and selling. Manufacturers' branches and offices are wholesaling operations conducted by nonwholesalers to bypass the wholesalers. Progressive wholesalers are adapting their services to the needs of target customers and seek cost-reducing methods of doing business.

# QUESTIONS FOR DISCUSSION

1. In deciding where to shop, many consumers value quality of service more than such factors as price or convenience. If this trend continues, what impact will it have on full-service and limited- service retailers?

2. Which would do more to increase a convenience store's sales—an increase in the length or the breadth of its product assortment?

3. Postal rate hikes make it more expensive to send direct mail, catalogs, and purchased products to consumers. How are direct-mail and catalog marketers likely to respond to an increase in postage rates?

4. Which retailing innovations can be explained by the wheel-of-retailing concept? Will retailing operations continue to evolve as described by this concept?

5. A typical "country store" in a farming community sells a variety of food and non-food items—snacks, staples, hardware, and many other types of goods. From what kinds of wholesalers do such stores obtain their products? Are they the same suppliers that a supermarket uses?

6. How would a small producer of lawn and garden tools prefer to sell its output—through a manufacturers' agent or through a selling agent?

7. When it comes to marketing decisions, are there any fundamental differences among retailers, wholesalers, and manufacturers? Give examples of the marketing decisions made by these three groups, showing key similarities and differences.

8. Why has the promotion area of marketing strategy traditionally been weak for wholesalers? How can they use promotion to improve competitive positions?

# KEY TERMS

**Agent** A wholesaler who represents buyers or sellers on a more permanent basis, performs only a few functions, and does not take title to goods.

**Automatic vending** Selling through coin-operated machines.

**Broker** A wholesaler who does not take title to goods and whose function is to bring buyers and sellers together and assist in negotiation.

**Catalog showroom** A retail operation that sells a wide selection of high-markup, fast-moving, brand-name goods at discount prices.

**Chain store** An organization operating four or more retail outlets in the same kind of business, under the same legal ownership.

**Combination store** Combined food and drug store.

**Convenience store** A small store, located near a residential area, open long hours seven days a week, and carrying a limited line of high-turnover convenience goods.

**Department store** A retail organization that carries a wide variety of product lines, each operated as a separate department managed by specialist buyers or merchandisers.

**Discount store** A retail institution that sells standard merchandise at lower prices by accepting lower margins and selling higher volume.

**Door-to-door retailing** Selling door-to-door, office-to-office, or at home sales parties.

**Franchise** A contractual association between a manufacturer, wholesaler, or service organization (a franchiser) and independent business people who buy the right to own and operate one or more units in the franchise system (franchisees).

**Manufacturers' sales branches and offices** Wholesaling done by sellers or buyers themselves, rather than through independent wholesalers.

**Merchant wholesaler** An independently owned business that takes title to the merchandise it handles.

**Retailers** Businesses whose sales come primarily from retailing.

**Retailing** All activities involved in selling goods or services directly to final consumers for their personal, nonbusiness use.

**Shopping center** A group of retail businesses planned, developed, owned, and managed as a unit.

**Specialty store** A retail store that carries a narrow product line with a deep assortment within that line.

**Supermarkets** Large, low-cost, low-margin, high-volume, self-service stores that carry a wide variety of food, laundry, and household maintenance products.

**Superstore** A store almost twice the size of a regular supermarket that carries a large assortment of routinely purchased food and nonfood items, and offers such services as laundry, dry cleaning, shoe repair, cheque cashing, bill paying, and bargain lunch counters.

**Telemarketing** Using the telephone to sell directly to consumers.

**Television marketing** Using television to market goods directly to consumers.

**Warehouse store** A no-frills, reduced-service store that seeks high volume through low prices.

**Wholesalers** Firms engaged primarily in wholesaling activity.

**Wholesaling** All the activities involved in selling goods and services to those buying for resale or business use.

# References

1. Mel S. Moyer and Hart E. Sernick, "The Decline of the Independent Store in Canada: Some Public Policy Questions," in Donald N. Thompson, et al., eds., *Macromarketing: A Canadian Perspective* (Chicago: American Marketing Association, Proceedings Series, 1980), pp. 124-46; Kenneth Kidd, "Store Was Forecast For Retail Trade," *Globe and Mail*, January 3, 1990, p. B1.

2. John Dart, "Voluntary Retail Groups: Performance and Promise," in Vernon J. Jones, ed., *Marketing ASAC Proceedings* (Montreal, 1980), pp. 117-25.

3. Anne Fletcher, "Woodward's Plans to Target Middle Market," *Financial Post*,

May 28, 1990, p. 31.

4. "Canadian Business 500," *Canadian Business*, June 1990.

5. Barry Nelson, "Co-op Takes on Giants in Calgary Food Fight," *Financial Times*, October 13, 1986, pp. 27.

6. Paul Goldstein, "Super-combos a Bitter Pill for Drug Giants," *Globe and Mail*, May 21, 1985, pp. B1, 4.

7. *Annual Report*, Leon's Furniture Ltd., 1989.

8. Jared Mitchell, "Nowhere to Hide," *Report on Business Magazine*, May 1990, pp. 65-72.

9. Murray Campbell, "Junk Mail," *Globe and Mail*, March 17, 1990, p. D1, D8.

10. Judith J. Marshall and Harrie Vredenburg, "Successfully Using Telemarketing in Industrial Sales," *Industrial Marketing Management*, 17, 1988, pp. 15-22.

11. Don Hogarth, "Loonie Fuels Vending Machine Fortunes," *Financial Post*, November 27, 1989, p. 1.

12. Ann Silversides, "Fine Line Separates Pyramids, Multi-Level Marketing," *Globe and Mail*, May 30, 1981, p. B1.

13. This definition is contained in *Retail Chain and Department Stores*, Statistics Canada, Catalogue 63-210.

14. *Ibid*.

15. Geoffrey York, "Co-op Grant Comes Out Swinging as Prairies Fight Economic Slump," *Globe and Mail*, December 21, 1989, p. B5.

16. For more on franchising in Canada, see J. Barry Mason, et al., *Canadian Retailing* (Homewood: IL, Irwin, 1990), Chap. 7.

17. "The Mall Overtakes Main Street," *Canadian Business*, December 1988, p. 10.

18. For more on retail site location, see Lewis A. Spaulding, "Beating the Bushes for New Store Locations," *Stores*, October 1980, pp. 30-35; R.L. Davies and D.S. Rogers, eds., *Store Location and Store Assessment Research* (New York: John Wiley, 1984); and Avijit Ghosh and C. Samuel Craig, "An Approach to Determining Optimal Locations for New Services," *Journal of Marketing Research*, November 1986, pp. 354-62.

19. Kenneth Kidd, "Store Wars Forecast for Retail Trade," *Globe and Mail*, January 3, 1990, p. B1.

20. See Malcolm P. McNair and Eleanor G. May, "The Next Revolution of the Retailing Wheel," *Harvard Business Review*, September-October 1978, pp. 81-91; and Ron J. Markin and Clovin P. Duncan, "The Transportation of Retailing Institutions: Beyond the Wheel of Retailing and Life Cycle Theories, *Journal of Marketing*, Spring 1981, pp. 58-66.

# CHAPTER 15

# Promoting Products: Communication and Promotion Strategy

## CHAPTER OBJECTIVES

After reading this chapter, you should be able to:
1. Name and define the four tools of the promotion mix.
2. Discuss the elements of the marketing communication process.
3. Explain the methods for setting the promotion budget.
4. Discuss the factors that affect the design of the promotion mix.

Many Quaker Oat brands have become staples in Canadian households. Quaker has leading products in hot cereals (Quaker Oats), nutritious snacks (Chewy Granola), ready-to-eat cereals (Quaker Oat Bran), baking mixes (Oatmeal Cookie), side dishes (Rice-a-Roni), and sports beverages (Gatorade) that are well positioned to appeal to health-conscious consumers. As well, Quaker is a major player in the pet food market with its Puss'n'Boots, Pep, and Ken-L Ration brands. All told, Quaker brands generate over $340 million in sales each year in Canada.

Quaker uses several promotion tools to communicate to consumers, retailers, the media, stockholders, employees, and other publics. As consumers we know a good deal about Quaker's advertising. Each year Quaker spends over $12 million on advertising to tell us about its brands and persuade us to buy them. Advertising for Quaker Oat Bran Hot Cereal helped triple sales in one year. Quaker also spends funds on consumer sales promotions such as coupons, premiums, and sweepstakes to encourage us further. Various promotions have helped keep Cap'N Crunch a leading brand in its category. Consumer advertising and sales promotions work directly to create consumer demand, and this demand "pulls" Quaker products through its channel.

But consumer advertising and sales promotions account for only a portion of Quaker's total promotion mix. The company spends more on behind-the-scenes promotion activities that "push" its products toward consumers. Personal selling and trade promotions are major weapons in Quaker's battle for retailer support. The company's main objective is shelf space in supermarkets, convenience stores, and corner groceries across Canada. Quaker's salespeople court retailers with strong service, trade allowances, attractive displays, and other trade promotions. Quaker has placed considerable marketing emphasis on building "partnership relationships" with national accounts and distributors. The company has organized its sales/marketing area to better serve the needs of retailers. These push-promotion activities work closely with pull-promotion efforts to build sales and market share. The pull activities persuade consumers to look for Quaker brands; the push activities ensure that Quaker products are available, easy to find, and effectively merchandised when consumers start looking.

In addition to advertising, sales promotion, and personal selling, Quaker communicates through publicity and public relations. The company's publicity department places newsworthy information about Quaker and its products in the news media. They prepare annual reports to communicate with investor and financial publics and hold press conferences to communicate with media publics. Quaker sponsors many public relations activities to promote the company as a good citizen. For example, Quaker conducts environmental impact studies for all its new products before they are introduced. As well, the company is actively engaged in waste reduction and recycling programs at its major manufacturing plant in Peterborough, Ontario. Quaker owes much of its success to quality products that appeal strongly to millions of consumers around the world. But success also depends on Quaker's skill in telling its publics about the company and its products. All of Quaker's promotion tools—advertising, personal selling, sales promotion, and public relations—must blend harmoniously into an effective communication program to tell the Quaker story.[1]

Modern marketing calls for more than developing a good product, pricing it attractively, and making it available to target customers. Companies must also communicate with their customers. What is communicated, however, should not be left to chance.

To communicate well, companies hire advertising agencies to develop effective ads, sales promotion specialists to design sales incentive programs, and public relations firms to develop the corporate image. They train their salespeople to be friendly, helpful, and persuasive. For most companies the question is not whether to communicate, but how much to spend and in what ways.

A modern company manages a complex marketing communications system (see Figure 15-1). The company communicates with its middlemen, consumers, and various publics. Its middlemen communicate with their consumers and publics. Consumers have word-of-mouth communication with each other and with other publics. Meanwhile each group provides feedback to every other group.

A company's total marketing communications program—called its **promotion mix**—consists of the specific blend of advertising, sales promotion, public relations, and personal selling that the company uses to pursue its advertising and marketing objectives. The four major promotion tools are defined below:

- **Advertising:** Any paid form of nonpersonal presentation and promotion of ideas, goods, or services by an identified sponsor.
- **Sales promotion:** Short-term incentives to encourage purchase or sales of a product or service.

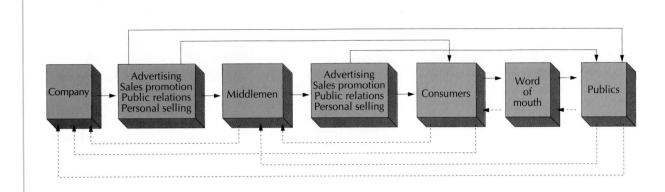

Figure 15-1 The Marketing Communications System

- **Public relations:** Building good relations with the company's various publics by obtaining favorable publicity, building a good "corporate image," and handling or heading off unfavorable rumors, stories, and events.
- **Personal selling:** Oral presentation in a conversation with one or more prospective purchasers for the purpose of making sales.[2]

Within the categories are specific tools such as sales presentations, point-of-purchase displays, specialty advertising, trade shows, fairs, demonstrations, catalogs, literature, press kits, posters, contests, premiums, and coupons. At the same time, communication goes beyond these specific tools. The product's design, its price, the package shape and color, and the salesperson's manner all communicate something to buyers. The whole marketing mix, not just the promotion mix, must be coordinated for greatest communication impact.

This chapter looks at two questions: What are the major steps in developing effective marketing communication? How should the promotion budget and mix be determined? Chapter 16 will look at mass communication tools—advertising, sales promotion, and public relations. Chapter 17 will look at the salesforce as a communication and promotion tool.

# Steps in Developing Effective Communication

Marketers need to understand how communication works. Communication involves the nine elements shown in Figure 15-2. Two elements are the major parties in a communication—sender and receiver. Another two are the major communication tools—message and media. Four are major communication functions—encoding, decoding, response, and feedback. The last element is noise in the system. These elements are defined below and applied to a McDonald's television ad:

- **Sender:** The party sending the message to another party—McDonald's.

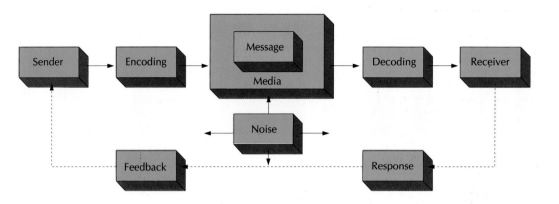

Figure 15-2 Elements in the Communication Process

- **Encoding:** The process of putting thought into symbolic form—McDonald's advertising agency assembles words and illustrations into an advertisement that will convey the intended message.
- **Message:** The set of symbols that the sender transmits—the actual McDonald's advertisement.
- **Media:** The communication channels through which the message moves from sender to receiver—in this case, television and the specific television programs that McDonald's selects.
- **Decoding:** The process by which the receiver assigns meaning to the symbols encoded by the sender—a consumer watches the ad and interprets the words and illustrations it contains.
- **Receiver:** The party receiving the message sent by another party—the consumer who watches the McDonald's ad.
- **Response:** The reactions of the receiver after being exposed to the message—any of hundreds of possible responses. For example, the consumer might like McDonald's better, be more likely to eat at McDonald's the next time he or she eats fast food, or do nothing.
- **Feedback:** The part of the receiver's response communicated back to the sender—the McDonald's research shows that consumers like and remember the ad.
- **Noise:** The unplanned static or distortion during the communication process that results in the receiver getting a different message than the sender sent—the consumer has poor TV reception or is distracted by noisy family members while watching the ad.

The model points out the key factors in good communication. Senders must know what audiences they want to reach and what responses they want. They must be good at encoding messages that take into account how the target audience decodes messages, and they must send the message through media that reach the target audience. Senders must develop feedback channels so that they can know the audience's response to the message.

Thus the marketing communicator must make the following decisions: (1) identify the target audience, (2) determine the response sought, (3) choose a message, (4) choose the media, (5) select the message source, and (6) collect feedback. We will now discuss each of these communication decisions.

# Identifying the Target Audience

A marketing communicator must start with a clear target audience in mind. The audience may be potential buyers, current users, those who make the buying decision, or those who influence it. The audience may be individuals, groups, special publics, or the general public. The target audience will affect the communicator's decisions on what will be said, how it will be said, when it will be said, where it will be said, and who is to say it.

# Determining the Response Sought

Once the target audience has been defined, the marketing communicator must decide what response is sought. Of course, the desired final response is purchase. But purchase is the result of a long process of consumer decision making. The marketing communicator needs to know where the target audience now stands and to which state it needs to be moved.

The target audience may be in any of the six **buyer readiness states**—awareness, knowledge, liking, preference, conviction, or purchase. These states are shown in Figure 15-3 and discussed below.

### AWARENESS

The communicator must first know how aware the target audience is of the product or organization. The audience may be unaware of it, know only its name, or know one or a few things about it. If most of the target audience is unaware, the communicator tries to build awareness, perhaps just name recognition. This can be done with simple messages that repeat the name. Even then, building awareness takes time. Suppose a small college in New Brunswick, Maritime College, seeks applicants from Nova Scotia but has no name recognition in that province. Suppose, in addition, that there are 30,000 high school graduates in Nova Scotia who may potentially be interested in Maritime College. The college might set the objective of making 70% of these students aware of Maritime's name within one year.

### KNOWLEDGE

The target audience might have company or product awareness, but not know much more. Maritime may want its target audience to know that it is a three-year college in the Saint John River Valley with excellent programs in English and language arts. Maritime College needs to learn how many people in the target audience have little, some, and much knowledge about Maritime. The college may decide to build up product knowledge as its first communication objective.

### LIKING

If the target audience knows the product, how do they feel about it? We can develop a scale covering degrees of liking—dislike very much, dislike somewhat, indifferent, like somewhat, like very much. If the audience looks unfavor-

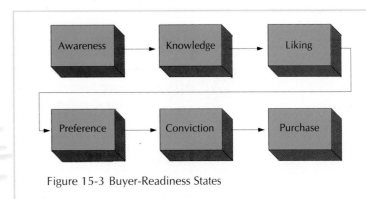

Figure 15-3 Buyer-Readiness States

ably on Maritime College, the communicator has to find out why and then develop a communications campaign to build up favorable feelings. If the unfavorable view is based on real problems of the college, then communications will not do the job. Maritime would have to fix its problems and then communicate its quality. Good public relations call for "good deeds followed by good words."

### PREFERENCE

The target audience might like the product, but prefer others. In this case, the communicator will try to build consumer preference. The communicator will promote the product's quality, value, performance, and other features. The campaign's success can be checked by the communicator by measuring the audience's preferences again after the campaign. If Maritime College finds that many high school graduates like Maritime but choose to attend other colleges, it will have to identify areas where its offerings are better than those of competing colleges. It must then promote its advantages to build preferences among prospective students.

### CONVICTION

A target audience might prefer the product but not develop a conviction about buying it. Thus some high school graduates may prefer Maritime, but may not be sure that they want to go to college. The communicator's job is to build conviction that going to college is the right thing to do.

### PURCHASE

Some members of the target audience might have conviction, but not quite get around to making the purchase. They may wait for more information or plan to act later. The communicator must lead these consumers to take the final step. This might include offering the product at a low price, offering a premium, or letting consumers try it on a limited basis. Maritime College might invite selected high school students to visit the campus or it might offer scholarships to deserving students.

The buyer readiness states are important to the marketing communicator. Buyers normally pass through these stages on their way to purchase. The communicator's task is to identify the stage most consumers are in and to develop a communication campaign that will move them to the next stage.

## Choosing a Message

Having defined the desired audience response, the communicator moves to developing an effective message. Ideally, the message should get Attention, hold Interest, arouse Desire, and obtain Action (known as the AIDA model). In practice, few messages take the consumer all the way from awareness to purchase, but the AIDA framework suggests the desirable qualities.

In putting together the message, the marketing communicator must solve three problems: what to say (message content), how to say it logically (message structure), and how to say it symbolically (message format).

### MESSAGE CONTENT

The communicator has to figure out an appeal or theme that will produce the desired response. There are three types of appeals. **Rational appeals** relate to the audience's self-interest. They show that the product will produce the claimed benefits. Examples would be messages showing a product's quality, economy, value, or performance. Ford's theme—"Quality is Job 1"—is an illustration of a rational appeal.

**Emotional appeals** attempt to stir up negative or positive emotions that will motivate purchase. These include fear, guilt, and shame appeals to people to do things they should (brush their teeth, have an annual health checkup) or stop doing things they shouldn't (smoke, drink too much, overeat). For example, Michelin tire ads that feature cute babies and suggest "Because so much is riding on your tires" may invoke mild fear. Communicators also use positive emotional appeals such as love, humor, pride, and joy.

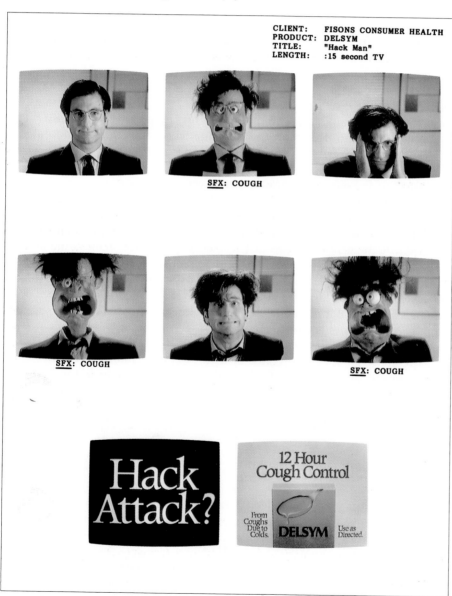

In this television ad, Delsym combines both humor and a mild fear appeal.

**Moral appeals** are directed to the audience's sense of what is right and proper. They are often used to urge people to support social causes such as a cleaner environment, equal rights for women, and assistance for the needy. An example is the appeal "God made you whole. Give to help those He didn't."

## MESSAGE STRUCTURE

The communicator has to decide on three message structure issues. The first is whether to draw a conclusion or leave it to the audience. Early research showed that drawing a conclusion was usually more effective. More recent research, however, suggests that in many cases, the advertiser is better off asking questions and letting the buyers come to their own conclusions. The second is whether to present a one-sided or two-sided argument. Usually a one-sided argument is more effective in sales presentations, except where the audiences are highly educated and negatively disposed. The third is whether to present the strongest arguments first or last. Presenting them first gets strong attention, but may lead to an anticlimactic ending.[3]

## MESSAGE FORMAT

The communicator must use a strong format for the message. In a print ad, the communicator has to decide on the headline, copy, illustration, and color. To attract attention, advertisers can use novelty and contrast, eye-catching pictures and headlines, distinctive formats, message size and position, and color, shape, and movement.[4] If the message is to be carried over the radio, the communicator has to choose words, sounds, and voices. The "sound" of an announcer promoting a used car has to be different from one promoting quality furniture.

If the message is to be carried on television or in person, then all these elements, plus body language, have to be planned. Presenters have to be aware of facial expressions, gestures, dress, posture, and hair style. If the message is carried on the product or its package, the communicator has to watch texture, scent, color, size, and shape. Color plays a major communication role in food preferences. When consumers sampled four cups of coffee that had been placed next to brown, blue, red, and yellow containers (all the coffee was identical, but this was unknown to the consumers), 75% felt that the coffee next to the brown container tasted too strong; nearly 85% judged the coffee next to the red container to be the richest; nearly everyone felt that the coffee next to the blue container was mild and the coffee next to the yellow container was weak. If a coffee company wants to communicate that its coffee is rich, it should probably use a red container along with label copy emphasizing the coffee's rich taste.

# Choosing Media

The communicator must now select channels of communication. There are two broad types of communication channels—personal and nonpersonal.

## PERSONAL COMMUNICATION CHANNELS

In **personal communication channels**, two or more people communicate directly with each other. They might communicate face to face, person to audience, over the telephone, or even through the mail. Personal communication channels are effective because they allow for personal addressing and feedback.

Most marketers use personal communication channels. For example, company salespeople contact buyers in the target market. However, other communicators may also reach buyers about the product. These might include independent experts making statements to target buyers—consumer advocates, consumer buying guides, and others. Neighbors, friends, family members, and associates may also talk to target buyers about the product. This last channel, known as word-of-mouth influence, has considerable effect in many product areas. As well, some consumers who are active, knowledgeable shoppers are used by others to obtain information on products they are about to purchase. These knowledgeable consumers—called market mavens—are potential targets for advertisers of low involvement products and retailers with a wide produce range.[5]

Personal influence carries great weight for products that are expensive or risky, or for products that are highly visible. Buyers of automobiles and major appliances go beyond mass-media sources to seek the opinions of knowledgeable people.

Companies can take several steps to put personal influence channels to work for them. They can identify influential people and companies and devote extra effort to them. Companies can create opinion leaders by supplying certain people with the product on attractive terms. Companies can work through community members such as disc jockeys, class presidents, and presidents of local organizations. They can also use influential people in testimonial advertising, or develop advertising that has high "conversation value."

## NONPERSONAL COMMUNICATION CHANNELS

**Nonpersonal communication channels** are media that carry messages without personal contact or feedback. They include mass and selective media, atmospheres, and events. **Mass and selective media** consist of print media (newspapers, magazines, direct mail), electronic media (radio, television), and display media (billboards, signs, posters). Mass media are aimed at large, often unsegmented audiences; selective media are aimed at smaller, selected audiences. **Atmospheres** are designed environments that create or reinforce the buyer's leanings toward consumption of the product. Thus lawyers' offices and banks are designed to communicate confidence and other qualities that might be valued by the clients. **Events** are occurrences staged to communicate messages to target audiences. Public relations departments arrange news conferences or grand openings to communicate with an audience.

Nonpersonal communication affects buyers directly. In addition, using mass media often helps to initiate more personal communication. Mass communication affects attitudes and behavior through a two-step flow-of-communication process. In this process, communications first flow from television, magazines, and other mass media to opinion leaders and from these to the less active sections of the population."[6] This two-step flow means the effect of mass media is not as direct, powerful, and automatic as one might think. Rather, opinion leaders, people whose product opinions are sought by others, step between the mass media and their audiences. The opinion leaders are more exposed to mass media, and they carry messages to people who are less exposed to media.

The two-step flow concept challenges the notion that people's buying decisions are affected by a "trickle-down" of opinions and information from higher social classes. Since people mostly interact with others in their own social class, they pick up their fashion opinions and other ideas from people like themselves who are opinion leaders. The two-step flow concept also suggests that mass communicators should direct their messages straight to opinion leaders, letting them carry the message to others. Thus pharmaceutical firms first try to promote their new drugs to the most influential doctors.

## SELECTING THE MESSAGE SOURCE

The message's impact on the audience is affected by how the audience views the sender. Messages delivered by highly credible sources are more persuasive. Pharmaceutical companies want doctors to tell consumers about their products' benefits because doctors are very credible. Marketers hire well-known actors and athletes to

Celebrities impart some of their own likability or fashionability to the products they endorse.

deliver their messages. Michael J. Fox tells us about Pepsi and Wayne Gretsky speaks for Coke.

What factors make a source credible? The three factors most often found are expertise, trustworthiness, and likability. Expertise is the degree to which the communicator appears to have the authority needed to back the claim. Doctors, scientists, and professors rank high on expertise in their fields. Trustworthiness is related to how objective and honest the source appears to be. Friends are trusted more than salespeople. Likability is the extent to which the source is attractive to the audience. People like sources who are open, humorous, and natural. Thus the most highly credible source would be a person who scored high on all three factors.[7]

## COLLECTING FEEDBACK

After sending the message, the communicator must research its effect on the target audience. This involves asking the target audience whether they remember the message, how many times they saw it, what points they recall, how they felt about the message, and their past and present attitudes toward the product and company. The communicator would also like to measure behavior resulting from the message, such as how many people bought the product and talked to others about it.

Figure 15-4 shows an example of feedback measurement. Looking at brand A,

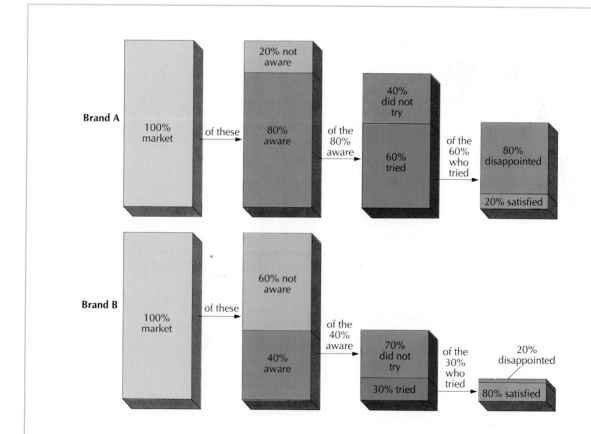

Figure 15-4 Current Consumer States for Two Brands

we find that 80% of the total market are aware of brand A, 60% of those who are aware have tried it, and only 20% of those who have tried it are satisfied. This suggests that the communication program is creating awareness, but that the product fails to give consumers what they expect. On the other hand, only 40% of the total market are aware of brand B, only 30% of those aware have tried it, but 80% of those who have tried it are satisfied. In this case, the communication program needs to be stronger to take advantage of the brand's power to obtain satisfaction.

# SETTING THE TOTAL PROMOTION BUDGET AND MIX

We have looked at the steps in planning and sending communications to a target audience. But how does the company decide on the total promotion budget and its division among the major promotional tools to create the promotion mix? We will now look at these questions.

## Setting the Total Promotion Budget

One of the hardest marketing decisions facing companies is how much to spend on promotion. John Wanamaker, the department store magnate, said: "I know that half of my advertising is wasted, but I don't know which half. I spent $2 million for advertising, and I don't know if that is half enough or twice too much."

Thus it is not surprising that industries and companies vary greatly in how much they spend on promotion. Promotion spending may be 20 to 30% of sales in the cosmetics industry and only five to ten percent in the industrial machinery industry.

Within a given industry, low- and high-spending companies can be found. Ford Canada, with sales over $14 billion, spends about $28 million on advertising. Chrysler Canada, with sales of $7 billion, spends about $20 million on advertising. Chrysler's larger expenditures as a percentage of sales are part of the company's efforts to gain market share.

How do companies decide on their promotion budget? We will look at four common methods used to set the total budget for advertising.

## Affordable Method

Many companies use the **affordable method**. They set the promotion budget at what they think the company can afford. One executive explained this method as follows: "Why it's simple. First, I go upstairs to the controller and ask how much they can afford to give this year. He says a million and a half. Later, the boss comes to me and asks how much we should spend and I say 'Oh, about a million and a half.'"[8]

This method of setting budgets completely ignores the effect of promotion on sales volume. It leads to an uncertain annual promotion budget, which makes long-range market planning difficult.

IS WHAT IS AVAILABLE TOO MUCH OR NOT ENOUGH.

# Percentage-of-Sales Method

Many companies use the **percentage-of-sales method**, setting their promotion budget at a certain percentage of current or forecasted sales. Alternatively, they can budget a percentage of the sales price. Automobile companies usually budget a fixed percentage for promotion based on the planned car price. Oil companies set the budget at some fraction of a cent for each litre of gasoline sold under their label.

A number of advantages are claimed for this method. First, the percentage-of-sales method means that promotion spending is likely to vary with what the company can "afford." Second, this method helps management to think about the relationship between promotion spending, selling price, and profit per unit. Third, this method creates competitive stability because competing firms tend to spend about the same percent of their sales on promotion.

In spite of these advantages, the percentage-of-sales method has little to justify it. It uses poor logic in viewing sales as the cause of promotion rather than as the result. As the budget is based on availability of funds rather than on opportunities, it prevents the increased spending sometimes needed to turn around falling sales. Because the budget varies with year-to-year sales, long-range planning is difficult. Finally, the method does not provide any basis for choosing the specific percentage, except what has been done in the past or what competitors are doing.

# Competitive-Parity Method

Some companies use the **competitive-parity method**, setting their promotion budgets to match competitors' outlays. They watch competitors' advertising, or get industry promotion spending estimates from publications or trade associations and set their budgets based on the industry average.

Two arguments support this method. One is that competitors' budgets represent the collective wisdom of the industry. The other is that spending the same amount as competitors helps prevent promotion wars. Neither argument is valid. There are no grounds for believing that the competition has a better idea of what a company should be spending on promotion. Companies differ greatly, and each has its own special promotion needs. In addition, there is no evidence that budgets based on competitive parity prevent promotion wars.

# Objective-and-Task Method

The most logical budget setting method is the **objective-and-task method**. Marketers develop their promotion budget by (1) defining specific objectives, (2) determining the tasks that must be performed to achieve these objectives, and (3) estimating the costs of performing these tasks. The sum of these costs is the proposed promotion budget.

The objective-and-task method makes management spell out its assumptions about the relationship between dollars spent and promotion results. However, it is also the most difficult method. It is often hard to figure out which specific task will achieve specific objectives. For example, suppose a company wants 95% awareness for its new product in the target market during a six-month introductory period.

What specific advertising messages and media schedule would be needed to attain this objective? Management should think about such questions even though they are difficult to answer. With the objective-and-task method, the company sets its promotion budget based on what it wants to accomplish with promotion. The overall answer to how large the promotion budget should be depends on where the company's products are in their life cycles, how much they differ from competing products, whether they are routinely needed or have to be "sold," and other factors.

## Setting the Promotion Mix

The company must now divide the total promotion budget among the major promotion tools—advertising, personal selling, sales promotion, and public relations. It must carefully blend the promotion tools into a coordinated promotion mix that will achieve its advertising and marketing objectives. Companies within the same industry may differ widely in how they design their promotion mixes. Avon spends most of its promotion funds on personal selling while Revlon spends heavily on advertising. In selling vacuum cleaners, Electrolux spends heavily on a door-to-door salesforce, while Hoover relies more on advertising. Thus it is possible to achieve a given sales level with various mixes of advertising, personal selling, sales promotion, and publicity.

Companies are always looking for ways to improve promotion by replacing one promotion tool with a more economical one. Many companies have replaced some field sales activity with telephone sales and direct mail. Other companies have increased their sales promotion spending in relation to advertising to gain quicker sales.

Designing the promotion mix is even more complex when one tool must be used to promote another. Thus when McDonald's decides to run Million Dollar Sweepstakes in its fast-food outlets (a sales promotion), it has to run ads to inform the public. When General Mills uses a consumer advertising/sales promotion campaign to back a new cake mix, it has to set aside money to promote this campaign to the resellers to win their support.

Many factors influence the marketer's choice of promotion tools. We will now look at these factors.

## Nature of Each Promotion Tool

Each promotion tool—advertising, personal selling, sales promotion, and public relations—has unique characteristics and costs. Marketers have to understand these characteristics in selecting the tools.

### ADVERTISING

Because of the many forms and uses of advertising, it is hard to generalize about its unique qualities as a part of the promotion mix. Yet several qualities can be noted. Advertising's public nature suggests that the product is standard and legitimate. Because many people see ads for the product, buyers know that purchasing the product will be publicly understood and accepted. Advertising also lets the seller repeat a message many times and it lets the buyer receive and compare the messages of various competitors. Large-scale advertising by a seller says something positive about the seller's size, popularity, and success.

Advertising is also expressive, letting the company dramatize its products through the artful use of print, sound, and color. On the one hand, advertising can be used to build up a long-term image for a product (such as Coca-Cola ads), and on the other, to trigger quick sales (as when Eaton's advertises a weekend sale). Advertising can reach masses of geographically spread-out buyers at a low cost per exposure.

Advertising also has some shortcomings. Although it reaches many people quickly, advertising is impersonal and cannot be as persuasive as a company salesperson. Advertising is able to carry on only a one-way communication with the audience, and the audience does not feel that it has to pay attention or respond. In addition, advertising can be very costly. Although some forms, such as newspaper and radio advertising, can be done on small budgets, other forms, such as network TV advertising, require very large budgets.

## PERSONAL SELLING

Personal selling is the most effective tool at certain stages of the buying process, particularly in building up a buyer's preference, conviction, and action. The reason is that personal selling, as compared with advertising, has several unique qualities. It involves personal interaction between two or more people, so each person can observe the other's needs and characteristics up close and make quick adjustments. Personal selling also lets all kinds of relationships spring up, ranging from a matter-of-fact selling relationship to a deep personal friendship. The effective salesperson keeps the customer's interests at heart in order to build a long-term relationship. Finally, the buyer feels a greater need to listen and respond, even if the response is a polite "no thank you."

These unique qualities come at a cost. A salesforce requires a longer-term commitment from a company than advertising—advertising can be turned on and off, but salesforce size is harder to change. As well, personal selling is the company's most expensive promotion tool, costing Canadian companies an average of over $150 a sales call.[9]

With personal selling, the customer feels a greater need to listen and respond.

### SALES PROMOTION

Sales promotion includes a wide assortment of tools—coupons, contests, premiums, and others—and these tools have many unique characteristics. They attract consumers and provide information that may lead the consumer to buy the product. They offer strong incentives to buy, by providing inducements or contributions that give additional value to consumers. They invite and reward quick response. While advertising says "buy our product," sales promotion says "buy it now."

Companies use sales promotion tools to create a stronger and quicker response. Sales promotion can be used to dramatize product offers and to boost sagging sales. Sales promotion effects are usually short-lived, however, and are not effective in building long-run brand preference.

### PUBLIC RELATIONS

Public relations offer several unique qualities. News stories and features seem more real and believable to readers than ads. Public relations can reach many prospects who may avoid salespeople and advertisement—the message gets to the buyers as news rather than as a sales-directed communication. Like advertising, public relations can dramatize a company or product.

Marketers tend to underuse public relations or use it as an after-thought. Yet a well-thought-out publicity campaign used along with the other promotion mix elements can be very effective and much less costly.

## Factors in Setting the Promotion Mix

Companies consider many factors when developing their promotion mixes. We will look at these factors below.

### TYPE OF PRODUCT/MARKET

The importance of the different promotion tools varies between consumer and industrial markets. The differences are shown in Figure 15-5. Consumer goods

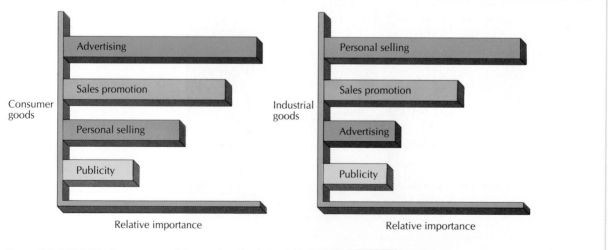

Figure 15-5 Relative Importance of Promotion Tools in Consumer Versus Industrial Markets

companies usually put more of their funds in advertising, followed by sales promotion, personal selling, and then public relations. Industrial goods companies put most of their funds in personal selling, followed by sales promotion, advertising, and public relations. In general, personal selling is more heavily used with expensive and risky goods and in markets with fewer and larger sellers.

Although advertising is less important than sales calls in industrial markets, it still plays an important role. Advertising can build product awareness and knowledge, develop sales leads, and reassure buyers.

Similarly, personal selling can strongly reinforce a consumer goods marketing effort. It is not simply the case that "salesmen put products on shelves and advertising takes them off." Well-trained consumer goods salespeople can sign up more dealers to carry the brand, convince them to give the brand more shelf space, and urge them to use special displays and promotions.

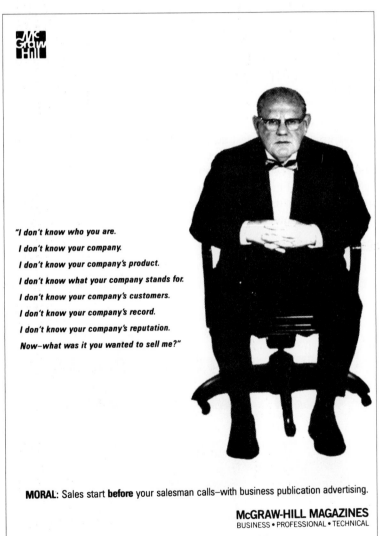

"I don't know who you are.

I don't know your company.

I don't know your company's product.

I don't know what your company stands for.

I don't know your company's customers.

I don't know your company's record.

I don't know your company's reputation.

Now–what was it you wanted to sell me?"

**MORAL:** Sales start **before** your salesman calls–with business publication advertising.

**McGRAW-HILL MAGAZINES**
BUSINESS • PROFESSIONAL • TECHNICAL

Advertising can play a dramatic role in industrial marketing, as shown in this classic McGraw-Hill ad.

## PUSH VERSUS PULL STRATEGY

The promotion mix is heavily affected by whether the company chooses a push or a pull strategy. The two strategies are contrasted in Figure 15-6. A **push strategy** calls for using the salesforce and trade promotion to push the product through the channels. Producers promote the product to wholesalers, wholesalers promote the product to retailers, and retailers promote the product to consumers.[10] A **pull strategy** calls for spending a lot of money on advertising and consumer promotion to build up consumer demand. Consumer demand then "pulls" the product through the channels. If the strategy is effective, consumers will ask retailers for the product, retailers will ask wholesalers for the product, and the wholesalers will ask the producers for the product.

Some small industrial goods companies use only push strategies; some direct marketing companies use only pull. Most large companies use some combination of push and pull. For example, Procter & Gamble uses mass-media advertising to pull its products, and a large salesforce and trade promotions to push its products through the channels. In recent years, consumer goods companies have been decreasing the pull portions of their promotion mixes in favor of more push [see Marketing Highlight 15-1].

## BUYER READINESS STAGE

Promotional tools vary in their effects at different stages of buyer readiness. In the awareness and knowledge stages, advertising, along with public relations, plays a more important role than that played by "cold calls" from salespeople. Customer liking, preference, and conviction are more affected by personal selling, followed closely by advertising. Finally, closing the sale is mostly done with sales calls and sales promotion. Given its high costs, personal selling should clearly focus on the later stages of the customer buying process.

## PRODUCT LIFE-CYCLE STAGE

The effects of different promotion tools also varies with stages of the product life cycle. In the introduction stage, advertising and publicity are good for producing

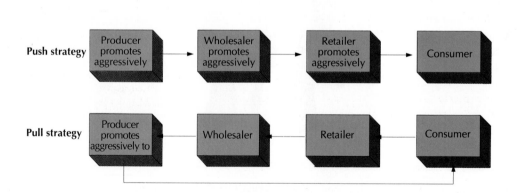

Figure 15-6 Push versus Pull Strategy

# MARKETING HIGHLIGHT 15-1

## Consumer Goods Companies Are Getting "Pushy"

Consumer packaged-goods companies like Procter & Gamble, General Foods, Quaker, and Campbell grew by using mostly pull promotion strategies. They advertised heavily to differentiate their products, build market share, and maintain customer loyalty. But during the past two decades, these companies have become more "pushy," de-emphasizing national advertising and putting more of their promotion budgets into personal selling and sales promotions. Trade promotions (trade allowances, displays, cooperative advertising) and consumer promotions (coupons, cents-off deals, premiums) are increasing, while the amount spent on advertising is declining.

Why are these companies shifting so heavily toward push strategies? One reason is that mass media campaigns are more expensive and less effective these days. Network television costs have risen while audiences have fallen off, making national advertising less cost-effective. As well, in these days of brand extensions and me-too products, companies sometimes have trouble finding meaningful product differences to feature in advertising. So they differentiate their products through price reductions, premium offers, coupons, and other push techniques.

Another factor speeding the shift from pull to push is greater strength of retailers. Today's retailers, like Loblaws, are larger and have more access to product sales and profit information. They have the power to demand and get what they want—and what they want is more push. While national advertising bypasses them on its way to the masses, push promotion benefits them directly. Consumer promotions give retailers an immediate sales boost, and cash from trade allowances pads retailer profits. Thus, producers must often use push just to obtain good shelf space and advertising support from important retailers.

However, many marketers are concerned that the reckless use of push will lead to fierce price competition and a never-ending spiral of price slashing and deal making. This situation would mean lower margins, and companies would have less to invest in the research and development, packaging, and advertising needed to improve products and maintain long-run consumer preference and loyalty. If used improperly, push promotion can mortgage a brand's future for short-term gains.

Yet push strategies are very important in packaged-goods marketing, where success often depends more on retailer support than on the producer's advertising. If they are well designed, push strategies can help rather than hinder in building long-run consumer preference. The company needs to blend both push and pull elements into an integrated promotion program that meets immediate consumer and retailer needs as well as long-run strategic needs.

**Sources:** Alvin A. Achenbaum and F. Kent Mitchel, "Pulling Away from Push Marketing," *Harvard Business Review*, May-June 1987, pp. 38-40; Robert D. Buzzell, John A. Quelch, and Walter J. Salmon, "The Costly Bargain of Trade Promotions," *Harvard Business Review*, March-April 1990, pp. 141-149; "The Battle Isn't Over," *Marketing*, June 12, 1989, p. 22; and Leonard Kubas, "Rethinking Promotions," *Marketing*, August 21, 1988, p.21.

high awareness, and sales promotion is useful in promoting early trial. Personal selling must be used to convince the trade to carry the product. In the growth stage, advertising and publicity continue to be powerful, while sales promotion can be reduced because fewer incentives are needed. In the mature stage, sales promotion again becomes important relative to advertising. Buyers know the brands and advertising is needed only to remind them. In the decline stage, advertising is kept at a reminder level, publicity is dropped, and salespeople give the product only a little attention. Sales promotion, however, might continue to be strong.[11]

# Responsibility for Marketing Communications Planning

Members of the marketing department often have different views on how to split the promotion budget. For example, a sales manager might prefer to hire two more salespeople than spend $100,000 on a single television commercial. The public relations manager may feel that he or she can do wonders with some money shifted from advertising to publicity.

In the past, companies left these decisions to different people. No one was responsible for thinking through the roles of the various promotion tools and coordinating the promotion mix. Today, companies are moving toward appointing a marketing communications director who is responsible for all of the company's marketing communications. This director develops policies for using the different promotion tools, keeps track of all promotion spending by product, tool, and results, and coordinates the promotion mix activities when major campaigns take place.

# SUMMARY

Promotion is one of the four major elements of the company's marketing mix. The main promotion tools—advertising, sales promotion, public relations, and personal selling—work together to achieve the company's communication objectives.

In preparing marketing communications, the communicator has to understand the nine elements of any communication process: sender, receiver, encoding, decoding, message, media, response, feedback, and noise. The communicator's first task is to identify the target audience and its characteristics. Next, the communicator has to define the response sought, whether it be awareness, knowledge, liking, preference, conviction, or purchase. Then a message should be constructed containing an effective content, structure, and format. Media must be selected, both for personal communication and nonpersonal communication. The message must be delivered by a credible source—someone who is an expert, trustworthy, and likable. Finally, the communicator must watch how much of the market becomes aware of the product, tries it, and is satisfied in the process.

The company has to decide how much to spend for promotion. The most popular approaches are to spend what the company can afford, use a percentage of sales, base promotion on competitors' spending, or base promotion on an analysis and costing of the communication objectives and tasks.

The company has to split the promotion budget among the major tools to create the promotion mix. Companies are guided by the characteristics of each promotion tool, the type of product/market, whether the company needs a push or a pull strategy, the buyer's readiness stage, and the product life-cycle stage. The different promotion activities require strong coordination for maximum impact.

# QUESTIONS FOR DISCUSSION

1. Which form of marketing communication does each of the following represent: (A) a U2 t-shirt sold at a concert, (b) a Rolling Stone interview with Bryan Adams arranged by his manager, (c) a scalper auctioning tickets at a Michael Jackson concert, (d) a record store selling Prince tapes at a two dollar discount during the week his latest movie opens?

2. Relate the six buyer-readiness states to (a) a product you bought on impulse at a grocery store and (b) your feelings about purchasing Coke, Coke Classic, and Pepsi.

3. Bill Cosby has appeared in ads for such products and companies as Jell-O, Coke, Texas Instruments, and E.F. Hutton. Is he a credible source for all these companies or does his credibility vary? Has he been chosen for his credibility or for some other characteristic?

4. How can an organization get feedback on the effects of its communication efforts? Describe the different ways in which (a) the Canadian Cancer Society and (b) Procter & Gamble can get such feedback.

5. When a decline in oil prices caused economic troubles in Alberta, Edmonton-based Western Convenience Stores stopped advertising to cut costs. Which of the four major budgeting approaches—affordable-method, percentage-of-sales-method, competitive-parity-method, or objective-and-task-method did the retailer use? What approach would you have recommended?

6. Why do some industrial marketers advertise on national television even though their target audience is only a fraction of the people they reach with their message? List some nonconsumer-oriented TV commercials and explain what the marketers were trying to accomplish.

7. How does the number of levels in the distribution channel influence the decision to use a push or a pull strategy? What other factors may be involved in this decision?

# KEY TERMS

**Advertising** Any paid form of nonpersonal presentation and promotion of ideas, goods, or services by an identified sponsor.

**Affordable method** Setting the promotion budget at what management thinks the company can afford.

**Atmospheres** Designed environments that create or reinforce the buyer's leanings toward consumption of a product.

**Buyer readiness states** The stages consumers normally pass through on their way to purchase, including awareness, knowledge, liking, preference, conviction, and purchase.

**Competitive-parity method** Setting the promotion budget to match competitors' outlays.

**Emotional appeals** Message appeals that attempt to stir up negative or positive emotions that will motivate purchase.

**Events** Occurrences staged to communicate messages to target audiences such as news conferences and grand openings.

**Mass and selective media** Print media, broadcast media, and display media aimed at large, unsegmented audiences (mass media) or at selected audiences (selective media).

**Moral appeals** Message appeals that are directed to the audience's sense of what is right and proper.

**Nonpersonal communication channels** Media that carry messages without personal contact or feedback, including mass and selective media, atmospheres, and events.

**Objective-and-task method** Developing the promotion budget by defining specific objectives, determining the tasks that must be performed, and estimating the costs of performing those tasks.

**Percentage-of-sales method** Setting the promotion budget at a certain percentage of current or forecasted sales, or as a percentage of the sales price.

**Personal communication channels** Channels through which two or more people communicate directly with each other, including face to face, person to audience, over the telephone, or through the mail.

**Personal selling** Oral presentation in a conversation with one or more prospective purchasers for the purpose of making sales.

**Promotion mix** The specific mix of advertising, personal selling, sales promotion, and public relations a company uses to pursue its advertising and marketing objectives.

**Public relations** Building good relations with the company's various publics by obtaining favorable publicity, building a good "corporate image," and handling or heading off unfavorable rumors, stories, and events.

**Pull strategy** A promotion strategy that calls for spending a lot on advertising and consumer promotion to build up consumer demand and "pull" the product through the channel.

**Push strategy** A promotion strategy that calls for using the salesforce and trade promotion to push the product through channels.

**Rational appeals** Message appeals that relate to the audience's self-interest and show that the product will produce the claimed benefits.

**Sales promotion** Short-term incentives to encourage purchase or sales of a product or service.

# REFERENCES

1. Quaker Oats Company of Canada, *Annual Report*, 1989.

2. These definitions, except for sales promotion, are from *Marketing Definitions: A*

*Glossary of Marketing Terms* (Chicago: American Marketing Association, 1960).

3. For more on message content and structure, see James F. Engel, Roger D. Blackwell, and Paul W. Miniard, *Consumer Behavior* (6th ed.) (Chicago: IL: Dryden, 1990), Chap. 13, and Gurprit S. Kindra, Michel Laroche, and Thomas E. Muller, *Consumer Behaviour in Canada* (Toronto: Nelson, 1989), Chap. 14.

4. For further discussion, see Engel, Blackwell, and Miniard, *Consumer Behavior*, Chap. 13.

5. Lawrence F. Feick and Linda L. Price, "The Market Maven; A Diffuser of Marketplace Information," *Journal of Marketing*, January 1987, pp. 83-97.

6. P.F. Lazarsfeld, B. Berelson, and H. Gaudet, *The People's Choice* (2nd ed.)(New York: Columbia University Press, 1948), p.151 and Engel, Blackwell, and Miniard, *Consumer Behavior*, Chap. 5.

7. For more on source credibility, see Kindra, Laroche, and Miniard, *Consumer Behavior in Canada*, pp. 476-479.

8. Quoted in Daniel Seligman, "How Much for Advertising?" *Fortune*, December 1956, p.123.

9. "The High Cost of a Personal Sales Pitch," *Marketing*, November 25, 1985, p.B11.

10. For more on push strategies, see Michael Levy, John Webster, and Roger Kerin, "Formulating Push Marketing Strategies: A Method and Application," *Journal of Marketing*, Winter 1983, pp.25-34; Alvin A. Achenbaum and F. Kent Mitchel, "Pulling Away from Push Marketing," *Harvard Business Review*, May-June 1987, pp. 38-40; and Robert D. Buzzell, John A. Quelch, and Walter J. Salmon, "The Costly Bargain of Trade Promotions," *Harvard Business Review*, March-April 1990, pp. 141-149.

11. For more on advertising and the product life cycle, see John E. Swan, and David R. Rink, "Fitting Market Strategy to Product Life Cycles," *Business Horizons*, January-February 1982, pp.60-67.

# CHAPTER 16

"Pop Art" by Pepsi. "Pepsi" and "Pepsi-Cola" are registered trademarks of PepsiCo, Inc.

# Promoting Products: Advertising, Sales Promotion, and Public Relations

## CHAPTER OBJECTIVES

After reading this chapter, you should be able to:

1. Define the roles of advertising, sales promotion, and public relations in the promotion mix.
2. Describe the major decisions in developing an advertising program.
3. Explain how sales promotion campaigns are developed and implemented.
4. Explain how companies use public relations to communicate with their publics.

Two of the leading advertisers in Canada are Coca-Cola and Pepsi. They each spend about $25 million in advertising each year persuading Canadians to buy their brands in the fast-growing soft drink market. But advertising is not the only weapon in their arsenal. Massive amounts are spent on sales promotions, from give-aways to contests, to switch consumers from one brand to another. As well, they are involved in extensive public relations campaigns to enhance their corporate images. Coca-Cola and Pepsi both recognize that the stakes are high in the $2 billion soft drink industry in Canada.

Coca-Cola is the leader, selling about half of all soft drinks sold in Canada. Its flagship brand, Coca-Cola Classic, is promoted as "The Official Soft Drink of Summer" through an integrated television, radio, print, and point-of-purchase campaign. In surveys of the most memorable advertisers across Canada, Coke consistently finishes in the top five. Diet Coke, the number one diet soft drink, has used extensive promotions including such campaigns as the "Spring Breakaway in L.A.," featuring Wayne Gretzky, and tie-ins with "Batman" to increase its market share. Diet Coke also sponsors the Player's Ltd. Tennis Championship and club tennis programs. Sprite, in the lemon-lime segment, has used the "I Like the Sprite in You" campaign with great success.

Coca-Cola is also involved in numerous community activities. It has sponsored training camps for young hockey players, recycling programs in a number of cities, and designated driver programs in Ontario.

Pepsi, the number two marketer, is just as aggressive. It matches Coke in advertising, and its "Pepsi Challenge" campaign has helped to maintain its share of the market. Among its more interesting campaigns is its relaunch of 7-Up (Pepsi owns this franchise in Canada). Using Fido Dido—a quirky, hip, black-and-white character, hair on end—the commercials ask "...are you up for it?" Pepsi's use of Fido Dido is part of the plan to position 7-Up as a distinctive alternative to mainstream colas. The marketing director for Pepsi-Cola Canada states that Fido Dido is an advertising alternative to the usual soft drink celebrity. "Fido Dido has a unique character, like the brand. And he'll appeal to our market's popular, independent spirit." Pepsi is counting on the Fido Dido concept to stand out in all the advertising clutter and help gain sales and share for 7-Up.

The battle in the soft drink industry is intense, and Coke and Pepsi will continue to market their products aggressively through advertising, sales promotion, and public relations.[1]

Fido Dido helps to position 7-Up as a fresh alternative to mainstream colas.

Companies must do more than make good products—they must inform consumers of product benefits, and carefully position products in consumers' minds. To do this they must skillfully use the mass-promotion tools of advertising, sales promotion, and public relations. These tools are examined in this chapter.

# ADVERTISING

We define **advertising** as any paid form of nonpersonal presentation and promotion of ideas, goods, or services by an identified sponsor. In 1990, advertising ran up a bill of over $10 billion.[2] The spenders included not only business firms, but museums, professionals, and social organizations that advertise their causes to various target publics. In fact, one of the largest advertising spenders is a nonprofit organization—the Canadian federal government. As well, two provincial governments, Ontario and Quebec, are among the top 25 advertisers in Canada.

Table 16-1 lists the top ten advertisers in 1990. The Thompson Group was the leading business spender with $76 million, or 1.2% of its total sales. The other major spenders were found in the auto, food, beer, and entertainment industries. Generally, advertising as a percentage of sales is low in the auto industry and high in food, drugs, toiletries, and cosmetics, followed by gum, candy, and soaps.

**TABLE 16-1**
**Top Ten National Advertisers in 1990**

| Rank | Company | Total Advertising (millions) | Total Sales (millions) | Advertising as a Percent of Sales |
|---|---|---|---|---|
| 1 | The Thompson Group | $ 76 | 6,259 | 1.2 |
| 2 | General Motors | 68 | 18,458 | .4 |
| 3 | Government of Canada | 67 | — | — |
| 4 | Procter & Gamble | 67 | 1,418 | 4.7 |
| 5 | Sears Canada | 64 | 4,571 | 1.4 |
| 6 | Molson Breweries | 53 | 2,122 | 2.5 |
| 7 | Paramount Communications | 45 | N/A | N/A |
| 8 | Unilever | 44 | 1,248 | 3.5 |
| 9 | Cineplex Odeon | 43 | 717 | 6.0 |
| 10 | John Labatt | 41 | 4,681 | .9 |

"Canada's Top Advertisers," *Marketing*, April 8, 1991, p.47. All advertising figures represent advertising expenditures in media measured in Canada by Media Measurement Services. The figures do not include media overflow from the United States, nor do they include retail or direct buys in broadcast. Sales figures from *The Financial Post*, Summer, 1991.

However, what Table 16-1 does not show is the tremendous spillover of advertising from the United States. Companies like Procter & Gamble, and General Motors are entirely owned by U.S. parent companies. These, and other heavy advertisers, benefit from U.S. advertising that "spills over" into the Canadian market. Over 60% percent of the top 50 commercial advertisers in Canada are foreign-owned and sell similar products in both Canada and the U.S.[3] The reason for the spillover is that most Canadians have access to U.S. television stations because they live close to the border and/or receive U.S. stations on cable (about 73% of Canadian households have cable TV; about 55% have converters allowing them to receive up to 30 channels).[4]

Many Canadian cable systems are now using a technique called simulcast, which reduces spillover by broadcasting only Canadian commercials when a television show is broadcast at the same time on both a Canadian and a U.S. station. However, a substantial number of Canadians watch U.S. television and view U.S. ads for many products that are sold in Canada. The same pattern holds true for radio. Probably the best example of the benefits of spillover was the introduction into Canada of Budweiser, a well-known American beer. It achieved a six percent national market share within a few months of being launched, and Labatt's could not keep up with demand.[5] Budweiser, Coors, and Miller are among the top selling brands in Canada.

In regard to magazines, Canada is the largest foreign market for U.S. magazine publishers, accounting for 72% of the sales (worth over $390 million annually) of periodicals exported by the U.S.[6] For example, *National Geographic* is one of the top selling periodicals in Canada, and *Sports Illustrated*, *Woman's Day*, *Family Circle* and *Newsweek* all have circulations of more than 100,000 in Canada.[7] Again, U.S. advertisers whose products are sold in both countries would benefit from ads in these magazines. Canadian magazine publishers have the advantages of Bill C-58, which prohibits the deduction for tax purposes of advertising expenditures made in media unless the media are at least 75% Canadian-owned and have at least 80% Canadian content.[8] While this bill has clearly helped Canadian consumer magazines, it has not stopped the sizeable U.S. magazine spillover in Canada.

Media decisions for companies operating in Canada are complicated because of the spillover from the U.S. and the fragmented audiences for particular media. Some markets are also difficult to reach because of lack of media alternatives, differences in language, and local market conditions. All told, advertising in Canada requires special consideration from those involved in the decision.

Advertising takes a wide variety of forms and may be used to achieve many different goals. Advertising dollars go into many media: magazines and newspapers, radio and television, outdoor, direct mail, and others. Advertising has many uses: to build an organization's image, build a brand, announce a sale, or support an idea or cause.

Organizations handle advertising in different ways. In small companies, advertising might be handled by someone in the sales department. Large companies set up advertising departments, whose job is to set the advertising budget, work with the ad agency, and handle direct mail advertising, dealer displays, and other advertising not done by the agency. Most large companies use an outside advertising agency because it offers several advantages (see Marketing Highlight 16-1).

# MARKETING HIGHLIGHT 16-1

## How Does an Advertising Agency Work?

An advertising agency is an organization of marketing, creative, and media people involved in the creation and placement of advertising. In Canada, many of the large advertising agencies are subsidiaries of U.S. parent firms. Companies like J. Walter Thompson, FCB, Ogilvy and Mather, McCann-Erickson, and Young and Rubicam have Canadian operations entirely owned by the U.S. parent. In many cases, the Canadian subsidiary will handle the Canadian advertising while the U.S. parent agency will handle the U.S. advertising to allow for consistency of advertising messages between the two countries. It has been estimated that close to 40% of the accounts handled by U.S.-owned agencies in Canada are also handled by the parent company. In fact, just three of Canada's top 15 advertising agencies are Canadian-owned and operated.

Even companies with a strong advertising department will use advertising agencies. The specialists at agencies can often perform advertising tasks better than the company's staff. Agencies also bring an outside point of view to solving the company's problems, along with considerable experience from working with different clients and situations. Agencies are paid partly from media discounts and often cost the firm very little. Since the firm can cancel its agency contract at any time, an agency works hard to do a good job.

Advertising agencies usually have four departments: creative, which develops and produces ads; media, which selects media and places ads; research, which studies audience characteristics and wants; and business, which handles the agency's business activities. Each account is supervised by an account executive, and people in each department are assigned to work on one or more accounts.

Agencies often attract new business through their reputation or size. Generally, however, a client invites a few agencies to make a presentation for its business and then selects one of them.

Ad agencies have traditionally been paid through commissions and some fees. Under this system, the agency usually receives 15% of the media cost as a rebate. Suppose the agency buys $60,000 of magazine space for a client. The magazine bills the advertising agency for $51,000 ($60,000 less 15%), and the agency bills the client for $60,000, keeping the $9,000 commission. If the client bought space directly from the magazine, it would have paid $60,000 because commissions are only paid to recognized advertising agencies.

Both advertisers and agencies have become unhappy with the commission system. Larger advertisers complain that they pay more than smaller ones for the same services simply because they place more advertising. Advertisers also believe that the commission system drives agencies away from low-cost media and short advertising campaigns. Agencies are unhappy because they perform extra services for an account without getting any more pay. The trend today in Canada is toward paying either a straight fee or a combination commission and fee.

Other trends are also hitting the advertising agency business. In recent years, as growth in advertising spending has slowed, many agencies have tried to keep growing by gobbling up other agencies, thus creating huge agency holding companies. The largest of these agency "supergroups," Saatchi & Saatchi PLC, includes several large agencies—Saatchi & Saatchi Compton, Ted Bates Worldwide, DFS Dorland Worldwide, and others—with combined billings (the dollar amount of advertising placed for clients) exceeding $13.5 billion. This includes over $128 million from its Canadian arm.

The introduction of fines or imprisonment for false or misleading advertising has resulted in some changes for advertising agencies. Many large agencies now have at least one person on staff whose job is to be familiar with all the laws and regulations governing advertising and to advise the agency accordingly. Most advertising in Canada is scrutinized, monitored, or regulated by some organization other than the advertiser and the agency. Canada has some extremely strict requirements for advertising that must be considered before any commercials are aired.

**Sources include:** Peter T. Zarry, "Advertising and Marketing Communication in Canada," in Donald N. Thompson and David S.R. Leighton, eds., *Canadian Marketing: Problems and Perspectives* (Toronto: Wiley, 1973), p. 241; Randy Scotland, "Commission System is Now on the Skids," *Marketing*, March 10, 1986, pp. 1, 7; "Canada's Top 100 Ad Agencies," *Marketing*, December 11, 1989, p. 23-29; Jennifer Wells, "Agencies Move From Commissions to Fees Gaining Momentum," *Financial Post*, March 9, 1987, p. 39; Martin Mehr, "Ad Cutback Not What It Seems," *Marketing*, March 26, 1990, p. 2; Randy Scotland, "Another Shop Goes Global," *Marketing*, November 27, 1989, pp. 1, 3; and Mark Evans, "Foreign Invasion," *The Financial Post 500*, Summer 1990, pp. 191-192.

# MAJOR DECISIONS IN ADVERTISING

Marketing management must make five important decisions in developing an advertising program. These decisions are listed in Figure 16-1 and discussed below.

## Setting Objectives

The first step in developing an advertising program is to set the advertising objectives. These objectives are based on past decisions about the target market, positioning, and marketing mix. The marketing positioning and mix strategy defines

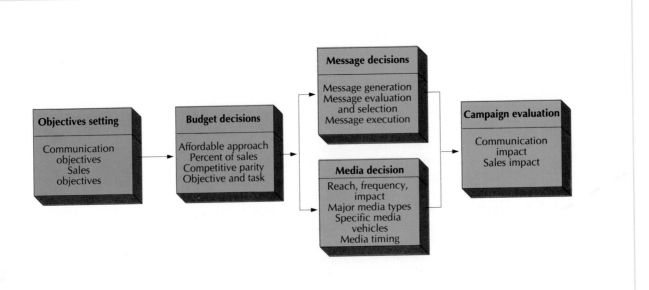

Figure 16-1 Major Decisions in Advertising

**TABLE 16-2**
**Possible Advertising Objectives**

Informative advertising:

| | |
|---|---|
| Telling the market about a new product | Describing available services |
| Suggesting new uses for a product | Correcting false impressions |
| Informing the market of a price change | Reducing consumers' fears |
| Explaining how the product works | Building a company image |

Persuasive advertising:

| | |
|---|---|
| Building brand preference | Persuading customer to purchase now |
| Encouraging switching to your brand | Persuading customer to receive a sales call |
| Changing customer's perception of product attributes | |

Reminder advertising:

| | |
|---|---|
| Reminding consumers that the product may be needed in the near future | Keeping it in their minds during off-seasons |
| Reminding them where to buy it | Maintaining its top-of-mind awareness |

the job that advertising must do in the total marketing program.

An **advertising objective** is a specific communication task to be accomplished with a specific target audience during a specific period of time. Advertising objectives can be classified as to whether their aim is to inform, persuade, or remind. Table 16-2 lists examples of these objectives. Informative advertising is used heavily when introducing a new product category, where the objective is to build primary demand. Thus, producers of compact disc players first informed consumers of the sound and convenience benefits of CDs. When Black & Decker took over the houseware products of Canadian General Electric, the company had to inform Canadian consumers that Black & Decker would maintain the reputation and quality of the brands. The first phase of the $15 million marketing campaign resulted in 80% of Canadians recognizing Black & Decker as a leader in small appliances.[9]

Persuasive advertising becomes more important as competition increases, and when a company's objective is to build selective demand. For example, one Fisher-Price ad attempts to persuade an audience of parents of babies that the new product line, the Activity Center, enhances a baby's learning skills.

Some persuasive advertising has become comparison advertising, which compares one brand directly or indirectly to one or more other brands. In its classic comparison campaign, Avis positioned itself against Hertz, the market leader, by claiming, "We're number two, but we try harder." Comparison advertising is used in Canada for such products as deodorants, toothpastes, detergents, automobiles, and tires.[10]

Reminder advertising is important for mature products, to keep the consumer thinking about the product. The purpose of expensive Coca-Cola ads in magazines is to remind people about Coca-Cola, not to inform or persuade them.

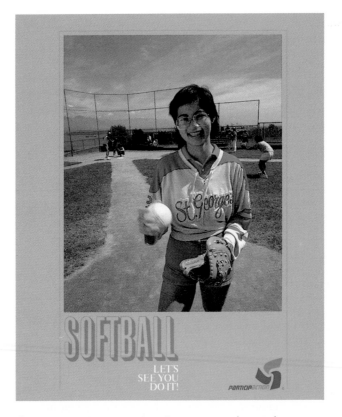

The Participaction campaign aims to persuade people to change their lifestyles.

## Budget Decision

After determining its advertising objectives, the company can next set its advertising budget for each product. The role of advertising is to affect demand for a product. The company wants to spend the amount needed to achieve the sales goal. Four methods for setting the advertising budget were discussed in Chapter 15. Here we will describe some specific factors that should be considered when setting the advertising budget:

- **Stage in the product life cycle.** New products typically need large advertising budgets to build awareness and to gain consumer trial. Mature brands usually require lower budgets as a ratio to sales.
- **Market share.** High-market-share brands usually need more advertising spending as a percentage of sales than low-share brands. Building the market or taking share from competitors requires greater advertising spending than simply maintaining current share.
- **Competition and clutter.** In a market with many competitors and high advertising spending, a brand must advertise more heavily to be heard above the noise in the market.
- **Advertising frequency.** When many repetitions are needed to put across the brand's message to consumers, the advertising budget must be larger.

- **Product differentiation.** A brand that closely resembles other brands in its product class (cigarettes, beer, soft drinks) requires heavy advertising to set it apart. When the product differs greatly from competitors', advertising can be used to point out the differences to consumers.[11]

# Message Decision

A large advertising budget does not guarantee a successful advertising campaign. No matter how big the budget, advertising can succeed only if messages gain attention and communicate well. Good advertising messages are especially important in today's costly and cluttered advertising environment. Take the situation facing network television advertisers. They typically pay $10,000 to $20,000 for 30 seconds of advertising time during prime-time TV on the CBC or CTV. In such cases, their ads are sandwiched in with a clutter of some 60 other commercials, announcements, and network promotions per hour.

The situation has gotten worse for advertisers. Until recently, television viewers were pretty much a captive audience for advertisers. With the growth in cable TV, VCRs, and remote-control units, today's viewers have many more options. They can actually avoid ads by watching commercial-free cable channels. They can "zap" commercials by pushing the fast-forward button during taped programs. With remote control, they can instantly turn off the sound during a commercial or "zip" around the channels to see what else is on.

Thus, just to gain and hold attention, today's advertising messages must be better planned, more imaginative, more entertaining, and more rewarding to consumers. Creative strategy will therefore play an increasingly important role in advertising success. Advertisers go through three steps to develop a creative strategy: message generation, message evaluation and selection, and message execution.

## MESSAGE GENERATION

Creative people use different methods to find ideas for advertising messages. Many creative people start by talking to consumers, dealers, experts, and competitors. Other people try to imagine consumers using the product, and to determine the benefits consumers seek when buying and using it. Generally, advertisers create many possible messages, only a few of which will be used.

## MESSAGE EVALUATION AND SELECTION

The advertiser must evaluate the possible messages. The appeals used in messages should have three characteristics. First, they should be meaningful, pointing out benefits that make the product more desirable or interesting to consumers. Second, appeals should be distinctive—they should tell how the product is better than competing brands. Finally, they must be believable. It may be hard to make the message believable as many consumers doubt the truth of advertising in general. One study found that, on average, consumers rate advertising messages as "somewhat unbelievable."[12] In general, Canadians have a more positive view of advertising today than five years ago.[13]

In Canada, the advertiser must also consider whether the message is suitable for both English and French audiences. Literal translations of messages from one language to the other may not be suitable. For example, when the English message for Budweiser, "This Bud's for you," was tested in Quebec, the response was very

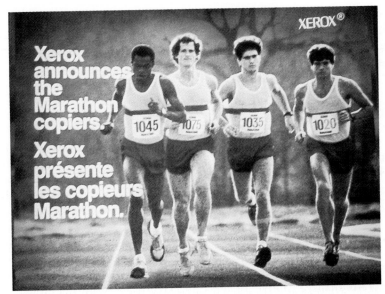

Xerox creates a visual pun on the name of its Marathon copiers to convey positive attributes.

negative. As a result, the English slogan was replaced with "toute une bière," which roughly translates as "one hell of a beer."[14]

## MESSAGE EXECUTION

The message's impact depends not only on what is said, but also on how it is said. The advertiser has to put the message across in a way that wins the target market's attention and interest.

The advertiser usually prepares a copy strategy statement describing the objective, content, support, and tone of the desired ad. Creative people then must find a style, tone, words, and format for executing the message. Any message can be presented in different execution styles, such as:

**Slice-of-life.** This shows one or more people using the product in a normal setting. A family seated at the dinner table might express satisfaction with Heinz Ketchup.

**Lifestyle.** This shows how a product fits in with a life style. A Dairy Bureau of Canada ad shows women exercising and talks about how milk adds to a healthy, active lifestyle.

**Fantasy.** This creates a fantasy around the product or its use. Revlon's first ad for Jontue showed a barefoot woman, wearing a chiffon dress, coming out of an old French barn, crossing a meadow, meeting a handsome young man on a white horse, and riding away with him.

**Mood or image.** This builds a mood or image around the product, such as beauty, love, or serenity. No claim is made about the product except through suggestion. Many coffee ads create mood.

**Musical.** This shows one or more people or cartoon characters singing a song about the product. Many cola ads have used this format.

**Personality symbol.** This creates a character that represents the product. The character might be animated (Green Giant, Cap'n Crunch, Mr. Clean) or real (Captain Highliner, Morris the Cat).

**Technical expertise.** This shows the company's expertise in making the product. Thus, Nabob shows that their coffee has been carefully prepared and packaged in a unique vacuum pack that preserves freshness for a year.

**Scientific evidence.** This presents survey or scientific evidence that the brand is better or better liked than one or more other brands. For years, Crest toothpaste has used scientific evidence to convince buyers that Crest is better at fighting cavities.

**Testimonial evidence.** This features a highly believable or likable source endorsing the product. It could be a celebrity like Wayne Gretzky (Diet Coke) or ordinary people saying how much they like the product.

The advertiser must also choose a tone for the ad. Procter & Gamble always uses a positive tone: Its ads say something very positive about the product. P&G avoids humor that might draw attention away from the message. On the other hand, Volkswagen's classic ads for its famous Beetle used humor and poked fun at the car ("the Ugly Bug").

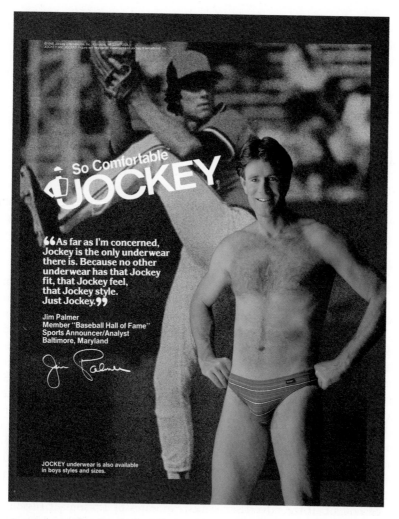

A member of the Baseball Hall of Fame endorses (and even models) Jockey's product.

Memorable and attention-getting words must be found. The theme listed below on the left would have had much less impact without the creative phrasing on the right:

| Theme | Creative Copy |
|---|---|
| • 7-Up is not a cola. | • "The Uncola." |
| • Instead of driving your car, let us drive you in our bus. | • "Take the bus, and leave the driving to us." |
| • Shop by turning the pages of the telephone directory. | • "Let your fingers do the walking." |
| • We don't rent as many cars, so we have to do more for our customers. | • "We're number 2, so we try harder." |

Format elements such as headlines, ad size, color, and illustration will make a difference in the impact as well as the cost of an ad. A small change in the way an ad is designed can make a big difference in its effect. Larger ads gain more attention, although the attention may not necessarily cover their difference in cost. Four-color ads, instead of black and white, increase both ad effectiveness and ad cost.

# Media Decision

The advertiser must next choose advertising media to carry the advertising message. The steps in media selection are (1) deciding on reach, frequency, and impact; (2) choosing among major media types; (3) selecting specific media vehicles; and (4) deciding on media timing.

### DECIDING ON REACH, FREQUENCY, AND IMPACT

To select media, the advertiser must decide what reach, frequency, and impact are needed to achieve advertising objectives. **Reach** is a measure of the percentage of people who are exposed to the ad campaign during a given period of time. For example, the advertiser might try to reach 70% of the target market during the first year. **Frequency** is a measure of how many times the average person in the target market is exposed to the message. For example, the advertiser might want an average exposure frequency of three. The advertiser must also decide on desired **media impact**, the qualitative value of a message exposure through a given medium. For example, messages on television may have more impact than messages on radio because television uses sight and sound, not just sound. The same message in one magazine (say, *Maclean's*) may be more believable than in another (say, *TV Times*).

Suppose the advertiser's product might appeal to a market of 1,000,000 consumers. The goal is to reach 700,000 consumers (1,000,000 x 70%). Since the average consumer should receive three exposures, 2,100,000 exposures (700,000 x 3) must be bought. If the advertiser wants exposures of 1.5 impact (assuming 1.0 impact is the average), a rated number of exposures of 3,150,000 (2,100,000 x 1.5) must be bought. If a thousand exposures with this impact cost $10, the advertising budget will have to be $31,500 (3,150 x $10). In general, the more reach, frequency, and impact the advertiser seeks, the higher the advertising budget will have to be.

## CHOOSING AMONG MAJOR MEDIA TYPES

The media planner has to know the reach, frequency, and impact of each of the major media types. The major advertising media are summarized in Table 16-3. In order of their advertising volume, the major media types are direct mail, newspapers, television, radio, outdoor, and magazines. Each medium has its advantages and limitations. Media planners consider many factors when making their media choices. The media habits of target customers will affect media choice—for example, radio and television are the best media for reaching teenagers. So will the nature of the product—dresses are best shown in color magazines, and Polaroid cameras are best demonstrated on television. Different types of messages may require different media. A message announcing a major sale tomorrow will require radio or newspapers; a message with a lot of technical data might require magazines or direct mailings. Cost is also a major factor in media choice. While television is very expensive, newspaper advertising costs much less. The media planner looks at both the total cost of using a medium and at the cost per thousand exposures—the cost of reaching 1,000 people using the medium.

Given these and other media characteristics, the media planner must decide how much of each media type to buy. For example, a firm launching a new shampoo might decide to spend $300,000 on daytime network television, $200,000 on women's magazines, and $100,000 on daily newspapers in 12 major markets.

If the company doing the advertising sold the product in both Canada and the U.S., the media planner might note how much the U.S. company was spending on advertising in the magazines that had high circulation in Canada. The planner might then consider this "spill-over" effect before making a final decision on where to spend the money in Canadian media.

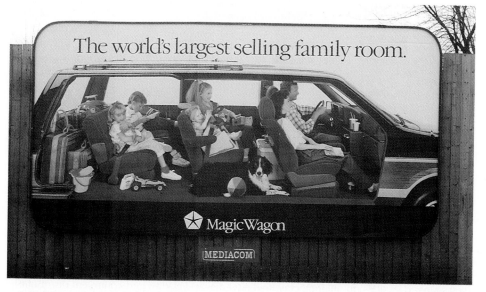

A billboard is an appropriate medium for this Magic Wagon ad, as it will be seen by motorists.

## TABLE 16-3
## Profiles of Major Media Types

| Medium | Volume in Millions | Example of Cost | Advantages | Limitations |
|---|---|---|---|---|
| Newspapers | $1,412 | $11,300 one-third page, weekday, in 17 Atlantic daily newspapers | Flexibility; timeliness; good local market coverage; broad acceptance; high believability | Short life; poor reproduction quality; small "pass-along" audience |
| Television | 1,248 | $23,500 for 30 seconds of prime time on 41 CBC stations | Combines sight, sound, and motion; appeals to the senses; high attention; high reach | High absolute cost; high clutter; fleeting exposure; less audience selectivity |
| Direct mail/ catalogs | 1,811 | Varies considerably | Audience selectivity; flexibility; no ad competition within the same medium; personalization | Relatively high cost; "junk mail" image |
| Radio | 681 | $7,000 for 60-second slots of prime time on four Toronto stations | Mass use; high geographic and demographic selectivity; low cost | Audio presentation only; lower attention than television; non-standardized rate structures; fleeting exposure |
| Magazines | 450 | $29,200 one page, four-color, in the English edition of *Chatelaine* | High geographic and demographic selectivity; credibility and prestige; high-quality reproduction; long life; good pass-along readership | Long ad purchase lead time; some waste circulation; no guarantee of position |
| Outdoor | 659 | $64,800 for 51 billboards covering Toronto/ Hamilton, Montreal, and Vancouver for one month | Flexibility; high repeat exposure; low cost; low competition | No audience selectivity; creative limitations |

**Note:** The data in column 2 is from *Canadian Advertising Rates and Data*, July 1990, p. 532. Newspaper data does not include classified advertising weeklies and controlled distribution; magazine data does not include farm publications or phone and city directories. The data in column 3 is from *Canadian Media Directors' Council Media Digest*, 1990/91.

## SELECTING SPECIFIC MEDIA VEHICLES

The media planner now chooses the best specific media vehicles. For example, if advertising is to be placed in magazines, the media planner looks up the circulation and costs of different ad sizes, color options, ad positions, and frequencies. The planner then evaluates the magazines on such factors as credibility, status, reproduction quality, editorial focus, and lead time. The media planner decides which vehicles give the best reach, frequency, and impact for the money.

Media planners compute the cost per thousand persons reached by a vehicle. If a full-page, four-color advertisement in *Maclean's* costs $21,700 and *Maclean's* readership is 620,000 people, the cost of reaching each one thousand persons is $35.00. The same advertisement in *Saturday Night* may cost $7,300 but reach only 115,000 people at a cost per thousand of $63.50. The media planner would rank each magazine by cost per thousand and initially favor those magazines with the lower cost per thousand.

The media planner must also consider the costs of producing ads for each medium. Newspaper ads may cost very little to produce, but the costs of television ads may run as high as $150,000. The media planner must add in production costs when computing the cost of using each medium.

The media planner must adjust these initial cost measures in several ways. First, the measures should be adjusted for audience quality. For a baby lotion advertisement, *Today's Parent* magazine would have a high exposure value; *Outdoor Canada* would have a low exposure value. Second, the exposure value should be adjusted for audience attention. Readers of *Chatelaine*, for example, may pay more attention to ads than readers of *Maclean's*. Third, the exposure value should be adjusted for the medium's editorial quality—*Maclean's* is more believable than the *National Enquirer*.

## DECIDING ON MEDIA TIMING

The advertiser has to decide how to schedule the advertising over the year. Suppose sales of a product peak in December and drop off in March. The firm can vary its advertising to follow the seasonal pattern, to oppose the seasonal pattern, or to be the same all year. Most firms do some seasonal advertising. Even with this choice, the firm still has to decide whether its advertising should come before or during a seasonal sale.

The advertiser also has to choose the pattern of the ads. **Continuity** means scheduling ads evenly within a given period. **Pulsing** means scheduling ads unevenly over the time period. Thus 52 ads could be scheduled at one per week during the year, or pulsed in several bursts. Those who favor pulsing feel that the audience will learn the message more completely and that money can be saved. Anheuser-Busch conducted research and found that Budweiser could drop advertising in a given market with no harm to sales for at least a year and a half.[15] Then the company could use a six-month burst of advertising and regain the past sales growth rate. This led Budweiser to adopt a pulsing strategy.

# Advertising Evaluation

The advertising program should regularly evaluate the communication effects and sales effects of advertising.

## MEASURING THE COMMUNICATION EFFECT

Measurement of the communication effect reveals whether an ad is communicating well. Called **copy testing**, it can be done before or after an ad is printed or broadcast. Before the ad is placed, the advertiser can show it to consumers, ask how they like it, and measure recall or attitude changes resulting from the ad. After the ad has run, the advertiser can measure how the ad affected consumer advertising recall, or product awareness, knowledge, and preference.

## MEASURING THE SALES EFFECT

What sales are caused by an ad that increases brand awareness by 20% and brand preference by ten percent? This sales effect of advertising is often harder to measure than the communication effect. Sales are affected by many factors besides advertising, such as product features, price, and availability.

One way to measure the sales effect of advertising is to compare past sales with past advertising expenditures. Another way is through experiments. Du Pont was one of the first companies to use advertising experiments.[16] Du Pont's paint department divided 56 sales territories into high, average, and low market share territories. In one-third of the group, Du Pont spent the normal amount for advertising; in another third, two and one-half times the normal amount; and in the remaining third, four times the normal amount. At the end of the experiment, Du Pont estimated how many extra sales had been created by higher levels of advertising expenditure. Du Pont found that higher advertising spending increased sales at a diminishing rate, and that the sales increase was weaker in Du Pont's high market share territories.[17]

To spend a large advertising budget wisely, advertisers must define their advertising objectives; make careful budget, message, and media decisions; and evaluate advertising's results. Advertising also draws much public attention, because of its power to affect life styles and opinions. Advertising faces increased regulation to ensure that it performs responsibly (see Marketing Highlight 16-2).

# SALES PROMOTION

Advertising is supplemented by two other mass-promotion tools, sales promotion and public relations. **Sales promotion** consists of short-term incentives to encourage purchase or sales of a product or service. Sales promotion includes a wide variety of promotion tools designed to stimulate earlier or stronger market response. It includes **consumer promotion** (samples, coupons, rebates, prices-off, premiums, contests, demonstrations), **trade promotion** (buying allowances, free goods, merchandise allowances, cooperative advertising, push money, dealer sales contests), and **salesforce promotion** (bonuses, contests, sales rallies).

Sales promotion tools are used by most organizations, including manufacturers, distributors, retailers, trade associations, and nonprofit institutions. Estimates of annual sales promotion spending run as high as $7 billion, and this spending has increased rapidly in recent years.[18]

Some sales promotion tools are "consumer franchise building"—they include a selling message along with the deal to build long-run consumer demand rather than temporary brand switching. These include samples; coupons, when they include a selling message; and premiums, when they are related to the product.[19]

# MARKETING HIGHLIGHT 16-2
## Advertising Decisions and Public Policy

The Canadian advertiser faces regulation from five sources: federal law, provincial law, municipal law, industry codes, and media acceptance or clearing policies. The advertiser faces over 100 federal and provincial statutes regulating advertising as well as city codes and industry codes. We will consider each in turn.

- **Federal laws.** The Competition Act covers such categories as misleading price advertising and misleading statements of fact. The Food and Drugs Act defines which drugs can and cannot be advertised and what can be said in drug advertising. The advertiser must be concerned with at least 15 federal statutes.

- **Provincial laws.** Each province has enacted its own laws dealing with advertising. Quebec probably has the most stringent laws including a ban on all advertising intended for children under 13 years, and language (French and English) specifications for ads. The provinces have a variety of laws concerning liquor advertising. Prince Edward Island bans liquor advertising in all media; Ontario has banned "lifestyle" beer and wine advertising.

- **City/municipal laws.** Various cities and municipalities have banned tobacco and liquor advertising in bus shelters and transit vehicles.

- **Industry codes.** The advertising industry, through the Canadian Advertising Foundation, has developed the Canadian Code of Advertising Standards which defines acceptable advertising practices. The purpose of this self-regulation is to set and maintain standards of honesty in advertising.

- **Broadcaster/media codes.** Most advertising media in Canada and particular broadcasters have established their own codes. For example, CBC has a commercial acceptance policy guideline and the Telecaster Committee, made up of independent TV stations, has developed a code specifying acceptable commercials.

The result of this regulation is that a new television commercial for a product like breakfast cereal is likely to take the following path before it is put on the air. First, it goes to the agency's legal department, then the client's legal department. Then it is sent to the Canadian Radio-television and Telecommunications Commission (CRTC) for clearance as to "good taste." The commercial is then sent to the health standards branch of the Department of Consumer and Corporate Affairs to ensure that it complies with the Food and Drugs Act and the Competition Act. Then the commercial goes to the CRTC's Children's Advertising Committee and also to the children's section of the Advertising Standards Council. The commercial must then go to Quebec to see if it is classified as an ad aimed at children. If it is, it cannot be shown. Assuming the commercial leaps these hurdles, it still must be approved by the CBC's Commercial Acceptance Department and the Telecaster Committee.

The legal environment for advertisers in Canada is fairly stringent. Expectations are that the future will continue to bring still more regulations into effect, thereby making companies more sensitive to the legalities of advertising.

**Sources:** Robert W. Sweitzer, et al., "Political Dimensions of Canadian Advertising Regulation," *The Canadian Marketer*, Fall 1979, pp. 3-8; "Quebec Led Provinces in Ad Legislation," *Marketing*, February 16, 1981, p. 35; Marq De Villiers, "The Great Toilet Paper Cover Up," *Canadian Business*, May 1978, pp. 46-49, 70-74; "Marketing's Guide to Liquor Advertising Regulations," *Marketing*, August 6, 1990, pp. 24-26; and Marina Strauss, "The Public Has a Right to Know When Ads Are Deemed Offensive," *Globe and Mail*, May 31, 1990, p. B15.

Sales promotion tools that are not consumer franchise building include price-off packs, consumer premiums not related to a product, contests and sweepstakes, refund offers, and trade allowances. Sellers frequently use franchise-building promotions because they have longer lasting effects.

Sales promotions seem most effective when used together with advertising. In one study, point-of-purchase displays related to current TV commercials were found to produce 15% more sales than similar displays not related to such advertising. In another, a heavy sampling approach along with TV advertising proved more successful than either TV alone or TV with coupons, in introducing a product.[20]

In using sales promotion, a company must set objectives; select the tools; develop the program; pretest, implement, and control it; and evaluate the results.[21]

## Setting Sales Promotion Objectives

Sales promotion objectives vary widely. For the consumer market, objectives include getting users to buy more of the product, building trial among nonusers, and attracting competitors' brand users. For the retail market, objectives include getting the retailer to carry new items and more inventory, getting them to advertise the product and give it more shelf space, and getting them to buy ahead. Concerning the salesforce, objectives include getting more salesforce support for current or new products, or getting salespeople to sign up new accounts.

## Selecting Sales Promotion Tools

Many tools can be used to accomplish the sales promotion objectives. The promotion planner should consider the type of market, sales promotion objectives, the competition, and the costs and effectiveness of each tool. The main consumer and trade promotion tools are described below.

## Consumer Promotion Tools

The main consumer promotion tools include samples, coupons, price packs, premiums, point-of-purchase displays, demonstrations, contests, sweepstakes, and games.

Samples are offers of a small amount or trial of a product. Some samples are free; for others the company charges a small amount to offset sampling costs. Samples might be delivered door-to-door, sent in the mail, picked up in the store, attached to another product, or offered in an ad. Sampling is the most effective but most expensive way to introduce a new product. Esprit shampoo was introduced to the Canadian market through sampling.

Coupons are certificates that give consumers a saving on the purchase of a product. Over 15 billion coupons are given out in Canada each year, and about two percent are redeemed.[22] Coupons can be mailed, included in other products, or placed in ads. They can stimulate sales of a mature brand and promote early trial of a new brand.

Price Packs (also called cents-off deals) offer consumers savings off the regular price of a product. The reduced prices are marked by the producer directly on the product's label or package. These can include single packages sold at a reduced

Over 15 billion coupons are given out in Canada each year.

price (such as two for the price of one). Or they might include two related products banded together (such as a toothbrush and toothpaste). Price packs are very effective—even more than coupons—for stimulating short-term sales.

Premiums are goods offered free or at low cost as an incentive to buy a product. A with-pack premium comes with the product, inside (in-pack) or outside (on-pack) the package. The package itself, if reusable, may serve as a premium. Premiums are sometimes mailed to consumers who send in a proof of purchase, such as a boxtop. Manufacturers now offer consumers all kinds of premiums bearing the companies' names.

Point-of-Purchase (POP) promotions include demonstrations that take place at the point of sale. An example would be a metre-high cardboard display of Cap'n Crunch next to Cap'n Crunch cereal boxes. Unfortunately, many retailers do not like to handle the hundreds of displays, signs, and posters they receive from manufacturers each year. Manufacturers are responding by offering better POP materials, tying them in with television or print messages, and offering to set them up. The L'eggs panty hose display is one of the most creative in the history of POP materials and a major factor in the success of this brand.

Contests, sweepstakes, and games give consumers, dealers, or salesforces the chance to win something—such as cash, trips, or goods—as a result of luck or extra effort. A contest calls for consumers to submit an entry such as a jingle, guess, or suggestion to be judged by a panel that will select the best entries. A sweepstakes calls for consumers to submit their names for a draw. A game gives consumers something every time they buy—bingo numbers, missing letters—which may help them win a prize. A sales contest urges dealers or the salesforce to increase their efforts, with prizes going to the top performers.

## TRADE PROMOTION TOOLS

More sales-promotion dollars are directed to retailers and wholesalers than to consumers.[23] Trade promotion can persuade retailers or wholesalers to carry a brand, give it shelf space, promote it in advertising, and push it to consumers. Shelf space is so scarce these days that manufacturers often have to offer price-offs, allowances, buy-back guarantees, or free goods to get on the shelf and, once there, to stay on it.

Manufacturers use several trade-promotion tools. Many of the tools used for consumer promotions—contests, premiums, displays—can also be used as trade promotions. Or the manufacturer may offer a straight discount off the list price on each case purchased during a stated period of time (also called a price-off, off-invoice, or off-list). The offer encourages dealers to buy in quantity or to carry a new item. Dealers can use the discount for immediate profit, for advertising, or for price reductions to their customers.

Manufacturers may also offer an allowance (usually a certain amount off per case) in return for the retailer's agreement to feature the manufacturer's products in some way. An advertising allowance compensates retailers for advertising the product. A display allowance compensates them for using special displays.

Manufacturers may offer free goods such as extra cases of merchandise to distributors who buy a larger quantity. They may offer push money, cash, or gifts to dealers or their salesforces to push the manufacturer's goods. Manufacturers may offer free specialty advertising items that carry the company's name, such as pens, pencils, calendars, paperweights, matchbooks, memo pads, and rulers.[24]

Industry associations organize annual conventions and may sponsor a trade show at the same time. Firms selling to the industry show their products at the trade show. The vendors who participate in Canadian industrial trade shows expect several benefits, including the opportunity to present new products, meet new buyers, maintain company visibility, and contact decision makers who might otherwise not be reached.[25]

## Developing the Sales Promotion Program

The marketer must make some other decisions to define the full sales promotion program. First, the marketer must decide on the size of the incentive. A certain minimum incentive is necessary if the promotion is to succeed. A larger incentive will produce more sales response. Some of the large firms that sell consumer packaged goods have a sales-promotion manager who studies past promotions and recommends incentive levels to brand managers.

The marketer must then decide how to promote and distribute the promotion program itself. A 50-cents-off coupon could be given out in a package, at the store, by mail, or in an advertisement. Each distribution method involves a different level of reach and cost. The length of the promotion is also important. If the sales promotion period is too short, many prospects who may not be buying during that time will not be able to take advantage of it. If the promotion runs too long, the deal will lose some of its "act now" force. Brand managers need to set calendar dates for the promotions. The dates will be used by production, sales, and distribution. Some unplanned promotions may also be needed, requiring cooperation on short notice.

Finally, the marketer has to decide on the sales promotion budget. It can be developed in two ways. The marketer can choose the promotions and estimate their total cost. However, the more common way is to use a percentage of the total budget for sales promotion. First, they do not consider cost effectiveness. Second, instead of spending to achieve objectives, they simply extend the previous year's spending, take a percentage of expected sales, or use the "affordable approach." Finally, advertising and sales-promotion budgets are too often prepared separately.[26]

## PRETESTING AND IMPLEMENTING

Whenever possible, sales promotion tools should be pretested to find out if they are appropriate and if they are of the right incentive size. Yet few promotions are ever tested ahead of time—most companies do not test sales promotions before starting them. Nevertheless, consumer sales promotions can be quickly and inexpensively pretested. For example, consumers can be asked to rate or rank different possible promotions, or promotions can be tried on a limited basis in selected geographic areas.

Companies should prepare implementation plans for each promotion, covering lead time and sell-off time. Lead time is the time necessary to prepare the program before launching it. Sell-off time begins with the launch and ends when the promotion ends.

# Evaluating the Results

Evaluation is also important. Yet many companies fail to evaluate their sales promotion programs and others evaluate them only superficially. Manufacturers can use one of many methods to evaluate sales promotions. The most common method is to compare sales before, during, and after a promotion. Suppose a company has a six percent market share before the promotion, which jumps to ten percent during the promotion, falls to five percent right after, and rises seven percent later on. The promotion seems to have attracted new triers and more buying from current customers. After the promotion, sales fell as consumers used up their inventories. The long-run rise to seven percent means that the company gained some new users. If the brand's share returned to the old level, then the promotion only changed the timing of demand rather than the total demand.

Consumer panel data reveals the kinds of people who responded to the promotion and what they did after the promotion. Consumer surveys can provide more information on how many consumers recall the promotion, what they thought of it, how many took advantage of it, and how it affected their buying. Sales promotions can also be evaluated through experiments that vary such factors as incentive value, length, and distribution method.

Clearly, sales promotion plays an important role in the total promotion mix. To use it well, the marketer must define the sales promotion objectives, select the best tools, design the sales promotion program, pretest it, implement it, and evaluate the results.

# PUBLIC RELATIONS

Another major mass-promotion tool is **public relations**—building good relations with the company's various publics by obtaining favorable publicity, building up a good "corporate image," and handling or heading off unfavorable rumors, stories, and events. The old name for marketing public relations was **publicity**, which was seen simply as activities to promote a company or its products by planting news about it in media not paid for by the sponsor. Public relations is a much broader concept that includes publicity and many other activities. Public relations departments use many different tools:

- **Press relations:** Placing newsworthy information into the news media to attract attention to a person, product, or service.
- **Product publicity:** Publicizing specific products.
- **Corporate communications:** Creating internal and external communications to promote understanding of the institution.
- **Lobbying:** Dealing with legislators and government officials to promote or defeat legislation and regulation.
- **Counseling:** Advising management about public issues and company positions and image.[27]

Public relations is used to promote products, people, places, ideas, activities, organizations, and even nations. Trade associations and marketing boards have used publicity to rebuild interest in declining commodities such as eggs, milk, and potatoes. Organizations have used publicity to attract attention or change a poor image. Nations have used publicity to attract more tourists, foreign investment, and international support.

Public relations is often described as a marketing stepchild because of its limited and scattered use. Yet public relations can have a strong impact on public awareness at a much lower cost than advertising. The company does not pay for the space or time in the media. It pays for a staff to develop and circulate the stories. If the company develops an interesting story, it could be picked by all the media, having the same effect as advertising that would cost millions of dollars. In addition, it would have more credibility than advertising.

In considering when and how to use product public relations, management should set PR objectives, choose PR messages and vehicles, implement the PR plan, and evaluate the results.

## Setting Public Relations Objectives

The first task is to set objectives for the public relations. The objectives are then turned into specific goals so that final results can be evaluated.

## Choosing Public Relations Messages and Vehicles

The organization next finds interesting stories to tell about the product. Suppose a little-known college wants more public recognition. It will search for possible stories. Do any faculty members have unusual backgrounds or are any working on unusual projects? Are any interesting new courses being taught, or any interesting events taking place on campus? Usually this search will uncover hundreds of stories, some of which can be fed to the press. The stories chosen should reflect the image this college wants.

If there are not enough stories, the college could sponsor newsworthy events. Here the organization creates news rather than finds it. Ideas include hosting major academic conventions, inviting well-known speakers, and holding news conferences. Each event creates many stories for many different audiences.

Event creation is very important in publicizing fundraising drives for nonprofit organizations. Fundraisers have developed a large set of special events such as art exhibits, auctions, benefit evenings, bingo games, book sales, cake sales, contests, dances, dinners, fairs, fashion shows, phoneathons, rummage sales, tours, and walkathons. No sooner is one type of event created, such as a walkathon, than competitors create new versions such as readathons, bikeathons, and jogathons.

## Implementing the Public Relations Plan

Implementing public relations requires care. Take the matter of placing stories in the media. A great story is easy to place. However, most stories are not great, and they may not get past busy editors. One of the main assets of public relations people is their personal relationships with media editors. Public relations people are often ex-journalists who know many media editors and know what they want. They view media editors as a market to satisfy so that these editors will continue to use their stories.

## Evaluating Public Relations Results

Public relations results are difficult to measure because PR is used with other promotion tools and its impact is indirect. If PR is used before the other tools come into action, its contribution is easier to evaluate.

The easiest measure of publicity effectiveness is the number of exposures in the media. Public relations people give the client a "clippings book" showing all the media that carried news about the product, and a summary such as the following:

> Media coverage included 350 column inches of news and photographs in 35 publications with a combined circulation of 8 million; 250 minutes of air time on 29 radio stations and an estimated audience of 7 million; and 66 minutes of air time on 16 television stations with an estimated audience of 9 million. If this time and space had been purchased at advertising rates, it would have amounted to $1,047,000.[28]

This exposure measure is not very satisfying. It does not tell how many people actually read or heard the message, and what they thought afterward. It does not give information on the net audience reached, since the media overlap in readership or audience.

A better measure of exposure involves finding out what change in product awareness/comprehension/attitude occurred as a result of the public relations campaign (after allowing for the impact of other promotional tools). This requires the use of survey methodology to measure the before-after levels of these variables.

Sales and profit impacts are the most satisfactory measures, if obtainable. This is often difficult because all elements of the marketing mix contribute to sales, and to attempt to estimate public relations' net contribution may not be possible.

# SUMMARY

Three major tools of mass promotion are advertising, sales promotion, and public relations. They are tools of mass marketing, as opposed to personal selling, which targets specific buyers.

Advertising—the use of paid media by a seller to inform, persuade, and remind about its products or organization—is a strong promotion tool. Canadian marketers spend over $10 billion each year on advertising, which takes many forms (national, regional, local; consumer, industrial, retail; product, brand, institutional). Advertising decision making is a five-step process consisting of setting objectives, budget decision, message decision, media decision, and evaluation. Advertisers should set clear goals as to whether the advertising is supposed to inform, persuade, or remind buyers. The advertising budget can be based on what is affordable, a percentage of sales, competitors' spending, or objectives and tasks. The message decision calls for designing messages, evaluating them, and executing them effectively. The media decision calls for defining reach, frequency, and impact goals; choosing major media types; selecting media vehicles; and scheduling the media. Finally, the communication and sales effects of advertising are evaluated before, during, and after the advertising is placed.

Sales promotion covers a wide variety of short-term incentive tools—coupons, premiums, contests, buying allowances—designed to stimulate consumers, the trade, and the company's own salesforce. Sales promotion spending has been growing faster than advertising spending in recent years. Sales promotion calls for setting sales promotion objectives; selecting tools; developing, pretesting, and implementing the sales promotion program; and evaluating results.

Public relations, which involves securing free editorial space or time, is the least used of the major promotion tools, although it has great potential for building awareness and preference. Public relations involves setting PR objectives, choosing PR messages and vehicles, implementing the PR plan, and evaluating PR results.

# Questions for Discussion

1. Is it feasible for an advertising agency to work for two competing clients at the same time? How much competition between such accounts is too much competition?

2. According to advertising expert Stuart Henderson Britt, good advertising objectives spell out the intended audience, the advertising message, the desired effects, and the criteria for determining whether the effects were achieved (for example, not just "increase awareness" but "increase awareness 20%"). Why should these components be part of the advertising objective? What are some effects that an advertiser wants a campaign to achieve?

3. What are some benefits and drawbacks of comparison advertising? Which has more to gain from using comparison advertising—the market-leading brand or a lesser brand?

4. What impact would a five percent national advertising tax have on advertising budgets? How would such a tax affect advertisers, consumers, the media, and the economy?

5. Describe several ads that you think are particularly effective and compare them with others you think are ineffective. How would you improve the less-effective ads?

6. What factors call for more frequency in an advertising media schedule? What

factors call for more reach? How can you increase one without either sacrificing the other or increasing your advertising budget?

7. A certain ad states that, except for homemade cookies, Almost Home cookies are the "moistest, chewiest, most perfectly baked cookies the world has ever tasted." If you think some other cookie is moister, chewier, or both, is the Almost Home claim false? Should such claims be regulated?

8. Which forms of sales promotion are most effective in getting consumers to try a product? Which are most effective in building loyalty to a product?

9. Why are many companies spending more on trade and consumer promotions than on advertising? Is heavy spending on sales promotion a good strategy for long-term profits?

# KEY TERMS

**Advertising** Any paid form of nonpersonal presentation and promotion of ideas, goods, or services by an identified sponsor.

**Advertising objective** A specific communication task to be accomplished with a specific target audience during a specific period of time.

**Consumer promotion** Sales promotion designed to stimulate consumer purchasing.

**Continuity** Scheduling ads evenly within a given period.

**Copy testing** Measuring the communication effect of an advertisement before or after it is printed or broadcast.

**Frequency** The number of times the average person in the target market is exposed to the advertising message during a given period.

**Media impact** The qualitative value of an exposure through a given medium.

**Public relations** Building good relations with the company's various publics by obtaining favorable publicity, building a good "corporate image," and handling or heading off unfavorable rumors, stories, and events.

**Publicity** Activities to promote a company or its products by planting news about it in media not paid for by the sponsor.

**Pulsing** Scheduling ads unevenly in bursts over a time period.

**Reach** The percentage of people in the target market exposed to an ad campaign during a given period.

**Sales promotion** Short-term incentives to encourage purchase or sales of a product or service.

**Salesforce promotion** Sales promotion designed to motivate the salesforce and make their selling efforts more effective.

**Trade promotion** Sales promotion designed to gain reseller support and to improve reseller selling efforts.

# REFERENCES

1. From various sources, including Marina Strauss, "7-Up Wagers Canada's Ready to Welcome Ads by Offbeat Fido," *Globe and Mail*, January 4, 1990, p. B5; Marina Strauss, "Pepsi Planning Expansion Into Flavored Soft-Drink Market," *Globe and Mail*, March 30, 1989, p. B7; Martin Mehr, "Coca-Cola Ads Sweep Nation and Big Screen," *Marketing*, November 3, 1989, p. 1, and Coca-Cola Beverages, *Annual Report*, 1989.

2. Martin Mehr, "Ad Revenues Projected to Top $10 Billion," *Marketing*, June 4, 1990, p. 1.

3. Based on a review of Canada's Top Advertisers, *Marketing*, April 8, 1991, p.47 and The *Financial Post*, Summer 1991.

4. *The Canadian Media Directors' Council Media Digest*, 1990/91.

5. Tracy Le May, "Can Bud Lead Labatt To the Top?" *Financial Times*, June 1, 1981, pp. 2, 14.

6. "U.S. Magazines Find a Hungry Market in Canada," *Marketing*, June 22, 1981, p. 34, and John Picton, "This Trivial Pursuit Designed Exclusively for Canadians," *Toronto Star*, April 15, 1984, p. A10.

7. *The Canadian Media Directors' Council Media Digest*, 1990/91.

8. For two perspectives on Bill C-58, see Vernon Jones and Sherry Monahan, "An Investigation Into the Effects of Bill C-58 on Advertising Media Decisions," in G.H.G. McDougall and R. Drolet, eds., *Marketing '77: The Canadian Perspective* (Fredericton: ASAC Proceedings, 1977), pp. 82-90; and I.A. Litvak and C.J. Maule, *The Impact of Bill C-58 on English Language Periodicals in Canada* (Ottawa: Secretary of State, 1978).

9. Michael Ryval, "Target: 600 Million Impressions," *Financial Times*, March 3, 1986, pp. 1, 6.

10. See William L. Wilkie and Paul W. Farris, "Comparison Advertising: Problems and Potential," *Journal of Marketing*, October 1975, pp. 7-15; Gordon H.G. McDougall, "Comparative Advertising in Canada: Practices and Consumer Reactions," *The Canadian Marketer*, Vol. 9, No. 2, 1978, pp. 14-20; and Auleen Carson and Marshall Rice, "The Incidence of Comparative Advertising: A Content Analysis of Canadian and American Magazines," in J. Liefeld, ed., *Marketing* (Whistler: ASAC Proceedings, 1990), pp. 65-73.

11. See Donald E. Schultz, Dennis Martin, and William P. Brown, *Strategic Advertising Campaigns* (Chicago: Crain Books, 1984), pp. 192-97.

12. Dik Warren Twedt, "How to Plan New Products, Improve Old Ones, and Create Better Advertising," *Journal of Marketing*, January 1969, pp. 53-57.

12. See "Ad Quality Good, Believability Low," *Advertising Age*, May 31, 1984, p. 3.

13. Martin Mehr, "Ads Have Better Image," *Marketing*, November 27, 1989, p. 1.

14. Dan Westall, "Quebec-Based Agencies Play Vital Function," *Globe and Mail*, April 15, 1981, p. B4.

15. Philip H. Dougherty, "Bud 'Pulses' the Market," *New York Times*, February 18, 1975, p. 40.

16. See Robert D. Buzzell, "E.I. Du Pont de Nemours & Co.: Measurement of Effects of Advertising," in his *Mathematical Models and Marketing Management* (Boston: Division of Research, Graduate School of Business Administration, Harvard University, 1964), pp. 157-79.

17. For some recent results on advertising and market share, see John Philip Jones, "Ad Spending: Maintaining Market Share," *Harvard Business Review*, January-February 1990, pp. 38-42 and James C. Schroer, "Ad Spending: Growing Market Share," *Harvard Business Review*, January-February 1990, pp. 44-48.

18. John Yokom, "Skeptical Look At Industry Figures," *Marketing*, April 23, 1990, pp. 11, 14, 26.

19. See Roger Strang, Robert M. Prentice, and Alden G. Clayton, *The Relationship Between Advertising and Promotion in Brand Strategy* (Cambridge, MA: Marketing Science Institute, 1975), Chap. 5; and P. Rajan Varadarajan, "Cooperative Sales Promotion: An Idea Whose Time Has Come," *Journal of Consumer Marketing*, Winter 1986, pp. 15-33.

20. Roger A. Strang, "Sales Promotion - Fast Growth, Faulty Management," *Harvard Business Review*, July-August, 1976, pp. 115-24.

21. For an interesting study of the effectiveness of various sales promotions in Canada, see Kenneth G. Hardy, "Key Success Factors for Manufacturers' Sales Promotions in Package Goods," *Journal of Marketing*, July 1986, pp. 13-23, and for some examples of point-of-purchase promotions, see Shelley Gillen, "How to Put More POP in your Sales," *Canadian Business*, February 1987, pp. 25-27.

22. Wayne Mouland, "More Exciting Times Ahead For the Consumer Promotion Industry," *Marketing*, February 20, 1989, pp. 6-7.

23. Yokom, "Skeptical Look At Industry Figures," pp. 11,14, 26.

24. For more on trade promotion, see John A. Quelch, "It's Time to Make Trade Promotion More Effective," *Harvard Business Review*, May-June 1983, pp. 130-36.

25. Peter M. Banting, "Industrial Trade Shows: A Comparative Perspective," in G.H.G. McDougall and R. Drolet, eds., *Marketing '77: The Canadian Perspective* (Fredericton: ASAC Proceedings, 1977), pp. 73-81.

26. Strang, "Sales Promotion," p. 119.

27. Adapted from Scott M. Cutlip, Allen H. Center, and Glen M. Brown, *Effective Public Relations*, 6th ed. (Englewood Cliffs, NJ: Prentice-Hall, 1985), pp. 7-17.

28. Arthur M. Merims, "Marketing's Stepchild: Product Publicity," *Harvard Business Review*, November-December 1972, pp. 111-112.

# CHAPTER 17

# Promoting Products: Personal Selling and Sales Management

## CHAPTER OBJECTIVES

After reading this chapter, you should be able to:
1. Discuss the role of a company's sales representatives.
2. Identify the major salesforce management decisions.
3. Explain how companies set salesforce objectives and strategy.
4. Tell how companies recruit, select, and train salespeople.
5. Describe how companies supervise salespeople and evaluate their effectiveness.

Many people would not consider a career in sales because of the negative images associated with this occupation. Salespeople are often viewed as fast-talking, pushy individuals who are only interested in making a quick dollar by peddling their products to a gullible public. A few of these types may still be around but most successful salespeople today are a far cry from the old stereotype. Consider the following examples:

- Telecommunication Terminal Systems (TTS) of Toronto sells complex corporate telephone systems ranging in price from $6,000 to millions of dollars. The competition includes Bell Information Systems and AT&T Canada. One of their top salespeople, who earns over $150,000 a year, puts her clients' needs first. As she says: "If you just forget about the commission and care about the client, I think that comes across." Or, as one buyer of a $3 million communication system from TTS commented, "she was able to coordinate her resources to meet our needs exceptionally well."

- ICL Computers of Montreal sells "point-of-sale" computer systems to large retail chains. One of ICL's top salespeople describes the process she goes through in making a sale that may take up to two years to complete. She never approaches a company without first researching its ownership, finances, and likely readiness to buy. Next, she meets with managers of the company and learns what they would like in a computer system. Then she meets with ICL's technical experts to determine exactly how much ICL can deliver. Next, she works nights and weekends writing a proposal that is given to the client during a formal presentation. If ICL makes the short list, she conducts further negotiations until the contract is signed. She adds: "I don't neglect my client after the contract is signed. In fact, I work even harder to see that they come back to ICL."

- Xerox Canada sells photocopy machines in the highly competitive office copier market. The company is well known and regarded for its sales training program and professional sales force. The top sales performers at Xerox are experts on their products and competitive offerings. They have a high business ethics level and are extremely motivated. They build long-term relationships based on trust and a knowledge of the customer's needs. As one Xerox salesperson said: "I get to know my customers well and if I think a competitor's machine will meet their needs better, I tell them."

Today's professional salespeople are sincere, hard-working individuals who identify and meet customer needs by listening carefully and delivering what they promise. As good salespeople know, satisfied customers are the key to their success.[1]

Robert Louis Stevenson noted that "everyone lives by selling something." Salesforces are found in nonprofit as well as profit organizations. University recruiters are the university's salesforce for attracting students. Churches use membership committees to attract new members. Agriculture Canada sends agricultural specialists to sell farmers on using new farming methods. Hospitals and museums use fundraisers to contact and raise money from donors.

There are many stereotypes of salespeople. "Salesmen" may bring to mind the image of Arthur Miller's pitiable Willy Loman in *Death of a Salesman* or Meredith Willson's cigar-smoking, back-slapping, joke-telling Harold Hill in *The Music Man*. Salespeople are typically pictured as sociable—although many salespeople are not particularly outgoing. They are blamed for forcing goods on people—although buyers often search out salespeople.

The term **salesperson** covers a wide range of positions, where the differences are often greater than the similarities. Here is one popular classification of sales positions:

- Positions in which the salesperson's job is largely to deliver the product—milk, bread, fuel, oil.
- Positions in which the salesperson is largely an inside order taker—such as the department store salesperson standing behind the counter, or an outside order taker such as the packing house or soap salesperson.
- Positions where the salesperson is not expected or permitted to take an order but only builds goodwill or educates buyers—the distiller's "missionary person" or the "detailer" for a pharmaceutical company.
- Positions where the major emphasis is placed on technical knowledge—the engineering salesperson who is mostly a consultant to client companies.
- Positions that demand the creative sale of tangible products like appliances, encyclopedias, houses, or technical equipment, or of intangibles, such as insurance, advertising services, or education.[2]

This list ranges from the least to the most creative types of selling. The jobs at the top of the list call for servicing accounts and taking orders, while the last ones call for locating buyers and persuading them to buy. We will focus on the more creative types of selling, and on the process of building and managing an effective salesforce. We define **salesforce management** as the analysis, planning, implementation, and control of salesforce activities. It includes setting salesforce objectives; designing salesforce strategy; and recruiting, selecting, training, supervising, and evaluating the firm's salespeople. The major salesforce management decisions are shown in Figure 17-1 and discussed in the following sections.[3]

# SETTING SALESFORCE OBJECTIVES

Companies set different objectives for their salesforces. IBM's salespeople are to "sell, install, and upgrade" customer computer equipment; Bell Canada salespeople should "develop, sell, and protect" accounts. Salespeople usually perform one or more of a variety of tasks for their companies. They find and develop new customers and communicate information about the company's products and services. They sell products by approaching, presenting, answering objections, and closing sales with customers. Salespeople provide services to customers, carry out market research and intelligence work, and fill in call reports.

Some companies are very specific about their salesforce objectives and activities. One company advises its salespeople to spend 80% of their time with current customers and 20% with prospects; and 85% of their time on current products and 15% on new products. If norms are not set, salespeople tend to spend most of their time selling current products to current accounts, while neglecting new products and new prospects.[4]

The old view is that salespeople should worry about sales and the company should worry about profit. The newer view is that salespeople should know how to produce customer satisfaction and company profit.

They should know how to look at sales data, measure market potential, gather market intelligence, and develop marketing strategies and plans. Salespeople need marketing analysis skills, especially at higher levels of sales management. A market-oriented rather than a sales-oriented salesforce will be more effective in the long run. This is particularly important for Canadian consumer goods manufacturers. The shift in channel power to retailers has meant that sales managers must consider the changing needs of Canada's large retailers.[5]

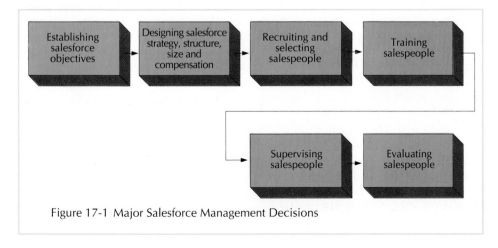

Figure 17-1 Major Salesforce Management Decisions

# Designing Salesforce Strategy

Once the company has set its salesforce objectives, it is ready to   face questions of salesforce strategy, structure, size, and compensation.

## Salesforce Strategy

Every company competes with others to get orders from customers. It must base its strategy on an understanding of the customer buying process. The company can use one or more of several sales approaches to contact customers. A salesperson talks to a prospect or customer in person or over the phone. Or the salesperson makes a sales presentation to a buying group. A sales team (such as a company executive, a salesperson, and a sales engineer) can make a sales presentation to a buying group. In conference selling a salesperson brings resource people from the company to meet with one or more buyers to discuss problems and opportunities. In seminar selling, company teams conduct an educational seminar for technical people in a customer company about state-of-the-art developments. Thus the salesperson often acts as an "account manager" who arranges contacts between people in the buying and selling companies. Selling calls for teamwork. Salespeople need help from others in the company, including top management (especially when major sales are at stake), technical people who provide customer services, and office staff such as sales analysts, order processors, and secretaries.

## Salesforce Structure

The company must also decide on how to structure its salesforce. This is simple if the company sells one product line to one industry with customers in many locations—here the company would use a territorial salesforce function. If the company sells many products to many types of customers, it might need a product salesforce structure or customer salesforce structure. These three structures are discussed below.

### TERRITORIAL SALESFORCE STRUCTURE

In the **territorial salesforce structure**, each salesperson is given an exclusive territory in which to sell the company's full line. This salesforce structure is the simplest sales organization and has many advantages. It clearly defines the salesperson's job, and because only one salesperson works the territory, she or he gets all the credit or blame for territory sales. The territorial structure also increases the salesperson's desire to build local business ties that, in turn, improve the salesperson's selling effectiveness. Finally, travel expenses are lower, since each salesperson travels within a smaller area.

Territorial sales organization is often supported by many levels of sales management positions. Several territories will be headed up by a district sales manager, several districts by a regional sales manager, and several regions by a national sales manager or sales vice-president.

### PRODUCT SALESFORCE STRUCTURE

Salespeople must know their products, especially when the products are numerous, unrelated, and complex. This, together with the trend toward product management, has led many companies to the **product salesforce structure**, in which the salesforce sells along product lines. The product structure, however, can lead to problems if many of the company's products are bought by the same customers. For example, many companies have several product divisions, each with its own salesforce. It is possible that several salespeople from the same company could call on the same customer on the same day. This means that they travel over the same routes, and each waits to see the customer's purchasing agents. These extra costs must be compared to the benefits of better product knowledge and attention to individual products.

## CUSTOMER SALESFORCE STRUCTURE

Companies often use a **customer salesforce structure**, in which they organize the salesforce along customer lines. Separate salesforces may be set up for different industries, for major industries, for major versus regular accounts, and for serving current customers versus finding new ones. The main advantage of customer specialization is that each salesforce can know more about specific customer needs. The major disadvantage arises when customers are scattered across the country, resulting in a lot of travel by all of the company's salesforce.

In Canada, sales managers of multiple-product firms face a dilemma. On the one hand, the wide geographic distribution of Canadian markets suggests that territorial-structured sales forces should be used to lower selling costs. On the other hand, the ready availability of new products, particularly for the Canadian subsidiaries of U.S. manufacturers, can result in product lines that are so broad as to spread the salesperson's efforts too thinly to be effective. The decision as to what structure to use can be assisted by an analytic approach based on a sales response function.[6]

# Salesforce Size

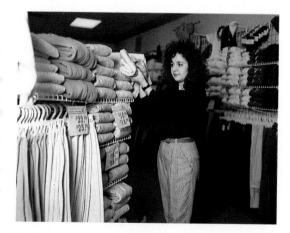

Once the company has set its strategy and structure, it is ready to consider salesforce size. Salespeople are one of the company's most productive and expensive assets. Increasing their number will increase both sales and costs.

Many companies use the workload approach to establish salesforce size. Under this approach, a company groups accounts into different size classes and then figures out how many salespeople are needed to call on

Salesforce size is a key management consideration.

them the desired number of times. The company might think as follows: Suppose we have 1,000 Type A accounts and 2,000 Type B accounts in Canada. Type A accounts require 36 calls a year and Type B accounts 12 calls a year. This means the company needs a salesforce that can make 60,000 calls a year. Suppose the average salesperson can make 1,000 calls a year. The company would need 60 salespeople.

## Salesforce Compensation

To attract the needed salespeople, the company has to have an attractive compensation plan. These plans vary considerably by industry and by company within the same industry. The level of compensation must be close to the "going rate" for the type of sales job and skills needed.

Compensation is made up of several elements—a fixed amount, a variable amount, expenses, and fringe benefits. The fixed amount, usually a salary, gives the salesperson some stable income. The variable amount, which might be commissions or bonuses, rewards the salesperson for greater effort. Expense allowances let the salespeople undertake needed and desirable selling efforts. Fringe benefits, such as paid vacations, sickness or accident benefits, pensions, and life insurance, provide job security and satisfaction. Management must decide what mix of these compensation elements makes the most sense for each sales job. Different combinations of fixed and variable compensation give rise to four basic types of compensation plans—straight salary, straight commission, salary plus bonus, and salary plus commissions.

# RECRUITING AND SELECTING SALESPEOPLE

Having set the strategy, structure, size, and compensation for the salesforce, the company now must set up systems for recruiting and selecting, training, supervising, and evaluating salespeople.

## Importance of Careful Selection

At the heart of successful salesforce operation is the selection of good salespeople. The performance levels of an average and a top salesperson can be quite different. In a typical salesforce, the top 30% of the salespeople might bring in over 60% of the sales. Careful selection of salespeople can greatly increase overall salesforce performance.

Beyond the differences in sales performance, poor selection results in costly turnover. One study found an average annual salesforce turnover rate for all industries of almost 20%. The costs of high turnover can be great. The company must spend more to hire and train replacements, and a salesforce with many new people is less productive.[7]

## What Makes a Good Salesperson?

Selecting salespeople would not be a problem if the company knew what traits to look for. If all good salespeople were outgoing, aggressive, and energetic, these characteristics could be checked in applicants. However, many successful salespeople are also bashful, mild mannered, and relaxed.

Still, the search continues for the magic list of traits that spells sure-fire sales ability. Many lists have been drawn up. One survey suggests that good salespeople have lots of enthusiasm, persistence, initiative, self-confidence, and job commitment. They are committed to sales as a way of life and have a strong customer orientation.[8] Another study concluded that the effective salesperson has at least two basic qualities: (1) empathy, the ability to feel as the customer does; and (2) ego drive, a strong personal need to make the sale.[9] These two traits led in predicting good subsequent performance of applicants for sales positions in three different industries. Charles Garfield found that good salespeople are goal-directed risk takers who identify strongly with their customers (see Marketing Highlight 17-1).

Empathy with the customer and a personal need to make a sale are qualities associated with good salespeople.

How can a company find out what traits salespeople in its industry should have? Job duties suggest some of the traits to look for. Is there a lot of paper work? Does the job call for much travel? Will the salesperson face a lot of rejections? The company should also look at the traits of its most successful salespeople for clues on needed traits.

## Recruiting Procedures

After management has decided on needed traits, it must recruit. The personnel department looks for applicants by getting names from current salespeople, using employment agencies, placing job ads, and contacting college students. If successful, recruiting will attract many applicants, and the company must select the best ones. The selection procedure can vary from a single informal interview to lengthy testing and interviewing. Many companies give formal tests to sales applicants. Test scores provide only one piece of information in a set that includes personal characteristics, references, past employment history, and interviewer reactions.

# TRAINING SALESPEOPLE

Many companies used to send their new salespeople into the field almost right away after hiring them. They would be given samples, order books, and instructions to "sell west of Regina." Training programs were luxuries. A training program meant spending a lot for instructors, materials, and space; paying a person who was not yet selling; and losing opportunities because he or she was not in the field.

Today's new salespeople may spend a few weeks to many months in training. The median training period is 17 weeks in industrial products companies, and 20 in consumer products companies. At IBM, new salespeople are not on their own for

# MARKETING HIGHLIGHT 17-1

## What Makes a Good Salesperson?

Charles Garfield, clinical professor of psychology at the University of California, San Francisco School of Medicine, claims his 20-year analysis of more than 1,500 superachievers in every field of endeavor is the longest running to date. *Peak Performance—Mental Training Techniques of the World's Greatest Athletes*, the book Garfield wrote about his findings, has been ordered by many companies (such as IBM, which took 3,000 copies) for their sales forces. Garfield says that the complexity and speed of change in today's business world means that to be a peak performer in sales requires greater mastery of different fields than to be one in science, sports, or the arts. The following are the most common characteristics he has found in peak sales performance:

- Supersalespeople are always taking risks and making innovations. Unlike most people, they stay out of the "comfort zone" and try to surpass their previous levels of performance.
- Supersalespeople have a powerful sense of mission and set the short-, intermediate-, and long-term goals necessary to fulfill that mission. Their personal goals are always higher than the sales quotas set by their managers. Supersalespeople also work well with managers, especially if the managers are also interested in peak performance.
- Supersalespeople are more interested in solving problems than in placing blame or bluffing their way out of situations. Because they view themselves as professionals in training, they are always upgrading their skills.
- Supersalespeople see themselves as partners with their customers, and as team players rather than adversaries. Peak performers believe their task is to communicate with people, while mediocre salespeople psychologically change their customers into objects and talk about the number of calls and closes they made as if it had nothing to do with human beings.
- Supersalespeople take each rejection as information they can learn from, whereas mediocre salespeople personalize rejection.
- The most surprising finding is that, like peak performers in sports and the arts, supersalespeople use mental rehearsal. Before every sale they review it in their mind's eye, from shaking the customer's hand when they walk in to discussing his problems and asking for the order.

Source: "What Makes a Supersalesperson?" *Sales and Marketing Management*, August 13, 1984, p. 86.

two years! IBM also expects its salespeople to spend 15% of their time each year in additional training.[10]

Training programs have several goals. Because salespeople need to know and identify with the company, most companies spend the first part of the training program describing the company's history and objectives, its organization, its financial structure and facilities, and its chief products and markets. Because salespeople need to know the company's products, sales trainees are shown how products are produced and how they work in various uses. Because salespeople need to know customers' and competitors' characteristics, they learn about the different types of customers and their needs, buying motives, buying habits, and about the company's and competitors' strategies. Salespeople also need to know how to make effective presentations, so they get training in the principles of salesmanship, and the company outlines the major sales arguments for each product. Finally, salespeople need to understand field procedures and responsibilities. They learn how to divide time between active and potential accounts, and how to use the expense account, prepare reports, and route communications effectively.

# Principles of Salesmanship

One of the major objectives of training programs is to teach salespeople the art of selling. Companies spend millions of dollars on seminars, books, cassettes, and other materials. Almost a million copies of books on selling are purchased every year, with such tantalizing titles as *How to Outsell the Born Salesman, How to Sell Anything to Anybody, The Power of Enthusiastic Selling, How Power Selling Brought Me Success in 6 Hours, Where Do You Go from No.1,* and *1000 Ways a Salesman Can Increase His Sales.* One of the most enduring books is Dale Carnegie's *How to Win Friends and Influence People.*

All of the training approaches try to convert a salesperson from being a passive order taker to being an active order getter. Order takers assume that customers know their own needs, would resent any attempt at influence, and prefer salespeople who are polite and reserved. An example of an order taker would be a salesperson who calls on a dozen customers each day, simply asking if the customer needs anything.

There are two approaches to training salespeople to be order getters—a sales-oriented approach and a customer-oriented approach. The first one trains the salesperson in high-pressure selling techniques, such as those used in selling encyclopedias or automobiles. This form of selling assumes the customers will not buy except under pressure, that they are influenced by a slick presentation, and that they will not be sorry after signing the order, or if they are, it doesn't matter.

The consumer-oriented approach, the one most often used in today's professional selling, trains salespeople in customer problem solving. The salesperson learns how to identify customer needs and find good solutions. This approach assumes that customer needs provide sales opportunities, that customers appreciate good suggestions, and that customers will be loyal to salespeople who have their long-term interests at heart. In one survey, purchasing agents described the following qualities as the ones they most disliked in salespeople: pushy, arrogant, unreliable, too talkative, fails to ask about needs. The qualities they valued most included reliability and credibility, integrity, innovativeness in solving problems, and product knowledge.[11] The problem solver salesperson fits better with the marketing concept than the hard seller or order taker.

# The Selling Process

Most training programs view the **selling process** as consisting of several steps that the salesperson must master. These steps are shown in Figure 17-2 and discussed below.[12]

## PROSPECTING AND QUALIFYING

The first step in the selling process is to identify prospects. The salesperson must approach many prospects to get a few sales. In one segment of the insurance industry, only one out of nine prospects becomes a customer. In the computer business,

125 phone calls result in 25 interviews leading to five demonstrations and one sale.[13] Although the company supplies leads, salespeople need skills to help find their own leads. Salespeople can obtain leads many ways. They can ask current customers for the names of prospects. They can build referral sources, such as suppliers, dealers, noncompeting salespeople, and bankers. They can join organizations to which prospects belong, or engage in speaking and writing activities that will draw attention. Using newspapers or directories they can search for names, and use the telephone and mail to track down leads. Or they can drop in unannounced on various offices (cold calling).

Sales representatives need to know how to qualify leads, that is, how to identify the good ones and screen out the poor ones. Prospects can be qualified by looking at their financial ability, volume of business, special needs, location, and possibilities for growth.

### PREAPPROACH

Before calling on a prospect, the salesperson should learn as much as possible about the organization (what it needs, who is involved in the buying) and its buyers (their characteristics and buying styles). The salesperson can consult standard sources (*Financial Post Survey of Industrials*, *Dun and Bradstreet*), acquaintances, and others to learn about the company. The salesperson should set call objectives, which might be to qualify the prospect, gather information, or make an immediate sale. Another task is to decide on the best approach, which might be a personal visit, a phone call, or a letter. The best timing should be thought out because many prospects are busy at certain times. Finally, the salesperson should give thought to an overall sales strategy for the account.

### APPROACH

During the approach step, the salesperson should know how to meet and greet the buyer to get the relationship off to a good start. This step involves the salesperson's appearance, the opening lines, and the follow-up remarks. Opening lines should be positive, such as "Mr. Smith, I am Yolanda Jones from the ABC Company. My company and I appreciate your willingness to see me. I will do my best to make this visit profitable and worthwhile for you and your company." This opening might be

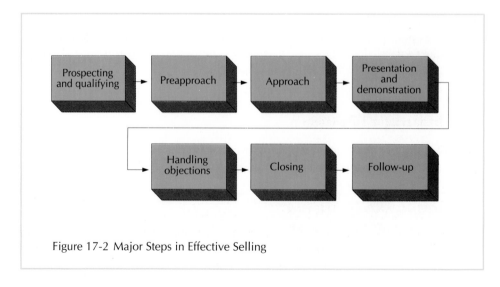

Figure 17-2 Major Steps in Effective Selling

followed by some key questions to learn more about the customers' needs, or by the showing of a display or sample to attract the buyer's attention and curiosity.

## PRESENTATION AND DEMONSTRATION

During the presentation step of the selling process, the salesperson now tells the product "story" to the buyer, showing how the product will make or save money. The salesperson describes the product features but concentrates on selling the customer benefits.

Companies use three styles of sales presentation. The oldest is the canned approach, which is a memorized sales talk covering the seller's main points. This approach has limited usefulness in industrial selling, but scripted presentations can be effective in some telephone-selling situations. A properly prepared and rehearsed script should sound natural and move the salesperson smoothly through the presentation. With electronic scripting, computers can lead a salesperson through a sequence of selling messages tailored on the spot to a prospect's responses.

Using the formula approach, the salesperson first identifies the buyer's needs, attitudes, and buying style. Then the salesperson moves into a formula presentation that shows how the product will satisfy that buyer's needs. Although not canned, the presentation follows a general plan.

The need-satisfaction approach starts with a search for the customer's real needs by getting the customer to do most of the talking. This approach calls for good listening and problem solving skills. One marketing director describes the approach this way:

> [High-performing salespeople] make it a point to understand customer needs and goals before they pull anything out of their product bag. Such salespeople spend the time needed to get an in-depth knowledge of the customer's business, asking questions that will lead to solutions our systems can address.[14]

Any style of sales presentation can be improved with demonstration aids such as booklets, flip charts, slides, movies, and product samples. If buyers can see or handle the product, they will better remember its features and benefits.

## HANDLING OBJECTIONS

Customers almost always have objections during the presentation or when asked to place an order. The problem can be logical or psychological. In handling objections, the salesperson should use a positive approach, ask the buyer to clarify the objection, take objections as opportunities to provide more information to the buyer, and turn objections into reasons for buying. Every salesperson needs training in the skills of handling objections.[15]

## CLOSING

The salesperson now tries to close the sale. Some salespeople do not get around to closing or do not handle it well. They may lack confidence, feel guilty about asking for the order, or not recognize the right moment to close the sale. Salespeople should know how to recognize closing signals from the buyer, including physical actions, comments, and questions. Salespeople can use one of several closing techniques. They can ask for the order, review the points of agreement, offer to help write up the order, ask whether the buyer wants this model or that one, or note

A telephone call can be an appropriate way to reach potential customers.

that the buyer will lose out if the order is not placed now. The salesperson may offer the buyer special reasons to close, such as a lower price or an extra quantity at no charge.

### FOLLOW-UP

This last step in the selling process, follow-up, is necessary if the salesperson wants to ensure customer satisfaction and repeat business. Right after closing, the salesperson should complete any details on delivery time, purchase terms, and other matters. The salesperson should schedule a follow-up call when the initial order is received to make sure there is proper installation, instruction, and servicing. This visit would show any problems, assure the buyer of the salesperson's interest, and reduce any buyer concerns that might have arisen since the sale.

# SUPERVISING SALESPEOPLE

New salespeople need more than a territory, compensation, and training—they need supervision. Through supervision, the company directs and motivates the salesforce to do a better job.

## Directing Salespeople

Companies vary in how closely they supervise their salespeople. Salespeople who are paid mostly on commission and who are expected to hunt down their own prospects are generally left on their own. Those who are salaried and must cover assigned accounts are usually more closely supervised.

An effective salesperson can use several closing techniques.

## Developing Customer Targets and Call Norms

Most companies classify customers into A, B, and C accounts, based on the account's sales volume, profit potential, and growth potential. They set the desired number of calls per period on each account class. Thus A accounts may receive nine calls a year; B accounts six, and C accounts three. The call norms depend upon competitive call norms and profits expected from the account.

## Developing Prospect Targets and Call Norms

Companies often specify how much time their salesforce should spend prospecting for new accounts. For example, a company may want its salespeople to spend 25% of their time prospecting, and to stop calling on a prospect after three unsuccessful calls. Companies set up prospecting standards for several reasons. If left alone, many salespeople will spend most of their time with current customers. Current customers are better-known quantities. Salespeople can depend on them for some business, whereas a prospect may never deliver any business. Unless salespeople are rewarded for opening new accounts, they may avoid new account development. Some companies rely on a special salesforce to open new accounts.

## Using Sales Time Efficiently

Salespeople need to know how to use their time efficiently. One tool is the annual call schedule showing which customers and prospects to call on in which months, and which activities to carry out. The activities include taking part in trade shows, attending sales meetings, and carrying out marketing research.

The other tool is time-and-duty analysis. In addition to time spent selling, the salesperson spends time traveling, waiting, eating and taking breaks, and doing administrative chores. Actual selling time may amount to as little as 15% of total working time. If selling time could be raised from 15 to 20%, this would be a 33% increase in the time spent selling. Companies are always looking for ways to save time—using phones instead of traveling, simplifying recordkeeping forms, finding better call and routing plans, and supplying more and better customer information.

Advances in technological equipment—desktop and laptop computers, videocassette recorders, videodiscs, automatic dialers, teleconferencing—have allowed dramatic breakthroughs in improving salesforce productivity. Salespeople have truly gone "electronic." Salespeople use computers to profile customers and prospects, analyze and forecast sales, schedule sales calls, enter orders, check inventories and order status, prepare sales and expense reports, process correspondence, and carry out many other activities. In a recent survey, salesforces using PCs reported an average 43% productivity gain.[16]

## Motivating Salespeople

Some salespeople will do their best without any special urging from management. To them, selling is the most fascinating job in the world. Nevertheless, the selling job often involves frustration. Salespeople usually work alone, and they are sometimes away from home. They may face aggressive, competing salespeople and difficult customers. They sometimes lack the authority to do what is needed to win a sale, and they may lose large orders they have worked hard to obtain. Thus salespeople often need special encouragement to work at their best level. Management can boost salesforce morale and performance through its organizational climate, sales quotas, and positive incentives.

## Organizational Climate

Organizational climate describes the feeling that the salespeople have about their opportunities, value, and rewards for a good performance. Some companies treat salespeople as if they are not very important. Other companies treat their salespeople as the prime movers and allow unlimited opportunity for income and promotion. The company's attitude toward its salespeople affects their behavior. If they are held in low esteem, there is high turnover and poor performance. If they are held in high esteem, there is little turnover and high performance.

Treatment from the salesperson's immediate superior is important. A good sales manager keeps in touch with the salesforce through letters and phone calls, visits in the field, and evaluation sessions in the home office. At different times the sales manager acts as the salesperson's boss, companion, coach, and confessor.

## Sales Quotas

Many companies set quotas for their salespeople stating what they should sell by product line and by product during the year. Compensation is often related to how well salespeople meet their quotas.

Sales quotas are set when the annual marketing plan is developed. The company first decides on a sales forecast that is reasonably achievable. Based on this forecast, management plans production, workforce size, and financial needs. It then sets sales quotas for its regions and territories. Generally, sales quotas are set higher than the sales forecast to encourage sales managers and salespeople to make their best effort. If they fail to make their quotas, the company may still make its sales forecast.

## Positive Incentives

Companies use several incentives to increase salesforce effort. Sales meetings provide a social occasion, a break from routine, a chance to meet and talk with "company brass," and a chance to air feelings and to identify with a larger group. Companies also sponsor sales contests to spur the salesforce to make a selling effort above what would normally be expected. Other incentives include honors, awards, and profit-sharing plans.

# EVALUATING SALESPEOPLE

We have described how management communicates what the salespeople should be doing and motivates them to do it. However, this communication requires good feedback. Good feedback also means getting regular information from salespeople to evaluate their performance.

## Sources of Information

Management gets information about its salespeople in several ways. The most important source is sales reports. Additional information comes from personal observation, customers' letters and complaints, customer surveys, and talks with other salespeople.

Sales reports are divided into plans for future activities and write-ups of completed activities. The best example of the first is the work plan, which salespeople submit a week or month in advance. The plan describes intended calls and routing. This report leads the salesforce to plan and schedule activities, informs management of their whereabouts, and provides a basis for comparing plans and performance. Salespeople can be evaluated on their ability to "plan their work and work their plan." Sometimes, management contacts individual salespeople after receiving their plans to suggest improvements.

Companies are beginning to require their salespeople to draft an annual territory marketing plan in which they outline their plans for building new accounts and increasing sales from existing accounts. The formats vary a lot—some ask for general ideas on territory development and others ask for detailed sales and profit estimates. This type of report casts salespeople into the role of marketing managers and profit centers. Their managers study these plans, make suggestions, and use them to develop sales quotas.

Salespeople write up their completed activities on call reports. Call reports keep sales management informed of the salesperson's activities, show what is happening with each customer's account, and provide information that might be useful in later calls. Salespeople also turn in expense reports for which they are partly or wholly repaid. Some companies also ask for reports on new business, reports on lost business, and reports on local business and economic conditions.

These reports supply the raw data from which sales management can evaluate salesforce performance. Are salespeople making too few calls per day? Are they spending too much time per call? Are they spending too much on entertainment? Are they closing enough orders per hundred calls? Are they finding enough new customers and holding on to the old customers?

## Formal Evaluation of Performance

Using the salesforce reports and other information, sales management evaluates members of the salesforce. Formal evaluation produces three benefits. First, management must establish and communicate clear standards for judging performance. Second, management must gather well-rounded information about each salesperson. Finally, salespeople know they will have to sit down one morning with the sales manager and explain their performance.

## Comparing Salespeople's Performance

One type of evaluation is to compare and rank the sales performance of the different salespeople. Such comparisons, however, can be misleading. Salespeople may perform differently because of differences in factors such as territory potential, workload, level of competition, and company promotion effort. Furthermore, sales are not usually the best indicator of achievement. Management should be more interested in how much each salesperson contributes to net profits. This requires looking at each salesperson's sales mix and sales expenses.

## Comparing Current Sales With Past Sales

A second type of evaluation is to compare a salesperson's current performance with past performance. This should directly indicate the person's progress. The comparison can show trends in sales and profits over the years for the salesperson. It can also show the salesperson's record on making calls and building new accounts. It cannot, however, tell why the salesperson's performance is moving in one direction or another.

## Qualitative Evaluation of Salespeople

The evaluation usually looks at the salesperson's knowledge of the company, products, customers, competitors, territory, and tasks. Personal traits can be rated, such as general manner, appearance, speech, and temperament. The sales manager can also review any problems in motivation or compliance. Each company must decide what would be most useful to know. It should communicate these criteria to the salespeople so that they understand how their performance is evaluated and can make an effort to improve it.

# SUMMARY

Most companies use salespeople, and many companies assign them the key role in the marketing mix. The high cost of the salesforce calls for an effective sales management process consisting of six steps: setting salesforce objectives; designing salesforce strategy, structure, size, and compensation; recruiting and selecting; training; supervising; and evaluating.

As an element of the marketing mix, the salesforce is very effective in achieving certain marketing objectives and carrying on certain activities such as prospecting, communicating, selling and servicing, and information gathering. A marketing-oriented salesforce needs skills in marketing analysis and planning in addition to the traditional selling skills.

Once the salesforce objectives have been set, strategy answers the questions of what type of selling would be most effective (solo selling, team selling), what type of salesforce structure would work best (territorial, product, or customer structured), how large the salesforce should be, and how the salesforce should be compensated in terms of salary, commission, bonus, expenses, and fringe benefits.

Salespeople must be recruited and selected carefully to hold down the high costs of hiring the wrong people. Training programs familiarize new salespeople with the company's history, its products and policies, the characteristics of the market and competitors, and the art of selling. The art of selling involves a seven-step sales process: prospecting and qualifying, preapproach, approach, presentation and demonstration, handling objections, closing, and follow-up. Salespeople need supervision and continual encouragement because they must make many decisions and face many frustrations. Periodically, the company must evaluate their performance to help them do a better job.

# QUESTIONS FOR DISCUSSION

1. Media representatives sell advertising space or time for newspapers, radio stations, and other advertising media. How creative is this type of selling?

2. Describe the advantages to IBM of each of the three different salesforce structures. Which structure do you think would be most appropriate?

3. In general, how does a company's salesforce size relate to its spending on other forms of promotion?

4. Why do so many salesforce compensation plans combine salary with bonus or commission? What are the advantages and disadvantages of using bonuses instead of commissions as incentives?

5. What two personal characteristics do you think are most important to success in a sales career? What tests can be used to detect these characteristics in a salesforce applicant?

6. Many people feel they do not have the ability to be a successful salesperson. What role does training play in helping to develop selling ability?

7. How would you apply the seven different steps in the selling process to a summer job selling encyclopedias door to door? Would these steps be applied in the

same way to selling copiers for Xerox?

8. What kinds of companies would benefit from an inside salesforce? What major factors determine which companies benefit?

9. The surest way to become a salesforce manager is to be an outstanding salesperson. What are the advantages and disadvantages of promoting top salespeople to management positions? Why might an outstanding salesperson decline promotion?

10. Good salespeople are familiar with their competitors' products as well as their own. What would you do if your company expected you to sell a product you thought was inferior to that of the competition?

# KEY TERMS

**Customer salesforce structure** A salesforce organization under which salespeople specialize in selling only to certain customers or industries.

**Product salesforce structure** A salesforce organization under which salespeople specialize in selling only a portion of the company's products or lines.

**Salesforce management** The analysis, planning, implementation, and control of salesforce activities.

**Salesperson** An individual acting for a company who performs one or more of the following activities: prospecting, communicating, servicing, and information gathering.

**Selling process** The steps that the salesperson follows when selling, including prospecting and qualifying, preapproach, approach, presentation and demonstration, handling objections, closing, and follow-up.

**Territorial salesforce structure** A salesforce organization that assigns each salesperson to an exclusive geographic territory in which that salesperson carries the company's full line.

# REFERENCES

1. From various sources, including David Silburt, "Secrets of the Super Sellers," *Canadian Business*, January 1987, pp. 54-59 and Rona Maynard, "Depth of a Saleswoman," *Financial Post Magazine*, December 1, 1985, pp. 26-32.

2. Robert N. McMurry, "The Mystique of Super-Salesmanship," *Harvard Business Review*, March-April 1961, p. 114. For a comparison of several classifications, see William C. Moncrief III, "Selling Activity and Sales Position Taxonomies for Industrial Salesforces," *Journal of Marketing Research*, August 1986, pp. 261-70.

3. For a review of the strategic, tactical, and operational decisions in sales management, see Adrian B. Ryans and Charles B. Weinberg, "Sales Force Manage-

ment: Integrating Research Advances," *California Management Review*, Fall 1981, pp. 75-89.

4. See Terry Deutscher, Judith Marshall, and David Burgoyne, "The Process of Obtaining New Accounts," *Industrial Marketing Management*, 11, 1982, pp. 173-181.

5. Gary Grundman, David Burgoyne, and Terry Deutscher, "Market Realities Demand New Sales Management Approaches," *Business Quarterly*, Summer 1981, pp. 34-39.

6. Ronald E. Turner, "Sales Force Specialization," *Journal of the Academy of Marketing Science*, Winter 1975, pp. 99-108.

7. For more on salesforce turnover costs, see René Y. Darmon, "Identifying Sources of Turnover Costs: A Segmentation Approach," *Journal of Marketing*, April 1990, pp. 46-56; and George H. Lucas Jr., A. Parasuraman, Robert A. Davis, and Ben M. Enis, "An Empirical Study of Salesforce Turnover," *Journal of Marketing*, July 1987, pp. 34-59.

8. Thayer C. Taylor, "Anatomy of a Star Salesperson," *Sales & Marketing Management*, May 1986, pp. 49-51.

9. David Mayer and Herbert M. Greenberg, "What Makes a Good Salesman?" *Harvard Business Review*, July-August 1964, pp. 119-25.

10. See "Survey of Selling Costs: 1987," *Sales & Marketing Management*, February 16, 1987, p. 2; and Patricia Sellers, "How IBM Teaches Techies to Sell," *Fortune*, June 6, 1988, pp. 141-46.

11. "PAs Examine the People Who Sell to Them," *Sales & Marketing Management*, November 11, 1985, pp. 38-41.

12. Some of the following discussion is based on W.J.E. Crissy, William H. Cunningham, and Isabella C.M. Cunningham, *Selling: The Personal Force in Marketing* (New York: Wiley, 1977), pp. 119-29.

13. Vincent L. Zirpoli, "You Can't 'Control' the Prospect, So Manage the Presale Activities to Increase Performance," *Marketing News*, March 16, 1984, p. 1.

14. Taylor, "Anatomy of a Star Salesperson," p. 50. Also see Harvey B. Mackay, "Humanize Your Selling Strategy," *Harvard Business Review*, March-April 1988, pp. 36-47.

15. See Thomas C. Keiser, "Negotiating With A Customer You Can't Afford to Lose," *Harvard Business Review*, November-December 1988, pp. 30-34.

16. Thayer C. Taylor, "Computers in Sales and Marketing: S&MM's Survey Results," *Sales & Marketing Management*, May 1987, pp. 50-53. Also see Jonathan B. Levine, "If Only Willy Loman Had Used a Laptop," *Business Week*, October 12, 1987, p. 137.


Promoting Products: Personal Selling and Sales Management

# Chapter 18

# International Marketing

## CHAPTER OBJECTIVES

After reading this chapter, you should be able to:
1. Discuss how foreign trade, economic, political-legal, and cultural environments affect a company's international marketing decisions.
2. Describe three key approaches to entering foreign markets.
3. Explain how companies might adapt their marketing mixes for foreign markets.
4. Identify the three forms of international marketing organization.

In early 1989 Canada entered the Free Trade Agreement (FTA) with the United States, its largest trading partner (75% of Canada's exports go to the U.S. and 70% of our imports come from the U.S.). The FTA will, over a ten-year period, eliminate duties on most goods and services between the two countries, creating one large market. The attitude of many Canadian companies toward the FTA is reflected in a statement from Forsyth, a leading Canadian shirt manufacturer: "The FTA is bringing both massive export opportunities and substantial competitive threats domestically from large U.S. competitors." The implication is clear—to grow and prosper, Canadian firms must take advantage of the U.S. market as well as defend their position in Canada from increased competition.

For commodity-type businesses like steel or glass containers, there is a need to manufacture a competitively priced product. Consumer Packaging, the largest manufacturer of glass and package containers in Canada and the third largest in North America, has declared that it must be a low-cost competitor of glass containers to grow. For some companies like Air Canada, Canadian National, and Canadian Pacific, the FTA will increase the north-south movement of people, goods, and services and provide opportunities for expansion. For U.S. multinationals operating in Canada, like Du Pont Canada and IBM Canada, opportunities exist for more mandates to develop, produce, and market selected products around the world. For Canadian multinationals like Bombardier, Northern Telecom, Alcan, Moore, Noranda, and Dominion Textile, the FTA should be beneficial as it reduces barriers to a market where they already have a major presence. For example, Dominion Textile regards the FTA as an important challenge and an opportunity to build and maintain an efficient North American production base on both sides of the border. The company sees its competitive advantage in areas where technical know-how, low labor content, and transportation costs matter. Five years ago, Dominion Textile had 65% of its sales in Canada—today it is 30%, with the other 70% in the U.S. (40%) or the rest of the world (30%). Dominion Textiles has doubled its sales over that five-year period.

For other Canadian companies, the FTA offers the opportunity to continue pursuing niche strategies—gaining a large share of a specialized market. These Canadian companies have a specialized product line or expertise they can sell to a world market—like Royal Trust in personal banking, DMR Group of Montreal for information systems consulting, Cascades Inc. in paper products, and the Lavalin Group in engineering.

Canadian companies need to consider the international arena as the world's trade barriers come tumbling down. Europe '92 promises a single market of 320 million customers and Japan has a further 120 million consumers. Future growth and prosperity will depend on Canadian firms who "think globally and act locally."[1]

The first step for Canadian companies entering international marketing is usually the U.S. market, which is roughly ten times the size of the Canadian market and has a similar social, political, economic, and technological environment. As noted, the U.S. is Canada's main trading partner and with the Free Trade Agreement will continue as Canada's most important foreign market. Two other major markets where Canadian companies operate are Japan and Europe. All told, these three markets account for 90% of Canada's exports and 88% of Canada's imports (Table 18-1). Among the fastest growing markets for Canada are the Newly Industrialized Countries (NICs) of Taiwan, Hong Kong, South Korea, and Singapore, referred to as the "Four Tigers." Substantial growth in trade with the emerging NICs—Indonesia, Thailand, Malaysia, and the Philippines—is also occurring. These trends reflect, in part, the patterns in world trade. The majority of world trade is between the developed nations, in particular the Triad—the three major trading blocs of Canada/U.S., Japan, and Europe.[2] However, the NICs and the emerging NICs are rapidly becoming significant international traders. Marketing in most of these countries requires managers to learn another language, deal with a different currency, face political and legal uncertainties, and often adapt the product to a different set of needs and expectations.

Canada's trade reflects its substantial natural resources. The country generates a large trade surplus in resource-based industries: forestry, mining, energy, and grain. Most of Canada's exports in finished products are in cars and trucks, which are exported to the U.S. as part of the Auto Pact. Canada imports large quantities of machinery and equipment, fruits, vegetables, textiles, and clothing.[3] This trade pattern reflects Canada's resource base and the fact that foreign-owned companies account for more than 50% of industrial output in Canada.[4] The Canadian federal government has encouraged companies to expand their activities abroad in order to earn more foreign exchange and increase employment in Canada. In addition to establishing trade missions in most foreign markets, the Canadian government organized the Export Development Corporation, a crown corporation that primarily

## TABLE 18-1
## Canada's Major Trading Partners

Growth in exports and imports 1979-89

| | Exports To | | Imports From | |
|---|---|---|---|---|
| | % change 1979-89 | $millions 1989 | % change 1979-89 | $millions 1989 |
| U.S. | +130 | 103,732 | +110 | 93,322 |
| EUROPE | | | | |
| Switzerland | +290 | 719 | +86 | 600 |
| Norway | +127 | 635 | +780 | 785 |
| France | +103 | 1,260 | +159 | 2,017 |
| Belgium/Luxembourg | +84 | 1,231 | +135 | 567 |
| Sweden | +84 | 319 | +145 | 939 |
| Spain | +83 | 398 | +220 | 567 |
| Italy | +50 | 1,096 | +216 | 2,012 |
| Netherlands | +42 | 1,533 | +227 | 823 |
| Britain | +41 | 3,538 | +145 | 4,604 |
| West Germany | +30 | 1,777 | +138 | 3,708 |
| AUSTRALIA | +85 | 1,032 | +34 | 618 |
| JAPAN | +117 | 8,472 | +291 | 8,262 |
| NEWLY INDUSTRIALIZED COUNTRIES (NICs) | | | | |
| Taiwan | +750 | 882 | +350 | 2,352 |
| Hong Kong | +637 | 1,014 | +172 | 1,161 |
| South Korea | +336 | 1,592 | +427 | 2,441 |
| Singapore | +112 | 243 | +207 | 503 |
| EMERGING NICs | | | | |
| Indonesia | +371 | 295 | +356 | 192 |
| Thailand | +289 | 340 | +1,224 | 420 |
| Malaysia | +235 | 219 | +232 | 320 |
| Philippines | +159 | 219 | +162 | 205 |
| OTHER | | | | |
| Mexico | +154 | 600 | +706 | 1,680 |
| China | +85 | 1,116 | +606 | 1,182 |
| Saudi Arabia | +34 | 337 | -80 | 253 |
| India | +32 | 297 | +140 | 224 |
| Brazil | +24 | 521 | +261 | 1,130 |
| U.S.S.R. | -11 | 685 | +83 | 118 |
| Algeria | -26 | 292 | -66 | 30 |
| TOTAL | +112 | 138,934 | +120 | 134,255 |

**Source:** *The Financial Post 500*, Summer 1990, p. 21.

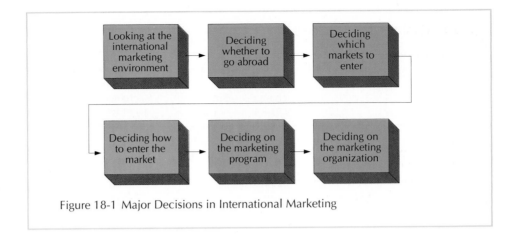

Figure 18-1 Major Decisions in International Marketing

assists small and medium-sized businesses in financing foreign sales.[5] In recent years Canadian firms have been investing in foreign markets at an accelerating rate. Most of this investment is in the United States, and Canada is now the fourth-largest investor in that country.[6]

Because future opportunities for many Canadian firms lie in the international arena, it is important to understand how to approach these markets. We might ask: Does international marketing, particularly for Canadian firms operating in the U.S., involve any new principles? In general the answer is no—the principles of marketing objectives, choosing target markets, developing marketing positions and mixes, and carrying out marketing control still apply. The principles are not new, but the differences between nations can be so great that the international marketer needs to understand foreign countries and how people in different countries respond to marketing efforts.

We will now look at the six decisions that a company faces in international marketing, as shown in Figure 18-1.

# LOOKING AT THE INTERNATIONAL MARKETING ENVIRONMENT

Before deciding whether to sell abroad, a company must thoroughly understand the international marketing environment. That environment has changed considerably in the last two decades and dramatically in the last few years, creating both new opportunities and new problems. World trade and investment have grown rapidly, with many attractive markets opening up in Western and Eastern Europe, the USSR, and elsewhere. There has been a growth of global brands in automobiles, food, clothing, electronics, and many other product categories. The number of **multinational companies**—companies that operate in many countries and have a major part of their operations outside their home countries—has grown dramatically. Countries such as Japan and West Germany have increased their economic power in world markets (see Marketing Highlight 18-1). The international financial system has become more complex and fragile, and Canadian companies in some instances face increasing trade barriers designed to protect domestic markets against foreign competition.

# MARKETING HIGHLIGHT 18-1

## The World's Champion Marketers: The Japanese?

Few dispute that the Japanese have performed an economic miracle since World War II. In a short time, they have achieved global market leadership in many industries: automobiles, motorcycles, watches, cameras, optical instruments, and consumer electronics. Some credit the global success of Japanese companies to their unique business and management practices. Others point to the help they get from Japan's government, powerful trading companies, and banks. Still others say Japan's success is based on low wage rates and unfair dumping policies.

One of the main keys to Japan's success is its skillful use of marketing. The Japanese know how to select a market, enter it in the right way, build market share, and protect their share against competitors.

### SELECTING MARKETS

The Japanese work hard to identify attractive global markets. First, they look for industries that require high skills and high labor intensity, but few natural resources. These include consumer electronics, cameras, watches, motorcycles, and pharmaceuticals. Second, they like markets where consumers around the world would be willing to buy the same product designs. Finally, they look for industries where the market leaders are weak or complacent.

### ENTERING MARKETS

Japanese study teams spend several months in the target country evaluating a target market, searching for market niches that are not being satisfied. Sometimes they start with a low-price, stripped-down version of a product, sometimes with a product that is as good as that of the competition but priced lower, sometimes with a product with higher quality or new features. The Japanese line up good distribution channels in order to provide quick service. They also use effective advertising to bring products to the consumer's attention. Their basic entry strategy is to build market share rather than early profits. The Japanese are often willing to wait as long as a decade before realizing their profits.

### BUILDING MARKET SHARE

Once Japanese firms gain a market foothold, they begin to expand their market share. They pour money into product improvements and new models so that they can offer more and better features than the competition. They spot new opportunities through market segmentation, develop markets in new countries, and work to build a network of world markets and production locations.

### PROTECTING MARKET SHARE

Once the Japanese achieve market leadership, they become defenders rather than attackers. Their defense strategy is a continuous product development and refined market segmentation.

**Sources:** See Philip Kotler, Liam Fahey, and Somkid Jatusripitak, *The New Competition* (Englewood Cliffs, NJ: Prentice Hall, 1985); Vernon R. Alden, "Who Says You Can't Crack Japanese Markets?" *Harvard Business Review*, January-February 1987, pp. 52-56; and Joel Dreyfuss, "How to Beat the Japanese at Home," *Fortune*, August 31, 1987, pp. 80-83.

# The International Trade System

The Canadian company looking abroad must start by understanding the international trade system. When selling to another country, the Canadian firms may face various trade restrictions. The most common is the **tariff**, which is a tax levied by a foreign government against certain imported products. The tariff may be designed to raise revenue or to protect domestic firms. The exporter may also face a **quota**,

McDonald's has made the world its market.

which sets limits on the amount of goods that the importing country will accept in certain product categories. The purpose of the quota is to conserve on foreign exchange and protect local industry and employment. An **embargo**, under which some kinds of imports are totally banned, is the strongest form of quota. Canadian firms may face exchange controls which limit the amount of foreign exchange and the exchange rate against other currencies. The company may also face nontariff barriers, such as bias against Canadian company bids, and product standards that go against Canadian product features. For example, the Dutch government bans tractors that run faster than 16 kilometers an hour, which means that most Canadian-made tractors are barred. As another example, consider the following:

> One of the cleverest ways the Japanese have found to keep foreign manufacturers out of their domestic market is to plead "uniqueness." Japanese skin is different, the government argues, so foreign cosmetics companies must test their products in Japan before selling there. The Japanese say their stomachs are small and have room for only the mikan, the local tangerine, so imports of oranges are limited. Now the Japanese have come up with what may be the flakiest argument yet: Their snow is different, so ski equipment should be too.[7]

At the same time, certain forces help trade between nations, or at least between some nations. Certain countries have formed economic communities—a group of nations organized to work toward common goals in the regulation of international trade. The most important such community is the European Community (EC, also known as the Common Market). The EC's members are the major Western European nations, with a combined population of over 320 million people. It works to create a single European market by reducing physical, financial, and technical barriers to trade among member nations. It eliminates restrictions on its members while setting uniform tariffs and other restrictions on trade with non-member nations.

Founded in 1957, the European Community in its early years did not achieve the true "common market" originally envisioned. In 1985, however, member countries renewed their push to integrate economically. They jointly enacted the Single European Act, which commits each member nation to a target date of 1992 for completing the process of making Europe "an area without internal frontiers in which the free movement of goods, persons, services, and capital is ensured." Thus, the year 1992 has come to symbolize the complete transformation of the European economy. The European economy will be the second largest market in the world, after the United States, and followed by Japan (Table 18-2).[8] Other economic communities that have been formed include the Latin American Free Trade Association (LAFTA), the Central American Common Market (CACM), the Council for Mutual Economic Assistance (CMEA) (Eastern European countries), and the Association of South East Asian Nations (ASEAN).

Each nation has unique features that must be understood. A nation's readiness for different products and services, and its attractiveness as a market to foreign firms, depend on its economic, political-legal, and cultural environments.

**TABLE 18-2**
**Vital Statistics—European Community, United States, and Japan**

| | Total Area (000 sq. km) | Population 1987 (millions) | Unemployment Rate 1988 (%) | 1988 GDP at Current Prices ($ Billion) | GDP per Capita at Current Prices ($) |
|---|---|---|---|---|---|
| Belgium | 30.5 | 9.83 | 10.2 | 147.5 | 14,071 |
| Denmark | 43.1 | 5.13 | 5.6 | 107.2 | 19,730 |
| France | 547.0 | 55.63 | 10.3 | 941.9 | 15,818 |
| West Germany | 248.6 | 61.20 | 6.2 | 1,204.6 | 18,280 |
| Greece | 132.0 | 9.99 | 7.4 | 53.0 | 4,719 |
| Ireland | 70.3 | 3.54 | 17.6 | 31.3 | 8,297 |
| Italy | 301.2 | 57.33 | 11.9 | 826.0 | 13,224 |
| Luxembourg | 2.6 | .37 | 1.7 | 6.3 | 16,138 |
| Netherlands | 37.3 | 14.67 | 9.5 | 227.2 | 14,530 |
| Portugal | 92.1 | 10.27 | 7.0 | 41.9 | 3,761 |
| Spain | 504.8 | 38.83 | 20.1 | 339.3 | 7,449 |
| United Kingdom | 224.8 | 56.93 | 8.3 | 805.6 | 11,765 |
| Total | 2,254.3 | 323.72 | --- | 4,731.8 | --- |
| United States | 9,372.6 | 243.92 | 5.4 | 4,805.5 | 18,338 |
| Japan | 372.3 | 122.09 | 2.5 | 2,853.0 | 19,437 |

**Source:** OECD, *Statistics on the Member Countries,* 1989 Edition.

# Economic Environment

In looking at foreign markets, the international marketer must study each country's economy. Two economic factors reflect the country's attractiveness as a market. The first is the country's industrial structure. The industrial structure of a country shapes its product and service needs, income levels, and employment levels. There are four types of industrial structures:

- **Subsistence economies.** In a subsistence economy the vast majority of people engage in simple agriculture. They consume most of their output and barter the rest for simple goods and services. They offer few market opportunities.
- **Raw-material exporting economies.** These economies are rich in one or more natural resources but poor in other ways. Much of their revenue comes from exporting these resources. Examples are Chile (tin and copper), Zaire (rubber), and Saudi Arabia (oil). These countries are good markets for large equipment, tools and supplies, and trucks. If there are many foreign residents and a wealthy upper class, they are also a market for luxury goods.
- **Industrializing economies.** In an industrializing economy, manufacturing accounts for between 10 and 20% of the country's economy. Examples include Egypt, the Philippines, India, and Brazil. As manufacturing increases, the country needs more imports of raw textile materials, steel, and heavy machinery, and fewer imports of finished textiles, paper products, and automobiles. Industrialization typically creates a new wealthy class and a small but growing middle class, both demanding new types of imported goods.
- **Industrial economies.** Industrial economies are major exporters of manufactured goods and investment funds. They trade goods among themselves and also export them to other types of economies for raw materials and semifinished goods. The varied manufacturing activities of these industrial nations and their large middle class make them rich markets for all sorts of goods.

The second economic factor is the country's income distribution. The international marketer might find countries with five different income distribution patterns: (1) very low family incomes; (2) mostly low family incomes; (3) very low and very high family incomes; (4) low, medium, high family incomes; and (5) mostly medium family incomes. Consider the market for the Lamborghini, an automobile costing more than $130,000. The market would be very small in countries with Type 1 or Type 2 income patterns. Most Lamborghinis are sold in large markets like the United States, Europe, and Japan, which have large segments of high-income consumers, or in small but wealthy countries like Saudi Arabia.

# Political-Legal Environment

Nations differ greatly in their political-legal environments. At least four such factors should be considered in deciding whether to do business in a given country.

## ATTITUDES TOWARD INTERNATIONAL BUYING

Most nations are very receptive to foreign firms; others are very hostile. For example, Mexico for many years has been attracting foreign businesses by offering investment incentives and site-location services. On the other hand, India has created obstacles for foreign businesses with import quotas, currency restrictions, and limits on the number of non-nationals in the management team. IBM and Coca-Cola decided to leave India because of all the "hassles." Pepsi, on the other hand, took positive steps to persuade the Indian government to allow it to do business in that country on reasonable terms.

## POLITICAL STABILITY

Stability is another issue. Governments change hands, sometimes violently. Even without a change, a government may decide to respond to new popular feelings. The foreign company's property may be taken over, its currency holdings may be blocked, or import quotas or new duties may be set. International marketers may still find it profitable to do business in an unstable country, but the situation will affect how they handle business and financial matters.

## MONETARY REGULATIONS

Sellers want to take their profits in a currency of value to them. Ideally, the buyer can pay in the seller's currency or in other world currencies. Short of this, sellers might accept a blocked currency—one whose removal from the country is restricted by the buyer's government—if they can buy other goods in that country that they need or can sell elsewhere for a needed currency. In the worst case they have to take their money out of the host country in the form of less marketable products that they can sell elsewhere only at a loss. Besides currency limits, a changing exchange rate also creates high risks for the seller.

Most international trade involves cash transactions. Yet many nations have too little hard currency to pay for their purchases from other countries. They want to pay with other items instead of cash. This situation has led to a growing practice called countertrade, which now accounts for about 25% of all world trade. Countertrade takes several forms. Barter involves the direct exchange of goods or services, as when a Canadian company supplies oil drilling equipment to Russia in exchange for oil. Another form is compensation (or buyback), whereby the seller sells a plant, equipment, or technology to another country and agrees to take payment in the resulting products. Another form is counterpurchase—the seller receives full payment in cash but agrees to spend some portion of the money in the other country within a stated time period.

## GOVERNMENT BUREAUCRACY

A fourth factor is the extent to which the host government runs an efficient system for helping foreign companies: efficient customs handling, good market information, and other factors that aid in doing business.

# Cultural Environment

Each country has its own folkways, norms, and taboos. The way foreign consumers think about and use certain products must be checked by the seller before planning the marketing program. Here are samples of some of the surprises in the consumer market:

- The average Frenchman uses almost twice as many cosmetics and beauty aids as does his wife.
- The Germans and the French eat more packaged, branded spaghetti than the Italians.

- Italian children like to eat a chocolate bar between two slices of bread as a snack.
- Women in Tanzania will not give their children eggs for fear of making them bald or impotent.

Business norms and behavior also vary from country to country. Here are some examples of different foreign business behavior:

- South Americans like to sit or stand very close to each other when they talk business—in fact, almost nose to nose. A Canadian business executive would back away as a South American moves closer. Both may end up being offended.
- In face-to-face communications, Japanese business executives rarely say no to a Canadian business executive. Canadians are frustrated by this behavior, as they like to know where they stand. Canadians also tend to come to the point quickly. Japanese business executives find this offensive.
- In France, wholesalers don't want to promote a product. They ask their retailers what they want, and deliver it. If a Canadian company builds its strategy around the French wholesaler's cooperation in promotions, it is likely to fail.
- In Muslim countries it is not proper to give anyone anything with your left hand. If you hand a person a pen with your left hand to sign a contract, he might not do it.[9]

Each country and region has cultural traditions, preferences, and taboos that the marketer must study.

# DECIDING WHETHER TO GO ABROAD

Not all companies need to venture into foreign markets to survive. For example, many companies are local businesses that need to market well only in the local marketplace. Other companies, however, operate in global industries in which their strategic positions in major markets are strongly affected by their overall global positions. As a company in a global industry, Northern Telecom must organize globally if it is to gain purchasing, manufacturing, financial, and marketing advantages. Firms in a global industry must compete on a worldwide basis if they are to succeed.

Companies get involved in international marketing in one of two ways. Someone—a domestic exporter, a foreign importer, a foreign government—asks the company to sell abroad. Or the company starts to think on its own about going abroad. It might face overcapacity or see better marketing opportunities in other countries than at home. For example, in one study of small and medium-size Canadian manufacturers, 30% got into international marketing through unsolicited orders, while most of the rest entered because they saw good opportunities in other countries.[10]

Before going abroad, the company should try to define its international marketing objectives and policies. It should determine if it can meet foreign wants and needs, with a long-term profit. First, it should decide what volume of foreign sales it wants. Most companies start small when they go abroad. Some plan to stay small, seeing foreign sales as a small part of their business. Other companies have bigger plans, seeing foreign business as equal to or even more important than their domestic business.

Second, the company must choose between marketing in a few countries and marketing in many countries. Third, the company must decide on the types of countries to enter. Which countries are attractive will depend on the product, geographical factors, income and population, political climate, and other factors. The seller may prefer certain groups of countries or parts of the world.

# DECIDING WHICH MARKETS TO ENTER

After listing possible export markets, the company will have to screen and rank them. The countries should be ranked on several factors such as market size, market growth, cost of doing business, competitive advantage, and risk level. Information on these factors may be obtained from the Canadian federal government, which offers a wide range of services to exporters including information on foreign markets, assistance in visiting foreign markets, and identification of potential customers.[11] The goal is to figure out the market potential of each market, using indicators such as those shown in Table 18-1. Then the marketer must decide which markets will offer the greatest long-run return on investment.

# DECIDING HOW TO ENTER THE MARKET

Once a company has decided to sell to a country, it must determine the best mode of entry. Its major choices are exporting, joint venturing, and direct investment

**TABLE 18-1**
**Indicators of Market Potential**

1. **Demographic characteristics**
   Size of population
   Rate of population growth
   Degree of urbanization
   Population density
   Age structure and composition
   of the population

2. **Geographic characteristics**
   Physical size of a country
   Topographical characteristics
   Climate conditions

3. **Economic factors**
   GNP per capita
   Income distribution
   Rate of growth of GNP
   Ratio of investment to GNP

4. **Technological factors**
   Level of technological skill
   Existing production technology
   Existing consumption technology
   Education levels

5. **Sociocultural factors,**
   **dominant values**
   Life-style patterns
   Ethnic groups
   Linguistic fragmentation

6. **National goals and plans**
   Industry priorities
   Infrastructure investment plans

**Source:** Susan P. Douglas, C. Samual Craig, and Warren Keegan, "Approaches to Assessing International Marketing Opportunities for Small and Medium-Sized Business," *Columbia Journal of World Business*, Fall 1982, pp. 26-32.

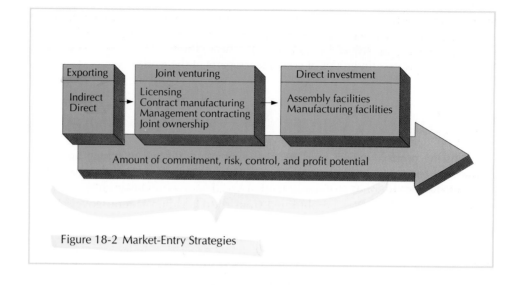

Figure 18-2 Market-Entry Strategies

abroad. As the figure shows, each succeeding strategy involves more commitment and risk, but also more control and potential possible profits. These three market-entry strategies are shown in Figure 18-2, along with the options under each.

# Exporting

The simplest way to enter a foreign market is through **exporting**. The company may passively export its surpluses from time to time, or it may actively make a commitment to expand exports to a particular market. In either case the company produces all its goods in its home country. It may or may not modify them for the export market. Exporting involves the least change in the company's product lines, organization, investments, or mission. Because the U.S. market is so close and has a similar environment to the Canadian market, many Canadian firms engage in occasional or active exporting to the U.S.

Companies typically start with indirect exporting, working through independent international marketing distributors. Indirect exporting involves less investment because the firm does not need an overseas salesforce or set of contacts. It also involves less risk. International marketing middlemen—domestic-based export merchants or agents, cooperative organizations, export-management companies—bring know-how and services to the relationship, and so the seller normally makes fewer mistakes.

## DIRECT EXPORT

Sellers may eventually move into direct exporting, handling their own exports. The investment and risk are somewhat greater, but so is the potential return.

The company can carry on direct exporting in several ways. First, it can set up a domestic export department that carries out export activities. Or it can set up an overseas sales branch that handles sales, distribution, and perhaps promotion. The sales branch gives the seller more presence and program control in the foreign market and it often serves as a display center and customer service center. Alternatively, the company can send home-based sales representatives abroad at certain times to find business. Finally, the company can do its exporting through foreign-based distributors who buy and own the goods, or through foreign-based agents who sell the goods on behalf of the company. In one study of Canadian exporters, most of the firms used the direct method. Smaller firms tended to use indirect methods, probably because of the high working capital costs of sales branches.[12]

# Joint Venturing

A second method of entering a foreign market is through **joint venturing**, joining with foreign companies to produce or market the products or services. Joint venturing differs from exporting in that the company joins with a partner to sell or market abroad. It differs from direct investment in that an association is formed with someone in the foreign country. There are four types of joint venture.[13]

## LICENSING

**Licensing** is a simple way for a manufacturer to enter international marketing. The company enters an agreement with a licensee in the foreign market, offering the right to use a manufacturing process, trademark, patent, trade secret, or other item of value for a fee or royalty. The company gains entry into the market at little risk; the licensee gains production expertise, or a well-known product or name, without having to start from scratch. Coca-Cola carries out its international marketing by licensing bottlers around the world and supplying them with the syrup needed to produce the product.

Licensing has potential disadvantages. The firm has less control over the licensee than if it had set up its own production facilities. If the licensee is very successful, the firm has given up these profits, and if and when the contract ends, the firm may find that it has created a competitor.

## CONTRACT MANUFACTURING

Another option is **contract manufacturing**, contracting with manufacturers in the foreign market to produce the product. Contract manufacturing has the drawback of less control over the manufacturing process and the loss of potential profits on manufacturing. On the other hand, it offers the company a chance to start faster with less risk, and with the opportunity to form a partnership with or to buy out the local manufacturer later.

## MANAGEMENT CONTRACTING

Under **management contracting**, the domestic firm supplies the management know-how to a foreign company that supplies the capital. The domestic firm is exporting management services rather than products. Hilton uses this arrangement in managing hotels around the world.

Management contracting is a low-risk method of getting into a foreign market, and it yields income from the beginning. The arrangement is very attractive if the contracting firm has an option to buy some share in the managed company later on. On the other hand, the arrangement is not sensible if the company can put its scarce management talent to better uses or if it can make greater profits by undertaking the whole venture. Management contracting prevents the company from setting up its own operations for a period of time.

## JOINT OWNERSHIP

**Joint ownership** ventures consist of the company joining with foreign investors to create a local business in which they share joint ownership and control. The company may buy an interest in a local firm, or the two parties may form a new business venture.[14]

A jointly owned venture may be needed for economic or political reasons. The firm may lack the financial, physical, or managerial resources to undertake the venture alone. Or the foreign government may require joint ownership as a condition for entry. For example, many Canadian firms are entering the Japanese market on a joint venture basis. The advantages for the Canadian firms include gaining an understanding of the complex Japanese business system, synergistic advantages, the availability of competent and reliable partners, and the diversification of risk and return. For the Japanese firms the main advantage is gaining access to technology or knowhow which the Japanese companies themselves do not possess.[15]

Joint ownership has certain drawbacks. The partners may disagree over investment, marketing, or other policies. Where many Canadian firms like to reinvest earnings for growth, local firms often like to take out these earnings. Where Canadian firms give a large role to marketing, local investors may rely on selling.

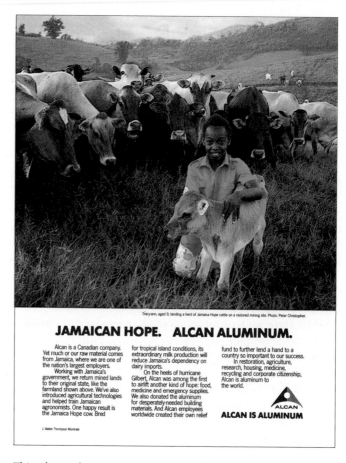

This Alcan ad encompasses all four aspects of direct investment.

# Direct Investment

The biggest involvement in a foreign market comes through **direct investment**, developing foreign-based assembly or manufacturing facilities. As a company gains experience in exporting, and if the foreign market is large enough, foreign production facilities offer many advantages. First, the firm may have lower costs in the form of cheaper labor or raw materials, foreign government investment incentives, and freight savings. Second, the firm will gain a better image in the host country because it creates jobs. Third, the firm develops a deeper relationship with government, customers, local suppliers, and distributors, letting it adapt its products better to the local market. Fourth, the firm keeps full control over the investment and can therefore develop manufacturing and marketing policies that serve its long-term international objectives. Canadian firms are increasingly using the direct investment method of operating in foreign markets. Direct investment by Canadian firms in the U.S. alone is estimated at over $4 billion annually and total direct investment by Canadian firms in the U.S. exceeds $30 billion.[16]

The main disadvantage is that the firm faces many risks in certain countries, such as restricted or devalued currencies, falling markets, or government takeover. In some cases, the firm has no choice but to accept these risks if it wants to operate in the host country.

# DECIDING ON THE MARKETING PROGRAM

Companies that operate in one or more foreign markets must decide how much, if at all, to adapt their marketing mixes to local conditions. At one extreme are companies that use a **standardized marketing mix** worldwide. Standardization of the product, advertising, distribution channels, and other elements of the marketing mix promises the lowest costs because no major changes have been introduced.

At the other extreme is a **customized marketing mix**. The producer adjusts the marketing mix elements to each target market, bearing more costs but hoping for a larger market share and return. Between these two extremes, many possibilities exist (see Marketing Highlight 18-2).

We will now look at possible changes in a company's product, promotion, price, and distribution as it goes abroad.[17]

# Product

There are five strategies for adapting product and promotion to a foreign market (see Figure 18-3).[18] Here we will look at the three product strategies, and later look at the two promotion strategies.

Straight product extension means marketing the product in the foreign market without any change. Top management tells its marketing people: "Take the product as is and find customers for it." The first step, however, should be to find out whether the foreign consumers use that product and what form they prefer.

Straight extension has been successful in some cases but a disaster in others. Massey-Ferguson designed a large-horsepower tractor with standard 74-inch treads and had little success selling it to corn farmers in the United States. The reason was that the corn is planted in 30-inch rows there, and 74-inch treads would have

# MARKETING HIGHLIGHT 18-2

## Customization or Standardization?

Companies disagree on how much they should standardize products and marketing programs across world markets. However, most marketers believe that because consumers in different countries vary so much, marketing programs will be more effective if tailored to specific market needs. They point out that countries differ in economic, political, legal, and cultural respects. Consumers in different countries have varied geographic, demographic, economic, and cultural characteristics—resulting in different needs and wants, spending power, product preferences, and shopping patterns. Because most marketers believe that these differences are hard to change, they customize their products, prices, distribution channels, and promotion approaches to fit unique consumer desires in each country. They argue that too much standardization places a company at a disadvantage against competitors who produce the goods that consumers want.

Recently, however, many companies have moved toward global standardization. They have created so-called "world brands" that are manufactured and marketed in much the same way worldwide. These marketers believe that advances in communication, transportation, and travel are turning the world into a common marketplace. They claim that people around the world want basically the same products and lifestyles. Everyone wants things that make life easier and increase both free time and buying power. Common needs and wants thus create global markets for standardized products.

Instead of focusing on differences between markets and customizing products to meet these differences, marketers who standardize globally sell more or less the same product the same way to all consumers. They agree that there are differences in consumer wants and buying behavior and that these differences cannot be entirely ignored. But they argue that wants are changeable. Despite what consumers say they want, all consumers want good products at lower prices. They argue that if the price is low enough, consumers will take highly standardized world products, even if these aren't exactly what mother said was suitable, what immemorial custom decreed was right, or what market research asserted was preferred.

Thus, the global corporation customizes products and marketing programs only when local wants cannot be changed or avoided. Standardization results in lower production, distribution, marketing, and management costs, letting the company offer consumers high quality and more reliable products at lower prices.

So which approach is best—customization or standardization? Clearly, global standardization is not an all-or-nothing proposition, but rather a matter of degree. Companies are justified in looking for more standardization to help keep costs and prices down. But they must remember that although standardization saves money, competitors are always ready to offer more of what consumers in each country want and that they might pay dearly for replacing long-run marketing thinking with short-run financial thinking. One international marketer suggests that companies should "think globally but act locally to give the individual consumer more to say in what he or she wants." The corporate level gives strategic direction; local units focus on the individual consumer differences. Global marketing, yes; global standardization, no.

**Sources:** See John A. Quelch and Edward J. Hoff, "Customizing Global Marketing," *Harvard Business Review*, May-June 1986, pp. 59-68; "Modular Marketing Cracks International Markets," *Marketing News*, April 27, 1984, p. 10; Julie Skur Hill and Joseph H. Winski, "Goodbye Global Ads," *Advertising Age*, November 16, 1987, p. 22; Yoram Wind and Susan P. Douglas, "The Myth of Globalization," *Journal of Consumer Marketing*, Spring 1986, pp. 23-6; A. Tansu Barker and Niza-mettin Aydin, "Globalization vs. Adaptation: A Marketing Perspective" in John Liefeld, ed., *Marketing* (Whistler, ASAC, 1990), pp. 25-32;

and Theodore Levitt, "The Globalization of Markets," *Harvard Business Review*, May-June 1983, pp. 92-102. Excerpt reprinted by permission of the *Harvard Business*

trampled every third row.[19] Straight extension is tempting because it involves no additional product development costs, manufacturing changes, or new promotion. However, it can be costly in the long run if products fail to satisfy foreign consumers.

Product adaptation involves changing the product to meet local conditions or wants. Heinz varies its baby-food products: in Australia it sells a baby food made from strained lamb brains and in the Netherlands, a baby food made from strained brown beans. General Foods blends different coffees for the British (who drink their coffee with milk), the French (who drink their coffee black), and Latin Americans (who want a chicory taste).

Product invention consists of creating something new for the foreign market. This strategy can take two forms. Product invention might mean reintroducing earlier product forms that happen to be well-adapted to the needs of that country. The National Cash Register Company reintroduced its crank-operated cash register selling at half the price of a modern cash register and sold large numbers in Asia, Latin America, and Spain. Or the company might create a brand new product to meet a need in another country. There is an enormous need in less-developed countries for low-cost, high-protein foods.

## Promotion

Companies can adopt the same promotion strategy they used in the home market or change it for each local market.

Consider the message. Many multinational companies use a standardized advertising theme around the world. Exxon used "Put a tiger in your tank" and gained international recognition. The copy is varied in a minor way, such as changing the colors to avoid taboos in other countries. Purple is associated with death in most of Latin America; white is a mourning color in Japan; and green is associated with jungle sickness in Malaysia. Even names have to be changed. In Germany, scotch (Scotch tape) means "schmuck."

Other companies ask their international divisions to develop their own ads. For example, when Moosehead beer was launched in the U.S. market, both the package and promotion were changed. These changes along with catchy slogans like "It

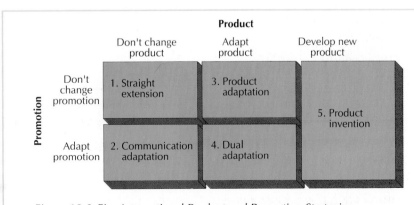

Figure 18-3 Five International Product and Promotion Strategies

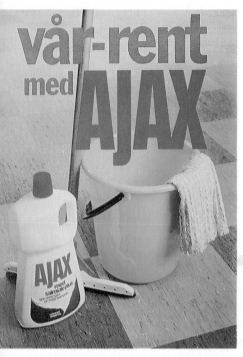

A Norwegian ad for Ajax.

stands head and antlers above the rest" and "The moose is loose" made it one of the top ten selling import beers in the U.S.[20]

Media must also be adapted internationally because media availability varies from country to country. Commercial TV time is available for one hour each evening in Germany, and advertisers must buy time months in advance. In Sweden, there is no commercial TV time. There is no commercial radio in France and Scandinavia. Magazines are a major medium in Italy and a minor one in Austria. Newspapers are national in the United Kingdom and local in Spain.

## Price

Companies also face many problems in setting their international prices. For example, how might a company set its prices globally? It could set a uniform price all around the world. But this amount would be too high in poor countries and not high enough in rich ones. It could charge what consumers in each country will bear. But this strategy ignores differences in the actual cost from country to country. Finally, the company could use a standard markup of its costs everywhere. But this approach might price the product out of the market in countries where costs are high.

Regardless of how companies go about pricing their products, their foreign prices will probably be higher than their domestic prices. They have to add the cost of transportation, tariffs, importer margin, wholesaler margin, and retailer margin to factory prices. Depending on these added costs, the product may have to sell for two to five times as much in another country to make the same profit.

Another problem involves setting a price for goods that a company ships to its foreign subsidiaries. If the company charges a foreign subsidiary too much, it may end up paying higher tariff duties even while paying lower income taxes in that country. If the company charges its subsidiary too little, it can be charged with dumping. Dumping occurs when a company either charges less than its costs or less than it charges in its home market. Various governments are always watching for dumping abuses and often force companies to set the price charged by other competitors for the same or similar products.

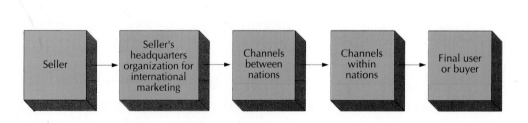

Figure 18-4 Whole-Channel Concept for International Marketing

# Distribution Channels

The international company must take a whole-channel view of the problem of distributing products to final consumers. Figure 18-4 shows the three major links between the seller and the final buyer. The first link, the seller's headquarters organization, supervises the channels and is part of the channel itself. The second link, channels between nations, gets the products to the borders of the foreign nations. The third link, channels within nations, gets the products from their foreign entry point to the final consumers. Too many Canadian manufacturers think their job is done once the product leaves their hands. They would do well to pay more attention to how it is handled within the foreign country.

Within-country channels of distribution vary a lot from country to country. There are large differences in the numbers and types of distributors serving each foreign market. To get soap into Japan, a company has to work through what may be the most complex distribution system in the world. It must sell to a general wholesaler, who sells to a basic product specialty wholesaler, who sells to a specialty wholesaler, who sells to a regional wholesaler, who sells to a local wholesaler, who finally sells to retailers. All these distribution levels may double or triple the consumer's price over the importer's price.

Another difference lies in the size and character of retail units abroad. Where large-scale retail chains dominate the Canadian scene, most foreign retailing is done by many small independent retailers. In India, millions of retailers operate tiny shops or sell in open markets. Their markups are high, but the real price is brought down through price haggling. Supermarkets could offer lower prices, but they are difficult to set up because of many economic and cultural barriers. People's incomes are low, and they prefer to shop daily for small amounts rather than weekly for large amounts. They lack storage and refrigeration to keep food for several days. Packaging is not well developed because it would add too much to the cost. These and other factors have kept large-scale retailing from spreading rapidly in developing countries.

# DECIDING ON THE MARKETING ORGANIZATION

Companies manage their international marketing activities in at least three different ways. Most companies first organize an export department, then create an international division, and finally become a multinational organization.

## Export Department

A firm normally gets into international marketing by simply shipping out its goods. If its international sales expand, the company organizes an export department with a sales manager and a few assistants. As sales increase, the export department expands to include various marketing services so that it can actively go after business. If the firm moves into joint ventures or direct investment, the export department will no longer be adequate.

## International Division

Many companies get involved in several international markets and ventures. A company may export to one country, license to another, have a joint ownership venture in a third, and own a subsidiary in a fourth. Sooner or later it will create an international division or subsidiary to handle all its international activity.

## Multinational Organization

Several firms have passed beyond the international division stage and become truly multinational organizations. They stop thinking of themselves as national marketers who sell abroad and start thinking of themselves as global marketers. The top corporate management and staff plan worldwide manufacturing facilities, marketing policies, financial flows, and logistical systems. The global operating units report directly to the chief executive or executive committee, not to the head of an international division. Executives are trained in worldwide operations, not just domestic or international operations. The company recruits from many countries, buys components and supplies where they cost the least, and invests where the expected returns are greatest.

Major companies must become more global in the 1990s if they hope to compete. As foreign companies successfully invade the domestic market, Canadian companies must move more aggressively into foreign markets.[21] They will have to change from companies that treat their foreign operations as secondary to companies that view the entire world as a single borderless market.[22]

# Summary

Companies today can no longer afford to pay attention only to their domestic market, no matter how large it is. Many industries are global industries, and those firms that operate globally achieve lower costs and higher brand awareness. At the same time, global marketing is risky because of variable exchange rates, unstable governments, protectionist tariffs and trade barriers, and several other factors. Given the potential risks and gains of international marketing, companies need a systematic way to make their international marketing decisions.

First, the company must understand the international marketing environment, especially the international trade system. It must assess each foreign market's economic, political-legal, and cultural characteristics. Second, the company must consider what level of foreign sales it will seek, whether it will do business in a few or many countries, and what types of countries it wants to market in. Third, the company must decide which specific markets to enter. This decision calls for weighing the probable rate of return on investment against the level of risk. Fourth, the company has to decide how to enter each chosen market, whether through exporting, joint venturing, or direct investment.

Many companies start as exporters, move to joint venturing, and finally make a direct investment in foreign markets. Companies must next decide how much their products, promotion, price, and channels should be adapted for each foreign market. Finally, the company must develop an effective organization for international marketing. Most firms start with an export department and graduate to an international division. A few pass to a multinational organization, which means that worldwide marketing is planned and managed by the top officers of the company.

# QUESTIONS FOR DISCUSSION

1. With all the problems facing companies that "go global," why are so many companies choosing to expand internationally? What are the major advantages of expanding beyond the domestic market?

2. When exporting goods to a foreign country, a marketer may be faced with various trade restrictions. Discuss the possible effects of the following on an exporter's marketing mix: (a) tariffs; (b) quotas; and (c) embargoes.

3. Which of these will have the greatest impact on a soft drink manufacturer's appraisal of a foreign nation as an attractive market: the economic environment, the political-legal environment, or the cultural environment?

4. Discuss the steps an advertising agency could take in entering a foreign market. What types of joint venture would be worth considering?

5. Which combination of product and promotion strategies would you recommend to Campbell Soup in marketing canned soups in Brazil? Why?

6. Although the price of an exported product is often higher in foreign markets than in the domestic market, there are occasions when foreign prices are lower than domestic prices. Under what conditions can these situations develop?

7. "Dumping" leads to price savings for the consumer. Why, then, do many governments make dumping illegal? What are the disadvantages to consumers of dumping by foreign firms?

8. Which type of international marketing organization would you suggest for the following companies: (a) Huffy Bicycles, selling three models in the Far East; (b) a small manufacturer of toys, marketing its products in Europe; (c) Dodge, planning to sell its full line of cars and trucks in Egypt?

# KEY TERMS

**Contract manufacturing** Joint-venturing to enter a foreign market by contracting with manufacturers in the foreign market to produce the product.

**Customized marketing mix** An international marketing strategy of adjusting the marketing mix elements to each international target market, bearing more costs but hoping for a larger market share and return.

**Direct investment** Entering a foreign market by developing foreign-based assembly or manufacturing facilities.

**Economic community** A group of nations organized to work toward common goals in the regulation of international trade.

**Embargo** A ban on the import of a certain product.

**Exporting**   Entering a foreign market by exporting products and selling them through international marketing middlemen (indirect exporting) or through the company's own department, branch, or sales representatives or agents (direct exporting).

**Joint ownership**   Entering a foreign market by joining with foreign investors to create a local business in which the company shares joint ownership and control.

**Joint venturing**   Entering foreign markets by joining with foreign companies to produce and market a product or service.

**Licensing**   A method of entering a foreign market in which the company enters an agreement with a licensee in the foreign market, offering the right to use a manufacturing process, trademark, patent, trade secret, or other item of value for a fee or royalty.

**Management contracting**   A joint venture in which the domestic firm supplies the management knowhow to a foreign company that supplies the capital; the domestic firm exports management services rather than products.

**Multinational company**   A company that operates in many countries and that has a major part of its operations outside its home country.

**Quota**   A limit on the amount of goods that an importing country will accept in certain product categories, designed to conserve on foreign exchange and protect local industry and employment.

**Standardized marketing mix**   An international marketing strategy of using basically the same product, advertising, distribution channels, and other elements of the marketing mix in all the company's international markets.

**Tariff**   A tax levied by a government against certain imported products designed to raise revenue or protect domestic firms.

# REFERENCES

1. Sources include "Going Global," *Financial Post 500*, Summer 1990, pp. 10-61; Kevin Dougherty, "Domtex Denim May Put Soviets in Top-line Jeans," *Financial Post*, February 16, 1990, p. 31; *Dominion Textiles Annual Report*, 1989; Forsyth Ltd., *Annual Report*, 1989; and Catherine Harris, "Signs Point to Trade Upswing," *Financial Post*, September 25, 1989, pp. 35, 37.

2. Kenichi Ohmae, *Triad Power: The Coming Shape of Global Competition* (New York: The Free Press, 1985).

3. Catherine Harris, "Signs Point to Trade Upswing," *Financial Post*, September 25, 1989, p. 35.

4. "Going Global," *Financial Post 500*, Summer, 1990, pp. 10-61.

5. For more information, see Export Development Corporation, *Annual Report*, various issues.

6. Jennifer Lewington, "Investment in U.S. Hits $390 Billion," *Globe and Mail*, March 14, 1990, p. B1.

7. "The Unique Japanese," *Fortune*, November 24, 1986, p. 8. Also see Rahul

Jacob, "Export Barriers the U.S. Hates Most," *Fortune*, February 27, 1989, pp. 88-89.

8. For information on the marketing implications of Europe '92, see John K. Ryans, Jr. and Pradeep A. Rau, *Marketing Strategies For the New Europe* (Chicago: American Marketing Association, 1990).

9. Len Butcher, "Passport to Profit," *Financial Post Magazine*, March 1, 1984, pp. 66-68.

10. Paul W. Beamish and Hugh Munro, "The Export Performance of Small and Medium-Sized Canadian Manufacturers," *Canadian Journal of Administrative Sciences*, June 1986, pp. 29-40.

11. F.H. Rolf Seringhaus, "The Impact of Government Export Marketing Assistance," *International Marketing Review*, Summer 1986, pp. 55-66. Also see F.H. Rolf Seringhaus and Philip J. Rosson, *Government Export Promotion: A Global Perspective* (London: Routledge, 1990).

12. Harold Crookell and Ian Graham, "International Marketing and Canadian Industrial Strategy," *The Business Quarterly*, Spring 1979, pp. 28-34.

13. For more on joint ventures, see Paul W. Beamish, J. Peter Killing, Donald L. Lecraw, and Harold Crookell, *International Management: Text and Cases* (Chicago: IL, Irwin, 1990), Chapters 4 and 5; and Barry Critchley, "Wanted: A Partner," *Financial Post 500*, Summer 1990, pp. 46-53.

14. For an interesting discussion of joint ventures, see Paul W. Beamish, *Multinational Joint Ventures in Developing Countries* (London: Routledge, 1988).

15. Richard W. Wright, "Canadian Joint Ventures in Japan," *The Business Quarterly*, Spring 1979, pp. 28-34.

16. Jennifer Lewington, "Investment in U.S. Hits $390 Billion," *Globe and Mail*, March 14, 1990, p. B1.

17. For strategic views of international marketing strategies, see Igal Ayal and Jehiel Zif, "Market Expansion Strategies in Multinational Marketing," *Journal of Marketing*, Spring 1979; and Subhash C. Jain, "Standardization of International Marketing Strategy: Some Research Hypotheses," *Journal of Marketing*, January 1989, pp. 70-79.

18. See Warren J. Keegan, *Multinational Marketing Management*, 3rd ed. (Englewood Cliffs, NJ: Prentice-Hall, 1984), pp. 317-24.

19. Diane Francis, "Bailing Out the Titanic," *Canadian Business*, June 1981, pp. 47-50, 132, 137-142.

20. Edith Terry, "A Canadian Suds Feud Runneth Over," *Business Week*, April 18, 1988, pp. 82-83.

21. For some examples of successful Canadian companies in international markets, see Catharine F. Johnston, *Globalization: Canadian Companies Compete*, Conference Board of Canada, Report 50-90-E, February, 1990. For an interesting study of Canadian companies entering the Japanese market, see Adrian B. Ryans, "Strategic Market Entry Factors and Market Share Achievement in Japan," *Journal of International Business Studies*, Fall 1988, pp. 389-409.

22. See Kenichi Ohmae, "Managing in a Borderless World," *Harvard Business Review*, May-June 1989, pp. 152-61.

# CHAPTER 19

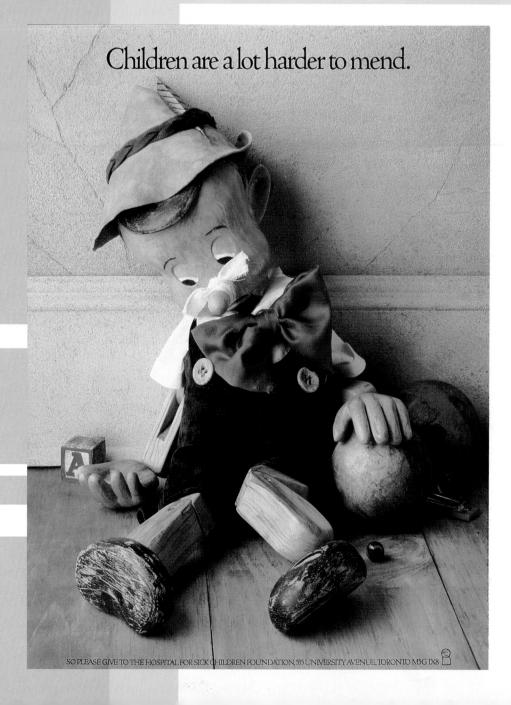

Children are a lot harder to mend.

# Services Marketing and Nonprofit Marketing

## CHAPTER OBJECTIVES

After reading this chapter, you should be able to:
1. Define service and describe four characteristics that affect the marketing of a service.
2. Explain how organizations market themselves.
3. Discuss person and place marketing.
4. Define social marketing and tell how social ideas are marketed.

Hospitals across Canada increasingly rely on fund-raising campaigns to meet their financial budgets. They need to raise millions to provide quality medical treatment for their patients. As well, hospitals get involved in special projects—such as Operation Herbie—a charity which flies children from all over the world for lifesaving surgery at the Hospital for Sick Children in Toronto. In entering the fund-raising sweepstakes these hospitals are in competition against each other, as well as against universities, orchestras, dance companies, and a host of charitable organizations.

Overall, the prospects are less than rosy for the cash-seeking hospitals. The federal government is cutting costs and handing out less money. Corporate donors are being approached by more and more sources: their alma mater universities from Newfoundland to British Columbia are trying to raise over $1 billion through fund-raising campaigns, the arts are linking corporate responsibility (and donations) to the development of cultural and artistic endeavors, and the charities are becoming increasingly sophisticated in their marketing, organization, and implementation strategies.

The hospitals face the problem of trying to market a voluntary donation fund in a very competitive market. The questions are: How do you differentiate yourself from the competition? What is your appeal? What philanthropic nerve are you trying to hit? What determines your approach to the target donors and specifically who are your donor groups? In light of fund-raising needs and difficulties, the hospitals are forced to look at the vast complexity of their marketing challenges. A hospital has to understand exactly what the health needs of the community are, what image this community has of different hospitals, how their own patients feel about the hospital's service and care, what impression the physical facilities make, and so on.

To compete in the fund-raising market, hospitals are pursuing a variety of strategies, including:

- Hiring full-time fund-raising experts. Many Canadian hospitals now have fund raisers on staff who hold conferences on ways to raise money.
- Employing advertising agencies to design professional promotion campaigns. The results include commer-

cials on TV and radio, selling T-shirts and using slogans like "Help Us Care. Help Us Cure" and "Be A Saint. Give to St. Mike's."

Wherever the donations come from, a few things appear to be clear in the successful marketing of a fund-raising campaign: (1) recognition of the volunteers in the campaign and of the donors as a primary motivating force; (2) selection of key volunteers and donors; and (3) a comprehensive marketing strategy.[1]

Initially, marketing was developed for selling physical products such as toothpaste, cars, steel, and equipment. But this traditional focus on physical products may cause people to overlook the many other types of goods that are marketed. In this chapter we will look at the special marketing requirements for services, organizations, persons, places, and ideas.

# Services Marketing

One of the major trends in Canadian business has been the rapid growth of services. The service sector is the fastest-growing segment of the Canadian economy; in the past ten years, new jobs in the service sector accounted for 94% of all jobs created.[2] Seven out of every ten working Canadians are employed in service industries. This growth is the result of rising incomes, more leisure time, and the growing complexity of products that require servicing.

Service industries vary greatly. The government sector offers services with its courts, employment services, hospitals, loan agencies, military services, police and fire departments, postal service, regulatory agencies, and schools. The private non-profit sector offers services with its museums, charities, churches, colleges, foundations, and hospitals. A good part of the business sector offers services with its airlines, banks, hotels, insurance companies, consulting firms, medical and law practices, entertainment companies, real estate firms, advertising and research agencies, and retailers.

Not only are there traditional service industries, but new types keep popping up all the time, including services that offer to baby-sit your plants, walk your dog, pick-up and deliver your laundry, or perform a host of other activities that they claim will save you time and make your life easier.

Some service businesses are large, with sales and assets in the billions. Table 19-1 shows the five largest service companies in each of five service categories. These, and thousands of other smaller service companies, compete in the over $200 billion service industry. Selling services presents some special problems calling for special marketing solutions.[3] We will now look at the nature of services and their great variety, how the major characteristics of services affect their marketing, and how service firms can increase their differentiation, quality, and productivity.

**TABLE 19-1**
**The Largest Canadian Service Companies**

| Commercial Banking | Life Insurance | Retailing | Utilities | Food and Hospitality |
|---|---|---|---|---|
| Royal Bank of Canada | Sun Life | Loblaws | Bell Canada | Scott's Hospitality |
| Canadian Imperial Bank of Commerce | Manufacturer's Life | Hudson's Bay Company | Ontario Hydro | Canadian Pacific Hotels |
| Bank of Montreal | Great-West Life | Sears Canada | Hydro-Quebec | VS Services |
| Bank of Nova Scotia | Confederation | Safeway | Trans. Canada | Cara Operations |
| Toronto Dominion Bank | Canada Life | Canadian Tire | B.C. Hydro | Four Seasons Hotels |

**Source:** *The Financial Post,* Summer 1991. Ranked by sales or operating revenue.

# Nature and Characteristics of a Service

We define a **service** as any activity or benefit that one party can offer to another that is essentially intangible and does not result in the ownership of anything; its production may or may not be tied to a physical product. Renting a hotel room, depositing money in a bank, traveling on an airplane, visiting a psychiatrist, getting a haircut, having a car repaired, watching a professional sport, seeing a movie, having clothes cleaned at a dry-cleaners, getting advice from a lawyer—all involve buying a service.

The company must consider four service characteristics when designing marketing programs: intangibility, inseparability, variability, and perishability. We will look at each of these characteristics in the following sections.

## INTANGIBILITY

Services are intangible. They cannot be seen, tasted, felt, heard, or smelled before they are bought.[4] People having cosmetic surgery cannot see the result before the purchase, and airline passengers have nothing but a ticket and the promise of safe delivery to their destinations.

To reduce uncertainty, buyers look for signs of service quality. They draw conclusions about quality from the place, people, equipment, communication material, and price that they can see. Therefore, the service provider's task is to make the service tangible in one or more ways. Whereas product marketers try to add intangibles to their tangible offers, service marketers try to add tangibles to their intangible offers.[5]

Consider a bank that wants to convey the idea that its service is quick and efficient. It must make this positioning strategy tangible in every aspect of customer contact. The bank's physical setting must suggest quick and efficient service: Its exterior and interior should have clean lines, internal traffic flow should be planned carefully, waiting lines should seem short, and background music should be light and upbeat. The bank's people should be busy and properly dressed. Its equipment—computers, copy machines, desks—should look modern. The bank's ads and other communications should suggest efficiency, with clean and simple designs and carefully chosen words and photos that communicate the bank's positioning. The bank should choose a name and symbol for its service that suggest speed and efficiency. Its pricing for various services should be kept simple and clear.

## INSEPARABILITY

Physical goods are produced, then stored, later sold, and still later consumed. But services are first sold, then produced and consumed at the same time. Thus, services are inseparable from their providers, whether the providers be people or machines. If a person provides the service, then that person is a part of the service. Because the client is also present when the service is produced, provider-client interaction is a special feature of services marketing. Both the provider and the client affect the service outcome.

In the case of entertainment and professional services, buyers care a great deal about who provides the service. It is not the same service at a Bryan Adams concert if Adams gets sick and is replaced by Anne Murray. When clients have strong provider preferences, price is used to ration the limited supply of the preferred provider's time.

Several strategies exist for getting around the problem of service- provider time limitations. The service provider can learn to work with larger groups. Some psychotherapists have moved from one-on-one therapy to small-group therapy to groups of over 300 people gathered in a larger hotel ballroom to be "therapized." The service provider can learn to work faster—the psychotherapist can spend 30 minutes with each patient instead of 50 minutes and can see more patients. The service organization can train more service providers and build up client confidence, as H & R Block has done with its national network of trained tax consultants.

## VARIABILITY

Services are highly variable—their quality depends on who provides them and when, where, and how they are provided. For example, some hotels have reputations for providing better service than others. Within a given hotel, one registration desk employee may be cheerful and efficient while another standing just a few feet away may be unpleasant and slow. Even the quality of a single employee's service will vary with his or her energy and frame of mind at the time of each customer contact.

Service firms can take several steps toward quality control.[6] First, they can carefully select and train their personnel. Airlines, banks, and hotels spend large sums to train their employees to give good service. Consumers should find the same sort of friendly and helpful personnel in every Canadian Pacific Hotel. Second, service firms can also provide employee incentives that emphasize quality, such as employee-of-the-month awards or bonuses based on customer feedback. Third, they can make service employees more visible and accountable to consumers—auto dealerships can let customers talk directly with the mechanics working on their cars. Finally, a firm can regularly check customer satisfaction through suggestion and complaint systems, customer surveys, and comparison shopping. When poor service is found, it can be corrected. How a firm handles problems resulting from

Because demand fluctuates, transit companies must own extra equipment to meet rush-hour demands.

service variability can dramatically affect customer perceptions of service quality.

## PERISHABILITY

Services are perishable—they cannot be stored for later sale or use. The reason many dentists charge patients for missed appointments is that the service value only existed at that point when the patient did not show up. The perishability of services is not a problem when demand is steady, because it is easy to staff the services in advance. When demand fluctuates, service firms often have difficulties. For example, because of rush hour demand, public transportation companies have to own much more equipment than they would need if demand were even throughout the day.

Service firms can use several strategies for producing a better match between demand and supply in a service business.[7] On the demand side, charging different prices at different times will shift some demand from peak to off-peak periods. Examples include low early-evening or special discount-day movie prices and weekend discount prices for car rentals. Or nonpeak demand can be increased. McDonald's developed its Egg McMuffin breakfast to draw customers in earlier in the day, and hotels have developed mini-vacation weekends. Complementary services can be offered during peak time to provide alternatives to waiting customers, such as cocktail lounges to sit in while waiting for a table in a restaurant, and automatic tellers in banks. Reservation systems can help to manage the demand level. Airlines, hotels, and physicians use them regularly.

On the supply side, part-time employees can be hired to serve peak demand. Universities add part-time teachers when enrollment goes up, and restaurants call in part-time waiters and waitresses when needed. Peak time demand can be handled more efficiently by having employees do only essential tasks during peak periods. Some tasks can be shifted to consumers, as when consumers fill out their own medical records or bag their own groceries. Providers can share services, as when several hospitals share an expensive piece of medical equipment. Finally, a firm can plan ahead for expansion, as when an amusement park buys surrounding land for later development.

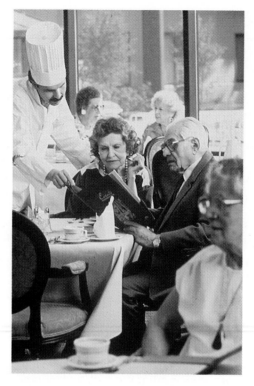

Restaurant reservations can help to manage shifting demand levels.

# Marketing Strategies For Service Firms

Service firms typically lag behind manufacturing firms in their use of marketing.[8] In many small service businesses (shoe repair, hair salons), the owners may think that marketing is too costly or is unneeded. There are also some service businesses (law, medical, and accounting practices), that still believe that it is unprofessional to use marketing. Other services businesses (colleges, hospitals) had steady demand or had sufficient funding, so that they did not need marketing until recently.

Furthermore, service businesses are more difficult to manage when they use only traditional marketing approaches. In a product business, products are fairly standardized and sit on shelves waiting for customers. In a service business, the customer interacts with a service provider whose service quality is less certain and more variable. The service outcome is affected not just by the service provider but by the whole supporting production process. Thus, service marketing requires more than just the traditional four P's of marketing. In addition, it requires both internal marketing and interactive marketing.[9]

Internal marketing means that the service firm must effectively train and motivate its customer-contact employees and all the supporting service people to work as a team to provide customer satisfaction. For the firm to deliver consistently high service quality, everyone must practice customer orientation. It is not enough to have a marketing department doing traditional marketing while the rest of the company goes its own way. Marketers must also get everyone else in the organization to practice marketing.[10]

Interactive marketing means that perceived service quality depends heavily on the quality of the buyer-seller interaction. In product marketing, product quality seldom depends on how the product is obtained. But in services marketing, service quality depends both on the service deliverer and on the quality of the delivery, especially in professional services. The customer judges service quality not just on technical quality (say, the success of the surgery) but also on its functional quality (whether the doctor showed concern and inspired confidence). Thus, professionals cannot assume that they will satisfy the client simply by providing good technical service. They must also master interactive marketing skills or functions.

Today, as competition increases, costs rise, productivity drops, and service quality falls off, more service firms are taking an interest in marketing. Service companies face three major marketing tasks. They want to increase their competitive differentiation, service quality, and productivity.

## Managing Differentiation

In these days of intense price competition, service marketers often complain that it is hard to differentiate their services from those of competitors. To the extent that customers view the services of different providers as similar, they care less about the provider than the price.

The solution to price competition is to develop a differentiated offer and image. A service firm can add innovative features to set its offer apart. For example, airlines have introduced such innovations as in-flight movies, advanced seating, air-to-ground telephone service, and frequent-flyer programs to differentiate their offers. Unfortunately, most service innovations are easily copied. Still, the service company that regularly finds desired service innovations will usually gain a succession of temporary advantages and may, by earning an innovative reputation, keep customers who want to go with the best.

Service companies can also work on differentiating their images through symbols and branding. The Royal Bank of Canada uses a lion as its symbol and Canada Trust has a "friendly loan" program with a Panda as its symbol. Branding services, such as the Money Builder bank account or the Green Machine automatic teller, provide the customer with a particular image that is difficult for competitors to duplicate.

## Managing Service Quality

One of the major ways to differentiate a service firm is for the firm to deliver consistently higher quality than its competitors. Many companies are finding that outstanding service quality can give them a potent competitive advantage leading to superior sales and profit performance. The key is to meet or exceed customers' service-quality expectations. These expectations are based on past experiences, word of mouth, and service firm advertising. Customers often compare the perceived ser-

**IT WAS YOUR ONLY CHANCE TO IMPRESS THOSE PEOPLE.**

If you want to make a good impression, send it Federal Express. Delivery by 10:30 AM the next business day to most major Canadian cities and on time delivery to 118 countries worldwide or your money back. And all of it backed by exclusive COSMOS tracking that can tell you where your package is every step of the way.

**NEXT TIME, SEND IT FEDERAL EXPRESS.**

Service marketing strategies: Federal Express promises delivery on time or your money back.

vice of a given firm with their expected service: If the perceived service meets or exceeds expected service, customers are apt to use the provider again.

The service provider thus needs to identify the expectations of target customers concerning service quality. Unfortunately, service quality is harder to define and judge than product quality. It is harder to get agreement on the quality of a haircut than on the quality of a hair dryer. Moreover, although greater service quality means greater customer satisfaction, it also means higher costs. Thus, service firms cannot always meet consumers' service-quality desires—they face trade-offs between customer satisfaction and company profitability. Whatever the level of service provided, it is important that the service provider clearly define and communicate that level so that its employees know what they must deliver and customers know what they will get. One approach to measuring service quality is by using the SERVQUAL scale (see Marketing Highlight 19-1).

Studies of well-managed service companies show that they share a number of virtues regarding service quality. First, they have a history of top management commitment to quality. Management at companies such as Four Seasons Hotels and McDonald's looks not only at financial performance but also at service performance. The best service providers set high service-quality standards. Swissair, for example, aims to have 96% or more of its passengers rate its service as good or superior; otherwise, it takes action. Top service firms also watch service performance closely—both their own and that of competitors. They use such methods as comparison shopping, customer surveys, and suggestion and complaint forms. Finally, well-managed service companies satisfy employees as well as customers. They believe that good employee relations will result in good customer relations. Management creates an environment of employee support, gives rewards for good service performance, and monitors employee job satisfaction.[11]

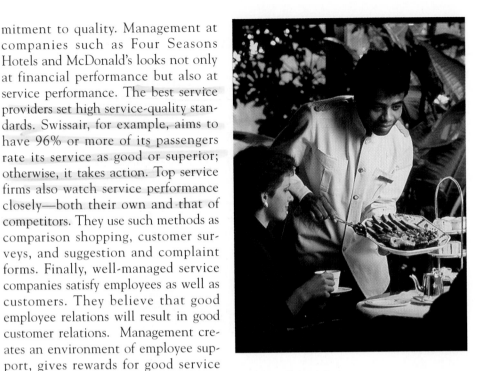

Four Seasons Hotels make service performance a high priority.

## Managing Productivity

With their costs rising rapidly, service firms are under great pressure to increase productivity. There are several ways to improve service productivity. First, service providers can better train current employees or hire new ones who will work harder or more skillfully for the same pay. Or service providers can increase the quantity of their service by giving up some quality. Providers can "industrialize" services by adding equipment and standardizing production, as in McDonald's assembly-line approach to fast-food retailing. Commercial dishwashing, jumbo jets, multiple-unit movie theaters—all represent technological expansions of service.

Service providers can also increase productivity by designing more effective services. How-to-quit-smoking clinics and recommendations for jogging may reduce the need for expensive medical services later on. Providers can also give customers incentives to substitute company labor with their own.

However, companies must avoid pushing productivity so hard that it reduces perceived quality. Some productivity steps can help to standardize quality, increasing customer satisfaction. But other productivity steps lead to too much standardization and rob consumers of customized service. In some cases, the service provider accepts reduced productivity to create more differentiation.[12]

## Organization Marketing

Organizations often carry out activities to "sell" the organization itself. **Organiza-**

# MARKETING HIGHLIGHT 19-1

## SERVQUAL: A Service Quality Measurement Scale

SERVQUAL is a service quality measurement scale that companies are using to increase their understanding of the service expectations and perceptions of their customers. Five service quality dimensions (tangibles, reliability, responsiveness, assurance, and empathy), which consumers use to evaluate a company's service, have been identified. A three-part questionnaire is used to measure: (1) consumers' expectations about service quality at an excellent company; (2) consumers' relative importance of each of the five dimensions, and (3) consumers' evaluation of service quality at the specific company. Examples of the questions used in the first part of the questionnaire are shown below. Consumers rate each statement on a seven-point scale from "Strongly Disagree" to "Strongly Agree."

**TANGIBLES**

1. Excellent companies have modern-looking equipment.
2. Employees at excellent companies will be neat-appearing.

**RELIABILITY**

1. When excellent companies promise to do something by a certain time, they will do so.
2. Excellent companies will perform the service right the first time.

**RESPONSIVENESS**

1. Employees in excellent companies will tell customers exactly when services will be performed.
2. Employees in excellent companies will give prompt service to customers.

**ASSURANCE**

1. The behavior of employees in excellent companies will instill confidence in customers.
2. Customers of excellent companies will feel safe in their transactions.

**EMPATHY**

1. Excellent companies will have the customer's best interests at heart.
2. The employees of excellent companies will understand the specific needs of their customers.

**Sources:** A. Parasuraman, Valarie A. Zeithaml, and Leonard L. Berry, "SERVQUAL: A Multiple-Item Scale for Measuring Consumer Perceptions of Service Quality," Journal of Retailing, Spring 1988, pp. 12-40 and Valarie A. Zeithaml, A. Parasuraman, and Leonard L. Berry, Delivering Quality Service (Free Press: New York), 1990.

tion marketing consists of activities undertaken to create, maintain, or change the attitudes and behavior of target audiences toward a organization. Both profit and nonprofit organizations practice organization marketing. Business firms sponsor public relations or corporate advertising campaigns to polish their images. Nonprofit organizations such as churches, colleges, charities, museums, and performing arts groups market their organizations in order to raise funds and attract members or patrons. Organization marketing calls for assessing the organization's current image and developing a marketing plan to improve its image.

## IMAGE ASSESSMENT

The first step in image assessment is to research the organization's current image among key publics. The way an individual or a group sees an organization is called its **organization image**. Different people can have different images of the same organization. The organization might be pleased with its public image or might find that it has serious image problems.

For example, suppose a bank does some marketing research to measure its image in the community. It finds its image to be that shown by the solid line in Figure 19-1. Thus current and potential customers view the bank as somewhat small, noninnovative, unfriendly, and unknowledgeable. The bank will want to change this image.

## IMAGE PLANNING AND CONTROL

Next the organization should figure out what image it would like to have and can achieve. For example, the bank might decide that it would like the image shown by the dashed line in Figure 19-1. It would like to be seen as a provider of more friendly and personal service, and as being more innovative, knowledgeable, and larger.

The firm now develops a marketing plan to shift its actual image toward the desired one. Suppose the bank first wants to improve its image so that it is perceived as giving friendly and personal service. The key step, of course, is to actually provide friendlier and more personal service. The bank can hire and train more personable and cooperative tellers and others who deal with customers. It can change its decor to make the bank seem warmer. When the bank is certain that it has improved performance on the important image measures, it can design a marketing program to communicate the new image to customers. Using public relations, the bank can sponsor community activities, send its executives to speak to local business and civic groups, offer public seminars on household finances, and issue press releases on newsworthy bank activities. In its advertising, the bank can position itself as "your friendly, personal bank."

The firm must resurvey its publics once in a while to see whether its activities are improving the firm's image. Images cannot be changed overnight because of limited funds and the "stickiness" of public images. If the firm is making no progress, either its marketing offer or its marketing program will have to be changed.[13]

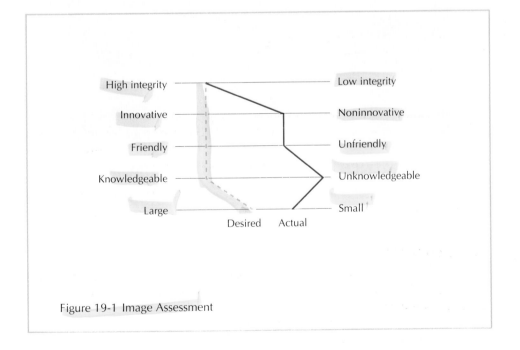

Figure 19-1 Image Assessment

# Person Marketing

People are also marketed. **Person marketing** consists of activities undertaken to create, maintain, or change attitudes or behavior toward a particular person. All kinds of people and organizations practice person marketing. Politicians market themselves to get votes and program support. Entertainers and sports figures use marketing to promote their careers and improve their incomes. Professionals such as doctors, lawyers, accountants, and architects market themselves in order to build reputations and increase business. Business leaders use person marketing as a strategic tool to develop their companies' fortunes as well as their own. Businesses, charities, sports teams, fine arts groups, religious groups, and other organizations also use person marketing. Creating, flaunting, or associating with well-known personalities often helps organizations to better achieve their goals.

The objective of person marketing is to create a "celebrity"—a well-known person whose name generates attention, interest, and action. Celebrities differ in

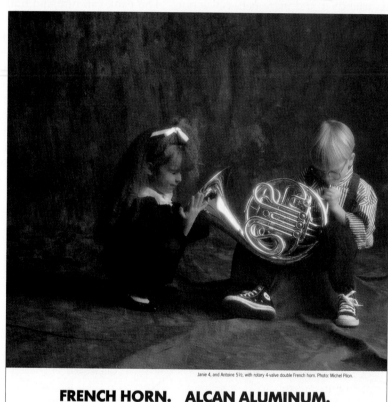

Janie 4, and Antoine 5½, with rotary 4-valve double French horn. Photo: Michel Pilon.

## FRENCH HORN.   ALCAN ALUMINUM.

Alcan is a Canadian company, in fact the largest aluminum producer in the world. But that doesn't mean we're strictly business. We are also involved as a corporate sponsor with hundreds of worthy causes, many of them in the arts.

From the children's Arts Umbrella in Vancouver, all the way to the mammoth Montreal International Jazz Festival,

Alcan sponsors more than 100 organizations and events in dance, opera, theatre, film and music.

Some of our sponsorships have brought top international performers to Canada. Others have helped introduce Canada's best talent to the world. And some are just there to encourage our youngest and neediest aspirants in taking that first tentative step on stage.

In the arts, automotive, aerospace, marine, packaging, housing, construction, medicine, research, design and corporate citizenship, Alcan is aluminum to the world.

**ALCAN IS ALUMINUM**

J. Walter Thompson Montreal

Corporate image advertising: Alcan advertises its sponsorship of the arts.

the scope of their visibility. Some are very well known, but only in limited geographic areas (a town mayor, a local businessperson, an area doctor) or specific segments (the president of the Canadian Dental Association, a company vice-president, a jazz musician with a small group of fans). Still others have broad national or international visibility (major entertainers, sports superstars, world political and religious leaders).

The person-marketing process is similar to the one used by product and service marketers. Person marketers begin with careful market research and analysis to discover consumer needs and market segments. Next comes product development—assessing the person's current qualities and image and transforming the person so as to better match market needs and expectations. Finally, the marketer develops programs to value, promote, and deliver the celebrity. Some people naturally possess the skills, appearances, and behaviors that target segments value. But for most, celebrity status in any field must be actively developed through sound person marketing.

# Place Marketing

**Place marketing** involves activities undertaken to create, maintain, or change attitudes or behavior toward particular places. Examples include business site marketing and vacation marketing.

## BUSINESS SITE MARKETING

Business site marketing involves developing, selling, or renting business sites such as factories, stores, offices, and warehouses. Large developers research companies' land needs and respond with real estate solutions, such as industrial parks, shopping centers, and new office buildings. Most provinces operate industrial development offices that try to sell companies on the advantages of locating new plants in their provinces. They spend large sums on advertising and offer to fly prospects to the site when necessary. Various cities, often through their Chamber of Commerce, attempt to do the same thing at the local level. Cities offer everything from lower housing prices to excellent transportation facilities to lower energy costs in trying to lure businesses to their area.

## VACATION MARKETING

Vacation marketing involves attracting vacationers to spas, resorts, cities, provinces, and even entire nations. The effort is carried on by travel agents, airlines, motor clubs, oil companies, hotels, motels, and governmental agencies. Tourism is a major industry in Canada worth over $24 billion a year. The federal and provincial governments spend millions trying to attract foreigners to Canada for a vacation. For example, the federal government developed a benefit segmentation of the tourist market in Canada, and designed marketing campaigns for selected segments.[14] Each year the federal government spends over $15 million in the United States to encourage Americans to visit "Canada—The World Next Door." The campaign focuses on three major benefits—a wild and open country, an old world rich in cultural heritage, and a new, exciting urban world—and attempts to market them separately. The overall theme has been "foreign but friendly" with the focus on "vive la difference."[15] One successful vacation campaign was Expo '86, which drew over 22 million people to the world's fair in Vancouver. In total, the provincial and federal governments spend over $40 million each year trying to attract tourists to Canada or encourage Canadians to spend their vacations "at home."[16]

## Idea Marketing

Ideas can also be marketed. In one sense, all marketing is the marketing of an idea, whether it be the idea of brushing your teeth or the idea that Crest is the most effective decay preventer. Here we will discuss only the marketing of social ideas, such as public health campaigns to reduce smoking, alcoholism, drug abuse, and overeating; environmental campaigns to promote wilderness protection, clean air, and conservation; and other campaigns such as family planning and human rights. This area has been called social marketing.[17] **Social marketing** is the design, implementation, and control of programs seeking to increase the acceptability of a social idea, cause, or practice among a target group.

Social marketers can pursue different objectives. They might want to produce understanding (knowing the nutritional value of different foods) or to trigger a one-time action (joining in a mass immunization campaign). They might want to

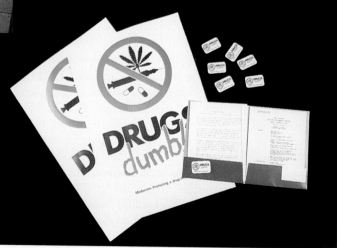

Social marketing: seeking to prevent the spread of AIDS and to discourage drug use.

# MARKETING HIGHLIGHT 19-2

## Can Social Marketing Reduce Cigarette Smoking?

Scientific evidence shows a link between cigarette smoking and lung cancer, heart disease, and emphysema. Most cigarette smokers know about the bad effects of cigarette smoking. The problem is to give them the means or the will to stop smoking. The four Ps suggest several possible approaches:

### PRODUCT

- Require manufacturers to add a tart or bitter ingredient to the tobacco.
- Cut down further on the tar and nicotine in cigarettes.
- Find a new type of tobacco for cigarettes that tastes as good but is safe.
- Promote other products that will help people relieve their tensions, such as chewing gum.

### PROMOTION

- Increase fear of early death among smokers.
- Create guilt or shame among cigarette users.
- Strengthen other goals of smokers and make them more important than smoking, such as the need for physical fitness.
- Urge smokers to cut down the number of cigarettes they smoke or to smoke only the first half of the cigarette.

### PLACE

- Make cigarettes harder to obtain or unavailable.
- Make it easier for cigarette smokers to attend antismoking clinics.
- Make it harder to find public places that allow cigarette smoking.

### PRICE

- Raise the price of cigarettes substantially.
- Raise the cost of life and health insurance to smokers.
- Offer a monetary or nonmonetary reward to smokers for each period they forgo smoking.

change behavior (auto seat-belt campaign) or change a basic belief (convincing employers that handicapped people can make a strong contribution in the work force).

In designing social change strategies, social marketers go through a normal marketing planning process. First, they define the social change objective—for example, "to reduce the percentage of teenagers who smoke from 35% to 25% within five years." Next they analyze the attitudes, beliefs, values, and behavior of teenagers, and the forces that encourage teenage smoking. They consider communication and distribution approaches that might prevent teenagers from smoking (see Marketing Highlight 19-2), develop a marketing plan, and build a marketing organization to carry out the plan. Finally, they evaluate and adjust the program to make it more effective.

Social marketing is fairly new and its effectiveness relative to other social change strategies is hard to evaluate. It is difficult to produce social change with any strategy, let alone one that relies on voluntary response. Social marketing has mainly been applied to family planning,[18] environmental protection,[19] energy conservation,[20] improved nutrition, auto driver safety,[21] and public transportation—and there have been some encouraging successes. But more applications are needed before we can fully assess social marketing's potential for producing social change.

# SUMMARY

Marketing has broadened in recent years to cover "marketable" entities other than products—namely, services, organizations, persons, places, and ideas.

As Canada moves toward a service economy, marketers need to know more about marketing services. Services are activities or benefits that one party can offer to another that are essentially intangible and do not result in the ownership of anything. They are intangible, inseparable, variable, and perishable. Marketers have to find ways to make services more tangible, to increase the productivity of providers who are inseparable from their products, to standardize quality in the face of variability, and to improve demand movements and supply capacities in the face of service perishability.

Service industries have typically lagged behind manufacturing firms in adopting and using marketing concepts, but this situation is now changing. Marketing strategy for services calls not only for external marketing but also for internal marketing to motivate employees and interactive marketing to create service-delivery skills among service providers. To succeed, service marketers must create competitive differentiation, offer high service quality, and find ways to increase service productivity.

Organizations can also be marketed. Organization marketing is undertaken to create, maintain, or change attitudes or behavior of target audiences toward an organization. It calls for assessing the organization's current image and developing a marketing plan for bringing about an improved image.

Person marketing consists of activities undertaken to create, maintain, or change attitudes or behavior toward particular people.

Place marketing involves activities to create, maintain, or change attitudes or behavior toward particular places. Examples include business site marketing and vacation marketing.

Idea marketing involves efforts to market ideas. In the case of social ideas it is called social marketing, and consists of the design, implementation, and control of programs seeking to increase the acceptability of a social idea, cause, or practice in a target group. The social marketer defines the social change objective, analyzes consumer attitudes and competitive forces, develops and tests alternative concepts, develops appropriate channels for the idea's communication and distribution, and finally, checks the results. Social marketing has been applied to family planning, environmental protection, energy conservation, antismoking campaigns, and other public issues.

# QUESTIONS FOR DISCUSSION

1. A "hot" concept in fast-food marketing is home delivery of everything from pizza to hamburgers to fried chicken. Why is this demand growing? How can marketers gain competitive advantages by satisfying the growing demand for increased services?

2. Many banks have begun hiring marketing executives with experience in consumer packaged-goods marketing. What benefits and problems might they experience as a result of this practice?

3. How can a theater deal with the intangibility, inseparability, variability, and perishability of its service? Give examples.

4. Retail stores sell tangible products rather than services. Is interactive marketing important to retailers? How can retailers use internal marketing to improve the quality of buyer-seller interactions?

5. Why do organizations want to "sell" themselves and not just their products? List several reasons for organization marketing and relate them to familiar promotional campaigns.

6. Reports of questionable, high-pressure tactics in the sale of vacation homes are common. For example, the "food processor" that one marketer used to attract prospects turned out to be a fork! Why do unethical practices appear to be so frequent in place marketing?

7. Social marketing is one approach to social change. What other methods are available? Compared with these other approaches, what advantages and disadvantages might social marketing have, for example, in attempting to reduce the amount of litter on the highways?

# KEY TERMS

**Organization image**  The way an individual or a group sees an organization.

**Organization marketing**  Activities undertaken to create, maintain, or change attitudes and behavior of target audiences toward an organization.

**Person marketing**  Activities undertaken to create, maintain, or change attitudes or behavior toward particular people.

**Place marketing**  Activities undertaken to create, maintain, or change attitudes or behavior toward particular places.

**Service**  Any activity or benefit that one party can offer to another that is essentially intangible and does not result in the ownership of anything.

**Social marketing**  The design, implementation, and control of programs seeking to increase the acceptability of a social idea, cause, or practice among a target group.

# REFERENCES

1. Sources include Louise Brown, "Why Metro Hospitals Are Pleading for Money," *Toronto Star*, January 18, 1987, pp. H1, H4; Rona Maynard, "Rebel with a Cause," *Report on Business Magazine*, March 1990, pp. 38-45; and Orland French, "Canadian Universities Fight to Turn That Old School Spirit Into Cold Cash Donations," *Globe and Mail*, June 7, 1989, p. A1.

2. Jennifer Lanthier, "Big Growth in Service Jobs Will Widen Disparities," *Financial Post*, March 5, 1990, p. 7.

3. See Leonard L. Berry, "Services Marketing is Different," *Services Marketing*, ed., Christopher H. Lovelock, Englewood Cliffs, N.J.: Prentice-Hall, 1984, 28-37; G. Lynn Shostock, "Service Positioning Through Structural Change," *Journal of Marketing*, January 1987, 34-43; and Valerie A. Zeithaml, A. Parasuraman, and Leonard L. Berry, "Problems and Strategies in Service Marketing," *Journal of Marketing*, Spring 1985, 33-46.

4. Gordon H.G. McDougall and Douglas W. Snetsinger, "The Intangibility of Services: Measurement and Competitive Perspectives," *Journal of Services Marketing*, Fall 1990, pp. 27-40.

5. See Theodore Levitt, "Marketing Intangible Products and Product Intangibles," *Harvard Business Review*, May-June 1981, pp. 94-102.

6. For more discussion, see James L. Heskett, "Lessons in the Service Sector," *Harvard Business Review*, March-April 1987, pp. 122-24.

7. See W. Earl Sasser, "Match Supply and Demand in Service Industries," *Harvard Business Review*, November-December 1976, pp. 133-40.

8. See A. Parasuraman, Leonard L. Berry, and Valerie A. Zeithaml, "Service Firms Need More Marketing," *Business Horizons*, November- December 1983, pp. 28-31.

9. See Christian Gronroos, "A Service Quality Model and Its Marketing Implications," *European Journal of Marketing*, 18, 4, 1984, pp. 36-44.

10. See Leonard L. Berry, "Big Ideas in Services Marketing," *Journal of Consumer Marketing*, Spring 1986, pp. 47-51.

11. For more on service quality, see A. Parasuraman, Valerie A. Zeithaml, and Leonard L. Berry, "A Conceptual Model of Service Quality and Its Implications for Future Research," *Journal of Marketing*, Fall 1985, pp. 41-50; Valerie A. Zeithaml, Leonard L. Berry, and A. Parasuraman, "Communication and Control Processes in the Delivery of Service Quality," *Journal of Marketing*, April 1988, pp. 35-48; and Patricia Sellers, "Getting Customers to Love You," *Fortune*, March 13, 1989, pp. 38-49.

12. For more on services marketing, see John E.G. Bateson, *Managing Services Marketing* (Hinsdale, IL; Dryden Press, 1989); and Christopher H. Lovelock, *Services Marketing*, 2nd ed., Englewood Cliffs, N.J.: Prentice-Hall, 1991.

13. For an example of image assessment in banking, see Michel Laroche and Thomas Taylor, "An Empirical Study of Major Segmentation Issues in Retail Banking," *International Journal of Bank Marketing*, 6, 1, 1988, pp. 31-48.

14. Shirley Young, Leland Ott, and Barbara Feigin, "Some Practical Considerations in Market Segmentation," *Journal of Marketing Research*, August 1978, pp. 405-12.

15. Carey French, "Foreign Mystique Reinforced In Latest Pitch to U.S. Travellers," *Globe and Mail*, April 17, 1990, p. B24.

16. Margaret Bream, "The Future at Stake," *Marketing*, July 3, 1989, pp. 8-9; Helga Loverseed, "Tourism Industry Faced With Selling Canada Anew," *Globe and Mail*, April 17, 1990, p. B24; and Barbara Wickens, "Go North, Please," *Maclean's*, March 19, 1990, p. 38.

17. See Philip Kotler and Gerald Zaltman, "Social Marketing: An Approach to Planned Social Change," *Journal of Marketing*, July 1971, pp. 3- 12.

18. See Eduardo Roberto, *Strategic Decision-Making in a Social Program: The Case of Family-Planning Diffusion* (Lexington, MA: Lexington Books, 1975).

19. See Karl E. Henion II, *Ecological Marketing* (Columbus, OH: Grid, 1976).

20. See John D. Claxton, C. Dennis Anderson, J.R. Brent Ritchie, and Gordon H.G. McDougall, eds. *Consumer and Energy Conservation* (New York: Praeger Publishers, 1981).

21. S. Brown and J.D. Forbes, "Social Marketing in Canada—The Seat- Belt Experience," in Robert D. Tamilia, ed., *Developments in Canadian Marketing* (Saskatoon: ASAC Proceedings, 1979), pp. 176-85.

# CHAPTER 20

# Marketing and Society

## CHAPTER OBJECTIVES

After reading this chapter, you should be able to:
1. List and respond to the social criticisms of marketing.
2. Define consumerism and environmentalism and explain how they affect marketing strategies.
3. Describe the principles of socially responsible marketing.
4. Discuss the role of ethics in marketing.

In a nationwide poll, Canadians were asked what was the most important issue facing Canada in the 1990s and the answer was the "environment." The 1990s are being referred to as the "decade of the environment" as people become concerned about environmental problems. Media attention has focused on various aspects of the situation and reported the following:

- The 25% of the world's population that lives in industrialized nations consumes 75% of the world's energy. Much of the carbon dioxide in the atmosphere comes from burning fossil fuels that provide this energy. Carbon dioxide is a major cause of the "greenhouse" effect (the warming of the world's climate). Canadians use more energy per capita than any other nation in the world and, among developed countries, Canada ranks first in energy use per unit of economic output. On average, every Canadian "produces" 15 tonnes of carbon dioxide each year.

- Western nations, the developed countries, are consumption-intensive whereas developing nations are not. For example, the per capita yearly consumption of paper is 120 kilograms in Western countries, eight kilograms in developing countries. The per capita yearly consumption of steel is 450 kilograms in Western countries, 48 kilograms in developing countries.

- The average Canadian generates one tonne of garbage each year.

- Each day, more than 40,000 trees are cut down to make the paper for Canada's daily newspapers.

- Canadians discard 1,500 tonnes of steel every day in food and drink cans.

- The average daily water use of each Canadian is 5,000 litres; the comparable figure for Britain is 840 litres and for Switzerland is 350 litres.

Based on their concern, more Canadians are becoming environmentally responsible and joining the "Green" revolution. In turn, businesses are responding. Consider the following:

- In July 1989, Loblaws introduced the G*R*E*E*N product line, a group of environmentally friendly products. In the first year, sales were approximately $60 million.
- Procter & Gamble launched their environmental compatible packages in September 1989. Company executives estimated that 15% to 25% of consumers of those products would choose to buy them in the new format.
- The Body Shop, which manufactures and markets only natural source skin and hair care products, has sales of over $40 million.
- Du Pont Canada has invested $24 million to build the world's first commercial plant to produce HCFC-133, a replacement for chlorofluorocarbons (FCs) in air conditioners.
- IBM Canada, in its Bromont, Quebec plant, has achieved the highest CFC recycling efficiency of all IBM establishments worldwide.

Some environmentalists say that these actions by business are not enough and have criticized companies like Loblaws, claiming that their advertising and products are misleading the public. Others are concerned that companies are merely jumping on the environmental bandwagon and not making any substantial changes in their products. Still others, remembering the energy crisis of the early 1970s, wonder if the environment is just the latest fad that will fade away when issues like unemployment or inflation become more pressing for Canadians.

Because the environmental problems are critical, it is likely that Canadians will continue to express their concerns. Today, marketers need to consider how their decisions will impact on society as a whole. By responding positively to the new realities of social responsibility, companies will improve the well-being of the consumer and society.[1]

Responsible marketers find out what consumers want and respond with the right products, priced to give good value to buyers and profit to the producer. The marketing concept is a philosophy of service and mutual gain. Its practice leads the economy by an invisible hand to satisfy the many and changing needs of millions of consumers.

Not all marketers follow the marketing concept. Some companies use questionable marketing practices. Some marketing actions that seem innocent in themselves strongly affect the larger society. Consider the sale of cigarettes. Ordinarily, companies should be free to sell cigarettes, and smokers should be free to buy them. However, this transaction affects the public interest. First, the smoker may be shortening his or her own life. Second, smoking places a burden on the smoker's family, and on society at large. Third, other people around the smoker may have to inhale the smoke and may suffer discomfort and harm. This is not to say that cigarettes should be banned. Rather, it shows that private transactions may involve larger questions of public policy.[2]

This chapter looks at the social effects of private marketing practices. It considers several questions: What are the most frequent social criticisms of marketing? What steps have private citizens taken to curb marketing ills? What steps have legislators and government agencies taken to curb marketing ills? What steps have enlightened companies taken to carry out socially responsible marketing?

# SOCIAL CRITICISMS OF MARKETING

Some social critics claim that marketing hurts individual consumers, society as a whole, and other business firms.

## Marketing's Impact on Individual Consumers

Consumer advocates, government agencies, and other critics have accused marketing of harming consumers through high prices, deceptive practices, high-pressure selling, shoddy or unsafe products, and planned obsolescence.

## High Prices

Many critics charge that the Canadian marketing system causes prices to be higher than they would be under more "sensible" systems. They point to three factors— high costs of distribution, high advertising and promotion costs, and excessive markups.

### HIGH COSTS OF DISTRIBUTION

A longstanding charge is that greedy middlemen mark up prices beyond the value of their services. Critics charge that there are too many middlemen or that middlemen are inefficient, provide unnecessary or duplicate services, and practice poor management and planning. As a result, distribution costs are too high, and consumers pay for these excessive costs in the form of higher prices.

How do retailers answer these charges? They argue as follows: First, middlemen do work that would otherwise have to be done by manufacturers or consumers. Second, the rising markup reflects improved services that consumers want—more convenience, larger stores and assortment, longer store hours, return privileges, and others. Third, the cost of operating stores keeps rising and forces retailers to raise their prices. Fourth, retail competition is so intense that margins are actually quite low. For example, supermarket chains are left with barely one percent profit on their sales after taxes.

### HIGH ADVERTISING AND PROMOTION COSTS

Modern marketing is also accused of pushing up prices because of heavy advertising and sales promotion. For example, a dozen tablets of a heavily-promoted brand of aspirin sell for the same price as 100 tablets of less- promoted brands. Critics feel that if many products were sold in bulk, their prices would be much lower. Differentiated products—cosmetics, detergents, toiletries—include packaging and promotion costs that can amount to 40% or more of the manufacturer's price to the retailer.[3] Critics charge that much of the packaging and promotion adds only psychological rather than functional value to the product. Retailers use additional promotion, such as advertising and displays, that add several cents more to retail prices.

Marketers answer these charges in several ways. First, consumers want more than the functional qualities of products. They also want psychological benefits such as feeling wealthy, beautiful, or special. Consumers can usually buy functional versions of products at lower prices, but they are often willing to pay more for products that also provide these psychological benefits. Second, branding gives buyers confidence. A brand name means a certain quality, and consumers are willing to pay for well-known brands even if they cost a little more. Third, heavy advertising is needed to inform the millions of potential buyers of the merits of a brand. Fourth, heavy advertising and promotion are necessary for the firm when competitors are doing it. A business would lose "share of mind" if it did not match competitive spending. At the same time, companies are very cost-conscious about promotion and try to spend their money wisely. Finally, heavy sales promotion is needed from time to time because goods are produced ahead of demand in a mass-production economy. Special incentives have to be offered in order to sell inventories.

## MARKUPS

Critics charge that some companies mark up goods excessively. They point to the drug industry, where a pill costing five cents to make may cost the consumer 40 cents. They point to the pricing tactics of funeral homes that prey on the emotions of bereaved relatives. The high charges of television and auto repair people are also criticized.

Marketers respond that most businesses try to deal fairly with consumers because they want repeat business. Most consumer abuses are unintentional. When shady marketers do take advantage of consumers, they should be reported to Better Business Bureaus and other consumer protection groups. Marketers also respond that consumers often do not understand the reason for high markups. For example, pharmaceutical markups must cover the costs of purchasing, promoting, and dis-

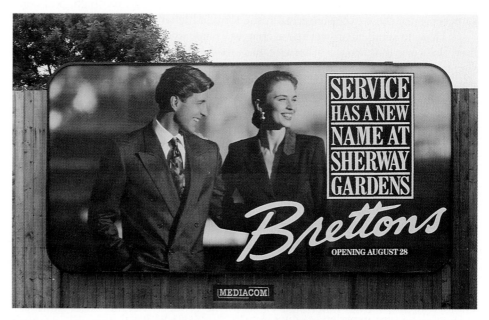

Markups cover services that consumers want, such as assortment, convenience, and personal service.

tributing existing medicines, and the high research and development costs of searching for new medicines.

# Deceptive Practices

Marketers are sometimes accused of deceptive practices that lead consumers to believe they will get more value than they actually do. Deceptive practices fall into three groups. Deceptive pricing includes such practices as falsely advertising "factory" or "wholesale" prices or advertising a large price reduction from a phony high list price. Deceptive promotion includes such practices as overstating the product's features or performance, luring the customer to the store for a bargain that is out of stock, and running rigged contests. Deceptive packaging includes exaggerating package contents through subtle design, not filling the package to the top, using misleading labeling, and describing size in misleading terms.

Deceptive practices have led to legislation and other consumer-protection actions. The Competition Act provides stiff penalties for those companies convicted of these practices.

Marketers argue that most companies avoid deceptive practices because such practices harm their business in the long run. If consumers do not get what they expect, they will switch to more reliable products. In addition, consumers usually protect themselves from deception. Most consumers recognize the marketer's selling intent and are careful when they buy, sometimes to the point of not believing completely true product claims.

# High-Pressure Selling

Salespeople are sometimes accused of high-pressure selling that gets people to buy goods they had no thought of buying. It is often said that encyclopedias, insurance, real estate, and jewelry are sold, not bought. The salespeople are trained to deliver smooth canned talks to entice purchase.[4] They sell hard because sales contests promise big prizes to those who sell the most.

Marketers know that buyers can often be talked into buying unwanted or unneeded things. Laws require door-to-door salespeople to announce that they are selling a product. Buyers in all provinces are allowed a "three-day cooling-off period" in which they can cancel a contract after rethinking it. In addition, consumers can complain to Better Business Bureaus or to provincial consumer protection agencies when they feel that undue selling pressure was applied.

# Shoddy or Unsafe Products

Another criticism is that products lack the quality they should have. One complaint is that products are not made well. Automobiles are the focus of many of the complaints—it seems that every new car has something wrong with it. Consumers grumble about rattles and pings, misalignments, dents, leaking, and creaking. Consumers have also experienced considerable problems with car rust. For five years Ford Motor Company of Canada designed cars that were prematurely rusting. After a number of class action suits were launched in four provinces, Ford settled out of court with the car owners. The Honda Motor Car Company also settled with consumers who had similar premature rusting problems.[5]

A second complaint is that some products deliver little benefit. Consumers got a shock on hearing that dry breakfast cereal may have little nutritional value. One nutrition expert stated: "In short, (the cereals) fatten but do little to prevent malnutrition .... The average cereal fails as a complete meal even with milk added."[6] The expert added that consumers could often get more nutrition by eating the cereal package than the contents.

A third complaint concerns product safety. For years, *Consumer Reports* and *Canadian Consumer* have reported various hazards in tested products—electrical dangers in appliances, carbon monoxide poisoning from room heaters, finger risks in lawnmowers, and faulty steering in automobiles. Product quality has been a problem for several reasons, including occasional manufacturer indifference, increased production complexity, poorly trained labor, and poor quality control.

On the other hand, most manufacturers want to produce good quality. Consumers who are unhappy with one of the firm's products may avoid its other products and talk other consumers into doing the same. The way a company deals with product quality and safety problems can damage or help its reputation. Companies selling poor-quality or unsafe products risk damaging conflicts with consumer groups. For example, Ford Motor Company received a considerable amount of unfavorable publicity when Phil Edmonston formed the Rusty Ford Owners Association and began class action suits against the automaker. In addition to consumer groups, various laws require local, provincial, and federal government agencies to protect consumers against poor or unsafe products.

## Planned Obsolescence

Critics have charged that some producers follow **planned obsolescence**, causing their products to become obsolete before they actually need replacement. In many cases, producers have been accused of continually changing consumer concepts of acceptable styles in order to encourage more and earlier buying. Producers have also been accused of holding back attractive functional features, then introducing them later to make older models obsolete. Critics claim that this practice is found in the consumer electronics industry. Finally, producers have been accused of using materials and components that will break, wear, rot, or rust sooner than they should. For example, many drapery manufacturers are using a higher percentage of rayon in their drapes. They argue that rayon reduces the price of the drapes and has better holding power. Critics claim that rayon will cause the drapes to fall apart sooner.

Marketers respond that consumers like style changes. They get tired of the old goods and want a new look in fashion or a new-styled car. No one has to buy the new look, and if not enough people like it, it will fail. Companies frequently do withhold new features when they are not fully tested, when they add more cost to the product than consumers are willing to pay, and for other good reasons. However, they do this at the risk of having a competitor introduce the new feature and steal the market. Furthermore, companies often put in new materials to lower their costs and prices. They do not design their products to break down earlier because they would lose their customers to other brands.

# Marketing's Impact on Society as a Whole

The Canadian marketing system has been accused of adding to several "evils" in society. Here we will examine claims that marketing creates false wants and too much materialism, too few social goods, and cultural pollution.

## FALSE WANTS AND TOO MUCH MATERIALISM

Critics have charged that the marketing system urges too much interest in material possessions. People are judged by what they own rather than by who they are. Some advertising gives the impression that to be considered successful, people must own a home, two cars, and the latest clothes and appliances.

Interest in goods and services is seen by critics not as a natural state of mind but rather as a set of false wants created by marketing. Business uses advertising to stimulate people's desires for goods. People work harder to earn the necessary money. Their purchases increase the output of Canadian industry and industry in turn uses advertising to stimulate more desire for the industrial output. Thus marketing is seen as creating false wants that benefit industry more than they benefit consumers.

These criticisms overstate the power of business to create wants. People have strong defenses against advertising and other marketing tools. Marketers are most effective when they appeal to existing needs rather than attempt to create new ones. Furthermore, people seek information when making important purchases and do not rely on single sources of information. Even minor purchases, which may be affected by advertising messages, lead to repeat purchases only if the product performs as promised. Finally, the high failure rate of new products shows that companies are not able to control demand.

On a deeper level, our wants and values are influenced not only by marketers, but also by family, peer groups, religion, ethnic background, and education. If Canadians are highly materialistic, these values arose out of basic socialization processes that go much deeper than business and mass media could produce alone.

## TOO FEW SOCIAL GOODS

Business has been accused of overselling private goods (such as automobiles) at the expense of public goods (the roads that the automobiles are driven on). As private goods increase, they require more public services that are usually not forthcoming. For example, an increase in automobile ownership (private good) requires more highways, traffic control, parking spaces, and police services (public goods). The overselling of private goods results in "social costs." In the case of cars, the social costs include excessive traffic congestion, air pollution, and deaths and injuries from car accidents.

A way must be found to restore a social balance between private and public goods. Producers could be made to bear the full social costs of their operations. In this way, they would build these costs into the price. If buyers found the price of the goods too high, the producers would disappear and resources would move to those users that could support the sum of the private and social costs.

## CULTURAL POLLUTION

Critics charge the marketing system with creating cultural pollution. People's senses are constantly being assaulted by advertising. Serious programs are interrupted

Cultural pollution: people's senses are sometimes assaulted by commercial messages.

by commercials; printed matter is lost between pages of ads; beautiful scenery is marred by billboards. These interruptions continuously pollute people's minds with images of sex, power, or status. Though most people do not find advertising very annoying (some even think it is the most interesting aspect of television), some critics call for sweeping changes.

Marketers answer the charges of "commercial noise" with these arguments: First, they hope that their ads primarily reach the target audience. Because of mass-communication channels, some ads are bound to reach people who have no interest in the product and are therefore bored or annoyed. People who buy magazines addressed to their interests—such as *Maclean's* or *Chatelaine* —rarely complain about the ads because they advertise products of interest. Second, the ads make radio and television free media and keep down the costs of magazines and newspapers. Most people think commercials are a small price to pay for this.

# Marketing's Impact on Other Businesses

Critics also charge that a company's marketing practices can harm other companies and reduce competition. Three problems are involved: acquisitions of competitors, marketing practices that create barriers to entry, and unfair competitive marketing practices.

Critics claim firms are harmed and competition is reduced when companies expand by acquiring competitors rather than by developing their own new products. This is of particular concern in Canada because of the sizable number of takeovers and mergers that had occurred in the early 1980s. While many of these mergers were of companies in unrelated industries, for example, Hiram-Walker (liquor) and Consumers Gas (oil and gas), and would not be considered anticompetitive acquisitions, others such as the Bay-Simpsons-Zellers merger are considered a "travesty" of competition.[7] The concentration of newspapers in a few chains such as Thompson Newspapers Ltd., whose papers account for 26% of the total circulation of daily newspapers in Canada, was described as "monstrous" by the Royal Commission on Newspapers.[8] Because of these types of business activity, there was considerable pressure, both inside and outside the federal government, to put some teeth into Canada's competition laws. The Competition Act of 1986 was designed to prohibit mergers and conspiracies that unduly lessen competition. Its purpose was "to maintain and encourage competition in Canada in order to promote the efficiency and adaptability of the Canadian economy."[9]

Since 1986, a number of mergers have been approved by the federal Bureau of Competition Policy, organized in 1986 as part of the Competition Act. These mergers include Canadian Airlines takeover of Wardair, Molson's takeover of Carling, Dofasco's takeover of Algoma, and Imperial Oil's takeover of Texaco. In some instances the Bureau required the companies to sell off some assets to ensure competition in the industry.[10]

Acquisition is a complex subject. Acquisitions can sometimes be good for a society. For example, the acquiring company may gain economies of scale leading to lower costs and lower prices. A well-managed company may take over a poorly managed company and improve its efficiency. An industry that was not very competitive might become more competitive after the acquisition. However, as acquisitions can sometimes be harmful, they are closely regulated by the government.

Critics have also charged that marketing practices add barriers to the entry of new companies into an industry. Large marketing companies can use heavy promotion spending, patents, and tie-ups of suppliers or dealers to keep out or drive out competitors. For example, as shopping center developers prefer dealing with chain stores, it is extremely difficult for an independent retailer to gain access to a shopping plaza. This is a formidable entry barrier for many independent retailers who wish to grow by expanding the number of their stores.

Finally, some firms have used unfair competitive marketing practices with the intention of hurting or destroying other firms. They may set their prices below costs, threaten to cut off business with suppliers, or discourage the buying of the competitor's products. While the Competition Act has a section dealing with predatory competition, the difficulty has been to establish that the intent or action was really predatory.

# CITIZEN ACTIONS TO REGULATE MARKETING

Because some people have viewed business as the cause of many economic and social ills, grassroots movements have arisen from time to time to keep business in line. The two major movements have been consumerism and environmentalism.

## Consumerism

Up until 1945, Canada experienced little of the consumer activity that was taking place in the U.S.[11] In the U.S. the first consumer movement took place in the early 1900s. It was fueled by rising prices, Upton Sinclair's writings on conditions in the meat industry, and ethical drug scandals. The second consumer movement, in the mid-1930s, was sparked by both an upturn in consumer prices during the Depression and another drug scandal.

Since 1945, the Consumers' Association of Canada (CAC) has been the leading force in consumerism in Canada. Much of the CAC's early activity was focused on relatively specific purchase problems with food products, drugs, and clothing.[12] In the mid-1960s, the CAC became more involved in broader issues concerning product safety, labeling, and rising prices.[13] Government activity in this area grew rapidly with the inception of the Department of Consumer and Corporate Affairs in 1967. At that time, the federal government defined four goals to be achieved on behalf of consumers: protection against fraud and deception, protection against accident and health hazards, ensuring that the market system is competitive, and representation of the consumer in the councils of government.[14] At the provincial level, most governments created departments of consumer affairs and increased the level of resources devoted to consumer protection. During the 1970s a considerable amount of legislation was enacted to safeguard consumer rights in the areas of deceptive advertising, door-to-door selling, defective products and services, credit financing, and rental accommodation.[15]

The consumer movement has spread internationally and has become very strong in many countries around the world. But what is the consumer movement? **Consumerism** is an organized movement of citizens and government to improve the rights and power of buyers in relation to sellers. The traditional sellers' rights include:

- The right to introduce any product in any size and style, provided it is not hazardous to personal health or safety; or, if it is, to include proper warnings and controls.
- The right to charge any price for a product, provided there is no discrimination among similar kinds of buyers.
- The right to spend any amount to promote a product, provided it is not defined as unfair competition.
- The right to use any product message, provided it is not misleading or dishonest in content or execution.
- The right to use any buying incentive schemes, provided they are not unfair or misleading.

The traditional buyers' rights include:

- The right not to buy a product that is offered for sale.
- The right to expect a product to be safe.
- The right to expect a product to perform as claimed.

Comparing these rights, many believe that the balance of power lies on the sellers' side. True, the buyer can refuse to buy. But critics feel that the buyer has too little information, education, and protection to make wise decisions when facing

Consumer desire for more information led to the listing of ingredients, and nutrition and dating information, on product labels.

sophisticated sellers. Consumer advocates call for the following additional consumer rights:

- The right to be well informed about important aspects of a product.
- The right to be protected against questionable products and marketing practices.
- The right to influence products and marketing practices in ways that will improve the "quality of life."

Each proposed right has led to more specific proposals by consumerists. The right to be informed includes the right to know the true interest on a loan (truth in lending), the true cost per unit of a brand (unit pricing), the ingredients in a product (ingredient labeling), the nutrition in foods (nutritional labeling), product freshness (open dating), and the true benefits of a product (truth in advertising). Proposals related to consumer protection include strengthening consumer rights in cases of business fraud, requiring greater product safety, and giving more power to government agencies. Proposals relating to quality of life include controlling the ingredients that go into certain products (detergents) and packaging (soft-drink containers), reducing the level of advertising "noise," and putting consumer representatives on company boards to protect consumer interests.

Consumers not only have rights, they also have responsibilities to protect themselves; they cannot leave this function to someone else. Consumers who feel they got a bad deal can take action by writing to the company president or to the media; contacting federal, provincial, or local agencies; and going to small-claims courts.

# Environmentalism

Where consumerists look at whether the marketing system is efficiently serving consumer wants, environmentalists look at how marketing affects the environment and at the costs of serving consumer needs and wants. In 1962, Rachel Carson's *Silent Spring* told about pesticide pollution of the environment.[16] It was no longer a matter of wasted resources, but of human survival. In 1970 the Ehrlichs coined the term "eco-catastrophe" to point out the harmful impact of certain business practices on the environment.[17] In 1972 the Meadowses published *The Limits to Growth*, which warned people that the quality of life would decline in the face of unchecked population growth, spreading pollution, and uncontrolled use of natural resources.[18] Pollution Probe, a Toronto-based environmental organization, has been very active in raising environmental concerns within Canada.[19]

These concerns are the basis for **environmentalism**—an organized movement of concerned citizens and government to protect and improve people's living environment and quality of life. Environmentalists are concerned with strip mining, forest depletion, factory smoke, billboards, and litter; with the loss of recreational areas; and with the increase in health problems caused by bad air and water, and chemically sprayed food.

Environmentalists are not against marketing and consumption; they simply want people and organizations to operate with more care for the environment. For example, Pollution Probe would like people to follow the "three Rs" rule: reduce consumption and waste, reuse by getting more out of items that people own, and recycle to conserve resources.[20] The marketing system's goal should not be to maximize consumption, consumer choice, or consumer satisfaction. The marketing system's goal should be to maximize life quality, which includes not only the quantity and quality of consumer goods and services, but also the quality of the environment. Environmentalists want environmental costs included in producer and consumer decision making.

Environmentalism has hit some industries hard. Steel companies and public utilities have had to invest millions of dollars in pollution-control equipment and costlier fuels. The auto industry has had to introduce expensive emission controls in cars. The packaging industry has had to find ways to reduce litter. The gasoline industry has had to create new low-lead and no-lead gasolines. These industries resent the extra costs represented by environmental regulations, especially when the regulations are imposed too rapidly to allow the companies to make the proper adjustments. These companies have absorbed large costs and have passed them on to buyers.

Thus, marketers' lives have become more complicated. Marketers must examine the ecological properties of their products and packaging. They must raise prices to cover environmental costs, knowing that the product will be harder to sell. Yet environmental issues have become so important in our society that there is no turning back to the time when few managers worried about the effects of product and marketing decisions on environmental quality.

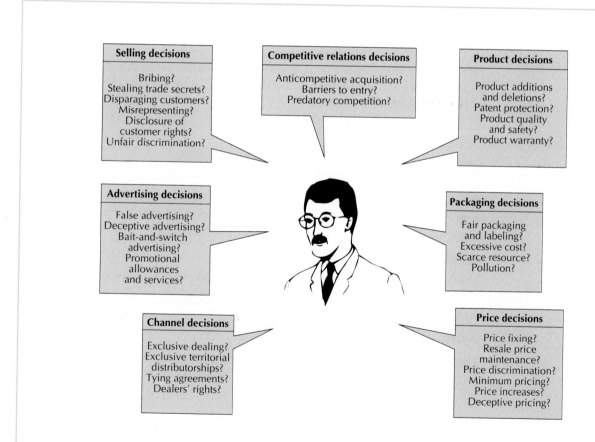

Figure 20-1 Major Marketing Decision Areas That May Be Called into Question under the Law

# PUBLIC ACTIONS TO REGULATE MARKETING

Citizen concerns about marketing practices will usually lead to public attention and legislative proposals. New bills will be debated—many will be defeated, others will be modified, and a few will become workable laws.

We listed many of the laws affecting marketing in Chapter 5. The task is to translate these laws into the language that marketing executives will understand as they make decisions about competitive relations, products, price, promotion, and channels of distribution. Figure 20-1 shows the major issues facing marketing management when making decisions.

# BUSINESS ACTIONS TOWARD SOCIALLY RESPONSIBLE MARKETING

At first, many companies opposed consumerism and environmentalism. They thought the criticisms were either unfair or unimportant. But by now, most companies have come around to accepting the new consumer rights in principle. They might oppose some pieces of legislation as not being the best way to solve certain consumer problems, but they recognize the consumer's right to information and protection. Many of these companies have responded positively to consumerism and environmentalism in order to better serve consumer needs. Here we will look at responsible business reactions to the changing marketing environment. We first outline a concept of enlightened marketing and then consider marketing ethics.

## A Concept of Enlightened Marketing

The concept of **enlightened marketing** holds that the company's marketing should support the best long-run performance of the marketing system. Enlightened marketing consists of five principles.

### CONSUMER-ORIENTED MARKETING

The company should view and organize its marketing activities from the consumers' point of view. It should work hard to sense, serve, and satisfy the needs of a defined group of customers.

### INNOVATIVE MARKETING

The company should continually seek real product and marketing improvements. The company that overlooks new and better ways to develop and market products will eventually lose out to a company that has found a better way.

### VALUE MARKETING

The company should put most of its resources into value-building marketing investments. Many marketing strategies such as one-shot sales promotions, minor packaging changes, and advertising puffery may raise sales in the short term, but add less long-term value than improvements in the product's quality, features, or

# MARKETING HIGHLIGHT 20-1

## The Body Shop: Practicing Societal Marketing

Societal marketing is successfully practiced today by many companies. One of the best examples is probably The Body Shop, a company that produces, distributes, and sells biodegradable skin and hair care products that have not been tested on animals, are sold in refillable and recyclable containers, and are never advertised or put on sale. During the past five years, sales in Canada have increased by 35% per year per store and total sales for 1989 will be approximately $40 million. Started in England, the Canadian operation is run by Margot Franssen. She made the following comments in a speech about the environment and The Body Shop:

We cannot expect to maintain economic prosperity unless we protect the environment. At the same time, economic growth and prosperity provide us with the ability to support wise resource management and protect environmental quality. Since The Body Shop's inception, it has operated on a non-exploitive approach. For instance, it does not sell or use products that: (1) consume a disproportionate amount of energy during manufacture or disposal; (2) cause unnecessary waste; (3) use materials derived from threatened species or from threatened environments; (4) involve cruelty to animals; or (5) adversely affect other countries, particularly in the Third World.

The most important thing about The Body Shop is that the foundation upon which we rest is not mere image. Our greatest danger at the moment is our success and the tremendous amount of press we have received. We must maintain our sincerity, integrity and, above all, values.

As The Body Shop illustrates, successful businesses can operate in nearly complete harmony with the environment.

**Source:** Margot Franssen, "Telling The Body Shop Story," *Marketing*, October 2, 1989, pp. 15-16.

The Body Shop: successful societal marketing.

convenience. Enlightened marketing calls for building long-term consumer loyalty by continually improving the value consumers receive from the firm's marketing offer.

### SENSE-OF-MISSION MARKETING

The company should define its mission in broad social terms rather than narrow

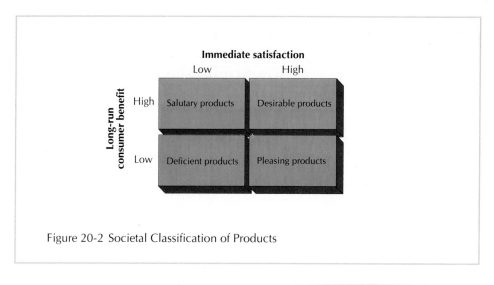

Figure 20-2 Societal Classification of Products

product terms. When a company defines a social mission, company people feel better about their work and have a clearer sense of direction.

## SOCIETAL MARKETING

An enlightened company makes marketing decisions by considering consumers' wants, the company's requirements, consumers' long-term interests, and society's long-term interests. The company is aware that neglecting the last two factors is a disservice to consumers and society (See Marketing Highlight 20-1).

A societally oriented marketer wants to design products that are not only pleasing but also beneficial. The difference is shown in Figure 20-2. Products can be classified according to their degree of immediate consumer satisfaction and long-term consumer benefit. **Desirable products** give both high immediate satisfaction and high long-term benefits, such as tasty, nutritious breakfast foods. **Pleasing products** give high immediate satisfaction but may hurt consumers in the long term, such as cigarettes. **Salutary products** have low appeal but benefit consumers in the long term, such as seat belts. Finally, **deficient products** have neither immediate appeal nor long-term benefits, such as bad-tasting yet ineffective medicine.

The challenge posed by pleasing products is that they sell very well, but may end up hurting the consumer. The product opportunity, therefore, is to add long-term benefits without reducing the product's pleasing qualities. The challenge posed by salutary products is to add some pleasing qualities so that they will become more desirable in the consumers' minds.

# Marketing Ethics

Conscientious marketers face many moral dilemmas. The best course of action is often unclear. Not every manager has a fine moral sensitivity, so companies need to develop corporate marketing policies, broad guidelines that everyone in the organization must follow. These policies should cover distributor relations, advertising standards, customer service, pricing, product development, and general ethical standards.

The finest guidelines cannot resolve all the challenging ethical situations the

**TABLE 20-1**
**Some Morally Difficult Situations in Marketing**

1. You work for a cigarette company and up to now have not been convinced that cigarettes cause cancer. A report comes across your desk that clearly shows the link between smoking and cancer. What would you do?

2. Your R&D department has changed one of your products slightly. It is not really "new and improved," but you know that putting this statement on the package and in advertising will increase sales. What would you do?

3. You have been asked to add a stripped-down model to your line that could be advertised to pull customers into the store. The product won't be very good, but salespeople will be able to switch buyers up to higher-priced units. You are asked to give the green light for this stripped-down version. What would you do?

4. You are thinking of hiring a product manager who just left a competitor's company. She would be more than happy to tell you all the competitor's plans for the coming year. What would you do?

5. One of your top dealers in an important territory has had recent family troubles and his sales have slipped. It looks like it will take him a while to straighten out his family trouble. Meanwhile you are losing many sales. Legally, you can terminate the dealer's franchise and replace him. What would you do?

6. You have a chance to win a big account that will mean a lot to you and your company. The purchasing agent hints that a "gift" would influence the decision. Your assistant recommends sending a fine color television set to the buyer's home. What would you do?

7. You have heard that a competitor has a new product feature that will make a big difference in sales. The competitor will demonstrate the feature in a private dealer meeting at the annual trade show. You can easily send a snooper to this meeting to learn about the new feature. What would you do?

8. You have to choose between three ad campaigns outlined by your agency. The first (A) is a soft-sell, honest information campaign. The second (B) used sex-loaded emotional appeals and exaggerates the product's benefits. The third (C) involves a noisy, irritating commercial that is sure to gain audience attention. Pretests show that the campaigns are effective in the following order: C, B, and A. What would you do?

9. You are interviewing a capable woman applicant for a job as a salesperson. She is better qualified than the men just interviewed. At the same time, you know that some of your important customers prefer dealing with men, and you may lose some sales if you hire her. What would you do?

10. You are sales manager in an encyclopedia company. Your competitor's salespeople are getting into homes by pretending to take a research survey. After they finish the survey, they switch to their sales pitch. This technique seems to be very effective. What would you do?

marketer faces. Table 20-1 lists some difficult ethical situations marketers could face during their careers. If marketers choose immediate sales-producing actions in all these cases, their marketing behavior might be described as immoral or amoral. If they refuse to go along with any of the actions, they might be ineffective as marketing managers and unhappy because of the constant moral tension. Managers need a set of principles that will help them figure out the moral importance of each situation and how far they can go in good conscience.

Each company and marketing manager must work out a philosophy of socially responsible and ethical behavior. Under the societal marketing concept, each manager must look beyond what is legal and allowed, and develop standards based on personal integrity, corporate conscience, and long-term consumer welfare.[21] A clear and responsible philosophy will help the marketing manager deal with the many knotty questions posed by marketing and other human activities.

Marketing executives of the 1990s will face even more challenges. They will have abundant marketing opportunities because of technological advances in solar energy, home computers and robots, cable television, modern medicine, and new forms of transportation, recreation, and communication. At the same time, forces in the socioeconomic environment will increase the limits under which marketing can be carried out. Those companies that are able to create new values and practice socially responsible marketing will have a world to conquer.

# Summary

A marketing system should sense, serve, and satisfy consumer needs and improve the quality of consumers' lives. In working to meet consumer needs, marketers may take some actions that are not to everyone's liking or benefit. Marketing managers should be aware of the main criticisms.

Marketing's impact on consumer welfare has been criticized for high prices, deceptive practices, high-pressure selling, shoddy or unsafe products, and planned obsolescence. Marketing's impact on society has been criticized for creating false wants and too much materialism, too few social goods, and cultural pollution. Marketing has also been accused of harming competitors and reducing competition through acquisitions, practices that create barriers to entry, and unfair competitive marketing practices.

These concerns about the marketing system have led to citizen action movements—consumerism and environmentalism. Consumerism is an organized social movement that aims to strengthen the rights and power of consumers relative to sellers. Alert marketers view it as an opportunity to serve consumers better by providing more consumer information, education, and protection. Environmentalism is an organized social movement seeking to minimize the harm done to the environment and quality of life by marketing practices. It calls for curbing consumer wants when the satisfaction of these wants would create too much environmental cost.

Citizen action has led to the passage of many laws to protect consumers in the area of product safety, truth-in-packaging, truth-in-lending, and truth-in-advertising.

Many companies at first opposed these social movements and laws, but most of them now recognize a need for positive consumer information, education, and protection. Some companies have followed a policy of enlightened marketing based on the principles of consumer orientation, innovation, value creation, social mission, and societal orientation. These companies have provided company policies and guidelines to help their managers deal with moral questions and marketing ethics.

# QUESTIONS FOR DISCUSSION

1. If regulators limited the allowable number of levels in a distribution channel or set a cap on the maximum markup that middlemen could add to the prices of products, would the cost of distribution increase or decrease? What impact would these regulations have on consumers?

2. Does advertising add an excessive amount to the price of products?

3. Does marketing create barriers to entry or reduce them? How, for example, could a small manufacturer of household cleaning products use advertising to compete with Procter & Gamble?

4. If you were a marketing manager at DuPont Canada, which would you prefer—government regulations on acceptable levels of air and water pollution, or a voluntary industry code for target levels of emissions?

5. Does Procter & Gamble practice the principles of enlightened marketing? Does your school?

6. Compare the marketing concept with the principle of societal marketing. Should marketers adopt the societal marketing concept?

7. Choose three of the situations described in Table 20-1 and explain what you would do in each case. Would you make the same decision if your company were having severe financial troubles? What if it had no stated policy supporting high ethical standards?

8. If you had the power to change our marketing system in any feasible way, what improvements would you make? What improvements can you make, either as a consumer or as an entry-level marketing practitioner?

# KEY TERMS

**Consumerism** An organized movement of citizens and government to improve the rights and power of buyers in relation to sellers.

**Deficient products** Products that have neither immediate appeal nor long-run benefits.

**Desirable products** Products that give both high immediate satisfaction and high long-run benefits.

**Enlightened marketing** A marketing philosophy that holds that the company's marketing should support the best long-run performance of the marketing system.

**Environmentalism** An organized movement of concerned citizens and government to protect and improve people's living environment and quality of life.

**Planned obsolescence** A strategy of causing products to become obsolete before they actually need replacement.

**Pleasing products** Products that give high immediate satisfaction but may hurt consumers in the long term.

**Salutary products** Products that have low appeal but benefit consumers in the long term.

# REFERENCES

1. Sources include Pollution Probe Foundation, *The Canadian Green Consumer Guide* (Toronto: McClelland and Stewart, 1989); "Greening of Corporate Canada," Special Report, *Financial Post*, June 4, 1990, pp. 33-40; and Gordon H.G. McDougall, "The Greening of Marketing: Fad, Fashion, or Good Business?" in John Liefeld, ed., *Marketing* (Whistler: ASAC Proceedings, 1990) pp. 206-217.

2. For an overview of some of the major public policy issues in marketing in Canada, see Stanley J. Shapiro and Louise Heslop, eds., *Marketplace Canada: Some Controversial Dimensions* (Toronto: McGraw- Hill Ryerson, 1982).

3. M. Dale Beckman, "An Analysis of Food Packaging Costs: Does Packaging Cost Too Much?" in J. M. Boisvert and R. Savitt, eds., *Marketing 1978* (London: ASAC Proceedings, 1978), pp.25-42.

4. For examples of these practices, see Ellen Roseman and Phil Edmonston, *Canadian Consumers' Survival Book* (Don Mills, Ont.: General Publishing, 1977).

5. Roseman and Edmonston, *Canadian Consumers' Survival Book*, p.157.

6. "The Breakfast of Fatties?" *Chicago Today*, July 24, 1970. For an example of some of the consequences of advertising to children, see Marvin E. Goldberg and Gerald J. Gorn, "Some Unintended Consequences of TV Advertising to Children," *Journal of Consumer Research*, June 1978, pp.22-29.

7. Amy Booth, "Empires—Old Sultanates and New," *Financial Post Magazine*, June 1981, pp.8-20.

8. Ross Laver, "Force Canada's Newspaper Chains to Sell Some Holdings, Inquiry Says," *Globe and Mail*, August 19, 1981, pp.1-2.

9. Peter Foster, "Takeover Horror," *Report on Business Magazine*, May 1989, pp. 55-65.

10. Peter Morton, "Imperial-Texaco Deal Stalled a Second Time," *Financial Post*, January 29, 1990, pp. 1, 4.

11. Maryon Brechin, "Consumer Protection," *Encyclopedia Canadiana* (Toronto: Grolier, 1970), pp. 94-98.

12. David S.R. Leighton, ed., *Canadian Marketing: Problems and Prospects* (Toronto: Wiley, 1973), pp.3-12.

13. For some examples of achievements of the Consumers' Association of Canada, see Maryon Brechin, "The Consumer Movement in Canada," in Vishnu H. Kirpalani and Ronald H. Rotenberg, eds., *Cases and Readings in Marketing* (Toronto: Holt Rinehart and Winston, 1974), pp.141-146.

14. Herb Gray, "Functions and Objectives of the Department of Consumer and Corporate Affairs," in Vishnu H. Kirpalani and Ronald H. Rotenberg, eds., *Cases and Readings in Marketing* (Toronto: Holt Rinehart and Winston, 1974), pp. 147-57.

15. See Michael J. Trebilcock, *Help! Handbook of Consumer Rights in Canada* (Toronto: CBC Learning Systems, 1978).

16. Rachel Carson, *Silent Spring* (Boston: Houghton Mifflin, 1962).

17. Paul R. Ehrlich and Ann H. Ehrlich, *Population, Resources, Environment: Issues in Human Ecology* (San Francisco: W.H. Freeman, 1970).

18. Donnella H. Meadows, Dennis L. Meadows, Jorgen Randers, and William W. Behrens III, *Tne Limits to Growth* (New York: Universe Books, 1972).

19. Pollution Probe Foundation, *The Canadian Green Consumer Guide* (Toronto: McClelland and Stewart, 1989).

20. *Ibid.*

21. Russell Abatt and Diane Sacks, "The Marketing Challenge: Towards Being Profitable and Socially Responsible," *Journal of Business Ethics*, July 1988, pp. 497-507.

# Appendix A: Marketing Arithmetic

One aspect of marketing not discussed within the text is marketing arithmetic. The calculation of sales, costs, and certain ratios is important for many marketing decisions. The purpose of this appendix is to describe four major areas of marketing arithmetic; the operating statement, analytic ratios, markups and markdowns, and cost-volume-profit analysis.

## OPERATING STATEMENT

The operating statement and the balance sheet are the two main financial statements used by companies. The balance sheet shows the assets, liabilities, and net worth of a company at a given time. The operating statement (also called profit and loss statement or income statement) is the more important of the two for marketing information. It shows company sales, cost of goods sold, and expenses during the time period. By comparing the operating statement from one time period to the next, the firm can spot favorable or unfavorable trends and take the appropriate action.

Table A-1 shows the 1991 operating statement for Sandra Parsons, a ladies-wear specialty store in New Brunswick. This statement is for a retailer; the operating statement for a manufacturer would be somewhat different. Specifically, the section "Cost of Goods Sold" would be replaced by "Cost of Goods Manufactured."

The outline of the operating statement follows a logical series of steps to arrive at the firm's $25,000 net profit figure:

| | |
|---|---|
| Net sales | $300,000 |
| Cost of goods sold | -175,000 |
| Gross margin | $125,000 |
| Expenses | -100,000 |
| Net profit | $ 25,000 |

We will now look at major parts of the operating statement separately.
The first part details the amount that Parsons received for the goods she sold

during the year. The sales figures consist of three items: gross sales, returns and allowances, and net sales. Gross sales is the total amount charged to customers during the year for merchandise purchased in Parsons's store. As expected, some customers returned merchandise because of damage or a change of mind. If the customer gets a full refund or full credit on another purchase, this is called a "return." If the customer decides to keep the item, provided Parsons reduces the price, this is called an "allowance." By subtracting returns and allowances from gross sales, we arrive at net sales—what Parsons earned in revenue from a year of selling merchandise:

| | |
|---|---|
| Gross sales | $325,000 |
| Returns and allowances | -25,000 |
| Net sales | $300,000 |

**TABLE A-1**
**Operating Statement for Sandra Parsons**
**for the Year Ending December 31, 1991**

| | | | |
|---|---|---|---|
| Gross Sales | | | $325,000 |
| Less: Sales returns and allowances | | | 25,000 |
| Net Sales | | | $300,000 |
| Cost of Goods Sold: | | | |
| Beginning inventory, January 1, at cost | | $ 60,000 | |
| Gross purchases | $165,000 | | |
| Less: Purchase discounts | 15,000 | | |
| Net purchases | $150,000 | | |
| Plus: Freight-in | 10,000 | | |
| Net cost of delivered purchases | | $160,000 | |
| Cost of goods available for sale | | $220,000 | |
| Less: Ending inventory, December 31, at cost | | $ 45,000 | |
| Cost of goods sold | | | $175,000 |
| Gross Margin | | | $125,000 |
| Expenses | | | |
| Selling expenses | | | |
| Sales, salaries, and commissions | $ 40,000 | | |
| Advertising | 5,000 | | |
| Delivery | 5,000 | | |
| Total selling expenses | | $ 50,000 | |
| Administrative expenses | | | |
| Office salaries | $ 20,000 | | |
| Office supplies | 5,000 | | |
| Miscellaneous (outside consultant) | 5,000 | | |
| Total administrative expenses | | $ 30,000 | |

General expenses

| | | |
|---|---:|---:|
| Rent | $ 10,000 | |
| Heat, light, telephone | 5,000 | |
| Miscellaneous (insurance, depreciation) | 5,000 | |
| Total general expenses | | $ 20,000 |
| Total expenses | | $100,000 |
| Net Profit | | $ 25,000 |

The second major part of the operating statement calculates the amount of sales revenue Sandra Parsons has left after paying the costs of the merchandise she sells. We start with the inventory in the store at the beginning of the year. During the year, Parsons bought $165,000 worth of dresses, slacks, blouses, handbags, jeans, and other goods. Suppliers gave the store discounts totaling $15,000, so that net purchases were $150,000. Because the store is located away from regular shipping routes, Parsons had to pay an additional $10,000 to get the products delivered, giving her a net cost of $160,000. Adding the beginning inventory, the cost of goods available for sale amounted to $220,000. The $45,000 ending inventory of clothes in the store on December 31 is then subtracted to come up with the figure $175,000 for cost of goods sold. Here again, we have followed a logical series of steps to figure out the cost of goods sold:

| | |
|---|---:|
| Amount Parsons started with (beginning inventory) | $ 60,000 |
| Net amount purchased | + 150,000 |
| Any added costs to obtain these purchases | + 10,000 |
| Total cost of goods Parsons had available for sale during year | $220,000 |
| Amount Parsons had left over (ending inventory) | - 45,000 |
| Cost of goods actually sold | $175,000 |

The difference between what Parsons paid for the merchandise ($175,000) and what she sold it for ($300,000) is called the gross margin ($125,000).

In order to show the profit Parsons cleared at the end of the year, we must subtract from the gross margin the expenses incurred while doing business. The selling expenses included two sales employees, local newspaper and radio advertising, and the cost of delivering merchandise to customers after alterations. Selling expenses added up to $50,000 for the year. Administrative expenses included the salary for an office manager, office supplies such as stationery and business cards, and miscellaneous expenses, including an administrative audit conducted by an outside consultant. Administrative expenses totalled $30,000 in 1987. Finally, the general expenses of rent, utilities, insurance, and depreciation came to $20,000. Total expenses were therefore $100,000 for the year. By subtracting expenses ($100,000) from the gross margin ($125,000), we arrive at the net profit of $25,000 for Parsons during 1991.

# ANALYTIC RATIOS

The operating statement provides the figures needed to compute some key ratios. These ratios are typically called operating ratios—the ratio of selected operating statement items to net sales. They let marketers compare the firm's performance in one year to that in previous years (or to industry standards and competitors in the same year). The most commonly used operating ratios are the gross margin percentage, the net profit percentage, the operating expense percentage, and the returns and allowances percentage.

| Ratio | Formula | Computation From Table A-1 | |
|---|---|---|---|
| Gross margin percentage | $= \dfrac{\text{gross margin}}{\text{net sales}}$ | $= \dfrac{\$125,000}{\$300,000}$ | $= 42\%$ |
| Net profit percentage | $= \dfrac{\text{net profit}}{\text{net sales}}$ | $= \dfrac{\$25,000}{\$300,000}$ | $= 8\%$ |
| Operating expense percentage | $= \dfrac{\text{total expenses}}{\text{net sales}}$ | $= \dfrac{\$100,000}{\$300,000}$ | $= 33\%$ |
| Returns and allowances percentages | $= \dfrac{\text{returns and allowances}}{\text{net sales}}$ | $= \dfrac{\$25,000}{\$300,000}$ | $= 8\%$ |

Another useful ratio is the stockturn rate. The stockturn rate is the number of times an inventory turns over or is sold during a specified time period (often one year). It may be computed on a cost, selling, or unit price basis. Thus the formula can be:

$$\text{Stockturn rate} = \frac{\text{cost of goods sold}}{\text{average inventory at cost}}$$

or

$$\text{Stockturn rate} = \frac{\text{selling price of goods sold}}{\text{average selling price of inventory}}$$

or

$$\text{Stockturn rate} = \frac{\text{sales in units}}{\text{average inventory units}}$$

We will use the first formula:

$$\frac{\$175,000}{\dfrac{\$60,000 + \$45,000}{2}} = \frac{\$175,000}{\$52,500} = 3.3$$

That is, Parsons's inventory turned over 3.3 times in 1991. Normally, the higher the stockturn rate, the higher management efficiency and company profitability.

Return on investment (ROI) is frequently used to measure managerial effectiveness. It uses figures from the firm's operating statement and balance sheet. A common formula for computing ROI is:

$$\text{ROI} = \frac{\text{net profit}}{\text{sales}} \times \frac{\text{sales}}{\text{investment}}$$

You may have two questions about this formula: Why use a two-step process when ROI could be computed simply as net profit divided by investment? What exactly is "investment"?

To answer these questions, let's look at how each component of the formula can affect the ROI. Suppose Sandra Parsons computed her ROI as follows:

$$\text{ROI} = \frac{\$25,000(\text{net profit})}{\$600,000(\text{sales})} \times \frac{\$300,000(\text{sales})}{\$150,000(\text{investment})}$$

$$8.3\% \quad \times \quad 2 \quad = 16.6\%$$

Suppose Parsons had worked to increase her share of market. She could have had the same ROI if her sales doubled while dollar profit and investment stayed the same. (She would accept a lower profit ratio to get a higher turnover and market share):

$$\text{ROI} = \frac{\$25,000(\text{net profit})}{\$600,000(\text{sales})} \times \frac{\$600,000(\text{sales})}{\$150,000(\text{investment})}$$

$$4.16\% \quad \times \quad 4 \quad = 16.6\%$$

Parsons might have increased her ROI by increasing net profit through more cost cutting and more efficient marketing:

$$\text{ROI} = \frac{\$50,000(\text{net profit})}{\$300,000(\text{sales})} \times \frac{\$300,000(\text{sales})}{\$150,000(\text{investment})}$$

$$16.6\% \quad \times \quad 2 \quad = 33.2\%$$

Another way to increase ROI is to find some way to get the same levels of sales and profits while decreasing investment (perhaps by cutting the size of Parsons's average inventory):

$$\text{ROI} = \frac{\$25,000(\text{net profit})}{\$300,000(\text{sales})} \times \frac{\$300,000(\text{sales})}{\$75,000(\text{investment})}$$

$$8.3\% \quad \times \quad 4 \quad = 33.2\%$$

What is "investment" in the ROI formula? Investment is often defined as the total assets of the firm. But many analysts now use other measures of return to assess performance. These measures include return on net assets (RONA), return on stockholders' equity (ROE), and return on assets managed (ROAM). Since investment is measured at a particular time, we usually compute ROI as the average investment between two time periods (say, January 1 and December 31 of the same year). We can also compute ROI as an "internal rate of return" by using discounted cash-flow analysis (see any financial textbook for more on this technique). The objective in using any of these measures is to figure out how well the company has been using its resources. As inflation, competitive pressures, and the cost of capital increase, the measures become increasingly important indicators of marketing and company performance.

# MARKUPS AND MARKDOWNS

Retailers and wholesalers must understand the concepts of markups and markdowns. They must make a profit to stay in business, and the markup percentage affects profits. Markups and markdowns are expressed as percentages.

There are two different ways to compute markups—on **cost** or on selling **price**:

$$\text{Markup percentage on cost} = \frac{\text{dollar markup}}{\text{cost}}$$

$$\text{Markup percentage on selling price} = \frac{\text{dollar markup}}{\text{selling price}}$$

Sandra Parsons must decide which formula to use. If Parsons bought blouses for $15 and wanted to mark them up $10, her markup percentage on cost would be $10/$15 = 67.7%. If she based markup on selling price, the percentage would be $10/$25 = 40%. In figuring markup percentage, most retailers use the selling price rather than the cost.

Suppose Parsons knew her cost ($12) and desired markup on price (25%) for a scarf, and wanted to compute the selling price. The formula is:

Selling price = cost ÷ (1 - margin)
Selling price = $12 ÷ .75 = $16

As a product moves through the channel of distribution, each channel member adds a markup before selling the product to the next member. This markup chain is shown for a dress purchased by a Parsons' customer for $200:

|  |  | $ Amount | % of Selling Price |
|---|---|---|---|
| Manufacturer | Cost | $108 | 90% |
|  | Markup | 12 | 10 |
|  | Selling price | $120 | 100% |
| Wholesaler | Cost | $120 | 80% |
|  | Markup | 30 | 20 |
|  | Selling price | $150 | 100% |
| Retailer | Cost | $150 | 75% |
|  | Markup | 50 | 25 |
|  | Selling price | $200 | 100% |

The retailer whose markup is 25% does not necessarily enjoy more profit than the manufacturer whose markup is 10%. Profit also depends on how many items with that profit margin can be sold (stockturn rate), as well as on operating efficiency (expenses).

Sometimes a retailer wants to convert markups based on selling price to markups based on cost, or vice versa. The formulas are:

$$\text{Markup percentage on selling price} = \frac{\text{markup percentage on cost}}{100\% + \text{markup percentage on cost}}$$

$$\text{Markup percentage on cost} = \frac{\text{markup percentage on selling price}}{100\% - \text{markup percentage on selling price}}$$

Suppose Parsons found that her competitor was using a markup of 30% based on cost, and she wanted to know what this would be as a percentage of selling price. The calculation would be:

$$\frac{30\%}{100\% + 30\%} = \frac{30\%}{130\%} = 23\%$$

Since Parsons was using a 25% markup on the selling price for dresses, she felt that her markup was suitable compared with that of the competitor.

Near the end of the summer Parsons found that she still had an inventory of summer slacks in stock. Thus she decided to use a markdown, a reduction from the original selling price. Before the summer, she had purchased 20 pairs of slacks at $10 each, and she had since sold ten pairs at $20 each. She marked down the other pairs to $15 and sold five pairs. We compute her markdown ratio as follows:

$$\text{Markdown percentage} = \frac{\text{dollar markdown}}{\text{total net sales in dollars}}$$

The dollar markdown is $25 (five pairs @ $5 each) and total net sales are $275 (ten pairs @ $20 + five pairs @ $15). The ratio, then, is $25/$275 = 9%.

Larger retailers usually compute markdown ratios for each department rather than for individual items. The ratios provide a measure of relative marketing performance for each department and can be calculated and compared over time. Markdown ratios can also be used to compare the performance of different buyers and salespeople in a store's various departments.

# COST-VOLUME-PROFIT ANALYSIS

The broad purpose of cost-volume-profit analysis is to examine the effects of changes in costs, prices, and volumes on profits. Sometimes referred to as sensitivity analysis, contribution analysis, or break-even analysis, it should be used whenever a decision is to be made that will alter existing costs or prices. The technique is useful in answering problems such as:

- How many additional units do we need to sell to break even, if we increase advertising expenditures by $5,000?
- What contribution would we make if the selling price was increased by $1.00?
- Which product, A or B, provides a greater contribution to the firm?

To use this technique, a number of terms must be understood:

- Variable costs—expenses that change with production or sales volume. Generally these costs vary directly with unit volume. For example, the costs of raw materials usually vary directly with production volume and sales commissions usually vary directly with sales volume.
- Fixed costs—expenses that remain constant regardless of production or sales volumes. For example, rent, depreciation, and advertising usually do not vary with production or sales volume.
- Contribution—the difference between selling price and variable costs.
- Break-even point—the point at which revenues equal expenses.

The analysis may be based on either sales volume or units. It will depend on the information available and the question to be answered. Illustrations of how cost-volume-profit analysis is determined through the use of break-even analysis and sensitivity analysis are shown below, using a simple example: A firm selling electric hair dryers at $15 per unit has fixed costs of $42,000 (administrative expenses of $30,000 and advertising expenses of $12,000). Variable costs are $8 per unit.

# BREAK-EVEN ANALYSIS

Objective: Determine how many units or what volume of sales are required to break even. General equation: Break-even = fixed costs/ (selling price per unit - variable costs per unit).

- The number of units required to break-even = $42,000/($15 - $8) = 6,000
- The sales volume required to break even = 6,000 x $15 = $90,000

The sales volume required to break-even could also be calculated as follows:

- Break-even = fixed costs/contribution percentage per unit where the contribution percentage per unit = (selling price - variable costs)/selling price
- Break-even = $42,000/($15 - $8)/$15 = $90,000

# CONTRIBUTION ANALYSIS

Objective: Determine the unit or volume contribution at some specified sales level. General equation: Contribution = selling price - variable costs. In the above example the contribution per unit is $7 (15 - $8). This is the amount that each unit sold will contribute toward covering fixed costs and profits. To illustrate, the question might be: What total contribution (expressed in units) is necessary to cover fixed costs and make a profit of $10,000?

- Total contribution necessary = $42,000 + $10,000 = $52,000
- Total contribution (in units) = $52,000/$7 = 7,429 units

The advantage in using contribution analysis is that it is relatively easy to determine the financial impact of changes in costs or prices. For example, assume the firm currently sells 10,000 hair dryers a year:

1. The advertising manager proposed an increase in advertising expenditures of $2,000 and expects sales to increase by 10%. What is the financial impact?
   Financial impact = additional contribution - additional expenses
   $$= \$7 \times 1000 - \$2,000 = \$5,000$$

2. The marketing manager proposed to increase the selling price from $15 to $17 and expects sales to decline by 5%. What is the financial impact?
   Financial impact = new contribution - previous contribution
   $$= \$9 \times 9,500 - \$7 \times 10,000 = \$15,500$$

# SENSITIVITY ANALYSIS

Objective: To determine unit or volume contribution or profit under various cost, price, and volume assumptions. General equation: Requires the application of break-even and/or contribution analysis.

Sensitivity analysis is often used to examine the financial impact of various alternatives at one time. For example, suppose the manufacturer of hair dryers was interested in the financial impact of a price change and a change in advertising expenditures at three different sales volumes. These alternatives can be handled in a contribution table as follows:

1. Assume that the two prices are low ($15) and high ($18).

2. Assume that the advertising expenditures are low ($12,000) and high ($20,000).

3. Assume that the three different sales volumes are low (8,000 units), medium (10,000 units), and high (12,000 units).

### Contribution Table (after advertising expenditures)

| | ADVERTISING | | | | | |
| | Low | | | High | | |
| Sales volume | 8,000 | 10,000 | 12,000 | 8,000 | 10,000 | 12,000 |
| Low price | $44,000 | $58,000 | $72,000 | $36,000 | $50,000 | $64,000 |
| High price | $68,000 | $88,000 | $108,000 | $60,000 | $80,000 | $100,000 |

The contribution table is the first step in assessing various alternatives. The next step would be to assign various probabilities to each alternative (e.g., what is the probability that the firm will achieve 8,000 unit sales with a low price and a low advertising budget?). Through the use of decision theory (which is not discussed here) the most suitable alternative can be determined. What is important here is to understand that sensitivity analysis is extremely useful in identifying the relationships between costs, volumes, and profits.

# Appendix B: Analyzing Cases

One of the objectives of the case method is to provide students with the opportunity to develop skills in critical thinking, an important factor in decision making. Cases, which are descriptions of business incidents and events, offer a range of situations for students to consider in order to gain knowledge and insights about the decision-making process.

To achieve the maximum benefits from the experience, students need to prepare each case to the best of their abilities. In preparing a case, the following guidelines and suggestions may be helpful. First, read the case quickly to get an idea of the problem, situation, company, industry, and environment. Second, read the case carefully and make notes on the important facts and the nature of the problem. It is here that you may find the problem-solving model useful (Exhibit 1).

The most important step in problem solving is the selection of the problem the student plans to solve. Distinguishing between a problem and a symptom of the problem is important. For example, "declining market share" is a symptom of a problem; the problem is what has caused this "decline in market share." At times, there may be more than one problem (in some cases there may be short-term and long-term problems, or, in other words, problems that require decisions by "tomorrow" and problems that require important decisions to be made about the future direction of the company). As a noted decision maker once said: "A problem well-defined is half solved."

The statement and analysis of the facts can be grouped under five broad headings. The purpose of these headings is to provide some structure for the analysis. The student might also consider drawing a list of implications for each section. As well, each section should contain a blend of both qualitative analysis (e.g., what needs are buyers satisfying?) and quantitative analysis (e.g., how many buyers are there?). During this analysis, the student may have to make some assumptions about data/facts that may or may not be in the case. In marketing, we live in an imperfect world where not all the information we may want is available. In these circumstances, it is often appropriate to make reasonable assumptions.

Based on the situational analysis, the student should be in a position to list the alternatives that could help address and solve the problem(s). One characteristic of the alternatives is that they should be mutually exclusive. That is, each alternative stands on its own and is not dependent on another. As well, only one alternative could be implemented, not two. Otherwise they are not alternatives. This part of the problem-solving model moves from the analysis to developing recommendations, preparing a plan of action, and implementing that plan. Finally, the student needs to consider how the decision should be evaluated after it has been implemented.

As a further suggestion on case analysis, Exhibit 2 provides some points that are often used by instructors to evaluate either an oral or written case analysis. In summary, a case analysis requires four major steps: (1) define the problem, (2) conduct a situational analysis, (3) list and evaluate alternatives, and (4) select, implement, and monitor the "best" alternative.

## EXHIBIT 1
## The Problem-Solving Model in Marketing

1. Statement of the Problem

2. Statement/Analysis of the Facts (Situational Analysis)
   A. Buyer Analysis
      - What needs are satisfied through the use of the product or service?
      - What is the buyer(s) decision-making process in purchasing the product/service?
   B. Segmentation Analysis
      - What are the possible ways the market could be segmented?
      - What appears to be the "best" way to segment the market?
      - Can these segments be quantified?
   C. Environmental Analysis
      - What opportunities and threats are present based on a review of the political, economic, social, and technological environment?
      - How important are these opportunities and threats for the company?
   D. Company/Competitive Analysis
      - What are the objectives, strengths, and weaknesses of this company?
      - What is this company's past, present, and probable future performance?
      - Who are the competitors? What are their strengths and weaknesses relative to those of the company?
   E. Industry/Market Analysis
      - What is the total market demand, current and future?
      - What are the current shares' sales, and profits of the companies in this industry?
      - What factors appear to be critical in a company's success in this industry?

3. Statement of Alternative Courses of Action
   - What are the options that are available to solve the problem?

4. Evaluation of Alternatives
   - What are the advantages and disadvantages of each alternative (quantitative and qualitative)?
   - What are the implications of each alternative in terms of company, competitor, trade, and buyer reaction?

5. Selection of the Best Alternative
   - Which alternative best addresses the problem? Why?

6. Implementation of Alternative
   - What resources will be required to implement this alternative?

- Who should be responsible for the implementation?
- When should the implementation take place (time frame)?

7. Evaluation of the Decision
   - How should performance be measured?
   - What corrective action, if any, should be taken?

**EXHIBIT 2**
**A Good Case Analysis: Some Suggestions**

The question naturally arises: In applying the outline such as that provided in Exhibit 1 to a case, how do I know when I have done a good analysis? The purpose of this section is to raise some points that are often used by instructors to evaluate either an oral or written analysis.

1. Be complete. It is imperative that the case analysis be complete. There are two dimensions to this issue. First is that each area of the situation analysis must be discussed. Second, each area must be covered in depth and with insight.

2. Avoid rehashing case facts. A good analysis uses facts that are relevant to the situation at hand to make summary points of analysis.

3. Make reasonable assumptions. A good case analysis must make realistic assumptions to fill in the gaps of information in the case. For example, the case may not describe the purchase decision process for the product of interest. A good analysis would attempt to present this purchase decision process.

4. Don't confuse symptoms with problems. In summarizing a firm's problems a poor analysis confuses the symptoms with real problems. Keep asking "why" until you are satisfied that you have identified the root problem.

5. Don't confuse opportunities with taking action. Decisions involve the complex trading-off of many problems and opportunities.

6. Deal with objectives realistically. Good analysis critically evaluates statements of objectives and revises them if necessary. Then it uses these revised objectives as part of the argument about which alternative to select.

7. Recognize alternatives. A good analysis explicitly recognizes and discusses alternative action plans.

8. Don't be impulsive. You must do your situation analysis and recognize alternatives before evaluating them and reaching a decision.

9. Discuss the pros and cons of each alternative. Every alternative always has pros and cons and a good analysis explicitly discusses these.

10. Make effective use of financial and other quantitative information. Financial data (such as break-even points and so on) and information derived from other quantitative analyses can add a great deal to a good case analysis.

11. Reach a clear decision.

12. Make good use of evidence developed in your situation analysis. A good analysis reaches a decision that is logically consistent with the situation analysis that was done. This is the ultimate test of an analysis. People should not be able to fault the logical connection between your situation analysis and decision.

**Source:** Kenneth L. Bernhardt and Thomas C. Kinnear, *Cases in Marketing Management,* Fourth Edition, Business Publications, Inc., Plano, Texas, 1988.

# Cases

The cases draw on aspects of marketing that are discussed in various chapters of the text. The following chart lists the chapters for which each case is most relevant.

| CASE NUMBER | CHAPTERS |
|---|---|
| 1. Bicycle Couriers Limited | 1, 3, 19 |
| 2. Campbell Soup Company Ltd. | 2, 3, 5 |
| 3. The Beer Battle: And The Winner Is? | 2, 3, 5, 18 |
| 4. E.D. Smith and Sons Limited | 2, 3, 10 |
| 5. Neidner Limited | 3, 7, 10 |
| 6. Family Service Agency | 4, 19 |
| 7. Atlantic Jeans | 4, 8 |
| 8. Canadian Population and Household Trends | 5, 6 |
| 9. Nutrasweet: Creative Marketing or Anti-Competitive Behavior? | 5, 20 |
| 10. Environmental Monitoring Limited | 5, 6, 20 |
| 11. Loctite Canada | 7, 10 |
| 12. Brand Loyalty | 9, 15, 16 |
| 13. Heritage Gift Shop | 11, 12, 14 |
| 14. Allied Chemical Canada Limited | 11, 12 |
| 15. Alliance Cosmetics | 11, 12 |
| 16. Video Movies | 11, 12 |
| 17. Valu Marketing - Turikan Stapler | 13, 14 |
| 18. Porsche Division - Volkswagen Canada Inc. | 13, 14 |
| 19. The Tot-Switch | 13, 15, 16 |
| 20. Camp Fortune Ski Resort | 15, 16 |
| 21. The Sales Promotion Challenge | 15, 16 |
| 22. J.T. Electronics | 17 |
| 23. EIT Limited | 18 |
| 24. Financial Exercises for Marketing | Appendix A |

# BICYCLE COURIERS LIMITED

Mr. Robert Jones, a successful entrepreneur, had been approached by Helen Smith with a proposal to invest in a bicycle courier business in Toronto. Ms. Smith had developed the idea after observing that the heavy traffic in Toronto made it difficult for courier vans to make deliveries in the city within a guaranteed two-hour delivery time. She felt she had a winning concept but needed an investor to provide funding for her venture. She had met Mr. Jones at a business entrepreneurs meeting, where Mr. Jones had discussed the criteria he used when deciding whether or not to invest in a new business. Ms. Smith thought her idea met these investment criteria and was hopeful that Mr. Jones would agree.

In large Canadian cities there are a substantial number of businesses that need to send letters, documents, and small parcels quickly to other firms within the city. For example, law firms need to send valuable legal documents to clients, frequently on a rush basis. They call a courier service that would guarantee a two-hour delivery at a price of $4.00 or $5.00. However, congested roads and traffic jams make the two-hour delivery difficult to achieve. Furthermore, the high cost of parking tickets (courier vans would often park illegally during pick-ups and deliveries), vehicle maintenance, and insurance made it difficult for the traditional courier company to make money on intracity business.

Ms. Smith had observed this dilemma while working for one of Canada's leading couriers. She knew that some firms in the United States and Europe were using bicycle couriers and she thought the idea could work in Canada. She felt that bicycles should be more efficient and economical than cars or trucks and that a bicycle service should be faster and cheaper. The total courier business in Canada, which included both intra- and intercity sales, was worth about $625 million each year and was growing at a rate of 15% annually. No actual data was available on what proportion of the total courier business was intracity (e.g., within Toronto) versus intercity (e.g., between Toronto and Montreal) but Ms. Smith thought that the intracity courier business in Toronto could be as low as $2 million or as high as $5 million each year. Based on the limited information and her experience and interests, she estimated that the total number of deliveries within Toronto on an average day was approximately 3,000. She felt that with the proper marketing plan she should be able to capture a large share of that business.

Ms. Smith then worked out some cost figures. The actual courier would be paid on a commission basis receiving 50% of the fees collected. However, they would be guaranteed a minimum wage of $5.50 per hour. If the business had a well-organized delivery system, a courier should be able to deliver up to three items per hour. A dispatcher would be required to organize delivery routes, at a cost of $250 per week. As well, the couriers would require bicycles ($300 each), weatherproof saddlebags ($100 each), and two-way radios ($200 each) to communicate with the dispatchers. Two telephone operators would be needed at $180 per week to handle the business calls. Office space located at the edge of the downtown core could be rented for $1,000 per month, and all other fixed costs (e.g., telephone, dispatch equipment, furnishings) were estimated at $20,000 per year.

Ms. Smith felt the key to the marketing plan was to offer cheaper, faster service than the traditional courier companies. She thought that she could guarantee a 1 1/2 hour delivery time at a base rate of $3.50. If faster delivery was required (i.e., under one hour), the charge would be $5.00. She did have three concerns about her proposed business:

1. Would companies entrust valuable documents to people who delivered on bicycles? Customers might not view this service as reliable.
2. Would winter conditions put a halt to her business? She did some checking and found that in Toronto there are only about ten days a year when there is snow on the roads.
3. How should she begin marketing her idea and to whom?

Ms. Smith thought she would have to start with at least 20 couriers, two telephone operators, and one dispatcher. She approached Mr. Jones with an offer of 40% of the business for an investment of $50,000. She outlined the idea, left the information, and Mr. Jones agreed to call her with his decision in two days.

## Questions

1. Would you recommend that Mr. Jones invest in the business?
2. Assume that Mr. Jones agrees to invest in the venture. Prepare a marketing plan for this service.

# 2. CAMPBELL SOUP COMPANY LTD.

David Clark, the president of Campbell Soup, plans to revolutionize the Canadian food business by dominating the "chilled" foods segment of the market. Chilled foods are short shelf-life, refrigerated foods that must be prepared a short time after their purchase. Faced with low growth and declining markets in soup and other products at the core of its business, Mr. Clark devised "Vision '93," a five-year plan introduced in 1988. "Vision '93" dedicates Campbell's to manufacturing food products that are as fresh as possible. As Mr. Clark puts it, this transition involves shortening the cycle from "gate (farm) to plate" through enhanced inventory management. The intended result is to squeeze costs out of production and distribution processes and encourage maximum freshness and quality for consumers. This is Mr. Clark's latest move toward his goal of making Campbell's the best food company in Canada.

## Background

The Campbell Soup Company of 1983 had been described as a stodgy, conservative company. It was losing share in the highly competitive packaged foods industry. The company showed little enthusiasm for change and no successful new product activity in an extremely dynamic and increasingly competitive business environment.

Conversely, the Campbell Soup Company of 1990 was described as an innovative company with the vision of providing food and beverage products that are as fresh as they possibly can be. David Clark, hired in 1983 to turn the company around, defined the corporate mission as operating in the "well-being" business and focusing on meeting the ever-changing needs of Canadian consumers. The food and beverage market had become variety- driven as consumers demanded new taste sensations and greater nutritional value. Long-term success in this business has been linked to aggressive anticipation of the changing environment.

Recent volume and profit performance at Campbell's (71% owned by Campbell's U.S. and 29% owned by Canadian investors) had been strong; between 1984 and 1989 sales increased by 42% and profits by 73% (Exhibit 1). Campbell's market share for soup was at a ten-year high because of increased research and development and marketing expenditures to support the launching of new products and the repositioning of existing products. In the past five years three brands had been added—Le Menu, Prego, and Home Cookin' Soup. Many products had been targeted at the growing health-conscious, convenience food market which was prepared to pay more for value-added, higher quality products.

# The Environment

There were several major macroenvironmental factors affecting Campbell's and other companies in the food industry:

- Canada's population was growing slowly and was aging.
- Each year, an increasing portion of Canadians exercised more, improved their eating habits, and quit smoking. As well, many Canadians planned to improve their exercise and eating patterns, but did not.
- Family size was declining as more Canadians married later in life and had fewer children.
- Family incomes were increasing as more married women entered the workforce.

Increased competition, shifting demographics, and changing consumer lifestyles provided constant opportunities and threats for Campbell's and its competitors in the soup market. There had been a flood of new products into the market and the primary weapon in the battle for share had been line extensions. With this strategy, soup companies had been trying to satisfy every imaginable customer preference. Whole new categories of soup, including dehydrated, microwaveable and, more recently, frozen and refrigerated, had been developed in attempts to expand the market in light of rapidly changing demographics and lifestyles.

# The Soup Market

In spite of the competitive activity and the new product introductions, total sales of soup in Canada had not increased in the past few years. During this time, the ready-to-serve market had grown faster than the market for condensed soup; it represented 20% of total sales, more than double the percentage of ten years ago.

Campbell Soup had been the soup market leader in every region of the country except for Quebec, which had traditionally been the weakest soup market. In 1989, by purchasing Habitant—Quebec's leading soup—Campbell's paid $69.5 million to gain a strong foothold in the Quebec market. Habitant brands were the premier choice of Quebec consumers and the plan was to increase national exposure.

Campbell's, along with Lipton and other competitors, faced the task of making soups more attractive in the current environment. Health and fitness concerns had created a demand for nutritional foods that contained no artificial ingredients and less salt. At the same time, the increasing number of dual-income families and single-parent families had increased the need for convenience in food products.

Lipton's "Cup-a-Soup" had continued to increase its share in the dehydrated segment as the line was extended to include "Cup-a-Soup Lite," which capitalized on consumers' need for convenience and controlled calories.

In the declining condensed soup segment, Campbell's advantage came from positioning itself as the "well-being company," and promoting its foods as conducive to good health with the slogan "Get Fresh!".

Campbell's had also put effort into increasing soup consumption by promoting it for different occasions (e.g. breakfast), new usages (e.g. cooking sauces), creative cookery (mixing two or more together) and by creating a ready-to-eat Chunky soup line for people who wanted to make soup an entire meal.

In addition to Campbell's Classic Red and White labeled soups, recent entries had been launched as line extensions to some of the newer brands and had assisted in the repositioning of older brands:

- Chunky Light—a ready-to-serve chunky soup targeted to health-conscious individuals
- Special Request Soups—low sodium (1/3 less salt than regular soup)
- Home Cookin'—hearty, ready-to-eat soups

In total, Campbell's marketed more than 200 different soups under five brand names: (1) Red and White condensed soups, (2) Chunky soups, (3) Habitant soups, (4) Home Cookin' soups, and (5) Special Request soups. As well, Campbell's continued to develop new and improved soups, including microwaveable soups and pasta soups, as well as new varieties of existing soups.

## The "Chilled" Market

Having successfully turned Campbell's into one of the more aggressive and profitable companies in Canada, David Clark's efforts were now directed at transforming the company from a producer of canned goods to one of fresh foods. The foray into "fresh foods" (also called the "chilled" market) had already begun for the packaged goods giants, and experts predicted that it could become a multi-billion dollar market as consumers increasingly looked for both freshness and convenience on the supermarket shelves. This would require a new focus on distribution—direct from the producer to the supermarket shelves to maintain freshness and product safety.

Catelli and Nestlé had beaten Campbell's to the "fresh food" shelves, each having launched fresh pasta products with average shelf-lives of six weeks. Both companies were predicting that the fresh pasta market would experience double-digit growth throughout the 1990s as consumers' eating habits changed and they became more self-indulgent in what they bought. Given this, the challenge lay in the creation of nutritional products with shorter shelf lives.

To coordinate its entrance into the fresh food category, Campbell's had set up a separate business unit by purchasing Quadelco—a company which sold refrigerated meats, cheese, salads, poultry products, and pasta to supermarkets and delis. Quadelco was Campbell's laboratory that would help the company manufacture, market, and distribute value-added, convenience short-shelf-life refrigerated products, while at the same time aggressively developing the company's current product lines.

To be successful in this business, Campbell's and its competitors would have to learn a totally different type of business, one that required a new distribution system where speed was crucial. In most cases, food products were delivered to central warehouses, and from there they were sent to local supermarket stores. With chilled foods, distribution usually had to be direct from the producer to the supermarket shelf. This would require a change in the entire distribution process.

As one expert noted:

> There has to be an integration of the manufacturing and distribution channels, which are currently out of sync in a lot of cases. When the first frozen foods came on the market, stores had some capacity, but not much. When products were delivered, people didn't always know what do with them, and they melted. That used to happen a lot. Now the major chains have frozen warehouses and send frozen trucks to special bays at their stores. The same type of thing has to happen with fresh foods.

*Marketing*, May 7, 1990

One other area of concern was the consumer's shopping patterns. Chilled foods were relatively common in parts of Europe where many consumers shopped on a daily basis looking for the freshest products possible. In Canada, most consumers shopped on a weekly basis, filling in occasionally throughout the week.

Mr. Clark was confident that the "chilled" market was where the future lay in the food business. He saw a gradual move by Canadian shoppers to the European model, as supermarkets created specialty departments within the store—seafood, meats, produce, deli counters, and dairy cabinets. In these areas the products were all refrigerated or short-shelf-life, while the traditional areas of the store—frozen and shelf-stable products—were shrinking.

Campbell's and its competitors had a vision of the future. How it would unfold would depend on their ability to plan and execute marketing strategies in the face of changing environmental and consumer patterns.

# Questions

1. Assess Campbell's recent responses to environmental forces affecting the market for soup.

2. Assess Campbell's strategy for the "chilled food" market.

3. Is there a market for "well-being" products? To develop the "well-being" strategy, how should new and existing product opportunities be evaluated?

4. Which new product ideas should Campbell's develop as part of the "well-being" strategy?

**Sources include:** "Foray Into Fresh Foods Begins," *Marketing*, May 7, 1990, pp. 11-12, and Campbell's Soup Company Ltd., *Annual Report*, 1989; and Oliver Bertin, "Campbell's Sloganeering Chairman Planning to Shift Into Fresh Foods," *Globe and Mail*, November 30, 1989, p. B13.

**EXHIBIT 1**
**Campbell Soup Company Ltd.**
**Selected Statistics 1984-1989 (in 000's)**

|  | 1989 | 1988 | 1987 | 1986 | 1985 | 1984 |
|---|---|---|---|---|---|---|
| Sales | $377,692 | 354,532 | 333,053 | 313,871 | 290,797 | 265,053 |
| Costs and expenses (excluding interest) | 343,229 | 321,931 | 299,722 | 285,401 | 268,352 | 245,559 |
| Interest and other income | 5,055 | 2,359 | 1,328 | 1,905 | 2,051 | 1,718 |
| Interest expense | 3,165 | 2,568 | 2,507 | 2,535 | 2,503 | 2,599 |
| Earnings before taxes and extraordinary item | 36,353 | 32,392 | 32,152 | 27,840 | 21,993 | 18,613 |
| Income taxes | 14,760 | 14,028 | 14,220 | 12,409 | 9,528 | 7,777 |
| Earnings before extraordinary item | 21,593 | 18,364 | 17,932 | 15,431 | 12,475 | 10,836 |
| Net earnings | 17,493 | 21,872 | 17,932 | 15,431 | 10,946 | 10,231 |

**Source:** Campbell Soup Company Ltd., *Annual Report,* 1989.

# 3. THE BEER BATTLE: AND THE WINNER IS?

The 1990s will be crucial for the beer business in Canada - an industry in transition. After nearly a decade of beer battles in the marketing arena, the big two (formerly the big three) brewers in Canada, Labatt and Molson, have nearly exhausted the possibilities of product, packaging, and promotional innovation, while beer consumption continues to decline.

The scenario: two major Canadian breweries competing for market share in a declining domestic market. The question is, who will win? And who is most strategically positioned to attack the global market?

## The Industry

The intensity of the beer wars has exhausted the combatants' "bag of tricks." New variations on the product—bock, dry, premium, light, shandy, and licensed—have fragmented the market but have not increased total sales. In fact, per capita consumption (based on the adult population) of beer in Canada has declined from about 107 litres in 1984 to a little over 103 litres in 1989. Packaging—tall bottles, twistoff caps, bottom bottle openers, aluminum cans, clear and painted glass—has moved beer from dowdy to upscale in image. In terms of promotion, the industry has pushed the legal limits in advertising and promotional tactics.

At the same time, the number two and three producers (Molson and Carling) have merged to take on the industry leader, Labatt. The expected outcome of the merger will be the creation of a more efficient industry in Canada, adding strength to marketing efforts abroad.

A major problem is the interprovincial trade barriers, which make Canadian brewers less competitive than their American counterparts. Because each province requires a brewery to set up a plant in that province if the brewery wants to sell beer there, many of the plants are relatively small. Every year, the average U.S. brewery produces around 1.1 billion litres of beer. In Canada, the largest brewery produces roughly 350 million litres annually.

The average size of each of the 36 breweries in Canada is slightly more than one million hectolitres and total production costs range from 25 to 50% higher than those of the major U.S. producers. All the major players agree that the future of the Canadian beer industry lies outside of Canada's borders.

# Labatt

In 1990, Labatt held a 42% share of the Canadian market and had sales of $1.92 billion. Labatt marketed 38 brands of beer in Canada through its 12 breweries, which were operating at close to capacity. (Exhibit 1 lists the major brands for each brewery.) Substantial capital investment programs would be required to add the necessary facilities to increase volume. As such, Labatt was generally opposed to free trade with the United States.

Labatt Breweries is a division of Labatt Brewing Group, which falls under the corporate umbrella of John Labatt Limited. John Labatt Limited is a diversified company which focuses on food and beverage industries. The entire brewing group makes up 36% of total corporate sales and 66% of its earnings (Exhibit 2). It is the most vertically integrated Canadian brewery with interests in both a malting company and a manufacturer of patented caps for bottled beverages.

Midway through 1990, Labatt's executive vice-president boasted "We're well over 42% (market share) but we're not at 43%." Even one-tenth of one percent increase in share is important in the brewing industry, where each percentage point of market share represents about $10.5 million in pretax operating profits.

On the negative side, Labatt's Blue, the most popular brand in Canada, had slipped behind Molson Canadian in the crucial Ontario market. There were two factors involved: first, Molson's aggressive attack on the Ontario market with its Molson Canadian brand, and second, the detrimental effects of Labatt's unsuccessful "Blue Zone" campaign. It was expected that Labatt's response would be a more concentrated focus on the Ontario market and some new advertising campaigns.

# Molson

The new Molson/Carling force in the Canadian brewing industry commands the leadership position with 52% of the market, having lost about one share point to small brewers as a result of the merger. However, the merger strategically positions Molson to maintain a strong presence in Canada and creates a base for North American and international expansion for brewing operations.

Previously, Molson operated 16 breweries in seven provinces at just under 80% capacity. The end result of the merger will see seven plants close across the country, allowing Molson's to compete more efficiently.

The Brewing Group is one of four groups within the Molson Companies' portfolio. The brewing operations comprised about 52% of total sales, and contributed 67% of operating profits in 1989 (Exhibit 3).

The Molson Companies is a diversified company across three industries, yet is not as vertically integrated as Labatt. A significant global presence has been achieved through Diversey Corporation, which supplies cleaning systems and products worldwide. Diversey operates 51 companies in 34 countries, with 85% of sales outside Canada.

In recognition of the complexities of the ever-changing international environment and the need to contain costs and maintain competitive advantages, Molson's objective is to build strategic alliances. It did that with Elders (the owner of Carling) when the Carling/Molson merger took place in 1989. Characterized by their large size, these alliances will enable innovation and development of products and markets to keep costs competitive.

## Recent Trends

As Canadians' lifestyles are becoming increasingly health-oriented, beer sales continue to stagnate (total volume in 1988 was slightly less than 1984). It appears likely that the near future will see more low- calorie and no-alcohol (containing less than one percent alcohol) products on the market, as this is one of the few growing sub-segments of the beer market. No-alcohol beer is aimed at satisfying consumer preferences for lighter, healthier products, as well as drinking and driving concerns. Most experts predict that low-alcohol beer will likely remain a niche product. The low- alcohol segment has reached a size of $15 million out of the $8,700 million beer market.

Labatt, now Canada's number two brewery, was the first major beer company to introduce a de-alcoholized beer, Labatt .5, containing only .5% alcohol. The product was launched in Quebec, where Labatt has established grocery-store distribution and has achieved .3% of the beer market. The new brand will be sold in grocery stores outside of Quebec because of the negligible alcohol content.

The level of competition between the Canadian breweries is reflected in the following events which occurred over a five-month period in late 1989 and early 1990.

> December 1989: Black Label introduces the painted bottle, others to follow.
> January 1990: Molson/Carling merger, to form #1 brewery in Canada.
> March 1990: Molson leads the way into the "Dry" beer segment with Molson Special Dry.
> Spring 1990: Labatt introduces the #1 brand in Canada, Labatt's Blue, in a new bottle with a painted label.
> April 1990: Labatt enters the "Dry" segment with Labatt's Dry.
> April 1990: Labatt launches a de-alcoholized beer, Labatt .5, into the Quebec market.

## Canada/United States Trade

Presently beer is almost exempt from the Free Trade Agreement between Canada and the United States, but if it were not, Canadian beer drinkers could expect better selection and lower prices. Since Canada was able to maintain its practices of regulating beer prices (with price floors) and imposing higher taxes on American beer, it is still possible to limit access of U.S. brands to the Canadian distribution channel.

However, in the summer of 1989, the domestic breweries suffered due to the importing of cheap U.S. beer, which knocked the premise of brand loyalty among Canadian beer drinkers. The price of a Canadian six-pack was $5.65 versus $4.30 to $4.55 for a six-pack from the U.S. The result was an increase in market share of U.S. beer in Ontario from about 2 percent to 7 percent.

The prospect of dismantling the interprovincial barriers could also lead to a greater volume of imported U.S. beer being sold in Canada. Imported beer volume has been growing steadily since 1986.

## The Future

Both Labatt and Molson are aggressively searching for new acquisition opportunities abroad. With a flat domestic market, exporting and expansion overseas is essential for growth. At this time, total exports of Canadian beer account for about ten percent of domestic production.

In 1990, Labatt's brands achieved ten percent volume growth in the U.S., and Labatt's Blue ranked as the fifth largest import beer in the U.S. Labatt's sales in the United Kingdom increased strongly in 1990 and Labatt lager became one of the top ten brands in the United Kingdom on-premise lager market. As well, Labatt purchased a regional brewery in Italy as part of its international expansion.

After the merger, the new Molson Breweries ranked third in sales in the imported beer market in the United States. Molson is Canada's leading exporter into the U.S. and shipped approximately 18 million cases to that market in 1990. A long-term goal is to make the Molson name internationally synonymous with Canadian beer. Molson considers the United Kingdom as the primary market for current expansion outside North America.

As the two breweries plan their future strategies, industry experts are uncertain as to who the winner will be, in either the domestic or international market. The exports are certain of one thing: the competition will be intense because the stakes are high.

## Questions

1. Which brewery is best positioned for the domestic market? Why?
2. Which brewery is best positioned for the international market? Why?

**EXHIBIT 1**
**Major Brands by Brewery**

## MOLSON BREWERIES

### BRANDS
Molson Export
Molson Canadian/Canadian Light
Coors/Coors Light
Molson Golden
Molson Special Dry
Old Vienna
O'Keefe Ale
Foster's Lager
Miller/Miller Lite

### NEW PRODUCT INTRODUCTIONS (1989)
1. Molson Canadian Light into "light beer" segment
2. Molson Special Dry first into new "dry" beer segment

## LABATT BREWERIES

### NATIONAL BRANDS
Labatt's Blue/Blue Light
Labatt's 50
Budweiser
John Labatt Classic
Carlsberg/Carlsberg Light

### REGIONAL BRANDS
Maritimes - Keith's, Schooner, Oland Export
Quebec - Légère
Ontario - Crystal
Manitoba/Alberta - Club
British Columbia - Kokanee, Lucky

### NEW PRODUCT INTRODUCTION (1989)
1. Labatt's Dry into new "dry" beer segment

**EXHIBIT 2**
**John Labatt**
**Selected Statistics - 1990 ($millions)**

|  | Total | Brewing Group | Food Group |
|---|---|---|---|
| Gross Sales | 5,274 | 1,920 | 3,354 |
| Earnings (before interest and taxes) | 264 | 174 | 90 |
| Assets Employed | 1,950 | 717 | 1,233 |
| Return on Assets Employed | 13.5% | 24.3% | 7.3% |

**Source:** John Labatt, *1990 Annual Report.*

**EXHIBIT 3**
**The Molson Companies**
**Selected Statistics - 1990 ($millions)**

|  | Total* | Brewing | Cleaning and Sanitizing | Retail Merchandising |
|---|---|---|---|---|
| Gross Sales | 2,550 | 1,322 | 763 | 394 |
| Earnings (before interest and taxes) | 193 | 129 | 53 | 28 |
| Total Assets | 1,842 | 798 | 540 | 302 |
| Return on Total Assets | 10.5% | 16.2% | 9.8% | 9.3% |

* "Other operations" not shown.

**Source:** The Molson Companies, *1990 Annual Report.*

# 4. E.D. Smith & Sons Limited

Written by Marvin Ryder, McMaster University

Chris Powell and Lee Ann Jessop of E.D. Smith and Sons Limited had just completed a review of the firm's line of jam and jelly products. As Marketing/Sales Manager-Grocery Products and Product Manager, respectively, they were responsible for determining the strategic plan for the product line. Among the issues they identified were: (1) the uncertainties created by the impending free trade agreement with the United States; (2) the lack of advertising support for the product line; and (3) trade rumors that shelf space for all jam, jelly, and marmalade products was about to decrease. As they began the meeting in early June, the plan of action for the remainder of 1988 and 1989 was far from certain.

## Company Background

In 1882, Ernest D'Israeli Smith, a fruit farmer in the fertile Niagara Escarpment area of Ontario known as Winona, was dissatisfied with the fact that shippers were taking part of growers' profits,. His solution was to ship his own fruit directly to the wholesaler. He was so successful that demand overtook his own farm's supply and he bought and shipped other farmers' fruit as well. At the turn of the century, this entrepreneur was faced with a glut of fruit in successive seasons which had caused a price drop and left excess fruit unsold. E.D. Smith decided to start making jams and jellies.

Up to 1903, all pure jams sold in Canada were imported from England. E.D. Smith's was the first pure jam ever produced commercially in Canada and, in 1905, a factory was built and the company went into full-scale jam production.

From these humble beginnings, E.D. Smith expanded into a variety of product lines including tomato ketchup, H.P. Sauce (produced under license), Worcestershire Sauce (under license), fruit pie fillings, and a variety of tomato-based products.

From 1956 to 1981, the company went through a major expansion plan that enabled them to compete with multinational food corporations in the Canadian market. A company organization based on the functional areas of business—marketing, sales, manufacturing, finance, and data processing—was adopted. Diet products, bulk pie fillings and Garden Cocktail vegetable juice were all introduced. In 1968, E.D. Smith purchased Ware Foods Limited of Hamilton, which produced a broad line of institutional products for the growing food service industry. In 1976, the company acquired McLarens Foods Limited of Hamilton, whose olives, pickles, and selected specialty products had an excellent reputation within Canada.

In 1986, a fourth generation of Smiths became President with the appointment of Llewellyn S. Smith. E.D. Smith remained, over 100 years later, a wholly Canadian-controlled and operated company.

## Company Operations

The company had kept pace with changing markets and new taste trends by means of a modern, efficient manufacturing capability, progressive management, and a dedicated group of over 200 employees. With the exception of sales offices, the entire E.D. Smith company operated from Winona, Ontario. The company continued to handle its own shipping. Products were carried by rail to Atlantic and western Canada while in Ontario and Quebec the E.D. Smith fleet of transport trailers handled deliveries.

Grocery products accounted for a major proportion of the Food Division business. E.D. Smith also marketed chili sauce relish under their own name, as well as H.P. Sauce and Lea & Perrins. Sales of these products were primarily handled by the 20-person National Grocery Sales Force who worked in all provinces except the Atlantic provinces, where a broker was retained.

Although the company's markets were mostly domestic, the firm had limited sales outside North America. Wherever possible, Canadian products were purchased as raw materials. Raspberries from British Columbia, blueberries from the Maritimes, rhubarb from Quebec, and apples and cherries from Ontario were examples of Canadian sourcing.

People were a key ingredient in E.D Smith's success. A team spirit was promoted and an open door policy was maintained to ensure good labor relations. Employees were encouraged to participate in "speak-up sessions" and in the company newsletter, *The Homestead*, which offered a forum for suggestions on maintaining and improving the company's standards. Employees were also encouraged to participate in subsidized courses both on and off the premises.

Automation and innovation had streamlined the production process. Modern methods preserved the products' natural goodness and ensured quality standards while maintaining stable prices. Computers assisted management in controlling operations from receipt of ingredients to order assembly for customer deliveries. While the company was busiest in the fall, production continued year-round with frozen and fresh fruit imported from the United States, British Columbia, and Europe. The seasonality and variety of products necessitated a complex scheduling system to ensure maximum efficiency and cost control.

# The Jam, Jelly, and Marmalade Market

Marketing research indicated that when consumers were asked what image the name E.D. Smith conjured in their mind, the answer most often given was jam. After all, E D. Smith was the first company to sell "pure" jam in Canada. Any product called "pure" jam had to contain a minimum of 45% fruit. The remainder of the product could contain sugar and natural preservatives such as citric acid. No additives, no artificial colors, and no chemicals could be added to "pure" jams.

E.D. Smith sold 80 to 85% of its pure jams and jellies in Ontario. Sales in Quebec were negligible due mostly to the preference of these consumers for sweeter, less thick jams. Likewise, sales in Canada's west were nearly negligible. The Maritimes accounted for the remainder of E.D. Smith's jam and jelly sales. Due to the concentration of sales in Ontario, Jessop and Powell decided to narrow their focus to this market.

In Ontario, the top six brands of jam, jelly, and marmalade accounted for 50.7% of the sales. Exhibit 1 provides information on the top six companies. This was a highly fragmented market with many companies vying for market share. Even foreign companies had some market share, although their jams were not classified as "pure" jams and were of low quality, containing large quantities of pectin (a natural substance used to solidify a jam, jelly, or marmalade). The heavy competition was surprising since demand for both jam and jelly had not grown in the last five years (annual changes in demand fluctuated between +1% and .1%) and demand for marmalade was declining at the rate of eight percent per year.

Theories to explain these declines were plentiful. Perhaps more and more people were not eating breakfast, or at least not eating breakfast in the home, but breakfast cereal and microwaveable breakfast sales were growing. Perhaps consumers had turned away from jam, jelly and marmalade in favor of honey, peanut butter, and other breakfast spreads, but these products had not shown any appreciable growth in sales. Certainly, people had not turned to making their own jam. The amount of homemade jam produced in Canada had been on a steady decline for the past 20 years.

The top selling brand in Ontario was Kraft, with 13.7% of the market. In fact, it was the best selling brand in Canada. Typical consumers of Kraft's products were children, who used the spread with peanut butter in a sandwich. Kraft was a large, diversified, processed food company which used a family branding approach. With a large advertising budget, Kraft was able to establish and maintain the brand name in the consumer's mind. Kraft's position was solidified by a product relaunch in 1988 with a change in packaging (from a round glass jar to a square glass jar), and labeling (giving new emphasis to the fruit).

The number two brand was Laura Secord, with 9.5% of the market. Laura Secord only sold "pure" jams and marmalades. A division of Catelli Foods, the company started selling jam and marmalade in 1977, making it the newest market entrant. Typical consumers of Laura Secord jams were "discriminating" shoppers. They were looking for a better product with a better taste. Independent taste tests indicated their flavor was better than Kraft's and equal to E.D. Smith's. The Laura Secord name was also a family brand, which was used for ice cream, chocolate, and pudding products. Rumors were afoot that Catelli's parent company, John Labatt Limited, was preparing to sell the Catelli division. These rumors were reinforced when it was announced that the Laura Secord name had been sold to Nestlé. Nestlé was interested in continuing the chocolate and milk products line but did not seem to have any interest in continuing the jam line. Catelli could soon begin the process of selling the jam production facilities and closing out this business.

The number three brand was Aylmer, with 9.3% of the market. This company sold mostly pectin jam and apple jelly. The former had far less fruit and far more pectin. Like Laura Secord and Kraft, Aylmer was a family brand spread over several product lines, including canned vegetables and soups. The typical consumers of this product were children and the value-conscious consumer.

E.D. Smith was fourth in the market, with 7.6% of the market. Like Laura Secord, typical E.D. Smith consumers were looking for a better product with a better flavor. The diet line of jams, introduced in 1978, accounted for 53% of E.D. Smith's market share figure. The diet jams contained no sugar but were sweetened with Sorbitol—a natural sweetener suitable for use in a low-sugar diet. The diet product line, including Apricot, Blueberry, Raspberry, and Strawberry/Rhubarb, had recently been reformulated using juice concentrates as sweeteners. The only competition in the "diet" line was Weight Watchers, but E.D. Smith's market share was 66% greater than Weight Watchers. Overall, E.D. Smith sold jam, diet jam, jelly, and a unique lemon spread that was especially popular in the Maritimes.

One quarter of the jam packaged at E.D. Smith used private labeling—the packaging of E.D. Smith product using different jars and labels. Typically, private labeling was done for a grocery store that had a house brand (e.g. Top Valu, Domino, President's Choice). In recent months, private labels had requested a change in the glass jars from the round shape used by E.D. Smith to a squarer shape similar to that used by Kraft. Kraft had never engaged in any private labeling.

Tied for fifth position was Welch's and Shiriff at 5.3% of the market each. Welch's competed in a narrow market niche—grape jams and jellies. In fact, Welch's was the number one seller in that niche. The Welch's family brand extended to grape juice and grape drinks in frozen concentrate, glass jar, and tetrabrick (cardboard box) forms. Shiriff was responsible for the "Good Morning" product line consisting of marmalades and mint jelly. In 1987, Shiriff Good Morning Marmalade was sold to Smucker's of the United States.

## The Situation at Hand

In 1983, E.D. Smith sold 250,000 cases of jam and jelly in Ontario—a $3.5 million business. By 1988, that figure had declined to 163,000 cases—an annual sales decrease of 11%. Without realizing it, E.D. Smith had been "milking a cash cow" because, at one time, E.D. Smith had been the market leader. The steady decline had been halted only twice during the last 20 years, with a relaunch of the product in 1974 and the introduction of diet jam in 1978. The relaunch consisted of a change in label design (emphasizing the fruit), accompanied by a couponing campaign on a newspaper/ magazine insert. In recent years, the jam line was given no advertising support as E.D. Smith had focused advertising dollars on other product opportunities.

During the recession of the early 1980s, E.D. Smith undertook cost-cutting moves which saw the amount of fruit used in the pure jam reduced to the minimum. Only a small quantity of fruit could be supplied by the E.D. Smith farms so, with purchasing budgets cut back, the quality of the imported fruit also suffered. A final cost-cutting measure saw the substitution of cheaper fructose sugar for glucose sugar—a savings of 36 cents per case of 12 jars. A side effect of using fructose in cooking the jam was a slight browning of the mixture. Glucose sugar not only improved the color of the mixture but improved the flavor as well.

The market was highly price-sensitive, and E.D. Smith was a price follower. Their strategy was simply to match Kraft's pricing policy, which had been a $2.19 price for the 250 ml container on the retail store shelf. This parity pricing policy was also followed by Laura Secord. Occasionally, to help move a volume of product, one of the three firms used a feature price of $1.99 at the retail store. However, it was not unusual to find all three brands moving to that price once one took the lead. E.D. Smith expected the regular price, set by Kraft, to increase soon as there had been no price increase during the previous three years.

Powell and Jessop were concerned with rumors/suggestions from wholesalers and retailers that the amount of shelf space devoted to jam, jelly, and marmalade in retail stores was about to be reduced. The argument made by the trade was that sales of these products had been declining and thus did not deserve as much exposure as they currently had. This meant either that the number of varieties carried by each store of each type of jam, jelly, and marmalade would be reduced or that some brand(s) would have to be eliminated. Both Aylmer and Laura Secord appeared to be vulnerable.

The approval in early 1989 of the Free Trade agreement between the United States and Canada would bring another set of problems. Smuckers, the number one producer of jam, jelly, and marmalade in the United States, had been trying to enter the Canadian market for some time. Though not prohibited from exporting product to Canada, Smuckers had not pursued the Canadian market because of perceived bureaucratic problems. With the Free Trade agreement in place, a new openness in terms of American investment in Canada, and the acquisition of Shiriff, Smuckers would likely succeed in opening a new Canadian operation.

## The Possibilities for E.D. Smith

Powell and Jessop could take a defensive posture and eliminate some of the varieties of jam and jelly produced by E.D Smith. Three varieties (strawberry, raspberry, and lemon spread) accounted for nearly 80% of the sales. These three could be kept in two sizes (250 ml and 500 ml). A different posture would be a flanking manoeuver that positioned the jam and jelly line as a product used in cooking/baking rather than as a breakfast spread. Jam could be used in cakes as a filling, in jelly rolls, on ice cream, over waffles, in tarts, in Christmas baking, as a sauce ingredient, or in muffins.

A different flanking manoeuver would focus on "peculiar" or unique flavors of specialty jams and jellies. At a current average price of $17.00 per case, a new flavor had to generate sales of at least 4,000 cases to break even. Coupled with this could be a price increase to establish a premium image. Though sales volume would likely fall, the profit margin on each jar would be greater and, presumably, profits could rise. A more offensive move would be to relaunch or even reformulate the product. In a relaunch, a company could change the packaging, the labeling, or the promotion of the product in such a way that it had a fresh, new image. Reformulation would mean a change in the basic product itself, either through a new jam recipe, a change in fruit, or a change in sugar. If a relaunch or reformulation were undertaken, how similar or dissimilar should the packaging, label, promotion, or recipe be to the other products on the market? Should the price be changed? Should E.D. Smith try to become the price leader?

Another offensive move would be to launch the product line in the United States. Informally, E.D. Smith liked to concentrate the firm's efforts within a 130 kilometre radius of Winona. Shipping costs increased price to a nearly non-competitive level outside of that area. Nonetheless, including the United States, 125 million people lived within a 130 kilometre radius of Winona.

Twenty years ago, E.D. Smith stopped selling Orange and Three Fruit marmalade. Perhaps the line could be revitalized. The ultimate offensive move would be the launch of a second E.D. Smith jam and jelly line. Like "New Coke" and "Classic Coke," E.D. Smith could have a regular and premium/ old-fashioned line of jams and jellies. These two lines would have different price points, packages, labels, and recipes and would require separate promotional support to build awareness and separation in the minds of the consumer.

## The Decision

The costing of the many options would have to come later. For now, Powell and Jessop were screening the alternatives from a strategic viewpoint. Equally of concern was the tactical plan that would have to be developed for any chosen strategies. Chris Powell loosened his tie and Lee Ann Jessop took off her jacket. There was plenty of work to be done.

## Questions

1. What are the threats and opportunities facing E.D. Smith?
2. What alternative courses of action are available?
3. What strategy would you recommend?

**EXHIBIT 1**
**Comparison of the Top Six Producers of Jam, Jelly, and Marmalade**

### Ontario Market

|  | Kraft | Laura Secord | Aylmer | E.D. Smith | Welch's | Shiriff |
|---|---|---|---|---|---|---|
| Market Share | 13.7% | 9.5% | 9.3% | 7.6% | 5.3% | 5.3% |
| Typical Retail Selling Price | $2.19 | $2.19 | $2.29 | $2.19 | $2.09 | $2.09 |
| Jam (250 ml) |  |  |  |  |  |  |
| Strawberry | X | X | X | X |  |  |
| Raspberry | X | X | X | X |  |  |
| Peach | X | X | X | X |  |  |
| Apricot | X | X |  | X |  |  |
| Cherry | X | X | X | X |  |  |
| Grape | X |  |  |  | X |  |

Continued on p. 535

(Exhibit 1 continued))

|  | Kraft | Laura Secord | Aylmer | E.D. Smith | Welch's | Shiriff |
|---|---|---|---|---|---|---|
| Damson Plum | X |  | X | X |  |  |
| Blueberry | X |  |  | X |  |  |
| Black Currant |  | X | X | X |  |  |
| Other Jam Flavors | Pineapple Red Currant | Kiwi Fieldberry | Red Plum | Seedless Raspberry |  |  |
| **Jelly (250 ml)** |  |  |  |  |  |  |
| Grape | X |  |  | X | X |  |
| Mint |  |  |  | X |  | X |
| Apple | X |  | X | X |  |  |
| Lemon Spread |  |  |  | X |  |  |
| Other Jelly Flavors | Raspberry Strawberry Red Currant Cherry Crabapple |  |  |  |  |  |
| **Marmalade** |  |  |  |  |  |  |
| Orange | X | X |  |  |  | X |
| Three Fruit | X | X |  |  |  | X |
| Pineapple |  |  |  |  |  | X |
| Seville Orange |  |  |  |  |  | X |
| Flavors Available in 500 ml jars | Raspberry Strawberry Apricot | Raspberry Strawberry Orange Marmalade |  | Raspberry Strawberry Lemon Spread | Grape Jam and Jelly | Orange Three Fruit |

* All of Aylmer's products were sold only in 500 ml jars.

# 5. NIEDNER LIMITED

Written by Robert M. MacGregor, Bishop's University

Mr. Robert Richardson, general manager of Niedner Limited, thought that 1986 would be the "break-through" year for sales of the firm, primarily because of a new product, the Snow Hose. Niedner Limited, located in Coaticook, Quebec, was the third largest manufacturer of industrial, municipal and fire hoses in North America. The Snow Hose, a recently developed product, was stronger, lighter, and more flexible than traditional hoses. Even at -60 degrees Fahrenheit, the Snow Hose remained flexible, which was a major benefit for ski hills where snow machines were used. Mr. Richardson believed the product was a winner because it fit the needs of the ski industry and related industries. The task was to determine a marketing strategy to capture the potential offered by the Snow Hose.

# The Company

Niedner Limited was a subsidiary of Wajax, a Canadian conglomerate with annual sales of $295 million and profits of $9,500,000 in 1985. Wajax Limited comprised a family of subsidiary companies engaged in the manufacturing, distribution, and servicing of industrial equipment and heavy machinery. These products were sold and serviced in the forestry, mining, steel, construction, oil and gas, utility, and municipal sectors. Each subsidiary operated as an autonomous profit center with its own management structure.

Wajax Limited expanded rapidly in the 1970s and early 1980s, acquiring a number of diverse companies. As a consequence, Wajax, through its subsidiaries, manufactured a wide range of products including Pitman cranes, digger derricks, and power line service vehicles. The distribution subsidiaries marketed and serviced products including off-highway trucks, conveyors for mines, paving finishers, Hyster vehicles, and underground drilling rigs.

Niedner Limited was purchased by Wajax in 1982 and became part of the manufacturing fire control group. This group manufactured and marketed a complete range of forest fire protection and municipal fire protection products. The product line included portable pumps, linen and synthetic hose, and a wide range of specialized accessory equipment including mobile slip-on tanks, back-pack pumps, helicopter accessories, and fire-retardant refilling stations. Approximately one-half of this group's sales were to municipal fire departments, forest product companies, and government agencies in North America. The other 50% of sales were to overseas customers for fire fighting equipment outside of North America. In the recent past, substantial orders were received from Senegal, Argentina, Australia, New Zealand, and Chile.

# Niedner Limited

After the purchase of Niedner Limited, Wajax invested in new equipment in order to produce a wide variety of hoses as efficiently as possible and to improve product quality. Recently, Niedner has introduced a number of new fire hoses to the market. New product features included weight reduction by as much as one-half, reduced storage space by one-third, flexibility, and an increased strength-to-weight ratio at extremely low temperatures. Neidner was the leading company in producing fire hoses for the Canadian market.

All of Neidner's products were manufactured at the Coaticook plant in Quebec. Robert Richardson was the general manager and was also responsible for the marketing of the product line. The plant employed 55 people who were involved in the various aspects of the hose-making operations.

One product feature that was recently developed was a new type of lining which has made it possible to manufacture exceptionally flexible, light, and compact space-saving hose. The new materials had extremely high strength allowing the hose manufacturer to reduce the thickness of the lining yielding the desirable characteristics of light weight and compactness without loss of physical properties of the hose. This led to a number of advantages for consumers (Exhibit 1).

# Snow Hose

As part of its continuing product development, Niedner had developed a lightweight municipal fire hose. This "superhose" had the following features: 100% more resistant (to abrasion) than the conventional rubber hose, 50% less weight than conventional rubber hoses; 33% less bulk; and at -60 degrees fahrenheit, the hose is still flexible. Mr. Richardson recognized that the product would fit the needs of ski slope operators who needed to "manufacture" snow for their hills. The product evolved into the line now called Snow Hose (see Exhibit 2). He decided to color the hose yellow so that it was fluorescent and, in fact, glowed at night and could be seen under snow. No other firm had even thought of this color innovation. With all the "super" benefits of the product, and with the new color feature, Mr. Richardson felt that the company had a winner on its hands.

The hose required a minimum pressure of 400 pounds per square inch to be operable. It was safely tested at 800 pounds per square inch, an important factor considering it would be used in close proximity to people on ski hills. Ski/snow-making equipment sometimes worked 24 hours non- stop, lay on rough terrain, and needed to have quick release and very durable couplings. All of these customer requirements were met by the Snow Hose.

The company named the first product The Snow Hose 1200. This referred to the fact that while the hose was rated at 800 pounds per square inch, the hose had an operating safety factor so that it would not burst under 1200 psi. Recent technological developments in snow-making equipment required even higher pressure and Niedner therefore introduced a superior Snow Hose to meet these requirements— Snow Hose 2000. This product had greater abrasion resistance and would not burst under 2000 psi. One of the first sales was made to the Canadian Olympic Committee for trial use on Mount Allan, site of the 1988 downhill Olympic skiing competition.

# Future Strategy

With the development of the Snow Hose completed, Mr. Richardson recognized that he would have to design a strategy for a market in which the company had virtually no experience. As a first step, he collected some data on ski resorts in North America. In total there were about 700 ski resorts in North America, of which approximately 320 used snow-making equipment. These were mainly in the eastern regions of North America.

In Canada, very few resorts in Alberta or British Columbia used snow-making equipment. However, as mentioned, Mount Allan was the main exception. The Olympic area would have 75 snow-making guns, costing $5 million. The Snow Hose was being used in the preparation stages. It was expected that the use of snow-making equipment could increase in the Western provinces and states in the next three to five years.

Snow-making equipment was far more prevalent in the Eastern provinces and states because the majority of skiers live in these areas and the potential for lost ski-days due to lack of snow was considerable. For example, the number of skier-days (the number of skiers times the number of days skiing was available) is over 5 million in Quebec, over 6 million in Ontario, and just under 4 million for all of Western Canada.

*[handwritten marginal notes:]* MAYBE A USE IN NORTHERN FIRE DEPTS FINLAND SWEDEN NORWAY NORTH-SEA DRILLING NORTHERN RUSSIA

*[handwritten marginal note:]* PROMOTE THIS ANGLE

As part of the initial marketing efforts for the Snow Hose, Mr. Richardson decided to demonstrate the hose at a trade show. In an early 1986 show in Nashville, the demonstration of the hose's durability and flexability greatly impressed the mainly American attendees. Pieces of the hose were immersed in dry ice to temperatures about minus 80 degrees fahrenheit, and then brought out. The hose was still flexible and operational.

Encouraged by the response, Mr. Richardson's task was to determine the most effective strategy to capture a large share of the snow-making hose market in North America. Specifically, he wanted to develop short, intermediate, and long-term strategies for the marketing of the Snow Hose. He knew, of course, that additional data would be required to develop such strategies but he did not want to get bogged down in a lot of paperwork for a product which had such obvious market appeal.

# Questions

1. What are Niedner's strengths, weaknesses, and objectives with regard to the Snow Hose?
2. What decisions are necessary for Mr. Richardson to make now?
3. What should Niedner do?

**EXHIBIT 1**
**Advantages of the New Niedner Lining**

*Reduces space requirements.* A rolled fire hose with the new Niedner lining occupies 30% less space than conventional hose.

*Low weight.* Due to the exceptional strength and processing methods, the amount of material used in the liner can be cut substantially, thus reducing the finished product weight as much as 50%.

*Very high tear strength and wear resistance.* Test results of the liner tear strength show the new Niedner liner is many times tougher than the conventional liners.

*Resistance to hydrolysis.* Results of elevated temperatures over long periods in hot air and water (NL 8103-80), showed no loss in physicals.

*Freedom from plasticizers.* No plasticizer in the New Niedner Liner to weaken adhesion or leach out to make lining stiff and crack.

*Resistance to microbial attack.* A two-year soil test was performed. The results show no change in physical properties. The resistance to aging and microbial attack was excellent.

**EXHIBIT 2**
**Promotion for the Snow Hose**

EXHIBIT 2

# NIEDNER
# SNOW HOSE®
## THE PROVEN PERFORMER

## The STANDARD By Which Others Are Judged

| | |
|---|---|
| LIGHTWEIGHT... | Half the weight of conventional hose used for snow-making. |
| FLEXIBLE... | Remains flexible down to −60°F. |
| HIGH WORKING PRESSURE... | Double jacket construction enables the use of higher working pressures while maintaining the margin of safety. |
| DURABLE... | Constructed of tough polyester yarns, designed for use under the most rugged conditions. |
| VISIBLE... | Day-Glo colour enhances visibility under all climatic conditions. |
| ENCAP®... | An exclusive NIEDNER process in which the polymer encapsulates each fibre to guarantee outstanding abrasion resistance and minimum moisture absorption. |
| COUPLING OPTIONS... | INTERNAL EXPANSION THREADED COUPLINGS CAM TYPE QUICK CONNECT COUPLINGS WITH SHANK |

### SPECIFICATIONS

| Catalog No. | Hose Size | Wt./50' Uncpld. | Test Press. | Burst Press. |
|---|---|---|---|---|
| 10015 | 1-1/2" | 10.5 lbs. | 800 PSI | 1200 PSI |
| 10020 | 2" | 13.0 lbs. | 800 PSI | 1200 PSI |
| 10025 | 2-1/2" | 17.5 lbs. | 800 PSI | 1200 PSI |
| 10030 | 3" | 23.0 lbs. | 800 PSI | 1200 PSI |
| 10040 | 4" | 36.0 lbs. | 500 PSI | 800 PSI |
| 10050 | 5" | 45.0 lbs. | 400 PSI | 500 PSI |

Developed and Manufactured by

## Ⓝ NIEDNER LIMITED
Distributed by

ALTHOUGH EACH LENGTH OF NIEDNER SNOW HOSE® IS HYDROSTATICALLY TESTED, THE INDICATED TEST PRESSURE APPLIES TO UNCOUPLED HOSE ONLY. TEST RATING MAY BE LOWER DEPENDING ON TYPE AND METHOD OF COUPLING ATTACHMENT. CAM TYPE COUPLINGS ARE RATED FOR SUBSTANTIALLY LOWER WORKING PRESSURES THAN HOSE. UNDER NORMAL CONDITIONS, THE WORKING PRESSURE IS CONSIDERED TO BE 50% OF THE TEST PRESSURE.

SNOW HOSE® and ENCAP® are the registered trademarks of Niedner Limited.          Printed in Canada

# 6. FAMILY SERVICE AGENCY

The Family Service Agency (FSA) was established in 1960 as a nonprofit organization. In 1970 the agency obtained United Appeal funding for the addition of a family counseling program. Since that time, the agency has expanded its services to include counseling, family-life education, and home health care.

In the summer of 1990, Ann Marek, director of community affairs, became concerned about the community's lack of knowledge regarding the available services of the agency. However, before embarking on an awareness campaign, she felt it necessary to assess the community's attitudes and perceptions toward FSA as well as attitudes and perceptions toward other agencies offering similar services.

Marek arranged for a local graduate student in marketing to assist with the project. Since the home health market was an important component of FSA's services, the project would involve a market research survey of the general public with emphasis on home health services. Marek also felt it was important to survey physicians because many of FSA's home health clients were referred by their doctors.

Telephone interviewing yielded 184 completed interviews from a random sample of 400 names drawn from the residence pages of the telephone directory. Respondents were first asked how they would rate the services provided by voluntary organizations in general. Ratings were on a scale of 1 to 5: 5 being "excellent" and 1 being "very poor." The results are shown in Exhibit 1.

Respondents were then asked if they were aware of several specific organizations. Awareness did not mean knowledge of services—only that respondents were aware of the organization's existence. Respondents were then asked to rate (on a scale of 1 to 5) the overall performance of all organizations of which they were aware. The results are shown in Exhibit 2. The 75 respondents aware of FSA were also asked what they considered to be the most important criterion in selecting a provider of counseling, home health, and educational services. The results are shown in Exhibit 3.

Telephone interviewing produced 102 completed interviews from a random list of 350 physicians. Each doctor was asked first to rate the efforts of home health organizations in general (on a scale of 1 to 5). The mean response was 3.82, with 80 "no responses."

Physicians were then asked if they were aware of several specific organizations. If aware of an organization, he or she was also asked to rate the performance of that organization. The results are shown in Exhibit 4.

The interviewer noted that although several doctors had heard of an organization, they did not know enough about it to rate it. Others, however, said that although they knew of an organization and had actually referred patients to it, they were unable to give a rating because they did not know how well the organization had served the patients.

Doctors were also asked to which home health organizations they usually referred their patients. Of the 102 physicians interviewed, 15 reported that they never referred to home health agencies. Of the remaining 87, 25 could not name any specific agency. Several of these 25 stated that they did not make the actual referral—that although they prescribed the needed services, a nurse or the hospital discharge planner actually selected the provider.

# Questions

1. How does the general public view the Family Service Agency and other agencies?
2. What are the marketing implications of Exhibit 3?
3. How do physicians view the Family Service Agency and other similar agencies?
4. What is the importance of the discrepancy between the number of physicians who were aware of an organization and the number who rated the organization?
5. What are the marketing implications of the 25 doctors who could not name the agency or agencies to which their patients were referred?
6. What recommendations would you make to the Family Service Agency?

**Source:** Based on a case written by Donna Legg.

**EXHIBIT 1**
**Overall Rating of Voluntary Organizations**

| Rating | Number |
|---|---|
| Excellent (5) | 38 |
| Good (4) | 87 |
| Fair (3) | 14 |
| Poor (2) | 1 |
| Very Poor (1) | 1 |
| No Rating | 43 |

Mean = 4.13
Standard deviation = .781

**EXHIBIT 2**
**Awareness and Ratings of Specific Organizations**

| Organization | Number Aware | Number Rated | Mean Rating |
|---|---|---|---|
| United Appeal | 160 | 128 | 3.70 |
| Home Health Services | 36 | 23 | 4.00 |
| Crisis Intervention | 118 | 79 | 3.84 |
| Family Service Agency | 75 | 48 | 3.90 |
| Meals on Wheels | 170 | 138 | 4.59 |
| Parenting Guidance Center | 100 | 69 | 4.12 |
| Visiting Nurses Assoc. | 107 | 72 | 4.31 |
| Mental Health/Mental Retardation | 154 | 108 | 4.11 |
| Home Care | 69 | 41 | 3.93 |

**EXHIBIT 3**
**Criteria for Selecting Provider of Services**

| Criteria | Number of Responses |
|---|---|
| Quality | 5 |
| Accreditation | 3 |
| Cost | 5 |
| Recommendations* | 23 |
| Image/reputation | 8 |
| Credentials/knowledge of staff | 9 |
| Supportive staff | 1 |
| Success rate | 2 |
| Needs/benefits | 2 |
| Tradition | 1 |
| Confidentiality | 1 |
| Communication | 1 |
| Christian organization | 1 |
| Don't know | 13 |

* Many respondents specified recommendations from doctors, ministers, school counsellors, friends, and relatives.

**EXHIBIT 4**
**Physicians' Awareness and Ratings of Specific Organizations**

| Organization | Number Aware | Number Rated | Mean Rating |
|---|---|---|---|
| United Appeal | 94 | 75 | 3.68 |
| Home Health Services | 52 | 35 | 3.86 |
| Crisis Intervention | 65 | 35 | 4.03 |
| Family Service Agency | 50 | 38 | 3.71 |
| Meals on Wheels | 89 | 68 | 4.25 |
| Parenting Guidance Center | 50 | 28 | 4.00 |
| Visiting Nurses Assoc. | 78 | 61 | 3.95 |
| Mental Health/Mental Retardation | 91 | 64 | 3.63 |
| Home Care | 57 | 41 | 3.76 |

# 7. ATLANTIC JEANS

Written by Arlene Bennett, Wilfrid Laurier University

Ms. Anne Jackson, the recently hired marketing manager for Atlantic Jeans, had just been given her first assignment. The president had met with her and made the following comments:

> Our company is in trouble. We've been using a strategy of mass marketing for our jeans and I think we should consider a change. We've been losing sales and market share for the last three years. I want you to assess the market and prepare a report outlining how we should or could segment the market and the implications for Atlantic Jeans of using a differentiated marketing strategy. As well, give me a proposal for a marketing mix that is based on the way you think the market should be segmented.

The first thing Ms. Jackson did was to look over her notes from the marketing course she had taken last year. She remembered that the instructor had provided a diagram which illustrated how a firm might approach segmenting, targeting, and positioning. She studied the diagram (Figure 1) and then started collecting information.

Then Ms. Jackson studied the marketing plan that had been used to support the company's mass marketing strategy. Atlantic currently produced a line of basic, durable blue jeans that appealed to a wide range of consumers. The jeans were priced within the typical retail price range for jeans—$25 to $40. The cost of goods for the line was approximately 60% of factory sales, and the promotion budget had fluctuated between $300,000 and $700,000 over the past five years.

Ms. Jackson then read published articles on the blue jean market. From various sources, including *Canadian Business*, *Financial Post*, *Business Week*, *Financial Times*, and *Report on Business*, she jotted down the following information:

- None of the major manufacturers, including Atlantic, Levi's, GWG, Lees and Blue Bell, had done well in the last two years because of changing demographics and intense competition from smaller jean manufacturers.
- Blue Bell Canada had recently launched a campaign in major urban markets for its Wrangler 909 jeans. The budget for only one part of the campaign, a one-month outdoor poster program, was $300,000. The target was adults in the 18-49 age group, and the emphasis was placed on form-fitting style. This was a change from Blue Bell's previous approach with Wrangler, which had been known for their wide-leg, western style and fit.
- Pantorama, a Montreal-based retailer, makes and sells Roberto jeans. They recently announced a major campaign to sell Roberto jeans across Canada, focusing on the youth market and emphasizing a young, trendy, and sexy image.
- Lee Canada did a market study and found that a Lee target market—women, aged 15 to 25—liked Lee jeans for quality but found them unexciting. Lee responded by designing a new line that included white and pastel Lees in non-blue jean materials such as twill and chambray. To promote the line, $1 million was spent on advertising, including billboards, subway posters, and a TV campaign.

Ms. Jackson's next step was to collect demographic data from Statistics Canada and other sources. She then prepared a series of tables (1 to 4). With this information she started writing the report. She knew she would have to make some assumptions but it was important to get the job done.

# Questions

1. What further information would you want before preparing the report?
2. Using the existing information, assume you are Ms. Jackson and prepare the report.

**Figure 1**
**Framework for Segmentation, Targeting, and Positioning**

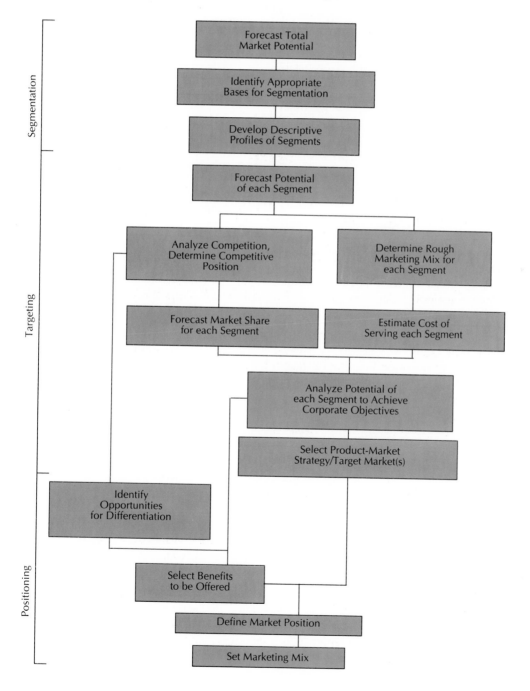

**TABLE 1**
**Projected Population by Province, 1991**
**(thousands of persons)**

| | |
|---|---:|
| Total, Canada | 26,610 |
| Newfoundland | 639 |
| Prince Edward Island | 133 |
| Nova Scotia | 911 |
| New Brunswick | 758 |
| Quebec | 6,786 |
| Ontario | 9,627 |
| Manitoba | 1,121 |
| Saskatchewan | 1,095 |
| Alberta | 2,374 |
| British Columbia | 3,091 |
| Yukon | 22 |
| Northwest Territories | 53 |

**Source:** Statistics Canada

**TABLE 2**
**Projected Population by Age Group and Sex, 1991**
**(thousands of persons)**

| Age | Male | Female |
|---|---:|---:|
| Total, Canada | 13,150 | 13,460 |
| Under 15 years | 2,757 | 2,619 |
| 15 - 19 | 925 | 879 |
| 20 - 24 | 1,008 | 964 |
| 25 - 29 | 1,212 | 1,171 |
| 30 - 34 | 1,196 | 1,199 |
| 35 - 39 | 1,087 | 1,105 |
| 40 - 44 | 1,007 | 1,016 |
| 45 - 49 | 800 | 802 |
| 50 - 54 | 648 | 657 |
| 55 - 59 | 599 | 613 |
| 60 - 64 | 569 | 604 |
| 65 and over | 1,342 | 1,831 |

**Source:** Statistics Canada

**TABLE 3**
**Income Distribution, 1986**

| Income Range | Number of People (000's) |
|---|---|
| Under $10,000 | 4,850 |
| $10,000 - 20,000 | 4,500 |
| $20,000 - 30,000 | 3,300 |
| $30,000 - 40,000 | 1,700 |
| $40,000 - 50,000 | 750 |
| $50,000 - 100,000 | 640 |
| Over $100,000 | 110 |
| Total | 15,800 |

**Source:** Woods Gordon and Revenue Canada (based on all tax returns)

**TABLE 4**
**Canadian Lifestyles**

| Lifestyle Category | % All Households |
|---|---|
| **Urban** | |
| Affluent | 1 |
| Upscale | 7 |
| Middle and Upper Middle Class | 16 |
| Working (Lower Middle) Class | 15 |
| Lower Class | 7 |
| Young Singles | 4 |
| Young Couples | 4 |
| Empty Nesters | 9 |
| Old and Retired | 4 |
| Ethnic | 3 |
| **Non-Urban** | |
| Upscale and Middle Class | 11 |
| Working and Lower Class | 16 |
| Farming | 3 |

**Source:** Compusearch Lifestyles Analysis

**Note:** There are approximately 9.3 million households in Canada. The lifestyle categories are determined by dividing the population into groups with shared attitudes and similar buying patterns.

# 8. Canadian Population and Household Trends

An important aspect of marketing is to determine the future implications of population and household trends. The three tables that follow provide past and future data on the Canadian population by age group, by geographic area, and by household.

## Questions

1. Analyze the tables and prepare a discussion of the marketing implications that are likely to occur in the decade from 1986 to 1996.

2. Contrast these changes with those that occurred in the decade from 1976 to 1986.

**TABLE 1**
**Population, Actual and Projected By Age Group**
**1951-2006 (Thousands)**

| Year | Population | Under 9 | 10-19 | 20-34 | 35-49 | 50-64 | 65 & Over |
|------|-----------|---------|-------|-------|-------|-------|-----------|
| Actual | | | | | | | |
| 1951 | 14,010 | 3,120 | 2,190 | 3,260 | 2,610 | 1,740 | 1,090 |
| 1956 | 16,080 | 3,790 | 2,600 | 3,540 | 3,020 | 1,890 | 1,240 |
| 1961 | 18,240 | 4,340 | 3,290 | 3,670 | 3,400 | 2,150 | 1,390 |
| 1966 | 20,020 | 4,500 | 3,930 | 3,950 | 3,630 | 2,470 | 1,540 |
| 1971 | 21,570 | 4,070 | 4,420 | 4,790 | 3,760 | 2,780 | 1,750 |
| 1976 | 22,990 | 3,620 | 4,620 | 5,760 | 3,850 | 3,140 | 2,000 |
| 1981 | 24,340 | 3,560 | 4,240 | 6,560 | 4,220 | 3,400 | 2,360 |
| 1986 | 25,600 | 3,630 | 3,730 | 6,940 | 4,980 | 3,590 | 2,730 |
| Projections | | | | | | | |
| 1991 | 26,610 | 3,570 | 3,610 | 6,750 | 5,820 | 3,690 | 3,170 |
| 1996 | 27,350 | 3,260 | 3,680 | 6,240 | 6,560 | 4,030 | 3,580 |
| 2001 | 27,820 | 2,880 | 3,620 | 5,770 | 6,910 | 4,760 | 3,880 |
| 2006 | 28,090 | 2,670 | 3,310 | 5,680 | 6,740 | 5,550 | 4,410 |

**Source:** *Marketing Research Handbook*, Statistics Canada, Catalogue 63-224, various years. Projections based on moderate fertility rates, average net international migration, and a migration flow within Canada that partially reflects the late 1960s pattern.

**TABLE 2**
**Population, Actual and Projected By Geographic Area**
**1951-2006 (Thousands)**

| Year | Total Population | Maritime Provinces | Quebec | Ontario | Prairie Provinces | B.C. & Yukon/NWT |
|------|-----------------|--------------------|--------|---------|-------------------|------------------|
| Actual | | | | | | |
| 1951 | 14,010 | 1,620 | 4,050 | 4,600 | 2,550 | 1,190 |
| 1956 | 16,080 | 1,760 | 4,630 | 5,410 | 2,850 | 1,430 |
| 1961 | 18,240 | 1,900 | 5,260 | 6,230 | 3,180 | 1,670 |
| 1966 | 20,020 | 1,980 | 5,780 | 6,960 | 3,380 | 1,920 |
| 1971 | 21,570 | 2,060 | 6,030 | 7,700 | 3,540 | 2,240 |
| 1976 | 22,990 | 2,180 | 6,240 | 8,260 | 3,780 | 2,530 |
| 1981 | 24,340 | 2,230 | 6,440 | 8,630 | 4,230 | 2,810 |
| 1986 | 25,600 | 2,320 | 6,630 | 9,110 | 4,510 | 3,030 |
| Projections | | | | | | |
| 1991 | 26,610 | 2,440 | 6,790 | 9,620 | 4,590 | 3,170 |
| 1996 | 27,350 | 2,520 | 6,880 | 9,950 | 4,730 | 3,270 |
| 2001 | 27,820 | 2,590 | 6,900 | 10,170 | 4,830 | 3,330 |
| 2006 | 28,090 | 2,630 | 6,890 | 10,280 | 4,910 | 3,380 |

**Source:** *Marketing Research Handbook*, Statistics Canada, Catalogue 63-224, various years. Projections based on moderate fertility rates, average net international migration, and a migration flow within Canada that partially reflects the late 1960s pattern.

**TABLE 3**
**Households, Actual and Projected By Geographic Area**
**1966-2001 (Thousands)**

| Year | Total Households | Maritime Provinces | Quebec | Ontario | Prairie Provinces | B.C. and Yukon/NWT |
|------|------------------|--------------------|--------|---------|-------------------|--------------------|
| Actual | | | | | | |
| 1966 | 5,180 | 450 | 1,390 | 1,880 | 910 | 550 |
| 1971 | 6,030 | 500 | 1,600 | 2,230 | 1,020 | 680 |
| 1976 | 7,170 | 600 | 1,900 | 2,640 | 1,190 | 840 |
| 1981 | 8,280 | 670 | 2,170 | 2,970 | 1,450 | 1,020 |
| 1986 | 9,220 | 750 | 2,340 | 3,430 | 1,590 | 1,110 |
| Projections | | | | | | |
| 1991 | 10,110 | 820 | 2,510 | 3,780 | 1,760 | 1,240 |
| 1996 | 10,680 | 860 | 2,590 | 4,020 | 1,870 | 1,340 |
| 2001 | 11,190 | 900 | 2,650 | 4,230 | 1,980 | 1,430 |

**Source:** *Marketing Research Handbook*, Statistics Canada, Catalogue 63-224, various years. Projections based on moderate fertility rates, average net international migration, and a migration flow within Canada that partially reflects the late 1960s pattern.

**Note:** Households include single-detached, single-attached, apartments and flats, and mobile homes.

# 9. NUTRASWEET: CREATIVE MARKETING OR ANTI-COMPETITIVE BEHAVIOR?

NutraSweet, the manufacturer of the artificial sweetener, aspartame, is in the middle of a sticky situation. It must defend its position in the $25 million Canadian artificial sweetener market to a Federal Competition Tribunal. The company faces allegations of aggressive anti-competitive business practices, which have allowed only one competitor to crack the Canadian market since NutraSweet's patent expired in 1987.

Marketing experts argue that the company has legitimately achieved its dominant position through years of superior marketing performance. Faced with patent expiration, competition from aspartame producers in Europe and Asia and the threat of new sweeteners arriving on the market, NutraSweet has engaged in a variety of marketing tactics to protect its business. The case is the latest battle in an ongoing war for global market share in aspartame, a key ingredient in the fast-growing and lucrative diet-food market.

The outcome of the court battle will set a precedent as to how the Canadian marketplace defines superior marketing performance versus unfair competition.

## The Company

Thirty years ago a researcher named G.D. Searle discovered the miracle substance "aspartame." The new product tasted like sugar, was low in calories, and was safe to eat and drink. It is 200 times sweeter than sugar, does not cause cavities, and adds just 1.2 calories to a can of diet cola, compared with 122 calories in a regular cola. In 1983, aspartame was approved by the Federal Drug Administration in the United States and Searle began its search for the most effective way to market the product to commercial food and beverage producers. Because industrial demand is derived from consumer demand for products that contain aspartame, Searle had to create brand awareness and preference among final consumers. Searle came up with a "branded ingredient" strategy. Instead of selling aspartame at the commercial level, Searle developed the brand name NutraSweet and launched a marketing campaign directed at the ultimate consumer, even though they could not directly buy the product.

The program was initiated with a direct mail campaign in which Searle's objective was to educate consumers. Searle mailed out thousands of gumballs sweetened with NutraSweet along with letters explaining that the product was low in calories, did not promote tooth decay, and contained nothing artificial. At the same time, Searle spent millions of dollars on advertising proclaiming that: "You can't buy it, but you're going to love it."

A simple red swirl became the logo on packaging that distinguished brands containing 100% NutraSweet. Success was achieved when Coca-Cola, Quaker, Kool-Aid, and others began to introduce products with NutraSweet. Demand actually increased for many flat product categories, such as powdered soft drinks and iced tea mixes.

The "branded ingredient" strategy has brought the company sweet success, with a dominant 95% share of the Canadian aspartame market, in light of the continual threat from European and Asian competitors and the risk of new sweetener products.

The biggest use of aspartame is the fast-growing diet soda market, in which less than $.01 of an $.80 can of pop covers the cost of aspartame. The two largest customers in this market are Coke and Pepsi.

# The Competition

Since the loss of its regulatory patent protection in 1987, NutraSweet has managed to keep a tight lock on the Canadian aspartame market, allowing its competitors only five percent of total sales. The anti-competitive conduct that NutraSweet is being charged with actually reflects the inability of other aspartame producers to crack NutraSweet's hold on the market.

Theoretically, many companies have the ability to compete with NutraSweet in Canada (although no company, including NutraSweet, manufactures the sweetener here) because their price is better and there is little difference in quality.

NutraSweet's primary competition comes from a Japanese-based producer, Tosoh Canada Ltd., which supplies three percent of the Canadian market. Tosoh instigated the investigation against NutraSweet because of the company's inability to further penetrate the Canadian market.

# The Court Battle

The primary hurdle faced by the competition is that the companies purchasing aspartame from NutraSweet display the company's swirl logo on their products. A change in suppliers would mean a costly change in packaging. NutraSweet argues that getting companies to display the trademark on products has been a significant marketing achievement that has been obtained fairly.

NutraSweet must also answer to allegations of unfair contract commitments, including granting trademark display allowances to customers, tied selling, volume discounts, and guaranteed lowest-price clauses in supply agreements.

It is alleged that NutraSweet further ensured its dominance in the market by signing a number of long-term exclusive supply contracts, prior to the expiry of the Canadian patent, with companies such as Coke and Pepsi, who are responsible for 60% of aspartame purchases.

The case against NutraSweet also raises questions about the principal purpose of competition legislation, about whether the objective is to provide a market for a competitor or the best prices and products to consumers. Among the allegations against NutraSweet are that prices in Canada have been set at such a low level that it is impractical for prospective competitors to enter the market. It has been suggested that prices charged to certain customers have been less that NutraSweet's costs, with the losses being subsidized from large profits in markets such as the United States, where NutraSweet is protected by patent regulation until 1992. The price of NutraSweet dropped to $50-75/kg. (depending on the customer) from $200/kg. when it was first introduced in 1981.

NutraSweet argues that they have been responding to increasing competitive pressure since patent rights have ceased to control the market. NutraSweet also argues that having invented the product and singlehandedly created a worldwide market for it, they have mastered aspects of the business that competitors cannot copy. The company stated: "We're not selling a molecule. We are selling a whole package of value to our customers and our customers' customers. NutraSweet's goal is to be able to keep customers even if a competitor offered sweetener for free."

## The Decision

In the end, the tribunal will have to decide whether NutraSweet is simply a clever, aggressive marketer that bested the competition fairly and squarely, or whether, in its zeal to hang on to the benefits that accompanied the invention of this low-calorie chemical, it simply went too far, too fast.

## Question

1. Is NutraSweet involved in creative marketing or anti-competitive behavior?

**Sources:** Brenda Dalglish, "The Test of Competition," *Maclean's,* July 16, 1990, pp. 30-32; "How Sweet It Is," *Management Review*, June 1985, p. 8; and Drew Fagan, "NutraSweet Case a Chance for Law to Show Its Teeth," *Globe and Mail*, January 22, 1990, p. B1.

# 10. ENVIRONMENTAL MONITORING LIMITED

On Earth Day, April 22, 1990, millions of people from 140 countries around the world expressed their concern about the environment by marching, speaking, and protesting. In one sense, it was a day of celebration for environmentalists who viewed the massive response to Earth Day as a major step forward in saving the planet from environmental destruction.

Howard Subins, the head of Environmental Monitoring Limited (EML), had been among the participants who marched in downtown Vancouver on Earth Day. EML, a non-profit organization, had recently been formed with two objectives in mind: (1) to encourage consumers to purchase environmentally friendly products, and (2) to encourage companies to produce and market these products. On April 22nd and in the weeks that followed, Mr. Subins was very optimistic as he felt that EML's objectives could be accomplished because of the increased public awareness and concern about the environment.

Seven months later, in November 1990, Mr. Subins was less optimistic as he read two items that appeared in the Vancouver *Sun*. The first, an ad from a paint manufacturer, claimed that consumers could help "Save the Environment" by purchasing its toxic-free paints. Mr. Subins was dismayed because the claim was exaggerated and toxic-free paints had been available for four years. He saw this as the latest example of a company jumping on the environmental bandwagon without any substantial change in their operations. The second item reported the results of a recent Canada-wide consumer survey; only seven percent of respondents listed the environment as the most important problem Canada faced, well behind the percentage who listed economic concerns and the goods and services tax. In a similar survey conducted one year earlier, 17% of respondents cited the environment as the most important issue. These two examples illustrated the problems facing his organization—marketers making dubious environmental claims and the apparent lack of consistent commitment of consumers to environmental issues. "Perhaps," Mr. Subins thought, "EML's strategy should be reviewed. In spite of these incidents, we have to determine effective ways of getting all Canadians, be they manufacturers, retailers, or consumers, to act in a more environmentally responsible manner." He then began preparing a memo to present to EML's board members to discuss the future direction of the organization.

## The Environmental Crisis

The chairman of the 1987 United Nations World Commission on Environment and Development offered an interesting two-choice scenario for the future. Ms. Brundtland stated that the world had to find sustainable forms of development or face environmental collapse. Simply put, the present economic course cannot be continued as it will result in an environmental catastrophe. Some examples of the current crisis are:

- The 25% of the world's population that lives in industrialized nations consumes 75% of the world's energy. Much of the carbon dioxide in the atmosphere comes from burning fossil fuels that provide this energy. Carbon dioxide is a major cause of the "greenhouse effect" (the warming of the world's climate). Canadians use more energy per capita than any other nation in the world and, among developed countries, Canada ranks first in energy use per unit of economic output. On average, every Canadian "produces" 15 tonnes of carbon dioxide each year.
- Western nations, the developed countries, are consumption-intensive whereas developing nations are not. For example, the per capita yearly consumption of paper is 120 kilograms in Western countries, 8 kilograms in developing countries. The per capita yearly consumption of steel is 450 kilograms in Western countries, 48 kilograms in developing countries.
- The average Canadian produces almost two kg of solid waste per day, more than any other citizen in the world, yet less than ten percent of Canada's solid waste is recycled.
- A Canadian family of five produces, on average, more than 2,000 litres of waste water each day.

The consequences of these activities are a host of environmental problems. On a collective basis, the citizens of the world are responsible. However, on a per capita basis, Canadians are major contributors to the greenhouse effect, acid rain, and air and water pollution. If Canadians, and other high per capita "contributors" do not change their consumption behavior, future generations will live in a dramatically different environment.

## Consumer Response

Today, most Canadians are aware that the world is facing an environmental crisis and when asked directly (e.g., "Are you concerned about the environment?"), they express concern. For some Canadians the concern has led to action, either individually or through organizations. Groups including Pollution Probe and the Consumers Association of Canada have had an impact in addressing environmental problems. New laws governing emission standards, product contents, and hazardous wastes have been enacted, often as a result of pressure from organized groups. Consumer response on an individual basis is also evident. A recycling program in Ontario, called the "Blue Box" program, is regarded as one of the best and largest in North America. About 1.5 million households in Ontario have been given a heavy-duty plastic box for regular pickup of cans, glass bottles, plastic soft-drink bottles, and newspapers. It is estimated that 80% to 90% of all households within the program boundaries have participated in the program.

However, it appears that many Canadians, while willing to express their concern, are not willing to purchase environmentally friendly products if it costs them money. That is, if faced with the choice of purchasing a higher-priced "friendly" product versus a lower-priced "regular" product, most Canadians choose the lower priced product. Groups and organizations such as EML were continually debating the most effective methods for getting more Canadians to act in an environmentally responsible manner.

## Business Response

Many business firms had responded to the environmental situation by introducing new products, modifying old products, and changing their marketing strategy. Consider the following examples:

- In July 1989, Loblaws launched the Green product line, a group of environmentally friendly products. In the first year, Loblaws sold $60 million worth of Green products.
- In September 1989, Procter & Gamble launched six of their products (e.g., Tide) in environpaks, environmentally compatible packages. One year later, approximately 25% of the sales of these products were in the new packages.
- In Fall 1989, Home Hardware Stores began marketing 40 of its low- toxicity paints and household cleaners under its new Earth Care logo.
- In early 1990, Eveready Canada began promoting its Energizer batteries as "environmentally safer."

While some people might be pleased with the above efforts, critics have made the following points:

- Environmentalists claim that many "green" labels are little more than promotion tools for products, from batteries to plastic bags, that may or may not be environmentally safe. Julia Langer, executive director of the Ottawa-based Canadian chapter of the Friends of the Earth has said: "Overconsumption got us into this mess. Switching brands is not going to solve it."
- Loblaws' Green line campaign has been dogged by controversy almost from its start. Colin Isaacs, executive director of the Toronto- based environmental group Pollution Probe, resigned after many associates complained of the organization's endorsement of several Loblaw's products, including a disposable diaper. Most environmental advocates contend that only cloth diapers are truly less harmful to the environment. Many environmental activists have complained that Loblaw's

Green line includes products devoid of any environmental benefit whatsoever, such as toxic cleaners carrying the Green label simply because they contain bitter-tasting additives meant to discourage children from swallowing them. Jenny Hillard, who chairs the Ottawa-based Consumers' Association of Canada environmental committee, has said "to call a product like that 'green' is the ultimate in marketing gall."

- With respect to Eveready's claims, Greenpeace campaigner Gordon Perks said that simply cutting down on mercury—which has been linked to nervous disorders in humans, and is one of several toxic metals used in batteries—does not make Eveready's product substantially safer.

One article on business and the environment captured the problem in the following quote:

> Corporate greening is a response to popular demand for ecologically benign products. People recognize that environmental problems are an increasing tax burden and health hazard and want to stop further pollution. Yet consumers lack the information to determine whether many products or their manufacturers are, in fact, "environmentally friendly."

> A market with strong demand for ecologically safe products, but little information, allows business to define "environmentally friendly" as synonymous with their goods. It's cheaper, after all, to hawk the same old products under green labels than to actually improve them.

Federal government officials at Consumer and Corporate Affairs have questioned whether biodegradable plastics are any better than regular plastics; whether disposable styrofoam plates, labeled as environmentally friendly, will not harm the Earth simply because they don't contain ozone- depleting CFCs (but still add to our garbage heaps); and whether environmentally friendly disposable diapers are much of an improvement over other disposables.

As Jacob Heilik, a senior policy officer with Consumer and Corporate Affairs, says: "We don't like the expression 'environmentally friendly' ... Generally the technical claims are true, but in the context of saving the environment, we're not sure if they're entirely useful for the consumer..."

"In my mind as a consumer, I believe I'm being misled to a certain extent by marketers who are looking to sell their products."

## The Task

EML had been formed in early 1989 by a group of concerned citizens and businesses with the broad mandate of collecting and disseminating information that would encourage both consumers and businesses to act in an environmentally responsible manner. To date, Mr. Subins had focused the efforts of EML on the positive aspects of the situation. For example, EML assisted in surveys which polled Canadians on their interest in the environmental issues and provided the results to newspapers. As well, EML provided numerous press releases of stories of consumers who had acted in ways to improve the environment. For example, Mr. Subins sent out a press release telling the story of a group of young people who had volunteered to spend their summer planting trees in an area that had been ravaged by a forest fire.

The idea was that businesses would recognize the opportunities of manufacturing and marketing products to an ever-growing environmentally- concerned segment of the population. As well, Mr. Subins had provided a monthly press release (which a number of newspapers used) that noted companies that had introduced environmentally friendly products. For example, in the latest press release, EML had identified five companies that had launched environmentally friendly products.

Now Mr. Subins wondered whether a different approach was called for. He wondered whether EML should continue just reporting "positive" news or whether EML should take more of a policing role. In this regard, he noted four possible options that EML could consider:

- The establishment of an EML "Seal of Approval" for products that were truly environmentally friendly. Mr. Subins had access to testing laboratories and experts in a number of areas who could evaluate the total environmental impact of products. The idea would be to evaluate products and those that "passed the test" would be given the EML Seal of Approval which companies could use in advertising their brands.
- The establishment of an environmentally responsible rating score for companies. Again, experts would evaluate company actions with respect to the environment. Those companies that had taken steps toward improving the environment and showed a genuine corporate concern for the environment would be given the EML Corporate Environmental Star Award, which they could use on their products.
- The establishment of a monitoring system that would rate new "friendly" products on the degree to which these products were, in fact, environmentally friendly. The ratings, from very negative (e.g., 0, not friendly) to very positive (e.g., 10, extremely friendly), would be provided to newspapers, or to anyone who asked for them. With this alternative, some firms would face negative ratings.
- A similar alternative would be to rate companies in the same manner on a scale from very negative to very positive and, again, provide the information to newspapers.

Mr. Subins was also wondering what could be done to encourage consumers to believe and act in an environmentally responsible manner. No immediate ideas came to mind but he wanted something to present to the board members at the next meeting.

# Questions

1. What strategies could EML pursue to encourage Canadians to act in an environmentally responsible manner?

2. Should EML adopt a strategy of "policing" versus "information/education" with respect to the actions of Canadian companies?

**Sources include:** Marina Strauss, "Ottawa Takes a Look at Claims of Environmental Friendliness," *Globe and Mail*, April 26, 1990, p. B6; Tom O'Brien, "What's Really Behind Those Green Labels?" *Globe and Mail*, January 28, 1990, p. A17; and David Todd, "Catering to New Concerns," *Maclean's*, April 30, 1990, pp. 52-53.

# 11. LOCTITE CANADA

When studying organizational markets, it is helpful to consider all the goods and services that businesses must buy in order to provide the consumers with products they want. Manufacturers buy from hundreds of suppliers—most of whom are little known to the consumers who buy the final product. Loctite Canada is one such organization.

Loctite Canada, a wholly-owned subsidiary of the U.S. corporation Loctite, is a manufacturer of adhesives and sealants, and related specialty chemicals. Loctite is the world's major manufacturer of anaerobic and cynocrylate adhesives and sealants, with annual sales of over $415 million. Canadian sales are just under $13 million. Recently, sales in both countries have grown by 25% per year. Consumers frequently use or own products that are held together by a Loctite product. Loctite adhesives are used in several sectors of the garment industry, including both clothing and shoes. Consumers may also buy Loctite products for their own use, including super glues such as "Glue Stick" and "Quick Gel" as well as several brands of household cement.

The original Loctite "anaerobic" adhesive was developed by Professor Vernon Krieble of Trinity College in 1953. This new product competed with the more traditional means of bonding materials, such as screws, nuts and bolts, riveting, and welding. Since that time, industrial designers and engineers have increasingly integrated Loctite products into thousands of production lines to assemble parts more quickly and efficiently. Products assembled with adhesives are lighter, safer, more reliable, and less costly. Loctite products are also used by maintenance workers to prevent mechanical parts from loosening, leaking, and wearing. Loctite adhesives and sealants ensure dependability and longer machine life.

Some specific Loctite industrial products and their uses include:

- Threadlocker adhesives: to prevent nuts, bolts, and screws from loosening because of shock and vibration.
- Pipe sealants: to prevent leakage from vibration loosening and extreme temperatures or pressure.
- Engineering adhesives: for assembly operations that require strong, durable adhesives that cure quickly at room temperature.
- Maintenance products: to maintain, repair, and overhaul machinery and equipment.

Today, adhesives are used to bond many products, including automobiles and airplanes. The Porsche 928, one of the world's fastest production autos, contains seven different Loctite adhesives and sealants with 24 different applications in 90 places. Lockheed now assembles and fastens airplane frames and skin parts using only adhesives, and the revolutionary new Lear business jet is also held together by adhesives.

The great success of Loctite can be attributed in part to its sales and distribution network. Loctite management realizes the importance of using the right product for the right application. Well-trained Loctite technical service personnel serve as customer problem solvers. Sixty percent of sales are made through independent distributors and the remaining 40% directly to end users. In order to provide technical assistance and support for the use of its products, the company maintains close and continued contact with both its distributors and major end users.

Recently, marketing executives at Loctite met to discuss a problem product, RC601—an engineering adhesive. Hoping to improve profitability, the company performed some marketing research on RC601, looking for new uses and new target markets for the product. Marketing executives are now trying to develop a new marketing strategy.

The traditional target market for RC601 has been design engineers. RC601 is a thin, liquid-retaining compound supplied in a red bottle. It fills small voids that remain when parts are bonded with cylindrical fasteners (such as bolts). Design engineers typically specify the use of RC601 in the production process to allow relaxation of machining tolerance for easier assembly and lower machining costs. In this way, RC601 compensates for the inexact fit of many parts used in numerous production processes.

Inclusion of a particular adhesive in the design of a product is typically a complex decision. Although design engineers actually make the buying decision, other individuals on the new-product development team may be involved—and agreement is not often easy. For example, purchasing agents are concerned with economy, engineers with performance, and production managers with prompt delivery. Factors such as the complexity of the production process and the long-term commitment made by specifying the adhesive in a production plan motivate decision makers to evaluate alternatives carefully.

Because design engineers are reluctant to consider new or different products, a Loctite sales representative's primary task in selling RC601 is to persuade them to buy the product for the first time. After RC601 is specified in the design of a product and the initial sale is made, almost all product requirements are bought through local distributors. Loctite used "Product Information Data" sheets as its primary promotion tool in marketing RC601.

Sales and profits of RC601 fell off when Loctite introduced newer products that appealed more to its target market. The new products have a tolerance to higher temperatures. In an effort to reverse the sales decline, Loctite marketers commissioned a marketing research study to find new potential users and customers for RC601.

Loctite always studies its products from the customer's point of view. The marketing research showed that the plant maintenance workers need a product that can keep broken-down machines running until replacement parts arrive. To satisfy this need, Loctite reformulated RC601 into a gel that can be applied between machinery parts to repair worn areas temporarily and restore correct fits. More important, RC601 gets equipment ready to run in one hour—compared with 12 hours for the most commonly used alternative method. Because the time and labor savings are so great, price is of less importance to buyers. In this situation they are more concerned with availability and performance. It is not unusual for maintenance workers to request a particular product by its brand name.

Loctite marketing executives are now trying to develop a marketing strategy for the changed product (gel-like reformulation of RC601) and the new target market (maintenance workers). They recognize that the new RC601 will probably need a new name, package, and promotion effort.

# Questions

1. Describe the decision-making process of design engineers and maintenance workers for Loctite products. Be sure to consider the type of buying situation facing each (straight rebuy, modified rebuy, or new task), the stages of the buying process, and the members of the organization who participate in the purchase-decision process.

2. What marketing strategy would you recommend to Loctite executives for the new market segment? Your recommendation should include a name for the product, packaging ideas, pricing strategy, and promotional suggestions.

# 12. Brand Loyalty

In late November, Jim Ashman, the brand manager for a leading Canadian shampoo, met with his superior, Susan Keller, to discuss the advertising and sales promotion budget for next year. Susan began the conversation. "Jim, I think we should consider changing the amount we spend on advertising. This year, we've spent $1,100,000 on advertising and have just held on to our 14% share of the market. On the other hand, we've spent only $800,000 on sales promotions. One half went to trade allowances—we sold the shampoo to retail chains at reduced prices. The other $400,000 was spent on price specials to the consumer, including selling the large size (400ml) for the price of the regular size (300ml). I think we should spend more of the budget on sales promotions and less on advertising. I don't think we get much brand loyalty with shampoo."

Jim responded, "No, I think we should spend the same amount on advertising and sales promotions as we did this year. Even though the competition is spending more on sales promotions and less on advertising than we are, we are holding our own. This is a product category where advertising can create brand loyalties." "I'm not sure," said Susan. "Look, there have been a number of articles written in the past few years on brand loyalty in the wake of the Coca-Cola change. Why don't you review the articles and then we'll discuss it again." Susan was referring to the fact that after the Coca-Cola Company changed the formulation of Coca-Cola and were forced to do an about-face and bring back the "Old Coke," the issue of brand loyalty had been examined by a number of writers and researchers.

Jim then left Susan's office and spent a day compiling the articles that had discussed brand loyalty. He then summarized the main points from the articles.

- Consumer loyalty to big-name brands is on the wane in several product categories, eroded by a wider selection and by price competition from aggressive name, generic, and store brands.
- Brand loyalty—that certain something that makes a consumer keep buying over and over again—is an elusive quality. It begins with the customer's preference for a product on the basis of objective reasons—the drink is sweeter, the paper towel more absorbent. The brand name is the customers' guarantee that they will get what they expect. But when a branded product has been around a long time and is heavily advertised, it can pick up emotional freight: it can become a part of a person's self-image or summon fond memories of days gone by.
- One study suggested that brand loyalties seem to be most intense with products

that are ingested or close to the skin. As well, the more closely a brand is bound to people's self-image, the more likely they will be to resist any change in it.

- Brand loyalties seem to be greater, the more emotionally involved the customer is with a given purchase. The higher the level of involvement, the stronger the brand loyalty.
- Many marketers are beginning to worry that generic and other bargain products are making brand loyalty a thing of the past among increasingly savvy and recession-weary consumers.
- A research study has shown that few customers favor a single brand. They choose from two or three, deciding in the store aisle, where display, price, and product availability are persuasive factors.
- The fact that many brands—Tide, Kleenex, and Kraft slices—have been the leading brands for many years suggests brand loyalty exists. However, some argue that people buy name brands out of habit, but do not necessarily feel loyal to them.
- One study of loyalty by an advertising agency provided some interesting results. The agency measured the degree of loyalty by asking people whether they would switch to another brand if it was sold at a 50% discount. The products where consumers most often said no were classed as high- loyalty products, those where consumers most often said yes were classed as low-loyalty products, and those in-between were classed as medium-loyalty products. The results are shown in Table 1.

**TABLE 1**

| High-Loyalty Products | Medium-Loyalty Products | Low-Loyalty Products |
| --- | --- | --- |
| cigarettes | cola drinks | paper towels |
| laxatives | margarine | crackers |
| cold remedies | shampoo | scouring powder |
| 35-mm film | hand lotion | plastic trash bags |
| toothpaste | furniture polish | facial tissues |

**TABLE 2**

| Brand Discrimination a | Brand Loyalty b | Products |
| --- | --- | --- |
| High | High | Coffee, power tools, gasoline, motor oil, color TV |
| High | Low | Men's cologne, cola drinks, fast-food restaurants |
| Low | High | Headache remedies, shaving cream |
| Low | Low | Cough remedies, light bulbs, disposable razors |

a   The question was: Do you feel that all brands are pretty much alike except for price? If consumer answered "yes" (pretty much alike), then the product was low brand discrimination.

b   The question was: Do you tend to buy just one brand, alternate between two or three brands that are acceptable to you, or do you switch around? If consumer answered "often switch around," then the product was low brand loyalty.

- Another study of loyalty by a marketing research firm looked at the relationship between brand discrimination (the perceived differences among competing brands) and brand loyalty. Over 2,000 consumers were asked about 13 product categories. The results are shown in Table 2.

   After reviewing his notes, Jim was uncertain as to what proportion of the budget should be spent on advertising or sales promotion. He thought the best thing he could do at this time would be to prepare a list of points for and against each method in preparation for the meeting.

## Questions

1. Which is more effective in marketing shampoo, advertising or sales promotions?
2. Prepare pros and cons for both sides of the argument.

**Sources include:** R.H. Bruskin, "New Study on Brand Loyalty," *Marketing Review*, June 1988, p. 25.

# 13. Heritage Gift Shop

The Heritage Gift Shop, located in downtown Banff, Alberta, specializes in hand-crafted artwork, made by local Canadian artists. Sally Carruthers, the owner of Heritage, has just returned from a buying trip and was interested to learn from the assistant store manager, Marg Green, how the sales of the stone carvings had gone. Several months ago, the store had received a selection of stone carvings. The selection included a wide range of items. Some of the pieces were very simple and others were more intricately carved.

   Sally had purchased the carvings at a very reasonable cost and was quite pleased with the distinctive artwork. She felt that the carvings would appeal particularly to the general souvenir buyer seeking an alternative to the paintings and wood carvings usually offered in the Banff area. She priced the carvings so that shoppers would receive a good value for their money but also added a sufficient markup to cover costs and allow for an average profit margin.

   After the items had been on display for about a month, Sally was disappointed with their sales. She decided to try several merchandising tactics that she had learned as a business student at the University of Alberta. For example, realizing that the location of an item in the store will often influence whether or not patrons will examine merchandise, she moved the carvings to a display unit to the right of the store entrance.

   When sales of the carvings still remained sluggish after the relocation, she decided to talk to the sales staff during their weekly meeting. Suggesting that they put more effort into "pushing" this particular product, she provided them with detailed descriptions of the carvings and the history of the artist. Unfortunately, this approach also failed. At this point, Sally was preparing to leave on a buying trip. Frustrated with the poor sales performance of the stone carvings and anxious to reduce current inventory to make room for newer selections that she would be buying, she decided to take drastic action. Sally would cut the price of the carvings in half. As she left the store, Sally hastily wrote a note for Marg Green. The note read:

Marg —
Everything in this
case x 1/2
Sally

Upon her return, Sally was pleasantly surprised to find that the entire selection of stone carvings had been sold. "I can't understand it," she said to Marg, "but the stone just didn't appeal to our customers. Next time I'll have to be more careful when I try to expand our product line." Marg responded that although she couldn't quite understand why Sally wanted to raise the price of slow-moving merchandise, she was surprised at how quickly it had sold at the higher price. Sally was puzzled. "What higher price?" she questioned, "My note said to cut the price in half." "In half?", replied Marg, "I thought your note said, prices on stone carvings times two!" As a result, Marg had doubled rather than lowered the price.

## Questions

1. Explain what happened in this situation. Why did the carvings sell so quickly at twice the normal price?
2. What assumption had Sally Carruthers made about the demand curve for the stone carvings? What did the demand curve for this particular product actually look like?
3. In what type of market is Heritage Gift Shop operating (pure competition, monopolistic competition, oligopolistic competition, or pure monopoly)? What leads you to this conclusion?
4. How would the concept of psychological pricing be useful to Sally Carruthers? How would you advise her about future pricing decisions?

# 14. ALLIED CHEMICAL CANADA LIMITED

Written by Thomas F. Funk, Nancy Brown, and William Braithwaite, University of Guelph

Bob Aitken knew he would have to make the decision today if Allied Chemical was to introduce its new line of micronutrient fertilizers to the Ontario and Quebec markets this spring. Micronutrients, a relatively new type of fertilizer, were applied to the leaves of crops such as apples and potatoes during their growth phase to improve the quality and yield of the crop. As manager of new product development, Mr. Aitken was responsible for initiating the launch of new and presumably profitable products for the company. While he had been very excited and enthusiastic about the micronutrient line initially, lately he had become less sure. Was the product really profitable enough to go with? At what price level should they enter the market?

Allied Chemical Canada Limited is a wholly owned subsidary of its United States parent. Although the U.S. company had long been involved in agriculture through its line of liquid fertilizers, the Canadian company had not yet entered this sector. Micronutrients would be the first agricultural product sold by Allied in Canada and could pave the way for other products in the future.

## The Micronutrient Market

Allied was proposing to enter the micronutrient market with two products imported from the U.S. company: Supergrow-M (Magnesium) and Supergrow-Z (Zinc). Although farmers could use up to 12 different micronutrients, the Allied line presently consisted of only magnesium and zinc. The two Allied products were in liquid form and designed for application at that point in a plant's growth when lack of these nutrients could limit the full development of grain or fruit. In simple terms, if a crop (e.g., potatoes) lacked micronutrients like magnesium or zinc during a stage of its growth, the result could be a lower yield (e.g., fewer potatoes per acre) or lower quality. In addition to the micronutrients, each Allied product also contained small amounts of nitrogen. This was included to give the crop a boost at a critical stage in its development as well as to promote a rich, green color. It was felt that the added greenness would be an indication to farmers that the product was in fact working. With the added nitrogen, however, it became important that the product be applied in precisely the right manner to avoid burning the crop. When applying these fertilizers during the growth phase of the crop, conventional soil tests for micronutrient deficiencies were of limited value in gauging the extent to which micronutrients were needed. Visual signs such as color changes in leaves were considered to be the best indicator of certain deficiencies, although these were far from being accurate.

Mr. Aitken felt the micronutrient market was questionable. Considerable debate had arisen recently as to the value of micronutrient fertilizer applications. While there was some industry evidence that the use of micronutrients could increase yields, most farmers had a very low awareness level of micronutrient deficiencies and products. What information was available to farmers from provincial departments of agriculture and Agriculture Canada did not, in general, support the use of micronutrients (Exhibit 1). As well, the University of Guelph, which farmers look to for technical information, was not promoting or recommending the use of micronutrients, and the university's soil testing lab did not include analysis for micronutrients in their soil testing service. As a result, many farmers were sending their soil samples to private testing labs in the United States where micronutrient tests were performed.

On the other hand, some of the more progressive farmers were anxious to use micronutrients and considered these institutions to be too conservative in their approach. A recent survey revealed that ten percent of all farmers in Ontario and Quebec had used micronutrients at one time or another during the past five years.

Another interesting conclusion of this study was that farmers normally required a 5:1 benefit to cost ratio for chemical products. That is, for every dollar invested in chemical products, farmers wanted a minimum increase of $5 in revenue.

The survey also revealed that farmers and fertilizer dealers had a number of positive and negative attitudes concerning micronutrients. On the positive side, the most common attitude was:

- lack of micronutrients could be a limiting factor which, when corrected, could dramatically increase yield potential.

On the negative side, the most common attitudes were:

- micronutrients are not as important as other management practices;
- it is very difficult to know when real deficiencies exist;
- some companies are pushing micronutrients without knowing what the real needs are; and
- foliar application (i.e. application to the leaves of the plant) of micronutrients may cause some burning of plants in hot weather, and does not result in lasting benefits. This method of application was not widely used by farmers in Ontario and Quebec.

From the market research done by Allied's new products group, Mr. Aitken knew the following:

- The total long-run market potential for magnesium and zinc in Ontario and Quebec was conservatively estimated to be 2.5 million gallons. Market potential was defined as the total gallons of product which could be sold if every deficient acre of every crop was treated with the recommended application rate.
- The potential for magnesium sales was much larger than for zinc.
- Industry sales for micronutrients had been growing rapidly.
- It was estimated that only ten percent of the long-run market potential for magnesium, and less than five percent of the long-run market potential for zinc had been developed at the present time.
- It was expected that 80% of the long-run market potential for both magnesium and zinc would be reached within a five-year period. Magnesium was expected to grow rapidly at first and then level off, while zinc was expected to grow more slowly at first, and then more rapidly later on.

## Distribution

All micronutrients in Ontario and Quebec are sold to farmers through local retail fertilizer dealers. Many of these dealers are directly controlled by large organizations such as Cyanamid, Agrico, and the Co-op, while others are independently owned and operated. Of the approximately 500 such outlets serving farmers in Ontario and Quebec, over half are branch operations of ten major chain organizations. Micronutrient sales are currently a relatively small, but growing part of overall dealer sales. There is considerable variation among retail outlets, even within the same organization, in their interest in and knowledge of micronutrients. Decisions to add new products by large fertilizer organizations are made at both the head office and branch levels. The major factors considered in assessing a new product are margins, performance, testing, information, and technical back-up.

# Competition

Mr. Aitken had managed to gain considerable intelligence about the current competition. There were four companies selling micronutrients in Ontario and Quebec. The companies and their approximate market shares were Stoller Chemical Company (60%), Frit Industries (30%), Eastman Kodak (five percent), and Duval Sales Corporation (five percent).

Mr. Aitken knew that Stoller had developed a very good reputation in the micronutrient market. They distributed a full line of micronutrients in Eastern Canada with a well-conceived and executed marketing plan. The products were attractively and conveniently packaged to meet the needs of specific growers. (As an example, Stoller sold "Apple-Grow," which was a pre-mix of all the micronutrients needed for apple production. The micronutrients in this product included magnesium, zinc, manganese, copper, boron, and sulphur.) Stoller products were well-supported with technical backup, product literature, sales people, and effective advertising. Their products sold in the vicinity of $9 per gallon, and could be purchased in both dry and liquid form.[1] Canadian prices were substantially above current U.S. prices for the same products. Stoller was headquartered in Indiana and sold its products in Canada through Niagara Chemical Company, a major agricultural chemical distributor. Niagara, in turn, sold to local fertilizer dealers who then sold to farmers. Niagara operated on a 10% margin. Stoller was one of the leading suppliers of micronutrients in the U.S. market.

Frit Industries also distributed a full line of micronutrients, but they were restricted to selling indirectly through local fertilizer dealers. They supplied dry products which were mixed in bulk fertilizers by the local dealer upon his recommendation or the farmer's request. As such, Frit had a very low profile with farmers. Their products were sold on the basis of price, with little or no technical backup or marketing support. When expressed in comparable terms with Stoller and Allied, Frit products would sell for slightly less than $6.00 per gallon.

Of the two major companies selling micronutrients in Canada, Stoller clearly had the most products, and therefore was considered by Mr. Aitken to be the main competitor.

# Allied's Plan

Allied's tentative plan was to enter the market in the six crop segments they felt had the greatest short-run potential for the company's line of micronutrients. These were apples, tomatoes, potatoes, soybeans, tobacco, and vegetables. The segments were selected on the basis of potential volume, anticipated willingness of farmers to try new products, and concentration of production in small areas to facilitate initial distribution. According to a survey conducted by Allied, the total long-run market potential in the six crop segments was 471,000 gallons of magnesium and 54,000 gallons of zinc (Exhibit 2).

Mr. Aitken was aware that Allied's ability to penetrate these markets would very likely depend on price. A recent Allied study on the benefits of micronutrients for various crops revealed a considerable difference in the marginal value of the product among the six target crops. The details of the study results are shown in Exhibit 3. Opinions concerning Allied's ability to penetrate these markets over the next five years were varied. He believed Allied would have no difficulty gaining ten percent market share for the six target crops in the first year if they were priced in line with Stoller. He hoped that within five years they would be able to capture 40% of the market. This would depend, to some extent, on the pricing strategy adopted. Allied was considering three possible price levels for the micronutrients: $6, $9, and $12 per gallon.

Mr. Aitken felt that Allied had three distribution options available: follow Stoller and sell through a chemical distributor, sell direct to fertilizer dealers in key market areas, or sell direct to farmers. Of the three, he favored the second alternative of working directly with local dealers. He estimated that 50 key dealers would provide good coverage in the six crop areas selected as initial targets.

Mr. Aitken also had estimated various costs associated with entering the market. He knew dealers would require a 20% margin on retail selling price. On top of this he would need to spend $40,000 a year for a sales representative's salary and expenses to handle the product line, and another $50,000 a year on advertising, promotion, and market testing. To date, he had invested $20,000 in market research for the product line. In addition, Allied would have to purchase a local warehouse and convert it into a product formulation and packaging plant (Allied would purchase the chemicals in bulk from their U.S. plant and then mix and package them into retail lots). The cost of purchase and conversion of the warehouse would be $300,000. The plant could be depreciated for taxation purposes at ten percent per year.

Allied's product costs were $1.90 a gallon for Supergrow-M and $2.00 a gallon for Supergrow-Z. These costs included raw materials, transportation, and the direct costs of mixing and packaging. Aitken knew that Allied required all new projects to be profitable and to return 20% on investment after tax within five years of launch. Allied's tax rate was 48%.

## The Decision

Mr. Aitken knew that pricing was a key issue in this decision. However, he was still concerned about whether he should recommend entering the micronutrient market. It would be Allied's first venture into this sector. With these thoughts in mind he began working through the information again. By four o'clock he would make the decision and present it to the president.

¹ A product such as Apple-Grow actually sold for more than nine dollars a gallon because it contained several other micronutrients. The nine dollar price refers only to magnesium and zinc.

## Questions

1. How large is the market for magnesium and zinc micronutrients in Eastern Canada?
2. How should Allied analyze their pricing decision? What pricing strategy should they adopt?
3. Should Allied market the micronutrients in Eastern Canada?
4. Develop a complete marketing plan including estimates of sales and profits for the line of products.

## EXHIBIT 1
## No Substitutes for Rotation
## By Pat Lynch and John Heard

This past year there has been a lot of interest in Perth and Huron counties about micronutrients. At one meeting in Huron County we were told a lot about micronutrients. There are numerous plots out this year with different formulations and mixes and ways of application, both on corn and beans. We are sure there will be a lot of discussion this winter about the subject.

Some things are becoming evident about micronutrients, at least we think they are. The first is that you cannot expect dramatic yield increases with micronutrients in any big field. You can get dramatic increases with individual nutrients on small areas.

Second, none of the micronutrient sales staff has been able to explain to us the problem of overapplying micronutrients. They suggest that if you put on too much potash you tie up magnesium. If you put on too much phosphorus, you may need to put on more zinc and manganese. With our variable soils, we believe that in some fields you can put on too much zinc and manganese.

Finally, these micronutrients seem to be most attractive to growers with poor crop rotations. Some of your neighbors have gone to poor crop rotations and their yields have cropped. (You know they are the ones that think Pioneer corn followed by Cargill corn is crop rotation.) Now they are searching for something to pull their yield back to former highs. Micronutrients appear to them to be an answer.

What puzzles us is why some of you are willing to spend large sums of money on products you are not sure will work: shot-gun micronutrients. We both know what the problem is. You have to get more crops into the rotation, especially perennial forages. I suppose the bottom line is when you hear your neighbor talking about all the micronutrients he is using. That's just a polite way for him to tell you he has a terrible crop rotation.

Mr. Lynch is a soils and crops specialist with the Ontario Ministry of Agriculture and Food. Mr. Heard is an assistant agricultural representative in Perth County.

## EXHIBIT 2
## Long-run Market Potential for
## Micronutrients by Segment

|  | Supergrow-M (gallons) | Supergrow-Z (gallons) |
|---|---|---|
| Apples | 126,000 | 500 |
| Potatoes | 62,000 | 2,000 |
| Tomatoes | 12,000 | 1,000 |
| Soybeans | 133,000 | 50,000 |
| Tobacco | 136,000 | 0 |
| Vegetables | 2,000 | 500 |
| Total | 471,000 | 54,000 |

**EXHIBIT 3**
**Economics of Using Magnesium and Zinc**

| Crops | Recommended Application Rates (gallons/acre) | Gross Revenue per acre without Micro nutrients | Gross Revenue per acre with Micro nutrients | Major Benefit to Farmers |
|---|---|---|---|---|
| SUPERGROW-M | | | | |
| Apples | 7.0 | $4,791 | $5,257 | Improved Quality |
| Potatoes | 3.0 | 1,029 | 1,192 | Improved Yield |
| Tomatoes | 2.5 | 1,707 | 1,835 | Improved Yield |
| Soybeans | 2.0 | 361 | 430 | Improved Yield |
| Tobacco | 4.0 | 2,047 | 2,402 | Improved Quality |
| Vegetables | 2.0 | 1,468 | 1,593 | Improved Quality |
| | | | | |
| SUPERGROW-Z | | | | |
| Apples | 1.0 | 4,791 | 4,824 | Improved Quality |
| Potatoes | 0.75 | 1,029 | 1,066 | Improved Yield |
| Tomatoes | 0.6 | 1,707 | 1,737 | Improved Yield |
| Soybeans | 0.5 | 361 | 376 | Improved Yield |
| Tobacco | 0.25 | 2,047 | 2,069 | Improved Quality |
| Vegetables | 0.5 | 1,468 | 1,501 | Improved Quality |

# 15. ALLIANCE COSMETICS

Alliance Cosmetics, a small cosmetics manufacturer in Manitoba, has a well-positioned set of mid-price-range facial cosmetic products. The quality of this product line, which retails in the $4 to $7 price range, is slightly above that of the major competitors such as Max Factor and Bonne Belle. The firm had sought and gained distribution through the major pharmacy stores in Ontario and Manitoba, and chains such as Shoppers Drug Mart had responded well to its product line.

The line's success was due to more than just the slightly higher quality-price relationship. The firm had initially contracted representation from an aggressive set of manufacturer's agents. This was necessary to get quick high-volume distribution which appeared to be possible only through the drug mart chains. The majority of the agents had long- term relationships with the chain buyers and were able to open the doors for the firm's products. This rapid and fairly intensive distribution was a key factor.

Drug mart chains are interested in high turnover and good margins. Therefore, above-average retail mark-ups—in the neighborhood of 120% versus the more typical 100% on cost to retailer—were offered. In addition, the firm spent $200,000 on advertising in the introductory three-month launch of the initial product line three years ago and has since spent about $600,000 per year on advertising.

With the success of the current mid-price-range product line, three drug chains had recently expressed an interest in the firm's producing top-of-the-line facial cosmetics. The firm had the following major facts to consider in pursuing this opportunity:

1. The plant had ample capacity. It could produce an extra 1,000,000 product units without overstraining the capacity of the equipment.
2. The fixed costs the company now faces per year are estimated at $650,000. This would likely increase by $175,000 with an additional product line.
3. The current average retail price of the company's product is $5.50. The company has an average selling price to retailers of $2.50 per unit.
4. The direct manufacturing costs per unit for the current line are $0.80. The direct overhead costs of the new line would be $1.00 per unit. Agent's commissions are four percent of the company's selling price.
5. Total advertising for all lines would be in the neighborhood of $1 million in the year the product is launched.
6. The average retail price of the line would have to be a minimum of $7.75 for it to be perceived as a high-quality good.
7. Some product samples had been produced and these were very well accepted by cosmeticians and models who had tried them.

This firm faces some interesting pricing problems. Price is often equated with quality in products like cosmetics. Here the consumer is purchasing, in a very real sense, "the total product concept." Cosmetics represent much more than the physical attributes of the product to the consumer. They represent glamor, beauty, and hope! Many buyers see price as a significant determinant of the quality of a product. To signify a premium-range product, a premium price has to be set. Unfortunately, as this premium price strategy is constrained by the firm's advertising budget, it cannot match the dollar volume of the large competitors in the industry. The higher the price, the greater the need for heavy and extensive advertising and promotional push. The company must have an advertising budget that will allow it to convince the public to pay the high price. The basic question is whether the planned $1 million in advertising expenditures is enough to support both product lines.

## Questions

1. What pricing approach would you recommend for the new product line?
2. What price would you set for the new line? Why?

# 16. VIDEO MOVIES

It is often difficult to set a price for a product or service. Trying to balance all the components—objectives, demand and cost analysis, competition, the effect on the company's other products or services, and legal considerations—and arrive at an optimum price requires considerable skill. Many of these components are relevant for the movie industry when it attempts to set prices for movies released on video cassettes for the home market.

A new market opened up for movie studios with the introduction of the video cassette recorder (VCR). Instead of just having one market for movies—the movie theater audience—multiple markets were now available. In fact, a movie studio can maximize the profits from films by reaching four markets: movie theaters, pay T.V., network T.V., and cassette sales for re-sale or rental. In particular, the rapid growth of VCRs in North America created a large market for the re-sale or rental of movies. In Canada, approximately 45,000 VCRs were sold in 1980; by the end of 1984, 23% of Canadian households had a VCR; by the end of 1985, 36%; by the end of 1987, 50%; and by the end of 1990 it was estimated that over 60% of the 9.3 million households in Canada had a VCR. A similar sales pattern and household ownership was experienced in the United States.

Accompanying the growth in VCR sales was the establishment of video rental stores, which sprung up all over North America. Because it was one of the easiest businesses to get into (very low costs to enter), both new stores and existing retailers (e.g., convenience stores) entered the video rental business. Because of the proliferation of these businesses it is difficult to determine how large the total retail market is or how many stores are in existence at one time. However, it was estimated that in 1984 there were approximately 35,000 video stores in North America (3,500 in Canada and 31,500 in the U.S.). By 1987 approximately 80,000 video stores were in operation (8,000 in Canada and 72,000 in the U.S.). By 1990, estimates were that there were about 90,000 video stores (8,400 in Canada and 81,600 in the U.S.). Against this backdrop the movie studios have a pricing decision to make when releasing movies for the VCR market.

Your task is to analyze each of the following two decisions.

## DECISION A

In early 1984, two video cassettes were released in the same week, *Raiders of the Lost Ark* and *Tootsie*. *Raiders of the Lost Ark* was one of the most popular movies of all time, an action-adventure film that appealed to people of all ages. With this movie, the studio had an objective of getting a greater share of the retail revenue generated by the home video market. It decided to use a penetration pricing strategy with *Raiders*. The movie was sold to wholesalers for a price of $25.00, and it retailed (to both consumers and video stores) for $39.95. Previously, most video movies had been priced at $50 wholesale and $79.95 retail. *Tootsie* also had considerable success at the box office although the comedic story—of an unemployed actor (played by Dustin Hoffman) who gets a part in a daily soap opera as a female—attracted a more adult, upscale audience than *Raiders*. This movie was released at the traditional wholesale price of $50 and retail price of $79.95.

## DECISION B

In early 1987, two video cassettes were released during the same week, *Top Gun* and *Stand By Me*. *Top Gun* was the top-grossing movie of 1986. This adventure-action story of navy pilots at a flight competition appealed to a broad audience, although it was heavily skewed to the teenage market. *Top Gun* sold for a retail price of $27 and a wholesale price of $16. At this time, many movies were being sold at retail for $30. *Top Gun* reduced its price to $27 because Pepsi paid $3 per cassette to have a commercial for Pepsi included at the start of the film. *Stand By Me*, the poignant story of four young boys and their adventures over a few summer days, did reasonably well at the box office. It attracted a diverse audience, many of whom went because of the very favorable reviews received by the movie. *Stand By Me* sold for $90 retail and $55 wholesale, a higher price than usual in the market.

## Questions

1. What factors should be considered in setting the price for a movie released on video cassette?
2. For each of the two examples, who do you think made the best pricing decision? Why?
3. For each decision, which of the two movies generated the largest total revenue for the studios?

# 17. VALU MARKETING COMPANY— TURIKAN STAPLER

Written by Susan Hain and C. Dennis Anderson, University of Manitoba.

In May of 1989, Al Stamler, president of Valu Marketing, was reassessing his marketing plans for a new product he had been importing and selling for about six months. The product was the Turikan Stapler, a unique device that worked like a stapler, but also attached hooks and loop clips to anything that could normally be stapled (Exhibit 1). This product appeared to offer a number of potential uses such as displaying merchandise in stores, affixing posters to bulletin boards, and hanging signs. The clips it produced were even sturdy enough to hang pictures on. Mr. Stamler felt certain that the Turikan Stapler had strong market potential. However, he needed to develop a marketing and distribution strategy to improve the product's lagging sales.

## Background Information

Mr. Stamler was a successful small business entrepreneur who specialized in finding products overseas that he could market in North America. A year ago, while studying the Japanese Trade Directory, he discovered the Turikan Stapler, manufactured by I.K. International Co. Ltd., of Tokyo. After some negotiations, Mr. Stamler was able to secure exclusive distribution rights for the product for Canada and the eastern United States. He did not have to pay a fee for the distribution rights; rather, he was granted exclusive rights by virtue of his willingness to stock large quantities of inventory.

# The Turikan Stapler

The Turikan Stapler attached loops or clips to anything that could be stapled. Exhibit 1 provides an illustration of both the stapler and the clips. The device was as easy to use and worked on the same principle as an ordinary stapler. In essence, it could staple a clip onto almost any item. The sturdy construction of both the stapler and the clips meant that clips could be attached to, and would support the weight of heavy items.

This product had many uses. It was an excellent means of displaying merchandise in retail outlets when used in conjunction with peg boards or racks. The Turikan Stapler could also be used in classrooms. It eliminated the need for thumbtacks, map tacks, pins, and Scotch tape when displaying posters, art work, and booklets. A Turikan Stapler hook clip attached to a wall or a bulletin board could be bent to a 90 degree angle. Items to which loop clips were then attached could be hung from the hook clips and would lie flat against the wall. Removal and replacement of the displayed items were thus greatly simplified. In offices or industrial plants, the product was useful for the display of such things as job sheets and scheduling notices. The clips were also sturdy enough to be used in place of tiny nails when stringing or hanging pictures. Many other craft-related and household uses existed for this product.

The Turikan Stapler could be purchased by itself or in a blister pack along with one package of loop clips and one package of hook clips. Refills of loop clips could also be purchased by themselves in packages of 100.

# Distribution

As a first step in marketing the stapler, Mr. Stamler successfully negotiated distribution deals with two Canadian firms. In January 1989, he granted exclusive western Canadian distribution rights for the Turikan Stapler to Christie's School Supplies. Christie's had stores in Calgary, Winnipeg, and Brandon, and operated a toll-free phone service line for customers in Saskatchewan, Manitoba, and northwestern Ontario. It employed 12 salespeople who called on school divisions and offices in the cities where retail outlets were located.

In addition to personal sales, Christie's promoted its products in catalogs and brochures. In April, the Turikan Stapler was advertised in a brochure the company distributed to about 30,000 potential customers (Exhibit 2). Christie's regular price for the Turikan Stapler was $24.95, while the sale price was $18.95. Discounts were available for volume purchases. Mr. Stamler felt that the initial order for the product by Christie's was somewhat disappointing, since the firm only ordered 100 blister packs and 200 refills of each type of clip. He felt that the small order was due to the fact that the product was new but he was hopeful for better results in the future.

In March, Mr. Stamler granted exclusive distribution rights for eastern Canada to Versa Hanger Systems. Versa carried a new type of pegboard display system and was pleased to pick up the Turikan Stapler, since the two products were complimentary. Versa promoted its product line primarily through personal sales. The firm employed two salespeople who called on stationery, hardware, and retail outlets. It also sold distribution rights to independent salespeople who traveled throughout eastern Canada. The firm had had opportunities to export its product to the United States, but had declined, preferring instead to limit distribution to eastern Canada so it could ensure that its customers were well serviced.

Sales to Versa had been a bit more encouraging than sales to Christie's. Since the firm began carrying the product in March, it had ordered 210 blister packs, 420 refills of each type of clip, and 300 staplers. Although Mr. Stamler recognized that these orders were modest in size, he felt that they indicated that Versa was at least working to sell the product.

The exclusive rights agreement Stamler had with Christie's was a verbal one and was to be reviewed at the end of June. The Versa agreement was a written one, but it could be terminated by either party. In keeping with the spirit of these agreements for exclusive distribution rights, Mr. Stamler referred all orders he received for the product to the appropriate distributor. He would not sell direct under any circumstances.

Mr. Stamler had also found a distributor to sell the Turikan Stapler in Puerto Rico by responding to an advertisement he found in a newsletter published by the United Association of Manufacturers' Representatives (UAMR). The ad had been placed by a Puerto Rican manufacturers' representative who was looking for new products to add to his product line of office and school supplies and educational products. His initial order early in 1989 consisted of 1,000 blister packs. Although he included the Turikan Stapler in a display he established at an office and school supply trade show in San Juan in March, he did not receive any orders as a result of the exhibit. He had been able to move about 500 units quickly through personal selling; however, sales had slowed after that point.

Mr. Stamler also wanted to establish a distribution system for the Turikan Stapler in the eastern United States. To accomplish that, he had advertised for a distributor in the UAMR newsletter on four occasions in December, 1988, and January, 1989. He had received several inquiries in response to the ad, and had begun negotiations with a firm in Chicago. Mr. Stamler had sent the company a few blister packs and about 100 brochures, and was awaiting its decisions.

# Promotion

Mr. Stamler had undertaken various types of promotion for the Turikan Stapler since his firm had begun distributing it. He had a two-color (8 1/2 X 14") poster printed, which he distributed in person and by mail and which he provided to his distributors for their use (Exhibit 3). Mr. Stamler had also engaged in a concerted personal selling effort to stimulate demand for the product, although he always referred potential customers to Christie's or Versa if they were interested in ordering. Mr. Stamler had made presentations to a variety of school divisions, teachers associations, and provincial government departments. He had also been successful in obtaining some publicity in the form of a short newspaper article which appeared in the New Products column of the Winnipeg Free Press on April 22, 1989 (Exhibit 4).

# Costs and Inventory

When calculating his cost for the Turikan Stapler, Mr. Stamler had to include exchange costs since the manufacturer demanded payment in American currency.

Other costs to be considered included federal sales tax (ten percent) and duty (12.5 percent). These costs are all included in the cost figures set out in Exhibit 5. Not included in these figures was a monthly interest payment of $150.00 which had to be made on a loan of $12,000.00 which Mr. Stamler borrowed to purchase his initial inventory. An income statement prepared after one year of operation is included in Exhibit 6. It also includes information regarding potential sales for the next year and a proposed budget for promotion. Stamler had to observe minimum order size requirements set by the Japanese manufacturer when he ordered inventory. He had to import either 1,000 blister packs or 1,000 staplers and 6,000 boxes of refills at one time. In turn, Stamler tried to encourage his distributors to order by the case, although he would occasionally make exceptions. Blister packs were sold in cases of 20, refills in cases of 200, and staplers alone in cases of 100.

As of June 30, 1989, Mr. Stamler had the following inventory on hand: 690 blister packs, 987 staplers, 5,370 refills of loop clips, and 3,370 refills of hook clips.

## Competition

Several products provided competition for the Turikan Stapler, although none was a direct competitor. Because the product was so versatile, it could be used to replace map tacks, thumb tacks, straight pins, picture hanging hardware, regular staples, plastic hooks, and premanufactured metal loops or hooks. It competed with any products that performed any of those functions.

Exhibit 7 contains the price ranges for some of the competitive products. These were compiled by examining the prices for each item at Willson's Stationers Ltd., General Stationery and Furniture Ltd., Christie's School Supplies, the University of Manitoba Bookstore, Sears, The Bay, and Coles Bookstore. The markup on cost for these items was generally 75 percent.

## Future Marketing Plans

Mr. Stamler considered looking for a distributor to take over sales in western Canada since he was disappointed with Christie's performance. He had also considered hiring a commissioned salesperson to sell the product.

In general, however, Mr. Stamler was uncertain of exactly what steps he should take to expand his business. Although he realized that a sound marketing strategy was a prerequisite for success, he was unsure of which segment(s) to market to and what marketing mix to employ for each identified segment. Clearly, Mr. Stamler had a number of crucial decisions to make in the immediate future.

## Questions

1. What are the reasons for the disappointing sales, to date, of the Turikan Stapler?
2. What distribution options are available for the Turikan Stapler?
3. What marketing strategy should be pursued by Mr. Stamler?

**EXHIBIT 1**
**The Turikan Stapler**

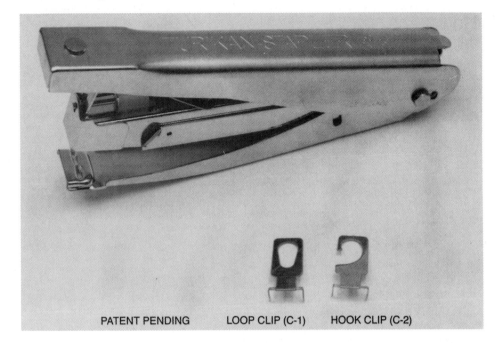

PATENT PENDING  LOOP CLIP (C-1)  HOOK CLIP (C-2)

**EXHIBIT 2**
**The Turikan Stapler as Featured in the Christie's Brochure**

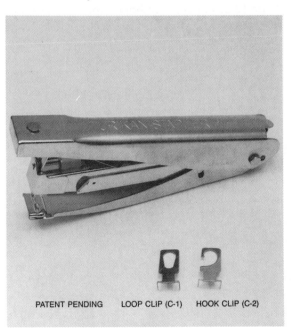

PATENT PENDING  LOOP CLIP (C-1)  HOOK CLIP (C-2)

**EXHIBIT 3**
**Valu Marketing Company's Promotional Poster**

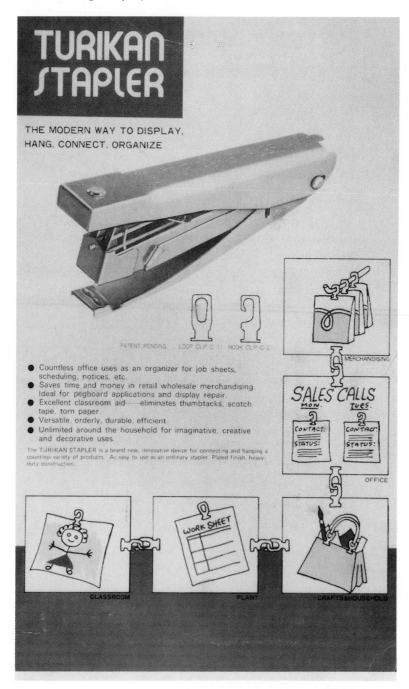

**EXHIBIT 4**
**Publicity**
**Winnipeg Free Press**

## VERSATILE STAPLER

Valu Marketing Co., of Winnipeg, features a stapler manufactured in Tokyo by I.K. International Co. Ltd. The Turikan Stapler releases book and loop clips and is advertised as "the modern way to display, hang, connect, organize."

Promotional material claims the clips have countless office uses for organizing job sheets, schedules, reports and charts. The clips also are designed to save time and money in merchandising.

The clips are billed as ideal for pegboard displays and package repair. In classrooms, they eliminate thumbtacks, pins, torn paper and are good for booklets and posters. Household uses are said to be unlimited.

Further information may be obtained by telephoning Valu Marketing president Al Stamler.

**EXHIBIT 5**
**Cost and Pricing Information**

| Product | Cost to Valu Marketing | Cost to Distributor | Suggested Retail Price |
|---|---|---|---|
| Blister Packs | $7.00 | $8.09 | $24.95 |
| Refill of Staples | $1.08 | $1.29 | $ 2.49 |
| Stapler | $4.84 | $5.51 | $20.00 |

**EXHIBIT 6**
**Financial Information for the Turikan Stapler**
**For April 1 to June 30, 1989**

| | | |
|---|---|---|
| New revenue from sales | $4182 | |
| Cost of merchandise sold | $3619 | |
| Gross profit on sales | | $    563 |
| Operating Expenses: | | |
| Advertising material | $268 | |
| Interest expense | $500 | |
| Miscellaneous expenses | $301 | |
| Total Expenses | | $ 1,069 |
| Loss on operations | | $ 506 |
| Unsold inventory cost | | $16,943 |

At presently stated prices to customers, total gross revenue possible from remaining inventory is $19,582, for a $2,132.74 possible gross profit.

A line of credit can be maintained at our bank as long as interest is paid on the loan of $12,000. Interest is $150 per month.

**EXHIBIT 7**
**Price Ranges of Competitive Products**

| Product | Retail Price Range (1) |
|---|---|
| Thumb Tacks (100) | $ .59 - $ .90 |
| Map Tacks (100) | $2.75 - $ 3.25 |
| Push Pins    ( 30) | $ .55 - $ .65 |
|                  (100) | $1.45 - $ 1.49 |
| Paper Clips (100) | $ .39 - $ .50 |
| Bulldog (Spring) Clips (1) | $ .27 - $ 1.10 |
| Fold-back Clips (12) | $1.55 - $ 7.55 |
| Magnetic Clips (2) | $1.00 - $ 1.18 |
| Plier-style Hole Punch (1) | $1.49 - $ 1.98 |
| Picture Hangers - 6X10  lb. | $ .95 |
|                            3X30  lb. | $2.00 |
|                            3X50  lb. | $ .95 |
|                            2X100 lb. | $ .95 |
| Staplers (1) | $4.95 - $32.50 |
| Mini-staplers with Refills (1) | $2.20 - $ 2.95 |
| Staples   (1,000) | $ .60 - $ 1.35 |
|                (5,000) | $1.65 - $ 2.25 |
| Transparent Tape  (25 meters) | $1.35 |
|                            (33 meters) | $2.25 - $ 4.20 |
| Invisible Tape      (33 meters) | $1.85 - $ 4.25 |
| Reinforcements (100) | $ .59 - $   .96 |

# 18. Porsche Division-Volkswagen Canada Inc.

Written by Marvin Ryder, McMaster University

Mr. Fred Dubee, General Manager of the Porsche Division of Volkswagen Canada Inc., was reviewing five proposals to establish new dealerships in Canada. As a preliminary screening move, Mr. Dubee had to make an assessment of the market potential and the qualifications of the person applying. He knew that any proposal that moved beyond the screening process would require several months of work, both on the part of the applicant and the company. He was not committed to the idea of opening a new dealership but he needed to have his assessment finished for the June 1, 1989 quarterly meeting to be held at the Scarborough headquarters one week from today.

## Company History

Porsche began in the early 1930s as a design firm. The company helped design and develop pumpers for the Vienna Fire Department, mortar tows for the Austrian artillery, tanks for the German army, Prince Henry touring cars, Sascha racing cars, and the Mercedes SSK for the Daimler-Benz corporation. The most famous of all these vehicles was the Volkswagen. In 1931, Porsche designed the first Volkswagen "Beetle" and full production of the car began in 1938.

In 1948, the first sports car to carry the Porsche name was designed and built in Austria—based on Volkswagen parts. This car, called the 356, was never intended to compete in races, yet that same year it won a race in Innsbruck, Austria, reaching a speed of 140 kilometres per hour. In 1950, the company returned to Stuttgart-Zuffenhausen, West Germany, after its exile in Austria, and full-scale production began. By 1954, 5,000 Porsches had been built. In 1955, the first engine developed for and by Porsche went into production. When the American actor James Dean died in a Porsche during an automobile accident in Paso Robles, California on September 30, 1955, the car acquired a certain mystique. In 1963, with more than 60,000 Type 356 Porsches having been built, its successor, the Porsche 911, was introduced.

In 1989, Porsche commercially manufactured three automobiles: the 911, the 928 (introduced in 1978), and the 944 (introduced in 1982). Sales were not evenly divided between the three models— the Porsche 944 accounted for 54% of sales, the 911 accounted for 30%, and the 928 accounted for 10%. North America was the major market for the cars (United States at 54%, Canada at 2%), though European purchases had been gaining steadily (Western Germany at 21%, other European countries and the rest of the world at 23%). Both latent demand (desire of people to some day own a Porsche) and true demand for Porsches was growing. With only a few exceptions in its history, demand for Porsches always outstripped supply. In 1985 Porsche sold 52,000 cars, a record for the company. However, in 1986 Porsche decided to cut back its production volume to ensure both quality and exclusivity, and produced 48,000 cars. Production was continually reduced and in 1989, Porsche would produce approximately 32,000 cars.

# The History of Porsche in Canada

United States and Canada were, from the beginning, the primary market for the Porsche. When the first Porsches were commercially produced in 1950, individual car dealers imported them to the United States. Canadian distribution evolved in a different direction. In 1952, Volkswagen established its first "daughter" company in Canada. It was responsible for the import of the Volkswagen car. As demand for Porsches in Canada at that time could be measured in single digits, it was convenient and less expensive for Porsche to "piggyback" efforts with Volkswagen Canada. To this day, the import of Porsches is handled through Volkswagen Canada.

For the average person on the street, the relationships between Porsche, Volkswagen, and Audi were confusing. Along with doing design work for Volkswagen, Porsche had also done design work for Audi. Audi assembled 944's for Porsche under contract, and in the mid 1970s Audi was purchased by Volkswagen. With increased sales in the 1970s, a dedicated Porsche presence emerged and in 1982 a separate Porsche division of Volkswagen Canada was created. It was responsible for marketing and technical support while Volkswagen Canada was responsible for logistic and administrative support.

In Canada, approximately 1,000,000 new automobiles were sold annually. Of that number, only 1.1% were luxury/sports cars and Porsche captured ten percent of those purchases. Like the parent company, Porsche Canada had reduced the number of cars it sold from 1,200 in 1986 to 820 in 1988 with a goal of selling 750 cars in 1989. But while volume declined, the average retail price of a Porsche sold in Canada had climbed from $50,000 in 1986 to $92,000 in 1988, with a projection of $100,000 in 1990. The increase in average retail price had been achieved through efforts to sell more six and eight cylinder automobiles and by providing better customer service in line with the 1989 business goals (Table 1). Remarkably, this increase in average retail price had occurred in the face of "hostile" changes to the tax act which made it more difficult to write-off the costs of a company car. As the average Porsche purchaser was a self-employed, entrepreneurial person between the ages of 30 and 55 with an above-average income, tax implications were an important influence on the purchase decision.

## The Product Line

It was difficult to describe the three basic models. Their shape and style were unique in the world of fine automobiles. Along with a coupe, cars were often available as a cabriolet (convertible) or targa (center section of roof was removable). The description of three of the nine cars that comprised the Porsche product line, taken from its 1989 brochure, gives one a sense of the type of automobile available.

- The 911 Carrera. "Ever since its debut in 1963, the Porsche 911 has been steadily refined by its designers, stylists, and engineers into an undeniable classic. The rear-mounted, high performance engine, exceptionally solid body structure, high production quality, and elegant lines combine beautifully to characterize the timeless appeal of this universally desirable concept. Available in Coupe, Targa, and Cabriolet form. Newly standard equipment for 1989: 16 inch forged wheels and ZR tires, new alarm system, sunroof, and new Blaupunkt radio."
- The 928 S4. "Very high performance delivered in a comfortable environment was the original design target for the Porsche 928. A design target escalated, and

achieved, time after time in its advancing evolution. The stunning 1989 edition of this outstanding sports car continues to distinguish itself from its competition by advanced technology and materials throughout, resulting in astonishing performance capabilities. With its Weissach axle the 928 S4 continues to set new cornering standards, while the 316 hp 32-valve engine and ABS braking maximize performance with safety. New for 1989: refined back-lit instrumentation and revised automatic transmission ratios, electronic diagnostic system and driving computer, and improved stereo and alarm systems."

- The 944 Turbo. "This automobile continues to embody the very latest advances in production car turbocharging and aerodynamic technology. Chronicled throughout motoring journals everywhere as nothing less than the current standard for high-performance sports cars, last year's limited edition 944 Turbo S inspired this year's 944 Turbo. Effortless acceleration, superb roadhandling, and exemplary comfort combine to provide the 944 Turbo owner with an unparalleled driving experience. New for 1989: 2.5 liter, 247 bhp engine, Sport suspension, brakes and transmission, and substantially expanded standard equipment."

## Distribution Decisions

In 1975, the 72 authorized Porsche dealers in Canada (all of whom also sold Audi and Volkswagen cars) sold 226 cars. The number of Volkswagen dealers carrying Porsche had grown quickly as Porsches provided an incremental source of profits. In the early days, with "Beetles" retailing at $2,000 each, an average Porsche might contribute $2,000 of gross profit to the dealership. With a slight downturn in the automotive market, the demise of the Porsche 914 (the low-priced, so-called "Volks-Porsche") and marketing research which showed Porsche purchasers wanted fewer barriers/ interfaces between them and the company, Porsche Division saw a chance to reduce some of the dealerships which sold only a few Porsches per year. In 1976, the number of Porsche dealers in Canada had been reduced to 33 and by 1979 that number was further reduced to 14. Over the next ten years, only two additional dealerships had been added (Table 2 lists the current dealer locations).

The 16 existing dealerships ranged from selling only Porsche to combining its sale with Volkswagen, Audi, Mercedes, BMW, Jaguar, Saab, and Volvo. The primary reason for keeping the smaller number of dealers was customer satisfaction. The best dealers were often "fanatic" Porsche lovers dedicated to the line and offering the best service. Dealers who carried Porsche as a side line were unable properly to sell and service the car. A mechanic had to be properly trained to service a Porsche and if only a few Porsches were serviced each month, the mechanic would quickly lose his edge.

The financial structure of each dealership was quite different. The larger the investment, the larger the acceptable profit level. A Porsche- only dealership with a large service business could sell only 20 to 30 new and used Porsches to earn acceptable profits. Another dealership with a smaller service business would have to sell 75 new and used Porsches. To reduce overhead, the "dual" dealerships listed above were born of necessity. Regardless, Mr. Dubee felt that any new dealership should be capable of selling 45 to 55 new and used Porsches annually. To maintain a service support edge, at least 100 to 200 cars per year had to come into the shop.

Within the last three weeks, Mr. Dubee had received proposals for five new dealerships. In evaluating a proposal, Mr. Dubee looked both at the market potential and at the person making the proposal. He felt that, at most, one dealership could be added while maintaining the 1989 Porsche business goals. When looking at market potential, he considered customer needs particularly in terms of technical service, geographic coverage of the dealership, possibility of cannibalizing business from existing dealers, and a potential for selling an adequate volume of new and used cars. If this analysis was positive, he examined the person making the proposal by checking his or her references, his or her past experience in the car industry (especially in the used car department), and the financial resources at the person's disposal. In particular, one would need $1 to 2 million to open a dealership exclusive of the land and the building.

Attitude was an important consideration in the examination of a dealership applicant. A Porsche purchaser, to acquire his or her car, would spend as much as many people would spend on a home. An average car salesperson, thinking that someone spending this much money on a car was quite foolish, would have a hard time communicating to a customer. Thus a good potential dealer had to be a lover of fine cars and of Porsches in particular.

# Proposals for New Dealerships

Mr. Dunbee prepared summary comments on each of the five proposals.

1. Trois Rivières, Quebec
   - nearest dealerships - Quebec City and Montreal - each about 110 kilometres away
   - population - 50,122
   - number of new and used cars sold - 20-25,000
   - number of Porsches in the area - 25
   - may need to use lower price to entice customer purchases
   - proposal submitted by a father and son team aged 28 and 56 - father had owned the top Chrysler dealership in the region but sold out after a heart attack three years ago—son just finished a four-year term in the army after completing a degree at the Royal Military College
   - basically father would supply the capital and son would run the dealership— father would be involved in promotion, however
   - pair had $800,000 to invest and felt they could get by without any additional financing

2. St. John's, Newfoundland
   - nearest dealership—Halifax—about 860 kilometres away
   - population—96,216
   - number of new and used cars sold—15-20,000
   - no Porsche dealers in Newfoundland or eastern Quebec
   - number of Porsches in the area—12
   - proposal submitted by two former fishermen aged 48 and 52—each had 20 years work experience in fish processing plants attaining levels of Marketing Manager and Production Manager respectively—plant had recently closed and both took early retirement
   - one had worked for two years at a Ford dealership 25 years ago and the other had some experience as a mechanic on a fishing trawler nearly 30 ago
   - pair had $300.000 to invest and felt that they could get government and bank financing for $1,000,000

3. Oakville, Ontario
   - nearest dealership—Toronto—about 35 kilometres away
   - population—83,214
   - number of new and used cars sold—45-50,000
   - hard to know buying habits as consumers were very mobile in the Golden Horseshoe area
   - number of Porsches in the area—250-400
   - have excellent market penetration
   - proposal submitted by three women between the ages of 35 and 43—each had worked for ten years prior to leaving the work force to have children—one had worked at a car dealership, one was a lawyer, and one was a pay equity consultant
   - proposal would see each of the three women working in the dealership but for less than 30 hours per week so that they could spend time with their young children
   - group had $200,000 to invest and felt that they could get a bank loan for $800,000

4. London, Ontario
   - nearest dealership—St. Catharines—about 170 kilometres away
   - population— 276,000
   - number of new and used cars sold—45-50,000
   - number of Porsches in the area—250-300
   - large number of independent unauthorized service centers in southwestern Ontario—problem for Porsche Canada
   - proposal submitted by a group of seven recent MBA grads between the ages of 27 and 30—each had two to three years work experience in packaged goods firms like Procter and Gamble or Colgate-Palmolive
   - three of the group would work at the dealership, the other four would be silent partners
   - group had $105,000 to invest and felt that they could get a line of credit for $900,000

5. Regina, Saskatchewan
   - nearest dealership—Saskatoon—about 225 kilometres away
   - population—175,064
   - number of new and used cars sold—35-40,000
   - number of Porsches in the area—30-50
   - proposal submitted by a former member of legislative assembly aged 45—had been in the assembly for 15 years attaining level of Assistant Minister of Industry and Trade—had owned a chain of hardware stores which had recently been sold
   - had $10,000,000 to invest and felt that this would be one of a number of new ventures for him

## The Decision

As Mr. Dubee leafed through the proposals, he thought about the Porsche Division's goal of wanting to sell and service all new and used Porsches in Canada. He was aware that some of these proposals would only contribute marginally to sales, could take away sales from existing dealers, might eliminate some unauthorized Porsche service centers, and could lead to poor customer service in the smaller territories. Locating dealerships in high traffic areas or "automotive rows" was unnecessary as Porsche dealerships were a destination for a shopping trip. If only increased sales were needed, he could work with existing dealers to improve the situation.

The decision was not an easy one. He began the task of preparing his assessment for the quarterly meeting next week.

# Questions

1. What criteria should be used to evaluate a potential dealer?

2. Using these criteria, what is the rank order of the five potential dealers?

3. Would you recommend giving any of these potential dealers a dealership? If yes, who? If no, why not?

**TABLE 1**
**Porsche Division: Key Business Goals**

Ensure that:

- The Customer Comes First

  The most valuable capital Porsche has is its band of loyal customers with their sense of Porsche responsibility.

- Porsches Are Serviced Only By Porsche

  Porsche's commitment to every owner and to each Porsche extends for the life of the car.

- Porsche Controls the Used Porsche Business

  A Porsche is a Porsche is a Porsche.

- Each Potential Porsche Person is Introduced to the Marque With Care

  There are many people who would like to drive a Porsche if the idea were presented to them properly.

**TABLE 2**
**List Of Dealer Locations**

| British Columbia | Manitoba | Quebec |
|---|---|---|
| • Vancouver | • Winnipeg | • Montreal (2) |
| • Victoria | | • Quebec City |
| | Ontario | |
| Alberta | • Toronto | New Brunswick |
| • Edmonton | • Scarborough | • Moncton/Dieppe |
| • Calgary | • Newmarket | |
| | • St. Catharines | Nova Scotia |
| Saskatchewan | • Ottawa | • Halifax |
| • Saskatoon | | |

# 19. THE TOT-SWITCH

Written by Robert Wyckham, Simon Fraser University

Jim Halstrum, the inventor of the Tot-Switch, was confronted with an interesting and perplexing dilemma. He was faced with the choice of leaving his product in the hands of Innovation Promotions Limited or using legal means to obtain control over Tot-Switch and finding another method of producing and marketing it.

The Tot-Switch was created by Mr. Halstrum to solve a problem he had observed in his own home. While recuperating from an illness, he noticed how often his two children, aged two and three years, asked their mother to turn lights on. He also noticed that the lights were left on as the children moved from one area to another in the house to play. He thought that if he could devise some method whereby the youngsters could turn the lights on and off he would save his wife innumerable steps and perhaps cut his hydro bill.

After tinkering with pulleys and switches, Mr. Halstrum was able to develop the prototype of the Tot-Switch. A string-and-pulley system allowed the children to operate the light switches. He put a number of these crude attachments on light switches throughout his house and immediately discovered a bonus. The children were able to light their own way to the bathroom at night.

Mr. Halstrum received encouragement from friends who were impressed by the system. Some asked him to put together sets for their homes. During the next few months he made numerous changes in design and materials until the light switch system was durable, easy to install, and easy to use.

After ten months of experimentation, Mr. Halstrum took two major steps. First, he made arrangements to patent his invention. He took out patents on five different designs in Canada. He also applied for patents in the United States and Japan. The total cost of his patents in the three countries was $4,050. Second, he consulted with Dr. Roger Vergin, a professor of business administration at Simon Fraser University. Professor Vergin agreed to install the switch system in two day-care centers with which he was associated in Bellingham, Washington.

Six months of heavy use by the children in the two daycare centers indicated that the switch systems worked very well. They did not break down, and the youngsters found them easy to use. At this point Professor Vergin recommended to Mr. Halstrum that he try to sell the concept to a manufacturer.

## Initial Marketing Efforts

Jim Halstrum's next step was to mail 50 prototypes of his switch to manufacturers and distributors across Canada. Over the next month or so he received a varied response:

1. McDonald's restaurant chain expressed interest in the switch as a promotional item. They would be willing to purchase 2.5 million units if Halstrum could sell the units for eight cents apiece.

2. A number of electric utility companies were favorably disposed toward the product. They were orienting their promotion toward conservation, and the switches

fit this theme. However, because of federal regulations, none of the utilities was able to help develop and market the product.

3. A sizable number of small manufacturers and distributors felt the product had merit. They wrote asking for additional information.

At this point, a friend told Mr. Halstrum about a company called Innovation Promotions Limited. Innovation Promotions had been formed recently by a lawyer, John Pobst, and an engineer, Fred Jamison, for the purpose of new product development. In their separate professional practices, Pobst and Jamison had observed the problems that inventors have in exploiting their new products. They decided that they could assist inventors and build a healthy business in new product development. At the time that Mr. Halstrum contacted Innovation Promotions, the company had one product under contract for development.

## The Contract

After a number of meetings with Pobst and Jamison, Mr. Halstrum agreed to a contract which would give Innovation Promotions Limited control over the product for five years. The contract, which was signed in October, contained the following conditions:

1. Innovation Promotions would research the market, develop the product for mass production, promote, and handle sales of the product.

2. Mr. Halstrum was to receive a royalty of 25 cents on each unit sold.

3. Innovation Promotions must sell a minimum of 30,000 units in the first year and 450,000 units over the next four years.

4. If at any time Innovation Promotions failed to fulfill their agreement, Mr. Halstrum would regain control over the product.

During the late fall, Innovation Promotions contracted with a plastics manufacturer in Vancouver to produce the product. The switch was modified and engineered to allow mass production. A two-cavity model was produced at a cost of $5,600. This resulted in a production cost of $.27 per unit. An eight-cavity model, which would have cost $18,000, would have reduced production costs to $.10 per unit.

A creative director from an advertising agency was hired to develop a name for the product and to design the package. The name chosen was the Tot-Switch. It was selected because it described the product in use and was catchy. The package design was executed by a local packaging firm. Mr. Jamison decided to use an innovative skin-tight plastic-coated package, which, although expensive ($.35 per unit), was thought to be a selling feature to the trade.

It was decided that the Tot-Switch should retail for $4.99. Up to this point no market or consumer research had been done. Pobst and Jamison were of the opinion that the six-month test at the daycare centers was an adequate evaluation of the worth of the product.

An initial production run of 2,500 units was completed by the end of January. The costs of production and markups for the first production run are shown in Table 1.

**TABLE 1**
**Selling Price and Costs**

|  | Per Unit |
|---|---|
| Retail selling price | $4.99 |
| Retail margin | 2.50 |
| Wholesale selling price | $2.49 |
| Production cost | .27 |
| Packaging cost | .35 |
| Royalty to Halstrum | .25 |
| Taxes | .16 |
| Royalty to Innovation Promotions, Shipping, and Advertising* | 1.46 |
|  | $2.49 |

As a first thrust into the marketplace, Innovation Promotions decided to use a mail-order marketing approach. An advertisement was prepared and placed in the Ontario, British Columbia, and Alberta regional editions of *TV Guide* for the first and third weeks in February. The advertisement encouraged multiple purchases by offering a quantity discount. Prices, including mailing and handling costs, were as follows: one, $5.49; two, $4.75 per unit; three, $4.58 per unit; five or more, $3.75 per unit.

## Mr. Halstrum's Reaction

Mr. Halstrum was very disappointed with the performance of Innovation Promotions Limited. He felt that the $4.99 price was much too high. His original idea was to sell the product for about $1.99. Although he could understand the benefits of using mass advertising to make people aware of the Tot-Switch, he felt that the mail order idea was a waste of time. Only about 500 units had been sold on the basis of the *TV Guide* ads. In discussing the situation with a friend, he made the following comments:

> They are never going to sell the required 30,000 units by September. Sales at the Thunderbird Electrical stores are not going well. I understand a California manufacturer has shown interest, but he wants national advertising support. Pobst and Jamison are negotiating with a local wholesaler on a deal for 300,000 units, but I can't see anything resulting from the discussions. They have also talked with the Paraplegic Society of British Columbia. Apparently the society wants to promote the product through their magazine and is asking for a 50-cent fee for each unit sold. As far as I'm concerned they just haven't been able to put the thing together. They probably should have gone the traditional route through the department stores. McDonald's is still interested, and if I could get the production costs down and McDonald's' price up I might be able to move a fantastic number of units in one quick sale.

Mr. Halstrum wondered what he should do. He felt only two options existed at this time, to hope for the best and leave the product with Innovation Promotions, or to use legal means to regain control of Tot-Switch and design a new marketing strategy for the product.

## Questions

1. What options are open to an inventor in bringing a new product to the market?
2. What steps can be taken to determine the size of the market for a new product?
3. Evaluate the current marketing mix for the Tot-Switch.
4. Assume Mr. Halstrum regains control of the Tot-Switch. What would you recommend as a future strategy?

# 20. Camp Fortune Ski Resort

Written by Sadrudin A. Ahmed and David Litvack, University of Ottawa

In August 1983, while most Canadians had their minds on enjoying the summer heat, Cindy Lawrence was thinking about skiing. As the newly hired marketing manager of Ottawa's Camp Fortune Ski Resort, Ms. Lawrence was concerned with reversing the decline in use of Camp Fortune over the past four years, particularly the poor attendance levels on weekdays and evenings. In the past, Camp Fortune had employed a marketing/sales person during only the fall and winter months; however, this year the Board had decided that more attention to marketing was needed and had hired Ms. Lawrence on a full-time basis. While her main goal was to establish a promotion policy for the 1983/84 skiing season, there was still time available for her to make changes in other areas, such as pricing.

## Background

Camp Fortune was situated in the heart of the Gatineau area of Western Quebec, 18 kilometres north of Ottawa-Hull, a metropolitan area with a population of 718,000, of which one-third was French speaking and two-thirds English speaking. The resort, established in 1909, was the oldest ski development in the area. It had been publicly owned by the nonprofit Ottawa Ski Club since 1921. The club's membership of approximately 3,000, mainly Anglophone, had remained fairly constant for the past six years.

The Ottawa Ski Club was incorporated as a nonprofit club to provide recreational facilities and opportunities for its members. Participation in the club required only the payment of nominal annual fees. Membership reached a peak of 14,000 in 1971 but had declined since then to 3,000.

The club was governed by an elected Board of Directors, comprising 16 volunteer members. At the Annual General Meeting in November of each year, half the board positions came up for election or re-election. In addition to board volunteers, many other members served on a variety of volunteer committees responsible for competitions, special events, and social activities.

The club staff was responsible for the day-to-day operation of the club, while the board provided general guidelines and made policy decisions. Regular monthly management meetings held during the fall and winter helped to ensure that board-staff communications were clear and that membership needs were being satisfied.

## Staff

The number of employees required to operate and maintain the club's 300 acres of land varied according to the amount of snowfall and the weather conditions. A good season required a staff of 75 full-time employees (day and night), with an additional 50 part-timers for weekends, and approximately 100 instructors for the ski school. A poor season could lead to a reduction in staff by as much as 50%, due to the closure of various trails. During the summer months, a skeleton staff operated various concessions at outdoor concerts, rented day lodges, catered banquets, and rented space for recreational purposes such as field days, company picnics, or fun runs.

## Facilities

With its wide variety of slopes, Camp Fortune could cater to all levels of skiers from novice to expert downhiller. In addition, the club had access to 220 kilometres of well-groomed and patrolled cross-country trails that radiated into the Gatineau Park. (Camp Fortune owned 20 kilometres of these trails, while the other 200 kilometres belonged to the National Capital Commission.) Alpine (downhill) skiers at the club were taken quickly and smoothly to the top of the runs on eight lifts: one triple-chair, one double-chair, four T-bars, one poma, and one rope tow. Total uphill capacity was 8,000 skiers per hour. On a good weekend, over 5,000 skiers could be on the slopes.

For office employees or students unable to get away during the day, Camp Fortune had trails open for night skiing from 4:30 to 10:30 p.m. Like other hills in the area, Camp Fortune had snowmaking equipment that could keep 90% of the trails adequately covered for most of the four-month ski season.

Camp Fortune's ski school, with over 100 highly qualified instructors, offered a number of programs ranging from teaching basics to beginners to helping more advanced skiers perfect their style. Alpine and cross-country skiing classes were available in both group and private sessions during the day, evenings, and weekends. Skiers could enjoy the hills with the knowledge that the Ottawa Ski Club Aid and Rescue Service (OSCARS) was available to assist them in the event of an accident. For the convenience of its skiers, the club ran a bus service which left from various locations in the City of Ottawa twice a day during the week. A babysitting service for parents with young children was also available.

One of Camp Fortune's most appealing features was its proximity to the Ottawa-Hull area. Historically, upper-middle-class English-speaking families accounted for the greatest portion of its season pass holders, while daily and nightly passes were bought primarily by students, professionals, or shift workers whose schedules were flexible.

# Food and Bar Facilities at Fortune

The club operated two major lodges for its skiers. Lockberg Lodge, situated at the base of the 60-metre jump and slalom hill, housed Le Loft, the main bar of the club. Le Loft was on the second floor of the lodge and could accommodate 75 people. In spite of the lodge's rustic look, its atmosphere was not very cosy; it was furnished with cafeteria-style tables and chairs, and its lighting was non-decorative. On the other hand, the lodge's ground floor, which could accommodate 100 people, offered skiers the warmth and ambience of a large fireplace while they munched on nachos and sandwiches or ate from the elaborate but reasonably priced salad bar and full buffet.

Lockberg Lodge was open from 9:30 a.m. to 11:00 p.m. on Saturdays, Sundays, and holidays, and between 11:00 a.m. and 11:30 p.m. on weekdays, but would remain open longer if so desired by its patrons. The club's management was disappointed with the turnout at the lodge. Although Lockberg was fairly busy during the day and after 9:00 p.m., it was virtually empty from 6:00 to 9:00 p.m. The amount of food and beverages sold was also disappointing. In an effort to encourage people to remain at the bar longer, the management experimented by providing disco and live entertainment for a two-week period during 1982. This experiment did not prove very successful and was abandoned.

Management was also concerned about the location and visibility of the bar. From the base of Fortune Valley the lodge was hidden behind thick trees and was easily accessible only to slalom trail skiers on their way down the mountain. Skiers who took other trails or who were returning ski equipment to the rental shop were unlikely to climb back up the hill to go to the bar, and those who did wish to venture back up the hill were often uncertain as to which of the chalet-like structures was the bar. In fact, the ski patrol's cabin was often mistaken for the lodge.

Alexander Lodge, the well-located main cafeteria, was essentially a meeting and eating place for skiers. Many families that skied the hill brought bag lunches and only bought drinks. This cafeteria could comfortably accommodate 240 people.

Camp Fortune also operated other minor lodges for the convenience of its cross-country and downhill skiers. Management was satisfied with the performance of these lodges.

# Promotion

Of the funds allocated to promotion and advertising during the past year, over one-third (36%) was spent on 30-second spot radio commercials. Another 36% was spent on printed material such as brochures, posters, and WOW passes (see Exhibit 1).[1] An additional 8% was used to place advertisements in newspapers (both English and French), and university and college newspapers. University and college papers advertised specials during spring break - coupons offering discounts for the bar, bus trips, etc. The remainder of the advertising budget was spent on magazine advertising, special promotions, and miscellaneous advertising.

Management felt that most of its potential clients were reached with this media mix. Ad themes and frequency varied during the year. For example, extensive advertising was employed throughout October to sell season passes. These sales were crucial to minimize losses that might be incurred if snow conditions were poor. Discounts ranging from 15 to 18% were offered for purchases made before

November 1. Smaller discounts were also offered if the passes were purchased in November. Exhibit 2 provides the expected prices for 1983 of passes at the major ski hills in the area. Most season passes were bought before November 1.

Since an estimated 30% of Camp Fortune's business occurred between Christmas and New Year's Day, a big advertising blitz was aimed at that period. In addition, several special campaigns were run during the rest of the skiing season. The WOW pass (Exhibit 1) was designed to encourage occasional skiers to return to Camp Fortune. This package contained lift tickets for holiday and weekend skiing and coupons for various Camp Fortune services, such as the Fortune Ski Bus and Cuspidor Day. Special package deals for lessons were also promoted before the Christmas season to attract all types of skiers over the holidays. The $5 *Ski 88* booklet, a promotional effort designed to increase skiing during the non-peak period, offered 25 coupons with a total value of $88. This promotion had the additional objective of raising money for skiers who hoped to be members of the 1988 Canadian Olympic ski team, so that they could train at Camp Fortune.

National Ski Week (January 21-28), with many skiing events, programs, and promotions, was organized by the local ski industry to persuade non- skiers thinking about skiing to actually try it. To entice non-skiers, Camp Fortune offered the Five-80 Ski evening with radio station CFRA, and the Learn-to-Ski package ($12 for one half-hour introductory lesson, one half-day of skiing, and rental of ski equipment). Advertisements were to be placed in university newspapers prior to the study break in February and in local newspapers before the March school break.[2] Camp Fortune's main advertising theme was "closer, bigger, better value" (Exhibit 3).

## The Skiing Market

According to the Canada Fitness Survey of 1981, most alpine skiers (about 81%) skied infrequently, limiting their skiing to less than once a month or fewer than 11 occasions per year. Among adult skiers aged 25 and over, 54% reported annual family incomes of at least $25,000 and 64% were married. Most alpine skiers were under 40 years of age, and 60% were male. Fifteen percent of alpine skiers between the ages of 10 and 19 were occasional skiers; 13% were regular skiers. Cross-country skiers tended to be older, married, and to have a slightly lower income than downhill skiers.

Alpine skiing appealed to many Canadians. The major obstacles faced by those who said they wanted to learn alpine skiing were cost (30%), lack of time (20%), and no facilities or equipment (14%). Seven percent of the alpine skiers reported stopping in the past year; 56% of these were females. Among these females, illness or injury was the leading reason given for stopping, while males were most likely to stop, they reported, because of lack of time.

When asked to describe why a person decides to go skiing, Ms. Lawrence said that fun, excitement, physical exercise, after-ski social activities, impressing friends, and becoming an expert were some of the benefits sought by skiers. The criteria used to select a ski resort depended on the benefits sought, as well as factors such as price, distance from home or work, safety, crowds, after-ski activities, availability of ski schools, babysitting services, number and quality of ski runs, and discounts offered.

# The Industry

In the past few years, unusually mild winters had caused financial problems for the local ski industry. Although all the ski operators in the Western Quebec-Gatineau region had snowmaking equipment and could keep at least a few hills adequately covered with snow, it was difficult to persuade city dwellers to go skiing when they could not see any snow on the ground at home. The worst period for the industry within the last five years had been the 1982-83 ski season. The warm December weather had ruined Christmas holiday skiing, which normally accounted for 25 to 33% of an operator's annual earnings. Camp Fortune's management estimated that it had made only 50% of its normal ticket sales during this period.

# Competition

There were four other ski hills in the Western Quebec-Gatineau area: Edelweiss, Vorlage, Mont Cascades, and Mont Ste. Marie. Exhibit 4 provides a comparison of the ski hills on a number of features and Exhibit 5 provides information on pricing at the hills.

Edelweiss was regarded as the main competition. The size of the Edelweiss ski area and its amenities were similar to those of Camp Fortune, except that it had just one main lodge which served as a central meeting place. Edelweiss's chalet-style lodge had a huge fireplace and bar that lent it a very pleasant après-ski ambience. This was believed to be one of the main reasons for its popularity with teenagers. It would cost over $300,000 in 1984 to build such a chalet at Camp Fortune. Edelweiss had a 25% share of the market and was 15 kilometres further from the city of Ottawa than Camp Fortune. Tow tickets were about the same price at both Edelweiss and Camp Fortune.

Vorlage, located a short distance from Edelweiss (35 kilometres from Ottawa), was known as the industry price cutter. Facilities at the resort were regarded as adequate. It was a family-oriented resort and had a ten percent share of the market. Its ski area was much smaller than that of Camp Fortune or Edelweiss.

Mont Cascades, located 20 kilometres from Ottawa, had a 15% market share. Although the facilities at Mont Cascades were adequate, the resort did not offer the diversity of runs needed to challenge the better skier.

Mont St. Marie, the highest mountain in the area, attracted the more dedicated and serious skier. Its picturesque location and hotel facilities also attracted many conference-goers. It was the farthest hill from Ottawa (88 kilometres), but captured 25% of the market. Its one main lodge had a chalet theme and included a fireplace, bar, restaurant, and cafeteria. The tow rates at Mont Ste. Marie were the highest in the region.

# The Marketing Plan

**Promotion:** In designing her marketing plan, Ms. Lawrence felt that promotional activities were important in attracting more people to the resort. She wondered if she should change her main advertising theme and/or media mix. She knew that for the 1983/84 skiing season, she could only afford a five to ten percent increase in her promotion budget of $60,000. To help her decide what might be a suitable approach to take, she collected some information regarding the Ottawa market and the costs and coverage of the local media vehicles (Appendix 1).

Next, she reviewed the promotional strategy for the past year. For the 1982/83 skiing season, the types of skiing to be promoted to various target groups through advertising messages were:

**TABLE 1**

| Target Group | Types of Skiing Promoted |
|---|---|
| Young Adult Segment (20-24 years old) | Night |
| Adult Segment (25-34 years old) | Weekday, Night |
| Family Segment (35-54 years old) | Weekends |
| Old and Retired Segment (55-64 years old) | Weekdays, Weekends |

Sixty percent of the advertising budget was spent between the first of October and 15th of December, 28% during the Christmas holidays, and 12% during the February break. Eight percent of the budget was spent on regular newspapers, with 20 advertisements in the *Citizen*, 15 in *Sunday Herald*, and five in *Le Droit*. Total cost of these print advertisements was $4,800 (40 advertisements at $120 each).

Thirty-six percent of the budget was spent on radio announcements. CHEZ-FM, CFGO, CFRA, CBO, and CIMF-FM (French) radio stations would broadcast ads from 7:00 a.m. to 10:00 p.m. The spots were directed at the adult segment during the early morning, the family segment during the day, and young adults in the evening. The detailed breakdown of the radio-broadcast plan is shown below.

Thirty-six percent of the budget was spent on printing brochures, posters, and WOW passes. Posters were put at the point of sale of ski equipment in sports shops to reach the adult segment and in the student residences to reach students. Brochures were made available in the hotels and restaurants of the capital (to inform the adult segment) and at the Rideau Centre.

**Table 2**
**Advertising Schedule and Number of Advertisements**

| | Period Oct 1-Dec 19 | Period Dec 20-Jan 4 | Period Feb 20-Feb 28 | Total |
|---|---|---|---|---|
| CHEZ-FM | 60 ads | 28 ads | 12 ads | 100 ads |
| CFGO | 75 | 36 | 14 | 125 |
| CFRA | 57 | 26 | 12 | 95 |
| CBO | 15 | 7 | 3 | 25 |
| Q 101 | 45 | 9 | 21 | 75 |
| CIFM-FM | 30 | 14 | 6 | 50 |
| | | | | 470 |

Cost: 470 advertisements at $46 each = $21,620

Nine percent of the advertising budget was spent on magazine advertising (for example, *Voyageur*) and 11% on special promotions and miscellaneous advertising.

**Segmentation**: Ms. Lawrence considered focusing on the teen market as Edelweiss had done. This segment, however, was under the drinking age. The 25 to 35-year-old adult group was another alternative. This age group was the one most likely to spend money on food and beverages. Due to the proximity of numerous government offices and the flexible working hours of government employees, she felt she could attract some of this market for weekday skiing. She also considered assessing the potential of each market segment to increase its attendance on weekdays and evenings. As well, she thought she could devote some effort to turning the occasional skier into a "regular" at Camp Fortune and wondered what kind of promotional schemes might accomplish this. She wondered, too, if serious thought and greater effort should be given to generating more revenue during the summer.

**Pricing**: While prices had been set before Ms. Lawrence was hired, there was still time to make changes as no passes had yet been sold. She had considerably more flexibility, however, with regard to promotional pricing.

**Low Snowfall**: Finally, she asked herself what plan of action should be followed to attract skiers to the hills if there were low snowfall this year. Should she rally the whole ski industry for a joint promotional campaign? What type of publicity campaign would be likely to persuade skiers to ski on hills covered with only artificial snow?

[1] The resort's printed material, which consisted of a series of brochures on features offered at Camp Fortune, such as prices, season passes, lessons and bus schedules, was distributed to some of the ski and sport stores in the Ottawa-Hull area.

[2] Camp Fortune also had a mailing list made up of approximately 20,000 names compiled from lists such as ski schools, WOW pass buyers, group mailings, members, and hotels.

## Questions

1. How could/should the skiing market in Ottawa be segmented?
2. What are the strengths and weaknesses of Camp Fortune Ski Resort?
3. What positioning strategy would you recommend for Camp Fortune?
4. Develop a promotion and pricing plan for the forthcoming year.

**EXHIBIT 1**
**WOW Pass Advertisement**

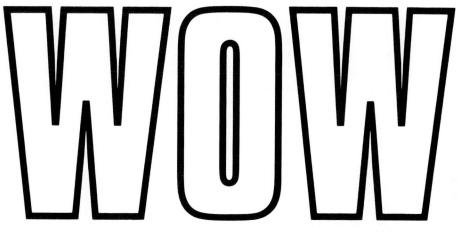

# A SUPER STOCKING STUFFER

# CAMP FORTUNE WOW PASS

**ONLY**
**$39** adults
**$34** students (17 & under)
**$24** junior (13 & under)

DISCOUNTS OF UP TO **38%**.
FOR **5** GREAT SKIING
EXPERIENCES!
Includes other important
cash savers.

**GIVE THE GIFT OF GREAT SKIING**
Order the Camp Fortune WOW pass
for your favourite skier.
Delivery guaranteed by Christmas.
Mastercharge and Visa accepted on
phone orders.

SKI CAMP FORTUNE

CALL CAMP FORTUNE 827-1717, ALSO AVAILABLE AT MOST SPORT SHOPS.

**EXHIBIT 2**
**Expected Prices of Season Passes for 1983**

| | Camp Fortune | | | Cascades | | Edelweiss | | Mt. Ste. Marie | Vorlage | |
|---|---|---|---|---|---|---|---|---|---|---|
| | A. | B. | C. | D. | E. | F. | G | H. | I. | J. |
| Family (4 persons) | | | | $500 | $575 | $500 | $575 | $560 | $430 | $495 |
| Additional members | | | | 75 | 100 | 75 | 100 | 100 | 50 | 60 |
| Maximum | $700 | $735 | $800 | 675 | 775 | 675 | 775 | 910 | 580 | 675 |
| Married Couple | | | | 390 | 425 | 390 | 425 | 710 | 340 | 380 |
| Adult | 210 | 220 | 250 | 215 | 235 | | | 395 | 195 | 220 |
| Student (16-21) | 190 | *200* | 230* | 185 | 200 | 185 | 200 | 340 + | 165 | 195 |
| (13-15) | 170 | 180 | 200 | 165 | 180 | 165 | 180 | | 165 | 195 |
| Junior (12 and under) | 140 | 150 | 170 | 130 | 140 | 130 | 140 | 280 + | 120 | 140 |
| Senior Citizen (65 and over) | 140 | 150 | 170 | | | | | 280 | 120 | 140 |
| Children under six | Free | Free | 20 | Free | Free | Free | Free | Free | Free | Free |
| Night Passes All ages | 105 | 110 | 125 | N/A | N/A | N/A | N/A | N/A | N/A | N/A |

A: Before Nov. 1
B: Nov. 1 - Nov. 30
C: Regular
D: Preseason
+ Ages 16 and under
* Ages 16-17
Family discount plan: Add up the value of the family application and apply the following discounts, based on the total number of passes purchased.
> Two passes 10% off
> Three passes 15% off
> Four passes 17.5% off
> Five passes or more 20.2% off

**Season Cross Country Ski Pass**

| | Fortune | | | Cascades $ | Edelweiss $ | Mt. St. Marie $ | Vorlage $ |
|---|---|---|---|---|---|---|---|
| | Before Nov. 1 | Nov. 1- Nov. 30 | Dec. ($) | | | | |
| Adult | 55 | 60 | 75 | | | 70 | |
| Junior and Student | 30 | 35 | 45 | Free | Free | 50 | N/A |
| Family Maximum | 150 | 160 | 180 | | | 110 | |

**EXHIBIT 3**
**Sample Advertising**

**12 MINUTES FROM OTTAWA**

## CAMP FORTUNE IS BETTER RELATIVE VALUE THAN EVER

## COMPARE . . . SEASON PASS COSTS**

| | Camp Fortune | Edelweiss | Mont Cascades | Vorlage | Mont Ste. Marie |
|---|---|---|---|---|---|
| ADULT | $160 | $165 | $145 | $140 | $240 |
| STUDENT | 150 | 145 | 120 | 120 | 165 |
| YOUTH | 130 | 125 | 120 | 120 | 165 |
| JUNIOR | 120 | 100 | 80 | 80 | 165 |
| MARRIED COUPLE | 295 | 290 | 260 | 250 | 390 |
| FAMILY OF FOUR | 485 | 425 | 375 | 375 | 605 |

*OUR PASS IS THE MEMBER/PASS—includes many other benefits—and discounts at other ski areas and ski shops.

## COMPARE                                              CLOSER

Camp Fortune is just 12 minutes from the Macdonald–Cartier Bridge in Ottawa to our Skyline parking lot.
Visits to Camp Fortune this winter could save a smart family
. . . ? hours of driving time
. . . ? kilometres of gas consumption and vehicle wear and tear
. . . Or for those not driving, 28 convenient bus departures per week every day and night

## COMPARE                                              BIGGER

Sixteen runs, eight lifts, six lodges, now 6 hills lighted for night skiing, 70 member bilingual professional ski school, 90% of area covered by snow-making facilities and the best access to 220 kilometres of groomed cross-country trails.

## OUR CONCLUSION                          BETTER VALUE

Camp Fortune provides its member/pass holders the best relative ski value in the national capital . . . and you are an owner of the Ottawa Ski Club. No one profits from your skiing at Camp Fortune but yourself—be an owner . . . join Camp Fortune.

## TO RESERVE YOUR MEMBER/PASS
## CALL 827-1717

### VISIT OUR SKI EXCHANGE ON WEEKENDS
### —OUR TRADING POST

**FROM PUBLISHED MATERIAL

**EXHIBIT 4**
**Main Features of the Gatineau Area Ski Resorts**

| Features | Fortune | Cascades | Edelweiss | Mt. Ste. Marie | Vorlage |
|---|---|---|---|---|---|
| Trails | 17 | 11 | 17 | 16 | 12 |
| Number of Easiest | 5 | 1 | | | 1 |
| more difficult | 5 | 8 | | | 9 |
| most difficult | 7 | 2 | | | 2 |
| Vertical drop | 192 m (630') | 152 m (500') | 198m (650') | 381 m (1250') | 142 m (465') |
| Length | 2146 m (7040') | 1219 m (4000') | 1829 m (6000') | 3658 m (12000') | 1609 m (5280') |
| Tow Service | | | | | |
| Triple chair | 1 | 1 | — | — | — |
| Double chair | 1 | 1 | 2 | — | 1 |
| T-bar | 4 | 2 | 2 | — | 4 |
| Poma | 1 | 1 | 2 | — | — |
| Rope | 1 | — | — | — | — |
| Cross-Country Skiing | yes | yes | yes | yes | no |
| Snowshoeing | no | no | no | no | no |
| Equipment Rental | yes | yes | yes | yes | yes |
| Ski School | yes | yes | yes | yes | yes |
| Night School | yes | yes | yes | no | yes |
| Snowmaking | yes | yes | yes | yes | yes |
| Lounge | yes | yes | yes | yes | yes |
| Bus Service | yes | yes | yes | — | yes |
| Restaurant | yes | yes | yes | yes | yes |
| Bar | yes | yes | yes | yes | yes |
| Lodging | no | no | yes | yes | no |
| Baby Sitting | yes | — | — | — | yes |
| Distance from Ottawa-Hull area | 18 km | 20 km | 35 km | 88 km | 35 km |
| Music Concerts | yes | — | — | — | — |
| Waterslide | — | yes | — | — | — |

**EXHIBIT 5**
**Prices of Daily and Nightly Passes by Age Group[1]**

| | Camp Fortune | | Cascades | | Edelweiss | |
|---|---|---|---|---|---|---|
| | Weekday | Weekend | Weekday | Weekend | Weekday | Weekend |
| **Adult** | | | | | | |
| - all day | $12.00 | $15.00 | $11.00 | $14.00 | $11.00 | $14.00 |
| - after 1:00 p.m. | 10.00 | 12.00 | 11.00 | 14.00 | 11.00 | 14.00 |
| - night | 10.00 | 10.00 | — | — | 11.00 | 12.00 |

Continued on p. 599

(Exhibit 5 continued))

|  | Camp Fortune | | Cascades | | Edelweiss | |
|---|---|---|---|---|---|---|
|  | Weekday | Weekend | Weekday | Weekend | Weekday | Weekend |
| **Youth (13-16 years)** | | | | | | |
| - all day | 11.00 | 14.00 | 11.00 | 14.00 | 11.00 | 14.00 |
| - after 1:00 p.m. | 9.00 | 11.00 | 11.00 | 14.00 | 11.00 | 14.00 |
| - night | 9.00 | 9.00 | — | — | 11.00 | 12.00 |
| **Junior (6-12 years)** | | | | | | |
| - all day | 9.00 | 12.00 | 8.00 | 8.00 | 8.00 | 8.00 |
| - after 1:00 p.m. | 7.00 | 8.00 | 8.00 | 8.00 | 8.00 | 8.00 |
| - night | 7.00 | 7.00 | — | — | 8.00 | 8.00 |

|  | Mt. Ste. Marie | | Vorlage [2] | |
|---|---|---|---|---|
|  | Weekday | Weekend | Weekday | Weekend |
| **Adult** | | | | |
| - all day | $12.00 | $15.00 | $11.00 | $14.00 |
| - after 1:00 p.m. | 10.00 | 12.00 | 11.00 | 11.00 |
| - night | * | * | 8.00 | 8.00 |
| **Youth (13-16 years)** | | | | |
| - all day | 12.00 | 12.00 | 11.00 | 14.00 |
| - after 1:00 p.m. | 10.00 | 8.00 | 11.00 | 11.00 |
| - night | * | * | 8.00 | 8.00 |
| **Junior (6-12 years)** | | | | |
| - all day | 12.00 | 12.00 | 8.00 | 9.00 |
| - after 1:00 p.m. | 10.00 | 8.00 | 8.00 | 9.00 |
| - night | * | * | 6.00 | 6.00 |

[1] Children under six years of age were admitted at all times.
[2] Night skiing at Vorlage only Wednesday, Thursday, Friday and Saturday, 3:30 to 10:00 p.m.
* No night skiing.

**APPENDIX 1**
**Radio Station Data**

| Station | Market | Format | Mon-Sun 5 a.m.-1 a.m. All Persons 7+ Years Old Weekly Reach % | Average Hours Listened Per Week |
|---|---|---|---|---|
| All Stations | | | 93 | 20.1 |
| CHEZ-FM1 | Ottawa-Hull | Adult Oriented Rock | 30 | 8.9 |
| CFMO-FM | " | Easy Listening | 22 | 12.3 |
| CFRA | " | Contemp. MOR[2] | 38 | 6.5 |
| CKBY-FM | " | Contemp. Country | 19 | 9.4 |
| *CIMF-FM | " | Popular, Traditional | 17 | 9.9 |
| CFGO | " | Adult Contemp. | 20 | 7.7 |
| CBO | " | Multi-format | 14 | 9.8 |
| CKCH* | " | Contemp. Music for general public | 11 | 9.6 |
| CJRC* | " | Contemp. Music for general public | 9 | 8.3 |
| CKOY | " | Adult, MOR | 10 | 5.7 |
| CBO-FM | " | Multi-format | 6 | 5.4 |
| CISB | " | Adult Contemp. MOR | 4 | 7.4 |
| CBOF | " | Multi-format | 4 | 7.7 |
| CBOF-FM | " | Multi-format | 3 | 5.1 |
| CKU-FM | Ottawa | Varied, News, Public Affairs | 4 | 3.3 |
| CKO | Ottawa-Hull | News, Sports | 3 | 2.9 |

[1] On average, 30% of the residents in Ottawa-Hull area listen to CHEZ-FM at least once during a week. Similarly, the average listener of CHEZ-FM listens to the station for 8.9 hours a week.
[2] MOR = Middle of the Road
Typical Advertising Costs - Station CFGO, from 6:00 to 10:00 a.m., 30 seconds, $67; from 7:00 to 10:00 p.m., 30 seconds $46.00.

*Broadcast in French

**APPENDIX 2**
**TV Station Data**

| Station | Market | Network Affiliation | Mon-Sun 6 a.m.-2 a.m. All Persons 2+ Years Old Weekly Reach % | Average Hours Watched Per Week |
|---|---|---|---|---|
| All Stations[1] | | | 98 | 20.6 |
| CJOH | Ottawa | CTV | 80 | 6.0 |
| CBOT | Ottawa | CBC | 75 | 3.9 |
| CKGN | Toronto | Global | 60 | 3.3 |
| CBOFT* | Ottawa | CBC | 27 | 6.0 |
| CHOT* | Hull | TVA | 25 | 6.3 |
| CHRO | Pembroke | CBC | 29 | 2.6 |

* Broadcast in French.
Typical Advertising Costs - Station CJOH: from 12:30 to 6:00 p.m., 30 seconds, $375; from 7:00 to 10:00 p.m., 30 seconds, $615.

[1]98% of the residents of Ottawa-Hull area watched television at least once a week, and on average turned on their TV 20.6 hours a week.

**Statistics: Ottawa/Hull Market**
**1982 Population (in thousands)**

| Age Groups (Years) | Male | Female |
|---|---|---|
| 0-4 | 24 | 23 |
| 5-9 | 25 | 24 |
| 10-14 | 28 | 26 |
| 15-19 | 35 | 34 |
| 20-24 | 35 | 38 |
| 25-34 | 66 | 69 |
| 35-44 | 48 | 48 |
| 45-54 | 38 | 38 |
| 55-64 | 37 | 33 |
| 65-69 | 9 | 12 |
| 70-over | 14 | 24 |
| TOTAL | 359 | 369 |

Daily Newspapers
(circulation in thousands)

| | |
|---|---|
| *Citizen* | |
| Circulation, Total(M+F) | 184 |
|    City area | 146 |
|    Outside Ottawa-Hull area | 38 |
| *Sunday Herald* | |
| Circulation, Total-Sundays | 50 |
|    City Area | 40 |
|    Outside Ottawa-Hull area | 10 |
| *Le Droit* (French) | |
| Circulation, Total(M+F) | 44 |
|    City area | 30 |
|    Outside Ottawa-Hull area | 14 |
| Typical Advertising Costs - Citizen - 4" x 4" space = $120 per insertion | |

**Sources:** *Canadian Advertising Rates & Data*, MacLean Hunter, Toronto, *Canadian Markets, Financial Post*, MacLean Hunter, Toronto

# 21. THE SALES PROMOTION CHALLENGE

Written by John Yokom, President, Checkmate Marketing Resources, Toronto

You are the product manager at a large bank and your marketing manager has presented you with a problem. The latest "deposit share" results indicate that your bank's share of the total funds on deposit in the total Canadian market has continued to decline. Trust companies are becoming more aggressive with advertising, promotion, and longer hours of service. Senior management at your bank has decided to use a promotional contest to try to stop the erosion and is willing to spend the funds needed if an exciting promotion can be implemented.

You have been working on the "deposits" problem for some time and have just received the results of a major bank industry study suggesting that "seniors" (defined as those 50 years old and above) are the key to deposits. In fact, across Canada this age group accounts for roughly 20% of bank customers but over 60% of the funds on deposit. The question: How do you motivate seniors to transfer deposit dollars to your bank?

You know this is a difficult challenge. A lot of noise and promotional clutter must be overcome if your promotion is to work. To succeed, you will need a powerful promotion. More important, you know that you are going to have to reach out to the target market and motivate them on a personal level. You want them to transfer at least $5,000 to an account at your bank.

You call in three agencies that specialize in running promotions, brief them on the challenge, and ask them to come back with their proposals in a week. Budgets for each promotion are virtually identical so the cost of the campaigns is not the issue. One week later, the following promotions are submitted:

Promotion Agency #1: Procter & Gamble (U.S.) and General Motors ran a tie-in promotion, "Win One of 750 Chevrolets" with a "key" packed in specially marked Procter & Gamble products. This agency has built on this concept to develop a promotion. It's "Here's Your Key to Win a Mercedes-Benz." The plan is to mail special Mercedes-Benz keys to seniors who live near each of your branches. Seniors will be invited to come into the branch and transfer a $5,000 deposit from another bank. If they do, they will get to try their key in the special Mercedes-Benz lock. If it opens, they win the car.

Promotion Agency #2: Based on its experience, the agency believes that seniors like bank passbooks. In fact, in this electronic age of the automatic teller machine, agency personnel think that seniors have become quite concerned that many banks seem to be moving away from this "old-fashioned" concept. To capitalize on this trend, the second agency has developed the "Passbook to Paradise" promotion.

Seniors in each branch trading area will receive a real bank passbook with a special account number. To win, all a senior needs to do is transfer $5,000 to the branch, then match his/her passbook number against the prize numbers at the branch. Prizes include a two-week trip for two to a South Pacific island plus $5,000 in cash. Other prizes are five one-week Caribbean cruises for two, and 20,000 other cash prizes, ranging from $1 to $1,000. The agency notes that it has run many successful sweepstakes promotions using this formula of one "big" grand prize plus lots of "smaller" prizes.

Promotion Agency #3: Scratch-and-win promotions have proven to be consistent winners. This agency's past experience with campaigns aimed at seniors suggests that this segment likes the fun and excitement of the instant-win concept. This agency proposes such a program. Seniors in each branch trading area will be mailed a "Double Your Deposit or Double Your Savings" scratch-and-win game card. To win, a senior must transfer $5,000 to the branch, and then scratch the card in front of a bank employee. Five depositors will instantly win double their deposits. The remaining contestants can enter a second-chance "Double Your Savings" sweepstakes. Five more double-your-account-balance prizes will be awarded.

The agency summarizes its presentation by saying "This promotion has fun and excitement combined with the most powerful motivator known—cash!"

## The Decision

Now that you have received the three proposals, the task is to select the one that you think will deliver the largest business gain (i.e. increase in share of seniors' deposits). To help in this selection, the marketing research department at the bank has prepared a summary of research findings on seniors (Appendix 1).

## Questions

1. Rank order the three promotions and provide the rationale for your ranking.
2. Would you recommend any modifications to the "best" promotion? If yes, what modifications? If no, why not?

# Appendix 1

## A NOTE ON SENIOR CITIZENS

Articles describing the expanding consumer segment of senior citizens have been increasing over the past few years. Marketers are now realizing that seniors are a very lucrative market. Canadians over 50 years of age represent 55% of the discretionary spending power of Canadians, and control 80% of all assets—physical and financial. However, only a small portion of all media spending is aimed directly at this segment. Marketers now recognize that they must develop campaigns aimed at seniors, who represent 35% of the Canadian adult population.

Canadians over 50 are among the heaviest consumers of expensive lifestyle products. They travel widely and are the leading purchasers of luxury condominiums, large cars, and such convenience products as microwave ovens. They are also living longer, healthier lives. They are among the largest consumers of newspapers and magazines, and their buying power helps to support several Canadian publications specifically for those over 50, including Toronto-based *Today's Seniors* and Vancouver-based *Maturity*.

Seniors should not be stereotyped into a homogeneous group. Lifestyle research has been undertaken to identify the sub-groups in this important sector of the population. It is the attitudes, actions, and activities within the demographic groups that are the real marketing trends. Based on a study by Grey Advertising, New York, three target groups among seniors are the following:

Master Consumers (the largest and most important) are fit, active, secure, and fulfilled. Rather than seeking a fountain of youth, they are looking forward to their future and see retirement as a time to do all the things they put off in the past.

Maintainers are financially comfortable, not as active as they could be, and lack the sense of purpose needed to push them beyond the status quo.

Simplifiers are older, less affluent, less active, and relatively light consumers.

The agency offers the following guidelines when advertising to the 50-plus market:

- Don't use euphemistic name tags, such as the "golden-harvest gang," which they dislike.
- Treat them like adults. They have been around long enough to know what they want. Hype, fluff, and a patronizing attitude will turn them off.
- Show how your product meets 50-plus needs, not how needy you find 50-plus consumers.
- Be fresh, but not frenetic. Think linear, be more literal and less abstract.
- Capture their spirit. They believe life goes on and keeps getting better.
- Sex—yes. The libido lives on after 50 and so does romance.
- Tune them in. Music can be the bridge that spans generations—if it is the right music.
- As consumers, they are the voice of authority, so make them your spokespeople and role models.

When designing campaigns targeted to older demographic groups, creative people should keep in mind that what works for younger target groups will not always have the right appeal for the 50-plus market. Once advertising industry expert recommends the following when targeting the older demographic groups:

- Show older consumers being active, not sitting down.
- Use actors ten years younger than the target group for the ad, since mature consumers think of themselves as younger than they really are.
- Do not use cartoons or negative selling messages.
- Steer clear of muted browns and grays, loud oranges, reds, and yellows. Mature consumers associate loud tones with garishness. They like cool blues and greens.

# 22. J.T. Electronics

Jack Booth, sales manager for J.T. Electronics, had just finished reviewing selected performance measures for 1991. He was concerned because market share had declined and there seemed to be a major problem in the Ontario region. He wondered if he should consider changing the compensation plan for the salesforce, or at least talk to the salespeople in Ontario. "Something has to be done," he thought, "but I'm not sure what."

J.T. Electronics was a leading manufacturer and marketer of quality stereo equipment in Canada. The product line included stereos (receivers and amplifiers), compact disc players, and cassette decks. The company was jointly owned by a Canadian firm and a Japanese firm. The Japanese partner manufactured most of the product line and the Canadian partner was responsible for distributing and marketing the products in Canada. One major task was to get distribution through the large department stores (e.g., Eaton's) and specialty sound equipment stores (e.g., Majestic Sound). J.T. Electronics used a salesforce to accomplish this job.

For any stereo manufacturer, distribution was difficult because of the intense competition in the industry. At least eight large manufacturers and over 20 smaller companies competed in this market. Thus, retailers had a wide range of manufacturers they could choose to do business with and, for this reason, they often could dictate terms to any manufacturer. Retailers could demand larger margins, request co-op advertising (where the manufacturer paid part of the retailer's advertising cost when that manufacturer's brands were advertised), and seek favorable credit terms.

The task for the J.T. Electronics salesforce was to work closely with retailers, particularly the large chains, and encourage them to carry, promote, and sell J.T. Electronics products. It was in this area that Jack Smith felt there could be a problem. He knew, based on market research studies, that J.T. Electronics products were well regarded by the stereo buying consumer, that the prices charged by J.T. were perceived as fair, and that the products were being carried by a reasonable number of stores. Even so, Jack Smith thought that possibly the salespeople were perhaps not establishing a strong working relationship with the retailers and that, as a result, the retailers were promoting competing brands rather than J.T. brands. "Maybe if the salespeople were put on commission or a combination of commission and salary, instead of straight salary, we'd do better," he thought. With that, he began reviewing the data again.

As Jack Booth looked through the tables (1 to 4) he thought about the three salespeople in the Ontario region. He felt that Phil Gowing had the most difficult territory (primarily Western Ontario), where a lot of travel was involved. Jack knew that Phil was a very conscientious individual and a "self-starter" who was fairly motivated. Martin Abell was a different type of individual. Jack felt that

Martin had a very good sales presentation and manner but was a rather easy-going individual who had the attitude of a "fair day's work for a fair day's pay." Martin had a territory in Central Ontario and little overnight traveling was involved. The third salesperson, Lucy Johnson, had an engaging personality and seemed well suited to a career in sales. However, Jack felt she could be more forceful in some of her sales presentations. She was a diligent worker and covered her territory in Eastern Ontario in a very efficient manner.

Jack Booth knew that something had to be done. He debated whether he should collect more data or talk to the salespeople now.

## Question

1. What course of action would you recommend for Jack Booth?

**TABLE 1**
**J.T. Electronics - Market Share**

| Year | J.T. Electronics Sales (millions) | Industry Sales (millions) | J.T. Electronics (Market Share) |
|------|-----------------------------------|---------------------------|---------------------------------|
| 1991 | $ 30.6 | $ 180.0 | 17% |
| 1990 | 31.5 | 175.0 | 18% |
| 1989 | 26.6 | 140.0 | 19% |
| 1988 | 25.7 | 135.0 | 19% |
| 1987 | 25.1 | 132.0 | 19% |

**TABLE 2**
**J.T. Electronics - Sales Performance, By Region, 1991**

| Region | Buying Power Index ( % ) | Sales Target | Actual Sales | Percentage Difference | Dollar Difference |
|--------|--------------------------|--------------|--------------|-----------------------|-------------------|
| Maritimes | 8.1 | $ 2,575,000 | $ 2,500,000 | 97 | $- 75,000 |
| Quebec | 24.8 | 7,880,000 | 8,100,000 | 103 | + 220,000 |
| Ontario | 38.5 | 12,240,000 | 10,710,000 | 88 | -1,530,000 |
| Prairies | 17.4 | 5,530,000 | 5,490,000 | 99 | - 40,000 |
| B.C. | 11.2 | 3,575,000 | 3,800,000 | 106 | + 225,000 |
| Total | 100.0 | $31,800,000 | $30,600,000 | 96 | $-1,200,000 |

**Note:** Sales target based on Buying Power Index. The Buying Power Index was based on personal disposable income by region.

**TABLE 3**
**J.T. Electronics - Sales Performance, By Product Line, Ontario**

| Product | Sales Target | Actual Sales | Percentage Difference | Dollar Difference |
|---|---|---|---|---|
| Stereos | $ 7,640,000 | $ 6,770,000 | 89 | $ - 870,000 |
| Compact Disc Players | 1,300,000 | 1,160,000 | 89 | - 140,000 |
| Cassette Decks | 3,300,000 | 2,780,000 | 84 | - 520,000 |
| | $ 12,240,000 | $ 10,710,000 | 88 | $ -1,530,000 |

**TABLE 4**
**J.T. Electronics - Sales Performance, By Sales Representative, Ontario**

| Sales Representative | Sales Target | Actual Sales | Percentage Differences | Dollar Differences |
|---|---|---|---|---|
| **Phil Gowing** | | | | |
| - Stereos | $2,570,000 | $2,560,000 | 100 | $ - 10,000 |
| - Compact Disc Players | 400,000 | 410,000 | 103 | + 10,000 |
| - Cassette Decks | 1,200,000 | 1,080,000 | 90 | - 120,000 |
| | $4,170,000 | $4,050,000 | 97 | $ - 120,000 |
| **Martin Abell** | | | | |
| - Stereos | $2,400,000 | $1,940,000 | 81 | $ - 460,000 |
| - Compact Disc Players | 500,000 | 410,000 | 82 | - 90,000 |
| - Cassette Decks | 1,100,000 | 860,000 | 78 | - 240,000 |
| | $4,000,000 | $3,210,000 | 80 | $ - 790,000 |
| **Lucy Johnson** | | | | |
| - Stereos | $2,670,000 | $2,270,000 | 85 | $ - 400,000 |
| - Compact Disc Players | 400,000 | 340,000 | 85 | - 60,000 |
| - Cassette Decks | 1,000,000 | 840,000 | 84 | - 160,000 |
| | $4,070,000 | $3,450,000 | 85 | $ - 620,000 |

# 23. EIT LIMITED

Mr. Jacques Martin, marketing manager of EIT, had just been given an interesting assignment—to identify the export opportunities for the firm's new product line of pollution reduction equipment. The request had come from the company's president, Paul Coton, who felt that the new line could be successfully sold to industrial customers in foreign markets.

Mr. Martin had little experience in international marketing. Most of the firm's sales to date had come from the Canadian and, to a lesser degree, the United States oil refinery business, where EIT had sold oil processing equipment. With the new line, EIT had an opportunity to enter export markets outside North America. Mr. Martin saw his task as twofold: (1) to identify a list of criteria that could be used to evaluate foreign markets; and (2) to apply these criteria to the foreign markets in order to select the best prospects.

## The Company

EIT, located in Montreal, was a successful manufacturer of process equipment for oil refineries. With the increased concern about the environment, EIT engineers had developed a product line, consisting of scrubbers, pipes, valves, and controls, that could be used by various processing industries (e.g., oil refineries, steel mills, pulp and paper plants, chemical plants) to reduce the level of pollutants entering the atmosphere. The product line had been completed and the first sale, for approximately $500,000, had been made to an oil refinery in Sarnia, Ontario. From the research and development engineers to the president, everyone at EIT was enthusiastic about the sale and the new product line. At issue was capturing market share in a rapidly changing market, which an ever-increasing number of competitors were entering. EIT, with sales of $50 million and profits of $6 million, had the resources to enter and compete in a limited number of foreign markets.

## The Industry

By the late 1980s, most governments in the Western industrialized nations had enacted some form of legislation requiring manufacturing firms to reduce the amount of pollutants that entered the atmosphere. Often referred to as "smokestack" industries because of the smoke that could be seen belching into the atmosphere, these companies had been responding, sometimes reluctantly, by installing pollution reduction equipment in their manufacturing facilities. The rate at which these manufacturing firms performed this upgrading depended on the requirements of the legislation and the environmental responsibility of the company. The legislation requirements ranged from strict compliance based on tough emission standards to moral suasion by government agencies. The environmental responsibility ranged from companies who readily complied and exceeded emission standards to companies who could best be described as "foot draggers."

Competition in the industry had been increasing as more firms entered this growing market. Some of these firms specialized in environmental upgrade systems for one industry (e.g., chemicals) whereas others, like EIT, had developed systems that could be used across industries (e.g., steel, chemicals, oil refineries, pulp and paper mills). Because of the company's experiences, the EIT system was particularly suited for oil refineries but could be applied, with some modifications, to other industries. EIT engineers felt that the modifications would be most readily adapted for the steel industry.

Regardless of the industry, Mr. Martin knew that extensive personal selling would be required to complete a sale. Both the technical complexity of the system and the selling price (ranging from $200,000 to $5 million, depending on the options and the size of the plant) meant that considerable effort would be needed to generate sales.

## The Task

Mr. Martin felt that the company had sufficient resources to establish five sales offices in foreign markets over the next two years. EIT currently had four offices in the United States which he considered sufficient to cover this market. As he thought further about the task, Mr. Martin decided that he should first determine what criteria to use to rank order the markets, then he should rank order them. Based on the rankings, he would prepare a short list of markets. For these markets that held the most promise, he would determine what detailed information would be needed to make the final decision: whether or not to open an office in that country. With these thoughts in mind, he began preparing the criteria.

## Question

1. Assume you are Mr. Martin and prepare a report for the president.

# 24. Financial Exercises for Marketing

Written by the Marketing Faculty, Wilfrid Laurier University

1. Mr. Johnson, owner of Johnson's Fine Furniture, is preparing for a year-end performance review of his two stores. He opened the downtown store 15 years ago; the suburban store (located in a shopping mall) was opened five years ago. The following financial data has been collected.

|  | Downtown Store | Suburban Store |
|---|---|---|
| Purchases at cost | $461,000 | $623,000 |
| Depreciation | 4,000 | 6,000 |
| Advertising | 8,000 | 78,000 |
| Returns and Allowances | 34,000 | 76,000 |
| Rent and Utilities | 10,000 | 40,000 |
| Beginning Inventory | 103,000 | 282,000 |
| Administrative Salaries | 30,000 | 42,000 |
| Telephone | 1,500 | 1,500 |
| Commissions | 44,000 | 112,000 |
| Salesforce Salaries | — | 95,000 |
| Office Expenses | 8,000 | 11,000 |
| Ending Inventory | 131,000 | 220,000 |
| Sales | 636,000 | 1,250,000 |
| Investment | 420,000 | 800,000 |

a) Prepare operating statements for each store.
b) Using ratio analysis, compare the performance of the two stores. What are the implications of this analysis?

c) What shop would you close if forced to close one? Why?

2. Jennifer Smith makes hand-braided mats, at a cost of $40 per mat, to sell at local craft shows. She has 30 mats on hand for the next show, and expects to sell them all for a total of $1,800. What is Jennifer's:
   a) mark-up percent on selling?
   b) mark-up on cost?
   c) margin?

3. A new multi-purpose clamp, the Vice-Master, has a retail selling price of $20. The retail margin is 40%, and the wholesale margin is 15%. The manufacturer's cost per unit is four dollars.
   a) What dollar mark-up does each channel member receive?
   b) Which channel member receives the greatest margin? Is this reasonable? Why?

4. Bill Rogers, owner of Roger's Jewelery, purchased a large shipment of watches for $20 each. He expected to sell each watch for $50, but a major competitor is now advertising the same watch for $40. John feels he must match this price. What is his markdown percentage if he reduces the price on the entire shipment?

5. The Ontario Electronics Company (OEC) manufactures portable cassette players. The factory selling price of the cassette player is $130. Variable cost per unit is $60 and total fixed costs are $230,000. How many units must OEC sell to:
   a) break-even?
   b) make $60,000 profit?

6. New Tech Corporation has completed development of a new electronic toy. It expects to get a 15% market share in the first year; a 25% market share in the second year. The total market size is forecast at 100,000 units per year for each of the next two years. The following financial and sales data have been assembled.

| | |
|---|---|
| Retail selling price | $70 |
| Retail margin | 50% |
| Material cost/unit | $5.00 |
| Labor cost/unit | $6.50 |
| Packaging cost/unit | $ .50 |
| Sales force salaries and expenses | $150,000 |
| Manufacturing overhead | $ 76,000 |
| Administrative expenses | $ 70,000 |
| Sales promotion (first year only) | $ 40,000 |

Prepare a two-year financial summary for the new toy, including: variable cost per unit, contribution per unit, total contribution, total fixed costs, break-even volume, gross margin, and net profit.

7. CTA Manufacturing, located in Dartmouth, Nova Scotia, holds a six percent share of a total market of 95,000 FAX machines that are sold each year. CTA provides its retailers with a margin of 35% on a retail price of $2,500 per FAX machine.

   Joyce Pango, CTA's controller, estimates that variable production costs amount to $825 per FAX machine and fixed manufacturing costs total $280,000 per year. In addition, shipping and packaging costs of $45 per unit are be paid by CTA. Management costs are $95,000 and the annual advertising budget is $120,000.

The company employs one sales representative at a salary of $65,000 a year.

a) What are CTA's fixed costs?
b) What are CTA's variable costs per unit?
c) What is the unit contribution?
d) What is the breakeven volume for CTA (in units)?
e) What market share is needed to achieve this volume?
f) What are CTA's current profits?
g) If establishing CTA involved an investment of $1,200,000 and the company requires a return of 16% on its capital, is the FAX machine line still profitable? Justify your answer.
h) What are the profits after allowing for the required return on capital?
i) Chuck Batton, the firm's vice-president for marketing, estimates CTA can sell six percent more FAX machines than it does presently by increasing its advertising budget from $120,000 to $140,000. Alternately, if he reduces the advertising budget by $20,000, he expects to sell 95 fewer units. Should CTA raise or lower its advertising budget? Why?
j) What would be the breakeven level (in units) if the advertising budget were raised?
k) What would be the breakeven level (in units) if the advertising budget were lowered?
l) As an alternative to the change in advertising, CTA is considering offering packages of FAX paper with every FAX machine sold. These packages cost CTA $60 each. If this offer can increase FAX machine sales by 180 units, what would be the change in total profits?

8. The Canadian Chocolate Company is preparing to introduce a new low- calorie chocolate bar, Choco-lite. Two alternative marketing plans have been developed. The first plan positions the new product directly against all regular chocolate bars. The second plan positions Choco-lite as an exclusive alternative to high-calorie regular bars. The total chocolate bar market in Canada is 200 million bars each year. Which plan should be adopted? Why?

|  | Plan 1 | Plan 2 |
|---|---|---|
| Retail selling price | $0.65 | $1.10 |
| Factory selling price | $0.39 | $0.64 |
| Materials/labor | $0.20/unit | $0.20/unit |
| Packaging | $0.08/unit | $0.12/unit |
| Total overhead | $200,000 | $200,000 |
| Advertising and promotion | $600,000 | $1,200,000 |
| Projected market share | 5% | 3% |

9. Montreal Gloves (MG) is considering the addition of a new line of waterproof gloves ("Water Smart") next year to its existing brand "Stay Dry." First-year sales of the new line are projected at 350,000 pair. Table 1 provides price and cost data. The sources of these sales are expected to be 20% from new customers, 40% from competitors' customers, and 40% (of the 350,000) from previous buyers of MG's other brand, Stay Dry. Sales of Stay Dry totalled 230,000 pair this year and are expected to remain at this level if the new line is not introduced. Ben Nadson, manager of the Gloves Division, is concerned about the cannibalization of Stay Dry sales by the new line. Should the new line be introduced?

**TABLE 1**

|  | Current | Year 1 with New Line | |
|---|---|---|---|
|  | Stay Dry | Stay Dry | Water Smart |
| Factory Selling Price | $24.00 | $24.00 | $29.50 |
| Variable Costs | 16.50 | 16.50 | 22.00 |
| Fixed Costs | $840,000 | $660,000 | $1,530,000 |

10. Greg Ross, the marketing manager of Electric Motor Company (EMC), was considering changing the company's distribution structure in Ontario. EMC was a medium size manufacturer of standard electric motors. The motors, ranging in size from 1/4 horsepower to 50 horsepower, were sold to a variety of industrial customers across Canada. EMC motors were sold primarily on the basis of price and reliability. Total company sales in the past year were $7,500,000 ($3,000,000 in Ontario).

Mr. Ross was considering replacing the six sales agents in Ontario with three company salespeople. The sales agents, who earned eight percent commission on sales, sold EMC's product line as well as a number of complementary products. It was estimated that EMC's motors accounted for about 25% of the agents' total sales. Mr. Ross felt that sales in Ontario could be increased by hiring three salespeople who focused exclusively on EMC's products. He estimated that if the three salespeople were hired there was a 50% chance that sales would remain the same, a 20% chance that sales would increase by 10%, and a 30% chance that sales would increase by 20%. The cost for each person would be $75,000 ($50,000 in salary and $25,000 in expenses).

Mr. Ross discussed his plan with the president of EMC, Laura Jeffries. Ms. Jeffries replied, "I'm not sure about your estimates. Rather than a 50% chance of sales remaining the same, I think there's only a 30% chance that they will stay the same and a 20% chance that sales will decline by 20% if we go with our own sales force. This is because the sales agents will pick up another line of motors and compete with our own sales force. I agree with the rest of the estimates. However, I think if we offer the sales agents a bonus for increased sales, they might push our product a little harder. Why don't you work out some alternatives and we'll talk again."

a. As Mr. Ross, prepare and evaluate alternatives.

b. What would you recommend?

# Glossary

**Action program** A detailed program that shows what must be done, who will do it, and how decisions and actions will be coordinated to implement marketing plans and strategy.

**Administered VMS** A vertical marketing system that coordinates successive stages of production and distribution, not through common ownership or contractual ties, but through the size and power of one of the parties.

**Advertising** Any paid form of nonpersonal presentation and promotion of ideas, goods, or services by an identified sponsor.

**Advertising objective** A specific communication task to be accomplished with a specific target audience during a specific period of time.

**Affordable method** Setting the promotion budget at what management thinks the company can afford.

**Agent** A wholesaler who represents buyers or sellers on a more permanent basis, performs only a few functions, and does not take title to goods.

**Annual plan control** Evaluation and corrective action to ensure that the company achieves the sales, profits, and other goals set out in its annual plan.

**Atmospheres** Designed environments that create or reinforce the buyer's leanings toward consumption of a product.

**Attitude** A person's consistently favorable or unfavorable evaluations, feelings, and tendencies toward some object or idea.

**Automatic vending** Selling through coin-operated machines.

**Baby boom** The major increase in the annual birthrate following World War II and lasting until the early 1960s.

**Basing-point pricing** A geographic pricing strategy in which the seller designates some city as a basing point and charges all customers the freight cost from that city to the customer location, regardless of the city from which the goods are actually shipped.

**Behavior segmentation** Dividing a market into groups based their knowledge, attitudes, uses, or responses to a product.

**Belief** A descriptive thought a person has about something.

**Brand** A name, term, sign, symbol, or design, or a combination of them intended to identify the goods or services of one seller or group of sellers and to differentiate them from those of competitors.

**Brand mark** That part of a brand that can be recognized but is not utterable, such as a symbol, design, or distinctive coloring or lettering.

**Brand name** That part of a brand that can be vocalized.

**Breakeven pricing** Setting price to break even on the costs of making and marketing a product.

**Broker** A wholesaler who does not take title to goods and whose function is to bring buyers and sellers together and assist in negotiation.

**Business analysis** A review of the sales, costs, and profit projections for a new product to find out whether they satisfy the company's objectives.

**Business portfolio** The collection of businesses and products that make up the company.

**Buyer readiness states** The stages consumers normally pass through on their way to purchase, including awareness, knowledge, liking, preference, conviction, and purchase.

**Buying center** All the individuals and groups that participate in the organizational buying decision process.

**Capital items** Industrial goods that enter the finished product partly, including installations and accessory equipment.

**Cash cows** Low-growth, high-share businesses or products—established and successful units that generate cash that the company uses to pay its bills and support other business units that need investment.

**Cash discount** A price reduction to buyers who pay their bills promptly.

**Catalog showroom** A retail operation that sells a wide selection of high-markup, fast-moving, brand-name goods at discount prices.

**Causal research** Marketing research to test hypotheses about cause-and-effect relationships.

**Chain store** An organization operating four or more retail outlets in the same kind of business, under the same legal ownership.

**Cognitive dissonance** Postpurchase consumer discomfort caused by after-purchase conflict.

**Combination store** Combined food and drug store.

**Commercialization** Introducing a new product into the market.

**Company culture** A system of values and beliefs shared by people in an organization, the company's collective identity and meaning.

**Company marketing opportunity** An attractive arena for marketing action in which the company would enjoy a competitive advantage.

**Competitive-parity method** Setting the promotion budget to match competitors' outlays.

**Concept testing** Testing new product concepts with a group of target consumers to find out if the concepts have strong consumer appeal.

**Consumer goods** Goods bought by final consumers for personal consumption.

**Consumer market** The set of all final consumers–individuals and households who buy goods and services for personal consumption.

**Consumer promotion** Sales promotion designed to stimulate consumer purchasing.

**Consumerism** An organized movement of citizens and government to improve

the rights and power of buyers in relation to sellers.

**Continuity** Scheduling ads evenly within a given period.

**Contract manufacturing** Joint-venturing to enter a foreign market by contracting with manufacturers in the foreign market to produce the product.

**Contractual VMS** A vertical marketing system in which independent firms at different levels of production and distribution join together through contracts to obtain more economies or sales impact than they could achieve alone.

**Convenience goods** Consumer goods that the customer usually buys frequently, immediately, and with the minimum of comparison and buying effort.

**Convenience store** A small store, located near a residential area, open long hours seven days a week, and carrying a limited line of high-turnover convenience goods.

**Conventional distribution channel** A channel consisting of an independent producer(s), wholesaler(s), and retailer(s), each a separate business seeking to maximize its own profits, even at the expense of profits for the system as a whole.

**Copy testing** Measuring the communication effect of an advertisement before or after it is printed or broadcast.

**Copyright** The exclusive legal right to reproduce, publish, and sell the matter and form of a literary, musical, or artistic work.

**Corporate VMS** A vertical marketing system that combines successive stages of production and distribution under single ownership.

**Cost-plus pricing** Adding a standard markup to the cost of the product.

**Cultural environment** Institutions and other forces that affect society's basic values, perceptions, preferences, and behaviors.

**Culture** The set of basic values, perceptions, wants, and behaviors learned by a member of society from family and other important institutions.

**Customer salesforce structure** A salesforce organization under which salespeople specialize in selling only to certain customers or industries.

**Customized marketing mix** An international marketing strategy of adjusting the marketing mix elements to each international target market, bearing more costs but hoping for a larger market share and return.

**Decline stage** The product life cycle stage in which a product's sales decline.

**Deficient products** Products that have neither immediate appeal nor long-run benefits.

**Demand curve** A curve that shows the number of units the market will buy in a given time period at different prices that might be charged.

**Demands** Human wants that are backed by buying power.

**Demographic segmentation** Dividing the market into groups based on demographic variables such as age, sex, family size, family life cycle, income, occupation, education, religion, race, and nationality.

**Demography** The study of human populations in terms of size, density, location, age, sex, race, occupation, and other statistics.

**Department store** A retail organization that carries a wide variety of product lines, each operated as a separate department managed by specialist buyers or merchandisers.

**Descriptive research** Marketing research to better describe marketing problems, situations, or markets—such as the market potential for a product, or the demographics and attitudes of consumers.

**Desirable products** Products that give both high immediate satisfaction and high long-run benefits.

**Direct investment** Entering a foreign market by developing foreign-¹ ased assembly or manufacturing facilities.

**Discount store** A retail institution that sells standard merchandise at lower prices by accepting lower margins and selling higher volume.

**Discriminatory pricing** Selling a product or service at two or more prices, where the difference in prices is not based on differences in costs.

**Distribution channel** The set of firms and individuals that take title, or assist in transferring title, to a good or service as it moves from the producer to the consumer or industrial user.

**Diversification** A strategy for expanding company growth by starting up or acquiring businesses outside the company's current products and markets.

**Dogs** Low-growth, low-share businesses and products that may generate enough cash to maintain themselves, but do not promise to be a large source of cash.

**Door-to-door retailing** Selling door-to-door, office-to-office, or at home sales parties.

**Durable goods** Tangible goods that normally survive many uses.

**Economic community** A group of nations organized to work toward common goals in the regulation of international trade.

**Economic environment** Factors that affect consumer purchasing power and spending patterns.

**Embargo** A ban on the import of a certain product.

**Emotional appeals** Message appeals that attempt to stir up negative or positive emotions that will motivate purchase.

**Enlightened marketing** A marketing philosophy that holds that the company's marketing should support the best long-run performance of the marketing system.

**Environmentalism** An organized movement of concerned citizens and government to protect and improve people's living environment and quality of life.

**Events** Occurrences staged to communicate messages to target audiences such as news conferences and grand openings.

**Exchange** The act of obtaining a desired object from someone by offering something in return.

**Exclusive distribution** Giving a limited number of dealers the exclusive right to distribute the company's products in their territories.

**Experimental research** The gathering of primary data by selecting matched groups of subjects, giving them different treatments, controlling related factors, and checking for differences in group responses.

**Exploratory research** Marketing research to gather preliminary information that will help to better define problems and suggest hypotheses.

**Exporting** Entering a foreign market by exporting products and selling them through international marketing middlemen (indirect exporting) or through the company's own department, branch, or sales representatives or agents (direct exporting).

**Family life cycle** The stages through which families might pass as they mature over time.

**Fixed costs** Costs that do not vary with production or sales level.

**FOB origin pricing** A geographic pricing strategy in which goods are placed free on board a carrier, and the customer pays the freight from the factory to the destination.

**Franchise** A contractual association between a manufacturer, wholesaler, or service organization (a franchiser) and independent business people who buy the right to own and operate one or more units in the franchise system (franchisees).

**Freight absorption pricing** A geographic pricing strategy in which the company absorbs all or part of the actual freight charges in order to get the business.

**Frequency** The number of times the average person in the target market is exposed to the advertising message during a given period.

**Functional discount** A price reduction offered by the seller to trade channel members who perform certain functions such as selling, storing, and record keeping.

**Functional organization** An organization structure in which marketing specialists are in charge of different marketing activities or functions such as advertising, marketing research, sales management, and others.

**Geographic organization** An organization structure in which a company's national sales force (and perhaps other functions) specializes by geographic area.

**Geographic segmentation** Dividing a market into different geographical units such as nations, provinces, regions, counties, cities, or neighborhoods.

**Going-rate pricing** Setting price based largely on following competitors' prices rather than on company cost or demand.

**Government market** Governmental units—federal, provincial, and municipal—that purchase or rent goods and services for carrying out the main functions of government.

**Growth stage** The product life cycle stage when the product's sales start climbing quickly.

**Human need** A state of felt deprivation in a person.

**Human want** The form taken by a human need as it is shaped by culture and individual personality.

**Idea generation** The systematic search for new product ideas.

**Idea screening** Screening new product ideas in order to spot good ideas and drop poor ones as soon as possible.

**Industrial goods** Goods bought by individuals and organizations for further processing or for use in conducting a business.

**Industrial market** All the individuals and organizations that acquire goods and services that enter into the production of other products and services that are in turn sold, rented, or supplied to others.

**Intensive distribution** Stocking the product in as many outlets as possible.

**Introduction stage** The product life cycle stage in which the new product is first distributed and made available for purchase.

**Joint ownership** Entering a foreign market by joining with foreign investors to create a local business in which the company shares joint ownership and control.

**Joint venturing** Entering foreign markets by joining with foreign companies to produce and market a product or service.

**Learning** Changes in an individual's behavior arising from experience.

**Licensing** A method of entering a foreign market in which the company enters an agreement with a licensee in the foreign market, offering the right to use a manufacturing process, trademark, patent, trade secret, or other item of value for a fee or royalty

**Life style** A person's pattern of living as expressed in his or her activities, interests, and opinions.

**Macroenvironment** The larger societal forces that affect the whole microenvironment—demographic, economic, natural, technological, political, and cultural forces.

**Management contracting** A joint venture in which the domestic firm supplies the management knowhow to a foreign company that supplies the capital; the domestic firm exports management services rather than products.

**Managerial climate** The company climate resulting from the way managers work with others in the company.

**Manufacturers' sales branches and offices** Wholesaling done by sellers or buyers themselves, rather than through independent wholesalers.

**Market** The set of all actual and potential buyers of a product.

**Market development** A strategy for expanding company growth by identifying and developing new market segments for current company products.

**Market management organization** An organization structure in which market managers are responsible for developing plans for sales and profits in their specific markets.

**Market penetration** A strategy for expanding company growth by increasing sales of current products to current market segments without changing the product in any way.

**Market penetration pricing** Setting a low price for a new product in order to attract a large number of buyers and a large market share.

**Market positioning** Arranging for a product to occupy a clear, distinctive, and desirable place relative to competing products in the minds of target consumers: formulating a competitive positioning for a product and a detailed marketing mix.

**Market segment** A group of consumers who respond in a similar way to a given set of marketing stimuli.

**Market segmentation** The process of classifying customers into groups with different needs, characteristics, or behavior. Dividing a market into distinct groups of buyers who might require separate products or marketing mixes.

**Market skimming pricing** Setting a high price for a new product to skim maximum revenue from the segments willing to pay the high price.

**Market targeting** The process of evaluating each market segment's attractiveness and selecting one or more segments to enter. Evaluating each market segment's attractiveness and selecting one or more segments to enter.

**Marketing** A social and managerial process by which individuals and groups obtain what they need and want through creating and exchanging products and value with others.

**Marketing audit** A comprehensive, systematic, independent, and periodic examination of a company's environment, objectives, strategies, and activities to determine problem areas and opportunities and to recommend a plan of action to improve the company's marketing performance.

**Marketing concept** The philosophy that achieving organizational goals depends on determining the needs and wants of target markets and delivering the desired satisfactions more effectively and efficiently than competitors.

**Marketing control** The process of measuring and evaluating the results of marketing strategies and plans, and taking corrective action to ensure that marketing objectives are attained.

**Marketing environment** The actors and forces outside the firm that affect marketing management's ability to develop and maintain successful transactions with its target customers.

**Marketing implementation** The process that turns marketing strategies and plans into marketing actions in order to accomplish strategic marketing objectives.

**Marketing information system (MIS)** A structure of people, equipment, and procedures to gather, sort, analyze, evaluate, and distribute information that is relevant, timely, and accurate to marketing decision makers.

**Marketing intelligence** Everyday information about developments in the marketing environment that helps managers prepare and adjust marketing plans.

**Marketing intermediaries** Firms that help the company to promote, sell, and distribute its goods to final buyers; they include middlemen, physical distribution firms, marketing service agencies, and financial intermediaries.

**Marketing management** The analysis, planning, implementation, and control of programs designed to create, build, and maintain beneficial exchanges with target buyers for the purpose of achieving organizational objectives.

**Marketing mix** The set of controllable marketing variables that the firm blends to produce the response it wants in the target market.

**Marketing research** The function that links the consumer, customer, and public to the marketer through information—information used to identify and define marketing opportunities and problems; to generate, refine, and evaluate marketing actions; to monitor marketing performance; and to improve understanding of the marketing process.

**Marketing strategy** The marketing logic by which the business unit hopes to achieve its marketing objectives. Marketing strategy consists of specific strategies for target markets, marketing mix, and marketing expenditure level.

**Marketing strategy development** Designing an initial marketing strategy for a new product based on the product concept.

**Mass and selective media** Print media, broadcast media, and display media aimed at large, unsegmented audiences (mass media) or at selected audiences (selective media).

**Materials and parts** Industrial goods that enter the manufacturer's product completely, including raw materials and manufactured materials and parts.

**Maturity stage** The stage in the product life cycle where sales growth slows or levels off.

**Media impact** The qualitative value of an exposure through a given medium.

**Merchant wholesaler** An independently owned business that takes title to the merchandise it handles.

**Microenvironment** The forces close to the company that affect its ability to serve its customers—the company, market channel firms, customer markets, competitors, and publics.

**Mission statement** A statement of the organization's purpose, what it wants to accomplish in the larger environment.

**Monopolistic competition** A market in which many buyers and sellers trade over a range of prices rather than a single market price.

**Moral appeals** Message appeals that are directed to the audience's sense of what is right and proper.

**Motive (or drive)** A need that is sufficiently pressing to direct the person to seek satisfaction of the need.

**Multinational company** A company that operates in many countries and that has a major part of its operations outside its home country.

**Natural environment** Natural resources that are needed as inputs by marketers or that are affected by marketing activities.

**New product development** The development of original products, product improvements, product modifications, and new brands through the firm's own R&D efforts.

**Nondurable goods** Tangible goods normally consumed in one or a few uses.

**Nonpersonal communication channels** Media that carry messages without personal contact or feedback, including mass and selective media, atmospheres, and events.

**Objective-and-task method** Developing the promotion budget by defining specific objectives, determining the tasks that must be performed, and estimating the costs of performing those tasks.

**Observational research** The gathering of primary data by observing relevant people, actions, and situations.

**Oligopolistic competition** A market in which there are a few sellers who are highly sensitive to each other's pricing and marketing strategies.

**Organizational buying** The decision-making process by which formal organizations establish the need for purchased products and services, and identify, evaluate, and choose among alternative brands and suppliers.

**Organization image** The way an individual or a group sees an organization.

**Organization marketing** Activities undertaken to create, maintain, or change attitudes and behavior of target audiences toward an organization.

**Packaging** The activities of designing and producing the container or wrapper for a product.

**Perceived-value pricing** Setting price based on buyers' perception of value rather than on the seller's cost.

**Percentage-of-sales method** Setting the promotion budget at a certain percentage of current or forecasted sales, or as a percentage of the sales price.

**Perception** The process by which people select, organize, and interpret information to form a meaningful picture of the world.

**Person marketing** Activities undertaken to create, maintain, or change attitudes or behavior toward particular people.

**Personal communication channels** Channels through which two or more people communicate directly with each other, including face to face, person to audience, over the telephone, or through the mail.

**Personal selling** Oral presentation in a conversation with one or more prospective purchasers for the purpose of making sales.

**Personality** The unique psychological characteristics that lead to relatively consistent and lasting responses to one's own environment.

**Physical distribution** The tasks involved in planning, implementing, and controlling the physical flow of materials and final goods from points of origin to points of use to meet the needs of customers at a profit.

**Place marketing** Activities undertaken to create, maintain, or change attitudes or behavior toward particular places.

**Planned obsolescence** A strategy of causing products to become obsolete before they actually need replacement.

**Pleasing products** Products that give high immediate satisfaction but may hurt consumers in the long term.

**Political environment** Laws, government agencies, and pressure groups that influence and limit various organizations and individuals in society.

**Price** The amount of money charged for a product or service, or the sum of the values consumers exchange for the benefits of having or using the product or service.

**Price elasticity** A measure of the responsiveness of demand to changes in price.

**Primary data** Information collected for the specific purpose at hand.

**Product** Anything that can be offered to a market for attention, acquisition, use, or consumption, that might satisfy a want or need.

**Product concept** A detailed version of the new product idea stated in meaningful consumer terms.

**Product development** A strategy for expanding company growth by offering modified or new products to current market segments. Developing the product concept into a physical product in order to ensure that the product idea can be turned into a workable product.

**Product idea** An idea for a possible product that the company can see itself offering to the market.

**Product image** The way consumers picture an actual or potential product.

**Product life cycle (PLC)** The course of a product's sales and profits over its lifetime. It involves five distinct stages: product development, introduction, growth, maturity, and decline.

**Product line** A group of products that are closely related, either by function, customer group, retail outlet, or price range.

**Product management organization** An organization structure in which product managers are responsible for developing and implementing marketing strategies and plans for a specific product or brand.

**Product mix** The set of all product lines and items that a particular seller offers for sale to buyers.

**Product position** The way the product is defined by consumers on important attributes—the place the product occupies in consumers' minds relative to competing products.

**Product salesforce structure** A salesforce organization under which salespeople specialize in selling only a portion of the company's products or lines.

**Production concept** The philosophy that consumers will favor products that are available and highly affordable, and therefore management should focus on improving production and distribution efficiency.

**Profitability control** Evaluation and corrective action to ensure the profitability of a company's various products, territories, customer groups, trade channels, and order sizes.

**Promotion mix** The specific mix of advertising, personal selling, sales promotion, and public relations a company uses to pursue its advertising and marketing objectives.

**Promotional allowance** A payment or price reduction to reward dealers for participating in advertising and sales-support programs.

**Promotional pricing** Temporarily pricing products below the list price, and sometimes even below cost, to increase short-run sales.

**Psychological pricing** A pricing approach which considers the psychology of prices and not simply the economics - the price is used to say something about the product.

**Psychographic segmentation** Dividing a market into different groups based on social class, life style, or personality characteristics.

**Public** Any group that has an actual or potential interest in or impact on an organization's ability to achieve its objectives.

**Public relations** Building good relations with the company's various publics by obtaining favorable publicity, building a good "corporate image," and handling or heading off unfavorable rumors, stories, and events.

**Publicity** Activities to promote a company or its products by planting news about it in media not paid for by the sponsor.

**Pull strategy** A promotion strategy that calls for spending a lot on advertising and consumer promotion to build up consumer demand and "pull" the product through the channel.

**Pulsing** Scheduling ads unevenly in bursts over a time period.

**Pure competition** A market in which many buyers and sellers trade in a uniform commodity—no single buyer or seller has much effect on the going market price.

**Pure monopoly** A market in which there is a single seller—it may be a government monopoly, a private regulated monopoly, or a private nonregulated monopoly.

**Push strategy** A promotion strategy that calls for using the sales-force and trade promotion to push the product through channels.

**Quantity discount** A price reduction to buyers who buy large volumes.

**Question marks** Low-share business units in high-growth markets that require a lot of cash to hold their share or build into stars.

**Quota** A limit on the amount of goods that an importing country will accept in certain product categories, designed to conserve on foreign exchange and protect local industry and employment.

**Rational appeals** Message appeals that relate to the audience's self-interest and show that the product will produce the claimed benefits.

**Reach** The percentage of people in the target market exposed to an ad campaign during a given period.

**Reference groups** Groups that have a direct (face-to-face) or indirect influence on the person's attitudes or behavior.

**Reseller market** All the individuals and organizations that acquire goods for the purpose of reselling or renting them to others at a profit.

**Retailers** Businesses whose sales come primarily from retailing.

**Retailing** All activities involved in selling goods or services directly to final consumers for their personal, nonbusiness use.

**Role** The activities people are expected to perform according to the people around them.

**Sales promotion** Short-term incentives to encourage purchase or sales of a product or service.

**Salesforce management** The analysis, planning, implementation, and control of salesforce activities.

**Salesforce promotion** Sales promotion designed to motivate the salesforce and make their selling efforts more effective.

**Salesperson** An individual acting for a company who performs one or more of the following activities: prospecting, communicating, servicing, and information gathering.

**Salutary products** Products that have low appeal but benefit consumers in the long term.

**Sample** A segment of the population selected for marketing research to represent the population as a whole.

**Sealed-bid pricing** Setting price based on how the firm thinks competitors will price rather than on its own costs or demand—used when a company bids for jobs.

**Seasonal discount** A price reduction to buyers who buy merchandise or services out of season.

**Secondary data** Information that already exists somewhere, having been collected for another purpose.

**Selective distribution** The use of more than one but less than all the middlemen who are willing to carry the company's products.

**Selling concept** The idea that consumers will not buy enough of the organization's products unless the organization undertakes a large selling and promotion effort.

**Selling process** The steps that the salesperson follows when selling, including prospecting and qualifying, preapproach, approach, presentation and demonstration, handling objections, closing, and follow-up.

**Services** Activities, benefits, or satisfactions that are offered for sale. Any activities or benefits that one party can offer to another that are essentially intangible and do not result in the ownership of anything.

**Shopping center** A group of retail businesses planned, developed, owned, and managed as a unit.

**Shopping goods** Consumer goods that the customer, in the process of selection and purchase, usually compares on such bases as suitability, quality, price, and style.

**Social classes** Relatively permanent and ordered divisions in a society whose members share similar values, interests, and behaviors.

**Social marketing** The design, implementation, and control of programs seeking to increase the acceptability of a social idea, cause, or practice among a target group.

**Societal marketing concept** The idea that the organization should determine the needs, wants, and interests of target markets and deliver the desired satisfactions more effectively and efficiently than competitors in a way that maintains or improves the consumer's and society's well-being.

**Specialty goods** Consumer goods with unique characteristics or brand identification for which a significant group of buyers is willing to make a special purchase effort.

**Specialty store** A retail store that carries a narrow product line with a deep assortment within that line.

**Standardized marketing mix** An international marketing strategy of using basically the same product, advertising, distribution channels, and other elements of the marketing mix in all the company's international markets.

**Stars** High-growth, high-share businesses or products. They often require heavy investment to finance their rapid growth.

**Status** The general esteem given to a role by society.

**Strategic business unit (SBU)** A unit of the company that has a separate mission and objective, and which can be planned independently from other company businesses.

**Strategic control** A critical review of the company's overall marketing effectiveness.

**Strategic planning** The process of developing and maintaining a strategic fit between the organization's goals and capabilities and its changing marketing opportunities.

**Subculture** A group of people with shared value systems based on common life experiences and situations.

**Supermarkets** Large, low-cost, low-margin, high-volume, self-service stores that carry a wide variety of food, laundry,

and household maintenance products.

**Superstore** A store almost twice the size of a regular supermarket that carries a large assortment of routinely purchased food and nonfood items, and offers such services as laundry, dry cleaning, shoe repair, cheque cashing, bill paying, and bargain lunch counters.

**Suppliers** Firms and individuals that provide the resources needed by the company and its competitors to produce goods and services.

**Supplies and services** Industrial goods that do not enter the finished product at all.

**Survey research** The gathering of primary data by asking people questions about their knowledge, attitudes, preferences, and buying behavior.

**Systems buying** Buying a whole solution to a problem and not making all the separate decisions involved.

**Tariff** A tax levied by a government against certain imported products designed to raise revenue or protect domestic firms.

**Technological environment** Forces that create new technologies, creating new product and market opportunities.

**Telemarketing** Using the telephone to sell directly to consumers.

**Television marketing** Using television to market goods directly to consumers.

**Territorial salesforce structure** A salesforce organization that assigns each salesperson to an exclusive geographic territory in which that salesperson carries the company's full line.

**Test marketing** The stage of new product development in which the product and marketing program are tested in more realistic market settings.

**Total costs** The sum of the fixed and variable cost for any given level of production.

**Trade promotion** Sales promotion designed to gain reseller support and to improve reseller selling efforts.

**Trade-in allowance** A price reduction given for turning in an old item when buying a new one.

**Trademark** A brand or part of a brand that is given legal protection —it protects the seller's exclusive rights to use the brand name or brand mark.

**Transaction** A trade between two parties that involves at least two things of value—agreed-upon conditions—a time of agreement, and a place of agreement.

**Uniform delivered pricing** A geographic pricing strategy in which the company charges the same price plus freight to all customers regardless of their location.

**Unsought goods** Consumer goods that the consumer does not know about or knows about but does not normally think of buying.

**Value analysis** An approach to cost reduction in which components are carefully studied to determine if they can be redesigned or standardized or made by cheaper methods of production.

**Variable costs** Costs that vary directly with the level of production.

**Vertical marketing system (VMS)** A distribution channel structure in which the producer(s), wholesaler(s), and retailer(s) act as a unified system.

**Warehouse store** A no-frills, reduced-service store that seeks high volume through low prices.

**Wholesalers** Firms engaged primarily in wholesaling activity.

**Wholesaling** All the activities involved in selling goods and services to those buying for resale or business use.

**Zone pricing** A geographic pricing strategy in which the company sets up two or more zones—all customers within a zone pay the same total price, and this price is higher in the more distant zones.

# Author Index

# Company/Product Index

# Subject Index

# Photo Credits

CHAPTER 10

10.1a   Photo Courtesy of Bombardier Inc. (p. 248)
10.1b   Photo Courtesy of Bombardier Inc. (p. 248)
10.1c   Photo Courtesy of Bombardier Inc. (p. 248)
10.1d   Photo Courtesy of Bombardier Inc. (p. 248)
10.2a   Photo Courtesy of General Motors of Canada Ltd. (p. 256)
10.2b   Photo Courtesy of General Motors of Canada Ltd. (p. 256)
10.3a   Photo Courtesy of Bell Canada (p. 262)
10.3b   Photo Courtesy of Kraft General Foods of Canada Ltd. (p. 262)
10.4   Photo Courtesy of 3M Canada (p. 263)
10.5   Photo Courtesy of Sony of Canada Ltd. "Sony is a registered trademark of Sony Corporation Tokyo, Japan" (p. 264)

CHAPTER 11

11.1   Photo Courtesy of Sony of Canada Ltd. "Sony is a registered trademark of Sony Corporation, Tokyo, Japan" (p. 273)
11.2   Photo Courtesy of General Motors of Canada Ltd. (p. 277)
11.3   Photo Courtesy of Radio Shack (p. 279)
11.4   Photo Courtesy of Tip Top Tailors, Division of Dylex Ltd. (p. 280)

CHAPTER 12

12.1   Photo Courtesy of Hurtig Publishers Ltd. (p. 292)
12.2   Photo Courtesy of Sony of Canada Ltd. "Sony is a registered trademark of Sony Corporation, Tokyo, Japan" (p. 297)
12.3   Photo Courtesy of Whistler Resort Association (p. 299)
12.4   Photo Courtesy of Kathleen Bellesiles/Little Apple Studio (p. 301)
12.5   Photo Courtesy of Kathleen Bellesiles/Little Apple Studio (p. 302)

CHAPTER 13

13.1a   Photo Courtesy of ISTC (p. 313)
13.1b   Photo Courtesy of ISTC (p. 313)
13.1c   Photo Courtesy of ISTC (p. 313)
13.1d   Photo Courtesy of ISTC (p. 313)
13.2a   Photo Courtesy of ISTC (p. 324)
13.2b   Photo Courtesy of Ontario Ministry of Agriculture and Food (p. 324)
13.3   Photo Courtesy of Becker Milk Company Ltd. (p. 326)
13.4   Photo Courtesy of Canadian Tire Corporation Ltd. (p. 331)
13.5a   Photo Courtesy of CP Rail (p. 334)
13.5b   Photo Courtesy of ISTC (p. 334)
13.5c   Photo Courtesy of Air Canada (p. 334)
13.5d   Photo Courtesy of CP Trucks (p. 334)

CHAPTER 14

14.1   Photo Courtesy of Kathleen Bellesiles/Little Apple Studio (p. 340)
14.2   Photo Courtesy of Suzy Shier (p. 345)
14.3   Photo Courtesy of Loblaws Companies Ltd. (p. 347)
14.4   Photo Courtesy of Kathleen Bellesiles/Little Apple Studio (p. 349)
14.5   Photo Courtesy of Cara Operations Ltd. (p. 352)
14.6   Photo Courtesy of Cadillac Fairview Corporation Ltd. (p. 353)
14.7   Photo Courtesy of Kathleen Bellesiles/Little Apple Studio (p. 355)
14.8   Photo Courtesy of Kathleen Bellesiles/Little Apple Studio (p. 359)

CHAPTER 15

15.1   Photo Courtesy of Quaker Oats Company of Canada Ltd. (p. 369)
15.2   Photo Courtesy of Fisons Corporations Ltd. (p. 375)
15.3   Photo Courtesy of Pepsi-Cola Company (New York) (p. 378)
15.4   Photo Courtesy of Xerox Canada Inc. (p. 383)
15.5   Photo Courtesy of McGraw-Hill Magazines (p. 385)

CHAPTER 16

16.1   Photo Courtesy of Pepsi-Cola Company (New York) (p. 392)
16.2   Photo Courtesy of Copyright 1985 Fido Dido Inc. Lic. by United Feature Syndicate Inc. (p. 394)
16.3   Photo Courtesy of Participaction (p. 400)
16.4   Photo Courtesy of Xerox Canada Inc. (p. 402)
16.5   Photo Courtesy of Jockey International Inc. (p. 403)
16.6   Photo Courtesy of Chrysler Canada Ltd. (p. 405)
16.7   Photo Courtesy of Kathleen Bellesiles/Little Apple Studio (p. 411)

CHAPTER 17

17.1   Photo Courtesy of Kathleen Bellesiles/Little Apple Studio (p. 421)
17.2   Photo Courtesy of Kathleen Bellesiles/Little Apple Studio (p. 425)
17.3   Photo Courtesy of Kathleen Bellesiles/Little Apple Studio (p. 427)
17.4   Photo Courtesy of Kathleen Bellesiles/Little Apple Studio (p. 432)
17.5   Photo Courtesy of Kathleen Bellesiles/Little Apple Studio (p. 433)

CHAPTER 18

18.1   Photo Courtesy of Canapress Photo Service (p. 441)
18.2   Photo Courtesy of McDonald's Restaurants of Canada Ltd. (p. 446)
18.3   Photo Courtesy of Alcan Aluminum Ltd. (p. 454)
18.4   Photo Courtesy of MEDIACOM INC. (p. 458)

CHAPTER 19

19.1   Photo Courtesy of Hospital for Sick Children (p. 464)
19.2   Photo Courtesy of Toronto Transit Commission (p. 469)
19.3   Photo Courtesy of VS Services Ltd. (p. 470)
19.4   Photo Courtesy of Federal Express Corporation (p. 472)
19.5   Photo Courtesy of Four Seasons Hotels (p. 473)
19.6   Photo Courtesy of Alcan Aluminum Ltd. (p. 476)
19.7a   Photo Courtesy of Toronto Department of Public Health (p. 478)
19.7b   Photo Courtesy of MEDIACOM INC. (p. 478)

CHAPTER 20

20.1   Photo Courtesy of Loblaws Companies (p. 484)
20.2   Photo Courtesy of Brettons (p. 488)
20.3   Photo Courtesy of Kathleen Bellesiles/Little Apple Studio (p. 492)
20.4   Photo Courtesy of Kathleen Bellesiles/Little Apple Studio (p. 495)
20.5   Photo Courtesy of The Body Shop (p. 499)